THE NATIONAL HOCKEY LEAGUE

Stanley Cup
Playoffs Fact Guide
1996

TRIUMPH BOOKS

National Hockey League
Stanley Cup Playoffs Fact Guide 1996

All rights reserved. The use of information contained in this book by members of the media is encouraged. The use of any part of this publication reproduced, transmitted in any form or by any means, electronic, mechanical, photocopying, recording, or otherwise or stored in a retrieval system, without the prior written consent of the publisher – or in the case of photocopying or other reprographic copying, a licence from the Canadian Reprography Collective – is an infringement of copyright law.

© Copyright 1995 by the National Hockey League

Vice President, Public Relations: Arthur Pincus
Editor: Greg Inglis
Design, data management, production: Dan Diamond

Printed in Canada

Published and Distributed in the United States by
Triumph Books, 644 South Clark Street, Chicago, Illinois, 60605
312/939-3330; FAX 312/633-3557

ISBN 0-57243-045-1

About the Cover . . .

Eight Stanley Cup winners spanning 55 years of championship play are depicted on the front and back covers of this book.

Front cover: *Top left,* Mark Messier, New York Rangers, 1994; *bottom left,* Montreal Canadiens, 1966. *top right,* Scott Stevens, New Jersey Devils, 1995; *bottom right,* Kent Nilsson, Wayne Gretzky, Edmonton Oilers, 1987.

Back cover: *Top left,* Mario Lemieux, Pittsburgh Penguins, 1991; *bottom left,* New York Rangers, 1940; *top right,* Boston's Johnny Bucyk receives the Cup from NHL president Clarence Campbell, 1970; *bottom right,* Mike Bossy, New York Islanders, 1982.

The National Hockey League
Stanley Cup Playoffs Fact Guide
1996

•

Table of Contents

Introduction	page 5
The NHL's Playoff Format	6
History of NHL Playoff Formats	9
Stanley Cup Champions and Finalists	10

SECTION I .... TEAM PLAYOFF HISTORIES

Team-by-Team Playoff Results and Top 10 Scorers	15

SECTION II .... YEAR-BY-YEAR PLAYOFF SCORES AND HIGHLIGHTS

All-Time Playoff Scoring Leaders	32
Playoff Game Scores and Highlights, 1893 to 1995	33

SECTION III .... PLAYOFF RECORDS

Playoff Record Book	110
Playoff Hat-Tricks, Leading Scorers Year-by-Year	121
Overtime, Coaching Records, Penalty Shots	123
This Date in Playoff History	128

SECTION IV .... THE STANLEY CUP FINALS

Final Series Results, Top Five Scorers, Team-by-Team	140
Final Series Record Book	143
Final Series Scoring, Year-by-Year	153
Players on Championship Teams, 1893 to 1995	169
Coaching and Player Registers, Final Series	180
Goaltending Register, Final Series	176

SECTION V .... THE STANLEY CUP FINALS

Final Series Game Summaries, 1980 to 1995	183

THE ORIGINAL BOWL

The bowl that currently sits atop the Stanley Cup is a carefully constructed copy of the original bowl purchased by Lord Stanley in 1893. The original trophy was retired in 1969 because it had become brittle and easily damaged. It can still be viewed and studied at the Hockey Hall of Fame in Toronto.

THE GROWTH OF THE CUP

In the early days, players used to add their names to the trophy by scratching them onto the original bowl with a knife or a nail. From the 1890s to the 1930s, various bands were added to the bottom of the bowl to hold the names of the winning teams and their players. Throughout this time, the appearance of the Cup kept changing almost from year to year. In 1939, the Stanley Cup was given a standardized form as a long, cigar-shaped trophy. It stayed this way until 1948, when it was rebuilt as a two-piece trophy with a wide barrel-shaped base and a removable bowl and collar. The modern one-piece Cup was introduced in 1958.

THE STANLEY CUP

IT ALL STARTED ON MARCH 18, 1892, at a dinner of the Ottawa Amateur Athletic Association. Lord Kilcoursie, a player on the Ottawa Rebels hockey club from Goverment House, delivered the following message on behalf of Lord Stanley, the Earl of Preston and Governor General of Canada:

> "I have for some time been thinking that it would be a good thing if there were a challenge cup which should be held from year to year by the champion hockey team in the Dominion (of Canada).
>
> "There does not appear to be any such outward sign of a championship at present, and considering the general interest which matches now elicit, and the importance of having the game played fairly and under rules generally recognized, I am willing to give a cup which shall be held from year to year by the winning team."

Shortly thereafter, Lord Stanley purchased a silver cup measuring 7 1/2 inches high by 11 1/2 inches across for the sum of 10 guineas (approximately $50); appointed two Ottawa gentlemen, Sheriff John Sweetland and Philip D. Ross, as trustees of that cup; and set the following preliminary conditions to govern the annual competition:

- *The winners to return the Cup in good order when required by the trustees in order that it may be handed over to any other team which may win it.*
- *Each winning team to have the club name and year engraved on a silver ring fitted on the Cup.*
- *The Cup to remain a challenge competition and not the property of any one team, even if won more than once.*
- *The trustees to maintain absolute authority in all situations or disputes over the winner of the Cup.*
- *A substitute trustee to be named in the event that one of the existing trustees drops out.*

The first winner of the Stanley Cup was the Montreal Amateur Athletic Association (AAA) hockey club, champions of the Amateur Hockey Association of Canada for 1893.

Ironically, Lord Stanley never witnessed a championship game nor attended a presentation of his trophy, having returned to his native England in the midst of the 1893 season. Nevertheless, the quest for his trophy has become one of the world's most prestigious sporting competitions.

THE 1996 NHL PLAYOFF FORMAT

SIXTEEN NATIONAL HOCKEY LEAGUE TEAMS begin competition for North America's oldest team trophy, the Stanley Cup, on Tuesday, April 16, 1996 when the Conference Quarterfinals open.

All series will be played under a best four-of-seven format with home-ice advantage rotating on a 2-2-1-1-1 basis, with the exception of series involving a Central Division team versus a Pacific Division team. In such a series, the higher ranked team has the choice of playing a 2-2-1-1-1 or a 2-3-2 format. If the 2-3-2 format is selected, the higher ranked team will also have the choice of playing Games 1,2, 6 and 7 at home or Games 3, 4 and 5 at home.

CONFERENCE QUARTERFINALS

The four division regular season champions are ranked in the first two positions in their respective conferences, the one with the higher standing in the regular season being ranked first. The remaining six playoff clubs in each conference will be ranked based on regular season points.

EASTERN CONFERENCE
Series A - #1 (Division winner) vs. #8
Series B - #2 (Division winner) vs. #7
Series C - #3 vs. #6
Series D - #4 vs. #5

WESTERN CONFERENCE
Series E - #1 (Division winner) vs. #8
Series F - #2 (Division winner) vs. #7
Series G - #3 vs. #6
Series H - #4 vs. #5

CONFERENCE SEMIFINALS

The same criteria used in seedings for the Conference Quarterfinals (Division winners, followed by remaining clubs based on regular season points) will again be in effect. Following are possible scenarios:

If one division winner is eliminated in the Conference Quarterfinals:

The remaining division winner would be seeded first, followed by the three remaining teams in order of regular season points. The #1 seed would face the team with the fewest regular season points, while the second and third teams would meet.

If both division winners are eliminated in the Conference Quarterfinals:

The remaining four teams would be ranked based on regular season points. The #1 seed would face the #4 seed, while the #2 and #3 teams would meet.

CONFERENCE FINALS

The same criteria used in selection of order for the Conference Quarterfinals (Division winners, followed by remaining clubs based on regular season points) will again be in effect. Following is a possible scenario:

If a division winner meets a non-division winner with more regular season points:

The division winner would have home ice advantage.

STANLEY CUP CHAMPIONSHIP

The Eastern Conference champion versus the Western Conference champion. Home ice will be determined solely by the higher number of regular season points. Games will be played on a 2-2-1-1-1 basis. The latest possible date for the completion of the Stanley Cup Championship series is June 17, 1996.

TIE-BREAKING PROCEDURE

In the event that two or more teams are tied in points at the conclusion of the regular season, the standing of the teams in each conference will be determined in the following order:

1. The greater number of games won by the club.
2. The higher number of points earned in games against each other. If two teams are tied, and have not played an equal number of home games against each other, points earned in the first game played in the city that had the extra game shall not be included. If more than two teams are tied, the higher winning percentage in games among those teams shall be used to determine the standing.
3. The greater differential between goals scored for and against for the complete regular season.

STANLEY BEFORE CALDER

Tony Esposito and Danny Grant both won the Stanley Cup one year and the Calder the next with different teams. Grant was a member of the 1968 Cup-winning Montreal Canadiens before winning the Calder as the NHL's top rookie in 1969 with Minnesota. Tony Esposito won the Cup with the Canadiens in 1969 and the Calder the following season with the Chicago Black Hawks. A player remains eligible for the Calder if he has played 25-or-fewer NHL regular-season games.

All-Time NHL Playoff Formats

1917-18 — The regular-season was split into two halves. The winners of both halves faced each other in a two-game, total-goals series for the NHL championship and the right to meet the PCHA champion in the best-of-five Stanley Cup Finals.

1918-19 — Same as 1917-18, except that the Stanley Cup Finals was extended to a best-of-seven series.

1919-20 — Same as 1917-1918, except that Ottawa won both halves of the split regular-season schedule to earn an automatic berth into the best-of-five Stanley Cup Finals against the PCHA champions.

1921-22 — The top two teams at the conclusion of the regular-season faced each other in a two-game, total-goals series for the NHL championship. The NHL champion then moved on to play the winner of the PCHA-WCHL playoff series in the best-of-five Stanley Cup Finals.

1922-23 — The top two teams at the conclusion of the regular-season faced each other in a two-game, total-goals series for the NHL championship. The NHL champion then moved on to play the PCHA champion in the best-of-three Stanley Cup Semi-Finals, and the winner of the Semi-Finals played the WCHL champion, which had been given a bye, in the best-of-three Stanley Cup Finals.

1923-24 — The top two teams at the conclusion of the regular-season faced each other in a two-game, total-goals series for the NHL championship. The NHL champion then moved to play the loser of the PCHA-WCHL playoff (the winner of the PCHA-WCHL playoff earned a bye into the Stanley Cup Finals) in the best-of-three Stanley Cup Semi-Finals. The winner of this series met the PCHA-WCHL playoff winner in the best-of-three Stanley Cup Finals.

1924-25 — The first place team (Hamilton) at the conclusion of the regular-season was supposed to play the winner of a two-game, total goals series between the second (Toronto) and third (Montreal) place clubs. However, Hamilton refused to abide by this new format, demanding greater compensation than offered by the League. Thus, Toronto and Montreal played their two-game, total-goals series, and the winner (Montreal) earned the NHL title and then played the WCHL champion (Victoria) in the best-of-five Stanley Cup Finals.

1925-26 — The format which was intended for 1924-25 went into effect. The winner of the two-game, total-goals series between the second and third place teams squared off against the first place team in the two-game, total-goals NHL championship series. The NHL champion then moved on to play the WHL champion in the best-of-five Stanley Cup Finals.

After the 1925-26 season, the NHL was the only major professional hockey league still in existence and consequently took over sole control of the Stanley Cup competition.

1926-27 — The 10-team league was divided into two divisions — Canadian and American — of five teams apiece. In each division, the winner of the two-game, total-goals series between the second and third place teams faced the first place team in a two-game, total-goals series for the division title. The two division title winners then met in the best-of-five Stanley Cup Finals.

1928-29 — Both first place teams in the two divisions played each other in a best-of-five series. Both second place teams in the two divisions played each other in a two-game, total-goals series as did the two third place teams. The winners of these latter two series then played each other in a best-of-three series for the right to meet the winner of the series between the two first place clubs. This Stanley Cup Final was a best-of-three.

Series A: First in Canadian Division versus first in American (best-of-five)
Series B: Second in Canadian Division versus second in American (two-game, total-goals)
Series C: Third in Canadian Division versus third in American (two-game, total-goals)
Series D: Winner of Series B versus winner of Series C (best-of-three)
Series E: Winner of Series A versus winner of Series D (best of three) for Stanley Cup

1931-32 — Same as 1928-29, except that Series D was changed to a two-game, total-goals format and Series E was changed to best of five.

1936-37 — Same as 1931-32, except that Series B, C, and D were each best-of-three.

1938-39 — With the NHL reduced to seven teams, the two-division system was replaced by one seven-team league. Based on final regular-season standings, the following playoff format was adopted:

Series A: First versus Second (best-of-seven)
Series B: Third versus Fourth (best-of-three)
Series C: Fifth versus Sixth (best-of-three)
Series D: Winner of Series B versus winner of Series C (best-of-three)
Series E: Winner of Series A versus winner of Series D (best-of-seven)

1942-43 — With the NHL reduced to six teams (the "original six"), only the top four finishers qualified for playoff action. The best-of-seven Semi-Finals pitted Team #1 vs Team #3 and Team #2 vs Team #4. The winners of each Semi-Final series met in the best-of-seven Stanley Cup Finals.

1967-68 — When it doubled in size from 6 to 12 teams, the NHL once again was divided into two divisions — East and West — of six teams apiece. The top four clubs in each division qualified for the playoffs (all series were best-of-seven):

Series A: Team #1 (East) vs Team #3 (East)
Series B: Team #2 (East) vs Team #4 (East)
Series C: Team #1 (West) vs Team #3 (West)
Series D: Team #2 (West) vs Team #4 (West)
Series E: Winner of Series A vs winner of Series B
Series F: Winner of Series C vs winner of Series D
Series G: Winner of Series E vs Winner of Series F

1970-71 — Same as 1967-68 except that Series E matched the winners of Series A and D, and Series F matched the winners of Series B and C.

1971-72 — Same as 1970-71, except that Series A and C matched Team #1 vs Team #4, and Series B and D matched Team #2 vs Team #3.

1974-75 — With the League now expanded to 18 teams in four divisions, a completely new playoff format was introduced. First, the #2 and #3 teams in each of the four divisions were pooled together in the Preliminary round. These eight (#2 and #3) clubs were ranked #1 to #8 based on regular-season record:

Series A: Team #1 vs Team #8 (best-of-three)
Series B: Team #2 vs Team #7 (best-of-three)
Series C: Team #3 vs Team #6 (best-of-three)
Series D: Team #4 vs Team #5 (best-of-three)

The winners of this Preliminary round then pooled together with the four division winners, which had received byes into this Quarter-Final round. These eight teams were again ranked #1 to #8 based on regular-season record:

Series E: Team #1 vs Team #8 (best-of-seven)
Series F: Team #2 vs Team #7 (best-of-seven)
Series G: Team #3 vs Team #6 (best-of-seven)
Series H: Team #4 vs Team #5 (best-of-seven)

The four Quarter-Finals winners, which moved on to the Semi-Finals, were then ranked #1 to #4 based on regular season record:

Series I: Team #1 vs Team #4 (best-of-seven)
Series J: Team #2 vs Team #3 (best-of-seven)
Series K: Winner of Series I vs winner of Series J (best-of-seven)

1977-78 — Same as 1974-75, except that the Preliminary round consisted of the #2 teams in the four divisions and the next four teams based on regular-season record (not their standings within their divisions).

1979-80 — With the addition of four WHA franchises, the League expanded its playoff structure to include 16 of its 21 teams. The four first place teams in the four divisions automatically earned playoff berths. Among the 17 other clubs, the top 12, according to regular-season record, also earned berths. All 16 teams were then pooled together and ranked #1 to #16 based on regular-season record:

Series A: Team #1 vs Team #16 (best-of-five)
Series B: Team #2 vs Team #15 (best-of-five)
Series C: Team #3 vs Team #14 (best-of-five)
Series D: Team #4 vs Team #13 (best-of-five)
Series E: Team #5 vs Team #12 (best-of-five)
Series F: Team #6 vs Team #11 (best-of-five)
Series G: Team #7 vs Team #10 (best-of-five)
Series H: Team #8 vs Team #9 (best-of-five)

The eight Preliminary round winners, ranked #1 to #8 based on regular-season record, moved on to the Quarter-Finals:

Series I: Team #1 vs Team #8 (best-of-seven)
Series J: Team #2 vs Team #7 (best-of-seven)
Series K: Team #3 vs Team #6 (best-of-seven)
Series L: Team #4 vs Team #5 (best-of-seven)

The eight Quarter-Finals winners, ranked #1 to #4 based on regular-season record, moved on to the semi-finals:

Series M: Team #1 vs Team #4 (best-of-seven)
Series N: Team #2 vs Team #3 (best-of-seven)
Series O: Winner of Series M vs winner of Series N (best-of-seven)

1981-82 — The first four teams in each division earned playoff berths. In each division, the first-place team opposed the fourth-place team and the second-place team opposed the third-place team in a best-of-five Division Semi-Final series (DSF). In each division, the two winners of the DSF met in a best-of-seven Division Final series (DF). The two winners in each conference met in a best-of-seven Conference Final series (CF). In the Prince of Wales Conference, the Adams Division winner opposed the Patrick Division winner; in the Clarence Campbell Conference, the Smythe Division winner opposed the Norris Division winner. The two CF winners met in a best-of-seven Stanley Cup Final (F) series.

1986-87 — Division Semi-Final series changed from best-of-five to best-of-seven.

1993-94 — The NHL's playoff draw conference-based rather than division-based. At the conclusion of the regular season, the top eight teams in each of the Eastern and Western Conferences qualify for the playoffs. The teams that finish in first place in each of the League's divisions are seeded first and second in each conference's playoff draw and are assured of home ice advantage in the first two playoff rounds. The remaining teams are seeded based on their regular-season point totals. In each conference, the team seeded #1 plays #8; #2 vs. #7; #3 vs. #6; and #4 vs. #5. All series are best-of-seven with home ice rotating on a 2-2-1-1-1 basis, with the exception of matchups between Central and Pacific Division teams. These matchups will be played on a 2-3-2 basis to reduce travel. In a 2-3-2 series, the team with the most points will have its choice to start the series at home or on the road. The Eastern Conference champion will face the Western Conference champion in the Stanley Cup Final.

1994-95 — Same as 1993-94, except that in first, second or third-round playoff series involving Central and Pacific Division teams, the team with the better record has the choice of using either a 2-3-2 or a 2-2-1-1-1 format. When a 2-3-2 format is selected, the higher-ranked team also has the choice of playing games 1, 2, 6 and 7 at home or playing games 3, 4 and 5 at home. The format for the Stanley Cup Final remains 2-2-1-1-1.

STANLEY CUP CHAMPIONS AND FINALISTS

YEAR	WINNING TEAM	COACH	FINALIST	COACH
1995	New Jersey Devils	Jacques Lemaire	Detroit Red Wings	Scotty Bowman
1994	New York Rangers	Mike Keenan	Vancouver Canucks	Pat Quinn
1993	Montreal Canadiens	Jacques Demers	Los Angeles Kings	Barry Melrose
1992	Pittsburgh Penguins	Scotty Bowman	Chicago Blackhawks	Mike Keenan
1991	Pittsburgh Penguins	Bob Johnson	Minnesota North Stars	Bob Gainey
1990	Edmonton Oilers	John Muckler	Boston Bruins	Mike Milbury
1989	Calgary Flames	Terry Crisp	Montreal Canadiens	Pat Burns
1988	Edmonton Oilers	Glen Sather	Boston Bruins	Terry O'Reilly
1987	Edmonton Oilers	Glen Sather	Philadelphia Flyers	Mike Keenan
1986	Montreal Canadiens	Jean Perron	Calgary Flames	Bob Johnson
1985	Edmonton Oilers	Glen Sather	Philadelphia Flyers	Mike Keenan
1984	Edmonton Oilers	Glen Sather	New York Islanders	Al Arbour
1983	New York Islanders	Al Arbour	Edmonton Oilers	Glen Sather
1982	New York Islanders	Al Arbour	Vancouver Canucks	Roger Neilson
1981	New York Islanders	Al Arbour	Minnesota North Stars	Glen Sonmor
1980	New York Islanders	Al Arbour	Philadelphia Flyers	Pat Quinn
1979	Montreal Canadiens	Scotty Bowman	New York Rangers	Fred Shero
1978	Montreal Canadiens	Scotty Bowman	Boston Bruins	Don Cherry
1977	Montreal Canadiens	Scotty Bowman	Boston Bruins	Don Cherry
1976	Montreal Canadiens	Scotty Bowman	Philadelphia Flyers	Fred Shero
1975	Philadelphia Flyers	Fred Shero	Buffalo Sabres	Floyd Smith
1974	Philadelphia Flyers	Fred Shero	Boston Bruins	Armand 'Bep' Guidolin
1973	Montreal Canadiens	Scotty Bowman	Chicago Blackhawks	Billy Reay
1972	Boston Bruins	Tom Johnson	New York Rangers	Emile Francis
1971	Montreal Canadiens	Al MacNeil	Chicago Blackhawks	Billy Reay
1970	Boston Bruins	Harry Sinden	St. Louis Blues	Scotty Bowman
1969	Montreal Canadiens	Claude Ruel	St. Louis Blues	Scotty Bowman
1968	Montreal Canadiens	Hector 'Toe' Blake	St. Louis Blues	Scotty Bowman
1967	Toronto Maple Leafs	George 'Punch' Imlach	Montreal Canadiens	Hector 'Toe' Blake
1966	Montreal Canadiens	Hector 'Toe' Blake	Detroit Red Wings	Sid Abel
1965	Montreal Canadiens	Hector 'Toe' Blake	Chicago Blackhawks	Billy Reay
1964	Toronto Maple Leafs	George 'Punch' Imlach	Detroit Red Wings	Sid Abel
1963	Toronto Maple Leafs	George 'Punch' Imlach	Detroit Red Wings	Sid Abel
1962	Toronto Maple Leafs	George 'Punch' Imlach	Chicago Blackhawks	Rudy Pilous
1961	Chicago Blackhawks	Rudy Pilous	Detroit Red Wings	Sid Abel
1960	Montreal Canadiens	Hector 'Toe' Blake	Toronto Maple Leafs	George 'Punch' Imlach
1959	Montreal Canadiens	Hector 'Toe' Blake	Toronto Maple Leafs	George 'Punch' Imlach
1958	Montreal Canadiens	Hector 'Toe' Blake	Boston Bruins	Milt Schmidt
1957	Montreal Canadiens	Hector 'Toe' Blake	Boston Bruins	Milt Schmidt
1956	Montreal Canadiens	Hector 'Toe' Blake	Detroit Red Wings	Jimmy Skinner
1955	Detroit Red Wings	Jimmy Skinner	Montreal Canadiens	Dick Irvin
1954	Detroit Red Wings	Tommy Ivan	Montreal Canadiens	Dick Irvin
1953	Montreal Canadiens	Dick Irvin	Boston Bruins	Lynn Patrick
1952	Detroit Red Wings	Tommy Ivan	Montreal Canadiens	Dick Irvin
1951	Toronto Maple Leafs	Joe Primeau	Montreal Canadiens	Dick Irvin
1950	Detroit Red Wings	Tommy Ivan	New York Rangers	Lynn Patrick
1949	Toronto Maple Leafs	Clarence 'Hap' Day	Detroit Red Wings	Tommy Ivan
1948	Toronto Maple Leafs	Clarence 'Hap' Day	Detroit Red Wings	Tommy Ivan
1947	Toronto Maple Leafs	Clarence 'Hap' Day	Montreal Canadiens	Dick Irvin
1946	Montreal Canadiens	Dick Irvin	Boston Bruins	Aubrey 'Dit' Clapper
1945	Toronto Maple Leafs	Clarence 'Hap' Day	Detroit Red Wings	Jack Adams
1944	Montreal Canadiens	Dick Irvin	Chicago Blackhawks	Paul Thompson
1943	Detroit Red Wings	Jack Adams	Boston Bruins	Art Ross
1942	Toronto Maple Leafs	Clarence 'Hap' Day	Detroit Red Wings	Jack Adams
1941	Boston Bruins	Ralph 'Cooney' Weiland	Detroit Red Wings	Ebbie Goodfellow
1940	New York Rangers	Frank Boucher	Toronto Maple Leafs	Dick Irvin
1939	Boston Bruins	Art Ross	Toronto Maple Leafs	Dick Irvin
1938	Chicago Blackhawks	Bill Stewart	Toronto Maple Leafs	Dick Irvin
1937	Detroit Red Wings	Jack Adams	New York Rangers	Lester Patrick
1936	Detroit Red Wings	Jack Adams	Toronto Maple Leafs	Dick Irvin
1935	Montreal Maroons	Tommy Gorman	Toronto Maple Leafs	Dick Irvin

YEAR	WINNING TEAM	COACH	FINALIST	COACH
1934	Chicago Blackhawks	Tommy Gorman	Detroit Red Wings	Herbie Lewis
1933	New York Rangers	Lester Patrick	Toronto Maple Leafs	Dick Irvin
1932	Toronto Maple Leafs	Dick Irvin	New York Rangers	Lester Patrick
1931	Montreal Canadiens	Cecil Hart	Chicago Blackhawks	Dick Irvin
1930	Montreal Canadiens	Cecil Hart	Boston Bruins	Art Ross
1929	Boston Bruins	Cy Denneny	New York Rangers	Lester Patrick
1928	New York Rangers	Lester Patrick	Montreal Maroons	Eddie Gerard
1927	Ottawa Senators	Dave Gill	Boston Bruins	Art Ross

THE NATIONAL HOCKEY LEAGUE ASSUMED CONTROL OF STANLEY CUP COMPETITION AFTER 1926

YEAR	WINNING TEAM	COACH	FINALIST	COACH
1926	Montreal Maroons	Eddie Gerard	Victoria Cougars	Lester Patrick
1925	Victoria Cougars	Lester Patrick	Montreal Canadiens	Leo Dandurand
1924	Montreal Canadiens	Leo Dandurand	Calgary Tigers	—
			Vancouver Maroons	—
1923	Ottawa Senators	Pete Green	Edmonton Eskimos	—
			Vancouver Maroons	—
1922	Toronto St. Pats	Eddie Powers	Vancouver Millionaires	Frank Patrick
1921	Ottawa Senators	Pete Green	Vancouver Millionaires	Frank Patrick
1920	Ottawa Senators	Pete Green	Seattle Metropolitans	—
1919	No decision	Series between Montreal and Seattle cancelled due to influenza epidemic		
1918	Toronto Arenas	Dick Carroll	Vancouver Millionaires	Frank Patrick
1917	Seattle Metropolitans	—	Montreal Canadiens	—
1916	Montreal Canadiens	—	Portland Rosebuds	—
1915	Vancouver Millionaires	—	Ottawa Senators	—
1914	Toronto Blueshirts	—	Victoria Cougars	—
			Montreal Canadiens	—
1913	Quebec Bulldogs	—	Sydney Miners	—
1912	Quebec Bulldogs	—	Moncton Victories	—
1911	Ottawa Senators	—	Port Arthur Bearcats	—
			Galt	—
1910	Montreal Wanderers	—	Berlin Union Jacks	—
			Edmonton Eskimos	—
			Galt	—
1909	Ottawa Senators	—	(no challengers)	
1908	Montreal Wanderers	—	Edmonton Eskimos	—
			Toronto Trolley Leaguers	—
			Winnipeg Maple Leafs	—
			Ottawa Victorias	—
1907	Montreal Wanderers	—	Kenora Thistles	—
	Kenora Thistles	—	Montreal Wanderers	—
1906	Montreal Wanderers	—	New Glascow Cubs	—
			Ottawa Silver Seven	—
	Ottawa Silver Seven	—	Montreal Wanderers	—
			Smiths Falls	—
			Queenís University	—
1905	Ottawa Silver Seven	—	Rat Portage Thistles	—
			Dawson City Nuggets	—
1904	Ottawa Silver Seven	—	Brandon Wheat Kings	—
			Montreal Wanderers	—
			Toronto Marlboros	—
			Winnipeg Rowing Club	—
1903	Ottawa Silver Seven	—	Rat Portage Thistles	—
			Montreal Victorias	—
	Montreal AAA	—	Winnipeg Victorias	—
1902	Montreal AAA	—	Winnipeg Victorias	—
	Winnipeg Victorias	—	Toronto Wellingtons	—
1901	Winnipeg Victorias	—	Montreal Shamrocks	—
1900	Montreal Shamrocks	—	Halifax Crescents	—
			Winnipeg Victorias	—
1899	Montreal Shamrocks	—	Queen's University	—
	Montreal Victorias	—	Winnipeg Victorias	—
1898	Montreal Victorias	—	(no challengers)	
1897	Montreal Victorias	—	Ottawa Capitals	—
1896	Montreal Victorias	—	Winnipeg Victorias	—
	Winnipeg Victorias	—	Montreal Victorias	—
1895	Montreal Victorias	—	(no challengers)	
1894	Montreal AAA	—	Ottawa Generals	—
1893	Montreal AAA	—	(no challengers)	

PLAYOFF POSTPONEMENTS

The assassination of Dr. Martin Luther King, Jr. forced the postponement of three series games during the quarterfinal rounds of the 1968 Stanley Cup playoffs. Match-ups between the Rangers and Chicago, St. Louis and Philadelphia, and Minnesota and Los Angeles were delayed by a minimum of two days.

National Hockey League
Stanley Cup Playoffs
Fact Guide
1996

Section I
•
Team Playoff Histories

Team-by-Team Playoff Results and Top 10 Scorers .... page **15**

Stanley Cup-Winning Goals, 1980-1995

1980	Bob Nystrom, New York Islanders
1981	Wayne Merrick, New York Islanders
1982	Mike Bossy, New York Islanders
1983	Mike Bossy, New York Islanders
1984	Ken Linseman, Edmonton Oilers
1985	Paul Coffey, Edmonton Oilers
1986	Bobby Smith, Montreal Canadiens
1987	Jari Kurri, Edmonton Oilers.
1988	Wayne Gretzky, Edmonton Oilers
1989	Doug Gilmour, Calgary Flames
1990	Craig Simpson, Edmonton Oilers
1991	Ulf Samuelsson, Pittsburgh Penguins
1992	Ron Francis, Pittsburgh Penguins
1993	Kirk Muller, Montreal Canadiens
1994	Mark Messier, New York Rangers
1995	Sergei Brylin, New Jersey Devils

BOSTON BRUINS

Playoff History, Team-by-Team

Playoffs

	Series	W	L	GP	W	L	T	GF	GA	Last Mtg.	Round	Result
Buffalo	6	5	1	33	19	14	0	132	113	1993	DSF	L 0-4
Chicago	6	5	1	22	16	5	1	97	63	1978	QF	W 4-0
Dallas	1	0	1	3	0	3	0	13	20	1981	PR	L 0-3
Detroit	7	4	3	33	19	14	0	96	98	1957	SF	W 4-1
Edmonton	2	0	2	9	1	8	0	20	41	1990	F	L 1-4
Hartford	2	2	0	13	8	5	0	24	17	1991	DSF	W 4-2
Los Angeles	2	2	0	13	8	5	0	56	38	1977	QF	W 4-2
Montreal	28	7	21	139	52	87	0	339	430	1994	CQF	W 4-3
New Jersey	3	1	2	18	7	11	0	52	55	1995	CQF	L 1-4
NY Islanders	2	0	2	11	3	8	0	35	49	1983	CF	L 2-4
NY Rangers	9	6	3	42	22	18	2	114	104	1973	QF	L 1-4
Philadelphia	4	2	2	20	11	9	0	60	57	1978	SF	W 4-1
Pittsburgh	4	2	2	19	9	10	0	62	67	1992	CF	L 0-4
Quebec	2	1	1	11	6	5	0	37	36	1983	DSF	W 3-1
St. Louis	2	2	0	8	8	0	0	48	15	1972	SF	W 4-0
Toronto	13	5	8	62	30	31	1	153	150	1974	QF	W 4-0
Washington	1	1	0	4	4	0	0	15	6	1990	CF	W 4-0
Defunct Clubs	3	1	2	11	4	5	2	20	20			
Totals	97	46	51	471	227	238	6	1389	1400			

Playoff Results 1995-91

Year	Round	Opponent	Result	GF	GA
1995	CQF	New Jersey	L 1-4	5	14
1994	CSF	New Jersey	L 2-4	17	22
	CQF	Montreal	W 4-3	22	20
1993	DSF	Buffalo	L 0-4	12	19
1992	CF	Pittsburgh	L 0-4	7	19
	DF	Montreal	W 4-0	14	8
	DSF	Buffalo	W 4-3	19	24
1991	CF	Pittsburgh	L 2-4	18	27
	DF	Montreal	W 4-3	18	18
	DSF	Hartford	W 4-2	24	17

Abbreviations: Round: F – Final; **CF** – conference final; **CQF** – conference quarter-final; **CSF** – conference semi-final; **DF** – division final; **DSF** – division semi-final; **SF** – semi-final; **QF** – quarter-final; **PR** – preliminary round.

PLAYOFF SCORING LEADERS

	PLAYER	YEARS	GP	G	A	TP
1.	Ray Bourque	80-95	157	33	106	139
2.	Phil Esposito	68-75	71	46	56	102
3.	Rick Middleton	77-88	111	45	55	100
4.	John Bucyk	58-77	109	40	60	100
5.	Bobby Orr	68-75	74	26	66	92
6.	Wayne Cashman	68-83	145	31	57	88
7.	Cam Neely	87-94	81	53	32	85
8.	Ken Hodge	68-75	86	34	47	81
9.	Brad Park	76-83	91	23	55	78
10.	Peter McNab	77-83	79	38	36	74

SERIES RECORDS VERSUS OTHER CLUBS

Opponent	Year	Series	Winner	W	L	T	GF	GA
Buf.	1982	DSF	Bos.	3	1		17	11
Buf.	1983	DF	Bos.	4	3		33	23
Buf.	1988	DSF	Bos.	4	2		28	22
Buf.	1989	DSF	Bos.	4	1		16	14
Buf.	1992	DSF	Bos.	4	3		19	24
Buf.	1993	DSF	Buf.	0	4		12	19
Chi.	1927	QF*	Bos.	1	0	1	10	5
Chi.	1942	QF	Bos.	2	1		5	7
Chi.	1970	SF	Bos.	4	0		20	10
Chi.	1974	SF	Bos.	4	2		28	20
Chi.	1975	PRE	Chi.	1	2		15	12
Chi.	1978	QF	Bos.	4	0		19	9
Det.	1941	F	Bos.	4	0		12	6
Det.	1942	SF	Det.	0	2		5	9
Det.	1943	F	Det.	0	4		5	16
Det.	1945	SF	Det.	3	4		22	22
Det.	1946	SF	Bos.	4	1		16	10
Det.	1953	SF	Bos.	4	2		21	21
Det.	1957	SF	Bos.	4	1		15	14
Edm.	1988	F	Edm.	0	4		12	21
Edm.	1990	F	Edm.	1	4		8	20
Hfd.	1990	DSF	Bos.	4	3		23	21
Hfd.	1991	DSF	Bos.	4	2		24	17
L.A.	1976	QF	Bos.	4	3		26	14
L.A.	1977	QF	Bos.	4	2		30	24
Min.	1981	PRE	Min.	0	3		13	20

A Note Regarding the Atlanta Flames
Atlanta's NHL franchise shifted to Calgary in 1980-81. Atlanta's playoff record from 1973 to 1980 is included under Calgary's and is found on page 16.

** Calgary indicates that a club played at least one series against the Flames when the club was based in Atlanta.

Opponent	Year	Series	Winner	W	L	T	GF	GA
Mtl.	1929	SF	Bos.	3	0		5	2
Mtl.	1930	F	Mtl.	0	2		3	7
Mtl.	1931	SF	Mtl.	2	3		13	13
Mtl.	1943	SF	Bos.	4	1		18	17
Mtl.	1946	F	Mtl.	1	4		13	19
Mtl.	1947	SF	Mtl.	1	4		10	16
Mtl.	1952	SF	Mtl.	3	4		12	18
Mtl.	1953	F	Mtl.	1	4		9	16
Mtl.	1954	SF	Mtl.	0	4		4	16
Mtl.	1955	SF	Mtl.	1	4		9	16
Mtl.	1957	F	Mtl.	1	4		6	15
Mtl.	1958	F	Mtl.	2	4		14	16
Mtl.	1968	QF	Mtl.	0	4		8	15
Mtl.	1969	SF	Mtl.	2	4		16	15
Mtl.	1971	QF	Mtl.	3	4		26	28
Mtl.	1977	F	Mtl.	0	4		6	16
Mtl.	1978	F	Mtl.	2	4		13	18
Mtl.	1979	SF	Mtl.	3	4		20	25
Mtl.	1984	DSF	Mtl.	0	3		2	10
Mtl.	1985	DSF	Mtl.	2	3		17	19
Mtl.	1986	DSF	Mtl.	0	3		6	10
Mtl.	1987	DSF	Mtl.	0	4		11	19
Mtl.	1988	DF	Bos.	4	1		15	10
Mtl.	1989	DF	Mtl.	1	4		13	16
Mtl.	1990	DF	Bos.	4	1		16	12
Mtl.	1991	DF	Bos.	4	3		18	18
Mtl.	1992	DF	Bos.	4	0		14	8
Mtl.	1994	CQF	Bos.	4	3		22	20
N.J.	1988	CF	Bos.	4	3		30	19
N.J.	1994	CSF	N.J.	2	4		17	22
N.J.	1995	CQF	N.J.	1	4		5	14
NYI	1980	QF	NYI	1	4		14	19
NYI	1983	CF	NYI	2	4		21	30
NYR	1927	SF*	Bos.	1	0	1	3	1
NYR	1928	SF*	NYR	0	1	1	2	5
NYR	1929	F	Bos.	2	0		4	1
NYR	1939	SF	Bos.	4	3		14	12
NYR	1940	SF	NYR	2	4		9	15
NYR	1958	SF	Bos.	4	2		28	16
NYR	1970	QF	Bos.	4	2		25	16
NYR	1972	F	Bos.	4	2		18	16
NYR	1973	QF	NYR	1	4		11	22

Opponent	Year	Series	Winner	W	L	T	GF	GA
Phi.	1974	F	Phi.	2	4		13	15
Phi.	1976	SF	Phi.	1	4		12	19
Phi.	1977	SF	Bos.	4	0		14	8
Phi.	1978	QF	Bos.	4	1		21	15
Pit.	1979	QF	Bos.	4	0		16	7
Pit.	1980	PRE	Bos.	3	2		21	14
Pit.	1991	CF	Pit.	2	4		18	27
Pit.	1992	CF	Pit.	0	4		7	19
Que.	1982	DF	Que.	3	4		26	28
Que.	1983	DSF	Bos.	3	1		11	8
St.L	1970	F	Bos.	4	0		20	7
St.L	1972	SF	Bos.	4	0		28	8
Tor.	1933	SF	Tor.	2	3		27	9
Tor.	1935	SF	Tor.	1	3		2	7
Tor.	1936	QF*	Tor.	1	1		6	8
Tor.	1938	SF	Tor.	0	3		3	6
Tor.	1939	F	Bos.	4	1		12	6
Tor.	1941	F	Bos.	4	3		15	17
Tor.	1948	SF	Tor.	1	4		13	20
Tor.	1949	SF	Tor.	1	4		10	16
Tor.	1951	SF	Tor.	1	4	1	5	17
Tor.	1959	SF	Tor.	3	4		21	20
Tor.	1969	QF	Bos.	4	0		24	5
Tor.	1970	QF	Bos.	4	1		18	10
Tor.	1974	QF	Bos.	4	0		17	6
Wsh.	1990	CF	Bos.	4	0		15	6

DEFUNCT CLUBS

Mtl.M	1930	SF	Bos.	3	1		11	5
Mtl.M	1937	QF	Mtl.M	1	2		6	8
Ott.	1927	F	Ott.	0	2	2	3	7

* Total-goals series

BUFFALO SABRES

PLAYOFF SCORING LEADERS

	PLAYER	YEARS	GP	G	A	TP
1.	Gilbert Perreault	73-85	90	33	70	103
2.	Richard Martin	73-80	62	24	29	53
3.	Craig Ramsay	73-85	89	17	31	48
4.	Danny Gare	75-81	57	23	21	44
5.	Rene Robert	73-79	47	22	17	39
6.	Don Luce	73-80	62	17	19	36
7.	Dale Hawerchuk	91-94	28	9	25	34
8.	Dave Andreychuk	83-92	41	12	20	32
9.	Alexander Mogilny	89-95	31	14	16	30
10.	Ric Seiling	78-85	55	14	14	28

SERIES RECORDS VERSUS OTHER CLUBS

Opponent	Year	Series	Winner	W	L	GF	GA
Bos.	1982	DSF	Bos.	1	3	11	17
Bos.	1983	DF	Bos.	3	4	23	33
Bos.	1988	DSF	Bos.	2	4	22	28
Bos.	1989	DSF	Bos.	1	4	14	16
Bos.	1992	DSF	Bos.	3	4	24	19
Bos.	1993	DSF	Buf.	4	0	19	12
Chi.	1975	QF	Buf.	4	1	20	10
Chi.	1980	QF	Buf.	4	0	16	7
Min.	1977	PRE	Buf.	2	0	11	3
Min.	1981	QF	Min.	1	4	17	23

Playoffs

	Series	W	L	GP	W	L	T	GF	GA	Last Mtg.	Round	Result
Boston	6	1	5	33	14	19	0	113	132	1993	DSF	W 4-0
Chicago	2	2	0	9	8	1	0	36	17	1980	QF	W 4-0
Dallas	2	1	1	7	3	4	0	28	26	1981	QF	L 1-4
Montreal	6	2	4	31	13	18	0	94	114	1993	DF	L 0-4
New Jersey	1	0	1	7	3	4	0	14	14	1994	CQF	L 3-4
NY Islanders	3	0	3	16	4	12	0	45	59	1980	SF	L 2-4
NY Rangers	1	1	0	3	2	1	0	11	6	1978	PR	W 2-1
Philadelphia	3	0	3	16	4	12	0	36	53	1995	CQF	L 1-4
Pittsburgh	1	0	1	3	1	2	0	9	9	1979	PR	L 1-2
Quebec	2	0	2	8	2	6	0	27	35	1985	DSF	L 2-3
St. Louis	1	1	0	3	2	1	0	7	8	1976	PR	W 2-1
Vancouver	2	2	0	7	6	1	0	28	14	1981	PR	W 3-0
Totals	30	10	20	143	62	81	0	448	480			

Opponent	Year	Series	Winner	W	L	GF	GA
Mtl.	1973	QF	Mtl.	2	4	16	21
Mtl.	1975	SF	Buf.	4	2	21	29
Mtl.	1983	DSF	Buf.	3	0	8	2
Mtl.	1990	DSF	Mtl.	2	4	13	17
Mtl.	1991	DSF	Mtl.	2	4	24	29
Mtl.	1993	DF	Mtl.	0	4	12	16
N.J.	1994	CQF	N.J.	3	4	14	14
NYI	1976	QF	NYI	2	4	18	21
NYI	1977	QF	NYI	0	4	10	16
NYI	1980	SF	NYI	2	4	17	22
NYR	1978	PRE	Buf.	2	1	11	6

Playoff Results 1995-91

Year	Round	Opponent	Result	GF	GA
1995	CQF	Philadelphia	L 1-4	13	18
1994	CQF	New Jersey	L 3-4	14	14
1993	DF	Montreal	L 0-4	12	16
	DSF	Boston	W 4-0	19	12
1992	DSF	Boston	L 3-4	24	19
1991	DSF	Montreal	L 2-4	24	29

Abbreviations: Round: F – Final;
CF – conference final; **CQF** – conference quarter-final;
CSF – conference semi-final; **DF** – division final;
DSF – division semi-final; **SF** – semi-final;
QF – quarter-final; **PR** – preliminary round.

Opponent	Year	Series	Winner	W	L	GF	GA
Phi.	1975	F	Phi.	2	4	12	19
Phi.	1978	QF	Phi.	1	4	11	16
Phi.	1995	CQF	Phi.	1	4	13	18
Pit.	1979	PRE	Pit.	1	2	9	9
Que.	1984	DSF	Que.	0	3	5	13
Que.	1985	DSF	Que.	2	3	22	22
St.L	1976	PRE	Buf.	2	1	7	8
Van.	1980	PRE	Buf.	3	1	15	7
Van.	1981	PRE	Buf.	3	0	13	7

CALGARY FLAMES

PLAYOFF SCORING LEADERS

	PLAYER	YEARS	GP	G	A	TP
1.	Al MacInnis	84-94	95	25	77	102
2.	Paul Reinhart	81-88	76	21	51	72
3.	Joe Nieuwendyk	87-95	68	32	28	60
4.	Theoren Fleury	89-95	55	27	32	59
5.	Joel Otto	85-94	80	23	35	58
6.	Joe Mullen	86-90	61	35	20	55
7.	Hakan Loob	84-89	73	26	28	54
8.	Lanny McDonald	82-89	72	24	23	47
9.	Jim Peplinski	81-89	99	15	31	46
10.	Gary Suter	86-93	49	6	33	39

SERIES RECORDS VERSUS OTHER CLUBS

Opponent	Year	Series	Winner	W	L	GF	GA
Chi.	1981	PRE	Cgy.	3	0	15	9
Chi.	1989	CF	Cgy.	4	1	15	8
Det.	1978	PRE	Det.	0	2	5	8
Edm.	1983	DF	Edm.	1	4	13	35
Edm.	1984	DF	Edm.	3	4	27	33
Edm.	1986	DF	Cgy.	4	3	25	24
Edm.	1988	DF	Edm.	0	4	11	18
Edm.	1991	DSF	Edm.	3	4	20	22

Note: Includes series played by Atlanta Flames, 1973-80

Playoffs

	Series	W	L	GP	W	L	T	GF	GA	Last Mtg.	Round	Result
Chicago	2	2	0	8	7	1	0	30	17	1989	CF	W 4-1
Dallas	1	0	1	6	2	4	0	18	25	1981	SF	L 2-4
Detroit	1	0	1	2	0	2	0	5	8	1978	PR	L 0-2
Edmonton	5	1	4	30	11	19	0	96	132	1991	DSF	L 3-4
Los Angeles	6	2	4	26	13	13	0	102	105	1993	DSF	L 2-4
Montreal	2	1	1	11	5	6	0	32	31	1989	F	W 4-2
NY Rangers	1	0	1	4	1	3	0	8	14	1980	PR	L 1-3
Philadelphia	2	1	1	11	4	7	0	28	43	1981	QF	W 4-3
St. Louis	1	1	0	7	4	3	0	28	22	1986	CF	W 4-3
San Jose	1	0	1	7	3	4	0	35	26	1995	CQF	L 3-4
Toronto	1	0	1	2	0	2	0	5	9	1979	PR	L 0-2
Vancouver	5	3	2	25	13	12	0	82	80	1994	CQF	L 3-4
Winnipeg	3	1	2	13	6	7	0	43	45	1987	DSF	L 2-4
Totals	31	12	19	152	69	83	0	522	557			

Opponent	Year	Series	Winner	W	L	GF	GA
L.A.	1976	PRE	L.A.	0	2	1	3
L.A.	1977	PRE	L.A.	1	2	7	11
L.A.	1988	DSF	Cgy.	4	1	30	18
L.A.	1989	DF	Cgy.	4	0	22	11
L.A.	1990	DSF	L.A.	2	4	24	29
L.A.	1993	DSF	L.A.	2	4	28	33
Min.	1981	SF	Min.	2	4	18	25
Mtl.	1986	F	Mtl.	1	4	13	15
Mtl.	1989	F	Cgy.	4	2	19	16
NYR	1980	PRE	NYR	1	3	8	14
Phi.	1974	QF	Phi.	0	4	6	17
Phi.	1981	QF	Cgy.	4	3	22	26

Playoff Results 1995-91

Year	Round	Opponent	Result	GF	GA
1995	CQF	San Jose	L 3-4	35	26
1994	CQF	Vancouver	L 3-4	20	23
1993	DSF	Los Angeles	L 2-4	28	33
1991	DSF	Edmonton	L 3-4	20	22

Abbreviations: Round: F – Final;
CF – conference final; **CQF** – conference quarter-final;
CSF – conference semi-final; **DF** – division final;
DSF – division semi-final; **SF** – semi-final;
QF – quarter-final; **PR** – preliminary round.

Opponent	Year	Series	Winner	W	L	GF	GA
St.L	1986	CF	Cgy.	4	3	28	22
S.J.	1995	CQF	S.J.	3	4	35	26
Tor.	1979	PRE	Tor.	0	2	5	9
Van.	1982	DSF	Van.	0	3	5	10
Van.	1983	DSF	Cgy.	3	1	17	14
Van.	1984	DSF	Cgy.	3	1	14	13
Van.	1989	DSF	Cgy.	4	3	26	20
Van.	1994	CQF	Van.	3	4	20	23
Wpg.	1985	DSF	Wpg.	1	3	13	15
Wpg.	1986	DSF	Cgy.	3	0	15	8
Wpg.	1987	DSF	Wpg.	2	4	15	22

TEAM-BY-TEAM PLAYOFF HISTORY • 17

CHICAGO BLACKHAWKS

Playoffs

	Series	W	L	GP	W	L	T	GF	GA	Last Mtg.	Round	Result
Boston	6	1	5	22	5	16	1	63	97	1978	QF	L 0-4
Buffalo	2	0	2	9	1	8	0	17	36	1980	QF	L 0-4
Calgary	2	0	2	8	1	7	0	17	30	1989	CF	L 1-4
Dallas	6	4	2	33	19	14	0	119	119	1991	DSF	L 2-4
Detroit	14	8	6	69	38	31	0	210	190	1995	CF	L 1-4
Edmonton	4	1	3	20	8	12	0	77	102	1992	CF	W 4-0
Los Angeles	1	1	0	5	4	1	0	10	7	1974	QF	W 4-1
Montreal	17	5	12	81	29	50	2	185	261	1976	QF	L 0-4
NY Islanders	2	0	2	6	0	6	0	6	21	1979	QF	L 0-4
NY Rangers	5	4	1	24	14	10	0	66	54	1973	SF	W 4-1
Philadelphia	1	1	0	4	4	0	0	20	8	1971	QF	W 4-0
Pittsburgh	2	1	1	8	4	4	0	24	23	1992	F	L 0-4
St. Louis	9	7	2	45	27	18	0	166	129	1993	DSF	L 0-4
Toronto	9	3	6	38	15	22	1	89	111	1995	CQF	W 4-3
Vancouver	2	1	1	9	5	4	0	24	24	1995	CSF	W 4-0
Defunct Clubs	4	2	2	9	5	3	1	16	15			
Totals	86	39	47	390	179	206	5	1109	1227			

Playoff Results 1995-91

Year	Round	Opponent	Result	GF	GA
1995	CF	Detroit	L 1-4	12	13
	CSF	Vancouver	W 4-0	11	6
	CQF	Toronto	W 4-3	22	20
1994	CQF	Toronto	L 2-4	10	15
1993	DSF	St. Louis	L 0-4	6	13
1992	F	Pittsburgh	L 0-4	10	15
	CF	Edmonton	W 4-0	21	8
	DF	Detroit	W 4-0	11	6
	DSF	St. Louis	W 4-2	23	19
1991	DSF	Minnesota	L 2-4	16	23

Abbreviations: Round: F – Final;
CF – conference final; **CQF** – conference quarter-final;
CSF – conference semi-final; **DF** – division final;
DSF – division semi-final; **SF** – semi-final;
QF – quarter-final; **PR** – preliminary round.

PLAYOFF SCORING LEADERS

	PLAYER	YEARS	GP	G	A	TP
1.	Stan Mikita	60-78	155	59	91	150
2.	Denis Savard	81-90 & 95	115	60	70	130
3.	Bobby Hull	59-72	116	62	67	129
4.	Steve Larmer	83-93	107	45	66	111
5.	Doug Wilson	78-91	95	19	61	80
6.	Dennis Hull	65-77	104	33	34	67
7.	Jeremy Roenick	89-95	72	30	35	65
8.	Pierre Pilote	59-68	82	8	52	60
9.	Bob Murray	77-90	112	19	37	56
10.	Chico Maki	61-73	113	17	36	53

SERIES RECORDS VERSUS OTHER CLUBS

Opponent	Year	Series	Winner	W	L	T	GF	GA
Bos.	1927	*Q	Bos.	0	1	1	5	10
Bos.	1942	QF	Bos.	1	2		7	5
Bos.	1970	SF	Bos.	0	4		10	20
Bos.	1974	SF	Bos.	2	4		20	28
Bos.	1975	PRE	Chi.	2	1		12	15
Bos.	1978	QF	Bos.	0	4		9	19
Buf.	1975	QF	Buf.	1	4		10	20
Buf.	1980	QF	Buf.	0	4		7	16
Cgy.	1981	PRE	Cgy.	0	3		9	15
Cgy.	1989	CF	Cgy.	1	4		8	15
Det.	1934	F	Chi.	3	1		9	7
Det.	1941	SF	Det.	0	2		2	5
Det.	1944	SF	Chi.	4	1		17	8
Det.	1961	F	Chi.	4	2		19	12
Det.	1963	SF	Det.	2	4		19	25
Det.	1964	SF	Det.	3	4		18	24
Det.	1965	SF	Chi.	4	3		23	19
Det.	1966	SF	Det.	2	4		10	22
Det.	1970	QF	Chi.	4	0		16	8
Det.	1985	DSF	Chi.	3	0		23	8
Det.	1987	DSF	Det.	0	4		6	15
Det.	1989	DSF	Chi.	4	2		25	18
Det.	1992	DF	Chi.	4	0		11	6
Det.	1995	CF	Det.	1	4		12	13
Edm.	1983	CF	Edm.	0	4		11	25
Edm.	1985	CF	Edm.	2	4		25	44
Edm.	1990	CF	Edm.	2	4		20	25
Edm.	1992	CF	Chi.	4	0		21	8
L.A.	1974	QF	Chi.	4	1		10	7
Min.	1982	DSF	Chi.	3	1		14	14
Min.	1983	DF	Chi.	4	1		22	17
Min.	1984	DSF	Min.	2	3		14	18
Min.	1985	DF	Chi.	4	2		32	29
Min.	1990	DSF	Chi.	4	3		21	18
Min.	1991	DSF	Min.	2	4		16	23

Opponent	Year	Series	Winner	W	L	T	GF	GA
Mtl.	1930	QF*	Mtl.	0	1	1	2	3
Mtl.	1931	F	Mtl.	2	3		8	11
Mtl.	1934	QF*	Chi.	1	1		4	3
Mtl.	1938	QF	Chi.	2	1		11	8
Mtl.	1941	QF	Chi.	2	1		8	7
Mtl.	1944	F	Mtl.	0	4		8	16
Mtl.	1946	SF	Mtl.	0	4		7	26
Mtl.	1953	SF	Mtl.	3	4		14	18
Mtl.	1959	SF	Mtl.	2	4		16	21
Mtl.	1960	SF	Mtl.	0	4		6	14
Mtl.	1961	SF	Chi.	4	2		16	15
Mtl.	1962	SF	Chi.	4	2		19	13
Mtl.	1965	F	Mtl.	3	4		12	18
Mtl.	1968	SF	Mtl.	1	4		10	22
Mtl.	1971	F	Mtl.	3	4		18	20
Mtl.	1973	F	Mtl.	2	4		23	33
Mtl.	1976	QF	Mtl.	0	4		3	13
NYI	1977	PRE	NYI	0	2		3	7
NYI	1979	QF	NYI	0	4		3	14
NYR	1931	SF*	Chi.	2	0		3	0
NYR	1968	QF	Chi.	4	2		18	12
NYR	1971	SF	Chi.	4	3		21	14
NYR	1972	SF	NYR	0	4		9	17
NYR	1973	SF	Chi.	4	1		15	11
Phi.	1978	QF	Chi.	4	0		20	8
Pit.	1972	QF	Chi.	4	0		14	8
Pit.	1992	F	Pit.	0	4		10	15
St.L	1973	QF	Chi.	4	1		22	9
St.L	1980	PRE	Chi.	3	0		12	4
St.L	1982	DF	Chi.	4	2		23	19
St.L	1983	DSF	Chi.	3	1		16	10
St.L	1988	DSF	St.L	1	4		17	21
St.L	1989	DF	Chi.	4	1		19	12
St.L	1990	DF	Chi.	4	3		28	22
St.L	1992	DSF	Chi.	4	2		23	19
St.L	1993	DSF	St.L	0	4		6	13

Opponent	Year	Series	Winner	W	L	T	GF	GA
Tor.	1931	QF*	Chi.	1	0	1	4	3
Tor.	1932	QF*	Tor.	1	1		2	6
Tor.	1938	F	Chi.	3	1		10	8
Tor.	1940	QF	Tor.	0	2		3	5
Tor.	1962	F	Tor.	2	4		15	18
Tor.	1967	SF	Tor.	2	4		14	18
Tor.	1986	DSF	Tor.	0	3		9	18
Tor.	1994	CQF	Tor.	2	4		10	15
Tor.	1995	CQF	Chi.	4	3		22	20
Van.	1982	CF	Van.	1	4		13	18
Van.	1995	CSF	Chi.	4	0		11	6

DEFUNCT CLUBS

Opponent	Year	Series	Winner	W	L	T	GF	GA
Mtl.M	1934	SF*	Chi.	2	0		6	2
Mtl.M	1935	QF*	Mtl.M	0	1	1	0	1
NYA	1936	QF*	NYA	1	1		5	7
NYA	1938	SF	Chi.	2	1		5	5

* Total-goals series

TEAM-BY-TEAM PLAYOFF HISTORY

COLORADO AVALANCHE

PLAYOFF SCORING LEADERS

	PLAYER	YEARS	GP	G	A	TP
1.	Peter Stastny	81-87	64	24	57	81
2.	Michel Goulet	80-87	66	34	30	64
3.	Anton Stastny	81-87	66	20	32	52
4.	Dale Hunter	81-87	67	16	26	42
5.	Alain Cote	80-87	67	9	15	24
6.	Wilf Paiement	82-85	45	13	10	23
7.	Marian Stastny	82-85	29	5	17	22
8.	J.F. Sauve	84-86	29	7	10	17
9.	Mario Marois	81-85	45	2	15	17
10.	Paul Gillis	84-87	35	3	13	16

Playoffs

	Series	W	L	GP	W	L	T	GF	GA	Last Mtg.	Round	Result
Boston	2	1	1	11	5	6	0	36	37	1983	DSF	L 1-3
Buffalo	2	2	0	8	6	2	0	35	27	1985	DSF	W 3-2
Hartford	2	1	1	9	4	5	0	34	35	1987	DSF	W 4-2
Montreal	5	2	3	31	14	17	0	85	105	1993	DSF	L 2-4
NY Islanders	1	0	1	4	0	4	0	9	18	1982	CF	L 0-4
NY Rangers	1	0	1	6	2	4	0	19	25	1995	CQF	L 2-4
Philadelphia	2	0	2	11	4	7	0	29	39	1985	CF	L 2-4
Totals	15	6	9	80	35	45	0	247	286			

Playoff Results 1995-91

Year	Round	Opponent	Result	GF	GA
1995	CQF	NY Rangers	L 2-4	19	25
1993	DSF	Montreal	L 2-4	16	19

Abbreviations: Round: F – Final; **CF** – conference final; **CQF** – conference quarter-final; **CSF** – conference semi-final; **DF** – division final; **DSF** – division semi-final; **SF** – semi-final; **QF** – quarter-final; **PR** – preliminary round.

SERIES RECORDS VERSUS OTHER CLUBS

Opponent	Year	Series	Winner	W	L	GF	GA
Bos.	1982	DF	Que.	4	3	28	26
Bos.	1983	DSF	Bos.	1	3	8	11
Buf.	1984	DF	Que.	3	0	13	5
Buf.	1985	DSF	Que.	3	2	22	22
Hfd.	1986	DSF	Hfd.	0	3	7	16
Hfd.	1987	DSF	Que.	4	2	27	19
Mtl.	1982	DSF	Que.	3	2	11	16
Mtl.	1984	DF	Mtl.	2	4	13	20
Mtl.	1985	DF	Que.	4	3	24	24
Mtl.	1987	DF	Mtl.	3	4	21	26
Mtl.	1993	DSF	Mtl.	2	4	16	19
NYI	1982	CF	NYI	0	4	9	18
NYR	1995	CQF	NYR	2	4	19	25
Phi.	1981	PRE	Phi.	2	3	17	22
Phi.	1985	CF	Phi.	2	4	12	17

Note: Includes series played by Quebec Nordiques, 1981-95

DALLAS STARS

Playoffs

	Series	W	L	GP	W	L	T	GF	GA	Last Mtg.	Round	Result
Boston	1	1	0	3	3	0	0	20	13	1981	PR	W 3-0
Buffalo	2	1	1	7	4	3	0	26	28	1981	QF	W 4-1
Calgary	1	1	0	6	4	2	0	25	18	1981	SF	W 4-2
Chicago	6	2	4	33	14	19	0	119	119	1991	DSF	W 4-2
Detroit	2	0	2	12	4	8	0	29	40	1995	CQF	L 1-4
Edmonton	2	1	1	9	4	5	0	30	36	1991	CF	W 4-1
Los Angeles	1	1	0	7	4	3	0	26	21	1968	QF	W 4-3
Montreal	2	1	1	13	6	7	0	37	48	1980	QF	W 4-3
NY Islanders	1	0	1	5	1	4	0	16	26	1981	F	L 1-4
Philadelphia	2	0	2	11	3	8	0	26	41	1980	SF	L 1-4
Pittsburgh	1	0	1	6	2	4	0	16	28	1991	F	L 2-4
St. Louis	10	5	5	56	30	26	0	174	162	1994	CQF	W 4-0
Toronto	2	2	0	7	6	1	0	35	26	1983	DSF	W 3-1
Vancouver	1	0	1	5	1	4	0	11	18	1994	CSF	L 1-4
Totals	34	15	19	180	86	94	0	590	624			

Playoff Results 1995-91

Year	Round	Opponent	Result	GF	GA
1995	CQF	Detroit	L 1-4	10	17
1994	CSF	Vancouver	L 1-4	11	18
	CQF	St. Louis	W 4-0	16	10
1992	DSF	Detroit	L 3-4	19	23
1991	F	Pittsburgh	L 2-4	16	28
	CF	Edmonton	W 4-1	20	14
	DF	St. Louis	W 4-2	22	17
	DSF	Chicago	W 4-2	23	16

Abbreviations: Round: F – Final; **CF** – conference final; **CQF** – conference quarter-final; **CSF** – conference semi-final; **DF** – division final; **DSF** – division semi-final; **SF** – semi-final; **QF** – quarter-final; **PR** – preliminary round.

PLAYOFF SCORING LEADERS

	PLAYER	YEARS	GP	G	A	TP
1.	Brian Bellows	83-92	81	34	49	83
2.	Neal Broten	81-94	113	28	50	78
3.	Bobby Smith	80-83, 91-92	77	26	50	76
4.	Steve Payne	80-85	71	35	35	70
5.	Dino Ciccarelli	81-86	62	28	23	51
6.	Brad Maxwell	80-84	58	10	39	49
7.	Dave Gagner	90-95	51	22	24	46
8.	Al MacAdam	80-84	63	20	24	44
9.	Craig Hartsburg	80-86	61	15	27	42
10.	Mike Modano	89-94	48	19	18	37
	Bill Goldsworthy	68-73	40	18	19	37

SERIES RECORDS VERSUS OTHER CLUBS

Opponent	Year	Series	Winner	W	L	GF	GA
Bos.	1981	PRE	Min.	3	0	20	13
Buf.	1977	PRE	Buf.	0	2	3	11
Buf.	1981	QF	Min.	4	1	23	17
Cgy.	1981	SF	Min.	4	2	25	18
Chi.	1982	DSF	Chi.	1	3	14	14
Chi.	1983	DF	Chi.	1	4	17	22
Chi.	1984	DSF	Min.	3	2	18	14
Chi.	1985	DF	Chi.	2	4	29	32
Chi.	1990	DSF	Chi.	3	4	18	21
Chi.	1991	DSF	Min.	4	2	23	16
Det.	1992	DSF	Det.	3	4	19	23
Det.	1995	CQF	Det.	1	4	10	17
Edm.	1984	CF	Edm.	0	4	10	22
Edm.	1991	CF	Min.	4	1	20	14
L.A.	1968	QF	Min.	4	3	26	21
Mtl.	1971	SF	Mtl.	2	4	19	27
Mtl.	1980	QF	Min.	4	3	18	21
NYI	1981	F	NYI	1	4	16	26
Phi.	1973	QF	Phi.	2	4	12	14
Phi.	1980	SF	Phi.	1	4	14	27
Pit.	1991	F	Pit.	2	4	16	28
St.L	1968	SF	St.L	3	4	22	18
St.L	1970	QF	St.L	2	4	16	20
St.L	1971	QF	Min.	4	2	16	15
St.L	1972	QF	St.L	3	4	19	19
St.L	1984	DF	Min.	4	3	19	17
St.L	1985	DSF	Min.	3	0	9	5
St.L	1986	DSF	St.L	2	3	20	18
St.L	1989	DSF	St.L	1	4	15	23
St.L	1991	DF	Min.	4	2	22	17
St.L	1994	CQF	Dal.	4	0	16	10
Tor.	1980	PRE	Min.	3	0	17	8
Tor.	1983	DSF	Min.	3	1	18	18
Van.	1994	CSF	Van.	1	4	11	18

Note: Includes series played by Minnesota North Stars, 1968-92

DETROIT RED WINGS

Playoffs

	Series	W	L	GP	W	L	T	GF	GA	Last Mtg.	Round	Result
Boston	7	3	4	33	14	19	0	98	96	1957	SF	L 1-4
Calgary	1	1	0	2	2	0	0	8	5	1978	PR	W 2-0
Chicago	14	6	8	69	31	38	0	190	210	1995	CF	W 4-1
Dallas	2	2	0	12	8	4	0	40	29	1995	CQF	W 4-1
Edmonton	2	0	2	10	2	8	0	26	39	1988	CF	L 1-4
Montreal	12	7	5	62	29	33	0	149	161	1978	QF	L 1-4
New Jersey	1	0	1	4	0	4	0	7	16	1995	F	L 0-4
NY Rangers	5	4	1	23	13	10	0	57	49	1950	F	W 4-3
St. Louis	3	1	2	16	8	8	0	53	51	1991	DF	L 3-4
San Jose	2	1	1	11	7	4	0	51	27	1995	CSF	W 4-0
Toronto	23	11	12	117	59	58	0	321	311	1993	DSF	L 3-4
Defunct Clubs	4	3	1	10	7	2	1	21	13			
Totals	76	39	37	369	180	188	1	1021	1007			

Playoff Results 1995-91

Year	Round	Opponent	Result	GF	GA
1995	F	New Jersey	L 0-4	7	16
	CF	Chicago	W 4-1	13	12
	CSF	San Jose	W 4-0	24	6
	CQF	Dallas	W 4-1	17	10
1994	CQF	San Jose	L 3-4	27	21
1993	DSF	Toronto	L 3-4	30	24
1992	DF	Chicago	L 0-4	6	11
	DSF	Minnesota	W 4-3	23	19
1991	DSF	St. Louis	L 3-4	20	24

Abbreviations: Round: F – Final; **CF** – conference final; **CQF** – conference quarter-final; **CSF** – conference semi-final; **DF** – division final; **DSF** – division semi-final; **SF** – semi-final; **QF** – quarter-final; **PR** – preliminary round.

PLAYOFF SCORING LEADERS

	PLAYER	YEARS	GP	G	A	TP
1.	Gordie Howe	47-70	154	67	91	158
2.	Alex Delvecchio	52-70	121	35	69	104
3.	Ted Lindsay	45-65	123	46	44	90
4.	Steve Yzerman	84-95	75	31	47	78
5.	Norm Ullman	56-66	80	27	47	74
6.	Sergei Fedorov	90-95	49	17	40	57
7.	Sid Abel	39-52	93	28	28	56
8.	Syd Howe	36-45	68	17	27	44
9.	Bob Probert	87-93	56	13	28	41
10.	Carl Liscombe	39-46	57	22	18	40

SERIES RECORDS VERSUS OTHER CLUBS

Opponent	Year	Series	Winner	W	L	T	GF	GA
Atl.	1978	PRE	Det.	2	0		8	5
Bos.	1941	F	Bos.	0	4		6	12
Bos.	1942	SF	Det.	2	0		9	5
Bos.	1943	F	Det.	4	0		16	5
Bos.	1945	SF	Det.	4	3		22	22
Bos.	1946	SF	Bos.	1	4		10	16
Bos.	1953	SF	Bos.	2	4		21	21
Bos.	1957	SF	Bos.	1	4		14	15
Chi.	1934	F	Chi.	1	3		7	9
Chi.	1941	SF	Det.	2	0		5	2
Chi.	1944	SF	Chi.	1	4		8	17
Chi.	1961	F	Chi.	2	4		12	19
Chi.	1963	SF	Det.	4	2		25	19
Chi.	1964	SF	Det.	4	3		24	18
Chi.	1965	SF	Chi.	3	4		19	23
Chi.	1966	SF	Det.	4	2		22	10
Chi.	1970	QF	Chi.	0	4		8	16
Chi.	1985	DSF	Chi.	0	3		8	23
Chi.	1987	DSF	Det.	4	0		15	6
Chi.	1989	DSF	Chi.	2	4		18	25
Chi.	1992	DF	Chi.	0	4		6	11
Chi.	1995	CF	Det.	4	1		13	12
Dal.	1995	CQF	Det.	4	1		17	10
Edm.	1987	CF	Edm.	1	4		10	16
Edm.	1988	CF	Edm.	1	4		16	23
Min.	1992	DSF	Det.	4	3		23	19

Opponent	Year	Series	Winner	W	L	T	GF	GA
Mtl.	1937	SF	Det.	3	2		13	8
Mtl.	1939	QF	Det.	2	1		8	5
Mtl.	1942	QF	Det.	2	1		8	8
Mtl.	1949	SF	Det.	4	3		17	14
Mtl.	1951	SF	Mtl.	2	4		12	13
Mtl.	1952	F	Det.	4	0		11	2
Mtl.	1954	F	Det.	4	3		14	12
Mtl.	1955	F	Det.	4	3		27	20
Mtl.	1956	F	Mtl.	1	4		9	18
Mtl.	1958	SF	Mtl.	0	4		6	19
Mtl.	1966	F	Mtl.	2	4		14	18
Mtl.	1978	QF	Mtl.	1	4		10	24
N.J.	1995	F	N.J.	0	4		7	16
NYR	1933	SF*	NYR	0	2		3	6
NYR	1937	F	Det.	3	2		9	8
NYR	1941	QF	Det.	2	1		6	6
NYR	1948	SF	Det.	4	2		17	12
NYR	1950	F	Det.	4	3		22	17
St.L	1984	DSF	St.L	1	3		12	13
St.L	1988	DF	Det.	4	1		21	14
St.L	1991	DSF	St.L	3	4		20	24
S.J.	1994	CQF	S.J.	3	4		27	21
S.J.	1995	CSF	Det.	4	0		24	6

Opponent	Year	Series	Winner	W	L	T	GF	GA
Tor.	1929	QF*	Tor.	0	2		2	7
Tor.	1934	SF	Det.	3	2		11	12
Tor.	1936	F	Det.	3	1		18	11
Tor.	1939	SF	Tor.	1	2		8	10
Tor.	1940	SF	Tor.	0	2		2	5
Tor.	1942	F	Tor.	3	4		19	25
Tor.	1943	SF	Det.	4	2		20	17
Tor.	1945	F	Tor.	3	4		9	9
Tor.	1947	SF	Tor.	1	4		14	18
Tor.	1948	F	Tor.	0	4		7	18
Tor.	1949	F	Tor.	0	4		5	12
Tor.	1950	SF	Det.	4	3		10	11
Tor.	1952	SF	Det.	4	0		13	3
Tor.	1954	SF	Det.	4	1		15	8
Tor.	1955	SF	Det.	4	0		14	6
Tor.	1956	SF	Det.	4	1		14	10
Tor.	1960	SF	Tor.	2	4		16	20
Tor.	1961	SF	Det.	4	1		15	8
Tor.	1963	F	Tor.	1	4		10	17
Tor.	1964	F	Tor.	3	4		17	22
Tor.	1987	DF	Det.	4	3		20	18
Tor.	1988	DSF	Det.	4	2		32	20
Tor.	1993	DSF	Tor.	3	4		30	24

DEFUNCT CLUBS

Opponent	Year	Series	Winner	W	L	T	GF	GA
Mtl.M	1932	QF*	Mtl.M	0	1	1	1	3
Mtl.M	1933	QF*	Det.	2	0		5	2
Mtl.M	1936	SF	Det.	3	0		6	1
NYA	1940	QF	Det.	2	1		9	7

* Total-goals series

20 • TEAM-BY-TEAM PLAYOFF HISTORY

EDMONTON OILERS

PLAYOFF SCORING LEADERS

	PLAYER	YEARS	GP	G	A	TP
1.	Wayne Gretzky	80-88	120	81	171	252
2.	Mark Messier	80-91	166	80	135	215
3.	Jari Kurri	81-90	146	92	110	202
4.	Glenn Anderson	81-91	164	81	102	183
5.	Paul Coffey	81-87	94	36	67	103
6.	Esa Tikkanen	85-92	114	51	46	97
7.	Charlie Huddy	82-91	138	16	61	77
8.	Craig Simpson	88-92	67	36	32	68
9.	Kevin Lowe	80-92	170	9	43	52
10.	Randy Gregg	82-90	130	13	37	50

Playoffs

	Series	W	L	GP	W	L	T	GF	GA	Last Mtg.	Round	Result
Boston	2	2	0	9	8	1	0	41	20	1990	F	W 4-1
Calgary	5	4	1	30	19	11	0	132	96	1991	DSF	W 4-3
Chicago	4	3	1	20	12	8	0	102	77	1992	CF	L 0-4
Dallas	2	1	1	9	5	4	0	36	30	1991	CF	L 1-4
Detroit	2	2	0	10	8	2	0	39	26	1988	CF	W 4-1
Los Angeles	7	5	2	36	24	12	0	154	127	1992	DSF	W 4-2
Montreal	1	1	0	3	3	0	0	15	6	1981	PR	W 3-0
NY Islanders	3	1	2	15	6	9	0	47	58	1984	F	W 4-1
Philadelphia	3	2	1	15	8	7	0	49	44	1987	F	W 4-3
Vancouver	2	2	0	9	7	2	0	35	20	1992	DF	W 4-2
Winnipeg	6	6	0	26	22	4	0	120	75	1990	DSF	W 4-3
Totals	**37**	**29**	**8**	**180**	**120**	**60**	**0**	**770**	**579**			

Playoff Results 1995-91

Year	Round	Opponent	Result	GF	GA
1992	CF	Chicago	L 0-4	8	21
	DF	Vancouver	W 4-2	18	15
	DSF	Los Angeles	W 4-2	23	18
1991	CF	Minnesota	L 1-4	14	20
	DF	Los Angeles	W 4-2	21	24
	DSF	Calgary	W 4-3	22	20

Abbreviations: Round: F – Final;
CF – conference final; **CQF** – conference quarter-final;
CSF – conference semi-final; **DF** – division final;
DSF – division semi-final; **SF** – semi-final;
QF – quarter-final; **PR** – preliminary round.

SERIES RECORDS VERSUS OTHER CLUBS

Opponent	Year	Series	Winner	W	L	GF	GA
Bos.	1988	F	Edm.	4	0	21	12
Bos.	1990	F	Edm.	4	1	20	8
Cgy.	1983	DF	Edm.	4	1	35	13
Cgy.	1984	DF	Edm.	4	3	33	27
Cgy.	1986	DF	Cgy.	3	4	24	25
Cgy.	1988	DF	Edm.	4	0	18	11
Cgy.	1991	DSF	Edm.	4	3	22	20
Chi.	1983	CF	Edm.	4	0	25	11
Chi.	1985	CF	Edm.	4	2	44	25
Chi.	1990	CF	Edm.	4	2	25	20
Chi.	1992	CF	Chi.	0	4	8	21

Opponent	Year	Series	Winner	W	L	GF	GA
Det.	1987	CF	Edm.	4	1	16	10
Det.	1988	CF	Edm.	4	1	23	16
L.A.	1982	DSF	L.A.	2	3	23	27
L.A.	1985	DSF	Edm.	3	0	11	7
L.A.	1987	DSF	Edm.	4	1	32	20
L.A.	1989	DSF	L.A.	3	4	20	25
L.A.	1990	DF	Edm.	4	0	24	10
L.A.	1991	DF	Edm.	4	2	21	20
L.A.	1992	DSF	Edm.	4	2	23	18
Min.	1984	CF	Edm.	4	0	22	10
Min.	1991	CF	Min.	1	4	14	20
Mtl.	1981	PRE	Edm.	3	0	15	6

Opponent	Year	Series	Winner	W	L	GF	GA
NYI	1981	QF	NYI	2	4	20	29
NYI	1983	F	NYI	0	4	6	17
NYI	1984	F	Edm.	4	1	21	12
Phi.	1980	PRE	Phi.	0	3	6	12
Phi.	1985	F	Edm.	4	1	21	14
Phi.	1987	F	Edm.	4	3	22	18
Van.	1986	DSF	Edm.	3	0	17	5
Van.	1992	DF	Edm.	4	2	18	15
Wpg.	1983	DSF	Edm.	3	0	14	9
Wpg.	1984	DSF	Edm.	3	0	18	7
Wpg.	1985	DF	Edm.	4	0	22	11
Wpg.	1987	DF	Edm.	4	0	17	9
Wpg.	1988	DSF	Edm.	4	1	25	17
Wpg.	1990	DSF	Edm.	4	3	24	22

HARTFORD WHALERS

PLAYOFF SCORING LEADERS

	PLAYER	YEARS	GP	G	A	TP
1.	Kevin Dineen	86-91	38	17	14	31
2.	Dean Evason	86-91	38	8	15	23
3.	Ron Francis	86-90	33	8	14	22
4.	Dave Babych	86-90	31	7	13	20
5.	Ray Ferraro	86-90	33	7	11	18
6.	John Anderson	86-89	20	6	11	17
7.	Stewart Gavin	86-88	22	8	7	15
8.	Paul MacDermid	86-89	26	5	8	13
9.	John Cullen	91-92	13	4	8	12
10.	Brad Shaw	89-92	19	4	8	12

Playoffs

	Series	W	L	GP	W	L	T	GF	GA	Last Mtg.	Round	Result
Boston	2	0	2	13	5	8	0	38	47	1991	DSF	L 2-4
Montreal	5	0	5	27	8	19	0	70	96	1992	DSF	L 3-4
Quebec	2	1	1	9	5	4	0	35	34	1987	DSF	L 2-4
Totals	**9**	**1**	**8**	**49**	**18**	**31**	**0**	**143**	**177**			

Playoff Results 1995-91

Year	Round	Opponent	Result	GF	GA
1992	DSF	Montreal	L 3-4	18	21
1991	DSF	Boston	L 2-4	17	24

Abbreviations: Round: F – Final;
CF – conference final; **CQF** – conference quarter-final;
CSF – conference semi-final; **DF** – division final;
DSF – division semi-final; **SF** – semi-final;
QF – quarter-final; **PR** – preliminary round.

SERIES RECORDS VERSUS OTHER CLUBS

Opponent	Year	Series	Winner	W	L	GF	GA
Bos.	1990	DSF	Bos.	3	4	21	23
Bos.	1991	DSF	Bos.	2	4	17	24

Opponent	Year	Series	Winner	W	L	GF	GA
Mtl.	1980	PRE	Mtl.	0	3	8	18
Mtl.	1986	DF	Mtl.	3	4	13	16
Mtl.	1988	DSF	Mtl.	2	4	20	23
Mtl.	1989	DSF	Mtl.	0	4	11	18
Mtl.	1992	DSF	Mtl.	3	4	18	21

Opponent	Year	Series	Winner	W	L	GF	GA
Que.	1986	DSF	Hfd.	3	0	16	7
Que.	1987	DSF	Que.	2	4	19	27

LOS ANGELES KINGS

Playoffs

	Series	W	L	GP	W	L	T	GF	GA	Last Mtg.	Round	Result
Boston	2	0	2	13	5	8	0	38	56	1977	QF	L 2-4
Calgary	6	4	2	26	13	13	0	105	112	1993	DSF	W 4-2
Chicago	1	0	1	5	1	4	0	7	10	1974	QF	L 1-4
Dallas	1	0	1	7	3	4	0	21	26	1968	QF	L 3-4
Edmonton	7	2	5	36	12	24	0	124	150	1992	DSF	L 2-4
Montreal	1	0	1	5	1	4	0	12	15	1993	F	L 1-4
NY Islanders	1	0	1	4	1	3	0	10	21	1980	PR	L 1-3
NY Rangers	2	0	2	6	1	5	0	14	32	1981	PR	L 1-3
St. Louis	1	0	1	4	0	4	0	5	16	1969	SF	L 0-4
Toronto	3	1	2	12	5	7	0	31	41	1993	CF	W 4-3
Vancouver	3	2	1	17	9	8	0	66	60	1993	DF	W 4-2
Defunct Clubs	1	1	0	7	4	3	0	23	25			
Totals	**29**	**10**	**19**	**142**	**55**	**87**	**0**	**459**	**568**			

Playoff Results 1995-91

Year	Round	Opponent	Result	GF	GA
1993	F	Montreal	L 1-4	12	15
	CF	Toronto	W 4-3	22	23
	DF	Vancouver	W 4-2	26	25
	DSF	Calgary	W 4-2	33	28
1992	DSF	Edmonton	L 2-4	18	23
1991	DF	Edmonton	L 2-4	20	21
	DSF	Vancouver	W 4-2	26	16

Abbreviations: Round: F – Final; **CF** – conference final; **CQF** – conference quarter-final; **CSF** – conference semi-final; **DF** – division final; **DSF** – division semi-final; **SF** – semi-final; **QF** – quarter-final; **PR** – preliminary round.

PLAYOFF SCORING LEADERS

PLAYER	YEARS	GP	G	A	TP
1. Wayne Gretzky	89-93	60	29	65	94
2. Luc Robitaille	87-93	73	34	41	75
3. Dave Taylor	78-93	92	26	33	59
4. Tomas Sandstrom	90-93	50	17	28	45
5. Marcel Dionne	76-85	43	20	23	43
6. Steve Duchesne	87-91	43	13	26	39
7. Bernie Nicholls	82-89	34	16	21	37
8. Tony Granato	90-93	52	13	24	37
9. Mike Murphy	74-82	45	11	20	31
10. Mike Donnelly	91-93	42	12	11	23

SERIES RECORDS VERSUS OTHER CLUBS

Opponent	Year	Series	Winner	W	L	GF	GA
Atl.	1976	PRE	L.A.	2	0	3	1
Atl.	1977	PRE	L.A.	2	1	11	7
Bos.	1976	QF	Bos.	3	4	14	26
Bos.	1977	QF	Bos.	2	4	24	30
Cgy.	1988	DSF	Cgy.	1	4	18	30
Cgy.	1989	DF	Cgy.	0	4	11	22
Cgy.	1990	DSF	L.A.	4	2	29	24
Cgy.	1993	DSF	L.A.	4	2	33	28
Chi.	1974	QF	Chi.	1	4	7	10

Opponent	Year	Series	Winner	W	L	GF	GA
Edm.	1982	DSF	L.A.	3	2	27	23
Edm.	1985	DSF	Edm.	0	3	7	11
Edm.	1987	DSF	Edm.	1	4	20	32
Edm.	1989	DSF	L.A.	4	3	25	20
Edm.	1990	DF	Edm.	0	4	10	24
Edm.	1991	DF	Edm.	2	4	20	21
Edm.	1992	DSF	Edm.	2	4	18	23
Min.	1968	QF	Min.	3	4	21	26
Mtl.	1993	F	Mtl.	1	4	12	15
NYI	1980	PRE	NYI	1	3	10	21

Opponent	Year	Series	Winner	W	L	GF	GA
NYR	1979	PRE	NYR	0	2	2	9
NYR	1981	PRE	NYR	1	3	12	23
St.L	1969	SF	St.L	0	4	5	16
Tor.	1975	PRE	Tor.	1	2	6	7
Tor.	1978	PRE	Tor.	0	2	3	11
Tor.	1993	CF	L.A.	4	3	22	23
Van.	1982	DF	Van.	1	4	14	19
Van.	1991	DSF	L.A.	4	2	26	16
Van.	1993	DF	L.A.	4	2	26	25
Oak.	1969	QF	L.A.	4	3	23	25

MONTREAL CANADIENS

PLAYOFF SCORING LEADERS

	PLAYER	YEARS	GP	G	A	TP
1.	Jean Beliveau	54-71	162	79	97	176
2.	Jacques Lemaire	68-79	145	61	78	139
3.	Larry Robinson	73-89	203	25	109	134
4.	Guy Lafleur	72-84	124	57	76	133
5.	Henri Richard	56-75	180	49	80	129
6.	Yvan Cournoyer	65-78	147	64	63	127
7.	Maurice Richard	44-60	133	82	44	126
8.	Bernie Geoffrion	51-64	127	56	59	115
9.	Steve Shutt	73-84	96	50	48	98
10.	Dickie Moore	52-63	112	38	56	94

Playoffs

	Series	W	L	GP	W	L	T	GF	GA	Last Mtg.	Round	Result
Boston	28	21	7	139	87	52	0	430	339	1994	CQF	L 3-4
Buffalo	6	4	2	31	18	13	0	114	94	1993	DF	W 4-0
Calgary	2	1	1	11	6	5	0	31	32	1989	F	L 2-4
Chicago	17	12	5	81	50	29	2	261	185	1976	QF	W 4-0
Dallas	2	1	1	13	7	6	0	48	37	1980	QF	L 3-4
Detroit	12	5	7	62	33	29	0	161	149	1978	QF	W 4-1
Edmonton	1	0	1	3	0	3	0	6	15	1981	PR	L 0-3
Hartford	5	5	0	27	19	8	0	96	70	1992	DSF	W 4-3
Los Angeles	1	1	0	5	4	1	0	15	12	1993	F	W 4-1
NY Islanders	4	3	1	22	14	8	0	64	55	1993	CF	W 4-1
NY Rangers	13	7	6	55	32	21	2	171	139	1986	CF	W 4-1
Philadelphia	4	3	1	21	14	7	0	72	52	1989	CF	W 4-2
Quebec	5	3	2	31	17	14	0	105	85	1993	DSF	W 4-2
St. Louis	3	3	0	12	12	0	0	42	14	1977	QF	W 4-0
Toronto	15	8	7	71	42	29	0	215	160	1979	QF	W 4-0
Vancouver	1	1	0	5	4	1	0	20	9	1975	QF	W 4-1
Defunct Clubs	11*	6	4	28	15	9	4	70	71			
Totals	**130***	**84**	**45**	**617**	**374**	**235**	**8**	**1921**	**1518**			

* 1919 Final incomplete due to influenza epidemic.

Playoff Results 1995-91

Year	Round	Opponent	Result	GF	GA
1994	CQF	Boston	L 3-4	20	22
1993	F	Los Angeles	W 4-1	15	12
	CF	NY Islanders	W 4-1	16	11
	DF	Buffalo	W 4-0	16	12
	DSF	Quebec	W 4-2	19	16
1992	DF	Boston	L 0-4	8	14
	DSF	Hartford	W 4-3	21	18
1991	DF	Boston	L 3-4	18	18
	DSF	Buffalo	W 4-2	29	24

Abbreviations: Round: F – Final; **CF** – conference final; **CQF** – conference quarter-final; **CSF** – conference semi-final; **DF** – division final; **DSF** – division semi-final; **SF** – semi-final; **QF** – quarter-final; **PR** – preliminary round.

SERIES RECORDS VERSUS OTHER CLUBS

Opponent	Year	Series	Winner	W	L	T	GF	GA
Bos.	1929	SF	Bos.	0	3		2	5
Bos.	1930	F	Mtl.	2	0		7	3
Bos.	1931	SF	Mtl.	3	2		13	13
Bos.	1943	SF	Bos.	1	4		17	18
Bos.	1946	F	Mtl.	4	1		19	13
Bos.	1947	SF	Mtl.	4	1		16	10
Bos.	1952	SF	Mtl.	4	3		18	12
Bos.	1953	F	Mtl.	4	1		16	9
Bos.	1954	SF	Mtl.	4	0		16	4
Bos.	1955	SF	Mtl.	4	1		16	9
Bos.	1957	F	Mtl.	4	1		15	6
Bos.	1958	F	Mtl.	4	2		16	14
Bos.	1968	QF	Mtl.	4	0		15	8
Bos.	1969	SF	Mtl.	4	2		15	16
Bos.	1971	QF	Mtl.	4	3		28	26
Bos.	1977	F	Mtl.	4	0		16	6
Bos.	1978	F	Mtl.	4	2		18	13
Bos.	1979	SF	Mtl.	4	3		25	20
Bos.	1984	DSF	Mtl.	3	0		10	2
Bos.	1985	DSF	Mtl.	3	2		19	17
Bos.	1986	DSF	Mtl.	3	0		10	6
Bos.	1987	DSF	Mtl.	4	0		19	11
Bos.	1988	DF	Bos.	1	4		10	15
Bos.	1989	DF	Mtl.	4	1		16	13
Bos.	1990	DF	Bos.	1	4		12	16
Bos.	1991	DF	Bos.	3	4		18	18
Bos.	1992	DF	Bos.	0	4		8	14
Bos.	1994	CQF	Bos.	3	4		20	22
Buf.	1973	QF	Mtl.	4	2		21	16
Buf.	1975	SF	Buf.	2	4		29	21
Buf.	1983	DSF	Buf.	0	3		2	8
Buf.	1990	DSF	Mtl.	4	2		17	13
Buf.	1991	DSF	Mtl.	4	2		29	24
Buf.	1993	DF	Mtl.	4	0		16	12
Cgy.	1986	F	Mtl.	4	1		15	13
Cgy.	1989	F	Cgy.	2	4		16	19
Chi.	1930	QF*	Mtl.	1	0	1	3	2
Chi.	1931	F	Mtl.	3	2		11	8
Chi.	1934	QF*	Chi.	0	1	1	3	4
Chi.	1938	QF	Chi.	1	2		8	11
Chi.	1941	QF	Chi.	1	2		7	8
Chi.	1944	F	Mtl.	4	0		16	8
Chi.	1946	SF	Mtl.	4	0		26	7
Chi.	1953	SF	Mtl.	4	3		18	14
Chi.	1959	SF	Mtl.	4	2		21	16
Chi.	1960	SF	Mtl.	4	0		14	6
Chi.	1961	SF	Chi.	2	4		15	16
Chi.	1962	SF	Chi.	2	4		13	19
Chi.	1965	F	Mtl.	4	3		18	12
Chi.	1968	SF	Mtl.	4	1		22	10
Chi.	1971	F	Mtl.	4	3		20	18
Chi.	1973	F	Mtl.	4	2		33	23
Chi.	1976	QF	Mtl.	4	0		13	3
Det.	1937	SF	Det.	2	3		8	13
Det.	1939	QF	Det.	1	2		5	8
Det.	1942	QF	Det.	1	2		8	8
Det.	1949	SF	Det.	3	4		14	17
Det.	1951	SF	Mtl.	4	2		13	12
Det.	1952	F	Det.	0	4		2	11
Det.	1954	F	Det.	3	4		12	14
Det.	1955	F	Det.	3	4		20	27
Det.	1956	F	Mtl.	4	1		18	9
Det.	1958	SF	Mtl.	4	0		19	6
Det.	1966	F	Mtl.	4	2		18	14
Det.	1978	QF	Mtl.	4	1		24	10
Edm.	1981	PRE	Edm.	0	3		6	15
Hfd.	1980	PRE	Mtl.	3	0		18	8
Hfd.	1986	DF	Mtl.	4	3		16	13
Hfd.	1988	DSF	Mtl.	4	2		23	20
Hfd.	1989	DSF	Mtl.	4	0		18	11
Hfd.	1992	DSF	Mtl.	4	3		21	18
L.A.	1993	F	Mtl.	4	1		15	12
Min.	1971	SF	Mtl.	4	2		27	19
Min.	1980	QF	Min.	3	4		21	18
NYI	1976	SF	Mtl.	4	1		17	14
NYI	1977	SF	Mtl.	4	2		19	13
NYI	1984	CF	NYI	2	4		12	17
NYI	1993	CF	Mtl.	4	1		16	11
NYR	1930	SF	Mtl.	2	0		4	1
NYR	1932	SF	NYR	1	3		9	13
NYR	1933	QF*	NYR	0	1	1	5	8
NYR	1935	QF*	NYR	0	1	1	5	6
NYR	1950	SF	NYR	1	4		7	15
NYR	1956	SF	Mtl.	4	1		24	9
NYR	1957	SF	Mtl.	4	1		22	12
NYR	1967	SF	Mtl.	4	0		14	8
NYR	1969	QF	Mtl.	4	0		16	7
NYR	1972	QF	NYR	2	4		14	19
NYR	1974	QF	NYR	2	4		17	21
NYR	1979	F	Mtl.	4	1		19	11
NYR	1986	CF	Mtl.	4	1		15	9
Phi.	1973	SF	Mtl.	4	1		19	13
Phi.	1976	F	Mtl.	4	0		14	9
Phi.	1987	CF	Phi.	2	4		22	22
Phi.	1989	CF	Mtl.	4	2		17	8
Que.	1982	DSF	Que.	2	3		16	11
Que.	1984	DF	Mtl.	4	2		20	13
Que.	1985	DF	Que.	3	4		24	24
Que.	1987	DF	Mtl.	4	3		26	21
Que.	1993	DSF	Mtl.	4	2		19	16
St.L	1968	F	Mtl.	4	0		11	7
St.L	1969	F	Mtl.	4	0		12	3
St.L	1977	QF	Mtl.	4	0		19	4
Tor.	1918	NHLF*	Tor.	1	1		7	10
Tor.	1925	NHLF*	Mtl.	2	0		5	2
Tor.	1944	SF	Mtl.	4	1		23	6
Tor.	1945	SF	Tor.	2	4		21	15
Tor.	1947	F	Tor.	2	4		13	13
Tor.	1951	F	Tor.	1	4		10	13
Tor.	1959	F	Mtl.	4	1		18	12
Tor.	1960	F	Mtl.	4	0		15	5
Tor.	1963	SF	Tor.	1	4		6	14
Tor.	1964	SF	Tor.	3	4		14	17
Tor.	1965	SF	Mtl.	4	2		17	14
Tor.	1966	SF	Mtl.	4	0		15	6
Tor.	1967	F	Tor.	2	4		16	17
Tor.	1978	SF	Mtl.	4	0		16	6
Tor.	1979	QF	Mtl.	4	0		19	10
Van.	1975	QF	Mtl.	4	1		20	9

DEFUNCT CLUBS

				W	L	T	GF	GA
Mtl.M	1927	QF*	Mtl.	1	0	1	2	1
Mtl.M	1928	SF	Mtl.M	0	1	1	2	3
Ott.	1919	NHLF	Mtl.	4	1		26	18
Ott.	1923	NHLF*	Ott.	1	1		2	3
Ott.	1924	NHLF*	Mtl.	2	0		5	2
Ott.	1927	SF*	Ott.	0	1	1	1	5
Seattle	1919	F	—**	2	2	1	10	19
Van/Cgy	1924	F	Mtl.	4	0		14	4

* Total-goals series

** No decision. Series suspended due to Spanish influenza epidemic.

NEW JERSEY DEVILS

Playoffs

	Series	W	L	GP	W	L	T	GF	GA	Last Mtg.	Round	Result
Boston	3	2	1	18	11	7	0	55	52	1995	CQF	W 4-1
Buffalo	1	1	0	7	4	3	0	14	14	1994	CQF	W 4-3
Detroit	1	1	0	4	4	0	0	16	7	1995	F	W 4-0
NY Islanders	1	1	0	6	4	2	0	23	18	1988	DSF	W 4-2
NY Rangers	2	0	2	14	6	8	0	41	46	1994	CF	L 3-4
Philadelphia	2	1	1	8	4	4	0	23	20	1995	CF	W 4-2
Pittsburgh	3	1	2	17	8	9	0	47	56	1995	CSF	W 4-1
Washington	2	1	1	13	6	7	0	43	44	1990	DSF	L 2-4
Totals	15	8	7	87	47	40	0	262	257			

Playoff Results 1995-91

Year	Round	Opponent	Result	GF	GA
1995	F	Detroit	W 4-0	16	7
	CF	Philadelphia	W 4-2	20	14
	CSF	Pittsburgh	W 4-1	17	8
	CQF	Boston	W 4-1	14	5
1994	CF	NY Rangers	L 3-4	16	18
	CSF	Boston	W 4-2	22	17
	CQF	Buffalo	W 4-3	14	14
1993	DSF	Pittsburgh	L 1-4	13	23
1992	DSF	NY Rangers	L 3-4	25	28
1991	DSF	Pittsburgh	L 3-4	17	25

Abbreviations: Round: F – Final; **CF** – conference final; **CQF** – conference quarter-final; **CSF** – conference semi-final; **DF** – division final; **DSF** – division semi-final; **SF** – semi-final; **QF** – quarter-final; **PR** – preliminary round.

PLAYOFF SCORING LEADERS

	PLAYER	YEARS	GP	G	A	TP
1.	John MacLean	88-95	78	27	39	66
2.	Claude Lemieux	91-95	59	30	17	47
3.	Bruce Driver	88-95	82	10	32	42
4.	Stephane Richer	92-95	51	16	24	40
5.	Scott Stevens	92-95	52	7	19	26
6.	Peter Stastny	90-93	25	9	15	24
7.	Patrik Sundstrom	88-91	26	8	16	24
8.	Tommu Albelin	91-95	49	6	14	20
9.	Mark Johnson	88-90	20	10	8	18
10.	Scott Niedermayer	88-95	45	6	12	18

SERIES RECORDS VERSUS OTHER CLUBS

Opponent	Year	Series	Winner	W	L	GF	GA
Bos.	1988	CF	Bos.	3	4	19	30
Bos.	1994	CSF	N.J.	4	2	22	17
Bos.	1995	CQF	N.J.	4	0	14	5
Buf.	1994	CQF	N.J.	4	3	14	14
NYI	1988	DSF	N.J.	4	2	23	18

Note: Includes series played by Colorado Rockies, 1978.

Opponent	Year	Series	Winner	W	L	GF	GA
Det.	1995	F	N.J.	4	0	16	7
NYR	1992	DSF	NYR	3	4	25	28
NYR	1994	CF	NYR	3	4	16	18
Phi.	1978	PRE	Phi.	0	2	3	6
Phi.	1995	CF	N.J.	4	2	20	14

Opponent	Year	Series	Winner	W	L	GF	GA
Pit.	1991	DSF	Pit.	3	4	21	21
Pit.	1993	DSF	Pit.	1	4	13	23
Pit.	1995	CSF	N.J.	4	1	17	8
Wsh.	1988	DF	N.J.	4	3	25	23
Wsh.	1990	DSF	Wsh.	2	4	18	2

NEW YORK ISLANDERS

Playoffs

	Series	W	L	GP	W	L	T	GF	GA	Last Mtg.	Round	Result
Boston	2	2	0	11	8	3	0	49	35	1983	CF	W 4-2
Buffalo	3	3	0	16	12	4	0	59	45	1980	SF	W 4-2
Chicago	2	2	0	6	6	0	0	21	6	1979	QF	W 4-0
Dallas	1	1	0	5	4	1	0	26	16	1981	F	W 4-1
Edmonton	3	2	1	15	9	6	0	58	47	1984	F	L 1-4
Los Angeles	1	1	0	4	3	1	0	21	10	1980	PR	W 3-1
Montreal	4	1	3	22	8	14	0	55	64	1993	CF	L 1-4
New Jersey	1	0	1	6	2	4	0	18	23	1988	DSF	L 2-4
NY Rangers	8	5	3	39	20	19	0	129	132	1994	CQF	L 0-4
Philadelphia	4	1	3	25	11	14	0	69	83	1987	DF	L 3-4
Pittsburgh	3	3	0	19	11	8	0	67	58	1993	DF	W 4-3
Quebec	1	1	0	4	4	0	0	18	9	1982	CF	W 4-0
Toronto	2	1	1	10	6	4	0	33	20	1981	PR	W 3-0
Vancouver	2	2	0	6	4	0	0	26	14	1982	F	W 4-0
Washington	6	5	1	30	18	12	0	99	88	1993	DSF	W 4-2
Totals	43	30	13	218	128	90	0	748	650			

Playoff Results 1995-91

Year	Round	Opponent	Result	GF	GA
1994	CQF	NY Rangers	L 0-4	3	22
1993	CF	Montreal	L 1-4	11	16
	DF	Pittsburgh	W 4-3	24	27
	DSF	Washington	W 4-2	23	22

Abbreviations: Round: F – Final; **CF** – conference final; **CQF** – conference quarter-final; **CSF** – conference semi-final; **DF** – division final; **DSF** – division semi-final; **SF** – semi-final; **QF** – quarter-final; **PR** – preliminary round.

PLAYOFF SCORING LEADERS

	PLAYER	YEARS	GP	G	A	TP
1.	Bryan Trottier	76-90	175	64	106	170
2.	Denis Potvin	78-88	185	56	108	164
3.	Mike Bossy	78-87	129	85	75	160
4.	Clark Gillies	75-86	159	47	46	93
5.	Bob Bourne	75-86	129	38	54	92
6.	Bob Nystrom	75-85	157	39	44	83
7.	John Tonelli	79-85	113	28	55	83
8.	Butch Goring	80-84	99	28	40	68
9.	Brent Sutter	82-90	88	24	35	59
10.	Stefan Persson	78-85	102	7	50	57

SERIES RECORDS VERSUS OTHER CLUBS

Opponent	Year	Series	Winner	W	L	GF	GA
Bos.	1980	QF	NYI	4	1	19	14
Bos.	1983	CF	NYI	4	2	30	21
Buf.	1976	QF	NYI	4	2	21	18
Buf.	1977	QF	NYI	4	0	16	10
Buf.	1980	SF	NYI	4	2	22	17
Chi.	1977	PRE	NYI	2	0	7	3
Chi.	1979	QF	NYI	4	0	14	3
Edm.	1981	QF	NYI	4	2	29	20
Edm.	1983	F	NYI	4	0	17	6
Edm.	1984	F	Edm.	1	4	12	21
L.A.	1980	PRE	NYI	3	1	21	10
Min.	1981	F	NYI	4	1	26	16

Opponent	Year	Series	Winner	W	L	GF	GA
Mtl.	1976	SF	Mtl.	1	4	14	17
Mtl.	1977	SF	Mtl.	2	4	13	19
Mtl.	1984	CF	NYI	4	2	17	12
Mtl.	1993	CF	Mtl.	1	4	11	16
N.J.	1988	DSF	N.J.	2	4	18	23
NYR	1975	PRE	NYI	2	1	10	13
NYR	1979	SF	NYR	2	4	13	18
NYR	1981	SF	NYI	4	0	22	8
NYR	1982	DF	NYI	4	2	27	20
NYR	1983	DF	NYI	4	2	28	15
NYR	1984	DSF	NYI	3	2	13	14
NYR	1990	DSF	NYR	1	4	13	22
NYR	1994	CQF	NYR	0	4	3	22
Phi.	1975	SF	Phi.	3	4	16	19
Phi.	1980	F	NYI	4	2	26	25
Phi.	1985	DF	Phi.	1	4	11	16
Phi.	1987	DF	Phi.	3	4	16	23

Opponent	Year	Series	Winner	W	L	GF	GA
Pit.	1975	QF	NYI	4	3	21	18
Pit.	1982	DSF	NYI	3	2	22	13
Pit.	1993	DF	NYI	4	3	24	27
Que.	1982	CF	NYI	4	0	18	9
Tor.	1978	QF	Tor.	3	4	13	16
Tor.	1981	PRE	NYI	3	0	20	4
Van.	1976	PRE	NYI	2	0	8	4
Van.	1982	F	NYI	4	0	18	10
Wsh.	1983	DSF	NYI	3	1	19	11
Wsh.	1984	DF	NYI	4	1	20	13
Wsh.	1985	DSF	NYI	3	2	14	12
Wsh.	1986	DSF	Wsh.	0	3	4	11
Wsh.	1987	DSF	NYI	4	3	19	19
Wsh.	1993	DSF	NYI	4	2	23	22

TEAM-BY-TEAM PLAYOFF HISTORY • 23

NEW YORK RANGERS

PLAYOFF SCORING LEADERS

	PLAYER	YEARS	GP	G	A	TP
1.	Brian Leetch	88-95	56	25	47	72
2.	Rod Gilbert	62-75	79	34	33	67
3.	Mark Messier	92-95	44	22	35	57
4.	Don Maloney	79-87	85	22	35	57
5.	Walt Tkaczuk	69-80	93	19	32	51
6.	Steve Vickers	73-81	68	24	25	49
7.	Ron Greschner	75-90	84	17	32	49
8.	Ron Duguay	78-87	69	28	19	47
9.	Anders Hedberg	79-85	58	22	24	46
10.	Brad Park	69-75	64	12	32	44

Playoffs

	Series	W	L	GP	W	L	T	GF	GA	Last Mtg.	Round	Result
Boston	9	3	6	42	18	22	2	104	114	1973	QF	W 4-1
Buffalo	1	0	1	3	1	2	0	6	11	1978	PR	L 1-2
Calgary	1	1	0	4	3	1	0	14	8	1980	PR	W 3-1
Chicago	5	1	4	24	10	14	0	54	66	1973	SF	L 1-4
Detroit	5	1	4	23	10	13	0	49	57	1950	F	L 3-4
Los Angeles	2	2	0	6	5	1	0	32	14	1981	PR	W 3-1
Montreal	13	6	7	55	21	32	2	139	171	1986	CF	L 1-4
New Jersey	2	2	0	14	8	6	0	46	41	1994	CF	W 4-3
NY Islanders	8	3	5	39	19	20	0	132	129	1994	CQF	W 4-0
Philadelphia	9	4	5	42	19	23	0	140	137	1995	CSF	L 0-4
Pittsburgh	2	0	2	10	2	8	0	30	44	1992	DF	L 2-4
Quebec	1	1	0	6	4	2	0	25	19	1995	CQF	W 4-2
St. Louis	1	1	0	6	4	2	0	29	22	1981	QF	W 4-2
Toronto	8	5	3	35	19	16	0	86	86	1971	QF	W 4-2
Vancouver	1	1	0	7	4	3	0	21	19	1994	F	W 4-3
Washington	4	2	2	22	11	11	0	71	75	1994	CSF	W 4-1
Defunct	9	6	3	22	11	7	4	43	29			
Totals	81	39	42	360	169	183	8	1021	1041			

Playoff Results 1995-91

Year	Round	Opponent	Result	GF	GA
1995	CSF	Philadelphia	L 0-4	10	18
	CQF	Quebec	W 4-2	25	19
1994	F	Vancouver	W 4-3	21	19
	CF	New Jersey	W 4-3	18	16
	CSF	Washington	W 4-1	20	12
	CQF	NY Islanders	W 4-0	22	3
1992	DF	Pittsburgh	L 2-4	19	24
	DSF	New Jersey	W 4-3	28	25
1991	DSF	Washington	L 2-4	16	16

Abbreviations: Round: F – Final; **CF** – conference final; **CQF** – conference quarter-final; **CSF** – conference semi-final; **DF** – division final; **DSF** – division semi-final; **SF** – semi-final; **QF** – quarter-final; **PR** – preliminary round.

SERIES RECORDS VERSUS OTHER CLUBS

Opponent	Year	Series	Winner	W	L	T	GF	GA
Atl.	1980	PRE	NYR	3	1		14	8
Bos.	1927	SF*	Bos.	0	1	1	1	3
Bos.	1928	SF*	NYR	1	0	1	5	2
Bos.	1929	F	Bos.	0	2		1	4
Bos.	1939	SF	Bos.	3	4		12	14
Bos.	1940	SF	NYR	4	2		15	9
Bos.	1958	SF	Bos.	2	4		16	28
Bos.	1970	QF	Bos.	2	4		16	25
Bos.	1972	F	Bos.	2	4		16	18
Bos.	1973	QF	NYR	4	1		22	11
Buf.	1978	PRE	Buf.	1	2		6	11
Chi.	1931	SF*	Chi.	0	2		0	3
Chi.	1968	QF	Chi.	2	4		12	18
Chi.	1971	SF	Chi.	3	4		14	21
Chi.	1972	SF	NYR	4	0		17	9
Chi.	1973	SF	Chi.	1	4		11	15
Det.	1933	SF*	NYR	2	0		6	3
Det.	1937	F	Det.	2	3		8	9
Det.	1941	QF	Det.	1	2		6	6
Det.	1948	SF	Det.	2	4		12	17
Det.	1950	F	Det.	3	4		17	22
L.A.	1979	PRE	NYR	2	0		9	2
L.A.	1981	PRE	NYR	3	1		23	12
Mtl.	1930	SF	Mtl.	0	2		1	4
Mtl.	1932	SF	NYR	3	1		13	9
Mtl.	1933	QF*	NYR	1	0	1	8	5
Mtl.	1935	QF*	NYR	1	0	1	6	5
Mtl.	1950	SF	NYR	4	1		15	7
Mtl.	1956	SF	Mtl.	1	4		9	24
Mtl.	1957	SF	Mtl.	1	4		12	22
Mtl.	1967	SF	Mtl.	0	4		8	14
Mtl.	1969	QF	Mtl.	0	4		7	16
Mtl.	1972	QF	NYR	4	2		19	14
Mtl.	1974	QF	NYR	4	2		21	17
Mtl.	1979	F	Mtl.	1	4		11	19
Mtl.	1986	CF	Mtl.	1	4		9	15

Opponent	Year	Series	Winner	W	L	T	GF	GA
N.J.	1992	DSF	NYR	4	3		28	25
N.J.	1994	CF	NYR	4	3		18	16
NYI	1975	PRE	NYI	1	2		13	10
NYI	1979	SF	NYR	4	2		18	13
NYI	1981	SF	NYI	0	4		8	22
NYI	1982	DF	NYI	2	4		20	27
NYI	1983	DF	NYI	2	4		15	28
NYI	1984	DSF	NYI	2	3		14	13
NYI	1990	DSF	NYR	4	1		22	13
NYI	1994	CQF	NYR	4	0		22	3
Phi.	1974	SF	Phi.	3	4		17	22
Phi.	1979	QF	NYR	4	1		28	8
Phi.	1980	QF	Phi.	1	4		7	14
Phi.	1982	DSF	NYR	3	1		19	15
Phi.	1983	DSF	NYR	3	0		18	9
Phi.	1985	DSF	Phi.	0	3		10	14
Phi.	1986	DSF	NYR	3	2		18	15
Phi.	1987	DSF	Phi.	2	4		13	22
Phi.	1995	CSF	Phi.	0	4		10	18
Pit.	1989	DSF	Pit.	0	4		11	19
Pit.	1992	DF	Pit.	2	4		19	24
Que.	1995	CQF	NYR	4	2		25	19
St.L	1981	QF	NYR	4	2		29	22
Tor.	1929	SF	NYR	2	0		3	1
Tor.	1932	F	Tor.	0	3		10	18
Tor.	1933	F	NYR	3	1		11	5
Tor.	1937	QF	NYR	2	0		5	1
Tor.	1940	F	NYR	4	2		14	11
Tor.	1942	SF	Tor.	2	4		12	13
Tor.	1962	SF	Tor.	2	4		15	22
Tor.	1971	QF	NYR	4	2		16	15
Van.	1994	F	NYR	4	3		21	19
Wsh.	1986	DF	NYR	4	2		20	25
Wsh.	1990	DF	Wsh.	1	4		15	22
Wsh.	1991	DSF	Wsh.	2	4		16	16
Wsh.	1994	CSF	NYR	4	1		20	12

DEFUNCT CLUBS

Opponent	Year	Series	Winner	W	L	T	GF	GA
Mtl.M	1928	F	NYR	3	2		5	6
Mtl.M	1931	QF*	NYR	2	0		8	1
Mtl.M	1934	QF*	Mtl.M	0	1	1	1	2
Mtl.M	1935	SF*	Mtl.M	0	1	1	4	5
Mtl.M	1937	SF	NYR	2	0		5	0
NYA	1929	QF*	NYR	1	0	1	1	0
NYA	1938	QF	NYA	1	2		7	8
Ott.	1930	QF*	NYR	1	0	1	6	3
Pit.P	1928	QF*	NYR	1	1		6	4

* Total-goals series

PHILADELPHIA FLYERS

Playoffs

	Series	W	L	GP	W	L	T	GF	GA	Last Mtg.	Round	Result
Boston	4	2	2	20	9	11	0	57	60	1978	QF	L 1-4
Buffalo	3	3	0	16	12	4	0	53	36	1995	CQF	W 4-1
Calgary	2	1	1	11	7	4	0	43	28	1981	QF	L 3-4
Chicago	1	0	1	4	0	4	0	8	20	1971	QF	L 0-4
Dallas	2	2	0	11	8	3	0	41	26	1980	SF	W 4-1
Edmonton	3	1	2	15	7	8	0	44	49	1987	F	L 3-4
Montreal	4	1	3	21	6	15	0	52	72	1989	CF	L 2-4
New Jersey	2	1	1	8	4	4	0	20	23	1995	CF	L 2-4
NY Islanders	4	3	1	25	14	11	0	83	69	1987	DF	W 4-3
NY Rangers	9	5	4	42	23	19	0	137	140	1995	CSF	W 4-0
Pittsburgh	1	1	0	7	4	3	0	31	24	1989	DF	W 4-3
Quebec	2	2	0	11	7	4	0	39	29	1985	CF	W 4-2
St. Louis	2	0	2	11	3	8	0	20	34	1969	QF	L 0-4
Toronto	3	3	0	17	12	5	0	67	47	1977	QF	W 4-2
Vancouver	1	1	0	3	2	1	0	15	9	1979	PR	W 2-1
Washington	3	1	2	16	7	9	0	55	65	1989	DSF	W 4-2
Totals	**46**	**27**	**19**	**238**	**126**	**112**	**0**	**765**	**731**			

Playoff Results 1995-91

Year	Round	Opponent	Result	GF	GA
1995	CF	New Jersey	L 2-4	14	20
	CSF	NY Rangers	W 4-0	18	10
	CQF	Buffalo	W 4-1	18	13

Abbreviations: Round: F – Final;
CF – conference final; **CQF** – conference quarter-final;
CSF – conference semi-final; **DF** – division final;
DSF – division semi-final; **SF** – semi-final;
QF – quarter-final; **PR** – preliminary round.

PLAYOFF SCORING LEADERS

	PLAYER	YEARS	GP	G	A	TP
1.	Bobby Clarke	71-84	136	42	77	119
2.	Brian Propp	80-89	116	52	60	112
3.	Bill Barber	73-83	129	53	55	108
4.	Rick MacLeish	71-81	108	53	52	105
5.	Tim Kerr	81-89	73	39	31	70
6.	Reggie Leach	75-81	91	47	22	69
7.	Ken Linseman	79-82	41	11	42	53
8.	Mark Howe	83-89	82	8	45	53
9.	Paul Holmgren	77-83	67	19	31	50
10.	Rick Tocchet	85-89	71	22	26	48

SERIES RECORDS VERSUS OTHER CLUBS

Opponent	Year	Series	Winner	W	L	GF	GA
Atl.	1974	QF	Phi.	4	0	17	6
Bos.	1974	F	Phi.	4	2	15	13
Bos.	1976	SF	Phi.	4	1	19	12
Bos.	1977	SF	Bos.	0	4	8	14
Bos.	1978	QF	Bos.	1	4	15	21
Buf.	1975	F	Phi.	4	2	19	12
Buf.	1978	QF	Phi.	4	1	16	11
Buf.	1995	CQF	Phi.	4	1	18	13
Cgy.	1981	QF	Cgy.	3	4	26	22
Chi.	1971	QF	Chi.	0	4	8	20
Col.	1978	PRE	Phi.	2	0	6	3
Edm.	1980	PRE	Phi.	3	0	12	6
Edm.	1985	F	Edm.	1	4	14	21
Edm.	1987	F	Edm.	3	4	18	22
Min.	1973	QF	Phi.	4	2	14	12
Min.	1980	SF	Phi.	4	1	27	14

Opponent	Year	Series	Winner	W	L	GF	GA
Mtl.	1973	SF	Mtl.	1	4	13	19
Mtl.	1976	F	Mtl.	0	4	9	14
Mtl.	1987	CF	Phi.	4	2	22	22
Mtl.	1989	CF	Mtl.	2	4	8	17
N.J.	1995	CF	N.J.	2	4	14	20
NYI	1975	SF	Phi.	4	3	19	16
NYI	1980	F	NYI	2	4	25	26
NYI	1985	DF	Phi.	4	1	16	11
NYI	1987	DF	Phi.	4	3	23	16
NYR	1974	SF	Phi.	4	3	22	17
NYR	1979	QF	NYR	1	4	8	28
NYR	1980	QF	Phi.	4	1	14	7
NYR	1982	DSF	NYR	1	3	15	19
NYR	1983	DSF	NYR	0	3	9	18
NYR	1985	DSF	Phi.	3	0	14	10
NYR	1986	DSF	NYR	2	3	15	18
NYR	1987	DSF	Phi.	4	2	22	13
NYR	1995	CSF	Phi.	4	0	18	10

Opponent	Year	Series	Winner	W	L	GF	GA
Pit.	1989	DF	Phi.	4	3	31	24
Que.	1981	PRE	Phi.	3	2	22	17
Que.	1985	CF	Phi.	4	2	17	12
St.L	1968	QF	St.L	3	4	17	17
St.L	1969	QF	St.L	0	4	3	17
Tor.	1975	QF	Phi.	4	0	15	6
Tor.	1976	QF	Phi.	4	3	33	23
Tor.	1977	QF	Phi.	4	2	19	18
Van.	1979	PRE	Phi.	2	1	15	9
Wsh.	1984	DSF	Wsh.	0	3	5	15
Wsh.	1988	DSF	Wsh.	3	4	25	31
Wsh.	1989	DSF	Phi.	4	2	25	19

PITTSBURGH PENGUINS

Playoffs

	Series	W	L	GP	W	L	T	GF	GA	Last Mtg.	Round	Result
Boston	4	2	2	19	10	9	0	67	62	1992	CF	W 4-0
Buffalo	1	1	0	3	2	1	0	9	9	1979	PR	W 2-1
Chicago	2	1	1	8	4	4	0	23	24	1992	F	W 4-0
Dallas	1	1	0	6	4	2	0	28	16	1991	F	W 4-2
New Jersey	3	2	1	17	9	8	0	56	47	1995	CSF	L 1-4
NY Islanders	3	0	3	19	8	11	0	58	67	1993	DF	L 3-4
NY Rangers	2	2	0	10	8	2	0	43	30	1992	DF	W 4-2
Philadelphia	1	0	1	7	3	4	0	24	31	1989	DF	L 3-4
St. Louis	3	1	2	13	6	7	0	40	45	1981	PR	L 2-3
Toronto	2	0	2	6	2	4	0	13	21	1977	PR	L 1-2
Washington	4	3	1	25	14	11	0	85	86	1995	CQF	W 4-3
Defunct Clubs	1	1	0	4	4	0	0	13	6			
Totals	**27**	**14**	**13**	**137**	**74**	**63**	**0**	**459**	**444**			

Playoff Results 1995-91

Year	Round	Opponent	Result	GF	GA
1995	CSF	New Jersey	L 1-4	8	17
	CQF	Washington	W 4-3	29	26
1994	CQF	Washington	L 2-4	12	20
1993	DF	NY Islanders	L 3-4	27	24
	DSF	New Jersey	W 4-1	23	13
1992	**F**	**Chicago**	**W 4-0**	**15**	**10**
	CF	Boston	W 4-0	19	7
	DF	NY Rangers	W 4-2	24	19
	DSF	Washington	W 4-3	25	27
1991	**F**	**Minnesota**	**W 4-2**	**28**	**16**
	CF	Boston	W 4-2	27	18
	DF	Washington	W 4-1	19	13
	DSF	New Jersey	W 4-3	25	17

PLAYOFF SCORING LEADERS

	PLAYER	YEARS	GP	G	A	TP
1.	Mario Lemieux	89-94	66	56	66	122
2.	Kevin Stevens	89-95	86	43	57	100
3.	Ron Francis	91-95	75	27	55	82
4.	Larry Murphy	91-95	74	15	57	82
5.	Jaromir Jagr	91-95	75	31	36	67
6.	Rick Tocchet	92-94	32	15	22	37
7.	Mark Recchi	91	24	10	24	34
8.	Joe Mullen	91-95	61	16	15	31
9.	Paul Coffey	89-91	23	4	22	26
10.	Phil Bourque	89-92	56	13	12	25

SERIES RECORDS VERSUS OTHER CLUBS

Opponent	Year	Series	Winner	W	L	GF	GA
Bos.	1979	QF	Bos.	0	4	7	16
Bos.	1980	PRE	Bos.	2	3	14	21
Bos.	1991	CF	Pit.	4	2	27	18
Bos.	1992	CF	Pit.	4	0	19	7
Buf.	1979	PRE	Pit.	2	1	9	9
Chi.	1972	QF	Chi.	0	4	8	14
Chi.	1992	F	Pit.	4	0	15	10
Min.	1991	F	Pit.	4	2	28	16

Opponent	Year	Series	Winner	W	L	GF	GA
N.J.	1991	DSF	Pit.	4	3	21	21
N.J.	1993	DSF	Pit.	4	1	23	13
N.J.	1995	CSF	N.J.	1	4	8	17
NYI	1975	QF	NYI	3	4	18	21
NYI	1982	DSF	NYI	2	3	13	22
NYI	1993	DF	NYI	3	4	27	24
NYR	1989	DSF	Pit.	4	0	19	11
NYR	1992	DF	Pit.	4	2	24	19
Phi.	1989	DF	Phi.	3	4	24	31

Opponent	Year	Series	Winner	W	L	GF	GA
St.L	1970	SF	St.L	2	4	10	19
St.L	1975	PRE	Pit.	2	0	9	6
St.L	1981	PRE	St.L	2	3	21	20
Tor.	1976	PRE	Tor.	1	2	3	8
Tor.	1977	PRE	Tor.	1	2	10	13
Wsh.	1991	DF	Pit.	4	1	19	13
Wsh.	1992	DSF	Pit.	4	3	25	27
Wsh.	1994	CQF	Wsh.	2	4	12	20
Wsh.	1995	CQF	Pit.	4	3	29	26
Oak.	1970	QF	Pit.	4	0	13	6

ST. LOUIS BLUES

PLAYOFF SCORING LEADERS

	PLAYER	YEARS	GP	G	A	TP
1.	Bernie Federko	77-89	91	35	66	101
2.	Brett Hull	88-95	73	56	35	91
3.	Doug Gilmour	84-88	49	17	38	55
4.	Frank St. Marseille	68-72	61	19	24	43
5.	Brian Sutter	77-88	65	21	21	42
6.	Jeff Brown	90-93	42	10	28	38
7.	Adam Oates	90-91	25	9	25	34
8.	Red Berenson	68-77	55	21	12	33
9.	Gino Cavallini	86-91	67	14	19	33
10.	Larry Keenan	68-70	46	15	16	31

Playoffs

	Series	W	L	GP	W	L	T	GF	GA	Last Mtg.	Round	Result
Boston	2	0	2	8	0	8	0	15	48	1972	SF	L 0-4
Buffalo	1	0	1	3	1	2	0	8	7	1976	PR	L 1-2
Calgary	1	0	1	7	3	4	0	22	28	1986	CF	L 3-4
Chicago	9	2	7	45	18	27	0	129	166	1993	DSF	W 4-0
Dallas	10	5	5	56	26	30	0	162	174	1994	CQF	L 0-4
Detroit	3	2	1	16	8	8	0	51	53	1991	DSF	W 4-3
Los Angeles	1	1	0	4	4	0	0	16	5	1969	SF	W 4-0
Montreal	3	0	3	12	0	12	0	14	42	1977	F	L 0-4
NY Rangers	1	0	1	6	2	4	0	22	29	1981	QF	L 2-4
Philadelphia	2	2	0	11	8	3	0	34	20	1969	QF	W 4-0
Pittsburgh	3	2	1	13	7	6	0	45	40	1981	PR	W 3-2
Toronto	4	2	2	25	13	12	0	67	75	1993	DF	L 3-4
Vancouver	1	0	1	7	3	4	0	27	27	1995	CQF	L 3-4
Winnipeg	1	1	0	4	3	1	0	20	13	1982	DSF	W 3-1
Totals	**42**	**17**	**25**	**217**	**96**	**121**	**0**	**632**	**727**			

Playoff Results 1995-91

Year	Round	Opponent	Result	GF	GA
1995	CQF	Vancouver	L 3-4	27	27
1994	CQF	Dallas	L 0-4	10	16
1993	DF	Toronto	L 3-4	11	22
	DSF	Chicago	W 4-0	13	6
1992	DSF	Chicago	L 2-4	19	23
1991	DF	Minnesota	L 2-4	17	22
	DSF	Detroit	W 4-3	24	20

Abbreviations: Round: F – Final; **CF** – conference final; **CQF** – conference quarter-final; **CSF** – conference semi-final; **DF** – division final; **DSF** – division semi-final; **SF** – semi-final; **QF** – quarter-final; **PR** – preliminary round.

SERIES RECORDS VERSUS OTHER CLUBS

Opponent	Year	Series	Winner	W	L	GF	GA
Bos.	1970	F	Bos.	0	4	7	20
Bos.	1972	SF	Bos.	0	4	8	28
Buf.	1978	PRE	Buf.	1	2	8	7
Cgy.	1986	CF	Cgy.	3	4	22	28
Chi.	1973	QF	Chi.	1	4	9	22
Chi.	1980	PRE	Chi.	0	3	4	12
Chi.	1982	DF	Chi.	2	4	19	23
Chi.	1983	DSF	Chi.	1	3	10	16
Chi.	1988	DSF	St.L	4	1	21	17
Chi.	1989	DF	Chi.	1	4	12	19
Chi.	1990	DF	Chi.	3	4	22	28
Chi.	1992	DSF	Chi.	2	4	19	23
Chi.	1993	DSF	St.L	4	0	13	6
Dal.	1994	CQF	Dal.	0	4	10	16
Det.	1984	DSF	St.L	3	1	13	12
Det.	1988	DF	Det.	1	4	14	21
Det.	1991	DSF	St.L	4	3	24	20
L.A.	1969	SF	St.L	4	0	16	5
Min.	1968	SF	St.L	4	3	18	22
Min.	1970	QF	St.L	4	2	20	16
Min.	1971	QF	Min.	2	4	15	16
Min.	1972	QF	St.L	4	3	19	19
Min.	1984	DF	Min.	3	4	17	19
Min.	1985	DSF	Min.	0	3	5	9
Min.	1986	DSF	St.L	3	2	18	20
Min.	1989	DSF	St.L	4	1	23	15
Min.	1991	DF	Min.	2	4	17	22
Mtl.	1968	F	Mtl.	0	4	7	11
Mtl.	1969	F	Mtl.	0	4	3	12
Mtl.	1977	QF	Mtl.	0	4	4	19
NYR	1981	QF	NYR	2	4	22	29
Phi.	1968	QF	St.L	4	3	17	17
Phi.	1969	QF	St.L	4	0	17	3
Pit.	1970	SF	St.L	4	2	19	10
Pit.	1975	PRE	Pit.	0	2	6	9
Pit.	1981	PRE	St.L	3	2	20	21
Tor.	1986	DF	St.L	4	3	24	22
Tor.	1987	DSF	Tor.	2	4	12	15
Tor.	1990	DSF	St.L	4	1	20	16
Tor.	1993	DF	Tor.	3	4	11	22
Van.	1995	CQF	Van.	3	4	27	27
Wpg.	1982	DSF	St.L	3	1	20	13

SAN JOSE SHARKS

Playoffs

	Series	W	L	GP	W	L	T	GF	GA	Last Mtg.	Round	Result
Calgary	1	1	0	7	4	3	0	26	35	1995	CQF	W 4-3
Detroit	2	1	1	11	4	7	0	27	51	1995	CSF	L 0-4
Toronto	1	0	1	7	3	4	0	21	26	1994	CSF	L 3-4
Totals	**4**	**2**	**2**	**25**	**11**	**14**	**0**	**74**	**112**			

Playoff Results 1995-91

Year	Round	Opponent	Result	GF	GA
1995	CSF	Detroit	L 0-4	6	24
	CQF	Calgary	W 4-3	26	35
1994	CSF	Toronto	L 3-4	21	26
	CQF	Detroit	W 4-3	21	27

Abbreviations: Round: F – Final; **CF** – conference final; **CQF** – conference quarter-final; **CSF** – conference semi-final; **DF** – division final; **DSF** – division semi-final; **SF** – semi-final; **QF** – quarter-final; **PR** – preliminary round.

PLAYOFF SCORING LEADERS

	PLAYER	YEARS	GP	G	A	TP
1.	Igor Larionov	94-95	25	6	21	27
2.	Ulf Dahlen	94-95	25	11	6	17
3.	Sergei Makarov	94-95	25	11	5	16
4.	Sandis Ozolinsh	94-95	25	3	12	15
5.	Ray Whitney	94-95	25	4	8	12
6.	Tom Pederson	94-95	24	1	11	12
7.	Todd Elik	94-95	14	5	5	10
8.	Johan Garpenlov	94	14	4	6	10
9.	Jamie Baker	94-95	25	5	4	9
10.	Mike Rathje	94-95	12	5	2	7

SERIES RECORDS VERSUS OTHER CLUBS

Opponent	Year	Series	Winner	W	L	GF	GA
Cgy.	1995	CQF	S.J.	4	3	26	35
Det.	1994	CQF	S.J.	4	3	21	27
Det.	1995	CSF	Det.	0	4	6	24
Tor.	1994	CSF	Tor.	3	4	21	26

TORONTO MAPLE LEAFS

Playoffs

	Series	W	L	GP	W	L	T	GF	GA	Last Mtg.	Round	Result
Boston	13	8	5	62	31	30	1	150	153	1974	QF	L 0-4
Calgary	1	1	0	2	2	0	0	9	5	1979	PR	W 2-0
Chicago	9	6	3	38	22	15	1	111	89	1995	CQF	L 3-4
Dallas	2	0	2	7	1	6	0	26	35	1983	DSF	L 1-3
Detroit	23	12	11	117	58	59	0	311	321	1993	DSF	W 4-3
Los Angeles	3	2	1	12	7	5	0	41	31	1993	CF	L 3-4
Montreal	15	7	8	71	29	42	0	160	215	1979	QF	L 0-4
NY Islanders	2	1	1	10	4	6	0	20	33	1981	PR	L 0-3
NY Rangers	8	3	5	35	16	19	0	86	86	1971	QF	L 2-4
Philadelphia	3	0	3	17	5	12	0	47	67	1977	QF	L 2-4
Pittsburgh	2	2	0	6	4	2	0	21	13	1977	PR	W 2-1
St. Louis	4	2	2	25	12	13	0	75	67	1993	DF	W 4-3
San Jose	1	1	0	7	4	3	0	26	21	1994	CSF	W 4-3
Vancouver	1	0	1	5	1	4	0	9	16	1994	CF	L 1-4
Defunct	8	6	2	24	12	10	2	59	57			
Totals	95	51	44	438	208	226	4	1151	1209			

Playoff Results 1995-91

Year	Round	Opponent	Result	GF	GA
1995	CQF	Chicago	L 3-4	20	22
1994	CF	Vancouver	L 1-4	9	16
	CSF	San Jose	W 4-3	26	21
	CQF	Chicago	W 4-2	15	10
1993	CF	Los Angeles	L 3-4	23	22
	DF	St. Louis	W 4-3	22	11
	DSF	Detroit	W 4-3	24	30

Abbreviations: Round: F – Final; **CF** – conference final; **CQF** – conference quarter-final; **CSF** – conference semi-final; **DF** – division final; **DSF** – division semi-final; **SF** – semi-final; **QF** – quarter-final; **PR** – preliminary round.

PLAYOFF SCORING LEADERS

	PLAYER	YEARS	GP	G	A	TP
1.	Doug Gilmour	93-95	46	16	53	69
2.	Dave Keon	61-75	89	32	35	67
3.	Darryl Sittler	71-81	64	25	40	65
4.	Ted Kennedy	44-55	78	29	31	60
5.	George Armstrong	52-71	110	26	34	60
6.	Frank Mahovlich	59-67	84	24	36	60
7.	Wendel Clark	86-94	67	31	24	55
8.	Red Kelly	60-67	70	17	38	55
9.	Syl Apps	37-48	69	25	28	53
10.	Bob Pulford	59-69	89	25	26	51

SERIES RECORDS VERSUS OTHER CLUBS

Opponent	Year	Series	Winner	W	L	T	GF	GA
Atl.	1979	PRE	Tor.	2	0		9	5
Bos.	1933	SF	Tor.	3	2		9	7
Bos.	1935	SF	Tor.	3	1		7	2
Bos.	1936	QF*	Tor.	1	1		8	6
Bos.	1938	SF	Tor.	3	0		6	3
Bos.	1939	F	Bos.	1	4		6	12
Bos.	1941	SF	Bos.	3	4		17	15
Bos.	1948	SF	Tor.	4	1		20	13
Bos.	1949	SF	Tor.	4	1		16	10
Bos.	1951	SF	Tor.	4	1	1	17	5
Bos.	1959	SF	Tor.	4	3		20	21
Bos.	1969	QF	Bos.	0	4		5	24
Bos.	1972	QF	Bos.	1	4		10	18
Bos.	1974	QF	Bos.	0	4		9	17
Chi.	1931	QF*	Chi.	0	1	1	3	4
Chi.	1932	QF*	Tor.	1	1		6	2
Chi.	1938	F	Chi.	1	3		8	10
Chi.	1940	QF	Tor.	2	0		5	3
Chi.	1962	F	Tor.	4	2		18	15
Chi.	1967	SF	Tor.	4	2		18	14
Chi.	1986	DSF	Tor.	3	0		18	9
Chi.	1994	CQF	Tor.	4	2		15	10
Chi.	1995	CQF	Chi.	3	4		20	22
Det.	1929	QF*	Tor.	2	0		7	2
Det.	1934	SF	Det.	2	3		12	11
Det.	1936	F	Det.	1	3		11	18
Det.	1939	SF	Tor.	2	1		10	8
Det.	1940	SF	Tor.	2	0		5	2
Det.	1942	F	Tor.	4	3		25	19
Det.	1943	SF	Det.	2	4		17	10
Det.	1945	F	Tor.	4	3		9	9
Det.	1947	SF	Tor.	4	1		18	14
Det.	1948	F	Tor.	4	0		18	7
Det.	1949	F	Tor.	4	0		12	5
Det.	1950	SF	Det.	3	4		11	10
Det.	1952	SF	Det.	0	4		3	13
Det.	1954	SF	Det.	1	4		8	15
Det.	1955	SF	Det.	0	4		6	14
Det.	1956	SF	Det.	1	4		10	14
Det.	1960	SF	Tor.	4	2		20	16
Det.	1961	SF	Det.	1	4		8	15
Det.	1963	F	Tor.	4	1		17	10
Det.	1964	F	Tor.	4	3		22	17
Det.	1987	DF	Det.	3	4		18	20
Det.	1988	DSF	Det.	2	4		20	32
Det.	1993	DSF	Tor.	4	3		24	30
L.A.	1975	PRE	Tor.	2	1		7	6
L.A.	1978	PRE	Tor.	2	0		11	3
L.A.	1993	CF	L.A.	3	4		23	22
Min.	1980	PRE	Min.	0	3		8	17
Min.	1983	DSF	Min.	1	3		18	18
Mtl.	1918	NHLF*	Tor.	1	1		10	7
Mtl.	1925	NHLF*	Mtl.	0	2		2	5
Mtl.	1945	SF	Tor.	4	2		15	21
Mtl.	1944	SF	Mtl.	1	4		6	23
Mtl.	1947	F	Tor.	4	2		13	13
Mtl.	1951	F	Tor.	4	1		13	10
Mtl.	1959	F	Mtl.	1	4		12	18
Mtl.	1960	F	Mtl.	0	4		5	15
Mtl.	1963	SF	Tor.	4	1		14	6
Mtl.	1964	SF	Tor.	4	3		17	14
Mtl.	1965	SF	Mtl.	2	4		14	17
Mtl.	1966	SF	Mtl.	0	4		6	15
Mtl.	1967	F	Tor.	4	2		17	16
Mtl.	1978	SF	Mtl.	0	4		6	16
Mtl.	1979	QF	Mtl.	0	4		10	19
NYI	1978	QF	Tor.	4	3		16	13
NYI	1981	PRE	NYI	0	3		4	20
NYR	1929	SF	NYR	0	2		1	3
NYR	1932	F	Tor.	3	0		18	10
NYR	1933	F	NYR	1	3		5	11
NYR	1937	QF	NYR	0	2		1	5
NYR	1940	F	NYR	2	4		11	14
NYR	1942	SF	Tor.	4	2		13	12
NYR	1962	SF	Tor.	4	2		22	15
NYR	1971	QF	NYR	2	4		15	16
Phi.	1975	QF	Phi.	0	4		6	15
Phi.	1976	QF	Phi.	3	4		23	33
Phi.	1977	QF	Phi.	2	4		18	19
Pit.	1976	PRE	Tor.	2	1		8	3
Pit.	1977	PRE	Tor.	2	1		13	10
St.L	1986	DF	St.L	3	4		22	24
St.L	1987	DSF	Tor.	4	2		15	12
St.L	1990	DSF	St.L	1	4		16	20
St.L	1993	DF	Tor.	4	3		22	11
S.J.	1994	CSF	Tor.	4	3		26	21
Van.	1994	CF	Van.	1	4		9	16

DEFUNCT CLUBS

Opponent	Year	Series	Winner	W	L	T	GF	GA
Mtl.M	1932	SF*	Tor.	1	1		4	3
Mtl.M	1935	F	Mtl.M	0	3		4	10
NYA	1936	SF	Tor.	2	1		6	3
NYA	1939	QF	Tor.	2	0		6	0
Ott.	1921	NHLF*	Ott.	0	2		0	7
Ott.	1922	NHLF*	Tor.	1	0	1	5	4
Van.	1918	F	Tor.	3	2		18	21
Van.	1922	F	Tor.	3	2		16	9

*Total-goals series

VANCOUVER CANUCKS

PLAYOFF SCORING LEADERS

	PLAYER	YEARS	GP	G	A	TP
1.	Trevor Linden	89-95	73	26	46	72
2.	Pavel Bure	92-95	60	34	32	66
3.	Geoff Courtnall	91-95	65	26	35	61
4.	Cliff Ronning	91-95	66	24	32	56
5.	Thomas Gradin	79-86	38	17	21	38
6.	Jyrki Lumme	91-95	66	8	28	36
7.	Greg Adams	88-94	53	15	19	34
8.	Stan Smyl	79-89	41	16	17	33
9.	Dave Babych	92-95	60	9	18	27
10.	Murray Craven	93-94	34	8	15	23

Playoffs

	Series	W	L	GP	W	L	T	GF	GA	Last Mtg.	Round	Result
Buffalo	2	0	2	7	1	6	0	14	28	1981	PR	L 0-3
Calgary	5	2	3	25	12	13	0	80	82	1994	CQF	W 4-3
Chicago	2	1	1	9	4	5	0	24	24	1995	CSF	L 0-4
Dallas	1	1	0	5	4	1	0	18	11	1994	CSF	W 4-1
Edmonton	2	0	2	9	2	7	0	20	35	1992	DF	L 2-4
Los Angeles	3	1	2	17	10	7	0	60	66	1993	DF	L 2-4
Montreal	1	0	1	5	1	4	0	9	20	1975	QF	L 1-4
NY Islanders	2	0	2	6	0	6	0	14	26	1982	F	L 0-4
NY Rangers	1	0	1	7	3	4	0	19	21	1994	F	L 3-4
Philadelphia	1	0	1	3	1	2	0	9	15	1979	PR	L 1-2
St. Louis	1	1	0	7	4	3	0	27	27	1995	CQF	W 4-3
Toronto	1	1	0	5	4	1	0	16	9	1994	CF	W 4-1
Winnipeg	2	2	0	13	8	5	0	50	34	1993	DSF	W 4-2
Totals	**24**	**9**	**15**	**118**	**52**	**66**	**0**	**360**	**398**			

Playoff Results 1995-91

Year	Round	Opponent	Result	GF	GA
1995	CSF	Chicago	L 0-4	6	11
	CQF	St. Louis	W 4-3	27	27
1994	F	NY Rangers	L 3-4	19	21
	CF	Toronto	W 4-1	16	9
	CSF	Dallas	W 4-1	18	11
	CQF	Calgary	W 4-3	23	20
1993	DF	Los Angeles	L 2-4	25	26
	DSF	Winnipeg	W 4-2	21	17
1992	DF	Edmonton	L 2-4	15	18
	DSF	Winnipeg	W 4-3	29	17
1991	DSF	Los Angeles	L 2-4	16	26

Abbreviations: Round: F – Final;
CF – conference final; **CQF** – conference quarter-final;
CSF – conference semi-final; **DF** – division final;
DSF – division semi-final; **SF** – semi-final;
QF – quarter-final; **PR** – preliminary round.

SERIES RECORDS VERSUS OTHER CLUBS

Opponent	Year	Series	Winner	W	L	GF	GA
Buf.	1980	PRE	Buf.	1	3	7	15
Buf.	1981	PRE	Buf.	0	3	7	13
Cgy.	1982	DSF	Van.	3	0	10	5
Cgy.	1983	DSF	Cgy.	1	3	14	17
Cgy.	1984	DSF	Cgy.	1	3	13	14
Cgy.	1989	DSF	Cgy.	3	4	20	26
Cgy.	1994	CQF	Van.	4	3	23	20

Opponent	Year	Series	Winner	W	L	GF	GA
Chi.	1982	CF	Van.	4	1	18	13
Chi.	1995	CSF	Chi.	0	4	6	11
Dal.	1994	CSF	Van.	4	1	18	11
Edm.	1986	DSF	Edm.	0	3	5	17
Edm.	1992	DF	Edm.	2	4	15	18
L.A.	1982	DF	Van.	4	1	19	14
L.A.	1991	DSF	L.A.	2	4	16	26
L.A.	1993	DF	L.A.	2	4	25	26
Mtl.	1975	QF	Mtl.	1	4	9	20

Opponent	Year	Series	Winner	W	L	GF	GA
NYI	1976	PRE	NYI	0	2	4	8
NYI	1982	F	NYI	0	4	10	18
NYR	1994	F	NYR	3	4	19	21
Phi.	1979	PRE	Phi.	1	2	9	15
St.L.	1995	CQF	Van.	4	3	27	27
Tor.	1994	CF	Van.	4	1	16	9
Wpg.	1992	DSF	Van.	4	3	29	17
Wpg.	1993	DSF	Van.	4	2	21	17

WASHINGTON CAPITALS

Playoffs

	Series	W	L	GP	W	L	T	GF	GA	Last Mtg.	Round	Result
Boston	1	0	1	4	0	4	0	6	15	1990	CF	L 0-4
New Jersey	2	1	1	13	7	6	0	44	43	1990	DSF	W 4-2
NY Islanders	6	1	5	30	12	18	0	88	89	1993	DSF	L 2-4
NY Rangers	4	2	2	22	11	11	0	75	71	1994	CSF	L 1-4
Philadelphia	3	2	1	16	9	7	0	65	55	1989	DSF	L 2-4
Pittsburgh	4	1	3	25	11	14	0	86	85	1995	CQF	L 3-4
Totals	20	7	13	110	50	60	0	364	368			

Playoff Results 1995-91

Year	Round	Opponent	Result	GF	GA
1995	CSF	Pittsburgh	L 3-4	26	29
1994	CSF	NY Rangers	L 1-4	12	20
	CQF	Pittsburgh	W 4-2	20	12
1993	DSF	NY Islanders	L 2-4	22	23
1992	DSF	Pittsburgh	L 3-4	27	25
1991	DF	Pittsburgh	L 1-4	13	19
	DSF	NY Rangers	W 4-2	16	16

Abbreviations: Round: F – Final;
CF – conference final; **CQF** – conference quarter-final;
CSF – conference semi-final; **DF** – division final;
DSF – division semi-final; **SF** – semi-final;
QF – quarter-final; **PR** – preliminary round.

PLAYOFF SCORING LEADERS

	PLAYER	YEARS	GP	G	A	TP
1.	Dale Hunter	88-95	73	24	38	62
2.	Mike Ridley	87-94	76	19	41	60
3.	Scott Stevens	83-90	67	9	44	53
4.	Kevin Hatcher	85-94	83	16	32	48
5.	Michal Pivonka	83-95	76	16	31	47
6.	Kelly Miller	87-95	84	17	28	45
7.	Mike Gartner	83-88	47	16	27	43
8.	Calle Johansson	89-95	57	8	29	37
9.	Dave Christian	84-89	49	17	19	36
10.	Dino Ciccarelli	89-92	32	21	14	35

SERIES RECORDS VERSUS OTHER CLUBS

Opponent	Year	Series	Winner	W	L	GF	GA
Bos.	1990	CF	Bos.	0	4	6	15
N.J.	1988	DF	N.J.	3	4	23	25
N.J.	1990	DSF	Wsh.	4	2	21	18

Opponent	Year	Series	Winner	W	L	GF	GA
NYI	1983	DSF	NYI	1	3	11	19
NYI	1984	DF	NYI	1	4	13	20
NYI	1985	DSF	NYI	2	3	12	14
NYI	1986	DSF	Wsh.	3	0	11	4
NYI	1987	DSF	NYI	3	4	19	19
NYI	1993	DSF	NYI	2	4	22	23
NYR	1986	DF	NYR	2	4	25	20
NYR	1990	DF	Wsh.	4	1	22	15
NYR	1991	DSF	Wsh.	4	2	16	16
NYR	1994	CSF	NYR	1	4	12	20

Opponent	Year	Series	Winner	W	L	GF	GA
Phi.	1984	DSF	Wsh.	3	0	15	5
Phi.	1988	DSF	Wsh.	4	3	31	25
Phi.	1989	DSF	Phi.	2	4	19	25
Pit.	1991	DF	Pit.	1	4	13	19
Pit.	1992	DSF	Pit.	3	4	27	25
Pit.	1994	CQF	Wsh.	4	2	20	12
Pit.	1995	CQF	Pit.	3	4	26	29

WINNIPEG JETS

Playoffs

	Series	W	L	GP	W	L	T	GF	GA	Last Mtg.	Round	Result
Calgary	3	2	1	13	7	6	0	45	43	1987	DSF	W 4-2
Edmonton	6	0	6	26	4	22	0	75	120	1990	DSF	L 3-4
St. Louis	1	0	1	4	1	3	0	13	20	1982	DSF	L 1-3
Vancouver	2	0	2	13	5	8	0	34	50	1993	DSF	L 2-4
Totals	12	2	10	56	17	39	0	167	233			

Playoff Results 1995-91

Year	Round	Opponent	Result	GF	GA
1993	DSF	Vancouver	L 2-4	17	21
1992	DSF	Vancouver	L 3-4	17	29

Abbreviations: Round: F – Final;
CF – conference final; **CQF** – conference quarter-final;
CSF – conference semi-final; **DF** – division final;
DSF – division semi-final; **SF** – semi-final;
QF – quarter-final; **PR** – preliminary round.

PLAYOFF SCORING LEADERS

	PLAYER	YEARS	GP	G	A	TP
1.	Dale Hawerchuk	82-90	38	16	33	49
2.	Thomas Steen	82-93	56	12	32	44
3.	Paul MacLean	82-88	35	16	10	26
4.	Dave Ellett	85-90	33	4	16	20
5.	Fredrik Olausson	87-93	35	4	13	17
6.	Randy Carlyle	84-92	31	3	14	17
7.	Brian Mullen	83-87	26	7	9	16
8.	Moe Mantha	82-90	16	5	10	15
9.	Laurie Boschman	83-90	34	5	10	15
10.	Dave Babych	82-85	18	4	10	14

SERIES RECORDS VERSUS OTHER CLUBS

Opponent	Year	Series	Winner	W	L	GF	GA
Cgy.	1985	DSF	Wpg.	3	1	15	13
Cgy.	1986	DSF	Cgy.	0	3	8	15
Cgy.	1987	DSF	Wpg.	4	2	22	15
Edm.	1983	DSF	Edm.	0	3	9	14
Edm.	1984	DSF	Edm.	0	3	7	18
Edm.	1985	DF	Edm.	0	4	11	22
Edm.	1987	DF	Edm.	0	4	9	17
Edm.	1988	DSF	Edm.	1	4	17	25
Edm.	1990	DSF	Edm.	3	4	22	24

Opponent	Year	Series	Winner	W	L	GF	GA
St.L	1982	DSF	St.L	1	3	13	20
Van.	1992	DSF	Van.	3	4	17	29
Van.	1993	DSF	Van.	2	4	17	21

These NHL clubs have not appeared in the Stanley Cup playoffs:

MIGHTY DUCKS OF ANAHEIM

FLORIDA PANTHERS

OTTAWA SENATORS

TAMPA BAY LIGHTNING

CONN SMYTHE TROPHY UPDATE

A total of 26 different players have won the Conn Smythe Trophy, awarded to the most valuable player to his team in the playoffs. The trophy was first awarded in 1965. Five players — Bobby Orr, Bernie Parent, Wayne Gretzky, Mario Lemieux and Patrick Roy — have won the award twice.

Four players — Roger Crozier of the 1966 Detroit Red Wings, Glenn Hall of the 1968 St. Louis Blues, Reg Leach of the 1976 Philadelphia Flyers and Ron Hextall of the 1987 Philadelphia Flyers — have won the Conn Smythe Trophy as members of losing teams in the Finals.

20-year-old Patrick Roy of the 1986 Montreal Canadiens was the youngest player ever to win the Conn Smythe Trophy.

The Conn Smythe Trophy is voted upon by the Professional Hockey Writers Association (PHWA) at the conclusion of the final game of the Stanley Cup Finals.

National Hockey League
**Stanley Cup Playoffs
Fact Guide
1996**

Section II

•

Year-by-Year Playoff Scores and Highlights

All-Time Playoff Scoring Leaders... page **32**
Playoff Game Scores and Highlights, 1893 to 1995   **33**

32 • ALL-TIME PLAYOFF SCORING LEADERS

Denis Savard returned to the Chicago Blackhawks in April, 1995 and became the 10th player in NHL history to collect 100 post-season assists.

All-Time Playoff Goal Leaders since 1918
(40 or more goals)

Player	Teams	Yrs.	GP	G
* Wayne Gretzky	Edm., L.A.	14	180	110
* Jari Kurri	Edm., L.A.	12	174	102
* Mark Messier	Edm., NYR	15	210	102
* Glenn Anderson	Edm., Tor., NYR, St.L.	14	214	92
Mike Bossy	NY Islanders	10	129	85
Maurice Richard	Montreal	15	133	82
Jean Beliveau	Montreal	17	162	79
Bryan Trottier	NYI, Pit.	17	221	71
Gordie Howe	Det., Hfd.	20	157	68
* Dino Ciccarelli	Min., Wsh., Det.	13	124	67
* Denis Savard	Chi., Mtl.	14	153	65
Yvan Cournoyer	Montreal	12	147	64
Brian Propp	Phi., Bos., Min.	13	160	64
Bobby Smith	Min., Mtl.	13	184	64
Bobby Hull	Chi., Hfd.	14	119	62
Phil Esposito	Chi., Bos., NYR	15	130	61
Jacques Lemaire	Montreal	11	145	61
* Joe Mullen	St.L., Cgy., Pit.	14	142	60
Stan Mikita	Chicago	18	155	59
* Brett Hull	Cgy., St.L.	10	79	58
Guy Lafleur	Mtl., NYR	14	128	58
Bernie Geoffrion	Mtl., NYR	16	132	58
* Cam Neely	Van., Bos.	9	93	57
* Esa Tikkanen	Edm., NYR, St.L.	10	144	57
* Mario Lemieux	Pittsburgh	5	66	56
Steve Larmer	Chi., NYR	13	140	56
Denis Potvin	NY Islanders	14	185	56
Rick MacLeish	Phi., Pit., Det.	11	114	54
Bill Barber	Philadelphia	11	129	53
* Paul Coffey	Edm., Pit., L.A., Det.	13	155	53
* Stephane Richer	Mtl., N.J.	10	123	52
* Claude Lemieux	Mtl., N.J.	10	136	52
Frank Mahovlich	Tor., Det., Mtl.	14	137	51
Steve Shutt	Mtl., L.A.	12	99	50
Henri Richard	Montreal	18	180	49
* Doug Gilmour	St.L., Cgy., Tor.	11	130	48
Reggie Leach	Bos., Phi.	8	94	47
Ted Lindsay	Det., Chi.	16	133	47
Clark Gillies	NYI, Buf.	13	164	47
Dickie Moore	Mtl., Tor. St.L.	14	135	46
Rick Middleton	NYR, Bos.	12	114	45
Lanny McDonald	Tor., Cgy.	13	117	44
* Kevin Stevens	Pit.	6	86	43
Ken Linseman	Phi., Edm., Bos.	11	113	43
Bobby Clarke	Philadelphia	13	136	42
* Luc Robitaille	L.A., Pit.	8	85	41
* Brian Bellows	Min., Mtl.	10	105	41
John Bucyk	Det., Bos.	14	124	41
Tim Kerr	Phi., NYR	10	81	40
* Bernie Nicholls	L.A., NYR, Edm., N.J., Chi.	11	102	40
Peter McNab	Bos., Van.	10	107	40
Bob Bourne	NYI, L.A.	13	139	40
* Dale Hunter	Que., Wsh.	15	140	40
John Tonelli	NYI, Cgy., L.A.	13	172	40

* — Active player.

All-Time Playoff Assist Leaders since 1918
(60 or more assists)

Player	Teams	Yrs.	GP	A
* Wayne Gretzky	Edm., L.A.	14	180	236
* Mark Messier	Edm., NYR	15	210	170
* Jari Kurri	Edm., L.A.	12	174	120
* Paul Coffey	Edm., Pit., L.A., Det.	13	155	119
* Glenn Anderson	Edm., Tor., NYR, St.L.	14	214	117
Larry Robinson	Mtl., L.A.	20	227	116
Bryan Trottier	NYI, Pit.	17	221	113
Denis Potvin	NY Islanders	14	185	108
* Ray Bourque	Boston	16	157	106
* Denis Savard	Chi., Mtl.	14	153	105
* Doug Gilmour	St.L., Cgy., Tor.	11	130	104
Jean Beliveau	Montreal	17	162	97
Bobby Smith	Min., Mtl.	13	184	96
Gordie Howe	Det., Hfd.	20	157	92
Stan Mikita	Chicago	18	155	91
Brad Park	NYR, Bos., Det.	17	161	90
* Larry Murphy	L.A., Wsh., Min., Pit.	14	142	86
* Chris Chelios	Mtl., Chi.	12	148	84
Brian Propp	Phi., Bos., Min.	13	160	84
* Adam Oates	Det., St.L., Bos.	9	200	84
* Al MacInnis	Cgy., St.L.	11	102	82
Henri Richard	Montreal	18	180	80
Jacques Lemaire	Montreal	11	145	78
* Craig Janney	Bos., St.L., S.J.	8	101	78
Ken Linseman	Phi., Edm., Bos.	11	113	77
Bobby Clarke	Philadelphia	13	136	77
Guy Lafleur	Mtl., NYR	14	128	76
Phil Esposito	Chi., Bos., NYR	15	130	76
Mike Bossy	NY Islanders	10	129	75
Steve Larmer	Chi., NYR	13	140	75
John Tonelli	NYI, Cgy., L.A.	13	172	75
* Peter Stastny	Que., N.J., St.L.	12	93	72
Gilbert Perreault	Buffalo	11	90	70
* Ron Francis	Hfd., Pit.	10	108	69
Alex Delvecchio	Detroit	14	121	69
Bobby Hull	Chi., Hfd.	14	119	67
Frank Mahovlich	Tor., Det., Mtl.	14	137	67
* Mario Lemieux	Pittsburgh	5	66	66
Bobby Orr	Boston	8	74	66
Bernie Federko	St. Louis	11	91	66
Jean Ratelle	NYR, Bos.	15	123	66
* Scott Stevens	Wsh., St. L., N.J.	13	132	66
* Charlie Huddy	Edm., L.A., Buf.	13	170	66
Dickie Moore	Mtl., Tor., St.L.	14	135	64
Doug Harvey	Mtl., NYR, St.L.	15	137	64
* Dale Hunter	Que., Wsh.	15	140	64
Yvan Cournoyer	Montreal	12	147	63
John Bucyk	Det., Bos.	14	124	62
* Neal Broten	Min., Dal., N.J.	14	133	62
Doug Wilson	Chicago	12	95	61
* Bernie Nicholls	L.A., NYR, Edm., N.J., Chi.	11	102	60
* Brian Bellows	Min., Mtl.	10	105	60

All-Time Playoff Point Leaders since 1918
(100 or more points)

Player	Teams	Yrs.	GP	G	A	Pts
* Wayne Gretzky	Edm., L.A.	14	180	110	236	346
* Mark Messier	Edm., NYR	15	210	102	170	272
* Jari Kurri	Edm., L.A.	12	174	102	120	222
* Glenn Anderson	Edm., Tor., NYR, St.L.	14	214	92	117	209
Bryan Trottier	NYI, Pit.	17	221	71	113	184
Jean Beliveau	Montreal	17	162	79	97	176
* Paul Coffey	Edm., Pit., L.A., Det.	13	155	53	119	172
* Denis Savard	Chi., Mtl.	14	153	65	105	170
Denis Potvin	NY Islanders	14	185	56	108	164
Mike Bossy	NY Islanders	10	129	85	75	160
Gordie Howe	Det., Hfd.	20	157	68	92	160
Bobby Smith	Min., Mtl.	13	184	64	96	160
* Doug Gilmour	St.L., Cgy., Tor.	11	130	48	104	152
Stan Mikita	Chicago	18	155	59	91	150
Brian Propp	Phi., Bos., Min.	13	160	64	84	148
Larry Robinson	Mtl., L.A.	20	227	28	116	144
Jacques Lemaire	Montreal	11	145	61	78	139
* Ray Bourque	Boston	16	157	33	106	139
Phil Esposito	Chi., Bos., NYR	15	130	61	76	137
Guy Lafleur	Mtl, NYR	14	128	58	76	134
Steve Larmer	Chi., NYR	13	140	56	75	131
Bobby Hull	Chi., Hfd.	14	119	62	67	129
Henri Richard	Montreal	18	180	49	80	129
Yvan Cournoyer	Montreal	12	147	64	63	127
Maurice Richard	Montreal	15	133	82	44	126
Brad Park	NYR, Bos., Det.	17	161	35	90	125
* Mario Lemieux	Pittsburgh	5	66	56	66	122
Ken Linseman	Phi., Edm., Bos.	11	113	43	77	120
Bobby Clarke	Philadelphia	13	136	42	77	119
Bernie Geoffrion	Mtl., NYR	16	132	58	60	118
Frank Mahovlich	Tor., Det., Mtl.	14	137	51	67	118
* Larry Murphy	L.A., Wsh., Min., Pit.	14	142	30	86	116
John Tonelli	NYI, Cgy., L.A.	13	172	40	75	115
* Adam Oates	Det., St.L., Bos.	9	100	30	84	114
* Chris Chelios	Mtl., Chi.	12	148	28	84	112
* Dino Ciccarelli	Min., Wsh., Det.	13	124	67	43	110
Dickie Moore	Mtl., Tor., St.L.	14	135	46	64	110
* Esa Tikkanen	Edm., NYR, St.L.	10	144	57	52	109
* Al MacInnis	Cgy., St.L.	11	102	26	82	108
Bill Barber	Philadelphia	11	129	53	55	108
Rick MacLeish	Phi., Pit., Det.	11	114	54	53	107
* Joe Mullen	St.L., Cgy., Pit.	14	142	60	46	106
* Peter Stastny	Que., N.J., St.L.	12	93	72	105	
* Ron Francis	Hfd., Pit.	10	108	35	69	104
Alex Delvecchio	Detroit	14	121	35	69	104
* Dale Hunter	Que., Wsh.	15	140	40	64	104
Gilbert Perreault	Buffalo	11	90	33	70	103
John Bucyk	Det., Bos.	14	124	41	62	103
Bernie Federko	St. Louis	11	91	35	66	101
* Craig Janney	Bos., St. L., S.J.	8	101	23	78	101
* Brian Bellows	Min., Mtl.	10	105	41	60	101
* Kevin Stevens	Pit.	6	36	43	57	100
* Bernie Nicholls	L.A., NYR, Edm., N.J., Chi.	11	102	40	60	100
Rick Middleton	NYR, Bos.	12	114	45	55	100

MONTREAL AMATEUR ATHLETIC ASSOCIATION (AHA) — 1893

In accordance with Lord Stanley's terms, the Montreal AAA hockey club captured the inaugural Stanley Cup championship in honor of winning Canada's Amateur Hockey Association (AHA) title. The AAA squad skated to a 7-1-0 record to beat out the 6-2-0 Ottawa Generals, who had handed the Montrealers their lone defeat of the season on opening day. Harvie Routh led the newly-crowned champs with a league-high 12 goals in seven games.

Formed in 1886, the AHA was considered the top hockey league in all of Canada. Its schedule consisted of 20 games among its five-club membership, which included three Montreal teams — the AAA, Victorias and Crystals — as well as the Ottawa Generals and Quebec Bulldogs.

Once the AAA had been declared holders of the Cup, any Canadian hockey team could challenge for the trophy, but none dared. Consequently, the $50 silver bowl remained in Montreal.

MONTREAL AMATEUR ATHLETIC ASSOCIATION (AHA) — 1894

SCORES
Mar. 17	Mtl Victorias	2	at Mtl AAA	3
Mar. 22	Ottawa	1	at Mtl AAA	3

The 1894 AHA season ended precariously. Four of the five competing clubs — the Montreal AAA, Montreal Victorias, Ottawa Capitals and Quebec Bulldogs — finished with 5-3-0 records and shares of first place. The determination of a champion and winner of the Stanley Cup created many problems for the league's governors, who simply could not come to terms on a solution suitable to all involved. With two of the four finalists from Montreal, home-ice advantage became the major issue of contention. After Quebec ultimately withdrew, it was decided that all playoff games be staged in Montreal and that Ottawa would be given a bye since it was the sole away team.

In what must be termed the first Stanley Cup playoff game ever, the two Montreal clubs battled to a 3-2 decision in favor of the defending champions, who then downed Ottawa in the finale.

Forward Billy Barlow, who finished third overall with eight goals in eight regular-season games, scored twice in each post-season contest as the AAA successfully defended its title.

1895 MONTREAL VICTORIAS (AHA)

The Montreal Victorias wrapped up the AHA title on March 8, and were prepared to defend the Cup as league champions. However, trustees Sweetland and Ross had already accepted a Stanley Cup challenge match between the 1894 champion AAA club and Queen's University with the game set for March 9.

In one of the most unusual Stanley Cup situations ever, Sweetland and Ross maintained that if the AAA defeated Queen's, the Vics would be declared champions, but if Queen's won, the trophy would go to the university squad. The AAA won the game and the challenge, and in turn the Vics were awarded the Cup.

Clarence McKerrow, the first "ringer" in Stanley Cup history, scored once for the AAA in a winning effort.

SCORES
Mar. 9 Queen's U. 1 at Mtl AAA 5

1896 FEBRUARY WINNIPEG VICTORIAS (MHL)

The first east-west confrontation in Stanley Cup history pitted the defending Montreal Victorias against the Winnipeg Victorias, champions of the Manitoba Hockey League (MHL).

Merritt, the Winnipeg netminder, introduced the first set of goalies' pads to the Montrealers when he skated onto to the ice with a pair of white cricket pads and proceeded to register a shutout. Dan Bain scored the Cup-winning goal mid-way through the game, and C.J. Campbell added the other.

SCORES
Feb. 14 Wpg Victorias 2 at Mtl Victorias 0

MONTREAL VICTORIAS (AHA) — 1896 DECEMBER

SCORES
Dec. 30 Mtl Victorias 6 at Wpg Victorias 5

After winning the AHA championship with a 7-1-0 record, the recently dethroned Cup champion Montreal Vics wasted no time in requesting a challenge, but satisfactory ice could not be ensured and the game was put off until the following winter.

The long-awaited rematch was described as the greatest sporting event in Winnipeg history to date. Throngs of fans jammed the arena with many paying as much as $12 per seat. Back in Montreal, the Daily Star newspaper arranged a public gathering whereby fans received up-to-the-minute game reports via telegraph.

The Montrealers overcame a 4-2 halftime deficit to tie the game 5-5, before Ernie McLea, who posted the first Stanley Cup hat-trick, rifled his third goal of the night past Merritt, cricket pads and all, to win the game in the closing seconds.

MONTREAL VICTORIAS (AHA) — 1897

SCORES
Dec. 27 Ottawa 2 at Mtl Victorias 15

The Montreal Vics (7-1-0), champions of the AHA for a third straight season, accepted a challenge from the Ottawa Capitals, winners of the Central Canada Hockey Association title. Although this Stanley Cup confrontation was originally set as a best-of-three series, the trustees ended the affair after one game because the two teams were unevenly matched.

1898 MONTREAL VICTORIAS (AHA)

Despite the absence of a challenger, the Montreal Vics became the first undefeated and untied Stanley Cup champions with a perfect 8-0-0 record on the season. Vics' forward Cam Davidson headlined the cast of scoring leaders with 14 goals in seven regular-season games.

1899 MONTREAL VICTORIAS (CAHL)
FEBRUARY

The AHA had dissolved prior to the start of the season with the Canadian Amateur Hockey League (CAHL) taking its place as the top hockey league in the country. The five former AHA franchises now comprised the new league.

The Montreal Vics successfully defended the Cup with consecutive one-goal wins in this mid-season challenge against their perennial rivals from Winnipeg.

After narrowly winning the first game of the set, Montreal was given a boost when a record crowd of over 7,000 fans attended the second. Mid-way through the contest, Montreal's Bob McDougall slashed and injured Winnipeg's Tony Gingras, and the referee imposed a two-minute penalty, which Winnipeg refused to accept. The westerners walked off the ice.

Insulted by the incident, the referee left the arena. He reappeared over an hour after play had stopped. He gave Winnipeg five minutes to resume play, and upon their failure to return, the game was awarded to Montreal.

SCORES
Mar. 14 Queen's U. 2 at Mtl Shamrocks 6

MONTREAL SHAMROCKS (CAHL)

1899 MARCH

SCORES
Feb. 15 Wpg Victorias 1 at Mtl Victorias 2
Feb. 18 Wpg Victorias 2 at Mtl Victorias 3

Total Goals
         Mtl Victorias 5   Wpg Victorias 3

The Montreal Shamrocks, formerly the Crystals, captured the 1899 CAHL title and with it the Stanley Cup. Harry Trihey of the Irish netted a hat-trick, and Arthur Farrell posted two more en route to the club's first successful defense of the Cup.

MONTREAL SHAMROCKS (CAHL)

1900 FEBRUARY

SCORES
Feb. 12 Wpg Victorias 3 at Mtl Shamrocks 4
Feb. 14 Wpg Victorias 3 at Mtl Shamrocks 2
Feb. 16 Wpg Victorias 4 at Mtl Shamrocks 5

In mid-season, the Shamrocks faced Winnipeg in the first best-of-three to go the limit. The series was evenly played with only one goal separating the teams in each contest. Harry Trihey was the offensive star again with seven goals in three games, including three in the finale.

The Winnipeg club, which had become noted for its innovations, introduced a new hockey stick which had the upper edge of the blade tapered, making it much lighter and considerably more modern.

1900 MARCH — MONTREAL SHAMROCKS (CAHL)

At the end of the 1900 season, the Montreal Shamrocks soundly turned back an attempt by the Halifax Crescents of the Maritime Hockey League to take the Cup. Montreal's Arthur Farrell established a new Stanley Cup record with four goals in each game to lead the champs.

SCORES
| Mar. 5 | Halifax | 2 | at | Mtl Shamrocks | 10 |
| Mar. 7 | Halifax | 0 | at | Mtl Shamrocks | 11 |

1901 — WINNIPEG VICTORIAS (MHL)

After a five-year hiatus, the Winnipeg Vics regained the Stanley Cup from the eastern champions in consecutive victories. Forward Dan Bain, who scored the Cup-winning goal four minutes into overtime in Game Two, played both games with a mask as the Vics continued to surprise Montrealers with new innovations from the west.

SCORES
| Jan. 21 | Tor. Wellingtons | 3 | at | Wpg Victorias | 5 |
| Jan. 23 | Tor. Wellingtons | 3 | at | Wpg Victorias | 5 |

WINNIPEG VICTORIAS (MHL)

1902 JANUARY

SCORES
Jan. 29 Wpg Victorias 4 at Mtl Shamrocks 3
Jan. 31 Wpg Victorias 2 at Mtl Shamrocks 1 OT

The Cup trustees accepted a challenge from the Toronto Wellingtons of the Ontario Hockey Association, and the Vics easily won the Cup in two games. For unknown reasons, Toronto wore Winnipeg uniforms in the first match and their own in the second.

MONTREAL AMATEUR ATHLETIC ASSOCIATION (AHA)

1902 MARCH

SCORES
Mar. 13 Mtl AAA 0 at Wpg Victorias 1
Mar. 15 Mtl AAA 5 at Wpg Victorias 0
Mar. 17 Mtl AAA 2 at Wpg Victorias 1

Over 4,000 fans packed the Winnipeg Arena paying as much as $25 for $5 and $10 seats for this battle of the giants.

After the two rivals split the first two games, Montreal's Art Hooper and Jack Marshall scored early in the third to give the AAA the lead. But it was a stubborn defense which lifted the Montrealers to victory and earned them the monicker "Little Men of Iron", a nickname which became commonly associated with the Montreal Wanderers who later employed most of the AAA's star players.

1903 FEBRUARY
MONTREAL AMATEUR ATHLETIC ASSOCIATION (AHA)

The first game was a lopsided contest won by the AAA, but the Vics bounced back in the second. With the score tied 2-2 at midnight after 27 minutes of overtime in this Saturday night affair, the Mayor of Westmount refused to allow the game to continue into the Sabbath. The Cup trustees first decided to resume the overtime the following Monday but later realized it would be impossible to sell tickets to a game which might end after a few minutes or even a few seconds. Consequently, the game was replayed in its entirety.

Tom Phillips, one of the greatest players of the early era, made his Stanley Cup debut with three goals in four games.

The Winnipeg players all wore tube skates, the first time an entire team had appeared in the east so equipped.

SCORES
Jan.	29	Wpg Victorias	1	at Mtl AAA	8	
Jan.	31	Wpg Victorias	2	at Mtl AAA	2	OT
Feb.	2	Wpg Victorias	4	at Mtl AAA	2	
Feb.	4	Wpg Victorias	1	at Mtl AAA	5	

1903 MARCH
OTTAWA SILVER SEVEN (CAHL)

With the Ottawa Silver Seven (6-2-0), formerly the Generals, and the Montreal Victorias (6-2-0) deadlocked atop the CAHL at season's end, the two clubs played out a two-game, total-goals playoff for rights to the Cup.

After a tie in Game One, Ottawa's famed Gilmour brothers - Billy, Dave and Suddy - combined for five goals and Frank McGee added a hat-trick en route to the league championship and the Cup.

SCORES
Mar.	7	Silver Seven	1	at Mtl Victorias	1
Mar.	10	Mtl Victorias	0	at Silver Seven	8

Total Goals:
Silver Seven	9	Mtl Victorias	1

OTTAWA SILVER SEVEN (CAHL) 1903
MARCH

SCORES
Mar 12 Rat Portage 2 at Silver Seven 6
Mar 14 Rat Portage 2 at Silver Seven 4

The Rat Portage Thistles, playing with only one man over the age of 20, journeyed from northern Ontario to Ottawa to meet the Silver Seven. The game proved to be a springboard for the Ottawa club, which successfully defended the Cup for the first of nine straight times.

Billy and Dave Gilmour combined with Frank McGee for all 10 Ottawa goals in the two-game series.

OTTAWA SILVER SEVEN (CAHL) 1904
JANUARY

SCORES
Dec. 30 Wpg Rowing Club 1 at Silver Seven 9
Jan. 1 Wpg Rowing Club 6 at Silver Seven 2
Jan. 4 Wpg Rowing Club 0 at Silver Seven 2

Before resigning from the CAHL, the Ottawa Silver Seven successfully defended the Cup against a new Winnipeg team. Ottawa's "One-eyed" Frank McGee registered a hat-trick in the first game, but Captain Bill Breen rallied the challengers with two goals in the second. In the finale, goalie Bouse Hutton shut down Winnipeg completely, with McGee scoring the game-winner.

Prior to the opening contest, both teams agreed to paint what essentially became the first "goal line" in hockey history. A red line was drawn from goalpost to goalpost in order to aid the referee in awarding goals.

Joe Hall made his Stanley Cup debut with the underdog Rowing Club.

1904 FEBRUARY
OTTAWA SILVER SEVEN

On February 8, Ottawa pulled out of the CAHL over a dispute involving a make-up game with the Montreal Vics. As a result, the Quebec Bulldogs, who had won the league title, petitioned the trustees to strip the Silver Seven of the Cup. The request was denied, but while the debate continued, Ottawa faced a new challenger, the Toronto Marlboros of the Ontario Hockey Association, in defense of the Cup.

Frank McGee led the Silver Seven with three goals in the first game and the first five-goal performance ever recorded in Stanley Cup competition in the second to insure the sweep.

SCORES
Feb. 23 Tor. Marlies 3 at Silver Seven 6
Feb. 25 Tor. Marlies 2 at Silver Seven 11

1904 MARCH
OTTAWA SILVER SEVEN

The Montreal Wanderers, who had stripped their cross-city rival AAA club of its best players, skated to the inaugural Federal Amateur Hockey Association (FAHL) championship with a perfect 6-0-0 record and were granted a two-game, total-goals challenge for the Stanley Cup.

Following the first game which ended with a 5-5 deadlock, a new two-game series was scheduled to be played in Ottawa. However, the Wanderers refused to play unless one of the games would be staged in Montreal. As defenders of the Cup, the Silver Seven did not have to yield to such a demand, and the series was awarded to Ottawa.

SCORES
Mar. 2 Silver Seven 5 at Mtl Wanderers 5

OTTAWA SILVER SEVEN

1904 MARCH

SCORES
Mar. 9	Brandon	3	at Silver Seven	6
Mar. 11	Brandon	3	at Silver Seven	9

Ottawa faced Brandon, the champions of the Manitoba/Northwestern Hockey League, in their fourth Stanley Cup challenge of the season and won in consecutive games. Frank McGee scored eight goals in the two games, including five in the first to tie his own Stanley Cup record set earlier in the year. 21-year-old Lester Patrick starred for Brandon in his Cup debut.

OTTAWA SILVER SEVEN (FAHL)

1905 JANUARY

SCORES
Jan. 13	Dawson City	2	at Silver Seven	9
Jan. 16	Dawson City	2	at Silver Seven	23

Now a member of the FAHL, Ottawa took on Dawson City in a mid-season challenge for the Cup. The Nuggets, backed by Yukon prospector Colonel Joe Boyle, departed from Dawson City on December 19th to meet the famed Silver Seven nearly a month later. The 4,000-mile excursion included travel by dogsled, boat and train and set the club back by over $3,000.

Wearied from the long trek, the challengers were overwhelmed in the series. In the second game, Ottawa set Stanley Cup scoring records of every variety, including an unparalleled 14-goal outburst from Frank McGee.

1905 MARCH
OTTAWA SILVER SEVEN (FAHL)

Ottawa had lost Frank McGee for the series opener, and the fleet-footed Rat Portage cast skated to victory. Tom Phillips put on an show for the fans with the first five-goal performance in a Stanley Cup game by a player other than the high-scoring McGee.

Ottawa's rink crew flooded the ice in the remaining two games, and the move greatly slowed the Thistles' fast-paced attack. McGee returned to score three goals in both games, including the Cup-winner in the finale.

SCORES
Mar. 7	Rat Portage	9	at Silver Seven	3
Mar. 9	Rat Portage	2	at Silver Seven	4
Mar. 11	Rat Portage	4	at Silver Seven	5

1906 FEBRUARY
OTTAWA SILVER SEVEN (ECAHA)

The Silver Seven, who had now jumped to the upstart Eastern Canada Amateur Hockey Association (ECAHA), hosted Queen's University, which challenged for the third time.

Alf and Harry Smith, the best of seven brothers to have tried out for the Ottawa squad, led the Silver Seven to victory. Alf scored five goals in the first game, and Harry duplicated the feat in the second.

SCORES
| Feb. 27 | Queen's U. | 7 | at Silver Seven | 16 |
| Feb. 28 | Queen's U. | 7 | at Silver Seven | 12 |

OTTAWA SILVER SEVEN (ECAHA) 1906 MARCH

SCORES
Mar. 6 Smiths Falls 5 at Silver Seven 6
Mar. 8 Smiths Falls 2 at Silver Seven 8

The Cup trustees decided that Ottawa should defend the Cup against Smiths Falls, champions of the FAHL. Frank McGee notched nine goals in the two games, which would be the last of Ottawa's nine straight successful Cup defenses.

It is interesting to note that the title "Silver Seven" was given only to the team and not to any particular seven players. Ottawa's line-up included a total of 16 players during its Stanley Cup reign from 1903-1906.

MONTREAL WANDERERS (ECAHA) 1906 MARCH

SCORES
Mar 14 Silver Seven   1 at Mtl Wanderers 9
Mar 17 Mtl Wanderers 3 at Silver Seven   9

Total Goals:
Mtl Wanderers 12   Silver Seven 10

Ottawa and Montreal each concluded the regular-season at 9-1-0, leading to a two-game, total-goals series for the ECAHA championship and possession of the Stanley Cup.

In his Stanley Cup debut, Ernie Russell scored four goals to lift Montreal over Ottawa 9-1 in the first game, which left the defending champs with the task of outscoring the Wanderers by a minimum of nine goals in the second in order to retain the trophy.

After Montreal put up the first goal in the second game, Ottawa stormed to a 9-1 lead on the strength of Harry Smith's five-goal effort to tie the series. However, Montreal rover Lester Patrick scored two late goals for the Wanderers to lock up the club's first Stanley Cup.

1906 DECEMBER — MONTREAL WANDERERS (ECAHA)

A new ruling allowed professionals to play with the amateurs, and the Wanderers were quick to give contracts to Riley Hern, "Pud" Glass, Hod Stuart, Ernie Johnson and Jack Marshall - who became the first five pros in Stanley Cup competition. The challenging New Glasgow squad was strictly amateur.

Amidst the partially pro line-up, it was amateur rover Lester Patrick who led Montreal over New Glasgow with seven goals in the two games.

SCORES
Dec. 27 New Glasgow 3 at Mtl Wanderers 10
Dec. 29 New Glasgow 2 at Mtl Wanderers 7

Total Goals:
    Mtl Wanderers 17 New Glasgow 5

1907 JANUARY — KENORA THISTLES

Because no ice was available earlier in 1906, this east-west confrontation had to be delayed until the start of the 1907 schedule.

The Kenora Thistles, *a.k.a.* the Rat Portage Thistles, brought in Art Ross and Roxy Beaudro as ringers in an effort to beef up the line-up which had failed to win its Cup challenge in 1905.

Tom Phillips scored seven times in the two games, including all four Kenora goals in the first contest.

SCORES
Jan. 17 Kenora Thistles 4 at Mtl Wanderers 2
Jan. 21 Kenora Thistles 8 at Mtl Wanderers 6

Total Goals:
    Kenora Thistles 12 Mtl Wanderers 8

MONTREAL WANDERERS (ECAHA) 1907
MARCH

SCORES
Mar. 23 Mtl Wanderers 7 vs Kenora Thistles 2 *
Mar. 25 Mtl Wanderers 5 vs Kenora Thistles 6 *
* played in Winnipeg

Total Goals:
　　Mtl Wanderers 12 　Kenora Thistles 8

Immediately after capturing the ECAHA title, the Wanderers submitted a challenge to the Cup trustees, who accepted the bid.

After the departure of Art Ross, Kenora imported two more players, Alf Smith and Harry Westwick of the Ottawa Silver Seven, to face the Wanderers. Although Smith scored in each game, Montreal's Ernie Russell led a winning attack with four goals in the first game and added a single in the second.

Both games were played in Winnipeg as a result of unsatisfactory rink conditions in Kenora.

MONTREAL WANDERERS (ECAHA) 1908
JANUARY

SCORES
Jan. 9 Ottawa Victorias 3 at Mtl Wanderers 9
Jan. 13 Ottawa Victorias 1 at Mtl Wanderers 13

Total Goals:
　　Mtl Wanderers 22 　Ottawa Victorias 4

The Ottawa Victorias, the latest cast of challengers, had actually finished third in the FAHL in 1907, but were awarded the league championship when the first and second place clubs - Montagnards and Cornwall - withdrew from competition. Nevertheless, Ottawa's challenge was accepted by the Cup trustees.

Ernie Russell netted 10 goals in two games, including six in the second, as Montreal easily defended the trophy.

1908 MARCH
MONTREAL WANDERERS (ECAHA)

After retaining the ECAHA crown with an 8-2-0 record, the Wanderers faced the Winnipeg Maple Leafs, champions of the Manitoba Hockey League.

For the first time ever in Stanley Cup play, every man on the winning team except the goalie scored at least once as the Wanderers took the first game. In the the second, Bruce Stuart and Ernie Johnson each registered four goals to defeat Winnipeg in consecutive games.

SCORES
Mar. 10	Wpg Maple Leafs	5	at Mtl Wanderers	11
Mar. 12	Wpg Maple Leafs	3	at Mtl Wanderers	9

Total Goals:
Mtl Wanderers 20   Wpg Maple Leafs 8

1908 MARCH
MONTREAL WANDERERS (ECAHA)

The Toronto Trolley Leaguers, champions of the Ontario Professional Hockey League (OPHL, the first entirely pro hockey league ever formed), played the Wanderers in a one-game, sudden-death affair.

The see-saw battle included four ties until Ernie Johnson scored the Wanderers' game-winning goal and Bruce Stuart tallied an insurance marker.

In his premier Stanley Cup appearance, Newsy Lalonde scored twice for Toronto.

SCORES
Mar. 14 Toronto 4 at Mtl Wanderers 6

MONTREAL WANDERERS (ECAHA) — 1908 DECEMBER

SCORES
Dec. 28 Edmonton 3 at Mtl Wanderers 7
Dec. 30 Edmonton 7 at Mtl Wanderers 6

Total Goals:
Mtl Wanderers 13   Edmonton 10

Having defeated the Manitoba Hockey League champions earlier in the year, the Alberta Hockey League champion Edmonton Eskimos earned a challenge series with Montreal.

With six of its seven players brought in especially to face the Wanderers, Edmonton established a new record for ringers on a Cup challenger. Only rover Fred Whitcroft was legitimate. Lester Patrick, Tom Phillips and Pit Pitre headlined the cast of imports.

After dropping the first game, Edmonton replaced two of its ringers with two regulars, Deeton and Miller, who had made the trip to Montreal. Both responded, scoring three and two goals, respectively. It marked the Wanderers' first Stanley Cup loss in seven games.

Harry Smith scored six goals, including five in the first game, as the Wanderers successfully defended the Cup despite splitting the series.

OTTAWA SENATORS (ECHA) — 1909

Prior to the 1909 season Montreal's AAA and Victoria clubs, who were the last amateur teams in the ECAHA, dropped out of the league. Consequently, the ECAHA was renamed the Eastern Canada Hockey Association (ECHA) with "Amateur" dropped from title.

The Ottawa Senators, formerly the Silver Seven, posted a 10-2-0 record to capture the first all-pro, ECHA championship and the Stanley Cup.

Although a challenge from the Winnipeg Shamrocks had been accepted by the Cup trustees, the lateness of the season prevented the series from ever being played.

Fred "Cyclone" Taylor, who tallied eight goals in 11 games, made his debut on a Stanley Cup championship team with the Senators.

1910 JANUARY
OTTAWA SENATORS (NHA)

1910 marked the inauguration of the National Hockey Association (NHA), the forerunner of the National Hockey League, and the formation of the Montreal Canadiens, who would eventually become hockey's most prolific champions.

The Ottawa Senators, holders of the Stanley Cup and now members of the NHA, defended the trophy against Galt, the 1909 champions of the Ontario Professional Hockey League (OPHL). Marty Walsh scored six goals in the first game en route to a sweep over the challengers.

Concerned by the number of "ringers" imported by Cup contestants, the trustees ruled that only players who had skated with their teams during the regular-season could be eligible for the Stanley Cup competition.

SCORES
Jan. 5   Galt   3   at   Ottawa Senators   12
Jan. 7   Galt   1   at   Ottawa Senators   3

Total Goals:
         Ottawa Senators   15   Galt   4

1910 JANUARY
OTTAWA SENATORS (NHA)

After a strong Stanley Cup performance in 1909, Edmonton faced Ottawa in the Finals, but the eastern champions were too strong. In the two-game set, the Senators' Bruce Stuart and Gordie Roberts scored seven goals apiece, while Fred Whitcroft notched five for Edmonton.

SCORES
Jan. 18   Edmonton   4   at   Ottawa Senators   8
Jan. 20   Edmonton   7   at   Ottawa Senators   13

Total Goals:
         Ottawa Senators   21   Edmonton   11

MONTREAL WANDERERS (NHA)

1910 MARCH

SCORES
Mar. 12 Berlin   3 at Mtl Wanderers   7

With the 1910 NHA title in hand, the Montreal Wanderers took possession of the Stanley Cup from Ottawa and accepted a challenge from Berlin, 1910 champions of the OPHL. The Wanderers held on to take the one-game affair, with Ernie Russell (4) and Harry Hyland (3) scoring all seven goals for the winners.

OTTAWA SENATORS (NHA)

1911 MARCH

SCORES
Mar. 13 Galt   4 at Ottawa Senators 7

After defeating Waterloo for the OPHL crown, Galt downed Port Hope, champions of the Eastern Professional Hockey League, in what became the second of two playoff series leading up to a challenge for the Stanley Cup.

The NHA champion Senators (13-3-0), defeated the Galt squad 7-4 as Marty Walsh, who had first appeared in Stanley Cup play in 1906 with Queen's University, notched a hat-trick for the winners.

1911 MARCH
OTTAWA SENATORS (NHA)

Three days after defeating Galt, Ottawa took on the Ontario Hockey League champion Port Arthur Bearcats, who had beaten the Saskatchewan champions from Prince Albert to earn the challenge.

In the one-game confrontation, the Senators' Marty Walsh scored 10 goals to fall four short of the record set by Frank McGee in 1905.

SCORES
Mar. 16 Port Arthur 4 at Ottawa Senators 14

1912
QUEBEC BULLDOGS (NHA)

The Stanley Cup trustees introduced two major rule changes at the outset of 1912. Teams were required to play for the first time with six men per side instead of seven, and all challenges for the Cup had to take place after the conclusion of the regular-season.

The Quebec Bulldogs, who posted a league-high 10-8-0 record, successfully defended the newly acquired trophy against Moncton of the Maritime Professional Hockey League. Jack McDonald contributed nine and Joe Malone five of Quebec's 17 goals in the best-of-three series.

Although the famed Patrick brothers, Frank and Lester, had started the Pacific Coast Hockey Association, not one of the three original PCHA teams challenged for the Stanley Cup. The Patricks introduced the first artificial ice surface in Canada at the new 10,000-seat Vancouver Arena.

SCORES
Mar. 11 Moncton 3 at Quebec Bulldogs 9
Mar. 13 Moncton 0 at Quebec Bulldogs 8

QUEBEC BULLDOGS (NHA) 1913

SCORES

| Mar. 8 | Sydney Miners | 3 | at | Quebec Bulldogs | 14 |
| Mar. 10 | Sydney Miners | 2 | at | Quebec Bulldogs | 6 |

Quebec repeated as NHA champs and faced the Sydney Miners, the top Maritime club, in defense of the Stanley Cup. "Phantom" Joe Malone poured in nine goals in the first, and Joe Hall netted three in the second.

TORONTO BLUESHIRTS (NHA) 1914 MARCH

SCORES

| Mar. 7 | Tor. Blueshirts | 0 | at | Montreal | 2 |
| Mar. 11 | Montreal | 0 | at | Tor. Blueshirts | 6 |

Total Goals:
Tor. Blueshirts 6   Montreal 2

The Montreal Canadiens, making their first appearance in a Stanley Cup series, faced the Toronto Blueshirts in a two-game showdown for the NHA title and possession of the Cup.

Although each team posted a shutout on its home ice, the Blueshirts, who later became the NHL's Maple Leafs, outscored the Canadiens overall.

Game Two in Toronto was the first Stanley Cup matchup ever played on artificial ice.

1914 MARCH — TORONTO BLUESHIRTS (NHA)

In the first of 13 consecutive east-west confrontations for the Stanley Cup, Victoria of the PCHA traveled east to play Toronto but overlooked the formality of submitting a challenge. The trustees did not regard the series as legitimate, but it counted nevertheless as a successful title defense for Toronto.

Frank Foyston led the Blueshirts with three goals, including the Cup-winner in Game Three of this first best-of-five series.

SCORES
Mar. 14 Victoria Cougars 2 at Tor. Blueshirts 5
Mar. 17 Victoria Cougars 5 at Tor. Blueshirts 6 OT
Mar. 19 Victoria Cougars 1 at Tor. Blueshirts 2

1915 MARCH — VANCOUVER MILLIONAIRES (PCHA)

At the start of the season, an informal agreement had been reached between the NHA and PCHA for the two league's respective champions to meet each year to determine a Stanley Cup champion. The arrangement also included the Finals to be played alternately in the east and west, which explains why Vancouver hosted this year's games. For the first time, the competition for the Cup took place further west than Winnipeg.

Deadlocked with 13-7-0 records at the conclusion of the season, the Ottawa Senators and Montreal Canadiens played a two-game, total goals series for the NHA championship and the right to face the PCHA champions from Vancouver. Although the two clubs swapped shutouts to split the home-and-home series, the Senators outscored the Canadiens 4-1 and packed up for Vancouver.

Fred "Cyclone" Taylor notched six goals in three games to lead the Millionaires to a sweep of the best-of-five series.

SCORES
Mar. 22 Ottawa Senators 2 at Vancouver 6
Mar. 24 Ottawa Senators 3 at Vancouver 8
Mar. 26 Ottawa Senators 3 at Vancouver 12

MONTREAL CANADIENS (NHA) 1916

SCORES

Mar. 20	Portland	2	at	Montreal	0
Mar. 22	Portland	1	at	Montreal	2
Mar. 25	Portland	3	at	Montreal	6
Mar. 28	Portland	6	at	Montreal	5
Mar. 30	Portland	1	at	Montreal	2

For the first time, the Stanley Cup series came down to a fifth and final game after both participants split the first four games. Portland's Tommy Dunderdale put the Rosebuds ahead early, but the Canadiens bounced back. Skene Ronan tied the game, and seldom-used Goldie Prodgers netted the Cup-winner.

In his first Stanley Cup Finals, goaltender Georges Vezina backed the Canadiens with a 2.60 average in five games en route to the club's first championship.

SEATTLE METROPOLITANS (PCHA) 1917

SCORES

Mar. 17	Montreal	8	at	Seattle Mets	4
Mar. 20	Montreal	1	at	Seattle Mets	6
Mar. 23	Montreal	1	at	Seattle Mets	4
Mar. 25	Montreal	1	at	Seattle Mets	9

In only their second season, the Seattle Mets skated to the PCHA title to distinguish themselves as the first U.S. team to host a Stanley Cup series and the first American squad to capture the coveted trophy. Consequently, one of Lord Stanley's original conditions - that the trophy be held by the champion of the Dominion of Canada - had been eradicated.

Seattle's Bernie Morris, who finished second in the PCHA scoring race with 37 goals in 24 games, scored a team-high 14 times against Montreal, including six in the finale, to lead the Mets over the Canadiens.

1918 TORONTO ARENAS (NHL)

Prior to the start of the 1917-18 campaign, the NHA dissolved with the NHL taking its place. The new league started out with four teams - Montreal Canadiens, Montreal Wanderers, Ottawa Senators and Toronto Arenas - but the Wanderers withdrew after the Montreal Arena burned down.

After capturing the first NHL title, Toronto played host to Vancouver in the Finals, with the series alternating between eastern rules (6-man) in the odd games and western rules (7-man) in the even games. Because neither club seemed comfortable playing an unfamiliar style, Toronto won the series with the advantage of playing the final game under eastern rules.

Alf Skinner led the Arenas with eight goals in five games, while Fred "Cyclone" Taylor paced Vancouver with nine. Rookie coach Dick Carroll steered his team to the NHL's first Stanley Cup.

SCORES
Mar. 20	Vancouver	3	at	Toronto Arenas	5
Mar. 23	Vancouver	6	at	Toronto Arenas	4
Mar. 26	Vancouver	3	at	Toronto Arenas	6
Mar. 28	Vancouver	8	at	Toronto Arenas	1
Mar. 30	Vancouver	1	at	Toronto Arenas	2

1919 NO DECISION

Seattle's Frank Foyston and Montreal's Newsy Lalonde, two of the greatest scorers of the early 1900's, were at their best in this series. Foyston notched nine goals and Lalonde six as the two clubs stood even at two wins and one tie apiece after five games.

Several of the players became seriously sick with the flu, which had reached epidemic proportions throughout the country, and health officials were forced to cancel the remaining games. Canadiens' defenseman Joe Hall, hospitalized with a severe case, died tragically on April 5, 1919, in Seattle.

SCORES
Mar. 19	Montreal	0	at	Seattle Mets	7
Mar. 22	Montreal	4	at	Seattle Mets	2
Mar. 24	Montreal	2	at	Seattle Mets	7
Mar. 26	Montreal	0	at	Seattle Mets	0 OT
Mar. 30	Montreal	4	at	Seattle Mets	3 OT

SERIES CANCELLED DUE TO INFLUENZA EPIDEMIC

OTTAWA SENATORS (NHL) 1920

SCORES
Mar. 22 Seattle Mets 2 at Ottawa Senators 3
Mar. 24 Seattle Mets 0 at Ottawa Senators 3
Mar. 27 Seattle Mets 3 at Ottawa Senators 1
Mar. 30 Seattle Mets 5 vs Ottawa Senators 2*
Apr. 1 Seattle Mets 1 vs Ottawa Senators 6*
* played in Toronto

When the Mets arrived in Ottawa, it became apparent that their red, white and green barber pole uniforms were all too similar to the Senators' red, white and black pattern. Ottawa agreed to play in white jerseys.

Poor ice conditions marred the first three games, and the series was subsequently shifted to the artfifical surface at Toronto's Mutual Arena. Jack Darragh, who tallied the winning marker in Game One, lifted Ottawa to the championship with a hat-trick in the decisive game.

Pete Green became the second rookie coach in the NHL to win the Cup, joining Dick Carroll of the 1918 Toronto Arenas.

OTTAWA SENATORS (NHL) 1921

SCORES
Mar. 21 Ottawa Senators 1 at Vancouver 2
Mar. 24 Ottawa Senators 4 at Vancouver 3
Mar. 28 Ottawa Senators 3 at Vancouver 2
Mar. 31 Ottawa Senators 2 at Vancouver 3
Apr. 4 Ottawa Senators 2 at Vancouver 1

11,000 fans, the largest crowd ever to see a hockey game anywhere in the world at the time, jammed the Vancouver arena for the first game of this series, and an estimated record of 51,000 tickets were sold for the entire five-game series.

Jack Darragh was the hero for the second straight year, scoring both Ottawa goals in the finale as the Senators became the first NHL club to capture back-to-back Stanley Cups and the first team since the 1912-13 Quebec Bulldogs to repeat as champions.

1922 TORONTO ST. PATRICKS (NHL)

With the inception of the Western Canada Hockey League (WCHL) in 1921-22, a new playoff structure was designed to match the champions of the two west coast leagues against each other with the winner to meet the NHL champions for the Stanley Cup.

After defeating the WCHL's Regina Capitals in the preliminary series, the WCHA's Vancouver Millionaires set out for Toronto, where the NHL champion St. Pats awaited their arrival.

Cecil "Babe" Dye notched nine of his club's 16 goals, including two game-winners, and goaltender John Roach, who recorded the first Stanley Cup shutout ever by an NHL rookie, posted a 1.80 average as Toronto won its second Stanley Cup.

Jack Adams, who had been lured away from Toronto by Vancouver in 1920, returned in impressive fashion, scoring six goals in the series.

SCORES

Mar. 17	Vancouver	4	at	Toronto St. Pats	3
Mar. 20	Vancouver	1	at	Toronto St. Pats	2OT
Mar. 23	Vancouver	3	at	Toronto St. Pats	0
Mar. 25	Vancouver	0	at	Toronto St. Pats	6
Mar. 28	Vancouver	1	at	Toronto St. Pats	5

1923 OTTAWA SENATORS (NHL)

For the first time in Stanley Cup history, two brothers opposed each other in the Finals. In fact, two sets of brothers - Cy and Corb Denneny and George and Frank Boucher - stood on opposite sides of the center line for the opening face-off. Cy and George skated with Ottawa, while Corb and Frank suited up for Vancouver. Neither of the Dennenys scored in the series, but each of the Bouchers scored twice.

Ottawa's Harry Broadbent, who posted the only goal in Game One, scored five for the series to lead the Senators, whom Vancouver coach Frank Patrick called the greatest team he had ever seen.

The WCHL-PCHA playoff format was abandonned, but the WCHL champions were given the opportunity to compete directly for the Stanley Cup in this best-of-three series. The Eskimos gave the battle-weary Senators a difficult time, but Ottawa came through with one-goal victories in each game. Cy Denneny and Harry Broadbent scored the game-winners.

SCORES

Mar. 16	Ottawa Senators	1	at	Vancouver	0
Mar. 19	Ottawa Senators	1	at	Vancouver	4
Mar. 23	Ottawa Senators	3	at	Vancouver	2
Mar. 26	Ottawa Senators	5	at	Vancouver	1
Mar. 29	Ottawa Senators	2	vs	Edmonton	1OT*
Mar. 31	Ottawa Senators	1	vs	Edmonton	0*

* played in Vancouver

MONTREAL CANADIENS (NHL) 1924

SCORES
Mar. 18	Vancouver	2	at	Montreal	3
Mar. 20	Vancouver	1	at	Montreal	2
Mar. 22	Calgary Tigers	1	at	Montreal	6
Mar. 25	Calgary Tigers	0	vs	Montreal	3*

* played at Ottawa

Billy Boucher scored three of the Canadiens' five goals, including both game-winning tallies, to lift Montreal over Vancouver, which lost its chance at the Stanley Cup for the third straight year.

21-year-old, 160-pound rookie forward Howie Morenz paced the Montreal attack with a hat-trick in Game One and added another in Game Two as the Canadiens rolled past the Calgary Tigers to complete a sweep of both 1924 series.

Morenz, Aurel Joliat and Sylvio Mantha all made their first appearances on a Stanley Cup winner.

VICTORIA COUGARS (WCHL) 1925

SCORES
Mar. 21	Montreal	2	at	Victoria Cougars	5
Mar. 23	Montreal	1	vs	Victoria Cougars	3*
Mar. 27	Montreal	4	at	Victoria Cougars	2
Mar. 30	Montreal	1	at	Victoria Cougars	6

* played in Vancouver

The Victoria Cougars, who joined the WCHL after the PCHA folded, became the last non-NHL team ever to win the Stanley Cup and only the third west coast club to capture the trophy, joining the 1915 Vancouver Millionaires and the 1917 Seattle Metropolitans as champions.

Despite all eight Montreal goals from the Canadiens' Speedball Line of Howie Morenz, Aurel Joliat and Billy Boucher, Victoria posted a more balanced attack with eight different skaters combining for 16 goals.

1926 MONTREAL MAROONS (NHL)

The Maroons had a new home for 1925-26 in the newly constructed Montreal Forum, which had artificial ice enabling the Stanley Cup to start later than ever.

In his first career Stanley Cup series, defenseman Nels Stewart scored six of Montreal's 10 goals, and goaltender Clint Benedict recorded an unprecedented three shutouts en route to the Maroons' first Stanley Cup in the club's second NHL season.

With the NHL taking full control of the Stanley Cup following WCHL's demise soon after this series, the 1926 championship punctuated the most dynamic era in Stanley Cup history. Since 1893, Cup play had grown from an amateur challenge in eastern Canada to a professional competition involving teams from across the continent.

SCORES

Mar. 30	Victoria Cougars	0	at	Mtl Maroons	3
Apr. 1	Victoria Cougars	0	at	Mtl Maroons	3
Apr. 3	Victoria Cougars	3	at	Mtl Maroons	2
Apr. 6	Victoria Cougars	0	at	Mtl Maroons	2

1927 OTTAWA SENATORS

Since the WCHL folded and no other major professional league existed, the Stanley Cup now became sole property of the NHL.

The American Division champion Boston Bruins met the Canadian champion Ottawa Senators in what became the first Stanley Cup of the modern era.

Cy Denneny led the Senators with four of the team's seven total goals, including the game-winners in both victories.

QUARTER-FINALS

Mar. 29	Montreal	1	at	Mtl Maroons	1	
Mar. 31	Mtl Maroons	0	at	Montreal	1	OT

Montreal won total-goals series 2–1

Mar. 29	Boston	6	vs	Chicago	1	*
Mar. 31	Chicago	4	at	Boston	4	

* at New York

Boston won total-goals series 10–5

SEMI-FINALS

Apr. 2	Ottawa	4	at	Montreal	0
Apr. 4	Montreal	1	at	Ottawa	1

Ottawa won total-goals series 5–1

Apr. 2	NY Rangers	0	at	Boston	0
Apr. 4	Boston	3	at	NY Rangers	1

Boston won total-goals series 3–1

FINALS

Apr. 7	Ottawa	0	at	Boston	0	OT
Apr. 9	Ottawa	3	at	Boston	1	
Apr. 11	Boston	1	at	Ottawa	1	OT
Apr. 13	Boston	1	at	Ottawa	3	

Boston won best-of-five series 2-0-2

NEW YORK RANGERS 1928

QUARTER-FINALS
| Mar. 27 | Mtl Maroons | 1 | at | Ottawa | 0 |
| Mar. 29 | Ottawa | 1 | at | Mtl Maroons | 2 |

Maroons won total-goals series 3–1

| Mar. 27 | Pittsburgh | 0 | at | NY Rangers | 4 |
| Mar. 29 | Pittsburgh | 4 | at | NY Rangers | 2 |

Rangers won total-goals series 6–4

SEMI-FINALS
| Mar. 31 | Montreal | 2 | at | Mtl Maroons | 2 | |
| Apr. 3 | Mtl Maroons | 1 | at | Montreal | 0 | OT |

Maroons won total-goals series 3–2

| Mar. 31 | Boston | 1 | at | NY Rangers | 1 |
| Apr. 3 | NY Rangers | 4 | at | Boston | 1 |

Rangers won total-goals series 5–2

FINALS
Apr. 5	NY Rangers	0	at	Mtl Maroons	2	
Apr. 7	NY Rangers	2	at	Mtl Maroons	1	OT
Apr. 10	NY Rangers	0	at	Mtl Maroons	2	
Apr. 12	NY Rangers	1	at	Mtl Maroons	0	
Apr. 14	NY Rangers	2	at	Mtl Maroons	1	

Rangers won best-of-five series 3–2

When the Rangers moved into the Finals, the circus moved into New York's Madison Square Garden and took priority over the hockey team. As a result, club management decided to play the entire series in Montreal.

After losing goalie Lorne Chabot to an eye injury midway through Game Two, 45-year-old Rangers' coach and former defenseman Lester Patrick took over between the pipes, inspiring the New Yorkers to a 2-1 overtime victory. The following day the Rangers signed New York Americans' netminder Joe Miller, who responded with two wins including the second shutout by an NHL rookie in Stanley Cup history.

In only their second NHL season, the Rangers captured their first Stanley Cup and became only the second American team in history, joining the 1917 Seattle Metropolitans of the PCHA, to possess the trophy.

BOSTON BRUINS 1929

SERIES A - SEMI-FINALS
Mar. 19	Montreal	0	at	Boston	1
Mar. 21	Montreal	0	at	Boston	1
Mar. 23	Boston	3	at	Montreal	2

Boston won best-of-five series 3–0

SERIES B AND C - QUARTER-FINALS
| Mar. 19 | NY Rangers | 0 | at | NY Americans | 0 | |
| Mar. 21 | NY Americans | 0 | at | NY Rangers | 1 | OT |

Rangers won total-goals series 1–0

| Mar. 19 | Toronto | 3 | at | Detroit | 1 |
| Mar. 21 | Detroit | 1 | at | Toronto | 4 |

Toronto won total-goals series 7–2

SERIES D - SEMI-FINALS
| Mar. 24 | Toronto | 0 | at | NY Rangers | 1 | |
| Mar. 26 | NY Rangers | 2 | at | Toronto | 1 | OT |

Rangers won best-of-three series 2–0

FINALS
| Mar. 28 | NY Rangers | 0 | at | Boston | 2 |
| Mar. 29 | Boston | 2 | at | NY Rangers | 1 |

Boston won best-of-three series 2–0

When the Bruins met the Rangers in this series, it marked the first time in Stanley Cup history that two American teams clashed head-on in the Finals.

Goalie Cecil "Tiny" Thompson backstopped the Bruins to consecutive wins, allowing just one goal in the two games and posting the third Stanley Cup shutout ever by an NHL rookie as Boston captured its first Cup.

Dit Clapper and Harry Oliver scored the two game-winning goals.

1930 MONTREAL CANADIENS

The defending champion Boston Bruins, who skated to the NHL's top regular-season record in 1929-30 at 38-5-1, suffered their first back-to-back defeats all season long as the Canadiens won the Stanley Cup.

The Canadiens, losers of all four of their regular-season meetings with the Bruins, were led by captain Sylvio Mantha who tallied a goal in both final series games.

SERIES A - SEMI-FINALS
Mar. 20	Boston	2	at	Mtl Maroons	1	OT
Mar. 22	Boston	4	at	Mtl Maroons	2	
Mar. 25	Mtl Maroons	1	at	Boston	0	OT
Mar. 27	Mtl Maroons	1	at	Boston	5	

Boston won best-of-five series 3–1

SERIES B AND C - QUARTER-FINALS
| Mar. 23 | Montreal | 1 | at | Chicago | 0 | |
| Mar. 26 | Chicago | 2 | at | Montreal | 2 | OT |

Montreal won total-goals series 3–2

| Mar. 20 | NY Rangers | 1 | at | Ottawa | 1 | |
| Mar. 23 | Ottawa | 2 | at | NY Rangers | 5 | |

Rangers won total-goals series 6–3

SERIES D - SEMI-FINALS
| Mar. 28 | NY Rangers | 1 | at | Montreal | 2 | OT |
| Mar. 30 | Montreal | 2 | at | NY Rangers | 0 | |

Montreal won best-of-three series 2–0

FINALS
| Apr. 1 | Montreal | 3 | at | Boston | 0 | |
| Apr. 3 | Boston | 3 | at | Montreal | 4 | |

Montreal won best-of-three series 2–0

1931 MONTREAL CANADIENS

The Montreal Canadiens became the second NHL team ever to repeat as champions, duplicating the feat accomplished by the Ottawa Senators in 1920-21. Chicago's Dick Irvin made his coaching debut in the Finals against the team which he would later lead to three Stanley Cups.

Over 18,000 fans packed Chicago Stadium for Game Two to set a new record for the largest attendance in hockey history.

SEMI-FINALS
Mar. 24	Montreal	4	at	Boston	5	OT
Mar. 26	Montreal	1	at	Boston	0	
Mar. 28	Boston	3	at	Montreal	4	OT
Mar. 30	Boston	3	at	Montreal	1	
Apr. 1	Boston	2	at	Montreal	3	OT

Montreal won best-of-five series 3–2

SERIES B AND C - QUARTER-FINALS
| Mar. 24 | Chicago | 2 | at | Toronto | 2 | |
| Mar. 26 | Toronto | 1 | at | Chicago | 2 | OT |

Chicago won total-goals series 4–3

| Mar. 24 | Mtl Maroons | 1 | at | NY Rangers | 5 | |
| Mar. 26 | NY Rangers | 3 | at | Mtl Maroons | 0 | |

Rangers won total-goals series 8–1

SERIES D - SEMI-FINALS
| Mar. 29 | NY Rangers | 0 | at | Chicago | 2 | |
| Mar. 31 | Chicago | 1 | at | NY Rangers | 0 | |

Chicago won total-goals series 3–0

FINALS
Apr. 3	Montreal	2	at	Chicago	1	
Apr. 5	Montreal	1	at	Chicago	2	OT
Apr. 9	Chicago	3	at	Montreal	2	OT
Apr. 11	Chicago	2	at	Montreal	4	
Apr. 14	Chicago	0	at	Montreal	2	

Montreal won best-of-five series 3–2

TORONTO MAPLE LEAFS 1932

SERIES A - SEMI-FINALS
Mar. 24	NY Rangers	3	at	Montreal	4	
Mar. 26	NY Rangers	4	at	Montreal	3	OT
Mar. 27	Montreal	0	at	NY Rangers	1	
Mar. 29	Montreal	2	at	NY Rangers	5	

Rangers won best-of-five series 3–1

SERIES B AND C - QUARTER-FINALS
Mar. 27	Toronto	0	at	Chicago	1
Mar. 29	Chicago	1	at	Toronto	6

Toronto won total-goals series 6–2

Mar. 27	Mtl Maroons	1	at	Detroit	1
Mar. 29	Detroit	0	at	Mtl Maroons	2

Maroons won total-goals series 3–1

SERIES D - SEMI-FINALS
Mar. 31	Toronto	1	at	Mtl Maroons	1	
Apr. 2	Mtl Maroons	2	at	Toronto	3	OT

Toronto won total-goals series 4–3

FINALS
Apr. 5	Toronto	6	at	NY Rangers	4	
Apr. 7	Toronto	6	at	NY Rangers	2	*
Apr. 9	NY Rangers	4	at	Toronto	6	

* played in Boston

Toronto won best-of-five series 3–0

After losing to Toronto in Game One, the Rangers also lost the home-ice advantage because the circus had once again invaded Madison Square Garden. Game Two, originally set for New York, was moved to Boston.

Toronto's famed "Kid Line" - Harvey "Busher" Jackson, Charlie Conacher and Joe Primeau - made its Stanley Cup debut, combining for eight goals in three games.

The Leafs' Dick Irvin, who lost in the 1931 Finals with Chicago, earned his first title as a coach.

NEW YORK RANGERS 1933

SERIES A - SEMI-FINALS
Mar. 25	Toronto	1	at	Boston	2	OT
Mar. 28	Toronto	1	at	Boston	0	OT
Mar. 30	Boston	2	at	Toronto	1	OT
Apr. 1	Boston	3	at	Toronto	5	
Apr. 3	Boston	0	at	Toronto	1	OT

Toronto won best-of-five series 3–2

SERIES B AND C - QUARTER-FINALS
Mar. 25	Detroit	2	at	Mtl Maroons	0
Mar. 28	Mtl Maroons	2	at	Detroit	3

Detroit won total-goals series 5–2

Mar. 26	Montreal	2	at	NY Rangers	5
Mar. 28	NY Rangers	3	at	Montreal	3

Rangers won total-goals series 8–5

SERIES D - SEMI-FINALS
Mar. 30	Detroit	0	at	NY Rangers	2
Apr. 2	NY Rangers	4	at	Detroit	3

Rangers won total-goals series 6–3

FINALS
Apr. 4	Toronto	1	at	NY Rangers	5	
Apr. 8	NY Rangers	3	at	Toronto	1	
Apr. 11	NY Rangers	2	at	Toronto	3	
Apr. 13	NY Rangers	1	at	Toronto	0	OT

Rangers won best-of-five series 3–1

Again the circus forced the Rangers out of New York, with all but Game One contested on Toronto's home ice.

In the final match, the Rangers' Bill Cook became the first of 12 players ever to register a Cup-winning goal in overtime when he snapped a scoreless tie at 7:33 of the fourth period, and goalie Andy Aitkenhead posted the fourth shutout by an NHL rookie in the Finals.

1934 CHICAGO BLACK HAWKS

For the second year in a row, the Stanley Cup-winning goal was scored in overtime. When Chicago's Harold "Mush" March netted the series-winner at 30:05 of overtime, the Blackhawks captured their first Cup.

Chicago's Chuck Gardiner limited Detroit to two goals in his club's three victories, while Detroit's Wilf Cude led the Red Wings to their only win of the series in Game Three despite suffering a broken nose mid-way through the contest.

SERIES A - SEMI-FINALS
Mar. 22	Detroit	2 at Toronto	1	OT
Mar. 24	Detroit	6 at Toronto	3	
Mar. 26	Toronto	3 at Detroit	1	
Mar. 28	Toronto	5 at Detroit	1	
Mar. 30	Toronto	0 at Detroit	1	

Detroit won best-of-five series 3–2

SERIES B AND C - QUARTER-FINALS
| Mar. 22 | Chicago | 3 at Montreal | 2 | |
| Mar. 25 | Montreal | 1 at Chicago | 1 | OT |

Chicago won total-goals series 4–3

| Mar. 20 | NY Rangers | 0 at Mtl Maroons | 0 | |
| Mar. 25 | Mtl Maroons | 2 at NY Rangers | 1 | |

Maroons won total-goals series 2–1

SERIES D - SEMI-FINALS
| Mar. 28 | Chicago | 3 at Mtl Maroons | 0 | |
| Apr. 1 | Mtl Maroons | 2 at Chicago | 3 | |

Chicago won total-goals series 6–2

FINALS
Apr. 3	Chicago	2 at Detroit	1	OT
Apr. 5	Chicago	4 at Detroit	1	
Apr. 8	Detroit	5 at Chicago	2	
Apr. 10	Detroit	0 at Chicago	1	OT

Chicago won best-of-five series 3–1

1935 MONTREAL MAROONS

In the first All-Canadian Finals since 1926, the Maroons battled to their second Stanley Cup championship in nine seasons with a sweep of Toronto. Montreal netminder Alex Connell allowed four goals in three games.

Winning coach Tommy Gorman became the first and only coach ever to win successive Stanley Cups with two different teams. He had directed the Chicago Blackhawks to the title a year earlier. Gorman currently ranks as one of three NHL coaches (Dick Irvin and Scott Bowman are the others) to have led more than one team to the Cup.

SERIES A - SEMI-FINALS
Mar. 23	Toronto	0 at Boston	1	OT
Mar. 26	Toronto	2 at Boston	0	
Mar. 28	Boston	0 at Toronto	3	
Mar. 30	Boston	1 at Toronto	2	OT

Toronto won best-of-five series 3–1

SERIES B AND C - QUARTER-FINALS
| Mar. 23 | Chicago | 0 at Mtl Maroons | 0 | |
| Mar. 26 | Mtl Maroons | 1 at Chicago | 0 | OT |

Maroons won total-goals series 1–0

| Mar. 24 | Montreal | 1 at NY Rangers | 2 | |
| Mar. 26 | NY Rangers | 4 at Montreal | 4 | |

Rangers won total-goals series 6–5

SERIES D - SEMI-FINALS
| Mar. 28 | Mtl Maroons | 2 at NY Rangers | 1 | |
| Mar. 30 | NY Rangers | 3 at Mtl Maroons | 3 | |

Maroons won total-goals series 5–4

FINALS
Apr. 4	Mtl Maroons	3 at Toronto	2	OT
Apr. 6	Mtl Maroons	3 at Toronto	1	
Apr. 9	Toronto	1 at Mtl Maroons	4	

Maroons won best-of-five series 3–0

DETROIT RED WINGS 1936

SERIES A - SEMI-FINALS
Mar. 24 Detroit   1 at Mtl Maroons   0 OT
Mar. 26 Detroit   3 at Mtl Maroons   0
Mar. 28 Mtl Maroons   1 at Detroit   2
Detroit won best-of-five series 3–0

SERIES B AND C - QUARTER-FINALS
Mar. 24 Toronto   0 at Boston   3
Mar. 26 Boston   3 at Toronto   8
Toronto won total-goals series 8–6

Mar. 24 Chicago   0 at NY Americans 3
Mar. 26 NY Americans 4 at Chicago   5
Americans won total-goals series 7–5

SERIES D - SEMI-FINALS
Mar. 28 NY Americans 1 at Toronto   3
Mar. 31 Toronto   0 at NY Americans 1
Apr. 2 NY Americans 1 at Toronto   3
Toronto won best-of-three series 5–4

FINALS
Apr. 5 Toronto   1 at Detroit   3
Apr. 7 Toronto   4 at Detroit   9
Apr. 9 Detroit   3 at Toronto   4 OT
Apr. 11 Detroit   3 at Toronto   1
Detroit won best-of-five series 3–1

Under the coaching guidance of Jack Adams, the Detroit Red Wings captured their first Stanley Cup after 10 NHL seasons.

The series marked Frank "King" Clancy's sixth and final appearance as a player in the Finals. However, it would not be his last Stanley Cup series, for Clancy went on to earn prominence as an NHL referee, working 20 Finals games in that capacity.

DETROIT RED WINGS 1937

SERIES A - SEMI-FINALS
Mar. 23 Montreal   0 at Detroit   4
Mar. 25 Montreal   1 at Detroit   5
Mar. 27 Detroit   1 at Montreal   3
Mar. 30 Detroit   1 at Montreal   3
Apr. 1 Detroit   2 at Montreal   1 OT
Detroit won best-of-five series 3–2

SERIES B AND C - QUARTER-FINALS
Mar. 23 Boston   1 at Mtl Maroons 4
Mar. 25 Mtl Maroons   0 at Boston   4
Mar. 28 Mtl Maroons   4 at Boston   1
Maroons won best-of-three series 2–1

Mar. 23 NY Rangers 3 at Toronto   0
Mar. 25 Toronto   1 at NY Rangers 2 OT
Rangers won best-of-three series 2–0

SERIES D - SEMI-FINALS
Apr. 1 Mtl Maroons 0 at NY Rangers   1
Apr. 3 NY Rangers   4 at Mtl Maroons 0
Rangers won best-of-three series 2–0

FINALS
Apr. 6 Detroit   1 at NY Rangers 5
Apr. 8 NY Rangers 2 at Detroit   4
Apr. 11 NY Rangers 1 at Detroit   0
Apr. 13 NY Rangers 0 at Detroit   1
Apr. 15 NY Rangers 0 at Detroit   3
Detroit won best-of-five series 3–2

The Rangers, turned away from Madison Square Garden once again by the incoming circus after Game One, agreed to play the remainder of the series on Detroit's home ice.

First-year goaltender Earl Robertson, who would never play a regular-season game for the Red Wings during his career, became the first rookie netminder to post two shutouts in the Finals, blanking the Rangers in the last two games of the series.

With their second straight Stanley Cup, Detroit became the first U.S.-based squad to repeat as champions.

1938 CHICAGO BLACK HAWKS

The Blackhawks faced the start of the Finals without top goaltender Mike Karakas, who had played every game during the season but broke his big toe on April 3. Chicago was forced to sign the New York Americans' Alfred Moore, who played Game One and posted a win in his only Cup appearance.

Following the victory, NHL President Frank Calder ruled Moore ineligible for further play, and Chicago had to call on minor-league goalie Paul Goodman, who lost his first NHL start in Game Two.

Karakas finally returned with a steel-capped boot to protect his toe and won both starts, while teammate Doc Romnes wore a football helmet to guard a broken nose and scored the winning goal in Game Three before a record crowd of 18,497.

Eight Americans - Karakas, Romnes, Alex Levinsky, Carl Voss, Carl Dahlstrom, Roger Jenkins, Louis Trudel and Virgil Johnson - skated for the Blackhawks to set a new record for U.S. talent on a Cup-winning team.

SERIES A - SEMI-FINALS
Mar. 24	Boston	0	at Toronto	1	OT
Mar. 26	Boston	1	at Toronto	2	
Mar. 29	Toronto	3	at Boston	2	OT

Toronto won best-of-five series 3–0

SERIES B AND C - QUARTER-FINALS
Mar. 22	NY Americans	2	at NY Rangers	1	OT
Mar. 24	NY Rangers	4	at NY Americans	3	
Mar. 27	NY Americans	3	at NY Rangers	2	OT

Americans won best-of-three series 2–1

Mar. 22	Chicago	4	at Montreal	6	
Mar. 24	Montreal	0	at Chicago	4	
Mar. 26	Chicago	3	at Montreal	2	OT

Chicago won best-of-three series 2–1

SERIES D - SEMI-FINALS
Mar. 29	Chicago	1	at NY Americans	3	
Mar. 31	NY Americans	0	at Chicago	1	OT
Apr. 3	Chicago	3	at NY Americans	2	

Americans won best-of-three series 2–1

FINALS
Apr. 5	Chicago	3	at Toronto	1	
Apr. 7	Chicago	1	at Toronto	5	
Apr. 10	Toronto	1	at Chicago	2	
Apr. 12	Toronto	1	at Chicago	4	

Chicago won best-of-five series 3–1

1939 BOSTON BRUINS

The NHL expanded the Finals to a best-of-seven format, which pitted Boston against Toronto. Goaltender Frank Brimsek held the Toronto Maple Leafs to 6 goals in 5 games as the Boston Bruins took the Cup for the first time in 10 seasons.

Mel Hill of Boston, who earlier set an NHL record with three overtime goals in the first round of the playoffs, scored twice in the series, and Bill Cowley led all playoff scorers with 11 assists and 14 points to set modern records in both categories.

SERIES A - SEMI-FINALS
Mar. 21	Boston	2	at NY Rangers	1	OT
Mar. 23	NY Rangers	2	at Boston	3	OT
Mar. 26	NY Rangers	1	at Boston	4	
Mar. 28	Boston	1	at NY Rangers	2	
Mar. 30	NY Rangers	2	at Boston	1	OT
Apr. 1	Boston	1	at NY Rangers	3	
Apr. 2	NY Rangers	1	at Boston	2	OT

Boston won best-of-seven series 4–3

SERIES B AND C - QUARTER-FINALS
| Mar. 21 | NY Americans | 0 | at Toronto | 4 | |
| Mar. 23 | Toronto | 2 | at NY Americans | 0 | |

Toronto won best-of-three series 2–0

Mar. 21	Detroit	0	at Montreal	2	
Mar. 23	Montreal	3	at Detroit	7	
Mar. 26	Montreal	0	at Detroit	1	OT

Detroit won best-of-three series 2–1

SERIES D - SEMI-FINALS
Mar. 28	Detroit	1	at Toronto	4	
Mar. 30	Toronto	1	at Detroit	3	
Apr. 1	Detroit	4	at Toronto	5	OT

Toronto won best-of-three series 2–1

FINALS
Apr. 6	Toronto	1	at Boston	2	
Apr. 9	Toronto	3	at Boston	2	OT
Apr. 11	Boston	3	at Toronto	1	
Apr. 13	Boston	2	at Toronto	0	
Apr. 16	Toronto	1	at Boston	3	

Boston won best-of-seven series 4–1

NEW YORK RANGERS 1940

SERIES A - SEMI-FINALS
Mar. 19	Boston	0	at NY Rangers	4	
Mar. 21	NY Rangers	2	at Boston	4	
Mar. 24	NY Rangers	3	at Boston	4	
Mar. 26	Boston	0	at NY Rangers	1	
Mar. 28	NY Rangers	1	at Boston	0	
Mar. 30	Boston	1	at NY Rangers	4	

Rangers won best-of-seven series 4–2

SERIES B AND C - QUARTER-FINALS
| Mar. 19 | Chicago | 2 | at Toronto | 3 | OT |
| Mar. 21 | Toronto | 2 | at Chicago | 1 | |

Toronto won best-of-three series 2–0

Mar. 19	NY Americans	1	at Detroit	2	OT
Mar. 22	Detroit	4	at NY Americans	5	
Mar. 24	NY Americans	1	at Detroit	3	

Detroit won best-of-three series 2–1

SERIES D - SEMI-FINALS
| Mar. 26 | Detroit | 1 | at Toronto | 2 | |
| Mar. 28 | Toronto | 3 | at Detroit | 1 | |

Toronto won best-of-three series 2–0

FINALS
Apr. 2	Toronto	1	at NY Rangers	2	OT
Apr. 3	Toronto	2	at NY Rangers	6	
Apr. 6	NY Rangers	1	at Toronto	2	
Apr. 9	NY Rangers	0	at Toronto	3	
Apr. 11	NY Rangers	2	at Toronto	1	OT
Apr. 13	NY Rangers	3	at Toronto	2	OT

Rangers won best-of-seven series 4–2

With the circus heading towards New York, the Rangers were forced to play the first two games on consecutive nights before vacating Madison Square Garden for the rest of the playoffs.

Three of the Rangers' four game-winning goals were scored in overtime, including the Cup-winner by Bryan Hextall in Game Six. It marked the third time in NHL history that the last goal of the season had been tallied in a sudden-death situation.

Lynn and Murray Patrick skated for the winners to become the third and fourth members of the Patrick family, joining father (and Rangers' manager) Lester and uncle Frank, to have their names engraved on the Cup.

BOSTON BRUINS 1941

SERIES A - SEMI-FINALS
Mar. 20	Toronto	0	at Boston	3	
Mar. 22	Toronto	5	at Boston	3	
Mar. 25	Boston	2	at Toronto	7	
Mar. 27	Boston	2	at Toronto	1	
Mar. 29	Toronto	2	at Boston	1	OT
Apr. 1	Boston	2	at Toronto	1	
Apr. 3	Toronto	1	at Boston	2	

Boston won best-of-seven series 4–3

SERIES B AND C - QUARTER-FINALS
Mar. 20	NY Rangers	1	at Detroit	2	OT
Mar. 23	Detroit	1	at NY Rangers	3	
Mar. 25	NY Rangers	2	at Detroit	3	

Detroit won best-of-three series 2–1

Mar. 20	Montreal	1	at Chicago	2	
Mar. 22	Chicago	3	at Montreal	4	OT
Mar. 25	Montreal	2	at Chicago	3	

Chicago won best-of-three series 2–1

SERIES D - SEMI-FINALS
| Mar. 27 | Chicago | 1 | at Detroit | 3 | |
| Mar. 30 | Detroit | 2 | at Chicago | 1 | OT |

Detroit won best-of-three series 2–0

FINALS
Apr. 6	Detroit	2	at Boston	3	
Apr. 8	Detroit	1	at Boston	2	
Apr. 10	Boston	4	at Detroit	2	
Apr. 12	Boston	3	at Detroit	1	

Boston won best-of-seven series 4–0

In the third best-of-seven series ever played in the Finals, Boston became the first to win in four straight games. Since the National Hockey League was formed in 1917, only four teams — the 1929 Boston Bruins and 1930 Montreal Canadiens in two straight and the 1932 Toronto Maple Leafs and 1935 Montreal Maroons in three straight — had ever won the Cup in the fewest possible games.

1942 TORONTO MAPLE LEAFS

In the most remarkable comeback in Stanley Cup Finals history, Toronto rebounded from a 3-0 deficit to win the series in seven games. The feat has never been duplicated.

The Maple Leafs hosted the first crowd of over 16,000 in Canada in Game Seven.

SERIES A - SEMI-FINALS
Mar. 21	NY Rangers	1	at	Toronto	3
Mar. 22	Toronto	4	at	NY Rangers	2
Mar. 24	Toronto	0	at	NY Rangers	3
Mar. 28	NY Rangers	1	at	Toronto	2
Mar. 29	Toronto	1	at	NY Rangers	3
Mar. 31	NY Rangers	2	at	Toronto	3

Toronto won best-of-seven series 4–2

SERIES B AND C - QUARTER FINALS
Mar. 22	Boston	2	at	Chicago	1	OT
Mar. 24	Chicago	4	at	Boston	0	
Mar. 26	Chicago	2	at	Boston	3	

Boston won best-of-three series 2–1

Mar. 22	Montreal	1	at	Detroit	2
Mar. 24	Detroit	0	at	Montreal	5
Mar. 26	Montreal	2	at	Detroit	6

Detroit won best-of-three series 2–1

SERIES D - SEMI-FINALS
| Mar. 29 | Detroit | 6 | at | Boston | 4 |
| Mar. 31 | Boston | 1 | at | Detroit | 3 |

Detroit won best-of-three series 2–0

FINALS
Apr. 4	Detroit	3	at	Toronto	2
Apr. 7	Detroit	4	at	Toronto	2
Apr. 9	Toronto	2	at	Detroit	5
Apr. 12	Toronto	4	at	Detroit	3
Apr. 14	Detroit	3	at	Toronto	9
Apr. 16	Toronto	3	at	Detroit	0
Apr. 18	Detroit	1	at	Toronto	3

Toronto won best-of-seven series 4–3

1943 DETROIT RED WINGS

After losing the Stanley Cup in 1941 and 1942, the Red Wings' third straight trip to the Finals proved to be the charm as they swept the Bruins, winning twice in Detroit and twice in Boston.

Goaltender Johnny Mowers blanked the Bruins at Boston Garden in the last two games to ice the championship.

SEMI-FINALS
Mar. 21	Toronto	2	at	Detroit	4	
Mar. 23	Toronto	3	at	Detroit	2	OT
Mar. 25	Detroit	4	at	Toronto	2	
Mar. 27	Detroit	3	at	Toronto	6	
Mar. 28	Toronto	2	at	Detroit	4	
Mar. 30	Detroit	3	at	Toronto	2	OT

Detroit won best-of-seven series 4–2

Mar. 21	Montreal	4	at	Boston	5	OT
Mar. 23	Montreal	3	at	Boston	5	
Mar. 25	Boston	3	at	Montreal	2	OT
Mar. 27	Boston	0	at	Montreal	4	
Mar. 30	Montreal	4	at	Boston	5	OT

Boston won best-of-seven series 4–1

FINALS
Apr. 1	Boston	2	at	Detroit	6
Apr. 4	Boston	3	at	Detroit	4
Apr. 7	Detroit	4	at	Boston	0
Apr. 8	Detroit	2	at	Boston	0

Detroit won best-of-seven series 4–0

MONTREAL CANADIENS 1944

SEMI-FINALS
Mar. 21	Toronto	3	at	Montreal	1
Mar. 23	Toronto	1	at	Montreal	5
Mar. 25	Montreal	2	at	Toronto	1
Mar. 28	Montreal	4	at	Toronto	1
Mar. 30	Toronto	0	at	Montreal	11

Montreal won best-of-seven series 4–1

Mar. 21	Chicago	2	at	Detroit	1
Mar. 23	Chicago	1	at	Detroit	4
Mar. 26	Detroit	0	at	Chicago	2
Mar. 28	Detroit	1	at	Chicago	7
Mar. 30	Chicago	5	at	Detroit	2

Chicago won best-of-seven series 4–1

FINALS
Apr. 4	Chicago	1	at	Montreal	5	
Apr. 6	Montreal	3	at	Chicago	1	
Apr. 9	Montreal	3	at	Chicago	2	
Apr. 13	Chicago	4	at	Montreal	5	OT

Montreal won best-of-seven series 4–0

Making his Stanley Cup debut, Maurice "Rocket" Richard scored five goals, including the first of his NHL-record three career Finals hat-tricks in the Finals in Game Two. In total, the "Punch Line" of Elmer Lach, Toe Blake and Richard combined for 10 of the Canadiens' 16 goals in the series, including all five Montreal scores in the finale. Blake netted the Cup-winning goal at 9:12 of overtime in Game Four, marking the fourth time an NHL player had clinched the Cup with a sudden-death tally.

In that final overtime contest, Canadiens' goaltender Bill Durnan stonewalled Chicago's Virgil Johnson on the first penalty shot ever awarded in a Stanley Cup Final.

The victory gave the Canadiens their first Stanley Cup championship in 14 years.

TORONTO MAPLE LEAFS 1945

SEMI-FINALS
Mar. 20	Toronto	1	at	Montreal	0	
Mar. 22	Toronto	3	at	Montreal	2	
Mar. 24	Montreal	4	at	Toronto	1	
Mar. 27	Montreal	3	at	Toronto	4	OT
Mar. 29	Toronto	3	at	Montreal	10	
Mar. 31	Montreal	2	at	Toronto	3	

Toronto won best-of-seven series 4–2

Mar. 20	Boston	4	at	Detroit	3	
Mar. 22	Boston	4	at	Detroit	2	
Mar. 25	Detroit	3	at	Boston	2	
Mar. 27	Detroit	3	at	Boston	2	
Mar. 29	Boston	2	at	Detroit	3	OT
Apr. 1	Detroit	3	at	Boston	5	
Apr. 3	Boston	3	at	Detroit	5	

Detroit won best-of-seven series 4–3

FINALS
Apr. 6	Toronto	1	at	Detroit	0	
Apr. 8	Toronto	2	at	Detroit	0	
Apr. 12	Detroit	0	at	Toronto	1	
Apr. 14	Detroit	5	at	Toronto	3	
Apr. 19	Toronto	0	at	Detroit	2	
Apr. 21	Detroit	1	at	Toronto	0	OT
Apr. 22	Toronto	2	at	Detroit	1	

Toronto won best-of-seven series 4–3

Two rookie goaltenders — Toronto's Frank McCool and Detroit's Harry Lumley — manned the opposing nets in the Cup Finals for the first time. McCool, who never played in another Final series, posted shutouts in the each of the first three games to set a new Stanley Cup record, while Lumley rebounded with two of his own in Games Five and Six to knot the series at three games apiece.

1946 MONTREAL CANADIENS

Two high-scoring forward units met in the NHL's first post-World War II Stanley Cup Finals. Boston was led by the "Kraut Line" – Bobby Bauer, Milt Schmidt and Woody Dumart. The Canadiens featured the "Punch Line" of Maurice Richard, Elmer Lach and Toe Blake. In Game One, Richard scored the first of a record six overtime goals in his playoff career and the first of his record three career overtime tallies in the Finals.

The Canadiens won a close, hard-fought series in five games, with three contests requiring overtime.

SEMI-FINALS
Mar. 19	Chicago	2	at	Montreal	6	
Mar. 21	Chicago	1	at	Montreal	5	
Mar. 24	Montreal	8	at	Chicago	2	
Mar. 26	Montreal	7	at	Chicago	2	

Montreal won best-of-seven series 4–0

Mar. 19	Detroit	1	at	Boston	3	
Mar. 21	Detroit	3	at	Boston	0	
Mar. 24	Boston	5	at	Detroit	2	
Mar. 26	Boston	4	at	Detroit	1	
Mar. 28	Detroit	3	at	Boston	4	OT

Boston won best-of-seven series 4–1

FINALS
Mar. 30	Boston	3	at	Montreal	4	OT
Apr. 2	Boston	2	at	Montreal	3	OT
Apr. 4	Montreal	4	at	Boston	2	
Apr. 7	Montreal	2	at	Boston	3	OT
Apr. 9	Boston	3	at	Montreal	6	

Montreal won best-of-seven series 4–1

1947 TORONTO MAPLE LEAFS

The Toronto Maple Leafs were a "new look" club in 1946-47. Young players like Calder Trophy-winner Howie Meeker, Bill Barilko and Bill Ezinicki were new performers in the Leafs' overhauled line-up.

In the first all-Canadian Finals in 12 years, the Maple Leafs defeated the Canadiens in six games. Toronto's Ted "Teeder" Kennedy potted three goals in the series, including the Cup-winner in the closing match-up. The Leafs were the youngest NHL team to win the Stanley Cup.

SEMI-FINALS
Mar. 25	Boston	1	at	Montreal	3	
Mar. 27	Boston	1	at	Montreal	2	OT
Mar. 29	Montreal	2	at	Boston	4	
Apr. 1	Montreal	5	at	Boston	1	
Apr. 3	Boston	3	at	Montreal	4	OT

Montreal won best-of-seven series 4–1

Mar. 26	Detroit	2	at	Toronto	3	OT
Mar. 29	Detroit	9	at	Toronto	1	
Apr. 1	Toronto	4	at	Detroit	1	
Apr. 3	Toronto	4	at	Detroit	1	
Apr. 5	Detroit	1	at	Toronto	6	

Toronto won best-of-seven series 4–1

FINALS
Apr. 8	Toronto	0	at	Montreal	2	
Apr. 10	Toronto	4	at	Montreal	0	
Apr. 12	Montreal	2	at	Toronto	4	
Apr. 15	Montreal	1	at	Toronto	2	OT
Apr. 17	Toronto	1	at	Montreal	3	
Apr. 19	Montreal	1	at	Toronto	2	

Toronto won best-of-seven series 4–2

TORONTO MAPLE LEAFS 1948

SEMI-FINALS

Mar. 24	Boston	4	at	Toronto	5	OT
Mar. 27	Boston	3	at	Toronto	5	
Mar. 30	Toronto	5	at	Boston	1	
Apr. 1	Toronto	2	at	Boston	3	
Apr. 3	Boston	2	at	Toronto	3	

Toronto won best-of-seven series 4–1

Mar. 24	NY Rangers	1	at	Detroit	2
Mar. 26	NY Rangers	2	at	Detroit	5
Mar. 28	Detroit	2	at	NY Rangers	3
Mar. 30	Detroit	1	at	NY Rangers	3
Apr. 1	NY Rangers	1	at	Detroit	3
Apr. 4	Detroit	4	at	NY Rangers	2

Detroit won best-of-seven series 4–2

FINALS

Apr. 7	Detroit	3	at	Toronto	5
Apr. 10	Detroit	2	at	Toronto	4
Apr. 11	Toronto	2	at	Detroit	0
Apr. 14	Toronto	7	at	Detroit	2

Toronto won best-of-seven series 4–0

The series marked the beginning and end of two great Stanley Cup careers. For Detroit's Gordie Howe, it was an introduction to the rigors of championship competition. For Toronto's Syl Apps, who scored one goal in Game Four, it meant the conclusion of a Hall-of-Fame career.

Toronto became the fourth NHL team to repeat as Stanley Cup champions, joining the Ottawa Senators (1920-21), Montreal Canadiens (1930-31) and Detroit Red Wings (1936-37).

TORONTO MAPLE LEAFS 1949

SEMI-FINALS

Mar. 22	Montreal	1	at	Detroit	2	OT
Mar. 24	Montreal	4	at	Detroit	3	OT
Mar. 26	Detroit	2	at	Montreal	3	
Mar. 29	Detroit	3	at	Montreal	1	
Mar. 31	Montreal	1	at	Detroit	3	
Apr. 2	Detroit	1	at	Montreal	3	
Apr. 5	Montreal	1	at	Detroit	3	

Detroit won best-of-seven series 4–3

Mar. 22	Toronto	3	at	Boston	0	
Mar. 24	Toronto	3	at	Boston	2	
Mar. 26	Boston	5	at	Toronto	4	OT
Mar. 29	Boston	1	at	Toronto	3	
Mar. 30	Toronto	3	at	Boston	2	

Toronto won best-of-seven series 4–1

FINALS

Apr. 8	Toronto	3	at	Detroit	2	OT
Apr. 10	Toronto	3	at	Detroit	1	
Apr. 13	Detroit	1	at	Toronto	3	
Apr. 16	Detroit	1	at	Toronto	3	

Toronto won best-of-seven series 4–0

The Toronto Maple Leafs established two NHL records in this 1949 series. Most significantly, they captured their third straight Stanley Cup title, a feat last accomplished 44 years earlier by the Ottawa Silver Seven, and they won an unprecedented ninth straight game in the Finals dating back to April 19, 1947.

1950 DETROIT RED WINGS

Bumped from Madison Square Garden by the circus, the Rangers opted to play Games Two and Three in Toronto.

Gordie Howe failed to appear for the winners in this series as a result of a serious head injury sustained in the first game of the playoffs. After sliding head first into the boards, Howe required surgery to repair a fractured nose and cheekbone. Despite the seriousness of the injury, he resumed his career the following season.

Even without Howe, Detroit managed to capture the Cup in seven games, but not without a fight. New York battled Detroit to a 3-3 tie at the end of regulation in Game Seven, which the Red Wings' Pete Babando ultimately ended at the 28:31 mark of overtime. Babando's goal was the first sudden-death tally ever scored in the seventh game of a Final series.

New York's Don Raleigh set a record that would remain unmatched until 1993 when he scored two overtime goals in one Stanley Cup Final series.

SEMI-FINALS
Mar. 28	Toronto	5	at	Detroit	0	
Mar. 30	Toronto	1	at	Detroit	3	
Apr. 1	Detroit	0	at	Toronto	2	
Apr. 4	Detroit	2	at	Toronto	1	OT
Apr. 6	Toronto	2	at	Detroit	0	
Apr. 8	Detroit	4	at	Toronto	0	
Apr. 9	Toronto	0	at	Detroit	1	OT

Detroit won best-of-seven series 4–3

Mar. 29	Montreal	1	at	NY Rangers	3	
Apr. 1	NY Rangers	3	at	Montreal	2	
Apr. 2	Montreal	1	at	NY Rangers	4	
Apr. 4	NY Rangers	2	at	Montreal	3	OT
Apr. 6	NY Rangers	3	at	Montreal	0	

Rangers won best-of-seven series 4–1

FINALS
Apr. 11	NY Rangers	1	at	Detroit	4	
Apr. 13	Detroit	1	at	NY Rangers	3	*
Apr. 15	Detroit	4	at	NY Rangers	0	*
Apr. 18	NY Rangers	4	at	Detroit	3	OT
Apr. 20	NY Rangers	2	at	Detroit	1	OT
Apr. 22	NY Rangers	4	at	Detroit	5	
Apr. 23	NY Rangers	3	at	Detroit	4	OT

* played in Toronto

Detroit won best-of-seven series 4–3

1951 TORONTO MAPLE LEAFS

The 1951 series distinguished itself as the only Stanley Cup in which every game ended in overtime. Sid Smith, Ted Kennedy, Harry Watson and Bill Barilko notched the overtime winners for Toronto, while Maurice "Rocket" Richard, who scored goals in all five contests, netted one in Montreal's lone victory.

Richard's overtime tally was his second in a Final series and the fourth of his playoff career, breaking the record of three set by Boston's Mel Hill in 1939.

For Barilko, his overtime goal would be his last as the rugged defenseman died tragically in a plane crash during the summer.

SEMI-FINALS
Mar. 27	Montreal	3	at	Detroit	2	OT
Mar. 29	Montreal	1	at	Detroit	0	OT
Mar. 31	Detroit	2	at	Montreal	0	
Apr. 3	Detroit	4	at	Montreal	1	
Apr. 5	Montreal	5	at	Detroit	2	
Apr. 7	Detroit	2	at	Montreal	3	

Montreal won best-of-seven series 4–2

Mar. 28	Boston	2	at	Toronto	0	
Mar. 31	Boston	1	at	Toronto	1	OT*
Apr. 1	Toronto	3	at	Boston	0	
Apr. 3	Toronto	3	at	Boston	1	
Apr. 7	Boston	1	at	Toronto	4	
Apr. 8	Toronto	6	at	Boston	0	

* game called after one overtime period due to curfew.

Toronto won best-of-seven series 4–1

FINALS
Apr. 11	Montreal	2	at	Toronto	3	OT
Apr. 14	Montreal	3	at	Toronto	2	OT
Apr. 17	Toronto	2	at	Montreal	1	OT
Apr. 19	Toronto	3	at	Montreal	2	OT
Apr. 21	Montreal	2	at	Toronto	3	OT

Toronto won best-of-seven series 4–1

DETROIT RED WINGS 1952

SEMI-FINALS
Mar. 25	Toronto	0	at	Detroit	3
Mar. 27	Toronto	0	at	Detroit	1
Mar. 29	Detroit	6	at	Toronto	2
Apr. 1	Detroit	3	at	Toronto	1

Detroit won best-of-seven series 4–0

Mar. 25	Boston	1	at	Montreal	5	
Mar. 27	Boston	0	at	Montreal	4	
Mar. 30	Montreal	1	at	Boston	4	
Apr. 1	Montreal	2	at	Boston	3	
Apr. 3	Boston	1	at	Montreal	0	
Apr. 6	Montreal	3	at	Boston	2	OT
Apr. 8	Boston	1	at	Montreal	3	

Montreal won best-of-seven series 4–3

FINALS
Apr. 10	Detroit	3	at	Montreal	1
Apr. 12	Detroit	2	at	Montreal	1
Apr. 13	Montreal	0	at	Detroit	3
Apr. 15	Montreal	0	at	Detroit	3

Detroit won best-of-seven series 4–0

Terry Sawchuk made his debut in the Finals and rose to the occasion, recording two shutouts and limiting Montreal to just two goals in the four-game series. Meanwhile, Gordie Howe contributed his first two career goals in a Stanley Cup championship series.

The Red Wings set a new NHL record by winning all eight post-season games, including a four-game sweep over Toronto in the first round.

MONTREAL CANADIENS 1953

SEMI-FINALS
Mar. 24	Boston	0	at	Detroit	7	
Mar. 26	Boston	5	at	Detroit	3	
Mar. 29	Detroit	1	at	Boston	2	OT
Mar. 31	Detroit	2	at	Boston	6	
Apr. 2	Boston	4	at	Detroit	6	
Apr. 5	Detroit	2	at	Boston	4	

Boston won best-of-seven series 4–2

Mar. 24	Chicago	1	at	Montreal	3	
Mar. 26	Chicago	3	at	Montreal	4	
Mar. 29	Montreal	1	at	Chicago	2	OT
Mar. 31	Montreal	1	at	Chicago	3	
Apr. 2	Chicago	4	at	Montreal	2	
Apr. 4	Montreal	3	at	Chicago	0	
Apr. 7	Chicago	1	at	Montreal	4	

Montreal won best-of-seven series 4–3

FINALS
Apr. 9	Boston	2	at	Montreal	4	
Apr. 11	Boston	4	at	Montreal	1	
Apr. 12	Montreal	3	at	Boston	0	
Apr. 14	Montreal	7	at	Boston	3	
Apr. 16	Boston	0	at	Montreal	1	OT

Montreal won best-of-seven series 4–1

After goaltender Jacques Plante, who made his Finals debut, recorded a split decision in the first two games, Canadiens' coach Dick Irvin sent Gerry McNeil into the nets. The move resulted in two shutouts in the final three games, and Montreal regained the Cup after a seven-year layoff.

Elmer Lach scored the series-winning goal at 1:22 of overtime in the fifth and final game.

1954 DETROIT RED WINGS

Tony Leswick's Cup-winning tally was the second overtime goal ever scored in overtime in the seventh and deciding game of a Final series. Leswick, who notched the winner at 4:29 of the first extra period, matched the feat first accomplished by former Red Wing Pete Babando in 1950.

Marguerite Norris, President of the Detroit club, was presented with the Stanley Cup by NHL President Clarence Campbell at the conclusion of the series. Mrs. Norris became the first woman in history to have her name engraved into the Stanley Cup.

SEMI-FINALS

Mar. 23	Toronto	0	at	Detroit	5	
Mar. 25	Toronto	3	at	Detroit	1	
Mar. 27	Detroit	3	at	Toronto	1	
Mar. 30	Detroit	2	at	Toronto	1	
Apr. 1	Toronto	3	at	Detroit	4	OT

Detroit won best-of-seven series 4–1

Mar. 23	Boston	0	at	Montreal	2	
Mar. 25	Boston	1	at	Montreal	8	
Mar. 28	Montreal	4	at	Boston	3	
Mar. 30	Montreal	2	at	Boston	0	

Montreal won best-of-seven series 4–0

FINALS

Apr. 4	Montreal	1	at	Detroit	3	
Apr. 6	Montreal	3	at	Detroit	1	
Apr. 8	Detroit	5	at	Montreal	2	
Apr. 10	Detroit	2	at	Montreal	0	
Apr. 11	Montreal	1	at	Detroit	0	OT
Apr. 13	Detroit	1	at	Montreal	4	
Apr. 16	Montreal	1	at	Detroit	2	OT

Detroit won best-of-seven series 4–3

1955 DETROIT RED WINGS

On March 13, Maurice Richard had been suspended for the remainder of the regular-season and playoffs and the high-scoring right-winger's absence was sorely felt by the Canadiens.

In Game Two, Detroit's Ted Lindsay scored four times to set a modern record for goals in a championship game, and the Red Wings won their 15th consecutive contest to establish another NHL record.

Lindsay then tallied one assist, his last of the series, in Game Four to tie Elmer Lach's record of 12 playoff assists set in 1946.

Gordie Howe set two records in the series. He amassed a 5-7-12 tally in the Finals to establish a new mark and snapped Toe Blake's overall playoff record with a 9-11-20 scoring total in 11 games.

For the first time in a best-of-seven Finals, the home team won all seven games.

SEMI-FINALS

Mar. 22	Toronto	4	at	Detroit	7	
Mar. 24	Toronto	1	at	Detroit	2	
Mar. 26	Detroit	2	at	Toronto	1	
Mar. 29	Detroit	3	at	Toronto	0	

Detroit won best-of-seven series 4–0

Mar. 22	Boston	0	at	Montreal	2	
Mar. 24	Boston	1	at	Montreal	3	
Mar. 27	Montreal	2	at	Boston	4	
Mar. 29	Montreal	4	at	Boston	3	OT
Mar. 31	Boston	1	at	Montreal	5	

Montreal won best-of-seven series 4–1

FINALS

Apr. 3	Montreal	2	at	Detroit	4	
Apr. 5	Montreal	1	at	Detroit	7	
Apr. 7	Detroit	2	at	Montreal	4	
Apr. 9	Detroit	3	at	Montreal	5	
Apr. 10	Montreal	1	at	Detroit	5	
Apr. 12	Detroit	3	at	Montreal	6	
Apr. 14	Montreal	1	at	Detroit	3	

Detroit won best-of-seven series 4–3

MONTREAL CANADIENS 1956

SEMI-FINALS
Mar. 20	NY Rangers	1	at	Montreal	7	
Mar. 22	NY Rangers	4	at	Montreal	2	
Mar. 24	Montreal	3	at	NY Rangers	1	
Mar. 25	Montreal	5	at	NY Rangers	3	
Mar. 27	NY Rangers	0	at	Montreal	7	

Montreal won best-of-seven series 4–1

Mar. 20	Toronto	2	at	Detroit	3	
Mar. 22	Toronto	1	at	Detroit	3	
Mar. 24	Detroit	5	at	Toronto	4	OT
Mar. 27	Detroit	0	at	Toronto	2	
Mar. 29	Toronto	1	at	Detroit	3	

Detroit won best-of-seven series 4–1

FINALS
Mar. 31	Detroit	4	at	Montreal	6
Apr. 3	Detroit	1	at	Montreal	5
Apr. 5	Montreal	1	at	Detroit	3
Apr. 8	Montreal	3	at	Detroit	0
Apr. 10	Detroit	1	at	Montreal	3

Montreal won best-of-seven series 4–1

Two rookies played integral roles on this first of five consecutive Stanley Cup championship teams for the Montreal Canadiens. Former playing star Toe Blake took over for Dick Irvin behind the Canadiens' bench as coach, while rookie center Henri Richard joined his famous brother Maurice on the ice.

Their first Stanley Cup contest proved a success. Blake, who would become the 10th rookie coach in NHL history to win the Cup, won his first game in the Finals as a coach, and young Richard notched his first Stanley Cup goal.

Jean Beliveau scored seven times in the series, including at least one in each game, to set the all-time record for goals in the Finals and tie Maurice Richard's overall playoff record of 12 goals set in 1944.

MONTREAL CANADIENS 1957

SEMI-FINALS
Mar. 26	Boston	3	at	Detroit	1	
Mar. 28	Boston	2	at	Detroit	7	
Mar. 31	Detroit	3	at	Boston	4	
Apr. 2	Detroit	0	at	Boston	2	
Apr. 4	Boston	4	at	Detroit	3	

Boston won best-of-seven series 4–1

Mar. 26	Montreal	4	at	NY Rangers	1	
Mar. 28	Montreal	3	at	NY Rangers	4	OT
Mar. 30	NY Rangers	3	at	Montreal	8	
Apr. 2	NY Rangers	1	at	Montreal	3	
Apr. 4	NY Rangers	3	at	Montreal	4	OT

Montreal won best-of-seven series 4–1

FINALS
Apr. 6	Boston	1	at	Montreal	5
Apr. 9	Boston	0	at	Montreal	1
Apr. 11	Montreal	4	at	Boston	2
Apr. 14	Montreal	0	at	Boston	2
Apr. 16	Boston	1	at	Montreal	5

Montreal won best-of-seven series 4–1

The Boston Bruins were surprise finalists in 1957, eliminating the regular-season champion Detroit Red Wings in five games. Maurice "Rocket" Richard scored four times in Game One, including three goals in the second period, to equal Ted Lindsay's modern Stanley Cup record for goals in a game.

Jacques Plante held the Bruins to six goals in five games as Montreal won its second consecutive Stanley Cup championship. Fleming Mackell had four of the Boston's six goals.

1958 MONTREAL CANADIENS

The Canadiens and Bruins met for a second consecutive year in the Stanley Cup Finals. Once again, Boston was an upset winner in the semi-finals, eliminating the New York Rangers in a high-scoring six-game series.

In the finals, the Habs won the Sanley Cup in six games. The Canadiens' third straight Stanley Cup title equalled the NHL record set by the Toronto Maple Leafs in 1947-49.

Maurice Richard, the top overall playoff goal-scorer with 11, notched his third career overtime goal in the Finals and sixth overall in the playoffs in Game #5 to set all-time records in each category.

SEMI-FINALS
Mar. 25	Detroit	1	at	Montreal	8	
Mar. 27	Detroit	1	at	Montreal	5	
Mar. 30	Montreal	2	at	Detroit	1	OT
Apr. 1	Montreal	4	at	Detroit	3	

Montreal won best-of-seven series 4–0

Mar. 25	Boston	3	at	NY Rangers	5	
Mar. 27	Boston	4	at	NY Rangers	3	OT
Mar. 29	NY Rangers	0	at	Boston	5	
Apr. 1	NY Rangers	5	at	Boston	2	
Apr. 3	NY Rangers	1	at	Boston	6	
Apr. 5	NY Rangers	2	at	Boston	8	

Boston won best-of-seven series 4–1

FINALS
Apr. 8	Boston	1	at	Montreal	2	
Apr. 10	Boston	5	at	Montreal	2	
Apr. 13	Montreal	3	at	Boston	0	
Apr. 15	Montreal	1	at	Boston	3	
Apr. 17	Boston	2	at	Montreal	3	OT
Apr. 20	Montreal	5	at	Boston	3	

Montreal won best-of-seven series 4–2

1959 MONTREAL CANADIENS

The Canadiens skated to a fourth consecutive championship title, breaking the record of three they had shared with Toronto (1947-49). Maurice Richard was held off the scoresheet during the playoffs for the first time in his career. Injuries restricted his participation to four post-season games.

Led by newly-appointed general manager Punch Imlach, the Toronto Maple Leafs made their first Final Series appearance since 1951, rebounding from a last-place finish in 1957-58. The Leafs had a perfect record of three wins and no losses in overtime games in the post-season.

SEMI-FINALS
Mar. 24	Chicago	2	at	Montreal	4	
Mar. 26	Chicago	1	at	Montreal	5	
Mar. 28	Montreal	2	at	Chicago	4	
Mar. 31	Montreal	1	at	Chicago	3	
Apr. 2	Chicago	2	at	Montreal	4	
Apr. 4	Montreal	5	at	Chicago	4	

Montreal won best-of-seven series 4–2

Mar. 24	Toronto	1	at	Boston	5	
Mar. 26	Toronto	2	at	Boston	4	
Mar. 28	Boston	2	at	Toronto	3	OT
Mar. 31	Boston	2	at	Toronto	3	OT
Apr. 2	Toronto	4	at	Boston	1	
Apr. 4	Boston	5	at	Toronto	4	
Apr. 7	Toronto	3	at	Boston	2	

Toronto won best-of-seven series 4–3

FINALS
Apr. 9	Toronto	3	at	Montreal	5	
Apr. 11	Toronto	1	at	Montreal	3	
Apr. 14	Montreal	2	at	Toronto	3	OT
Apr. 16	Montreal	3	at	Toronto	2	
Apr. 18	Toronto	3	at	Montreal	5	

Montreal won best-of-seven series 4–1

MONTREAL CANADIENS 1960

SEMI-FINALS
Mar.	24	Chicago	3	at	Montreal	4	
Mar.	26	Chicago	3	at	Montreal	4	OT
Mar.	29	Montreal	4	at	Chicago	0	
Mar.	31	Montreal	2	at	Chicago	0	

Montreal won best-of-seven series 4–0

Mar.	23	Detroit	2	at	Toronto	1	
Mar.	26	Detroit	2	at	Toronto	4	
Mar.	27	Toronto	5	at	Detroit	4	OT
Mar.	29	Toronto	1	at	Detroit	2	OT
Apr.	2	Detroit	4	at	Toronto	5	
Apr.	3	Toronto	4	at	Detroit	2	

Toronto won best-of-seven series 4–2

FINALS
Apr.	7	Toronto	2	at	Montreal	4
Apr.	9	Toronto	1	at	Montreal	2
Apr.	12	Montreal	5	at	Toronto	2
Apr.	14	Montreal	4	at	Toronto	0

Montreal won best-of-seven series 4–0

The Canadiens retained the Stanley Cup for an unprecedented fifth straight season. No team has since matched the record-setting achievement.

Jacques Plante, who introduced the goal mask to the hockey world on November 1, 1959, in New York, sparkled with his self-designed face guard. His Stanley Cup performance, which included just five goals allowed in four games, played a large role in the acceptance of the mask by goaltenders world-wide.

Maurice Richard played in the last four games of his career. In Game Three, the "Rocket" scored his 34th goal in the Finals, still an all-time record.

CHICAGO BLACK HAWKS 1961

SEMI-FINALS
Mar.	21	Chicago	2	at	Montreal	6	
Mar.	23	Chicago	4	at	Montreal	3	
Mar.	26	Montreal	1	at	Chicago	2	OT
Mar.	28	Montreal	5	at	Chicago	2	
Apr.	1	Chicago	3	at	Montreal	0	
Apr.	4	Montreal	0	at	Chicago	3	

Chicago won best-of-seven series 4–2

Mar.	22	Detroit	2	at	Toronto	3	OT
Mar.	25	Detroit	4	at	Toronto	2	
Mar.	26	Toronto	0	at	Detroit	2	
Mar.	28	Toronto	1	at	Detroit	4	
Apr.	1	Detroit	3	at	Toronto	2	

Detroit won best-of-seven series 4–1

FINALS
Apr.	6	Detroit	2	at	Chicago	3
Apr.	8	Chicago	1	at	Detroit	3
Apr.	10	Detroit	1	at	Chicago	3
Apr.	12	Chicago	1	at	Detroit	2
Apr.	14	Detroit	3	at	Chicago	6
Apr.	16	Chicago	5	at	Detroit	1

Chicago won best-of-seven series 4–2

In their fifth appearance in the Finals, the Chicago Blackhawks captured their first Stanley Cup since 1938 and their third championship overall since joining the NHL in 1926-27.

Two of the greatest athletes in Chicago sports history - Bobby Hull and Stan Mikita - made their premier Stanley Cup appearances, and both figured prominently in the outcome. "The Golden Jet" sparkled in Game One with his first two Cup goals, including the game-winner, while Mikita scored the winner in Game Five.

1962 TORONTO MAPLE LEAFS

The Maple Leafs regained the Stanley Cup after 11 years, putting an end to the club's longest period without a championship in its 45-year NHL history through 1962.

In his Stanley Cup debut, 22-year-old Dave Keon scored a goal and added an assist in Game One.

Stan Mikita tallied two assists in Game Five to set new playoff records for assists (15) and points (21). The latter broke Gordie Howe's mark of 20 points set in the 1955 playoffs.

SEMI-FINALS

Mar. 27	Chicago	1	at	Montreal	2	
Mar. 29	Chicago	3	at	Montreal	4	
Apr. 1	Montreal	1	at	Chicago	4	
Apr. 3	Montreal	3	at	Chicago	5	
Apr. 5	Chicago	4	at	Montreal	3	
Apr. 8	Montreal	0	at	Chicago	2	

Chicago won best-of-seven series 4–2

Mar. 27	NY Rangers	2	at	Toronto	4	
Mar. 29	NY Rangers	1	at	Toronto	2	
Apr. 1	Toronto	4	at	NY Rangers	5	
Apr. 3	Toronto	2	at	NY Rangers	4	
Apr. 5	NY Rangers	2	at	Toronto	3	OT
Apr. 7	NY Rangers	1	at	Toronto	7	

Toronto won best-of-seven series 4–2

FINALS

Apr. 10	Chicago	1	at	Toronto	4	
Apr. 12	Chicago	2	at	Toronto	3	
Apr. 15	Toronto	0	at	Chicago	3	
Apr. 17	Toronto	1	at	Chicago	4	
Apr. 19	Chicago	4	at	Toronto	8	
Apr. 22	Toronto	2	at	Chicago	1	

Toronto won best-of-seven series 4–2

1963 TORONTO MAPLE LEAFS

Five different Maple Leafs - Bob Nevin, Dick Duff, Ron Stewart, Red Kelly and Dave Keon - recorded multiple-goal performances in Toronto's four victories, and 38-year-old goaltender Johnny Bower limited Detroit to 10 goals in five games.

Keon scored twice in Game Five with Toronto players in the penalty box, establishing a new playoff record for shorthanded goals in one game.

SEMI-FINALS

Mar. 26	Toronto	0	at	Montreal	2	
Mar. 28	Toronto	2	at	Montreal	1	
Mar. 31	Montreal	3	at	Toronto	2	
Apr. 2	Montreal	3	at	Toronto	5	
Apr. 4	Toronto	2	at	Montreal	4	
Apr. 7	Montreal	0	at	Toronto	3	
Apr. 9	Toronto	3	at	Montreal	1	

Toronto won best-of-seven series 4–3

Mar. 26	Detroit	1	at	Chicago	4	
Mar. 29	Detroit	5	at	Chicago	4	
Mar. 31	Chicago	0	at	Detroit	3	
Apr. 2	Chicago	3	at	Detroit	2	OT
Apr. 5	Detroit	2	at	Chicago	3	
Apr. 7	Chicago	2	at	Detroit	7	
Apr. 9	Detroit	4	at	Chicago	2	

Detroit won best-of-seven series 4–3

FINALS

Apr. 11	Detroit	2	at	Toronto	3	
Apr. 14	Detroit	4	at	Toronto	3	OT
Apr. 16	Toronto	3	at	Detroit	4	
Apr. 18	Toronto	4	at	Detroit	2	
Apr. 21	Detroit	2	at	Toronto	1	
Apr. 23	Toronto	4	at	Detroit	3	OT
Apr. 25	Detroit	0	at	Toronto	4	

Toronto won best-of-seven series 4–3

TORONTO MAPLE LEAFS 1964

SEMI-FINALS
Mar. 26	Montreal	1	at	Toronto	3
Mar. 28	Montreal	2	at	Toronto	3
Mar. 30	Toronto	2	at	Montreal	0
Apr. 2	Toronto	1	at	Montreal	3
Apr. 4	Montreal	0	at	Toronto	5

Toronto won best-of-seven series 4–1

Mar. 26	Detroit	4	at	Chicago	5
Mar. 28	Detroit	2	at	Chicago	5
Mar. 31	Chicago	2	at	Detroit	4
Apr. 2	Chicago	1	at	Detroit	4
Apr. 4	Detroit	4	at	Chicago	2
Apr. 7	Chicago	4	at	Detroit	7

Detroit won best-of-seven series 4–2

FINALS
Apr. 9	Detroit	2	at	Toronto	4
Apr. 11	Detroit	2	at	Toronto	4
Apr. 14	Toronto	2	at	Detroit	3
Apr. 16	Toronto	4	at	Detroit	2
Apr. 18	Detroit	1	at	Toronto	3

Toronto won best-of-seven series 4–1

Tying their club record set in 1947-49, Toronto captured the Cup for a third consecutive season.

In each of the first three games, the winning goal was scored in the last minute of play. After Toronto took Game One on Bob Pulford's goal with two seconds remaining in regulation, Detroit skated to consecutive last-minute victories with Larry Jeffrey netting the game-winner at 7:52 of overtime in Game Two and Alex Delvecchio potting the tie-breaker with 17 seconds to play in Game Three.

With the score tied 3-3 late in Game Six, Maple Leafs' defenseman Bobby Baun took a Gordie Howe slapshot on his skate and dropped to the ice with an apparently sprained ankle. After freezing and taping the injury, he returned for overtime and scored the winning goal at 2:43 of the extra period. On crutches for the next two days, he would later suit up for the series finale and never miss a shift as Toronto won the Cup. The following day, x-rays confirmed what Baun had known all along, that the ankle was in fact broken. The Leafs' blueliner spent two more months on crutches.

MONTREAL CANADIENS 1965

SEMI-FINALS
Apr. 1	Chicago	3	at	Detroit	4	
Apr. 4	Chicago	3	at	Detroit	6	
Apr. 6	Detroit	2	at	Chicago	5	
Apr. 8	Detroit	1	at	Chicago	2	
Apr. 11	Chicago	2	at	Detroit	4	
Apr. 13	Detroit	0	at	Chicago	4	
Apr. 15	Chicago	4	at	Detroit	2	

Chicago won best-of-seven series 4–3

Apr. 1	Toronto	2	at	Montreal	3	
Apr. 3	Toronto	1	at	Montreal	3	
Apr. 6	Montreal	2	at	Toronto	3	OT
Apr. 8	Montreal	2	at	Toronto	4	
Apr. 10	Toronto	1	at	Montreal	3	
Apr. 13	Montreal	4	at	Toronto	3	OT

Montreal won best-of-seven series 4–2

FINALS
Apr. 17	Chicago	2	at	Montreal	3
Apr. 20	Chicago	0	at	Montreal	2
Apr. 22	Montreal	1	at	Chicago	3
Apr. 25	Montreal	1	at	Chicago	5
Apr. 27	Chicago	0	at	Montreal	6
Apr. 29	Montreal	1	at	Chicago	2
May 1	Chicago	0	at	Montreal	4

Montreal won best-of-seven series 4–3

Repeating the feat accomplished in 1955, the home teams won every game in the Finals. With the extra game at the Montreal Forum, the Canadiens treated their fans to all four victories.

Lorne "Gump" Worsley, appearing in his first Stanley Cup after 12 seasons in the NHL, recorded two shutouts in four starts, including one in Game Seven.

Jean Beliveau captured the inaugural Conn Smythe Trophy as the most valuable player for his team in the playoffs after amassing eight goals and eight assists in 13 games.

CONN SMYTHE TROPHY
Jean Beliveau - Center - Montreal Canadiens

1966 MONTREAL CANADIENS

The Canadiens repeated as champions to give coach Toe Blake his seventh title in 11 years behind the Montreal bench. Henri Richard, a member of each of those seven Stanley Cup teams, scored the game-winner in overtime in Game Six, marking the ninth time in history that a series-winning goal had been scored in overtime.

Despite his team's loss in the Finals, goaltender Roger Crozier received the Conn Smythe Trophy after posting a 2.17 average and one shutout in 12 playoff games.

SEMI-FINALS
Apr.	7	Toronto	3	at	Montreal	4
Apr.	9	Toronto	0	at	Montreal	2
Apr.	12	Montreal	5	at	Toronto	2
Apr.	14	Montreal	4	at	Toronto	1

Toronto won best-of-seven series 4–2

Apr.	7	Detroit	1	at	Chicago	2
Apr.	10	Detroit	7	at	Chicago	0
Apr.	12	Chicago	2	at	Detroit	1
Apr.	14	Chicago	1	at	Detroit	5
Apr.	17	Detroit	5	at	Chicago	3
Apr.	19	Chicago	2	at	Detroit	3

Detroit won best-of-seven series 4–2

FINALS
Apr.	24	Detroit	3	at	Montreal	2	
Apr.	26	Detroit	5	at	Montreal	2	
Apr.	28	Montreal	4	at	Detroit	2	
May	1	Montreal	2	at	Detroit	1	
May	3	Detroit	1	at	Montreal	5	
May	5	Montreal	3	at	Detroit	2	OT

Montreal won best-of-seven series 4–2

CONN SMYTHE TROPHY
Roger Crozier - Goaltender - Detroit Red Wings

1967 TORONTO MAPLE LEAFS

With an average age of over 31 years old, the Toronto Maple Leafs sported the oldest line-up ever to win a Stanley Cup. Goaltender Johnny Bower (42) and defenseman Allan Stanley (41) were the senior citizens of the squad, which included seven players over 35 and 12 members over 30.

27-year-old "youngster" Dave Keon, who scored a goal and assist in the series, captured the Conn Smythe Trophy on the basis of an outstanding defensive performance.

SEMI-FINALS
Apr.	6	Toronto	2	at	Chicago	5
Apr.	9	Toronto	3	at	Chicago	1
Apr.	11	Chicago	1	at	Toronto	3
Apr.	13	Chicago	4	at	Toronto	3
Apr.	15	Toronto	4	at	Chicago	2
Apr.	18	Chicago	1	at	Toronto	3

Toronto won best-of-seven series 4–2

Apr.	6	NY Rangers	4	at	Montreal	6	
Apr.	8	NY Rangers	1	at	Montreal	3	
Apr.	11	Montreal	3	at	NY Rangers	2	
Apr.	13	Montreal	2	at	NY Rangers	1	OT

Montreal won best-of-seven series 4–0

FINALS
Apr.	20	Toronto	2	at	Montreal	6	
Apr.	22	Toronto	3	at	Montreal	0	
Apr.	25	Montreal	2	at	Toronto	3	OT
Apr.	27	Montreal	6	at	Toronto	3	
Apr.	29	Toronto	4	at	Montreal	1	
May	2	Montreal	1	at	Toronto	3	

Toronto won best-of-seven series 4–2

CONN SMYTHE TROPHY
Dave Keon - Center - Toronto Maple Leafs

MONTREAL CANADIENS 1968

The NHL doubled in size with the addition of six expansion teams which comprised one of two new divisions. In the playoffs, Montreal won the East Division, and St. Louis won the West to earn a chance at the Stanley Cup. The Blues' line-up boasted several aging superstars, including the goalie tandem of former two-time Vezina Trophy winners Glenn Hall and Gump Worsley, two-time Art Ross Trophy winner Dickie Moore and seven-time Norris Trophy recipient Doug Harvey. The four were no strangers to playoff action with 50 years of post-season experience among them. Rookie defenseman Serge Savard, who would amass seven Stanley Cup rings in his career, scored his first two career playoff goals while shorthanded in Games Two and Three to tie a Final series record. Toe Blake retired after capturing his eighth Stanley Cup in 13 years as coach of the Canadiens and set a record as the first person to win a total of 11 Cups in a career. Blake also played on championship teams with the Montreal Maroons in 1926 and Canadiens in 1944 and 1946.

CONN SMYTHE TROPHY • Glenn Hall - Goaltender - St. Louis Blues

QUARTER-FINALS
Apr.	4	Boston	1	at	Montreal	2
Apr.	6	Boston	3	at	Montreal	5
Apr.	9	Montreal	5	at	Boston	2
Apr.	11	Montreal	3	at	Boston	2

Montreal won best-of-seven series 4–0

Apr.	4	Chicago	1	at	NY Rangers	3
Apr.	9	Chicago	1	at	NY Rangers	2
Apr.	11	NY Rangers	4	at	Chicago	7
Apr.	13	NY Rangers	1	at	Chicago	3
Apr.	14	Chicago	2	at	NY Rangers	1
Apr.	16	NY Rangers	1	at	Chicago	4

Chicago won best-of-seven series 4–2

Apr.	4	St. Louis	1	at	Philadelphia	0
Apr.	6	St. Louis	3	at	Philadelphia	4
Apr.	10	Philadelphia	2	at	St. Louis	3 OT
Apr.	11	Philadelphia	2	at	St. Louis	5
Apr.	13	St. Louis	1	at	Philadelphia	6
Apr.	16	Philadephia	2	at	St. Louis	1 OT
Apr.	18	St. Louis	3	at	Philadelphia	1

St. Louis won best-of-seven series 4–3

Apr.	4	Minnesota	1	at	Los Angeles	2
Apr.	6	Minnesota	0	at	Los Angeles	2
Apr.	9	Los Angeles	5	at	Minnesota	7
Apr.	11	Los Angeles	2	at	Minnesota	3
Apr.	13	Minnesota	2	at	Los Angeles	3
Apr.	16	Los Angeles	3	at	Minnesota	4 OT
Apr.	18	Minnesota	9	at	Los Angeles	4

Minnesota won best-of-seven series 4–3

SEMI-FINALS
Apr.	18	Chicago	2	at	Montreal	9
Apr.	20	Chicago	1	at	Montreal	4
Apr.	23	Montreal	4	at	Chicago	2
Apr.	25	Montreal	1	at	Chicago	2
Apr.	28	Chicago	3	at	Montreal	4 OT

Montreal won best-of-seven series 4–1

Apr.	21	Minnesota	3	at	St. Louis	5
Apr.	22	St. Louis	2	at	Minnesota	3 OT
Apr.	25	Minnesota	5	at	St. Louis	1
Apr.	27	Minnesota	3	at	St. Louis	4 OT
Apr.	29	Minnesota	2	at	St. Louis	3 OT
May	1	St. Louis	1	at	Minnesota	5
May	3	Minnesota	1	at	St. Louis	2 OT

St. Louis won best-of-seven series 4–3

FINALS
May	5	Montreal	3	at	St. Louis	2 OT
May	7	Montreal	1	at	St. Louis	0
May	9	St. Louis	3	at	Montreal	4 OT
May	11	St. Louis	2	at	Montreal	3

Montreal won best-of-seven series 4–0

1969 MONTREAL CANADIENS

Following in his predecessor's footsteps, Claude Ruel won the Stanley Cup in his first season behind the Canadiens' bench and became the 11th rookie coach in NHL history to go the distance with his team.

Goaltender Rogie Vachon limited St. Louis to three goals in four outings and registered his first career playoff and Stanley Cup shutout in the third game.

Serge Savard become the first defenseman to win the Conn Smythe Trophy.

CONN SMYTHE TROPHY • Serge Savard - Defenseman - Montreal Canadiens

QUARTER-FINALS
Apr.	2	NY Rangers	1	at	Montreal	3
Apr.	3	NY Rangers	2	at	Montreal	5
Apr.	5	Montreal	4	at	NY Rangers	1
Apr.	6	Montreal	4	at	NY Rangers	3

Montreal won best-of-seven series 4–0

Apr.	2	Toronto	0	at	Boston	10
Apr.	3	Toronto	0	at	Boston	7
Apr.	5	Boston	4	at	Toronto	3
Apr.	6	Boston	3	at	Toronto	2

Boston won best-of-seven series 4–0

Apr.	2	Philadelphia	2	at	St. Louis	5
Apr.	3	Philadelphia	0	at	St. Louis	5
Apr.	5	St. Louis	3	at	Philadelphia	0
Apr.	6	St. Louis	4	at	Philadelphia	1

St. Louis won best-of-seven series 4–0

Apr.	2	Los Angeles	5	at	Oakland	4 OT
Apr.	3	Los Angeles	2	at	Oakland	4
Apr.	5	Oakland	5	at	Los Angeles	2
Apr.	6	Oakland	2	at	Los Angeles	4
Apr.	9	Los Angeles	1	at	Oakland	4
Apr.	10	Oakland	3	at	Los Angeles	4
Apr.	13	Los Angeles	5	at	Oakland	3

Los Angeles won best-of-seven series 4–3

SEMI-FINALS
Apr.	10	Boston	2	at	Montreal	3 OT
Apr.	13	Boston	3	at	Montreal	4 OT
Apr.	17	Montreal	0	at	Boston	5
Apr.	20	Montreal	2	at	Boston	3
Apr.	22	Boston	2	at	Montreal	4
Apr.	24	Montreal	2	at	Boston	1 OT

Montreal won best-of-seven series 4–2

Apr.	15	Los Angeles	0	at	St. Louis	4
Apr.	17	Los Angeles	2	at	St. Louis	3
Apr.	19	St. Louis	5	at	Los Angeles	2
Apr.	20	St. Louis	4	at	Los Angeles	1

St. Louis won best-of-seven series 4–0

FINALS
Apr.	27	St. Louis	1	at	Montreal	3
Apr.	29	St. Louis	1	at	Montreal	3
May	1	Montreal	4	at	St. Louis	0
May	4	Montreal	2	at	St. Louis	1

Montreal won best-of-seven series 4–0

BOSTON BRUINS 1970

For the third straight year, the St. Louis Blues qualified for the Finals but faced new rivals in the Boston Bruins, who featured the first 100-point defenseman in NHL history in Norris Trophy recipient Bobby Orr.

After winning the first three by margins of five, four and three goals, respectively, the Bruins were extended into overtime in the fourth game. Conn Smythe Trophy winner Orr quickly ended the affair at the 40 second mark of overtime with his first goal of the series. With Orr literally flying through the air on the play, his winning tally has become one of the most memorable images in hockey history.

The series victory marked the Bruins' first Stanley Cup in 29 years, closing out the club's longest period without a championship.

CONN SMYTHE TROPHY • Bobby Orr - Defenseman - Boston Bruins

QUARTER-FINALS
Apr. 8	Detroit	2	at	Chicago	4
Apr. 9	Detroit	2	at	Chicago	4
Apr. 11	Chicago	4	at	Detroit	2
Apr. 12	Chicago	4	at	Detroit	2

Chicago won best-of-seven series 4–0

Apr. 8	NY Rangers	2	at	Boston	8
Apr. 9	NY Rangers	3	at	Boston	5
Apr. 11	Boston	3	at	NY Rangers	4
Apr. 12	Boston	2	at	NY Rangers	4
Apr. 14	NY Rangers	2	at	Boston	3
Apr. 16	Boston	4	at	NY Rangers	1

Boston won best-of-seven series 4–2

Apr. 8	Minnesota	2	at	St. Louis	6
Apr. 9	Minnesota	1	at	St. Louis	2
Apr. 11	St. Louis	2	at	Minnesota	4
Apr. 12	St. Louis	0	at	Minnesota	4
Apr. 14	Minnesota	3	at	St. Louis	6
Apr. 16	St. Louis	4	at	Minnesota	2

St. Louis won best-of-seven series 4–2

Apr. 8	Oakland	1	at	Pittsburgh	2
Apr. 9	Oakland	1	at	Pittsburgh	3
Apr. 11	Pittsburgh	5	at	Oakland	2
Apr. 12	Pittsburgh	3	at	Oakland	2 OT

Pittsburgh won best-of-seven series 4–0

SEMI-FINALS
Apr. 19	Boston	6	at	Chicago	3
Apr. 21	Boston	4	at	Chicago	1
Apr. 23	Chicago	2	at	Boston	5
Apr. 26	Chicago	4	at	Boston	5

Boston won best-of-seven series 4–0

Apr. 19	Pittsburgh	1	at	St. Louis	3
Apr. 21	Pittsburgh	1	at	St. Louis	4
Apr. 23	St. Louis	2	at	Pittsburgh	3
Apr. 26	St. Louis	1	at	Pittsburgh	2
Apr. 28	Pittsburgh	0	at	St. Louis	5
Apr. 30	St. Louis	4	at	Pittsburgh	3

St. Louis won best-of-seven series 4–2

FINALS
May 3	Boston	6	at	St. Louis	1
May 5	Boston	6	at	St. Louis	2
May 7	St. Louis	1	at	Boston	4
May 10	St. Louis	3	at	Boston	4 OT

Boston won best-of-seven series 4–0

1971 MONTREAL CANADIENS

After missing the playoffs for the first time in 22 years in 1970, the Canadiens rebounded in 1971 to win their 16th Stanley Cup. Brothers Frank and Peter Mahovlich were reunited in mid-season, and the two responded with a total of nine goals in the seven-game Finals. Frank also set a new playoff record with 14 goals and tied Phil Esposito's record 27-point performance of 1970. After Chicago went ahead 2-0 in Game Seven, Henri Richard scored the tying and winning goals to seal the victory. The hero of the playoffs and the Stanley Cup turned out to be rookie goaltender Ken Dryden, who appeared in all 20 post-season games after only six starts during the regular-season. Dryden's performance, which included a 12-8 record and 3.00 average, earned him the Conn Smythe Trophy. While the series heralded the beginning of Dryden's career in the Montreal nets, it also marked the conclusion of Jean Beliveau's playing days. Beliveau, who finished the playoffs with six goals and a record 16 assists, left the sport as the all-time leader in playoff assists (97) and points (176) and temporarily shared first place with Henri Richard in Stanley Cups won as a player at 10.

CONN SMYTHE TROPHY • Ken Dryden - Goaltender - Montreal Canadiens

QUARTER-FINALS
Date	Away			Home		
Apr. 7	Montreal	1	at	Boston	3	
Apr. 8	Montreal	7	at	Boston	5	
Apr. 10	Boston	1	at	Montreal	3	
Apr. 11	Boston	5	at	Montreal	2	
Apr. 13	Montreal	3	at	Boston	7	
Apr. 15	Boston	3	at	Montreal	8	
Apr. 18	Montreal	4	at	Boston	2	

Montreal won best-of-seven series 4–3

Apr. 7	Toronto	4	at	NY Rangers	5	
Apr. 8	Toronto	4	at	NY Rangers	1	
Apr. 10	NY Rangers	1	at	Toronto	3	
Apr. 11	NY Rangers	4	at	Toronto	2	
Apr. 13	Toronto	1	at	NY Rangers	3	
Apr. 15	NY Rangers	2	at	Toronto	1	OT

Rangers won best-of-seven series 4–2

Apr. 7	Philadelphia	2	at	Chicago	5	
Apr. 8	Philadelphia	2	at	Chicago	6	
Apr. 10	Chicago	3	at	Philadelphia	2	
Apr. 11	Chicago	6	at	Philadelphia	2	

Chicago won best-of-seven series 4–0

Apr. 7	Minnesota	3	at	St. Louis	2	
Apr. 8	Minnesota	2	at	St. Louis	4	
Apr. 10	St. Louis	3	at	Minnesota	0	
Apr. 11	St. Louis	1	at	Minnesota	2	
Apr. 13	Minnesota	4	at	St. Louis	3	
Apr. 15	St. Louis	2	at	Minnesota	5	

Minnesota won best-of-seven series 4–2

SEMI-FINALS
Apr. 20	Minnesota	2	at	Montreal	7	
Apr. 22	Minnesota	6	at	Montreal	3	
Apr. 24	Montreal	6	at	Minnesota	3	
Apr. 25	Montreal	2	at	Minnesota	5	
Apr. 27	Minnesota	1	at	Montreal	6	
Apr. 29	Montreal	3	at	Minnesota	2	

Montreal won best-of-seven series 4–2

Apr. 18	NY Rangers	2	at	Chicago	1	OT
Apr. 20	NY Rangers	0	at	Chicago	3	
Apr. 22	Chicago	1	at	NY Rangers	4	
Apr. 25	Chicago	7	at	NY Rangers	1	
Apr. 27	NY Rangers	2	at	Chicago	3	OT
Apr. 29	Chicago	2	at	NY Rangers	3	OT
May 2	NY Rangers	2	at	Chicago	4	

Chicago won best-of-seven series 4–3

FINALS
May 4	Montreal	1	at	Chicago	2	OT
May 6	Montreal	3	at	Chicago	5	
May 9	Chicago	2	at	Montreal	4	
May 11	Chicago	2	at	Montreal	5	
May 13	Montreal	0	at	Chicago	2	
May 16	Chicago	3	at	Montreal	4	
May 18	Montreal	3	at	Chicago	2	

Montreal won best-of-seven series 4–3

BOSTON BRUINS 1972

After 43 years of waiting, the New York Rangers finally got a chance to avenge their 1929 loss to the Boston Bruins in the Stanley Cup Finals. However, history would repeat itself as the Bruins defeated the Rangers in this six-game confrontation.

Bobby Orr, who scored his second Cup-winning goal in three years, became the first two-time winner of the Conn Smythe Trophy. With a 4-4-8 mark in the Finals, Orr raised his playoff totals to 5-19-24, breaking Jean Beliveau's assist mark set in 1971.

CONN SMYTHE TROPHY • Bobby Orr - Defenseman - Boston Bruins

QUARTER-FINALS
Apr.	5	Toronto	0	at Boston	5	
Apr.	6	Toronto	4	at Boston	3	OT
Apr.	8	Boston	2	at Toronto	0	
Apr.	9	Boston	5	at Toronto	4	
Apr.	11	Toronto	2	at Boston	3	

Boston won best-of-seven series 4–1

Apr.	5	Montreal	2	at NY Rangers	3
Apr.	6	Montreal	2	at NY Rangers	5
Apr.	8	NY Rangers	1	at Montreal	2
Apr.	9	NY Rangers	6	at Montreal	4
Apr.	11	Montreal	2	at NY Rangers	1
Apr	13	NY Rangers	3	at Montreal	2

Rangers won best-of-seven series 4–2

Apr.	5	Pittsburgh	1	at Chicago	3	
Apr.	6	Pittsburgh	2	at Chicago	3	
Apr.	8	Chicago	2	at Pittsburgh	0	
Apr.	9	Chicago	6	at Pittsburgh	5	OT

Chicago won best-of-seven series 4–0

Apr.	5	St. Louis	0	at Minnesota	3	
Apr.	6	St. Louis	5	at Minnesota	6	OT
Apr.	8	Minnesota	1	at St. Louis	2	
Apr.	9	Minnesota	2	at St. Louis	3	
Apr.	11	St. Louis	3	at Minnesota	4	
Apr.	13	Minnesota	2	at St. Louis	4	
Apr.	16	St. Louis	2	at Minnesota	1	OT

St. Louis won best-of-seven series 4–2

SEMI-FINALS
Apr.	18	St. Louis	1	at Boston	6
Apr.	20	St. Louis	2	at Boston	10
Apr.	23	Boston	7	at St. Louis	2
Apr.	25	Boston	5	at St. Louis	3

Boston won best-of-seven series 4–0

Apr.	16	NY Rangers	3	at Chicago	2
Apr.	18	NY Rangers	5	at Chicago	3
Apr.	20	Chicago	2	at NY Rangers	3
Apr	23	Chicago	2	at NY Rangers	6

Rangers won best-of-seven series 4–0

FINALS
Apr.	30	NY Rangers	5	at Boston	6
May	2	NY Rangers	1	at Boston	2
May	4	Boston	2	at NY Rangers	5
May	7	Boston	3	at NY Rangers	2
May	9	NY Rangers	3	at Boston	2
May	11	Boston	3	at NY Rangers	0

Boston won best-of-seven series 4–2

1973 MONTREAL CANADIENS

The Canadiens and Blackhawks met in a rematch of the 1971 Finals. Chicago's Tony Esposito and Montreal's Ken Dryden, former teammates in the noted 1972 Summit Series against the Soviet Union prior to the start of the season, now faced each other at opposite ends of the ice. Yvan Cournoyer, who recorded the game-winning tallies in the second and sixth contests, closed out the playoffs with a new record of 15 goals en route to winning the Conn Smythe Trophy. Cournoyer (6-6-12) and Jacques Lemaire (3-9-12) both tied Gordie Howe's record for points in the Finals, while the latter also set a new record for assists in the Finals with nine. Henri Richard became the first player ever to play for 11 Stanley Cup champions and tied the overall record held by Toe Blake, who played on three and coached eight more before retiring in 1968. After coaching the St. Louis Blues to three successive Finals from 1968 to 1970, Montreal's Scotty Bowman earned his first Stanley Cup championship.

CONN SMYTHE TROPHY • Yvan Cournoyer - Right Wing - Montreal Canadiens

QUARTER-FINALS
Apr. 4	Buffalo	1	at	Montreal	2
Apr. 5	Buffalo	3	at	Montreal	7
Apr. 7	Montreal	5	at	Buffalo	2
Apr. 8	Montreal	1	at	Buffalo	5
Apr. 10	Buffalo	3	at	Montreal	2 OT
Apr. 12	Montreal	4	at	Buffalo	2

Montreal won best-of-seven series 4–2

Apr. 4	NY Rangers	6	at	Boston	2
Apr. 5	NY Rangers	4	at	Boston	2
Apr. 7	Boston	4	at	NY Rangers	2
Apr. 8	Boston	0	at	NY Rangers	4
Apr. 10	NY Rangers	6	at	Boston	3

Rangers won best-of-seven series 4–1

Apr. 4	St. Louis	1	at	Chicago	7
Apr. 5	St. Louis	0	at	Chicago	1
Apr. 7	Chicago	5	at	St. Louis	2
Apr. 8	Chicago	3	at	St. Louis	5
Apr. 10	St. Louis	1	at	Chicago	6

Chicago won best-of-seven series 4–1

Apr. 4	Minnesota	3	at	Philadelphia	0
Apr. 5	Minnesota	1	at	Philadelphia	4
Apr. 7	Philadelphia	0	at	Minnesota	5
Apr. 8	Philadelphia	3	at	Minnesota	0
Apr. 10	Minnesota	2	at	Philadelphia	3 OT
Apr. 12	Philadelphia	4	at	Minnesota	1

Philadelphia won best-of-seven series 4–2

SEMI-FINALS
Apr. 14	Philadelphia	5	at	Montreal	4 OT
Apr. 17	Philadelphia	3	at	Montreal	4 OT
Apr. 19	Montreal	2	at	Philadelphia	1
Apr. 22	Montreal	4	at	Philadelphia	1
Apr. 24	Philadelphia	3	at	Montreal	5

Montreal won best-of-seven series 4–1

Apr. 12	NY Rangers	4	at	Chicago	1
Apr. 15	NY Rangers	4	at	Chicago	5
Apr. 17	Chicago	2	at	NY Rangers	1
Apr. 19	Chicago	3	at	NY Rangers	1
Apr. 24	NY Rangers	1	at	Chicago	4

Chicago won best-of-seven series 4–1

FINALS
Apr. 29	Chicago	3	at	Montreal	8
May 1	Chicago	1	at	Montreal	4
May 3	Montreal	4	at	Chicago	7
May 6	Montreal	4	at	Chicago	0
May 8	Chicago	8	at	Montreal	7
May 10	Montreal	6	at	Chicago	4

Montreal won best-of-seven series 4–2

PHILADELPHIA FLYERS 1974

Owning a 17-0-2 record in their previous 19 outings at home against Philadelphia, Boston was a heavy favorite with home-ice advantage coming into the Finals.

Flyers' captain Bobby Clarke ended his team's drought at the Garden in Game Two by scoring two goals, the second in sudden-death, and added one assist to overcome an early 2-0 deficit.

Goaltender Bernie Parent limited the Bruins to three goals in his three remaining wins, including a sixth game shutout as the Flyers became the first expansion team to win the Stanley Cup, after only seven years in the NHL.

Parent earned the Conn Smythe Trophy with a 12-5-0 record and 2.02 average in 17 playoff games.

CONN SMYTHE TROPHY • Bernie Parent - Goaltender - Philadelphia Flyers

QUARTER-FINALS
Apr. 10	Toronto	0	at	Boston	1
Apr. 11	Toronto	3	at	Boston	6
Apr. 13	Boston	6	at	Toronto	3
Apr. 14	Boston	4	at	Toronto	3 OT

Boston won best-of-seven series 4–0

Apr. 10	NY Rangers	4	at	Montreal	1
Apr. 11	NY Rangers	1	at	Montreal	4
Apr. 13	Montreal	4	at	NY Rangers	2
Apr. 14	Montreal	4	at	NY Rangers	6
Apr. 16	NY Rangers	3	at	Montreal	2 OT
Apr. 18	Montreal	2	at	NY Rangers	5

Rangers won best-of-seven series 4–2

Apr. 9	Atlanta	1	at	Philadelphia	4
Apr. 11	Atlanta	1	at	Philadelphia	5
Apr. 12	Philadelphia	4	at	Atlanta	1
Apr. 14	Philadelphia	4	at	Atlanta	3 OT

Philadelphia won best-of-seven series 4–0

Apr. 10	Los Angeles	1	at	Chicago	3
Apr. 11	Los Angeles	1	at	Chicago	4
Apr. 13	Chicago	1	at	Los Angeles	0
Apr. 14	Chicago	1	at	Los Angeles	5
Apr. 16	Los Angeles	0	at	Chicago	1

Chicago won best-of-seven series 4–1

SEMI-FINALS
Apr. 18	Chicago	4	at	Boston	2
Apr. 21	Chicago	6	at	Boston	8
Apr. 23	Boston	3	at	Chicago	4 OT
Apr. 25	Boston	5	at	Chicago	2
Apr. 28	Chicago	2	at	Boston	6
Apr. 30	Boston	4	at	Chicago	2

Boston won best-of-seven series 4–2

Apr. 20	NY Rangers	0	at	Philadelphia	4
Apr. 23	NY Rangers	2	at	Philadelphia	5
Apr. 25	Philadelphia	3	at	NY Rangers	5
Apr. 28	Philadelphia	1	at	NY Rangers	2 OT
Apr. 30	NY Rangers	1	at	Philadelphia	4
May 2	Philadelphia	1	at	NY Rangers	4
May 5	NY Rangers	3	at	Philadelphia	4

Philadelphia won best-of-seven series 4–3

FINALS
May 7	Philadelphia	2	at	Boston	3
May 9	Philadelphia	3	at	Boston	2 OT
May 12	Boston	1	at	Philadelphia	4
May 14	Boston	2	at	Philadelphia	4
May 16	Philadelphia	1	at	Boston	5
May 19	Boston	0	at	Philadelphia	1

Philadelphia won best-of-seven series 4–2

1975 PHILADELPHIA FLYERS

Two modern-era expansion teams met in the Finals for the time in 1975. The Flyers became the first to defend the Stanley Cup successfully, defeating the Buffalo Sabres in six games.

Bernie Parent's netminding highlighted the series as he allowed only 12 goals in six games and recorded his second consecutive Cup-winning shutout to defeat the Buffalo Sabres. Parent became the first player to win the Conn Smythe Trophy in consecutive years and joined Boston's Bobby Orr as the only players to win the award twice.

CONN SMYTHE TROPHY • Bernie Parent - Goaltender - Philadelphia Flyers

PRELIMINARY ROUND
Apr. 8	Toronto	2	at Los Angeles	3	OT
Apr. 10	Los Angeles	2	at Toronto	3	OT
Apr. 11	Toronto	2	at Los Angeles	1	

Toronto won best-of-three series 2–1

Apr. 8	Chicago	2	at Boston	8	
Apr. 10	Boston	3	at Chicago	4	OT
Apr. 11	Chicago	6	at Boston	4	

Chicago won best-of-three series 2–1

Apr. 8	St. Louis	3	at Pittsburgh	4	
Apr. 10	Pittsburgh	5	at St. Louis	3	

Pittsburgh won best-of-three series 2–0

Apr. 8	NY Islanders	3	at NY Rangers	2	
Apr. 10	NY Rangers	8	at NY Islanders	3	
Apr. 11	NY Islanders	4	at NY Rangers	3	OT

Islanders won best-of-three series 2–1

QUARTER-FINALS
Apr. 13	Toronto	3	at Philadelphia	6	
Apr. 15	Toronto	0	at Philadelphia	3	
Apr. 17	Philadelphia	2	at Toronto	0	
Apr. 19	Philadelphia	4	at Toronto	3	OT

Philadelphia won best-of-seven series 4–0

Apr. 13	Chicago	1	at Buffalo	4	
Apr. 15	Chicago	1	at Buffalo	3	
Apr. 17	Buffalo	4	at Chicago	5	OT
Apr. 20	Buffalo	6	at Chicago	2	
Apr. 22	Chicago	1	at Buffalo	3	

Buffalo won best-of-seven series 4–1

Apr. 13	Vancouver	2	at Montreal	6	
Apr. 15	Vancouver	2	at Montreal	1	
Apr. 17	Montreal	4	at Vancouver	1	
Apr. 19	Montreal	4	at Vancouver	0	
Apr. 22	Vancouver	4	at Montreal	5	OT

Montreal won best-of-seven series 4–1

Apr. 13	NY Islanders	4	at Pittsburgh	5	
Apr. 15	NY Islanders	1	at Pittsburgh	3	
Apr. 17	Pittsburgh	6	at NY Islanders	4	
Apr. 20	Pittsburgh	1	at NY Islanders	3	
Apr. 22	NY Islanders	4	at Pittsburgh	2	
Apr. 24	Pittsburgh	1	at NY Islanders	4	
Apr. 26	NY Islanders	1	at Pittsburgh	0	

Islanders won best-of-seven series 4–3

SEMI-FINALS
Apr. 29	NY Islanders	0	at Philadelphia	4	
May 1	NY Islanders	4	at Philadelphia	5	OT
May 4	Philadelphia	1	at NY Islanders	0	
May 7	Philadelphia	3	at NY Islanders	4	OT
May 8	NY Islanders	5	at Philadelphia	1	
May 11	Philadelphia	1	at NY Islanders	2	
May 13	NY Islanders	1	at Philadelphia	4	

Philadelphia won best-of-seven series 4–3

Apr. 27	Montreal	5	at Buffalo	6	OT
Apr. 29	Montreal	2	at Buffalo	4	
May 1	Buffalo	0	at Montreal	7	
May 3	Buffalo	2	at Montreal	8	
May 6	Montreal	4	at Buffalo	5	OT
May 8	Buffalo	4	at Montreal	3	

Buffalo won best-of-seven series 4–2

FINALS
May 15	Buffalo	1	at Philadelphia	4	
May 18	Buffalo	1	at Philadelphia	2	
May 20	Philadelphia	4	at Buffalo	5	OT
May 22	Philadelphia	2	at Buffalo	4	
May 25	Buffalo	1	at Philadelphia	5	
May 27	Philadelphia	2	at Buffalo	0	

Philadelphia won best-of-seven series 4–2

MONTREAL CANADIENS 1976

The Montreal Canadiens returned to the Stanley Cup Finals against the Flyers after a two-year absence. Guy Lafleur scored his first two goals in the Finals and both proved to be game-winners.

Philadelphia's Reggie Leach scored four times in the series to finish the playoffs with the all-time record of 19 post-season goals. Leach became the third player on a Stanley Cup loser to earn the Conn Smythe Trophy.

CONN SMYTHE TROPHY • Reggie Leach - Right Wing - Philadelphia Flyers

PRELIMINARY ROUND
Apr.	6	Buffalo	2	at	St. Louis	5	
Apr.	8	St. Louis	2	at	Buffalo	3	OT
Apr.	9	St. Louis	1	at	Buffalo	2	OT

Buffalo won best-of-three series 2–1

| Apr. | 6 | Vancouver | 3 | at | NY Islanders | 5 |
| Apr. | 8 | NY Islanders | 3 | at | Vancouver | 1 |

Islanders won best-of-three series 2–0

| Apr. | 6 | Atlanta | 2 | at | Los Angeles | 1 |
| Apr. | 8 | Los Angeles | 1 | at | Atlanta | 0 |

Los Angeles won best-of-three series 2–0

Apr.	6	Pittsburgh	1	at	Toronto	4
Apr.	8	Toronto	0	at	Pittsburgh	2
Apr.	9	Pittsburgh	0	at	Toronto	4

Toronto won best-of-three series 2–1

QUARTER-FINALS
Apr.	11	Chicago	0	at	Montreal	4
Apr.	13	Chicago	1	at	Montreal	3
Apr.	15	Montreal	2	at	Chicago	1
Apr.	18	Montreal	4	at	Chicago	1

Montreal won best-of-seven series 4–0

Apr.	12	Toronto	1	at	Philadelphia	4
Apr.	13	Toronto	1	at	Philadelphia	3
Apr.	15	Philadelphia	4	at	Toronto	5
Apr.	17	Philadelphia	3	at	Toronto	4
Apr.	20	Toronto	1	at	Philadelphia	7
Apr.	22	Philadelphia	5	at	Toronto	8
Apr.	25	Toronto	3	at	Philadelphia	7

Philadelphia won best-of-seven series 4–3

Apr.	11	Los Angeles	0	at	Boston	4	
Apr.	13	Los Angeles	3	at	Boston	2	OT
Apr.	15	Boston	4	at	Los Angeles	6	
Apr.	17	Boston	3	at	Los Angeles	0	
Apr.	20	Los Angeles	1	at	Boston	7	
Apr.	22	Boston	3	at	Los Angeles	4	OT
Apr.	25	Los Angeles	0	at	Boston	3	

Boston won best-of-seven series 4–3

Apr.	11	NY Islanders	3	at	Buffalo	5	
Apr.	13	NY Islanders	2	at	Buffalo	3	OT
Apr.	15	Buffalo	3	at	NY Islanders	5	
Apr.	17	Buffalo	2	at	NY Islanders	4	
Apr.	20	NY Islanders	4	at	Buffalo	3	
Apr.	22	Buffalo	2	at	NY Islanders	3	

Islanders won best-of-seven series 4–2

SEMI-FINALS
Apr.	27	NY Islanders	2	at	Montreal	3
Apr.	29	NY Islanders	3	at	Montreal	4
May	1	Montreal	3	at	NY Islanders	2
May	4	Montreal	2	at	NY Islanders	5
May	6	NY Islanders	2	at	Montreal	5

Montreal won best-of-seven series 4–1

Apr.	27	Boston	4	at	Philadelphia	2	
Apr.	29	Boston	1	at	Philadelphia	2	OT
May	2	Philadelphia	5	at	Boston	2	
May	4	Philadelphia	4	at	Boston	2	
May	6	Boston	3	at	Philadelphia	6	

Philadelphia won best-of-seven series 4–1

FINALS
May	9	Philadelphia	3	at	Montreal	4
May	11	Philadelphia	1	at	Montreal	2
May	13	Montreal	3	at	Philadelphia	2
May	16	Montreal	5	at	Philadelphia	3

Montreal won best-of-seven series 4–0

1977 MONTREAL CANADIENS

Winning their second consecutive Stanley Cup, the Canadiens extended their undefeated streak against Boston in the Finals to six straight series.

In Game Two, Ken Dryden posted his fourth shutout of the playoffs to tie the record shared by six goaltenders.

Jacques Lemaire, who scored three of Montreal's game-winning goals including the Cup-winner in overtime, joined Maurice Richard (3) and Don Raleigh (2) in recording more than one career overtime goal in a Stanley Cup championship series. Lemaire first scored in overtime against the St. Louis Blues in the 1968 Finals and duplicated the feat in the finale of this latest series.

Guy Lafleur won the Conn Smythe Trophy with a 9-17-26 mark in 14 playoff games.

CONN SMYTHE TROPHY • Guy Lafleur - Right Wing - Montreal Canadiens

PRELIMINARY ROUND
| Apr. 5 | Chicago | 2 | at | NY Islanders | 5 |
| Apr. 7 | Chicago | 1 | at | NY Islanders | 2 |

Islanders won best-of-three series 2–0

| Apr. 5 | Minnesota | 2 | at | Buffalo | 4 |
| Apr. 7 | Buffalo | 7 | at | Minnesota | 1 |

Buffalo won best-of-three series 2–0

Apr. 5	Atlanta	2	at	Los Angeles	5
Apr. 7	Los Angeles	2	at	Atlanta	3
Apr. 9	Atlanta	2	at	Los Angeles	4

Los Angeles won best-of-three series 2–1

Apr. 5	Toronto	4	at	Pittsburgh	2
Apr. 7	Pittsburgh	6	at	Toronto	4
Apr. 9	Toronto	5	at	Pittsburgh	2

Toronto won best-of-three series 2–1

QUARTER-FINALS
Apr. 11	St. Louis	2	at	Montreal	7
Apr. 13	St. Louis	0	at	Montreal	3
Apr. 16	Montreal	5	at	St. Louis	1
Apr. 17	Montreal	4	at	St. Louis	1

Montreal won best-of-seven series 4–0

Apr. 11	Toronto	3	at	Philadelphia	2
Apr. 13	Toronto	4	at	Philadelphia	1
Apr. 15	Philadelphia	4	at	Toronto	3 OT
Apr. 17	Philadelphia	6	at	Toronto	5 OT
Apr. 19	Toronto	0	at	Philadelphia	2
Apr. 21	Philadelphia	4	at	Toronto	3

Philadelphia won best-of-seven series 4–2

Apr. 11	Los Angeles	3	at	Boston	8
Apr. 13	Los Angeles	2	at	Boston	6
Apr. 15	Boston	7	at	Los Angeles	6
Apr. 17	Boston	4	at	Los Angeles	7
Apr. 19	Los Angeles	3	at	Boston	1
Apr. 21	Boston	4	at	Los Angeles	3

Boston won best-of-seven series 4–2

Apr. 11	Buffalo	2	at	NY Islanders	4
Apr. 13	Buffalo	2	at	NY Islanders	4
Apr. 15	NY Islanders	4	at	Buffalo	3
Apr. 17	NY Islanders	4	at	Buffalo	3

Islanders won best-of-seven series 4–0

SEMI-FINALS
Apr. 23	NY Islanders	3	at	Montreal	4
Apr. 26	NY Islanders	0	at	Montreal	3
Apr. 28	Montreal	3	at	NY Islanders	5
Apr. 30	Montreal	4	at	NY Islanders	0
May 3	NY Islanders	4	at	Montreal	3 OT
May 5	Montreal	2	at	NY Islanders	1

Montreal won best-of-seven series 4–2

Apr. 24	Boston	4	at	Philadelphia	3 OT
Apr. 26	Boston	5	at	Philadelphia	4 OT
Apr. 28	Philadelphia	1	at	Boston	2
May 1	Philadelphia	0	at	Boston	3

Boston won best-of-seven series 4–0

FINALS
May 7	Boston	3	at	Montreal	7
May 10	Boston	0	at	Montreal	3
May 12	Montreal	4	at	Boston	2
May 14	Montreal	2	at	Boston	1 OT

Montreal won best-of-seven series 4–0

MONTREAL CANADIENS 1978

The Canadiens lost just ten regular-season games in 1977-78 and were favored in the post-season. The Habs needed just nine games to reach the finals where they again met Boston in a rematch of the 1977 Finals. The Bruins also needed just nine games to advance, winning three overtime games en route to their date with the Canadiens.

Conn Smythe Trophy winner Larry Robinson led all playoff performers with 17 assists and tied teammate Guy Lafleur (10-11-21) for the overall playoff scoring lead with 21 points. Robinson was one of three Canadiens, including Doug Jarvis and Steve Shutt, to appear in all 95 games during the course of the season.

CONN SMYTHE TROPHY • Larry Robinson - Defenseman - Montreal Canadiens

PRELIMINARY ROUND
Apr. 11	Colorado	2	at	Philadelphia	3	OT
Apr. 13	Philadelphia	3	at	Colorado	1	

Colorado won best-of-three series 2–0

Apr. 11	NY Rangers	1	at	Buffalo	4	
Apr. 13	Buffalo	3	at	NY Rangers	4	OT
Apr. 15	NY Rangers	1	at	Buffalo	4	

Buffalo won best-of-three series 2–1

Apr. 11	Los Angeles	3	at	Toronto	7
Apr. 13	Toronto	4	at	Los Angeles	0

Toronto won best-of-three series 2–0

Apr. 11	Detroit	5	at	Atlanta	3
Apr. 13	Atlanta	2	at	Detroit	3

Detroit won best-of-three series 2–0

QUARTER-FINALS
Apr. 17	Detroit	2	at	Montreal	6	
Apr. 19	Detroit	4	at	Montreal	2	
Apr. 21	Montreal	4	at	Detroit	2	
Apr. 23	Montreal	8	at	Detroit	0	
Apr. 25	Detroit	2	at	Montreal	4	

Montreal won best-of-seven series 4–1

Apr. 17	Chicago	1	at	Boston	6	
Apr. 19	Chicago	3	at	Boston	4	OT
Apr. 21	Boston	4	at	Chicago	3	OT
Apr. 23	Boston	5	at	Chicago	2	

Boston won best-of-seven series 4–0

Apr. 17	Toronto	1	at	NY Islanders	4	
Apr. 19	Toronto	2	at	NY Islanders	3	OT
Apr. 21	NY Islanders	0	at	Toronto	2	
Apr. 23	NY Islanders	1	at	Toronto	3	
Apr. 25	Toronto	1	at	NY Islanders	2	OT
Apr. 27	NY Islanders	2	at	Toronto	5	
Apr. 29	Toronto	2	at	NY Islanders	1	OT

Toronto won best-of-seven series 4–3

Apr. 17	Buffalo	1	at	Philadelphia	4
Apr. 19	Buffalo	2	at	Philadelphia	3
Apr. 22	Philadelphia	1	at	Buffalo	4
Apr. 23	Philadelphia	4	at	Buffalo	2
Apr. 25	Buffalo	2	at	Philadelphia	4

Philadelphia won best-of-seven series 4–1

SEMI-FINALS
May 2	Toronto	3	at	Montreal	5
May 4	Toronto	2	at	Montreal	3
May 6	Montreal	6	at	Toronto	1
May 9	Montreal	2	at	Toronto	0

Montreal won best-of-seven series 4–0

May 2	Philadelphia	2	at	Boston	3	OT
May 4	Philadelphia	5	at	Boston	7	
May 7	Boston	1	at	Philadelphia	3	
May 9	Boston	4	at	Philadelphia	2	
May 11	Philadelphia	3	at	Boston	6	

Boston won best-of-seven series 4–1

FINALS
May 13	Boston	1	at	Montreal	4	
May 16	Boston	2	at	Montreal	3	OT
May 18	Montreal	0	at	Boston	4	
May 21	Montreal	3	at	Boston	4	OT
May 23	Boston	1	at	Montreal	4	
May 25	Montreal	4	at	Boston	1	

Montreal won best-of-seven series 4–2

1979 MONTREAL CANADIENS

The Montreal Canadiens captured their fourth straight Stanley Cup to record the second longest streak of championships in NHL history. Only the Canadiens' five-year stronghold on the Cup from 1956 to 1960 lasted longer.

Montreal's Game Five series-winning effort also marked the first time since 1968 that the Canadiens won the Cup on home ice. At the conclusion of the series, Jacques Lemaire, Yvan Cournoyer and Ken Dryden retired from the NHL. The trio left the game with a combined total of 24 Cups among them. Scotty Bowman, who had amassed his fifth Cup in seven seasons behind the Canadiens' bench, also made his farewell appearance with the team as he joined the Buffalo Sabres the following season.

CONN SMYTHE TROPHY • Bob Gainey - Left Wing - Montreal Canadiens

PRELIMINARY ROUND
Apr. 10	Vancouver	3	at	Philadelphia	2
Apr. 12	Philadelphia	6	at	Vancouver	4
Apr. 14	Vancouver	2	at	Philadelphia	7

Philadelphia won best-of-three series 2–1

Apr. 10	Los Angeles	1	at	NY Rangers	7
Apr. 12	NY Rangers	2	at	Los Angeles	1 OT

Rangers won best-of-three series 2–0

Apr. 10	Toronto	2	at	Atlanta	1
Apr. 12	Atlanta	4	at	Toronto	7

Toronto won best-of-three series 2–0

Apr. 10	Pittsburgh	4	at	Buffalo	3
Apr. 12	Buffalo	3	at	Pittsburgh	1
Apr. 14	Pittsburgh	4	at	Buffalo	3 OT

Pittsburgh won best-of-three series 2–1

QUARTER-FINALS
Apr. 16	Chicago	2	at	NY Islanders	6
Apr. 18	Chicago	0	at	NY Islanders	1 OT
Apr. 20	NY Islanders	4	at	Chicago	0
Apr. 22	NY Islanders	3	at	Chicago	1

Islanders won best-of-seven series 4–0

Apr. 16	Toronto	2	at	Montreal	5
Apr. 18	Toronto	1	at	Montreal	5
Apr. 21	Montreal	4	at	Toronto	3 OT
Apr. 22	Montreal	5	at	Toronto	4 OT

Montreal won best-of-seven series 4–0

Apr. 16	Pittsburgh	2	at	Boston	6
Apr. 18	Pittsburgh	3	at	Boston	4
Apr. 21	Boston	2	at	Pittsburgh	1
Apr. 22	Boston	4	at	Pittsburgh	1

Boston won best-of-seven series 4–0

Apr. 16	NY Rangers	2	at	Philadelphia	3 OT
Apr. 18	NY Rangers	7	at	Philadelphia	1
Apr. 20	Philadelphia	1	at	NY Rangers	5
Apr. 22	Philadelphia	0	at	NY Rangers	6
Apr. 24	NY Rangers	8	at	Philadelphia	3

Rangers won best-of-seven series 4–1

SEMI-FINALS
Apr. 26	NY Rangers	4	at	NY Islanders	1
Apr. 28	NY Rangers	3	at	NY Islanders	4 OT
May 1	NY Islanders	1	at	NY Rangers	3
May 3	NY Islanders	3	at	NY Rangers	2 OT
May 5	NY Rangers	4	at	NY Islanders	3
May 8	NY Islanders	1	at	NY Rangers	2

Rangers won best-of-seven series 4–2

Apr. 26	Boston	2	at	Montreal	4
Apr. 28	Boston	2	at	Montreal	5
May 1	Montreal	1	at	Boston	2
May 3	Montreal	3	at	Boston	4 OT
May 5	Boston	1	at	Montreal	5
May 8	Montreal	2	at	Boston	5
May 10	Boston	4	at	Montreal	5 OT

Montreal won best-of-seven series 4–3

FINALS
May 13	NY Rangers	4	at	Montreal	1
May 15	NY Rangers	2	at	Montreal	6
May 17	Montreal	4	at	NY Rangers	1
May 19	Montreal	4	at	NY Rangers	3 OT
May 21	NY Rangers	1	at	Montreal	4

Montreal won best-of-seven series 4–1

NEW YORK ISLANDERS 1980

In their eighth NHL season, the New York Islanders became the second expansion team to win the Stanley Cup. Two players, Billy Smith and Bob Nystrom, had been with the team since its inception in 1972.

In Game One, Denis Potvin recorded the first power-play goal ever scored in overtime in Stanley Cup history. The Flyers' Jimmy Watson went off at the 2:08 mark, and Potvin scored 1:59 later to end the game and give the Islanders their first win in the Finals. Nystrom also scored an overtime goal, the Cup-winner in Game Six, to raise his career total to four. Maurice "Rocket" Richard, who scored six overtime goals in the playoffs, owns the all-time record.

CONN SMYTHE TROPHY • Bryan Trottier - Center - New York Islanders

PRELIMINARY ROUND
Apr.	8	Edmonton	3	at Philadelphia	4	OT
Apr.	9	Edmonton	1	at Philadelphia	5	
Apr.	11	Philadelphia	3	at Edmonton	2	OT

Philadelphia won best-of-five series 3–0

Apr.	8	Vancouver	1	at Buffalo	2	
Apr.	9	Vancouver	0	at Buffalo	6	
Apr.	11	Buffalo	4	at Vancouver	5	
Apr.	12	Buffalo	3	at Vancouver	1	

Buffalo won best-of-five series 3–1

Apr.	8	Hartford	1	at Montreal	6	
Apr.	9	Hartford	4	at Montreal	8	
Apr.	11	Montreal	4	at Hartford	3	OT

Montreal won best-of-five series 3–0

Apr.	8	Pittsburgh	4	at Boston	2	
Apr.	10	Pittsburgh	1	at Boston	4	
Apr.	12	Boston	1	at Pittsburgh	4	
Apr.	13	Boston	8	at Pittsburgh	3	
Apr.	14	Pittsburgh	2	at Boston	6	

Boston won best-of-five series 3–2

Apr.	8	Los Angeles	1	at NY Islanders	8	
Apr.	9	Los Angeles	6	at NY Islanders	3	
Apr.	11	NY Islanders	4	at Los Angeles	3	OT
Apr.	12	NY Islanders	6	at Los Angeles	0	

Islanders won best-of-five series 3–1

Apr.	8	Toronto	3	at Minnesota	6	
Apr.	9	Toronto	2	at Minnesota	7	
Apr.	11	Minnesota	4	at Toronto	3	OT

Minnesota won best-of-five series 3–0

Apr.	8	St. Louis	2	at Chicago	3	OT
Apr.	9	St. Louis	1	at Chicago	5	
Apr.	11	Chicago	4	at St. Louis	1	

Chicago won best-of-five series 3–0

Apr.	8	Atlanta	1	at NY Rangers	2	OT
Apr.	9	Atlanta	1	at NY Rangers	5	
Apr.	11	NY Rangers	2	at Atlanta	4	
Apr.	12	NY Rangers	5	at Atlanta	2	

Rangers won best-of-five series 3–1

QUARTER-FINALS
Apr.	16	NY Rangers	1	at Philadelphia	2	
Apr.	17	NY Rangers	1	at Philadelphia	4	
Apr.	19	Philadelphia	3	at NY Rangers	0	
Apr.	20	Philadelphia	3	at NY Rangers	4	
Apr.	22	NY Rangers	1	at Philadelphia	3	

Philadelphia won best-of-seven series 4–1

Apr.	16	Chicago	0	at Buffalo	5	
Apr.	17	Chicago	4	at Buffalo	6	
Apr.	19	Buffalo	2	at Chicago	1	
Apr.	20	Buffalo	3	at Chicago	2	

Buffalo won best-of-seven series 4–0

Apr.	16	Minnesota	3	at Montreal	0	
Apr.	17	Minnesota	4	at Montreal	1	
Apr.	19	Montreal	5	at Minnesota	0	
Apr.	20	Montreal	5	at Minnesota	1	
Apr.	22	Minnesota	2	at Montreal	6	
Apr.	24	Montreal	2	at Minnesota	5	
Apr.	27	Minnesota	3	at Montreal	2	

Minnesota won best-of-seven series 4–3

Apr.	16	NY Islanders	2	at Boston	1	OT
Apr.	17	NY Islanders	5	at Boston	4	OT
Apr.	19	Boston	3	at NY Islanders	5	
Apr.	21	Boston	4	at NY Islanders	3	OT
Apr.	22	NY Islanders	4	at Boston	2	

Islanders won best-of-seven series 4–1

SEMI-FINALS
Apr.	29	Minnesota	6	at Philadelphia	5	
May	1	Minnesota	0	at Philadelphia	7	
May	4	Philadelphia	5	at Minnesota	3	
May	6	Philadelphia	3	at Minnesota	2	
May	8	Minnesota	3	at Philadelphia	7	

Philadelphia won best-of-seven series 4–1

Apr.	29	NY Islanders	4	at Buffalo	1	
May	1	NY Islanders	2	at Buffalo	1	OT
May	3	Buffalo	4	at NY Islanders	7	
May	6	Buffalo	7	at NY Islanders	4	
May	8	NY Islanders	0	at Buffalo	2	
May	10	Buffalo	2	at NY Islanders	5	

Islanders won best-of-seven series 4–2

FINALS
May	13	NY Islanders	4	at Philadelphia	3	OT
May	15	NY Islanders	3	at Philadelphia	8	
May	17	Philadelphia	2	at NY Islanders	6	
May	19	Philadelphia	2	at NY Islanders	5	
May	22	NY Islanders	3	at Philadelphia	6	
May	24	Philadelphia	4	at NY Islanders	5	OT

Islanders won best-of-seven series 4–2

1981 NEW YORK ISLANDERS

The New York Islanders captured a second consecutive Stanley Cup with a five-game series triumph over the Minnesota North Stars. For Minnesota, it marked the club's first trip to the Finals since joining the NHL in 1967-68.

New York's Mike Bossy shattered playoff records for points (17-18-35) and power-play goals (9) in his 18 post-season outings.

Dino Ciccarelli of Minnesota broke Don Maloney's rookie scoring record with 21 playoff points and Steve Christoff's rookie mark for playoff goals with 14.

CONN SMYTHE TROPHY • Butch Goring - Center - New York Islanders

PRELIMINARY ROUND
Apr.	8	Toronto	2	at	NY Islanders	9
Apr.	9	Toronto	1	at	NY Islanders	5
Apr.	11	NY Islanders	6	at	Toronto	1

Islanders won best-of-five series 3–0

Apr.	8	Pittsburgh	2	at	St. Louis	4
Apr.	9	Pittsburgh	6	at	St. Louis	4
Apr.	11	St. Louis	5	at	Pittsburgh	4
Apr.	12	St. Louis	3	at	Pittsburgh	6
Apr.	14	Pittsburgh	3	at	St. Louis	4 OT

St. Louis won best-of-five series 3–2

Apr.	8	Edmonton	6	at	Montreal	3
Apr.	9	Edmonton	3	at	Montreal	1
Apr.	11	Montreal	2	at	Edmonton	6

Edmonton won best-of-five series 3–0

Apr.	8	NY Rangers	3	at	Los Angeles	1
Apr.	9	NY Rangers	4	at	Los Angeles	5
Apr.	11	Los Angeles	3	at	NY Rangers	10
Apr.	12	Los Angeles	3	at	NY Rangers	6

Rangers won best-of-five series 3–1

Apr.	8	Vancouver	2	at	Buffalo	3 OT
Apr.	9	Vancouver	2	at	Buffalo	5
Apr.	11	Buffalo	5	at	Vancouver	3

Buffalo won best-of-five series 3–0

Apr.	8	Quebec	4	at	Philadelphia	6
Apr.	9	Quebec	5	at	Philadelphia	8
Apr.	11	Philadelphia	0	at	Quebec	2
Apr.	12	Philadelphia	3	at	Quebec	4 OT
Apr.	14	Quebec	2	at	Philadelphia	5

Philadelphia won best-of-five series 3–2

Apr.	8	Chicago	3	at	Calgary	4
Apr.	9	Chicago	2	at	Calgary	6
Apr.	11	Calgary	5	at	Chicago	4 OT

Calgary won best-of-five series 3–0

Apr.	8	Minnesota	5	at	Boston	4 OT
Apr.	9	Minnesota	9	at	Boston	6
Apr.	11	Boston	3	at	Minnesota	6

Minnesota won best-of-five series 3–0

QUARTER-FINALS
Apr.	16	Edmonton	2	at	NY Islanders	8
Apr.	17	Edmonton	3	at	NY Islanders	6
Apr.	19	NY Islanders	2	at	Edmonton	5
Apr.	20	NY Islanders	5	at	Edmonton	4 OT
Apr.	22	Edmonton	4	at	NY Islanders	3
Apr.	24	NY Islanders	5	at	Edmonton	2

Islanders won best-of-seven series 4–2

Apr.	16	NY Rangers	3	at	St. Louis	6
Apr.	17	NY Rangers	6	at	St. Louis	4
Apr.	19	St. Louis	3	at	NY Rangers	6
Apr.	20	St. Louis	1	at	NY Rangers	4
Apr.	22	NY Rangers	3	at	St. Louis	4
Apr.	24	St. Louis	4	at	NY Rangers	7

Rangers won best-of-seven series 4–2

Apr.	16	Minnesota	4	at	Buffalo	3 OT
Apr.	17	Minnesota	5	at	Buffalo	2
Apr.	19	Buffalo	4	at	Minnesota	6
Apr.	20	Buffalo	5	at	Minnesota	4 OT
Apr.	22	Minnesota	4	at	Buffalo	3

Minnesota won best-of-seven series 4–1

Apr.	16	Calgary	0	at	Philadelphia	4
Apr.	17	Calgary	5	at	Philadelphia	4
Apr.	19	Philadelphia	1	at	Calgary	2
Apr.	20	Philadelphia	4	at	Calgary	5
Apr.	22	Calgary	4	at	Philadelphia	9
Apr.	24	Philadelphia	3	at	Calgary	2
Apr.	26	Calgary	4	at	Philadelphia	1

Calgary won best-of-seven series 4–3

SEMI-FINALS
Apr.	28	NY Rangers	2	at	NY Islanders	5
Apr.	30	NY Rangers	3	at	NY Islanders	7
May	2	NY Islanders	5	at	NY Rangers	1
May	5	NY Islanders	5	at	NY Rangers	2

Islanders won best-of-seven series 4–0

Apr.	28	Minnesota	4	at	Calgary	1
Apr.	30	Minnesota	2	at	Calgary	3
May	3	Calgary	4	at	Minnesota	6
May	5	Calgary	4	at	Minnesota	7
May	7	Minnesota	1	at	Calgary	3
May	9	Calgary	3	at	Minnesota	5

Minnesota won best-of-seven series 4–2

FINALS
May	12	Minnesota	3	at	NY Islanders	6
May	14	Minnesota	3	at	NY Islanders	6
May	17	NY Islanders	7	at	Minnesota	5
May	19	NY Islanders	2	at	Minnesota	4
May	21	Minnesota	1	at	NY Islanders	5

Islanders won best-of-seven series 4–1

NEW YORK ISLANDERS 1982

The Islanders distinguished themselves as the first U.S.-based team in history to win three consecutive Stanley Cup championships with a sweep of the Vancouver Canucks.

The Canucks, meanwhile, became the first Vancouver team since the 1924 Maroons of the WCHL to appear in the Finals.

Mike Bossy won the Conn Smythe Trophy with seven goals in the four-game series, tying the record for most goals in the Finals set by Jean Beliveau in 1956.

Bryan Trottier tallied 32 playoff assists in 19 games to set a new record, while goalie Billy Smith amassed a 15-4-0 mark to equal his own record for playoff wins.

CONN SMYTHE TROPHY • Mike Bossy - Right Wing - New York Islanders

DIVISION SEMI-FINALS
Apr.	7	Quebec	1	at	Montreal	5
Apr.	8	Quebec	3	at	Montreal	2
Apr.	10	Montreal	1	at	Quebec	2
Apr.	11	Montreal	6	at	Quebec	2
Apr.	13	Quebec	3	at	Montreal	2 OT

Quebec won best-of-five series 3–2

Apr.	7	Buffalo	1	at	Boston	3
Apr.	8	Buffalo	3	at	Boston	7
Apr.	10	Boston	2	at	Buffalo	5
Apr.	11	Boston	5	at	Buffalo	2

Boston won best-of-five series 3–1

Apr.	7	Chicago	3	at	Minnesota	2 OT
Apr.	8	Chicago	5	at	Minnesota	3
Apr.	10	Minnesota	7	at	Chicago	1
Apr.	11	Minnesota	2	at	Chicago	5

Chicago won best-of-five series 3–1

Apr.	7	St. Louis	4	at	Winnipeg	3
Apr.	8	St. Louis	2	at	Winnipeg	5
Apr.	10	Winnipeg	3	at	St. Louis	6
Apr.	11	Winnipeg	2	at	St. Louis	8

St. Louis won best-of-five series 3–1

Apr.	7	Pittsburgh	1	at	NY Islanders	8
Apr.	8	Pittsburgh	2	at	NY Islanders	7
Apr.	10	NY Islanders	1	at	Pittsburgh	2 OT
Apr.	11	NY Islanders	2	at	Pittsburgh	5
Apr.	13	Pittsburgh	3	at	NY Islanders	4 OT

Islanders won best-of-five series 3–2

Apr.	7	Philadelphia	4	at	NY Rangers	1
Apr.	8	Philadelphia	3	at	NY Rangers	7
Apr.	10	NY Rangers	4	at	Philadelphia	3
Apr.	11	NY Rangers	7	at	Philadelphia	5

Rangers won best-of-five series 3–1

Apr.	7	Los Angeles	10	at	Edmonton	8
Apr.	8	Los Angeles	2	at	Edmonton	3 OT
Apr.	10	Edmonton	5	at	Los Angeles	6 OT
Apr.	12	Edmonton	3	at	Los Angeles	2
Apr.	13	Los Angeles	7	at	Edmonton	4

Los Angeles won best-of-five series 3–2

Apr.	7	Calgary	3	at	Vancouver	5
Apr.	8	Calgary	1	at	Vancouver	2 OT
Apr.	10	Vancouver	3	at	Calgary	1

Vancouver won best-of-five series 3–0

DIVISION FINALS
Apr.	15	Quebec	3	at	Boston	4
Apr.	16	Quebec	4	at	Boston	8
Apr.	18	Boston	2	at	Quebec	3 OT
Apr.	19	Boston	2	at	Quebec	7
Apr.	21	Quebec	4	at	Boston	3
Apr.	23	Boston	6	at	Quebec	5 OT
Apr.	25	Quebec	2	at	Boston	1

Quebec won best-of-seven series 4–3

Apr.	15	Chicago	5	at	St. Louis	4
Apr.	16	Chicago	1	at	St. Louis	3
Apr.	18	St. Louis	5	at	Chicago	6
Apr.	19	St. Louis	4	at	Chicago	7
Apr.	21	Chicago	2	at	St. Louis	3 OT
Apr.	23	St. Louis	0	at	Chicago	2

Chicago won best-of-seven series 4–2

Apr.	15	NY Rangers	5	at	NY Islanders	4
Apr.	16	NY Rangers	2	at	NY Islanders	7
Apr.	18	NY Islanders	4	at	NY Rangers	3 OT
Apr.	19	NY Islanders	5	at	NY Rangers	3
Apr.	21	NY Rangers	4	at	NY Islanders	2
Apr.	23	NY Islanders	5	at	NY Rangers	3

Islanders won best-of-seven series 4–2

Apr.	15	Los Angeles	2	at	Vancouver	3
Apr.	16	Los Angeles	3	at	Vancouver	2 OT
Apr.	18	Vancouver	4	at	Los Angeles	3 OT
Apr.	19	Vancouver	5	at	Los Angeles	4
Apr.	21	Los Angeles	2	at	Vancouver	5

Vancouver won best-of-seven series 4–1

CONFERENCE FINALS
Apr.	27	Quebec	1	at	NY Islanders	4
Apr.	29	Quebec	2	at	NY Islanders	5
May	1	NY Islanders	5	at	Quebec	4 OT
May	4	NY Islanders	4	at	Quebec	2

Islanders won best-of-seven series 4–0

Apr.	27	Vancouver	2	at	Chicago	1 OT
Apr.	29	Vancouver	1	at	Chicago	4
May	1	Chicago	3	at	Vancouver	4
May	4	Chicago	3	at	Vancouver	5
May	6	Vancouver	6	at	Chicago	2

Vancouver won best-of-seven series 4–1

FINALS
May	8	Vancouver	5	at	NY Islanders	6 OT
May	11	Vancouver	4	at	NY Islanders	6
May	13	NY Islanders	3	at	Vancouver	0
May	16	NY Islanders	3	at	Vancouver	1

Islanders won best-of-seven series 4–0

1983 NEW YORK ISLANDERS

The New York Islanders won their fourth straight Stanley Cup to become only the second NHL franchise in history to amass as many championships in a row. The Montreal Canadiens own the all-time record with five consecutive Cups from 1956 to 1960 and four more between 1976 and 1979.

Goaltender Billy Smith won the Conn Smythe Trophy after limiting the Edmonton Oilers to six goals in four games and shutting out the Campbell Conference champions in seven of 12 periods of play.

In his first appearance in the Finals, Wayne Gretzky tallied four assists on the Oilers' six goals.

CONN SMYTHE TROPHY • Billy Smith - Goaltender - New York Islanders

DIVISION SEMI-FINALS

Date	Away		At	Home		
Apr. 5	Quebec	3	at	Boston	4	OT
Apr. 7	Quebec	2	at	Boston	4	
Apr. 9	Boston	1	at	Quebec	2	
Apr. 10	Boston	2	at	Quebec	1	

Boston won best-of-five series 3–1

Apr. 6	Buffalo	1	at	Montreal	0
Apr. 7	Buffalo	3	at	Montreal	0
Apr. 9	Montreal	2	at	Buffalo	4

Buffalo won best-of-five series 3–0

Apr. 5	NY Rangers	5	at	Philadelphia	3
Apr. 7	NY Rangers	4	at	Philadelphia	3
Apr. 9	Philadelphia	3	at	NY Rangers	9

Rangers won best-of-five series 3–0

Apr. 6	Washington	2	at	NY Islanders	5
Apr. 7	Washington	4	at	NY Islanders	2
Apr. 9	NY Islanders	6	at	Washington	2
Apr. 10	NY Islanders	6	at	Washington	3

Islanders won best-of-five series 3–1

Apr. 6	St. Louis	4	at	Chicago	2
Apr. 7	St. Louis	2	at	Chicago	7
Apr. 9	Chicago	2	at	St. Louis	1
Apr. 10	Chicago	5	at	St. Louis	3

Chicago won best-of-five series 3–1

Apr. 6	Toronto	4	at	Minnesota	5	
Apr. 7	Toronto	4	at	Minnesota	5	OT
Apr. 9	Minnesota	3	at	Toronto	6	
Apr. 10	Minnesota	5	at	Toronto	4	OT

Minnesota won best-of-five series 3–1

Apr. 6	Winnipeg	3	at	Edmonton	6
Apr. 7	Winnipeg	3	at	Edmonton	4
Apr. 9	Edmonton	4	at	Winnipeg	3

Edmonton won best-of-five series 3–0

Apr. 6	Vancouver	3	at	Calgary	4	OT
Apr. 7	Vancouver	3	at	Calgary	5	
Apr. 9	Calgary	4	at	Vancouver	5	
Apr. 10	Calgary	4	at	Vancouver	3	OT

Calgary won best-of-five series 3–1

DIVISION FINALS

Apr. 14	Buffalo	7	at	Boston	4	
Apr. 15	Buffalo	3	at	Boston	5	
Apr. 17	Boston	3	at	Buffalo	4	
Apr. 18	Boston	6	at	Buffalo	2	
Apr. 20	Buffalo	0	at	Boston	9	
Apr. 22	Boston	3	at	Buffalo	5	
Apr. 24	Buffalo	2	at	Boston	3	OT

Boston won best-of-seven series 4–3

Apr. 14	NY Rangers	1	at	NY Islanders	4
Apr. 15	NY Rangers	0	at	NY Islanders	5
Apr. 17	NY Islanders	6	at	NY Rangers	7
Apr. 18	NY Islanders	1	at	NY Rangers	3
Apr. 20	NY Rangers	2	at	NY Islanders	7
Apr. 22	NY Islanders	5	at	NY Rangers	2

Islanders won best-of-seven series 4–2

Apr. 14	Minnesota	2	at	Chicago	5	
Apr. 15	Minnesota	4	at	Chicago	7	
Apr. 17	Chicago	1	at	Minnesota	5	
Apr. 18	Chicago	4	at	Minnesota	3	OT
Apr. 20	Minnesota	2	at	Chicago	5	

Chicago won best-of-seven series 4–1

Apr. 14	Calgary	3	at	Edmonton	6
Apr. 15	Calgary	1	at	Edmonton	5
Apr. 17	Edmonton	10	at	Calgary	2
Apr. 18	Edmonton	5	at	Calgary	6
Apr. 20	Calgary	1	at	Edmonton	9

Edmonton won best-of-seven series 4–1

CONFERENCE FINALS

Apr. 26	NY Islanders	5	at	Boston	2
Apr. 28	NY Islanders	1	at	Boston	4
Apr. 30	Boston	3	at	NY Islanders	7
May 3	Boston	3	at	NY Islanders	8
May 5	NY Islanders	1	at	Boston	5
May 7	Boston	4	at	NY Islanders	8

Islanders won best-of-seven series 4–2

Apr. 24	Chicago	4	at	Edmonton	8
Apr. 26	Chicago	2	at	Edmonton	8
May 1	Edmonton	3	at	Chicago	2
May 3	Edmonton	6	at	Chicago	3

Edmonton won best-of-seven series 4–0

FINALS

May 10	NY Islanders	2	at	Edmonton	0
May 12	NY Islanders	6	at	Edmonton	3
May 14	Edmonton	1	at	NY Islanders	5
May 17	Edmonton	2	at	NY Islanders	4

Islanders won best-of-seven series 4–0

EDMONTON OILERS 1984

The Edmonton Oilers, who joined the NHL in 1979-80 with the Hartford Whalers, Quebec Nordiques and Winnipeg Jets, became the first of the four former World Hockey Association (WHA) clubs to win the Stanley Cup.

In his first championship game, Oilers' goalie Grant Fuhr posted a shutout to hand the defending champion New York Islanders their first loss in 10 Final series games.

Four different Oilers - Kevin McClelland, Glenn Anderson, Mark Messier and Ken Linseman - scored game-winning goals.

Messier won the Conn Smythe Trophy with an 8-18-26 mark in 19 games.

CONN SMYTHE TROPHY • Mark Messier - Center - Edmonton Oilers

DIVISION SEMI-FINALS
Apr.	4	Montreal	2	at	Boston	1
Apr.	5	Montreal	3	at	Boston	1
Apr.	7	Boston	0	at	Montreal	5

Montreal won best-of-five series 3–0

Apr.	4	Quebec	3	at	Buffalo	2
Apr.	5	Quebec	6	at	Buffalo	2
Apr.	7	Buffalo	1	at	Quebec	4

Quebec won best-of-five series 3–0

Apr.	4	NY Rangers	1	at	NY Islanders	4
Apr.	5	NY Rangers	3	at	NY Islanders	0
Apr.	7	NY Islanders	2	at	NY Rangers	7
Apr.	8	NY Islanders	4	at	NY Rangers	1
Apr.	10	NY Rangers	2	at	NY Islanders	3 OT

Islanders won best-of-five series 3–2

Apr.	4	Philadelphia	2	at	Washington	4
Apr.	5	Philadelphia	2	at	Washington	6
Apr.	7	Washington	5	at	Philadelphia	1

Washington won best-of-five series 3–0

Apr.	4	Chicago	3	at	Minnesota	1
Apr.	5	Chicago	5	at	Minnesota	6
Apr.	7	Minnesota	4	at	Chicago	1
Apr.	8	Minnesota	3	at	Chicago	4
Apr.	10	Chicago	1	at	Minnesota	4

Minnesota won best-of-five series 3–2

Apr.	4	Detroit	2	at	St. Louis	3
Apr.	5	Detroit	5	at	St. Louis	3
Apr.	7	St. Louis	4	at	Detroit	3 OT
Apr.	8	St. Louis	3	at	Detroit	2 OT

St. Louis won best-of-five series 3–1

Apr.	4	Winnipeg	2	at	Edmonton	9
Apr.	5	Winnipeg	4	at	Edmonton	5 OT
Apr.	7	Edmonton	4	at	Winnipeg	1

Edmonton won best-of-five series 3–0

Apr.	4	Vancouver	3	at	Calgary	5
Apr.	5	Vancouver	2	at	Calgary	4
Apr.	7	Calgary	0	at	Vancouver	7
Apr.	8	Calgary	5	at	Vancouver	1

Calgary won best-of-five series 3–1

DIVISION FINALS
Apr.	12	Montreal	2	at	Quebec	4
Apr.	13	Montreal	4	at	Quebec	1
Apr.	15	Quebec	1	at	Montreal	2
Apr.	16	Quebec	4	at	Montreal	3 OT
Apr.	18	Montreal	4	at	Quebec	0
Apr.	20	Quebec	3	at	Montreal	5

Montreal won best-of-seven series 4–2

Apr.	12	Washington	3	at	NY Islanders	2
Apr.	13	Washington	4	at	NY Islanders	5 OT
Apr.	15	NY Islanders	3	at	Washington	1
Apr.	16	NY Islanders	5	at	Washington	2
Apr.	18	Washington	3	at	NY Islanders	5

Islanders won best-of-seven series 4–1

Apr.	12	St. Louis	1	at	Minnesota	2
Apr.	13	St. Louis	4	at	Minnesota	3 OT
Apr.	15	Minnesota	1	at	St. Louis	3
Apr.	16	Minnesota	3	at	St. Louis	2
Apr.	18	St. Louis	0	at	Minnesota	6
Apr.	20	Minnesota	0	at	St. Louis	4
Apr.	22	St. Louis	3	at	Minnesota	4 OT

Minnesota won best-of-seven series 4–3

Apr.	12	Calgary	2	at	Edmonton	5
Apr.	13	Calgary	6	at	Edmonton	5 OT
Apr.	15	Edmonton	3	at	Calgary	2
Apr.	16	Edmonton	5	at	Calgary	3
Apr.	18	Calgary	5	at	Edmonton	4
Apr.	20	Edmonton	4	at	Calgary	5 OT
Apr.	22	Calgary	4	at	Edmonton	7

Edmonton won best-of-seven series 4–3

CONFERENCE FINALS
Apr.	24	NY Islanders	0	at	Montreal	3
Apr.	26	NY Islanders	2	at	Montreal	4
Apr.	28	Montreal	2	at	NY Islanders	5
May	1	Montreal	1	at	NY Islanders	3
May	3	NY Islanders	3	at	Montreal	1
May	5	Montreal	1	at	NY Islanders	4

Islanders won best-of-seven series 4–2

Apr.	24	Minnesota	1	at	Edmonton	7
Apr.	26	Minnesota	3	at	Edmonton	4
Apr.	28	Edmonton	8	at	Minnesota	5
May	1	Edmonton	3	at	Minnesota	1

Edmonton won best-of-seven series 4–0

FINALS
May	10	Edmonton	1	at	NY Islanders	0
May	12	Edmonton	1	at	NY Islanders	6
May	15	NY Islanders	2	at	Edmonton	7
May	17	NY Islanders	2	at	Edmonton	7
May	19	NY Islanders	2	at	Edmonton	5

Edmonton won best-of-seven series 4–1

1985 EDMONTON OILERS

In the 1985 playoffs, Wayne Gretzky set new records for assists (30) and points (47) in one playoff year with a 17-30-47 mark in 18 games. Gretzky also tied the record shared by Montreal's Jean Beliveau (1956) and Mike Bossy (1982) for most goals in the Stanley Cup Finals with seven in five games. Jari Kurri scored 19 goals in 18 games to tie the record for goals in one playoff year. Kurri also broke teammate Mark Messier's record for most hat-tricks in a playoff year with four, including one four-goal game. Paul Coffey, who registered a 12-25-37 mark in 18 games, shattered the one-year playoff records for goals, assists and points by a defenseman. Coffey broke Boston Bruin Bobby Orr's records for goals (9 in 1970) and assists (19 in 1972) and New York Islander Denis Potvin's record for points (25 in 1981). Grant Fuhr tied New York Islanders' goaltender Billy Smith for most wins, 15, in a playoff year. Fuhr posted a 15-3 record in 18 games. Smith amassed 15 wins in both 1980 and 1982. For the first time in the Finals, two penalty shots were awarded in the same series. Both were stopped by the Oilers' Grant Fuhr.

CONN SMYTHE TROPHY • Wayne Gretzky - Center - Edmonton Oilers

DIVISION SEMI-FINALS
Date	Visitor			Home	
Apr. 10	Boston	5	at	Montreal	3
Apr. 11	Boston	3	at	Montreal	5
Apr. 13	Montreal	4	at	Boston	2
Apr. 14	Montreal	6	at	Boston	7
Apr. 16	Boston	0	at	Montreal	1

Montreal won best-of-five series 3–2

Apr. 10	Buffalo	2	at	Quebec	5
Apr. 11	Buffalo	2	at	Quebec	3
Apr. 13	Quebec	4	at	Buffalo	6
Apr. 14	Quebec	4	at	Buffalo	7
Apr. 16	Buffalo	5	at	Quebec	6

Quebec won best-of-five series 3–2

Apr. 10	NY Rangers	4	at	Philadelphia	5 OT
Apr. 11	NY Rangers	1	at	Philadelphia	3
Apr. 13	Philadelphia	6	at	NY Rangers	5

Philadelphia won best-of-five series 3–0

Apr. 10	NY Islanders	3	at	Washington	4 OT
Apr. 11	NY Islanders	1	at	Washington	2 OT
Apr. 13	Washington	1	at	NY Islanders	2
Apr. 14	Washington	4	at	NY Islanders	6
Apr. 16	NY Islanders	2	at	Washington	1

Islanders won best-of-five series 3–2

Apr. 10	Minnesota	3	at	St. Louis	2
Apr. 11	Minnesota	4	at	St. Louis	3
Apr. 13	St. Louis	0	at	Minnesota	2

Minnesota won best-of-five series 3–0

Apr. 10	Detroit	5	at	Chicago	9
Apr. 11	Detroit	1	at	Chicago	6
Apr. 13	Chicago	8	at	Detroit	2

Chicago won best-of-five series 3–0

Apr. 10	Los Angeles	2	at	Edmonton	3 OT
Apr. 11	Los Angeles	2	at	Edmonton	4
Apr. 13	Edmonton	4	at	Los Angeles	3 OT

Edmonton won best-of-five series 3–0

Apr. 10	Calgary	4	at	Winnipeg	5 OT
Apr. 11	Calgary	2	at	Winnipeg	5
Apr. 13	Winnipeg	0	at	Calgary	4
Apr. 14	Winnipeg	5	at	Calgary	3

Winnipeg won best-of-five series 3–1

DIVISION FINALS
Apr. 18	Quebec	2	at	Montreal	1 OT
Apr. 21	Quebec	4	at	Montreal	6
Apr. 23	Montreal	6	at	Quebec	7 OT
Apr. 25	Montreal	3	at	Quebec	1
Apr. 27	Quebec	5	at	Montreal	1
Apr. 30	Montreal	5	at	Quebec	2
May 2	Quebec	3	at	Montreal	2 OT

Quebec won best-of-seven series 4–3

Apr. 18	NY Islanders	0	at	Philadelphia	3
Apr. 21	NY Islanders	2	at	Philadelphia	5
Apr. 23	Philadelphia	5	at	NY Islanders	3
Apr. 25	Philadelphia	2	at	NY Islanders	6
Apr. 28	NY Islanders	0	at	Philadelphia	1

Philadelphia won best-of-seven series 4–1

Apr. 18	Minnesota	8	at	Chicago	5
Apr. 21	Minnesota	2	at	Chicago	6
Apr. 23	Chicago	5	at	Minnesota	3
Apr. 25	Chicago	7	at	Minnesota	6 OT
Apr. 28	Minnesota	5	at	Chicago	4 OT
Apr. 30	Chicago	6	at	Minnesota	5 OT

Chicago won best-of-seven series 4–2

Apr. 18	Winnipeg	2	at	Edmonton	4
Apr. 20	Winnipeg	2	at	Edmonton	5
Apr. 23	Edmonton	5	at	Winnipeg	4
Apr. 25	Edmonton	8	at	Winnipeg	3

Edmonton won best-of-seven series 4–0

CONFERENCE FINALS
May 5	Philadelphia	1	at	Quebec	2 OT
May 7	Philadelphia	4	at	Quebec	2
May 9	Quebec	2	at	Philadelphia	4
May 12	Quebec	5	at	Philadelphia	3
May 14	Philadelphia	2	at	Quebec	1
May 16	Quebec	0	at	Philadelphia	3

Philadelphia won best-of-seven series 4–2

May 4	Chicago	2	at	Edmonton	11
May 7	Chicago	3	at	Edmonton	7
May 9	Edmonton	2	at	Chicago	5
May 12	Edmonton	6	at	Chicago	8
May 14	Chicago	5	at	Edmonton	10
May 16	Edmonton	8	at	Chicago	2

Edmonton won best-of-seven series 4–2

FINALS
May 21	Edmonton	1	at	Philadelphia	4
May 23	Edmonton	3	at	Philadelphia	1
May 25	Philadelphia	3	at	Edmonton	4
May 28	Philadelphia	3	at	Edmonton	5
May 30	Philadelphia	3	at	Edmonton	8

Edmonton won best-of-seven series 4–1

MONTREAL CANADIENS 1986

The Montreal Canadiens set a new professional record for championships, winning their 23rd Stanley Cup title. Montreal had been tied with the New York Yankees, who have amassed 22 World Series titles in their history.

The series marked the first All-Canadian Finals since Montreal and Toronto faced each other in the 1967 Finals.

Brian Skrudland scored nine seconds into overtime in Game Two to set a new record for the fastest overtime goal in playoff history, eclipsing the old mark of 11 seconds set by J.P. Parise of the NY Islanders on April 11, 1975.

20-year-old goaltender Patrick Roy became the youngest player ever to earn the Conn Smythe Trophy in the 22-year history of the award. Roy posted a record-tying 15 playoff wins (15-5) and a 1.92 average in 20 post-season games.

CONN SMYTHE TROPHY • Patrick Roy - Goaltender - Montreal Canadiens

DIVISION SEMI-FINALS
Apr.	9	Hartford	3	at	Quebec	2 OT
Apr.	10	Hartford	4	at	Quebec	1
Apr.	12	Quebec	4	at	Hartford	9

Hartford won best-of-five series 3–0

Apr.	9	Boston	1	at	Montreal	3
Apr.	10	Boston	2	at	Montreal	3
Apr.	12	Montreal	4	at	Boston	3

Montreal won best-of-five series 3–0

Apr.	9	NY Rangers	6	at	Philadelphia	2
Apr.	10	NY Rangers	1	at	Philadelphia	2
Apr.	12	Philadelphia	2	at	NY Rangers	5
Apr.	13	Philadelphia	7	at	NY Rangers	1
Apr.	15	NY Rangers	5	at	Philadelphia	2

Rangers won best-of-five series 3–2

Apr.	9	NY Islanders	1	at	Washington	3
Apr.	10	NY Islanders	2	at	Washington	5
Apr.	12	Washington	3	at	NY Islanders	1

Washington won best-of-five series 3–0

Apr.	9	Toronto	5	at	Chicago	3
Apr.	10	Toronto	6	at	Chicago	4
Apr.	12	Chicago	2	at	Toronto	7

Toronto won best-of-five series 3–0

Apr.	9	St. Louis	2	at	Minnesota	1
Apr.	10	St. Louis	2	at	Minnesota	6
Apr.	12	Minnesota	3	at	St. Louis	4
Apr.	13	Minnesota	7	at	St. Louis	4
Apr.	15	St. Louis	6	at	Minnesota	3

St. Louis won best-of-five series 3–2

Apr.	9	Vancouver	3	at	Edmonton	7
Apr.	10	Vancouver	1	at	Edmonton	5
Apr.	12	Edmonton	5	at	Vancouver	1

Edmonton won best-of-five series 3–0

Apr.	9	Winnipeg	1	at	Calgary	5
Apr.	10	Winnipeg	4	at	Calgary	6
Apr.	12	Calgary	4	at	Winnipeg	3 OT

Calgary won best-of-five series 3–0

DIVISION FINALS
Apr.	17	Hartford	4	at	Montreal	1
Apr.	19	Hartford	1	at	Montreal	3
Apr.	21	Montreal	4	at	Hartford	1
Apr.	23	Montreal	1	at	Hartford	2 OT
Apr.	25	Hartford	3	at	Montreal	5
Apr.	27	Montreal	0	at	Hartford	1
Apr.	29	Hartford	1	at	Montreal	2 OT

Montreal won best-of-seven series 4–3

Apr.	17	NY Rangers	4	at	Washington	3 OT
Apr.	19	NY Rangers	1	at	Washington	8
Apr.	21	Washington	6	at	NY Rangers	3
Apr.	23	Washington	5	at	NY Rangers	6 OT
Apr.	25	NY Rangers	4	at	Washington	2
Apr.	27	Washington	1	at	NY Rangers	2

Rangers won best-of-seven series 4–2

Apr.	18	Toronto	1	at	St. Louis	6
Apr.	20	Toronto	3	at	St. Louis	0
Apr.	22	St. Louis	2	at	Toronto	5
Apr.	24	St. Louis	7	at	Toronto	4
Apr.	26	Toronto	3	at	St. Louis	4 OT
Apr.	28	St. Louis	3	at	Toronto	5
Apr.	30	Toronto	1	at	St. Louis	2

St. Louis won best-of-seven series 4–3

Apr.	18	Calgary	4	at	Edmonton	1
Apr.	20	Calgary	5	at	Edmonton	6 OT
Apr.	22	Edmonton	2	at	Calgary	3
Apr.	24	Edmonton	7	at	Calgary	4
Apr.	26	Calgary	4	at	Edmonton	1
Apr.	28	Edmonton	5	at	Calgary	2
Apr.	30	Calgary	3	at	Edmonton	2

Calgary won best-of-seven series 4–3

CONFERENCE FINALS
May	1	NY Rangers	1	at	Montreal	2
May	3	NY Rangers	2	at	Montreal	6
May	5	Montreal	4	at	NY Rangers	3 OT
May	7	Montreal	0	at	NY Rangers	2
May	9	NY Rangers	1	at	Montreal	3

Montreal won best-of-seven series 4–1

May	2	St. Louis	3	at	Calgary	2
May	4	St. Louis	2	at	Calgary	8
May	6	Calgary	5	at	St. Louis	3
May	8	Calgary	2	at	St. Louis	5
May	10	St. Louis	2	at	Calgary	4
May	12	Calgary	5	at	St. Louis	6 OT
May	14	St. Louis	1	at	Calgary	2

Calgary won best-of-seven series 4–3

FINALS
May	16	Montreal	2	at	Calgary	5
May	18	Montreal	3	at	Calgary	2 OT
May	20	Calgary	3	at	Montreal	5
May	22	Calgary	0	at	Montreal	1
May	24	Montreal	4	at	Calgary	3

Montreal won best-of-seven series 4–1

1987 EDMONTON OILERS

After a year's absence, the Edmonton Oilers returned to Finals action and captured their third Stanley Cup in four seasons.

The two teams carried the championship series to a full seven games for the first time since the Montreal Canadiens - Chicago Blackhawks Final series in 1971. Philadelphia goaltender Ron Hextall received the Conn Smythe Trophy, joining Roger Crozier (1966 Detroit Red Wings), Glenn Hall (1968 St. Louis Blues) and Reg Leach (1976 Philadelphia Flyers) as the only players on a losing club to be so honored.

CONN SMYTHE TROPHY • Ron Hextall - Goaltender - Philadelphia Flyers

DIVISION SEMI-FINALS

Apr. 8	Quebec	2	at	Hartford	3 OT
Apr. 9	Quebec	4	at	Hartford	5
Apr. 11	Hartford	1	at	Quebec	5
Apr. 12	Hartford	1	at	Quebec	4
Apr. 14	Quebec	7	at	Hartford	5
Apr. 16	Hartford	4	at	Quebec	5 OT

Quebec won best-of-seven series 4–2

Apr. 8	Boston	2	at	Montreal	6
Apr. 9	Boston	3	at	Montreal	4 OT
Apr. 11	Montreal	5	at	Boston	4
Apr. 12	Montreal	4	at	Boston	2

Montreal won best-of-seven series 4–0

Apr. 8	NY Rangers	3	at	Philadelphia	0
Apr. 9	NY Rangers	3	at	Philadelphia	8
Apr. 11	Philadelphia	3	at	NY Rangers	0
Apr. 12	Philadelphia	3	at	NY Rangers	6
Apr. 14	NY Rangers	1	at	Philadelphia	3
Apr. 16	Philadelphia	5	at	NY Rangers	0

Philadelphia won best-of-seven series 4–2

Apr. 8	NY Islanders	3	at	Washington	4
Apr. 9	NY Islanders	3	at	Washington	1
Apr. 11	Washington	2	at	NY Islanders	0
Apr. 12	Washington	4	at	NY Islanders	1
Apr. 14	NY Islanders	4	at	Washington	2
Apr. 16	Washington	4	at	NY Islanders	5
Apr. 18	NY Islanders	3	at	Washington	2 OT

Islanders won best-of-seven series 4–3

Apr. 8	Toronto	1	at	St. Louis	3
Apr. 9	Toronto	3	at	St. Louis	2 OT
Apr. 11	St. Louis	5	at	Toronto	3
Apr. 12	St. Louis	1	at	Toronto	2
Apr. 14	Toronto	2	at	St. Louis	1
Apr. 16	St. Louis	0	at	Toronto	4

Toronto won best-of-seven series 4–2

Apr. 8	Chicago	1	at	Detroit	3
Apr. 9	Chicago	1	at	Detroit	5
Apr. 11	Detroit	4	at	Chicago	3 OT
Apr. 12	Detroit	3	at	Chicago	1

Detroit won best-of-seven series 4–0

Apr. 8	Los Angeles	5	at	Edmonton	2
Apr. 9	Los Angeles	3	at	Edmonton	13
Apr. 11	Edmonton	6	at	Los Angeles	5
Apr. 12	Edmonton	6	at	Los Angeles	3
Apr. 14	Los Angeles	4	at	Edmonton	5

Edmonton won best-of-seven series 4–1

Apr. 8	Winnipeg	4	at	Calgary	2
Apr. 9	Winnipeg	3	at	Calgary	2
Apr. 11	Calgary	3	at	Winnipeg	2 OT
Apr. 12	Calgary	3	at	Winnipeg	4
Apr. 14	Winnipeg	3	at	Calgary	4
Apr. 16	Calgary	1	at	Winnipeg	6

Winnipeg won best-of-seven series 4–2

DIVISION FINALS

Apr. 20	Quebec	7	at	Montreal	5
Apr. 22	Quebec	2	at	Montreal	1
Apr. 24	Montreal	7	at	Quebec	2
Apr. 26	Montreal	3	at	Quebec	2 OT
Apr. 28	Quebec	2	at	Montreal	3
Apr. 30	Montreal	2	at	Quebec	3
May 2	Quebec	3	at	Montreal	5

Montreal won best-of-seven series 4–3

Apr. 20	NY Islanders	2	at	Philadelphia	4
Apr. 22	NY Islanders	2	at	Philadelphia	1
Apr. 24	Philadelphia	4	at	NY Islanders	1
Apr. 26	Philadelphia	6	at	NY Islanders	4
Apr. 28	NY Islanders	2	at	Philadelphia	1
Apr. 30	Philadelphia	2	at	NY Islanders	4
May 2	NY Islanders	1	at	Philadelphia	5

Philadelphia won best-of-seven series 4–3

Apr. 21	Toronto	4	at	Detroit	2
Apr. 23	Toronto	7	at	Detroit	2
Apr. 25	Detroit	4	at	Toronto	2
Apr. 27	Detroit	2	at	Toronto	3 OT
Apr. 29	Toronto	0	at	Detroit	3
May 1	Detroit	4	at	Toronto	2
May 3	Toronto	0	at	Detroit	3

Detroit won best-of-seven series 4–3

Apr. 21	Winnipeg	2	at	Edmonton	3 OT
Apr. 23	Winnipeg	3	at	Edmonton	5
Apr. 25	Edmonton	5	at	Winnipeg	2
Apr. 27	Edmonton	4	at	Winnipeg	2

Edmonton won best-of-seven series 4–0

CONFERENCE FINALS

May 4	Montreal	3	at	Philadelphia	4 OT
May 6	Montreal	5	at	Philadelphia	2
May 8	Philadelphia	4	at	Montreal	3
May 10	Philadelphia	6	at	Montreal	3
May 12	Montreal	5	at	Philadelphia	2
May 14	Philadelphia	4	at	Montreal	3

Philadelphia won best-of-seven series 4–2

May 5	Detroit	3	at	Edmonton	1
May 7	Detroit	1	at	Edmonton	4
May 9	Edmonton	2	at	Detroit	1
May 11	Edmonton	3	at	Detroit	2
May 13	Detroit	3	at	Edmonton	6

Edmonton won best-of-seven series 4–1

FINALS

May 17	Philadelphia	2	at	Edmonton	4
May 20	Philadelphia	2	at	Edmonton	3 OT
May 22	Edmonton	3	at	Philadelphia	5
May 24	Edmonton	4	at	Philadelphia	1
May 26	Philadelphia	4	at	Edmonton	3
May 28	Edmonton	2	at	Philadelphia	3
May 31	Philadelphia	1	at	Edmonton	3

Edmonton won best-of-seven series 4–3

EDMONTON OILERS 1988

The Edmonton Oilers won their fourth Stanley Cup in five years with a 4-0 series victory over the Boston Bruins, who were making their first appearance in the Stanley Cup Finals in 10 years.

For the first time since 1927, a Stanley Cup Final game failed to determine a winner. During the fourth game of the series, a power failure at Boston Garden halted play at 16.37 of the second period with the teams tied 3-3. Under League By-Laws, the match was suspended, to be made up in its entirety only in the event that a seventh and deciding game was necessary.

Thus the series shifted back to Edmonton where the Oilers, still holding a 3-0 series lead, recorded a 6-3 victory to win the Cup. Wayne Gretzky was selected as the Conn Smythe Trophy winner for the second time in his career, establishing a Stanley Cup Final series record of 13 points (3-10-13).

CONN SMYTHE TROPHY • Wayne Gretzky - Center - Edmonton Oilers

DIVISION SEMI-FINALS
Apr.	6	Hartford	3	at	Montreal	4
Apr.	7	Hartford	3	at	Montreal	7
Apr.	9	Montreal	4	at	Hartford	3
Apr.	10	Montreal	5	at	Hartford	7
Apr.	12	Hartford	3	at	Montreal	1
Apr.	14	Montreal	2	at	Hartford	1

Montreal won best-of-seven series 4–2

Apr.	6	Buffalo	3	at	Boston	7
Apr.	7	Buffalo	1	at	Boston	4
Apr.	9	Boston	2	at	Buffalo	6
Apr.	10	Boston	5	at	Buffalo	6 OT
Apr.	12	Buffalo	4	at	Boston	5
Apr.	14	Boston	5	at	Buffalo	2

Boston won best-of-seven series 4–2

Apr.	6	New Jersey	3	at	NY Islanders	4 OT
Apr.	7	New Jersey	3	at	NY Islanders	2
Apr.	9	NY Islanders	0	at	New Jersey	3
Apr.	10	NY Islanders	5	at	New Jersey	4 OT
Apr.	12	New Jersey	4	at	NY Islanders	2
Apr.	14	NY Islanders	5	at	New Jersey	6

New Jersey won best-of-seven series 4–2

Apr.	6	Philadelphia	4	at	Washington	2
Apr.	7	Philadelphia	4	at	Washington	5
Apr.	9	Washington	3	at	Philadelphia	4
Apr.	10	Washington	4	at	Philadelphia	5 OT
Apr.	12	Philadelphia	2	at	Washington	5
Apr.	14	Washington	7	at	Philadelphia	2
Apr.	16	Philadelphia	4	at	Washington	5 OT

Washington won best-of-seven series 4–3

Apr.	6	Toronto	6	at	Detroit	2
Apr.	7	Toronto	2	at	Detroit	6
Apr.	9	Detroit	6	at	Toronto	3
Apr.	10	Detroit	8	at	Toronto	0
Apr.	12	Toronto	6	at	Detroit	5 OT
Apr.	14	Detroit	5	at	Toronto	3

Detroit won best-of-seven series 4–2

Apr.	6	Chicago	1	at	St. Louis	5
Apr.	7	Chicago	2	at	St. Louis	3
Apr.	9	St. Louis	3	at	Chicago	6
Apr.	10	St. Louis	6	at	Chicago	5
Apr.	12	Chicago	3	at	St. Louis	5

St. Louis won best-of-seven series 4–1

Apr.	6	Los Angeles	2	at	Calgary	9
Apr.	7	Los Angeles	4	at	Calgary	6
Apr.	9	Calgary	2	at	Los Angeles	5
Apr.	10	Calgary	7	at	Los Angeles	3
Apr.	12	Los Angeles	4	at	Calgary	6

Calgary won best-of-seven series 4–1

Apr.	6	Winnipeg	4	at	Edmonton	7
Apr.	7	Winnipeg	2	at	Edmonton	3
Apr.	9	Edmonton	4	at	Winnipeg	6
Apr.	10	Edmonton	5	at	Winnipeg	3
Apr.	12	Winnipeg	2	at	Edmonton	6

Edmonton won best-of-seven series 4–1

DIVISION FINALS
Apr.	18	Boston	2	at	Montreal	5
Apr.	20	Boston	4	at	Montreal	3
Apr.	22	Montreal	1	at	Boston	3
Apr.	24	Montreal	0	at	Boston	2
Apr.	26	Boston	4	at	Montreal	1

Boston won best-of-seven series 4–1

Apr.	18	New Jersey	1	at	Washington	3
Apr.	20	New Jersey	5	at	Washington	2
Apr.	22	Washington	4	at	New Jersey	10
Apr.	24	Washington	4	at	New Jersey	1
Apr.	26	New Jersey	3	at	Washington	1
Apr.	28	Washington	7	at	New Jersey	2
Apr.	30	New Jersey	3	at	Washington	2

New Jersey won best-of-seven series 4–3

Apr.	19	St. Louis	4	at	Detroit	5
Apr.	21	St. Louis	0	at	Detroit	6
Apr.	23	Detroit	3	at	St. Louis	6
Apr.	25	Detroit	3	at	St. Louis	1
Apr.	27	St. Louis	3	at	Detroit	4

Detroit won best-of-seven series 4–1

Apr.	19	Edmonton	3	at	Calgary	1
Apr.	21	Edmonton	5	at	Calgary	4 OT
Apr.	23	Calgary	2	at	Edmonton	4
Apr.	25	Calgary	4	at	Edmonton	6

Edmonton won best-of-seven series 4–0

CONFERENCE FINALS
May	2	New Jersey	3	at	Boston	5
May	4	New Jersey	3	at	Boston	2 OT
May	6	Boston	6	at	New Jersey	1
May	8	Boston	1	at	New Jersey	3
May	10	New Jersey	1	at	Boston	7
May	12	Boston	3	at	New Jersey	6
May	14	New Jersey	2	at	Boston	6

Boston won best-of-seven series 4–3

May	3	Detroit	1	at	Edmonton	4
May	5	Detroit	3	at	Edmonton	5
May	7	Edmonton	2	at	Detroit	5
May	9	Edmonton	4	at	Detroit	3 OT
May	11	Detroit	4	at	Edmonton	8

Edmonton won best-of-seven series 4–1

FINALS
May	18	Boston	1	at	Edmonton	2
May	20	Boston	2	at	Edmonton	4
May	22	Edmonton	6	at	Boston	3
May	24	Edmonton	3	at	Boston	3 *
May	26	Boston	3	at	Edmonton	6

* Game suspended at 16.37 of second period due to power failure.

Edmonton won best-of-seven series 4–0

1989 CALGARY FLAMES

The Calgary Flames won their first-ever Stanley Cup with a 4-2 series victory over the Montreal Canadiens, who had defeated Calgary in the 1986 Stanley Cup Championship. The Flames wrapped up the series with a 4-2 triumph over the Canadiens in Game #6, becoming the first visiting team ever to win the Stanley Cup on Montreal Forum ice.

Goaltender Mike Vernon tied an NHL playoff record by registering 16 wins during the post-season, tying the mark Edmonton Oilers' goaltender Grant Fuhr had set the previous year.

Al MacInnis became the fourth defenseman to win the Conn Smythe Trophy since the award was instituted in 1965. MacInnis joined Serge Savard (1969), Bobby Orr (1970 and 1972) and Larry Robinson (1978). MacInnis led the League in playoff scoring with 31 points (7-24-31) and amassed a 17-game consecutive point-scoring streak, the second longest in NHL playoff history and the longest ever among defensemen.

CONN SMYTHE TROPHY • Al MacInnis - Defense - Calgary Flames

DIVISION SEMI-FINALS

Date	Away	Score		Home	Score	
Apr. 5	Hartford	2	at	Montreal	6	
Apr. 6	Hartford	2	at	Montreal	3	
Apr. 8	Montreal	5	at	Hartford	4	OT
Apr. 9	Montreal	4	at	Hartford	3	OT

Montreal won best-of-seven series 4–0

Apr. 5	Buffalo	6	at	Boston	0	
Apr. 6	Buffalo	3	at	Boston	5	
Apr. 8	Boston	4	at	Buffalo	2	
Apr. 9	Boston	3	at	Buffalo	2	
Apr. 11	Buffalo	1	at	Boston	4	

Boston won best-of-seven series 4–1

Apr. 5	Philadelphia	2	at	Washington	3	
Apr. 6	Philadelphia	3	at	Washington	2	
Apr. 8	Washington	4	at	Philadelphia	3	OT
Apr. 9	Washington	2	at	Philadelphia	5	
Apr. 11	Philadelphia	8	at	Washington	5	
Apr. 13	Washington	3	at	Philadelphia	4	

Philadelphia won best-of-seven series 4–2

Apr. 5	NY Rangers	1	at	Pittsburgh	3	
Apr. 6	NY Rangers	4	at	Pittsburgh	7	
Apr. 8	Pittsburgh	5	at	NY Rangers	3	
Apr. 9	Pittsburgh	4	at	NY Rangers	3	

Pittsburgh won best-of-seven series 4–0

Apr. 5	Chicago	2	at	Detroit	3	
Apr. 6	Chicago	5	at	Detroit	4	OT
Apr. 8	Detroit	2	at	Chicago	4	
Apr. 9	Detroit	2	at	Chicago	3	
Apr. 11	Chicago	4	at	Detroit	6	
Apr. 13	Detroit	1	at	Chicago	7	

Chicago won best-of-seven series 4–2

Apr. 5	Minnesota	3	at	St. Louis	4	OT
Apr. 6	Minnesota	3	at	St. Louis	4	OT
Apr. 8	St. Louis	5	at	Minnesota	3	
Apr. 9	St. Louis	4	at	Minnesota	5	
Apr. 11	Minnesota	1	at	St. Louis	6	

St. Louis won best-of-seven series 4–1

Apr. 5	Vancouver	4	at	Calgary	3	OT
Apr. 6	Vancouver	2	at	Calgary	5	
Apr. 8	Calgary	4	at	Vancouver	0	
Apr. 9	Calgary	3	at	Vancouver	5	
Apr. 11	Vancouver	0	at	Calgary	4	
Apr. 13	Calgary	3	at	Vancouver	6	
Apr. 15	Vancouver	3	at	Calgary	4	OT

Calgary won best-of-seven series 4–3

Apr. 5	Edmonton	4	at	Los Angeles	3	
Apr. 6	Edmonton	2	at	Los Angeles	5	
Apr. 8	Los Angeles	0	at	Edmonton	4	
Apr. 9	Los Angeles	3	at	Edmonton	4	
Apr. 11	Edmonton	2	at	Los Angeles	4	
Apr. 13	Los Angeles	4	at	Edmonton	1	
Apr. 15	Edmonton	3	at	Los Angeles	6	

Los Angeles won best-of-seven series 4–3

DIVISION FINALS

Apr. 17	Boston	2	at	Montreal	3	
Apr. 19	Boston	2	at	Montreal	3	OT
Apr. 21	Montreal	5	at	Boston	4	
Apr. 23	Montreal	2	at	Boston	3	
Apr. 25	Boston	2	at	Montreal	3	

Montreal won best-of-seven series 4–1

Apr. 17	Philadelphia	3	at	Pittsburgh	4	
Apr. 19	Philadelphia	4	at	Pittsburgh	2	
Apr. 21	Pittsburgh	4	at	Philadelphia	3	OT
Apr. 23	Pittsburgh	1	at	Philadelphia	4	
Apr. 25	Philadelphia	7	at	Pittsburgh	10	
Apr. 27	Pittsburgh	2	at	Philadelphia	6	
Apr. 29	Philadelphia	4	at	Pittsburgh	1	

Philadelphia won best-of-seven series 4–3

Apr. 18	Chicago	3	at	St. Louis	1	
Apr. 20	Chicago	3	at	St. Louis	5	OT
Apr. 22	St. Louis	2	at	Chicago	5	
Apr. 24	St. Louis	2	at	Chicago	3	
Apr. 26	Chicago	4	at	St. Louis	2	

Chicago won best-of-seven series 4–1

Apr. 18	Los Angeles	3	at	Calgary	4	OT
Apr. 20	Los Angeles	3	at	Calgary	8	
Apr. 22	Calgary	5	at	Los Angeles	2	
Apr. 24	Calgary	5	at	Los Angeles	3	

Calgary won best-of-seven series 4–0

CONFERENCE FINALS

May 1	Philadelphia	3	at	Montreal	1	
May 3	Philadelphia	0	at	Montreal	3	
May 5	Montreal	5	at	Philadelphia	1	
May 7	Montreal	3	at	Philadelphia	0	
May 9	Philadelphia	2	at	Montreal	1	OT
May 11	Montreal	4	at	Philadelphia	2	

Montreal won best-of-seven series 4–2

May 2	Chicago	0	at	Calgary	3	
May 4	Chicago	4	at	Calgary	2	
May 6	Calgary	5	at	Chicago	2	
May 8	Calgary	2	at	Chicago	1	OT
May 10	Chicago	1	at	Calgary	3	

Calgary won best-of-seven series 4–1

FINALS

May 14	Montreal	2	at	Calgary	3	
May 17	Montreal	4	at	Calgary	2	
May 19	Calgary	3	at	Montreal	4	OT
May 21	Calgary	4	at	Montreal	2	
May 23	Montreal	2	at	Calgary	3	
May 25	Calgary	4	at	Montreal	2	

Calgary won best-of-seven series 4–2

EDMONTON OILERS 1990

The Oilers captured their fifth Stanley Cup in seven years, defeating Boston for their second Stanley Cup Finals triumph over the Bruins in three seasons.

The two teams battled for 55:13 of overtime in Game #1 at Boston Garden before Edmonton's Petr Klima ended the marathon encounter with the game-winner. It represented the longest game in Stanley Cup Finals history, edging the previous mark of 53:50 set in Game #3 of the 1931 Final between Chicago and Montreal.

Edmonton goaltender Bill Ranford, who posted all 16 Oilers' victories in the post-season, won the Conn Smythe Trophy as playoff MVP.

Seven players - Glenn Anderson, Grant Fuhr, Randy Gregg, Charlie Huddy, Jari Kurri, Kevin Lowe and Mark Messier - won their fifth Stanley Cup rings as members of the Oilers.

CONN SMYTHE TROPHY • Bill Ranford - Goaltender - Edmonton Oilers

DIVISION SEMI-FINALS

Apr. 5	Hartford	4	at	Boston	3
Apr. 7	Hartford	1	at	Boston	3
Apr. 9	Boston	3	at	Hartford	5
Apr. 11	Boston	6	at	Hartford	5
Apr. 13	Hartford	2	at	Boston	3
Apr. 15	Boston	2	at	Hartford	3 OT
Apr. 17	Hartford	1	at	Boston	3

Boston won best-of-seven series 4–3

Apr. 5	Montreal	1	at	Buffalo	4
Apr. 7	Montreal	3	at	Buffalo	0
Apr. 9	Buffalo	1	at	Montreal	2 OT
Apr. 11	Buffalo	4	at	Montreal	2
Apr. 13	Montreal	4	at	Buffalo	2
Apr. 15	Buffalo	2	at	Montreal	5

Montreal won best-of-seven series 4–2

Apr. 5	NY Islanders	1	at	NY Rangers	2
Apr. 7	NY Islanders	2	at	NY Rangers	5
Apr. 9	NY Rangers	3	at	NY Islanders	4 OT
Apr. 11	NY Rangers	6	at	NY Islanders	1
Apr. 13	NY Islanders	5	at	NY Rangers	6

Rangers won best-of-seven series 4–1

Apr. 5	Washington	5	at	New Jersey	4 OT
Apr. 7	Washington	5	at	New Jersey	6
Apr. 9	New Jersey	2	at	Washington	1
Apr. 11	New Jersey	1	at	Washington	3
Apr. 13	Washington	4	at	New Jersey	3
Apr. 15	New Jersey	2	at	Washington	3

Washington won best-of-seven series 4–2

Apr. 4	Minnesota	2	at	Chicago	1
Apr. 6	Minnesota	3	at	Chicago	5
Apr. 8	Chicago	2	at	Minnesota	1
Apr. 10	Chicago	0	at	Minnesota	4
Apr. 12	Minnesota	1	at	Chicago	5
Apr. 14	Chicago	3	at	Minnesota	5
Apr. 16	Minnesota	2	at	Chicago	5

Chicago won best-of-seven series 4–3

Apr. 4	Toronto	2	at	St. Louis	4
Apr. 6	Toronto	2	at	St. Louis	4
Apr. 8	St. Louis	6	at	Toronto	5 OT
Apr. 10	St. Louis	2	at	Toronto	4
Apr. 12	Toronto	3	at	St. Louis	4

St. Louis won best-of-seven series 4–1

Apr. 4	Los Angeles	5	at	Calgary	3
Apr. 6	Los Angeles	5	at	Calgary	8
Apr. 8	Calgary	1	at	Los Angeles	2 OT
Apr. 10	Calgary	4	at	Los Angeles	12
Apr. 12	Los Angeles	1	at	Calgary	5
Apr. 14	Calgary	3	at	Los Angeles	4 OT

Los Angeles won best-of-seven series 4–2

Apr. 4	Winnipeg	7	at	Edmonton	5
Apr. 6	Winnipeg	2	at	Edmonton	3 OT
Apr. 8	Edmonton	1	at	Winnipeg	2
Apr. 10	Edmonton	3	at	Winnipeg	4 OT
Apr. 12	Winnipeg	3	at	Edmonton	4
Apr. 14	Edmonton	4	at	Winnipeg	3
Apr. 16	Winnipeg	1	at	Edmonton	4

Edmonton won best-of-seven series 4–3

DIVISION FINALS

Apr. 19	Montreal	0	at	Boston	1
Apr. 21	Montreal	4	at	Boston	5 OT
Apr. 23	Boston	6	at	Montreal	3
Apr. 25	Boston	1	at	Montreal	4
Apr. 27	Montreal	1	at	Boston	3

Boston won best-of-seven series 4–1

Apr. 19	Washington	3	at	NY Rangers	7
Apr. 21	Washington	6	at	NY Rangers	3
Apr. 23	NY Rangers	1	at	Washington	7
Apr. 25	NY Rangers	3	at	Washington	4 OT
Apr. 27	Washington	2	at	NY Rangers	1 OT

Washington won best-of-seven series 4–1

Apr. 18	St. Louis	4	at	Chicago	3
Apr. 20	St. Louis	3	at	Chicago	5
Apr. 22	Chicago	4	at	St. Louis	5
Apr. 24	Chicago	3	at	St. Louis	2
Apr. 26	St. Louis	2	at	Chicago	3
Apr. 28	Chicago	2	at	St. Louis	4
Apr. 30	St. Louis	2	at	Chicago	8

Chicago won best-of-seven series 4–3

Apr. 18	Los Angeles	0	at	Edmonton	7
Apr. 20	Los Angeles	1	at	Edmonton	6
Apr. 22	Edmonton	5	at	Los Angeles	4
Apr. 24	Edmonton	6	at	Los Angeles	5 OT

Edmonton won best-of-seven series 4–0

CONFERENCE FINALS

May 3	Washington	3	at	Boston	5
May 5	Washington	0	at	Boston	3
May 7	Boston	4	at	Washington	1
May 9	Boston	3	at	Washington	2

Boston won best-of-seven series 4–0

May 2	Chicago	2	at	Edmonton	5
May 4	Chicago	4	at	Edmonton	3
May 6	Edmonton	1	at	Chicago	5
May 8	Edmonton	4	at	Chicago	2
May 10	Chicago	3	at	Edmonton	4
May 12	Edmonton	8	at	Chicago	4

Edmonton won best-of-seven series 4–2

FINALS

May 15	Edmonton	3	at	Boston	2 OT
May 18	Edmonton	7	at	Boston	2
May 20	Boston	2	at	Edmonton	1
May 22	Boston	1	at	Edmonton	5
May 24	Edmonton	4	at	Boston	1

Edmonton won best-of-seven series 4–1

1991 PITTSBURGH PENGUINS

The Penguins captured their first-ever Stanley Cup, defeating the Minnesota North Stars in six games. The North Stars were making their second career Finals appearance.

Pittsburgh center Mario Lemieux, despite missing one game in the series due to a back injury, recorded 12 points (5-7-12) in five games to lead all scorers. His overall playoff performance earned him Conn Smythe Trophy honors.

Penguins' defenseman Larry Murphy tallied 10 points (1-9-10) in six games, the second highest total for a defenseman in Stanley Cup Finals history.

Four Pittsburgh players - Bryan Trottier, Paul Coffey, Joe Mullen and Jiri Hrdina - won a Stanley Cup championship with their second team. Trottier won four previous titles with the New York Islanders, Coffey captured three with Edmonton, while Mullen and Hrdina were members of the 1989 Stanley Cup-champion Calgary Flames.

CONN SMYTHE TROPHY • Mario Lemieux - Center - Pittsburgh Penguins

DIVISION SEMI-FINALS

Date	Away	Score		Home	Score	
Apr. 3	Hartford	5	at	Boston	2	
Apr. 5	Hartford	3	at	Boston	4	
Apr. 7	Boston	6	at	Hartford	3	
Apr. 9	Boston	3	at	Hartford	4	
Apr. 11	Hartford	1	at	Boston	6	
Apr. 13	Boston	3	at	Hartford	1	

Boston won best-of-seven series 4–2

Apr. 3	Buffalo	5	at	Montreal	7	
Apr. 5	Buffalo	4	at	Montreal	5	
Apr. 7	Montreal	4	at	Buffalo	5	
Apr. 9	Montreal	4	at	Buffalo	6	
Apr. 11	Buffalo	3	at	Montreal	4	OT
Apr. 13	Montreal	5	at	Buffalo	1	

Montreal won best-of-seven series 4–2

Apr. 3	New Jersey	3	at	Pittsburgh	1	
Apr. 5	New Jersey	4	at	Pittsburgh	5	OT
Apr. 7	Pittsburgh	4	at	New Jersey	3	
Apr. 9	Pittsburgh	1	at	New Jersey	4	
Apr. 11	New Jersey	4	at	Pittsburgh	2	
Apr. 13	Pittsburgh	4	at	New Jersey	3	
Apr. 15	New Jersey	0	at	Pittsburgh	4	

Pittsburgh won best-of-seven series 4–3

Apr. 3	Washington	1	at	NY Rangers	2	
Apr. 5	Washington	3	at	NY Rangers	0	
Apr. 7	NY Rangers	6	at	Washington	0	
Apr. 9	NY Rangers	2	at	Washington	3	
Apr. 11	Washington	5	at	NY Rangers	4	OT
Apr. 13	NY Rangers	2	at	Washington	4	

Washington won best-of-seven series 4–2

Apr. 4	Minnesota	4	at	Chicago	3	OT
Apr. 6	Minnesota	2	at	Chicago	5	
Apr. 8	Chicago	6	at	Minnesota	5	
Apr. 10	Chicago	1	at	Minnesota	3	
Apr. 12	Minnesota	6	at	Chicago	0	
Apr. 14	Chicago	1	at	Minnesota	3	

Minnesota won best-of-seven series 4–2

Apr. 4	Detroit	6	at	St. Louis	3	
Apr. 6	Detroit	2	at	St. Louis	4	
Apr. 8	St. Louis	2	at	Detroit	5	
Apr. 10	St. Louis	3	at	Detroit	4	
Apr. 12	Detroit	1	at	St. Louis	6	
Apr. 14	St. Louis	3	at	Detroit	0	
Apr. 16	Detroit	2	at	St. Louis	3	

St. Louis won best-of-seven series 4–3

Apr. 4	Vancouver	6	at	Los Angeles	5	
Apr. 6	Vancouver	2	at	Los Angeles	3	OT
Apr. 8	Los Angeles	1	at	Vancouver	2	OT
Apr. 10	Los Angeles	6	at	Vancouver	1	
Apr. 12	Vancouver	4	at	Los Angeles	7	
Apr. 14	Los Angeles	4	at	Vancouver	1	

Los Angeles won best-of-seven series 4–2

Apr. 4	Edmonton	3	at	Calgary	1	
Apr. 6	Edmonton	1	at	Calgary	3	
Apr. 8	Calgary	3	at	Edmonton	4	
Apr. 10	Calgary	2	at	Edmonton	5	
Apr. 12	Edmonton	3	at	Calgary	5	
Apr. 14	Calgary	2	at	Edmonton	1	OT
Apr. 16	Edmonton	5	at	Calgary	4	OT

Edmonton won best-of-seven series 4–3

DIVISION FINALS

Apr. 17	Montreal	1	at	Boston	2	
Apr. 19	Montreal	4	at	Boston	3	OT
Apr. 21	Boston	3	at	Montreal	2	
Apr 23	Boston	2	at	Montreal	6	
Apr. 25	Montreal	1	at	Boston	4	
Apr. 27	Boston	2	at	Montreal	3	OT
Apr. 29	Montreal	1	at	Boston	2	

Boston won best-of-seven series 4–3

Apr. 17	Washington	4	at	Pittsburgh	2	
Apr. 19	Washington	6	at	Pittsburgh	7	OT
Apr. 21	Pittsburgh	3	at	Washington	1	
Apr. 23	Pittsburgh	3	at	Washington	1	
Apr. 25	Washington	1	at	Pittsburgh	4	

Pittsburgh won best-of-seven series 4–1

Apr. 18	Minnesota	2	at	St. Louis	1	
Apr. 20	Minnesota	2	at	St. Louis	5	
Apr. 22	St. Louis	1	at	Minnesota	5	
Apr. 24	St. Louis	4	at	Minnesota	8	
Apr. 26	Minnesota	2	at	St. Louis	4	
Apr. 28	St. Louis	2	at	Minnesota	3	

Minnesota won best-of-seven series 4–2

Apr. 18	Edmonton	3	at	Los Angeles	4	OT
Apr. 20	Edmonton	4	at	Los Angeles	3	OT
Apr. 22	Los Angeles	3	at	Edmonton	4	OT
Apr. 24	Los Angeles	2	at	Edmonton	4	
Apr. 26	Edmonton	2	at	Los Angeles	5	
Apr. 28	Los Angeles	3	at	Edmonton	4	OT

Edmonton won best-of-seven series 4–2

CONFERENCE FINALS

May 1	Pittsburgh	3	at	Boston	6	
May 3	Pittsburgh	4	at	Boston	5	OT
May 5	Boston	1	at	Pittsburgh	4	
May 7	Boston	1	at	Pittsburgh	4	
May 9	Pittsburgh	7	at	Boston	2	
May 11	Boston	3	at	Pittsburgh	5	

Pittsburgh won best-of-seven series 4–2

May 2	Minnesota	3	at	Edmonton	1	
May 4	Minnesota	2	at	Edmonton	7	
May 6	Edmonton	3	at	Minnesota	7	
May 8	Edmonton	1	at	Minnesota	5	
May 10	Minnesota	3	at	Edmonton	2	

Minnesota won best-of-seven series 4–1

FINALS

May 15	Minnesota	5	at	Pittsburgh	4	
May 17	Minnesota	1	at	Pittsburgh	4	
May 19	Pittsburgh	1	at	Minnesota	3	
May 21	Pittsburgh	5	at	Minnesota	3	
May 23	Minnesota	4	at	Pittsburgh	6	
May 25	Pittsburgh	8	at	Minnesota	0	

Pittsburgh won best-of-seven series 4–2

PITTSBURGH PENGUINS 1992

The Penguins captured their second consecutive Stanley Cup, winning the Championship in four consecutive games from the Chicago Blackhawks, who were making their first Finals appearance since 1973.

Both finalists established a new record for consecutive playoff wins with 11. The Blackhawks' victories spanned the first three rounds of the playoffs. The Penguins' 11 wins included their four-game Final Series sweep.

Mario Lemieux captured the Conn Smythe Trophy as playoff MVP for the second straight year, becoming just the second player in NHL history (Bernie Parent, 1974 and 1975) to accomplish the feat.

CONN SMYTHE TROPHY • Mario Lemieux - Center - Pittsburgh Penguins

DIVISION SEMI-FINALS

Date	Away			Home		
Apr. 19	Hartford	0	at	Montreal	2	
Apr. 21	Hartford	2	at	Montreal	5	
Apr. 23	Montreal	2	at	Hartford	5	
Apr. 25	Montreal	1	at	Hartford	3	
Apr. 27	Hartford	4	at	Montreal	7	
Apr. 29	Montreal	1	at	Hartford	2	OT
May 1	Hartford	2	at	Montreal	3	OT

Montreal won best-of-seven series 4–3

Apr. 19	Buffalo	3	at	Boston	2	
Apr. 21	Buffalo	2	at	Boston	3	OT
Apr. 23	Boston	3	at	Buffalo	2	
Apr. 25	Boston	5	at	Buffalo	4	OT
Apr. 27	Buffalo	2	at	Boston	0	
Apr. 29	Boston	3	at	Buffalo	9	
May 1	Buffalo	2	at	Boston	3	

Boston won best-of-seven series 4–3

Apr. 19	New Jersey	1	at	NY Rangers	2	
Apr. 21	New Jersey	7	at	NY Rangers	3	
Apr. 23	NY Rangers	1	at	New Jersey	3	
Apr. 25	NY Rangers	3	at	New Jersey	0	
Apr. 27	New Jersey	5	at	NY Rangers	6	
Apr. 29	NY Rangers	3	at	New Jersey	5	
May 1	New Jersey	4	at	NY Rangers	8	

Rangers won best-of-seven series 4–3

Apr. 19	Pittsburgh	1	at	Washington	3	
Apr. 21	Pittsburgh	2	at	Washington	6	
Apr. 23	Washington	4	at	Pittsburgh	6	
Apr. 25	Washington	7	at	Pittsburgh	2	
Apr. 27	Pittsburgh	5	at	Washington	2	
Apr. 29	Washington	4	at	Pittsburgh	6	
May 1	Pittsburgh	3	at	Washington	1	

Pittsburgh won best-of-seven series 4–3

Apr. 18	Minnesota	4	at	Detroit	3	
Apr. 20	Minnesota	4	at	Detroit	2	
Apr. 22	Detroit	5	at	Minnesota	4	OT
Apr. 24	Detroit	4	at	Minnesota	5	
Apr. 26	Minnesota	0	at	Detroit	3	
Apr. 28	Detroit	1	at	Minnesota	0	OT
Apr. 30	Minnesota	2	at	Detroit	5	

Detroit won best-of-seven series 4–3

Apr. 18	St. Louis	1	at	Chicago	3	
Apr. 20	St. Louis	5	at	Chicago	3	
Apr. 22	Chicago	4	at	St. Louis	5	OT
Apr. 24	Chicago	5	at	St. Louis	3	
Apr. 26	St. Louis	4	at	Chicago	6	
Apr. 28	Chicago	2	at	St. Louis	1	

Chicago won best-of-seven series 4–2

Apr. 18	Winnipeg	3	at	Vancouver	2	
Apr. 20	Winnipeg	2	at	Vancouver	3	
Apr. 22	Vancouver	2	at	Winnipeg	4	
Apr. 24	Vancouver	1	at	Winnipeg	3	
Apr. 26	Winnipeg	2	at	Vancouver	8	
Apr. 28	Vancouver	8	at	Winnipeg	3	
Apr. 30	Winnipeg	0	at	Vancouver	5	

Vancouver won best-of-seven series 4–3

Apr. 18	Edmonton	3	at	Los Angeles	1	
Apr. 20	Edmonton	5	at	Los Angeles	8	
Apr. 22	Los Angeles	3	at	Edmonton	4	
Apr. 24	Los Angeles	4	at	Edmonton	3	
Apr. 26	Edmonton	5	at	Los Angeles	2	
Apr. 28	Los Angeles	0	at	Edmonton	3	

Edmonton won best-of-seven series 4–2

DIVISION FINALS

May 3	Boston	6	at	Montreal	4	
May 5	Boston	3	at	Montreal	2	OT
May 7	Montreal	2	at	Boston	3	
May 9	Montreal	0	at	Boston	2	

Boston won best-of-seven series 4–0

May 3	Pittsburgh	4	at	NY Rangers	2	
May 5	Pittsburgh	2	at	NY Rangers	4	
May 7	NY Rangers	6	at	Pittsburgh	5	OT
May 9	NY Rangers	4	at	Pittsburgh	5	OT
May 11	Pittsburgh	3	at	NY Rangers	2	
May 13	NY Rangers	1	at	Pittsburgh	5	

Pittsburgh won best-of-seven series 4–2

May 2	Chicago	2	at	Detroit	1	
May 4	Chicago	3	at	Detroit	1	
May 6	Detroit	4	at	Chicago	5	
May 8	Detroit	0	at	Chicago	1	

Chicago won best-of-seven series 4–0

May 3	Edmonton	4	at	Vancouver	3	OT
May 4	Edmonton	0	at	Vancouver	4	
May 6	Vancouver	2	at	Edmonton	5	
May 8	Vancouver	2	at	Edmonton	3	
May 10	Edmonton	3	at	Vancouver	4	
May 12	Vancouver	0	at	Edmonton	3	

Edmonton won best-of-seven series 4–2

CONFERENCE FINALS

May 17	Boston	3	at	Pittsburgh	4	OT
May 19	Boston	2	at	Pittsburgh	5	
May 21	Pittsburgh	5	at	Boston	1	
May 23	Pittsburgh	5	at	Boston	1	

Pittsburgh won best-of-seven series 4–0

May 16	Edmonton	2	at	Chicago	8	
May 18	Edmonton	2	at	Chicago	4	
May 20	Chicago	4	at	Edmonton	3	OT
May 22	Chicago	5	at	Edmonton	1	

Chicago won best-of-seven series 4–0

FINALS

May 26	Chicago	4	at	Pittsburgh	5	
May 28	Chicago	1	at	Pittsburgh	3	
May 30	Pittsburgh	1	at	Chicago	0	
June 1	Pittsburgh	6	at	Chicago	5	

Pittsburgh won best-of-seven series 4–0

1993 MONTREAL CANADIENS

The Montreal Canadiens claimed their 24th Stanley Cup title, defeating the Los Angeles Kings in an exciting five-game series. The Kings, led by playoff scoring leader Wayne Gretzky, were making their first-ever appearance in the Finals. After dropping the opening game of the series at home, Montreal responded with four straight wins, including three in overtime.

The overtime wins capped a record-setting performance for Montreal in extra time. After losing their first overtime game of the playoffs at Quebec in Game #1 of the opening round, the club posted 10 straight wins in extra time, setting playoff records for most OT wins in one season and most consecutive OT wins. Of the 85 games played in the post-season, 28 were decided in overtime, smashing the previous playoff record of 16, set in 1982 and 1991.

Canadiens goaltender Patrick Roy was awarded the Conn Smythe Trophy as playoff MVP, posting a 16-4 record and 2.13 goals-against average in 20 games. Roy became the fifth multiple winner of the award, having previously won as a rookie in 1986.

CONN SMYTHE TROPHY • Patrick Roy - Goaltender - Montreal Canadiens

DIVISION SEMI-FINALS

Date	Away		at	Home		
Apr. 18	Buffalo	5	at	Boston	4	OT
Apr. 20	Buffalo	4	at	Boston	0	
Apr. 22	Boston	3	at	Buffalo	4	OT
Apr. 24	Boston	5	at	Buffalo	6	OT

Buffalo won best-of-seven series 4–0

Apr. 18	Montreal	2	at	Quebec	3	OT
Apr. 20	Montreal	1	at	Quebec	4	
Apr. 22	Quebec	1	at	Montreal	2	OT
Apr. 24	Quebec	2	at	Montreal	3	
Apr. 26	Montreal	5	at	Quebec	4	OT
Apr. 28	Quebec	2	at	Montreal	6	

Montreal won best-of-seven series 4–2

Apr. 18	New Jersey	3	at	Pittsburgh	6	
Apr. 20	New Jersey	0	at	Pittsburgh	7	
Apr. 22	Pittsburgh	4	at	New Jersey	3	
Apr. 25	Pittsburgh	1	at	New Jersey	4	
Apr. 26	New Jersey	3	at	Pittsburgh	5	

Pittsburgh won best-of-seven series 4–1

Apr. 18	NY Islanders	1	at	Washington	3	
Apr. 20	NY Islanders	5	at	Washington	4	OT
Apr. 22	Washington	3	at	NY Islanders	4	OT
Apr. 24	Washington	3	at	NY Islanders	4	OT
Apr. 26	NY Islanders	4	at	Washington	6	
Apr. 28	Washington	3	at	NY Islanders	5	

Islanders won best-of-seven series 4–2

Apr. 18	St. Louis	4	at	Chicago	3	
Apr. 21	St. Louis	2	at	Chicago	0	
Apr. 23	Chicago	0	at	St. Louis	3	
Apr. 25	Chicago	3	at	St. Louis	4	OT

St. Louis won best-of-seven series 4–0

Apr. 19	Toronto	3	at	Detroit	6	
Apr. 21	Toronto	2	at	Detroit	6	
Apr. 23	Detroit	2	at	Toronto	4	
Apr. 25	Detroit	2	at	Toronto	3	
Apr. 27	Toronto	5	at	Detroit	4	OT
Apr. 29	Detroit	7	at	Toronto	3	
May 1	Toronto	4	at	Detroit	3	OT

Toronto won best-of-seven series 4–3

Apr. 19	Winnipeg	2	at	Vancouver	4	
Apr. 21	Winnipeg	2	at	Vancouver	3	
Apr. 23	Vancouver	4	at	Winnipeg	5	
Apr. 25	Vancouver	3	at	Winnipeg	1	
Apr. 27	Winnipeg	4	at	Vancouver	3	OT
Apr. 29	Vancouver	4	at	Winnipeg	3	OT

Vancouver won best-of-seven series 4–2

Apr. 18	Los Angeles	6	at	Calgary	3	
Apr. 21	Los Angeles	4	at	Calgary	9	
Apr. 23	Calgary	5	at	Los Angeles	2	
Apr. 25	Calgary	1	at	Los Angeles	3	
Apr. 27	Los Angeles	9	at	Calgary	4	
Apr. 29	Calgary	6	at	Los Angeles	9	

Los Angeles won best-of-seven series 4–2

DIVISION FINALS

May 2	Buffalo	3	at	Montreal	4	
May 4	Buffalo	3	at	Montreal	4	OT
May 6	Montreal	4	at	Buffalo	3	OT
May 8	Montreal	4	at	Buffalo	3	OT

Montreal won best-of-seven series 4–0

May 2	NY Islanders	3	at	Pittsburgh	2	
May 4	NY Islanders	0	at	Pittsburgh	3	
May 6	Pittsburgh	3	at	NY Islanders	1	
May 8	Pittsburgh	5	at	NY Islanders	6	
May 10	NY Islanders	3	at	Pittsburgh	6	
May 12	Pittsburgh	5	at	NY Islanders	7	
May 14	NY Islanders	4	at	Pittsburgh	3	OT

Islanders won best-of-seven series 4–3

May 3	St. Louis	1	at	Toronto	2	OT
May 5	St. Louis	2	at	Toronto	1	OT
May 7	Toronto	3	at	St. Louis	4	
May 9	Toronto	4	at	St. Louis	1	
May 11	St. Louis	1	at	Toronto	5	
May 13	Toronto	1	at	St. Louis	2	
May 15	St. Louis	0	at	Toronto	6	

Toronto won best-of-seven series 4–3

May 2	Los Angeles	2	at	Vancouver	5	
May 5	Los Angeles	6	at	Vancouver	3	
May 7	Vancouver	4	at	Los Angeles	7	
May 9	Vancouver	7	at	Los Angeles	2	
May 11	Los Angeles	4	at	Vancouver	3	OT
May 13	Vancouver	3	at	Los Angeles	5	

Los Angeles won best-of-seven series 4–2

CONFERENCE FINALS

May 16	NY Islanders	1	at	Montreal	4	
May 18	NY Islanders	3	at	Montreal	4	OT
May 20	Montreal	2	at	NY Islanders	1	OT
May 22	Montreal	1	at	NY Islanders	4	
May 24	NY Islanders	2	at	Montreal	5	

Montreal won best-of-seven series 4–1

May 17	Los Angeles	1	at	Toronto	4	
May 19	Los Angeles	3	at	Toronto	2	
May 21	Toronto	2	at	Los Angeles	4	
May 23	Toronto	4	at	Los Angeles	2	
May 25	Los Angeles	2	at	Toronto	3	OT
May 27	Toronto	4	at	Los Angeles	5	OT
May 29	Los Angeles	5	at	Toronto	4	

Los Angeles won best-of-seven series 4–3

FINALS

June 1	Los Angeles	4	at	Montreal	1	
June 3	Los Angeles	2	at	Montreal	3	OT
June 5	Montreal	4	at	Los Angeles	3	OT
June 7	Montreal	3	at	Los Angeles	2	OT
June 9	Los Angeles	1	at	Montreal	4	

Montreal won best-of-seven series 4–1

NEW YORK RANGERS 1994

The New York Rangers ended their 54-year Stanley Cup drought with a stirring, seven-game series win over the Vancouver Canucks. The Rangers jumped out to a 3-1 series lead, only to see the Canucks storm back to tie the series, forcing a deciding game at Madison Square Garden. Viewed by a record television audience worldwide, the Rangers earned a 3-2 win and the Stanley Cup.

Both the Rangers and Canucks followed a difficult route to the Championship series. In the Eastern Conference Final, the Rangers were stretched to the limit by the New Jersey Devils before prevailing, four games to three with three games in the series decided in double overtime. The Canucks, meanwhile, had faced a 3-1 series deficit in their first-round series versus the Calgary Flames, but rallied to win the last three games of the series, all in overtime.

Rangers defenseman Brian Leetch became the first U.S.-born player to capture the Conn Smythe Trophy as playoff MVP. Leetch led all players in scoring during the postseason with 34 points (11-23- 34) in 23 games. Head coach Mike Keenan, in his first season behind the Rangers bench, captured his first Stanley Cup. He had previously made Championship series appearances with the Philadelphia Flyers (twice) and Chicago Blackhawks.

CONN SMYTHE TROPHY • Brian Leetch - Defenseman - New York Rangers

CONFERENCE QUARTERFINALS
Apr. 17 NY Islanders 0 at NY Rangers 6
Apr. 18 NY Islanders 0 at NY Rangers 6
Apr. 21 NY Rangers 5 at NY Islanders 1
Apr. 24 NY Rangers 5 at NY Islanders 2
NY Rangers won best-of-seven series 4-0

Apr. 17 Washington 5 at Pittsburgh 3
Apr. 19 Washington 1 at Pittsburgh 2
Apr. 21 Pittsburgh 0 at Washington 2
Apr. 23 Pittsburgh 1 at Washington 4
Apr. 25 Washington 2 at Pittsburgh 3
Apr. 27 Pittsburgh 3 at Washington 6
Washington won best-of-seven series 4-2

Apr. 17 Buffalo 2 at New Jersey 0
Apr. 19 Buffalo 1 at New Jersey 2
Apr. 21 New Jersey 2 at Buffalo 1
Apr. 23 New Jersey 3 at Buffalo 5
Apr. 25 Buffalo 3 at New Jersey 5
Apr. 27 New Jersey 0 at Buffalo 1 OT
Apr. 29 Buffalo 1 at New Jersey 2
New Jersey won best-of-seven series 4-3

Apr. 16 Montreal 2 at Boston 3
Apr. 18 Montreal 3 at Boston 2
Apr. 21 Boston 6 at Montreal 3
Apr. 23 Boston 2 at Montreal 5
Apr. 25 Montreal 2 at Boston 1 OT
Apr. 27 Boston 3 at Montreal 2
Apr. 29 Montreal 3 at Boston 5
Boston won best-of-seven series 4-3

Apr. 18 San Jose 5 at Detroit 4
Apr. 20 San Jose 0 at Detroit 4
Apr. 22 Detroit 3 at San Jose 2
Apr. 23 Detroit 3 at San Jose 4
Apr. 26 Detroit 4 at San Jose 6
Apr. 28 San Jose 1 at Detroit 7
Apr. 30 San Jose 3 at Detroit 2
San Jose won best-of-seven series 4-3

Apr. 18 Vancouver 5 at Calgary 0
Apr. 20 Vancouver 5 at Calgary 7
Apr. 22 Calgary 4 at Vancouver 2
Apr. 24 Calgary 3 at Vancouver 2
Apr. 26 Vancouver 2 at Calgary 1 OT
Apr. 28 Calgary 2 at Vancouver 3 OT
Apr. 30 Vancouver 4 at Calgary 3 OT
Vancouver won best-of-seven series 4-3

Apr. 18 Chicago 1 at Toronto 5
Apr. 20 Chicago 0 at Toronto 1 OT
Apr. 23 Toronto 4 at Chicago 5
Apr. 24 Toronto 3 at Chicago 4 OT
Apr. 26 Chicago 0 at Toronto 1
Apr. 28 Toronto 1 at Chicago 0
Toronto won best-of-seven series 4-2

Apr. 17 St. Louis 3 at Dallas 5
Apr. 20 St. Louis 2 at Dallas 4
Apr. 22 Dallas 5 at St. Louis 4 OT
Apr. 24 Dallas 2 at St. Louis 1
Dallas won best-of-seven series 4-0

CONFERENCE SEMIFINALS
May 1 Washington 3 at NY Rangers 6
May 3 Washington 2 at NY Rangers 5
May 5 NY Rangers 3 at Washington 0
May 7 NY Rangers 2 at Washington 4
May 9 Washington 3 at NY Rangers 4
NY Rangers won best-of-seven series 4-1

May 1 Boston 2 at New Jersey 1
May 3 Boston 6 at New Jersey 5 OT
May 5 New Jersey 4 at Boston 2
May 7 New Jersey 5 at Boston 4 OT
May 9 Boston 0 at New Jersey 2
May 11 New Jersey 5 at Boston 3
New Jersey won best-of-seven series 4-2

May 2 San Jose 3 at Toronto 2
May 4 San Jose 1 at Toronto 5
May 6 Toronto 2 at San Jose 5
May 8 Toronto 8 at San Jose 3
May 10 Toronto 2 at San Jose 5
May 12 San Jose 2 at Toronto 3 OT
May 14 San Jose 2 at Toronto 4
Toronto won best-of-seven series 4-3

May 2 Vancouver 6 at Dallas 4
May 4 Vancouver 3 at Dallas 0
May 6 Dallas 4 at Vancouver 3
May 8 Dallas 1 at Vancouver 2 OT
May 10 Dallas 2 at Vancouver 4
Vancouver won best-of-seven series 4-1

CONFERENCE FINALS
May 15 New Jersey 4 at NY Rangers 3 OT
May 17 New Jersey 0 at NY Rangers 4
May 19 NY Rangers 3 at New Jersey 2 OT
May 21 NY Rangers 1 at New Jersey 3
May 23 New Jersey 4 at NY Rangers 1
May 25 NY Rangers 4 at New Jersey 2
May 27 New Jersey 1 at NY Rangers 2 OT
NY Rangers won best-of-seven series 4-3

May 16 Vancouver 2 at Toronto 3 OT
May 18 Vancouver 4 at Toronto 3
May 20 Toronto 0 at Vancouver 4
May 22 Toronto 0 at Vancouver 2
May 24 Vancouver 3 at Vancouver 4 OT
Vancouver won best-of-seven series 4-1

STANLEY CUP FINALS
May 31 Vancouver 3 at NY Rangers 2 OT
June 2 Vancouver 1 at NY Rangers 3
June 4 NY Rangers 5 at Vancouver 1
June 7 NY Rangers 4 at Vancouver 2
June 9 Vancouver 6 at NY Rangers 3
June 11 NY Rangers 1 at Vancouver 4
June 14 Vancouver 2 at NY Rangers 3
NY Rangers won best-of-seven series 4-3

1995 NEW JERSEY DEVILS

After 21 seasons and two franchise relocations, the New Jersey Devils captured their first Stanley Cup title by downing the Detroit Red Wings in the championship final. Paced by the stellar goaltending of Martin Brodeur and the timely scoring of Claude Lemieux, the Devils upset the favored Red Wings in four straight games, outscoring, outshooting and outplaying Detroit in each encounter.

Both teams had a fairly easy road to the finals. Detroit lost only two games in the opening three rounds, although they did need a trio of overtime victories to subdue Chicago in the Western Conference finals. New Jersey dropped four games in the opening three rounds, including a pair to the Philadelphia Flyers in a stirring six-game Eastern Conference final.

New Jersey's Claude Lemieux, who scored only six times in the regular season, erupted for 13 goals in the post-season and was awarded the Conn Smythe Trophy. 14-year veteran Neal Broten, acquired by New Jersey late in the season from Dallas, notched four game-winning goals for the champions. Devils' coach Jacques Lemaire, who won 8 Stanley Cup rings as a player, became the fourth individual to score a Stanley Cup-winning goal and coach a Stanley Cup-winning team.

CONN SMYTHE TROPHY • Claude Lemieux - Right Wing - New Jersey Devils

CONFERENCE QUARTERFINALS
May	6	NY Rangers	4	at	Quebec	5
May	8	NY Rangers	8	at	Quebec	3
May	10	Quebec	3	at	NY Rangers	4
May	12	Quebec	2	at	NY Rangers	3 OT
May	14	NY Rangers	2	at	Quebec	4
May	16	Quebec	2	at	NY Rangers	4

NY Rangers won best-of-seven series 4-2

May	7	Buffalo	3	at	Philadelphia	4 OT
May	8	Buffalo	1	at	Philadelphia	3
May	10	Philadelphia	1	at	Buffalo	3
May	12	Philadelphia	4	at	Buffalo	2
May	14	Buffalo	4	at	Philadelphia	6

Philadelphia won best-of-seven series 4-1

May	6	Washington	5	at	Pittsburgh	4
May	8	Washington	3	at	Pittsburgh	5
May	10	Pittsburgh	2	at	Washington	6
May	12	Pittsburgh	2	at	Washington	6
May	14	Washington	5	at	Pittsburgh	6 OT
May	16	Pittsburgh	7	at	Washington	1
May	18	Washington	0	at	Pittsburgh	3

Pittsburgh won best-of-seven series 4-3

May	7	New Jersey	5	at	Boston	0
May	8	New Jersey	3	at	Boston	0
May	10	Boston	3	at	NewJersey	2
May	12	Boston	0	at	NewJersey	1 OT
May	14	New Jersey	3	at	Boston	2

New Jersey won best-of-seven series 4-1

May	7	Dallas	3	at	Detroit	4
May	9	Dallas	1	at	Detroit	4
May	11	Detroit	5	at	Dallas	1
May	14	Detroit	1	at	Dallas	4
May	15	Dallas	1	at	Detroit	3

Detroit won best-of-seven series 4-1

May	7	San Jose	5	at	Calgary	4
May	9	San Jose	5	at	Calgary	4 OT
May	11	Calgary	9	at	San Jose	2
May	13	Calgary	6	at	San Jose	4
May	15	San Jose	0	at	Calgary	5
May	17	Calgary	3	at	San Jose	5
May	19	San Jose	5	at	Calgary	4 OT

San Jose won best-of-seven series 4-3

May	7	Vancouver	1	at	St. Louis	2
May	9	Vancouver	5	at	St. Louis	3
May	11	St. Louis	1	at	Vancouver	6
May	13	St. Louis	5	at	Vancouver	2
May	15	Vancouver	6	at	St. Louis	5 OT
May	17	St. Louis	8	at	Vancouver	2
May	19	Vancouver	5	at	St. Louis	3

Vancouver won best-of-seven series 4-3

May	7	Toronto	5	at	Chicago	3
May	9	Toronto	3	at	Chicago	0
May	11	Chicago	3	at	Toronto	2
May	13	Chicago	3	at	Toronto	1
May	15	Toronto	2	at	Chicago	4
May	17	Chicago	4	at	Toronto	5 OT
May	19	Toronto	2	at	Chicago	5

Chicago won best-of-seven series 4-3

CONFERENCE SEMIFINALS
May	21	NY Rangers	4	at	Philadelphia	5 OT
May	22	NY Rangers	3	at	Philadelphia	4 OT
May	24	Philadelphia	5	at	NY Rangers	2
May	26	Philadelphia	4	at	NY Rangers	1

Philadelphia won best-of-seven series 4-0

May	20	New Jersey	2	at	Pittsburgh	3
May	22	New Jersey	4	at	Pittsburgh	2
May	24	Pittsburgh	1	at	New Jersey	5
May	26	Pittsburgh	1	at	New Jersey	2 OT
May	28	New Jersey	4	at	Pittsburgh	1

New Jersey won best-of-seven series 4-1

May	21	San Jose	0	at	Detroit	6
May	23	San Jose	2	at	Detroit	6
May	25	Detroit	6	at	San Jose	2
May	27	Detroit	6	at	San Jose	2

Detroit won best-of-seven series 4-0

May	21	Vancouver	1	at	Chicago	2 OT
May	23	Vancouver	0	at	Chicago	2
May	25	Chicago	3	at	Vancouver	2 OT
May	27	Chicago	4	at	Vancouver	3 OT

Chicago won best-of-seven series 4-0

CONFERENCE FINALS
June	3	New Jersey	4	at	Philadelphia	1
June	5	New Jersey	5	at	Philadelphia	2
June	7	Philadelphia	3	at	New Jersey	2 OT
June	10	Philadelphia	4	at	New Jersey	2
June	11	New Jersey	3	at	Philadelphia	2
June	13	Philadelphia	2	at	New Jersey	4

New Jersey won best-of-seven series 4-2

June	1	Chicago	1	at	Detroit	2 OT
June	4	Chicago	2	at	Detroit	3
June	6	Detroit	4	at	Chicago	3 OT
June	8	Detroit	2	at	Chicago	5
June	11	Chicago	1	at	Detroit	2 OT

Detroit won best-of-seven series 4-1

STANLEY CUP FINALS
June	17	New Jersey	2	at	Detroit	1
June	20	New Jersey	4	at	Detroit	2
June	22	Detroit	2	at	New Jersey	5
June	24	Detroit	2	at	New Jersey	5

New Jersey won best-of-seven series 4-0

National Hockey League
Stanley Cup Playoffs Fact Guide
1996

Section III
•
Playoff Records

Team Playoff Records	page **110**
Individual Playoff Records	**116**
Early Playoff Records	**120**
Playoff Hat-Tricks	**121**
Leading Playoff Scorers Year-by-Year	**122**
Overtime	**123**
Playoff Coaching Records	**126**
Penalty Shots	**127**
This Date in Stanley Cup Playoff History	**128**

Martin Brodeur led all post-season goaltenders in games (20), victories (16), minutes played (1222), goals-against average (1.67), save percentage (.927) and shutouts (3) as the New Jersey Devils became only the fourth team in the last 50 years to win the Stanley Cup in their first trip to the championship finals.

Team Records
1918-1995

MOST STANLEY CUP CHAMPIONSHIPS:
- **23 — Montreal Canadiens** 1924-30-31-44-46-53-56-57-58-59-60-65-66-68-69-71-73-76-77-78-79-86-93
- 13 — Toronto Maple Leafs 1918-22-32-42-45-47-48-49-51-62-63-64-67
- 7 — Detroit Red Wings 1936-37-43-50-52-54-55

MOST FINAL SERIES APPEARANCES:
- **32 — Montreal Canadiens** in 78-year history.
- 21 — Toronto Maple Leafs in 78-year history.
- 19 — Detroit Red Wings in 69-year history.

MOST YEARS IN PLAYOFFS:
- **69 — Montreal Canadiens** in 78-year history.
- 57 — Toronto Maple Leafs in 78-year history.
- 56 — Boston Bruins in 71-year history.

MOST CONSECUTIVE STANLEY CUP CHAMPIONSHIPS:
- **5 — Montreal Canadiens** (1956-57-58-59-60)
- 4 — Montreal Canadiens (1976-77-78-79)
  — NY Islanders (1980-81-82-83)

MOST CONSECUTIVE FINAL SERIES APPEARANCES:
- **10 — Montreal Canadiens** (1951-60, inclusive)
- 5 — Montreal Canadiens, (1965-69, inclusive)
  — NY Islanders, (1980-84, inclusive)

MOST CONSECUTIVE PLAYOFF APPEARANCES:
- **28 — Boston Bruins** (1968-95, inclusive)
- 26 — Chicago Blackhawks (1970-95, inclusive)
- 24 — Montreal Canadiens (1971-94, inclusive)
- 21 — Montreal Canadiens (1949-69, inclusive)
- 20 — Detroit Red Wings (1939-58, inclusive)

MOST GOALS BOTH TEAMS, ONE PLAYOFF SERIES:
- **69 — Edmonton Oilers, Chicago Blackhawks** in 1985 CF. Edmonton won best-of-seven series 4-2, outscoring Chicago 44-25.
- 62 — Chicago Blackhawks, Minnesota North Stars in 1985 DF. Chicago won best-of-seven series 4-2, outscoring Minnesota 33-29.
- 61 — Los Angeles Kings, Calgary Flames in 1993 DSF. Los Angeles won best-of-seven series 4-2, outscoring Calgary 33-28.
  — San Jose Sharks, Calgary Flames in 1995 CQF. San Jose won best-of-seven series 4-3, while being outscored 35-26.

MOST GOALS ONE TEAM, ONE PLAYOFF SERIES:
- **44 — Edmonton Oilers** in 1985 CF. Edmonton won best-of-seven series 4-2, outscoring Chicago 44-25.
- 35 — Edmonton Oilers in 1983 DF. Edmonton won best-of-seven series 4-1, outscoring Calgary 35-13.
  — Calgary Flames in 1995 CQF. Calgary lost best-of-seven series 3-4, outscoring San Jose 35-26.

MOST GOALS, BOTH TEAMS, TWO-GAME SERIES:
- **17 — Toronto St. Patricks, Montreal Canadiens** in 1918 NHL F. Toronto won two-game total goal series 10-7.
- 15 — Boston Bruins, Chicago Blackhawks in 1927 QF. Boston won two-game total goal series 10-5.
  — Pittsburgh Penguins, St. Louis Blues in 1975 PR. Pittsburgh won best-of-three series 2-0, outscoring St. Louis 9-6.

MOST GOALS, ONE TEAM, TWO-GAME SERIES:
- **11 — Buffalo Sabres** in 1977 PR. Buffalo won best-of-three series 2-0, outscoring Minnesota 11-3.
  — Toronto Maple Leafs in 1978 PR. Toronto won best-of-three series 2-0, outscoring Los Angeles 11-3.
- 10 — Boston Bruins in 1927 QF. Boston won two-game total goal series 10-5.

MOST GOALS, BOTH TEAMS, THREE-GAME SERIES:
- **33 — Minnesota North Stars, Boston Bruins** in 1981 PR. Minnesota won best-of-five series 3-0, outscoring Boston 20-13.
- 31 — Chicago Blackhawks, Detroit Red Wings in 1985 DSF. Chicago won best-of-five series 3-0, outscoring Detroit 23-8.
- 28 — Toronto Maple Leafs, NY Rangers in 1932 F. Toronto won best-of-five series 3-0, outscoring New York 18-10.

MOST GOALS, ONE TEAM, THREE-GAME SERIES:
- **23 — Chicago Blackhawks** in 1985 DSF. Chicago won best-of-five series 3-0, outscoring Detroit 23-8.
- 20 — Minnesota North Stars in 1981 PR. Minnesota won best-of-five series 3-0, outscoring Boston 20-13.
  — NY Islanders in 1981 PR. New York won best-of-five series 3-0, outscoring Toronto 20-4.

MOST GOALS, BOTH TEAMS, FOUR-GAME SERIES:
- **36 — Boston Bruins, St. Louis Blues** in 1972 SF. Boston won best-of-seven series 4-0, outscoring St. Louis 28-8.
  — Edmonton Oilers, Chicago Blackhawks in 1983 CF. Edmonton won best-of-seven series 4-0, outscoring Chicago 25-11.
  — Minnesota North Stars, Toronto Maple Leafs in 1983 DSF. Minnesota won best-of-five series 3-1; teams tied in scoring 18-18.
- 35 — NY Rangers, Los Angeles Kings in 1981 PR. NY Rangers won best-of-five series 3-1, outscoring Los Angeles 23-12.

PLAYOFF TEAM RECORDS • 111

MOST GOALS, ONE TEAM, FOUR-GAME SERIES:
28 — **Boston Bruins** in 1972 SF. Boston won best-of-seven series 4-0, outscoring St. Louis 28-8.

MOST GOALS, BOTH TEAMS, FIVE-GAME SERIES:
52 — **Edmonton Oilers, Los Angeles Kings** in 1987 DSF. Edmonton won best-of-seven series 4-1, outscoring Los Angeles 32-20.
50 — Los Angeles Kings, Edmonton Oilers in 1982 DSF. Los Angeles won best-of-five series 3-2, outscoring Edmonton 27-23.
48 — Edmonton Oilers, Calgary Flames in 1983 DF. Edmonton won best-of-seven series 4-1, outscoring Calgary 35-13.
— Calgary Flames, Los Angeles Kings in 1988 DSF. Calgary won best-of-seven series 4-1, outscoring Los Angeles 30-18.

MOST GOALS, ONE TEAM, FIVE-GAME SERIES:
35 — **Edmonton Oilers** in 1983 DF. Edmonton won best-of-seven series 4-1, outscoring Calgary 35-13.
32 — Edmonton Oilers in 1987 DSF. Edmonton won best-of-seven series 4-1, outscoring Los Angeles 32-20.
28 — NY Rangers in 1979 QF. NY Rangers won best-of-seven series 4-1, outscoring Philadelphia 28-8.
27 — Philadelphia Flyers in 1980 SF. Philadelphia won best-of-seven series 4-1, outscoring Minnesota 27-14.
— Los Angeles Kings, in 1982 DSF. Los Angeles won best-of-five series 3-2, outscoring Edmonton 27-23.

MOST GOALS, BOTH TEAMS, SIX-GAME SERIES:
69 — **Edmonton Oilers, Chicago Blackhawks** in 1985 CF. Edmonton won best-of-seven series 4-2, outscoring Chicago 44-25.
62 — Chicago Blackhawks, Minnesota North Stars in 1985 DF. Chicago won best-of-seven series 4-2, outscoring Minnesota 33-29.
61 — Los Angeles Kings, Calgary Flames in 1993 DSF. Los Angeles won best-of-seven series 4-2, outscoring Calgary 33-28.

MOST GOALS, ONE TEAM, SIX-GAME SERIES:
44 — **Edmonton Oilers** in 1985 CF. Edmonton won best-of-seven series 4-2, outscoring Chicago 44-25.
33 — Chicago Blackhawks in 1985 DF. Chicago won best-of-seven series 4-2, outscoring Minnesota 33-29.
— Montreal Canadiens in 1973 F. Montreal won best-of-seven series 4-2, outscoring Chicago 33-23.
— Los Angeles Kings in 1993 DSF. Los Angeles won best-of-seven series 4-2, outscoring Calgary 33-28.

MOST GOALS, BOTH TEAMS, SEVEN-GAME SERIES:
61 — **San Jose Sharks, Calgary Flames** in 1995 CQF. San Jose won best-of-seven series 4-3, while being outscored 35-26.
60 — Edmonton Oilers, Calgary Flames in 1984 DF. Edmonton won best-of-seven series 4-3, outscoring Calgary 33-27.

MOST GOALS, ONE TEAM, SEVEN-GAME SERIES:
35 — **Calgary Flames** in 1995 CQF. Calgary lost best-of-seven series 3-4, outscoring San Jose 35-26.
33 — Philadelphia Flyers in 1976 QF. Philadelphia won best-of-seven series 4-3, outscoring Toronto 33-23.
— Boston Bruins in 1983 DF. Boston won best-of-seven series 4-3, outscoring Buffalo 33-23.
— Edmonton Oilers in 1984 DF. Edmonton won best-of-seven series 4-3, outscoring Calgary 33-27.

FEWEST GOALS, BOTH TEAMS, TWO-GAME SERIES:
1 — **NY Rangers, NY Americans,** in 1929 SF. NY Rangers defeated NY Americans 1-0 in two-game, total-goal series.
— Mtl. Maroons, Chicago Blackhawks in 1935 SF. Mtl. Maroons defeated Chicago 1-0 in two-game, total-goal series.

FEWEST GOALS, ONE TEAM, TWO-GAME SERIES:
0 — **NY Americans** in 1929 SF. Lost two-game total-goal series 1-0 against NY Rangers.
— Chicago Blackhawks in 1935 SF. Lost two-game total-goal series 1-0 against Mtl. Maroons.
— Mtl. Maroons in 1937 SF. Lost best-of-three series 2-0 to NY Rangers while being outscored 5-0.
— NY Americans in 1939 QF. Lost best-of-three series 2-0 to Toronto while being outscored 6-0.

FEWEST GOALS, BOTH TEAMS, THREE-GAME SERIES:
7 — **Boston Bruins, Montreal Canadiens** in 1929 SF. Boston won best-of-five series 3-0, outscoring Montreal 5-2.
— Detroit Red Wings, Mtl. Maroons in 1936 SF. Detroit won best-of-five series 3-0, outscoring Mtl. Maroons 6-1.

FEWEST GOALS, ONE TEAM, THREE-GAME SERIES:
1 — **Mtl. Maroons** in 1936 SF. Lost best-of-five series 3-0 to Detroit and were outscored 6-1.

FEWEST GOALS, BOTH TEAMS, FOUR-GAME SERIES:
9 — **Toronto Maple Leafs, Boston Bruins** in 1935 SF. Toronto won best-of-five series 3-1, outscoring Boston 7-2.

FEWEST GOALS, ONE TEAM, FOUR-GAME SERIES:
2 — **Boston Bruins** in 1935 SF. Toronto won best-of-five series 3-1, outscoring Boston 7-2.
— Montreal Canadiens in 1952 F. Detroit won best-of-seven series 4-0, outscoring Montreal 11-2.

FEWEST GOALS, BOTH TEAMS, FIVE-GAME SERIES:
11 — **NY Rangers, Mtl. Maroons** in 1928 F. NY Rangers won best-of-five series 3-2, while outscored by Mtl. Maroons 6-5.

FEWEST GOALS, ONE TEAM, FIVE-GAME SERIES:
5 — **NY Rangers** in 1928 F. NY Rangers won best-of-five series 3-2, while outscored by Mtl. Maroons 6-5.

FEWEST GOALS, BOTH TEAMS, SIX-GAME SERIES:
22 — **Toronto Maple Leafs, Boston Bruins** in 1951 SF. Toronto won best-of-seven series 4-1 with 1 tie, outscoring Boston 17-5.

FEWEST GOALS, ONE TEAM, SIX-GAME SERIES:
5 — **Boston Bruins** in 1951 SF. Toronto won best-of-seven series 4-1 with 1 tie, outscoring Boston 17-5.

FEWEST GOALS, BOTH TEAMS, SEVEN-GAME SERIES:
18 — **Toronto Maple Leafs, Detroit Red Wings** in 1945 F. Toronto won best-of-seven series 4-3; teams tied in scoring 9-9.

FEWEST GOALS, ONE TEAM, SEVEN-GAME SERIES:
9 — **Toronto Maple Leafs,** in 1945 F. Toronto won best-of-seven series 4-3; teams tied in scoring 9-9.
— Detroit Red Wings, in 1945 F. Toronto won best-of-seven series 4-3; teams tied in scoring 9-9.

MOST GOALS, BOTH TEAMS, ONE GAME:
18 — **Los Angeles Kings, Edmonton Oilers** at Edmonton, April 7, 1982. Los Angeles 10, Edmonton 8. Los Angeles won best-of-five DSF 3-2.
17 — Pittsburgh Penguins, Philadelphia Flyers at Pittsburgh, April 25, 1989. Pittsburgh 10, Philadelphia 7. Philadelphia won best-of-seven DF 4-3.
16 — Edmonton Oilers, Los Angeles Kings at Edmonton, April 9, 1987. Edmonton 13, Los Angeles 3. Edmonton won best-of-seven DSF 4-1.
— Los Angeles Kings, Calgary Flames at Los Angeles, April 10, 1990. Los Angeles 12, Calgary 4. Los Angeles won best-of-seven DF 4-2.

MOST GOALS, ONE TEAM, ONE GAME:
13 — **Edmonton Oilers** at Edmonton, April 9, 1987. Edmonton 13, Los Angeles 3. Edmonton won best-of-seven DSF 4-1.
12 — Los Angeles Kings at Los Angeles, April 10, 1990. Los Angeles 12, Calgary 4. Los Angeles won best-of-seven DSF 4-2.
11 — Montreal Canadiens at Montreal, March 30, 1944. Montreal 11, Toronto 0. Canadiens won best-of-seven SF 4-1.
— Edmonton Oilers at Edmonton May 4, 1985. Edmonton 11, Chicago 2. Edmonton won best-of-seven CF 4-2.

MOST GOALS, BOTH TEAMS, ONE PERIOD:
9 — **NY Rangers, Philadelphia Flyers,** April 24, 1979, at Philadelphia, third period. NY Rangers won 8-3 scoring six of nine third-period goals.
— Los Angeles Kings, Calgary Flames at Los Angeles, April 10, 1990, second period. Los Angeles won game 12-4, scoring five of nine second-period goals.
8 — Chicago Blackhawks, Montreal Canadiens at Montreal, May 8, 1973, in the second period. Chicago won 8-7 scoring five of eight second-period goals.
— Chicago Blackhawks, Edmonton Oilers at Chicago, May 12, 1985 in the first period. Chicago won 8-6, scoring five of eight first-period goals.
— Edmonton Oilers, Winnipeg Jets at Edmonton, April 6, 1988 in the third period. Edmonton won 7-4, scoring six of eight third period goals.
— Hartford Whalers, Montreal Canadiens at Hartford, April 10, 1988 in the third period. Hartford won 7-5, scoring five of eight third period goals.

MOST GOALS, ONE TEAM, ONE PERIOD:
7 — **Montreal Canadiens,** March 30, 1944, at Montreal in third period, during 11-0 win against Toronto.

LONGEST OVERTIME:
116 Minutes, 30 Seconds — **Detroit Red Wings, Mtl. Maroons** at Montreal, March 24, 25, 1936. Detroit 1, Mtl. Maroons 0. Mud Bruneteau scored, assisted by Hec Kilrea, at 16:30 of sixth overtime period, or after 176 minutes, 30 seconds from start of game, which ended at 2:25 a.m. Detroit won best-of-five SF 3-0.

SHORTEST OVERTIME:
9 Seconds — **Montreal Canadiens, Calgary Flames,** at Calgary, May 18, 1986. Montreal won 3-2 on Brian Skrudland's goal and captured the best-of-seven F 4-1.
11 Seconds — NY Islanders, NY Rangers, at NY Rangers, April 11, 1975. NY Islanders won 4-3 on Jean-Paul Parise's goal and captured the best-of-three PR 2-1.

MOST OVERTIME GAMES, ONE PLAYOFF YEAR:
28 — **1993.** Of 85 games played, 28 went into overtime.
18 — 1994. Of 90 games played, 18 went into overtime.
— 1995. Of 81 games played, 18 went into overtime.

FEWEST OVERTIME GAMES, ONE PLAYOFF YEAR:
0 — **1963.** None of the 16 games went into overtime, the only year since 1926 that no overtime was required in any playoff series.

MOST OVERTIME-GAME VICTORIES, ONE TEAM, ONE PLAYOFF YEAR:
10 — **Montreal Canadiens, 1993.** Two against Quebec in the DSF; three against Buffalo in the DF; two against NY Islanders in the CF; and three against Los Angeles in the F. Montreal played 20 games.
6 — NY Islanders, 1980. One against Los Angeles in the PR; two against Boston in the QF; one against Buffalo in the SF; and two against Philadelphia in the F. Islanders played 21 games.
— Vancouver Canucks, 1994. Three against Calgary in the CQF; one against Dallas in the CSF; one against Toronto in the CF; and one against NY Rangers in the F. Vancouver played 24 games.

MOST OVERTIME GAMES, FINAL SERIES:
5 — **Toronto Maple Leafs,, Montreal Canadiens** in 1951. Toronto defeated Montreal 4-1 in best-of-seven series.

112 • PLAYOFF TEAM RECORDS

MOST OVERTIME GAMES, SEMI-FINAL SERIES:
4 — **Toronto Maple Leafs, Boston Bruins** in 1933. Toronto won best-of-five series 3-2.
— **Boston Bruins, NY Rangers** in 1939. Boston won best-of-seven series 4-3.
— **St. Louis Blues, Minnesota North Stars** in 1968. St. Louis won best-of-seven series 4-3.

MOST GAMES PLAYED BY ALL TEAMS, ONE PLAYOFF YEAR:
92 — **1991.** There were 51 DSF, 24 DF, 11 CF and 6 F games.
90 — **1994.** There were 48 CQF, 23 CSF, 12 CF and 7 F games.
87 — **1987.** There were 44 DSF, 25 DF, 11 CF and 7 F games.
86 — **1992.** There were 54 DSF, 20 DF, 8 CF and 4 F games.

MOST GAMES PLAYED, ONE TEAM, ONE PLAYOFF YEAR:
26 — **Philadelphia Flyers,** 1987. Won DSF 4-2 against NY Rangers, DF 4-3 against NY Islanders, CF 4-2 against Montreal, and lost F 4-3 against Edmonton.
24 — **Pittsburgh Penguins,** 1991. Won DSF 4-3 against New Jersey, DF 4-1 against Washington, CF 4-2 against Boston, and F 4-2 against Minnesota.
— **Los Angeles Kings,** 1993. Won DSF 4-2 against Calgary, DF 4-2 against Vancouver, CF 4-3 against Toronto, and lost F 4-1 against Montreal.
— **Vancouver Canucks,** 1994. Won CQF 4-3 against Calgary, CSF 4-1 against Dallas, CF 4-1 against Toronto, and lost F 4-3 against NY Rangers.

MOST ROAD VICTORIES, ONE TEAM, ONE PLAYOFF YEAR:
10 — **New Jersey Devils,** 1995. Won three at Boston in CQF; two at Pittsburgh in CSF; three at Philadelphia in CF; and two at Detroit in F series.
8 — **NY Islanders,** 1980. Won two at Los Angeles in PR; three at Boston in QF; two at Buffalo in SF; and one at Philadelphia in F series.
— **Philadelphia Flyers,** 1987. Won two at NY Rangers in DSF; two at NY Islanders in DF; three at Montreal in CF; and one at Edmonton in F series.
— **Edmonton Oilers,** 1990. Won one at Winnipeg in DSF; two at Los Angeles in DF; two at Chicago in CF and three at Boston in F series.
— **Pittsburgh Penguins,** 1992. Won two at Washington in DSF; two at NY Rangers in DF; two at Boston in CF; and two at Chicago in F series.
— **Vancouver Canucks,** 1994. Won three at Calgary in CQF; two at Dallas in CSF; one at Toronto in CF; and two at NY Rangers in F series.

MOST HOME VICTORIES, ONE TEAM, ONE PLAYOFF YEAR:
11 — Edmonton Oilers, 1988
10 — Edmonton Oilers, 1985 in 10 home-ice games.
— Montreal Canadiens, 1986
— Montreal Canadiens, 1993
9 — Philadelphia Flyers, 1974
— Philadelphia Flyers, 1980
— NY Islanders, 1981
— NY Islanders, 1983
— Edmonton Oilers, 1984
— Edmonton Oilers, 1987
— Calgary Flames, 1989
— Pittsburgh Penguins, 1991
— NY Rangers, 1994.

MOST ROAD VICTORIES, ALL TEAMS, ONE PLAYOFF YEAR:
46 — **1987.** Of 87 games played, road teams won 46 (22 DSF, 14 DF, 8 CF and 2 Stanley Cup final).

MOST CONSECUTIVE PLAYOFF GAME VICTORIES:
14 — **Pittsburgh Penguins.** Streak started May 9, 1992, at Pittsburgh with a 5-4 in fourth game of a DF series against NY Rangers, won by Pittsburgh 4-2. Continued with a four-game sweep over Boston in the 1992 CF and a four-game sweep over Chicago in the 1992 F. Pittsburgh then won the first three games of the 1993 DSF versus New Jersey. New Jersey ended the streak April 25, 1993, at New Jersey with a 4-1 win.
12 — Edmonton Oilers. Streak began May 15, 1984 at Edmonton with a 7-2 win over NY Islanders in third game of F series, and ended May 9, 1985 when Chicago defeated Edmonton 5-2 at Chicago. Included in the streak were three wins over the NY Islanders in 1984, three over Los Angeles, four over Winnipeg and two over Chicago, all in 1985.
11 — Montreal Canadiens. Streak began April 16, 1959, at Toronto with 3-2 win in fourth game of F series, won by Montreal 4-1, and ended March 23, 1961, when Chicago defeated Montreal 4-3 in second game of SF series. Included in streak were eight straight victories in 1960.
— Montreal Canadiens. Streak began April 28, 1968, at Montreal with 4-3 win in fifth game of SF series, won by Montreal 4-1, and ended April 17, 1969, at Boston when Boston defeated them 5-0 in third game of SF series. Included in the streak were four straight wins over St. Louis in the 1968 F and four straight wins over NY Rangers in 1969 QF series.
— Boston Bruins. Streak began April 14, 1970, at Boston with 3-2 victory over NY Rangers in fifth game of a QF series, won by Boston 4-2. It continued with a four-game victory over Chicago in the 1970 SF and a four-game win over St. Louis in the 1970 F. Boston then won the first game of a 1971 QF series against Montreal. Montreal ended the streak April 8, 1971, at Boston with a 7-5 victory.
— Montreal Canadiens. Streak started May 6, 1976, at Montreal with 5-2 win in fifth game of a SF series against NY Islanders, won by Montreal 4-1. Continued with a four-game sweep over Philadelphia in the 1976 F and a four-game win against St. Louis in the 1977 QF. Montreal won the first two games of a 1977 SF series against the NY Islanders before NY Islanders ended the streak, April 2, 1977 at New York with a 5-3 victory.
— Chicago Blackhawks. Streak started April 24, 1992, at St. Louis with a 5-3 win in fourth game of a DSF series against St. Louis, won by Chicago 4-2. Continued with a four-game sweep over Detroit in the 1992 DF and a four-game win over Edmonton in the 1992 CF. Pittsburgh ended the streak May 26, 1992, at Pittsburgh with a 5-4 victory.

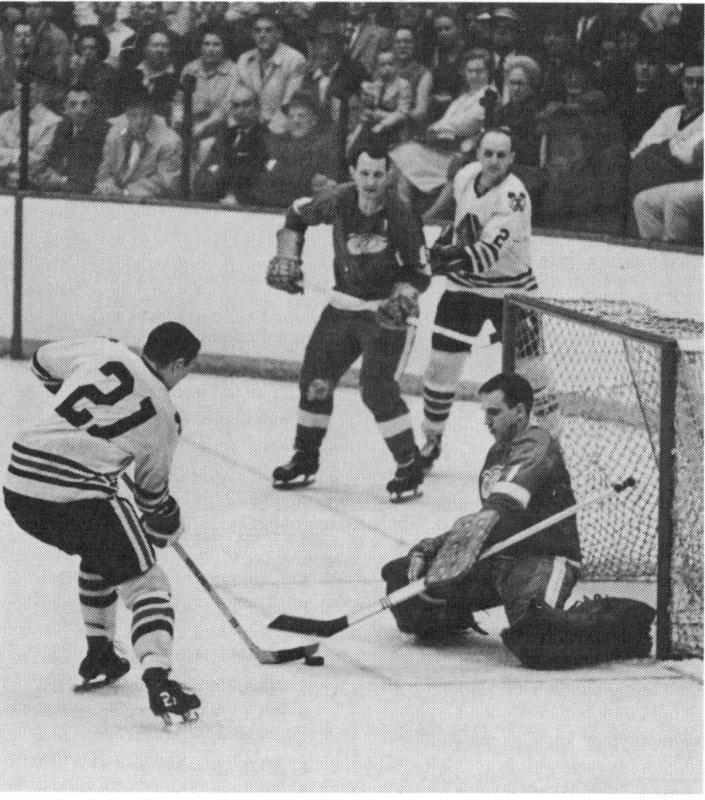

Doug Mohns (#2) and Bill Gadsby watch as Stan Mikita finds himself all alone in front of Detroit netminder Roger Crozier during game seven of the 1965 Stanley Cup semi-finals. A split-second later, Mikita deposited Mohns' pass behind Crozier to give the Black Hawks a 4-2 win and a berth in the 1965 finals.

MOST CONSECUTIVE VICTORIES, ONE PLAYOFF YEAR:
11 — **Chicago Blackhawks** in 1992. Chicago won last three games of best-of-seven DSF against St. Louis to win series 4-2 and then defeated Detroit 4-0 in best-of-seven DF and Edmonton 4-0 in best-of-seven CF.
— **Pittsburgh Penguins** in 1992. Pittsburgh won last three games of best-of-seven DF against NY Rangers to win series 4-2 and then defeated Boston 4-0 in best-of-seven CF and Chicago 4-0 in best-of-seven F.
— **Montreal Canadiens** in 1993. Montreal won last four games of best-of-seven DSF against Quebec to win series 4-2, defeated Buffalo 4-0 in best-of-seven DF and won first three games of CF against NY Islanders.

LONGEST PLAYOFF LOSING STREAK:
16 Games — **Chicago Blackhawks.** Streak started in 1975 QF against Buffalo when Chicago lost last two games. Then Chicago lost four games to Montreal in 1976 QF; two games to NY Islanders in 1977 PR; four games to Boston in 1978 QF and four games to NY Islanders in 1979 QF. Streak ended on April 8, 1980 when Chicago defeated St. Louis 3-2 in the opening game of their 1980 PR series.
12 Games — Toronto Maple Leafs. Streak started on April 16, 1979 as Toronto lost four straight games in a QF series against Montreal. Continued with three-game PR defeats versus Philadelphia and NY Islanders in 1980 and 1981 respectively. Toronto failed to qualify for the 1982 playoffs and lost the first two games of a 1983 DSF against Minnesota. Toronto ended the streak with a 6-3 win against the North Stars on April 9, 1983.
10 Games — NY Rangers. Streak started in 1968 QF against Chicago when NY Rangers lost last four games and continued through 1969 (four straight losses to Montreal in QF) and 1970 (two straight losses to Boston in QF) before ending with a 4-3 win against Boston, at New York, April 11, 1970.
— Philadelphia Flyers. Streak started on April 18, 1968, the last game in the 1968 QF series against St. Louis, and continued through 1969 (four straight losses to St. Louis in QF), 1971 (four straight losses to Chicago in QF) and 1973 (opening game loss to Minnesota in QF) before ending with a 4-1 win against Minnesota, at Philadelphia, April 5, 1973.
— Chicago Blackhawks. Streak started on May 26, 1992 as Chicago lost four straight games in the F to Pittsburgh. Continued with four straight losses to St. Louis in 1993 DSF. Chicago lost the first two games of 1994 CQF to Toronto before ending the streak with a 5-4 win against Toronto on April 23, 1994.

PLAYOFF TEAM RECORDS • 113

MOST SHUTOUTS, ONE PLAYOFF YEAR, ALL TEAMS:
16 — **1994.** Of 90 games played, NY Rangers and Vancouver had 4 each, Toronto had 3, Buffalo had 2, while Washington, Detroit and New Jersey had 1 each.
12 — **1992.** Of 86 games played, Detroit, Edmonton and Vancouver had 2 each, while Boston, Buffalo, Chicago, Montreal, NY Rangers and Pittsburgh had 1 each.

FEWEST SHUTOUTS, ONE PLAYOFF YEAR, ALL TEAMS:
0 — **1959.** 18 games played.

MOST SHUTOUTS, BOTH TEAMS, ONE SERIES:
5 — **1945 F, Toronto Maple Leafs, Detroit Red Wings.** Toronto had 3 shutouts, Detroit 2. Toronto won best-of-seven series 4-3.
— **1950 SF, Toronto Maple Leafs, Detroit Red Wings.** Toronto had 3 shutouts, Detroit 2. Detroit won best-of-seven series 4-3.

MOST PENALTIES, BOTH TEAMS, ONE SERIES:
219 — **New Jersey Devils, Washington Capitals** in 1988 DF won by New Jersey 4-3. New Jersey received 98 minors, 11 majors, 9 misconducts and 1 match penalty. Washington received 80 minors, 11 majors, 8 misconducts and 1 match penalty.

MOST PENALTY MINUTES, BOTH TEAMS, ONE SERIES:
656 — **New Jersey Devils, Washington Capitals** in 1988 DF won by New Jersey 4-3. New Jersey had 351 minutes; Washington 305.

MOST PENALTIES, ONE TEAM, ONE SERIES:
119 — **New Jersey Devils** in 1988 DF versus Washington. New Jersey received 98 minors, 11 majors, 9 misconducts and 1 match penalty.

MOST PENALTY MINUTES, ONE TEAM, ONE SERIES:
351 — **New Jersey Devils** in 1988 DF versus Washington. Series won by New Jersey 4-3.

MOST PENALTY MINUTES, BOTH TEAMS, ONE GAME:
298 Minutes — **Detroit Red Wings, St. Louis Blues,** at St. Louis, April 12, 1991. Detroit received 33 penalties for 152 minutes; St. Louis 33 penalties for 146 minutes. St. Louis won 6-1.
267 Minutes — **NY Rangers, Los Angeles Kings,** at Los Angeles, April 9, 1981. NY Rangers received 31 penalties for 142 minutes; Los Angeles 28 penalties for 125 minutes. Los Angeles won 5-4.

MOST PENALTIES, BOTH TEAMS, ONE GAME:
66 — **Detroit Red Wings, St. Louis Blues,** at St. Louis, April 12, 1991. Detroit received 33 penalties; St. Louis 33. St. Louis won 6-1.
62 — **New Jersey Devils, Washington Capitals,** at New Jersey, April 22, 1988. New Jersey received 32 penalties; Washington 30. New Jersey won 10-4.

MOST PENALTIES, ONE TEAM, ONE GAME:
33 — **Detroit Red Wings,** at St. Louis, April 12,1991. St. Louis won 6-1.
— **St. Louis Blues,** at St. Louis, April 12, 1991. St. Louis won 6-1.
32 — New Jersey Devils, at Washington, April 22,1988. New Jersey won 10-4.
31 — NY Rangers, at Los Angeles, April 9, 1981. Los Angeles won 5-4.
30 — Philadelphia Flyers, at Toronto, April 15, 1976. Toronto won 5-4.

MOST PENALTY MINUTES, ONE TEAM, ONE GAME:
152 — **Detroit Red Wings,** at St. Louis, April 12, 1991. St. Louis won 6-1.
146 — St. Louis Blues, at St. Louis, April 12, 1991. St. Louis won 6-1.
142 — NY Rangers, at Los Angeles, April 9, 1981. Los Angeles won 5-4.

MOST PENALTIES, BOTH TEAMS, ONE PERIOD:
43 — **NY Rangers, Los Angeles Kings,** April 9, 1981, at Los Angeles, first period. NY Rangers had 24 penalties; Los Angeles 19. Los Angeles won 5-4.

MOST PENALTY MINUTES, BOTH TEAMS, ONE PERIOD:
248 — **NY Islanders, Boston Bruins,** April 17, 1980, first period, at Boston. Each team received 124 minutes. Islanders won 5-4.

MOST PENALTIES, ONE TEAM, ONE PERIOD: (AND) MOST PENALTY MINUTES, ONE TEAM, ONE PERIOD:
24 Penalties; 125 Minutes — **NY Rangers,** April 9, 1981, at Los Angeles, first period. Los Angeles won 5-4.

FEWEST PENALTIES, BOTH TEAMS, BEST-OF-SEVEN SERIES:
19 — **Detroit Red Wings, Toronto Maple Leafs** in 1945 F, won by Toronto 4-3. Detroit received 10 minors. Toronto 9 minors.

FEWEST PENALTIES, ONE TEAM, BEST-OF-SEVEN SERIES:
9 — **Toronto Maple Leafs** in 1945 F, won by Toronto 4-3 against Detroit.

MOST POWER-PLAY GOALS BY ALL TEAMS, ONE PLAYOFF YEAR:
199 — **1988** in 83 games.

MOST POWER-PLAY GOALS, ONE TEAM, ONE PLAYOFF YEAR:
35 — **Minnesota North Stars,** 1991 in 23 games.
32 — Edmonton Oilers, 1988 in 18 games.
31 — NY Islanders, 1981, in 18 games.

MOST POWER-PLAY GOALS, BOTH TEAMS, ONE SERIES:
21 — **NY Islanders, Philadelphia Flyers** in 1980 F, won by NY Islanders 4-2. NY Islanders had 15 and Flyers 6.
— **NY Islanders, Edmonton Oilers** in 1981 QF, won by NY Islanders 4-2. NY Islanders had 13 and Edmonton 8.
— **Philadelphia Flyers, Pittsburgh Penguins** in 1989 DF, won by Philadelphia 4-3. Philadelphia had 11 and Pittsburgh 10.
— **Minnesota North Stars, Chicago Blackhawks** in 1991 DSF, won by Minnesota 4-2. Minnesota had 15 and Chicago 6.
20 — Toronto Maple Leafs, Philadelphia Flyers in 1976 QF series won by Philadelphia 4-3. Toronto had 12 power-pay goals; Philadelphia 8.

MOST POWER-PLAY GOALS, ONE TEAM, ONE SERIES:
15 — **NY Islanders** in 1980 F against Philadelphia. NY Islanders won series 4-2.
— **Minnesota North Stars** in 1991 DSF against Chicago. Minnesota won series 4-2.
13 — NY Islanders in 1981 QF against Edmonton. NY Islanders won series 4-2.
— Calgary Flames in 1986 CF against St. Louis. Calgary won series 4-3.
12 — Toronto Maple Leafs in 1976 QF series won by Philadelphia 4-3.

MOST POWER-PLAY GOALS, BOTH TEAMS, ONE GAME:
8 — **Minnesota North Stars, St. Louis Blues,** April 24, 1991 at Minnesota. Minnesota had 4, St. Louis 4. Minnesota won 8-4.
7 — **Minnesota North Stars, Edmonton Oilers,** April 28, 1984 at Minnesota. Minnesota had 4, Edmonton 3. Edmonton won 8-5.
— **Philadelphia Flyers, NY Rangers,** April 13, 1985 at New York. Philadelphia had 4, NY Rangers 3. Philadelphia won 6-5.
— **Edmonton Oilers, Chicago Blackhawks,** May 14, 1985 at Edmonton. Chicago had 5, Edmonton 2. Edmonton won 10-5.
— **Edmonton Oilers, Los Angeles Kings,** April 9, 1987 at Edmonton. Edmonton had 5, Los Angeles 2. Edmonton won 13-3.
— **Vancouver Canucks, Calgary Flames,** April 9, 1989 at Vancouver. Vancouver had 4, Calgary 3. Vancouver won 5-3.

MOST POWER-PLAY GOALS, ONE TEAM, ONE GAME:
6 — **Boston Bruins,** April 2, 1969, at Boston against Toronto. Boston won 10-0.

MOST POWER-PLAY GOALS, BOTH TEAMS, ONE PERIOD:
5 — **Minnesota North Stars, Edmonton Oilers,** April 28, 1984, second period, at Minnesota. Minnesota had 4 and Edmonton 1. Edmonton won 8-5.
— **Vancouver Canucks, Calgary Flames,** April 9, 1989, third period at Vancouver. Vancouver had 3 and Calgary 2. Vancouver won 5-3.
— **Minnesota North Stars, St. Louis Blues,** April 24, 1991, second period, at Minnesota. Minnesota had 4 and St. Louis 1. Minnesota won 8-4.

MOST POWER-PLAY GOALS, ONE TEAM, ONE PERIOD:
4 — **Toronto Maple Leafs,** March 26, 1936, second period against Boston at Toronto. Toronto won 8-3.
— **Minnesota North Stars,** April 28, 1984, second period against Edmonton at Minnesota. Edmonton won 8-5.
— **Boston Bruins,** April 11, 1991, third period against Hartford at Boston. Boston won 6-1.
— **Minnesota North Stars,** April 24, 1991, second period against St. Louis at Minnesota. Minnesota won 8-4.

MOST SHORTHAND GOALS BY ALL TEAMS, ONE PLAYOFF YEAR:
33 — **1988,** in 83 games.

MOST SHORTHAND GOALS, ONE TEAM, ONE PLAYOFF YEAR:
10 — **Edmonton Oilers 1983,** in 16 games.
9 — NY Islanders, 1981, in 19 games.
8 — Philadelphia Flyers, 1989, in 19 games.
7 — NY Islanders, 1980, in 21 games.
— Chicago Blackhawks, 1989, in 16 games.
— Vancouver Canucks, 1995, in 11 games.

Stefan Persson scored three of the New York Islanders' record-setting 15 powerplay goals during the 1980 Stanley Cup Finals against the Philadelphia Flyers.

MOST SHORTHAND GOALS, BOTH TEAMS, ONE SERIES:
7 — **Boston Bruins (4), NY Rangers (3),** in 1958 SF, won by Boston 4-2.
— **Edmonton Oilers (5), Calgary Flames (2),** in 1983 DF won by Edmonton 4-1.
— **Vancouver Canucks (6), St. Louis Blues (1),** in 1995 CQF won by Vancouver 4-3.

MOST SHORTHAND GOALS, ONE TEAM, ONE SERIES:
6 — **Calgary Flames** in 1995 against San Jose in best-of-seven CQF won by San Jose 4-3.
— **Vancouver Canucks** in 1995 against St. Louis in best-of-seven CQF won by Vancouver 4-3.
5 — Edmonton Oilers in 1983 against Calgary in best-of-seven DF won by Edmonton 4-1.
— NY Rangers in 1979 against Philadelphia in best-of-seven QF, won by NY Rangers 4-1.

MOST SHORTHAND GOALS, BOTH TEAMS, ONE GAME:
4 — **NY Islanders, NY Rangers,** April 17, 1983 at NY Rangers. NY Islanders had 3 shorthand goals, NY Rangers 1. NY Rangers won 7-6.
— **Boston Bruins, Minnesota North Stars,** April 11, 1981, at Minnesota. Boston had 3 shorthand goals, Minnesota 1. Minnesota won 6-3.
— **San Jose Sharks, Toronto Maple Leafs,** May 8, 1994 at San Jose. Toronto had 3 shorthanded goals, San Jose 1. Toronto won 8-3.
3 — Toronto Maple Leafs, Detroit Red Wings, April 5, 1947, at Toronto. Toronto had 2 shorthand goals, Detroit 1. Toronto won 6-1.
— NY Rangers, Boston Bruins, April 1, 1958, at Boston. NY Rangers had 2 shorthand goals, Boston 1. NY Rangers won 5-2.
— Minnesota North Stars, Philadelphia Flyers, May 4, 1980, at Minnesota. Minnesota had 2 shorthand goals, Philadelphia 1. Philadelphia won 5-3.
— Edmonton Oilers, Winnipeg Jets, April 9, 1988 at Winnipeg. Winnipeg had 2 shorthand goals, Edmonton 1. Winnipeg won 6-4.
— New Jersey Devils, NY Islanders, April 14, 1988 at New Jersey. NY Islanders had 2 shorthand goals, New Jersey 1. New Jersey won 6-5.

MOST SHORTHAND GOALS, ONE TEAM, ONE GAME:
3 — **Boston Bruins,** April 11, 1981, at Minnesota. Minnesota won 6-3.
— **NY Islanders,** April 17, 1983, at NY Rangers. NY Rangers won 7-6.
— **Toronto Maple Leafs,** May 8, 1994 at San Jose. Toronto won 8-3.

MOST SHORTHAND GOALS, BOTH TEAMS, ONE PERIOD:
3 — **Toronto Maple Leafs, Detroit Red Wings,** April 5, 1947, at Toronto, first period. Toronto had 2 shorthand goals, Detroit 1. Toronto won 6-1.
— **Toronto Maple Leafs, San Jose Sharks,** May 8, 1994, at San Jose, third period. Toronto had 2 shorthanded goals, San Jose 1. Toronto won 8-3.

MOST SHORTHAND GOALS ONE TEAM, ONE PERIOD:
2 — **Toronto Maple Leafs,** April 5, 1947, at Toronto against Detroit, first period. Toronto won 6-1.
— **Toronto Maple Leafs,** April 13, 1965, at Toronto against Montreal, first period. Montreal won 4-3.
— **Boston Bruins,** April 20, 1969, at Boston against Montreal, first period. Boston won 3-2.
— **Boston Bruins,** April 8, 1970, at Boston against NY Rangers, second period. Boston won 8-2.
— **Boston Bruins,** April 30, 1972, at Boston against NY Rangers, first period. Boston won 6-5.
— **Chicago Blackhawks,** May 3, 1973, at Chicago against Montreal, first period. Chicago won 7-4.
— **Montreal Canadiens,** April 23, 1978, at Detroit, first period. Montreal won 8-0.
— **NY Islanders,** April 8, 1980, at New York against Los Angeles, second period. NY Islanders won 8-1.
— **Los Angeles Kings,** April 9, 1980, at NY Islanders, first period. Los Angeles won 6-3.
— **Boston Bruins,** April 13, 1980, at Pittsburgh, second period. Boston won 8-3.
— **Minnesota North Stars,** May 4, 1980, at Minnesota against Philadelphia, second period. Philadelphia won 5-3.
— **Boston Bruins,** April 11, 1981, at Minnesota, third period. Minnesota won 6-3.
— **NY Islanders,** May 12, 1981, at New York against Minnesota, first period. NY Islanders won 6-3.
— **Montreal Canadiens,** April 7, 1982, at Montreal against Quebec, third period. Montreal won 5-1.
— **Edmonton Oilers,** April 24, 1983, at Edmonton against Chicago, third period. Edmonton won 8-4.
— **Winnipeg Jets,** April 14, 1985, at Calgary, second period. Winnipeg won 5-3.
— **Boston Bruins,** April 6, 1988 at Boston against Buffalo, first period. Boston won 7-3.
— **NY Islanders,** April 14, 1988 at New Jersey, third period. New Jersey won 6-5.
— **Detroit Red Wings,** April 29, 1993 at Toronto, second period. Detroit won 7-3.
— **Toronto Maple Leafs,** May 8, 1994 at San Jose, third period. Toronto won 8-3.
— **Calgary Flames,** May 11, 1995 at San Jose, first period. Calgary won 9-2.
— **Vancouver Canucks,** May 15, 1995 at St. Louis, second period. Vancouver won 6-5.

Chicago penalty-killing specialist Wayne Presley scored three short-handed goals during the 1989 playoffs.

A group of victorious Toronto Maple Leafs, from left to right: Bob Pulford, Brian Conacher, Pete Stemkowski, Larry Hillman, Milan Marcetta, Larry Jeffrey (with crutches), Marcel Pronovost and Mike Walton surround captain George Armstrong after the Leafs clinched the Stanley Cup on May 2, 1967.

FASTEST TWO GOALS, BOTH TEAMS:
5 Seconds — Pittsburgh Penguins, Buffalo Sabres at Buffalo, April 14, 1979. Gilbert Perreault scored for Buffalo at 12:59 and Jim Hamilton for Pittsburgh at 13:04 of first period. Pittsburgh won 4-3 and best-of-three PR 2-1.
8 Seconds — Minnesota North Stars, St. Louis Blues at Minnesota, April 9, 1989. Bernie Federko scored for St. Louis at 2:28 of third period and Perry Berezan at 2:36 for Minnesota. Minnesota won 5-4. St. Louis won best-of-seven DSF 4-1.
9 Seconds — NY Islanders, Washington Capitals at Washington, April 10, 1986. Bryan Trottier scored for New York at 18:26 of second period and Scott Stevens at 18:35 for Washington. Washington won 5-2, and won best-of-five DSF 3-0.
10 Seconds — Washington Capitals, New Jersey Devils at New Jersey, April 5, 1990. Pat Conacher scored for New Jersey at 8:02 of second period and Dale Hunter at 8:12 for Washington. Washington won 5-4, and won best-of-seven DSF 4-2.
— Calgary Flames, Edmonton Oilers at Edmonton, April 8, 1991. Joe Nieuwendyk scored for Calgary at 2:03 of first period and Esa Tikkanen at 2:13 for Edmonton. Edmonton won 4-3, and won best-of-seven DSF 4-3.

FASTEST TWO GOALS, ONE TEAM:
5 Seconds — Detroit Red Wings at Detroit, April 11, 1965, against Chicago. Norm Ullman scored at 17:35 and 17:40, second period. Detroit won 4-2. Chicago won best-of-seven SF 4-3.

FASTEST THREE GOALS, BOTH TEAMS:
21 Seconds — Edmonton Oilers, Chicago Blackhawks at Edmonton, May 7, 1985. Behn Wilson scored for Chicago at 19:22 of third period, Jari Kurri at 19:36 and Glenn Anderson at 19:43 for Edmonton. Edmonton won 7-3 and best-of-seven CF 4-2.
30 Seconds — Chicago Blackhawks, Pittsburgh Penguins at Chicago, June 1, 1992. Dirk Graham scored for Chicago at 6:21 of first period, Kevin Stevens for Pittsburgh at 6:33 and Graham for Chicago at 6:51. Pittsburgh won 6-5 and best-of-seven F 4-0.
31 Seconds — Edmonton Oilers, Philadelphia Flyers at Edmonton, May 25, 1985. Wayne Gretzky scored for Edmonton at 1:10 and 1:25 of first period, Derrick Smith scored for Philadelphia at 1:41. Edmonton won 4-3 and best-of-seven F 4-1.

FASTEST THREE GOALS, ONE TEAM:
23 Seconds — Toronto Maple Leafs at Toronto, April 12, 1979, against Atlanta Flames. Darryl Sittler scored at 4:04 of first period and again at 4:16 and Ron Ellis at 4:27. Leafs won 7-4 and best-of-three PR 2-0.
38 Seconds — NY Rangers at New York, April 12, 1986. Jim Wiemer scored at 12:29 of third period, Bob Brooke at 12:43 and Ron Grescher at 13:07. NY Rangers won 5-2 and best-of-five DSF 3-2.
56 Seconds — Montreal Canadiens at Detroit, April 6, 1954. Dickie Moore scored at 15:03 of first period, Maurice Richard at 15:28 and again at 15:59. Montreal won 3-1. Detroit won best-of-seven F 4-3.

FASTEST FOUR GOALS, BOTH TEAMS:
1 Minute, 33 Seconds — Philadelphia Flyers, Toronto Maple Leafs at Philadelphia, April 20, 1976. Don Saleski of Philadelphia scored at 10:04 of second period; Bob Neely, Toronto, 10:42; Gary Dornhoefer, Philadelphia, 11:24; and Don Saleski, 11:37. Philadelphia won 7-1 and best-of-seven QF series 4-3.
1 minute, 34 seconds — Montreal Canadiens, Calgary Flames at Montreal, May 20, 1986. Joel Otto of Calgary scored at 17:59 of first period; Bobby Smith, Montreal, 18:25; Mats Naslund, Montreal, 19:17; and Bob Gainey, Montreal, 19:33. Montreal won 5-3 and best-of-seven F series 4-1.
1 Minute, 38 Seconds — Boston Bruins, Philadelphia Flyers at Philadelphia, April 26, 1977. Gregg Sheppard of Boston scored at 14:01 of second period; Mike Milbury, Boston, 15:01; Gary Dornhoefer, Philadelphia, 15:16; and Jean Ratelle, Boston, 15:39. Boston won 5-4 and best-of-seven SF series 4-0.

FASTEST FOUR GOALS, ONE TEAM:
2 Minutes, 35 Seconds — Montreal Canadiens at Montreal, March 30, 1944, against Toronto. Toe Blake scored at 7:58 of third period and again at 8:37; Maurice Richard, 9:17; Ray Getliffe, 10:33. Montreal won 11-0 and best-of-seven SF 4-1.

FASTEST FIVE GOALS, BOTH TEAMS:
3 Minutes, 6 Seconds — Chicago Blackhawks, Minnesota North Stars, at Chicago April 21, 1985. Keith Brown scored for Chicago at 1:12, second period; Ken Yaremchuk, Chicago, 1:27; Dino Ciccarelli, Minnesota, 2:48; Tony McKegney, Minnesota, 4:07; and Curt Fraser, Chicago, 4:18. Chicago won 6-2 and best-of-seven DF 4-2.
3 Minutes, 20 Seconds — Minnesota North Stars, Philadelphia Flyers, at Philadelphia, April 29, 1980. Paul Shmyr scored for Minnesota at 13:20, first period; Steve Christoff, Minnesota, 13:59; Ken Linseman, Philadelphia, 14:54; Tom Gorence, Philadelphia, 15:36; and Linseman, 16:40. Minnesota won 6-5. Philadelphia won best-of-seven SF 4-1.
4 Minutes, 19 Seconds — Toronto Maple Leafs, NY Rangers at Toronto, April 9, 1932. Ace Bailey scored for Toronto at 15:07, third period; Fred Cook, NY Rangers, 16:32; Bob Gracie, Toronto, 17:36; Frank Boucher, NY Rangers, 18:26 and again at 19:26. Toronto won 6-4 and best-of-five F 3-0.

FASTEST FIVE GOALS, ONE TEAM:
3 Minutes, 36 Seconds — Montreal Canadiens at Montreal, March 30, 1944, against Toronto. Toe Blake scored at 7:58 of third period and again at 8:37; Maurice Richard, 9:17; Ray Getliffe, 10:33; and Buddy O'Connor, 11:34. Canadiens won 11-0 and best-of-seven SF 4-1.

MOST THREE-OR-MORE GOAL GAMES BY ALL TEAMS, ONE PLAYOFF YEAR:
12 — **1983** in 66 games.
— **1988** in 83 games.
11 — **1985** in 70 games.
— **1992** in 86 games.

MOST THREE-OR-MORE GOAL GAMES, ONE TEAM, ONE PLAYOFF YEAR:
6 — **Edmonton Oilers** in 16 games, 1983.
— **Edmonton Oilers** in 18 games, 1985.

Individual Records

Career

MOST YEARS IN PLAYOFFS:
20 — **Gordie Howe, Detroit, Hartford** (1947-58 incl.; 60-61; 63-66 incl.; 70 & 80)
 — **Larry Robinson, Montreal, Los Angeles** (1973-92 incl.)
19 — Red Kelly, Detroit, Toronto
18 — Stan Mikita, Chicago
 — Henri Richard, Montreal

MOST CONSECUTIVE YEARS IN PLAYOFFS:
20 — **Larry Robinson, Montreal, Los Angeles** (1973-1992, inclusive).
17 — Brad Park, NY Rangers, Boston, Detroit (1969-1985, inclusive).
16 — Jean Beliveau, Montreal (1954-69, inclusive).
 — Ray Bourque, Boston (1980-95, inclusive).

MOST PLAYOFF GAMES:
227 — **Larry Robinson, Montreal, Los Angeles**
221 — Bryan Trottier, NY Islanders, Pittsburgh
214 — Glenn Anderson, Edmonton, Toronto, NY Rangers, St. Louis
210 — Mark Messier, Edmonton, NY Rangers
202 — Kevin Lowe, Edmonton, NY Rangers

MOST POINTS IN PLAYOFFS (CAREER):
346 — **Wayne Gretzky, Edmonton, Los Angeles**, 110G, 236A
272 — Mark Messier, Edmonton, NY Rangers, 102G, 170A
222 — Jari Kurri, Edmonton, Los Angeles, 102G, 120A
209 — Glenn Anderson, Edmonton, Toronto, NY Rangers, St. Louis, 92G, 117A
184 — Bryan Trottier, NY Islanders, Pittsburgh 71G, 113A

MOST GOALS IN PLAYOFFS (CAREER):
110 — **Wayne Gretzky, Edmonton, Los Angeles**
102 — Jari Kurri, Edmonton, Los Angeles
102 — Mark Messier, Edmonton, NY Rangers
92 — Glenn Anderson, Edmonton, Toronto, NY Rangers, St. Louis
85 — Mike Bossy, NY Islanders

MOST ASSISTS IN PLAYOFFS (CAREER):
236 — **Wayne Gretzky, Edmonton, Los Angeles**
170 — Mark Messier, Edmonton, NY Rangers
120 — Jari Kurri, Edmonton, Los Angeles
119 — Paul Coffey, Edmonton, Pittsburgh, Los Angeles, Detroit
117 — Glenn Anderson, Edmonton, Toronto, NY Rangers, St. Louis

MOST OVERTIME GOALS IN PLAYOFFS (CAREER):
6 — **Maurice Richard, Montreal** (1 in 1946; 3 in 1951; 1 in 1957; 1 in 1958.)
4 — Bob Nystrom, NY Islanders
 — Dale Hunter, Quebec, Washington
 — Glenn Anderson, Edmonton, Toronto
 — Wayne Gretzky, Edmonton, Los Angeles
 — Stephane Richer, Montreal, New Jersey
3 — Mel Hill, Boston
 — Rene Robert, Buffalo
 — Danny Gare, Buffalo
 — Jacques Lemaire, Montreal
 — Bobby Clarke, Philadelphia
 — Terry O'Reilly, Boston
 — Mike Bossy, NY Islanders
 — Steve Payne, Minnesota
 — Ken Morrow, NY Islanders
 — Lanny McDonald, Toronto, Calgary
 — Peter Stastny, Quebec
 — Dino Ciccarelli, Minnesota, Washington
 — Russ Courtnall, Montreal
 — Kirk Muller, Montreal
 — Greg Adams, Vancouver
 — Joe Murphy, Edmonton, Chicago

MOST POWER-PLAY GOALS IN PLAYOFFS (CAREER):
35 — **Mike Bossy, NY Islanders**
30 — Wayne Gretzky, Edmonton, Los Angeles
28 — Dino Ciccarelli, Minnesota, Washington, Detroit
27 — Denis Potvin, NY Islanders
26 — Jean Beliveau, Montreal
25 — Jari Kurri, Edmonton, Los Angeles
 — Mario Lemieux, Pittsburgh
24 — Bobby Smith, Minnesota, Montreal
 — Cam Neely, Vancouver, Boston
23 — Glenn Anderson, Edmonton, Toronto, NY Rangers
 — Brian Propp, Philadelphia, Boston, Minnesota

MOST SHORTHAND GOALS IN PLAYOFFS (CAREER):
14 — **Mark Messier, Edmonton, NY Rangers**
11 — Wayne Gretzky, Edmonton, Los Angeles
9 — Jari Kurri, Edmonton, Los Angeles
8 — Ed Westfall, Boston, NY Islanders
 — Hakan Loob, Calgary

MOST GAME-WINNING GOALS IN PLAYOFFS (CAREER):
21 — **Wayne Gretzky, Edmonton, Los Angeles**
18 — Maurice Richard, Montreal
17 — Mike Bossy, NY Islanders
16 — Glenn Anderson, Edmonton, Toronto, NY Rangers
15 — Jean Beliveau, Montreal
 — Yvan Cournoyer, Montreal

MOST THREE-OR-MORE-GOAL GAMES IN PLAYOFFS (CAREER):
8 — **Wayne Gretzky, Edmonton.** Six three-goal games; two four-goal games.
7 — Maurice Richard, Montreal. Four three-goal games; two four-goal games; one five-goal game.
 — Jari Kurri, Edmonton. Six three-goal games; one four-goal game.
6 — Dino Ciccarelli, Minnesota, Washington, Detroit. Five three-goal games; one four-goal game.
5 — Mike Bossy, NY Islanders. Four three-goal games; one four-goal game.

MOST PENALTY MINUTES IN PLAYOFFS (CAREER):
637 — **Dale Hunter,** Quebec, Washington
541 — Chris Nilan, Montreal, NY Rangers, Boston
466 — Willi Plett, Atlanta, Calgary, Minnesota, Boston
455 — Dave Williams, Toronto, Vancouver, Los Angeles
436 — Glenn Anderson, Edmonton, Toronto, NY Rangers, St. Louis

MOST SHUTOUTS IN PLAYOFFS (CAREER):
15 — **Clint Benedict,** Ottawa, Mtl. Maroons
14 — Jacques Plante, Montreal, St. Louis
13 — Turk Broda, Toronto
12 — Terry Sawchuk, Detroit, Toronto, Los Angeles

MOST PLAYOFF GAMES APPEARED IN BY A GOALTENDER (CAREER):
132 — **Bill Smith, NY Islanders**
119 — Grant Fuhr, Edmonton, Buffalo
116 — Andy Moog, Edmonton, Boston, Dallas
115 — Glenn Hall, Detroit, Chicago, St. Louis
114 — Patrick Roy, Montreal
112 — Jacques Plante, Montreal, St. Louis, Toronto, Boston
 — Ken Dryden, Montreal

MOST MINUTES PLAYED BY A GOALTENDER (CAREER):
7,645 — **Bill Smith, NY Islanders**
7,002 — Grant Fuhr, Edmonton, Buffalo
6,964 — Patrick Roy, Montreal
6,899 — Glenn Hall, Detroit, Chicago, St. Louis
6,846 — Ken Dryden, Montreal

Single Playoff Year

MOST POINTS, ONE PLAYOFF YEAR:
47 — **Wayne Gretzky, Edmonton,** in 1985. 17 goals, 30 assists in 18 games.
44 — Mario Lemieux, Pittsburgh, in 1991. 16 goals, 28 assists in 23 games.
43 — Wayne Gretzky, Edmonton, in 1988. 12 goals, 31 assists in 19 games.
40 — Wayne Gretzky, Los Angeles, in 1993. 15 goals, 25 assists in 24 games.
38 — Wayne Gretzky, Edmonton, in 1983. 12 goals, 26 assists in 16 games.
37 — Paul Coffey, Edmonton, in 1985. 12 goals, 25 assists in 18 games.
35 — Mike Bossy, NY Islanders, in 1981. 17 goals, 18 assists in 18 games.
 — Wayne Gretzky, Edmonton, in 1984. 13 goals, 22 assists in 19 games.
 — Mark Messier, Edmonton, in 1988. 11 goals, 23 assists in 19 games.
 — Doug Gilmour, Toronto, in 1993. 10 goals, 25 assists in 21 games.
34 — Wayne Gretzky, Edmonton, in 1987. 5 goals, 29 assists in 21 games.
 — Mark Recchi, Pittsburgh, in 1991. 10 goals, 24 assists in 24 games.
 — Mario Lemieux, Pittsburgh, in 1992. 16 goals, 18 assists in 15 games.
 — Brian Leetch, NY Rangers, in 1994. 11 goals, 23 assists in 23 games.

MOST POINTS BY A DEFENSEMAN, ONE PLAYOFF YEAR:
37 — **Paul Coffey, Edmonton,** in 1985. 12 goals, 25 assists in 18 games.
34 — Brian Leetch, NY Rangers, in 1994. 11 goals, 23 assists in 23 games.
31 — Al MacInnis, Calgary, in 1989. 7 goals, 24 assists in 18 games.
25 — Denis Potvin, NY Islanders, in 1981. 8 goals, 17 assists in 18 games.
 — Ray Bourque, Boston, in 1991. 7 goals, 18 assists in 19 games.

MOST POINTS BY A ROOKIE, ONE PLAYOFF YEAR:
21 — **Dino Ciccarelli, Minnesota,** in 1981. 14 goals, 7 assists in 19 games.
20 — Don Maloney, NY Rangers, in 1979. 7 goals, 13 assists in 18 games.

LONGEST CONSECUTIVE POINT-SCORING STREAK, ONE PLAYOFF YEAR:
18 games — **Bryan Trottier, NY Islanders,** 1981. 11 goals, 18 assists, 29 points.
17 games — Wayne Gretzky, Edmonton, 1988. 12 goals, 29 assists, 41 points.
 — Al MacInnis, Calgary, 1989. 7 goals, 19 assists, 24 points.

LONGEST CONSECUTIVE POINT-SCORING STREAK, MORE THAN ONE PLAYOFF YEAR:
27 games — **Bryan Trottier, NY Islanders,** 1980, 1981 and 1982. 7 games in 1980 (3 G, 5 A, 8 PTS), 18 games in 1981 (11 G, 18 A, 29 PTS), and two games in 1982 (2 G, 3 A, 5 PTS). Total points, 42.
19 games — Wayne Gretzky, Edmonton, Los Angeles 1988 and 1989. 17 games in 1988 (12 G, 29 A, 41 PTS with Edmonton), 2 games in 1989 (1 G, 2 A, 3 PTS with Los Angeles). Total points, 44.
18 games — Phil Esposito, Boston, 1970 and 1971. 13 G, 20 A, 33 PTS.

PLAYOFF INDIVIDUAL RECORDS • 117

MOST GOALS, ONE PLAYOFF YEAR:
19 — **Reggie Leach, Philadelphia,** 1976. 16 games.
  — **Jari Kurri, Edmonton,** 1985. 18 games.
17 — Newsy Lalonde, Montreal, 1919. 10 games.
  — Mike Bossy, NY Islanders, 1981. 18 games.
  — Steve Payne, Minnesota, 1981. 19 games.
  — Mike Bossy, NY Islanders, 1982. 19 games.
  — Mike Bossy, NY Islanders, 1983. 19 games.
  — Wayne Gretzky, Edmonton, 1985. 18 games.
  — Kevin Stevens, Pittsburgh, 1991. 24 games.

MOST GOALS BY A DEFENSEMAN, ONE PLAYOFF YEAR:
12 — **Paul Coffey, Edmonton,** 1985. 18 games.
11 — Brian Leetch, NY Rangers, 1994. 23 games.
9 — Bobby Orr, Boston, 1970. 14 games.
  — Brad Park, Boston, 1978. 15 games.
8 — Denis Potvin, NY Islanders, 1981. 18 games.
  — Raymond Bourque, Boston, 1983. 17 games.
  — Denis Potvin, NY Islanders, 1983. 20 games.
  — Paul Coffey, Edmonton, 1984. 19 games

MOST GOALS BY A ROOKIE, ONE PLAYOFF YEAR:
14 — **Dino Ciccarelli, Minnesota,** 1981. 19 games.
11 — Jeremy Roenick, Chicago, 1990. 20 games.
10 — Claude Lemieux, Montreal, 1986. 20 games.
9 — Pat Flatley, NY Islanders, 1984. 21 games
8 — Steve Christoff, Minnesota, 1980. 14 games.
  — Brad Palmer, Minnesota, 1981. 19 games.
  — Mike Krushelnyski, Boston, 1983. 17 games.
  — Bob Joyce, Boston, 1988. 23 games.

MOST GAME-WINNING GOALS, ONE PLAYOFF YEAR:
5 — **Mike Bossy, NY Islanders,** 1983. 19 games.
  — **Jari Kurri, Edmonton,** 1987. 21 games.
  — **Bobby Smith, Minnesota,** 1991. 23 games.
  — **Mario Lemieux, Pittsburgh,** 1992. 15 games.

MOST OVERTIME GOALS, ONE PLAYOFF YEAR:
3 — **Mel Hill, Boston,** 1939. All against NY Rangers in best-of-seven SF, won by Boston 4-3.
  — **Maurice Richard, Montreal,** 1951. 2 against Detroit in best-of-seven SF, won by Montreal 4-2; 1 against Toronto best-of-seven F, won by Toronto 4-1.

MOST POWER-PLAY GOALS, ONE PLAYOFF YEAR:
9 — **Mike Bossy, NY Islanders,** 1981. 18 games against Toronto, Edmonton, NY Rangers and Minnesota.
  — **Cam Neely, Boston,** 1991. 19 games against Hartford, Montreal, Pittsburgh.
8 — Tim Kerr, Philadelphia, 1989. 19 games.
  — John Druce, Washington, 1990. 15 games
  — Brian Propp, Minnesota, 1991. 23 games.
  — Mario Lemieux, Pittsburgh, 1992. 15 games.
7 — Michel Goulet, Quebec, 1985. 17 games.
  — Mark Messier, Edmonton, 1988. 19 games.
  — Mario Lemieux, Pittsburgh, 1989. 11 games.
  — Brett Hull, St. Louis, 1990. 12 games.
  — Kevin Stevens, Pittsburgh, 1991. 24 games.

MOST SHORTHAND GOALS, ONE PLAYOFF YEAR:
3 — **Derek Sanderson, Boston,** 1969. 1 against Toronto in QF, won by Boston 4-0; 2 against Montreal in SF, won by Montreal, 4-2.
  — **Bill Barber, Philadelphia,** 1980. All against Minnesota in SF, won by Philadelphia 4-1.
  — **Lorne Henning, NY Islanders,** 1980. 1 against Boston in QF won by NY Islanders 4-1; 1 against Buffalo in SF, won by NY Islanders 4-2, 1 against Philadelphia in F, won by NY Islanders 4-2.
  — **Wayne Gretzky, Edmonton,** 1983. 2 against Winnipeg in DSF won by Edmonton 3-0; 1 against Calgary in DF, won by Edmonton 4-1.
  — **Wayne Presley, Chicago,** 1989. All against Detroit in DSF won by Chicago 4-2.

MOST THREE-OR-MORE GOAL GAMES, ONE PLAYOFF YEAR:
4 — **Jari Kurri, Edmonton,** 1985. 1 four-goal game, 3 three-goal games.
3 — Mark Messier, Edmonton, 1983. 3 three-goal games.
  — Mike Bossy, NY Islanders, 1983. 1 four-goal game, 2 three-goal games
2 — Newsy Lalonde, Montreal, 1919. 1 five-goal game, 1 four-goal game.
  — Maurice Richard, Montreal, 1944. 1 five-goal game; 1 three-goal game.
  — Doug Bentley, Chicago, 1944. 2 three-goal games.
  — Norm Ullman, Detroit, 1964. 2 three-goal games.
  — Phil Esposito, Boston, 1970. 2 three-goal games.
  — Pit Martin, Chicago, 1973. 2 three-goal games.
  — Rick MacLeish, Philadelphia, 1975. 2 three-goal games.
  — Lanny McDonald, Toronto, 1977. 1 three-goal game; 1 four-goal game.
  — Wayne Gretzky, Edmonton, 1981. 2 three-goal games.
  — Wayne Gretzky, Edmonton, 1983. 2 four-goal games.
  — Wayne Gretzky, Edmonton, 1985. 2 three-goal games.
  — Petr Klima, Detroit, 1988. 2 three-goal games.
  — Cam Neely, Boston, 1991. 2 three-goal games.

LONGEST CONSECUTIVE GOAL-SCORING STREAK, ONE PLAYOFF YEAR:
9 Games — Reggie Leach, Philadelphia, 1976. Streak started April 17 at Toronto and ended May 9 at Montreal. He scored one goal in each of seven games; two in one game; and five in another; a total of 14 goals.

MOST ASSISTS, ONE PLAYOFF YEAR:
31 — **Wayne Gretzky, Edmonton,** 1988. 19 games.
30 — Wayne Gretzky, Edmonton, 1985. 18 games.
29 — Wayne Gretzky, Edmonton, 1987. 21 games.
28 — Mario Lemieux, Pittsburgh, 1991. 23 games.
26 — Wayne Gretzky, Edmonton, 1983. 16 games.
25 — Paul Coffey, Edmonton, 1985. 18 games.
  — Wayne Gretzky, Los Angeles, 1993. 24 games.
  — Doug Gilmour, Toronto, 1993. 21 games.

MOST ASSISTS BY A DEFENSEMAN, ONE PLAYOFF YEAR:
25 — **Paul Coffey, Edmonton,** 1985. 18 games.
24 — Al MacInnis, Calgary, 1989. 22 games.
23 — Brian Leetch, NY Rangers, 1994. 23 games.
19 — Bobby Orr, Boston, 1972. 15 games.
18 — Ray Bourque, Boston, 1988. 23 games.
  — Ray Bourque, Boston, 1991. 19 games.
  — Larry Murphy, Pittsburgh, 1991. 23 games.

MOST MINUTES PLAYED BY A GOALTENDER, ONE PLAYOFF YEAR:
1,544 — **Kirk McLean, Vancouver,** 1994. 24 games.
1,540 — Ron Hextall, Philadelphia, 1987. 26 games.
1,477 — Mike Richter, NY Rangers, 1994. 23 games.
1,401 — Bill Ranford, Edmonton, 1990. 22 games.
1,381 — Mike Vernon, Calgary, 1989. 22 games.

MOST WINS BY A GOALTENDER, ONE PLAYOFF YEAR:
16 — **Grant Fuhr, Edmonton,** 1988. 19 games.
  — **Mike Vernon, Calgary,** 1989. 22 games.
  — **Bill Ranford, Edmonton,** 1990. 22 games.
  — **Tom Barrasso, Pittsburgh,** 1992. 21 games.
  — **Patrick Roy, Montreal,** 1993. 20 games.
  — **Mike Richter, NY Rangers,** 1994. 23 games.
  — **Martin Brodeur, New Jersey,** 1995. 20 games.
15 — Bill Smith, NY Islanders, 1980. 20 games.
  — Bill Smith, NY Islanders, 1982. 18 games.
  — Grant Fuhr, Edmonton, 1985. 18 games.
  — Patrick Roy, Montreal, 1986. 20 games.
  — Ron Hextall, Philadelphia, 1987. 26 games.
  — Kirk McLean, Vancouver, 1994. 24 games.

MOST CONSECUTIVE WINS BY A GOALTENDER, ONE PLAYOFF YEAR:
11 — **Ed Belfour, Chicago,** 1992. 3 wins against St. Louis in DSF, won by Chicago 4-2; 4 wins against Detroit in DF, won by Chicago 4-0; and 4 wins against Edmonton in CF, won by Chicago 4-0.
  — **Tom Barrasso, Pittsburgh,** 1992. 3 wins against NY Rangers in DF, won by Pittsburgh 4-2; 4 wins against Boston in CF, won by Pittsburgh 4-0; and 4 wins against Chicago in F, won by Pittsburgh 4-0.
  — **Patrick Roy, Montreal,** 1993. 4 wins against Quebec in DSF, won by Montreal 4-2; 4 wins against Buffalo in DF, won by Montreal 4-0; and 3 wins against NY Islanders in CF, won by Montreal 4-1.

MOST SHUTOUTS, ONE PLAYOFF YEAR:
4 — **Clint Benedict, Mtl. Maroons,** 1926. 8 games.
  — **Clint Benedict, Mtl. Maroons,** 1928. 9 games.
  — **Dave Kerr, NY Rangers,** 1937. 9 games.
  — **Frank McCool, Toronto,** 1945. 13 games.
  — **Terry Sawchuk, Detroit,** 1952. 8 games.
  — **Bernie Parent, Philadelphia,** 1975. 17 games.
  — **Ken Dryden, Montreal,** 1977. 14 games.
  — **Mike Richter, NY Rangers,** 1994. 23 games.
  — **Kirk McLean, Vancouver,** 1994. 24 games.

MOST CONSECUTIVE SHUTOUTS:
3 — **Clint Benedict, Mtl. Maroons,** 1926. Benedict shut out Ottawa 1-0, Mar. 27; he then shut out Victoria twice, 3-0, Mar. 30; 3-0, Apr. 1. Mtl. Maroons won NHL F vs. Ottawa 2 goals to 1 and won the best-of-five F vs. Victoria 3-1.
  — **John Roach, NY Rangers,** 1929. Roach shutout NY Americans twice, 0-0, Mar. 19; 1-0, Mar. 21; he then shutout Toronto 1-0, Mar. 24. NY Rangers won QF vs. NY Americans 1 goal to 0 and won the best-of-three SF vs. Toronto 2-0.
  — **Frank McCool, Toronto,** 1945. McCool shut out Detroit 1-0, April 6; 2-0, April 8; 1-0, April 12. Toronto won the best-of-seven F 4-3.

LONGEST SHUTOUT SEQUENCE:
248 Minutes, 32 Seconds — **Norm Smith, Detroit,** 1936. In best-of-five SF, Smith shut out Mtl. Maroons 1-0, March 24, in 116:30 overtime; shut out Maroons 3-0 in second game, March 26; and was scored against at 12:02 of first period, March 29, by Gus Marker. Detroit won SF 3-0.

Left: The Philadelphia Flyers mob goaltender Bernie Parent after blanking the Boston Bruins 1-0 to win the 1974 Stanley Cup Finals. The Flyers were the first Cup winner from the "Second Six" teams that joined the NHL in 1967. Below: George Armstrong sealed the fate of the Detroit Red Wings when he slipped this shot past Terry Sawchuk at the 15:26 mark of the third period to give the Leafs a commanding 4-0 lead in the seventh and deciding game of the 1964 Stanley Cup Finals.

One-Series Records

MOST POINTS IN FINAL SERIES:
13 — **Wayne Gretzky, Edmonton,** in 1988, 4 games plus suspended game vs. Boston. 3 goals, 10 assists.
12 — Gordie Howe, Detroit, in 1955, 7 games vs. Montreal. 5 goals, 7 assists.
 — Yvan Cournoyer, Montreal, in 1973, 6 games vs. Chicago. 6 goals, 6 assists.
 — Jacques Lemaire, Montreal, in 1973, 6 games vs. Chicago. 3 goals, 9 assists.
 — Mario Lemieux, Pittsburgh, in 1991, 5 games vs. Minnesota. 5 goals, 7 assists.

MOST GOALS IN FINAL SERIES:
9 — **Babe Dye, Toronto,** in 1922, 5 games vs. Van. Millionaires.
8 — Alf Skinner, Toronto, in 1918, 5 games vs. Van. Millionaires.
7 — Jean Beliveau, Montreal, in 1956, during 5 games vs. Detroit.
 — Mike Bossy, NY Islanders, in 1982, during 4 games vs. Vancouver.
 — Wayne Gretzky, Edmonton, in 1985, during 5 games vs. Philadelphia.

MOST ASSISTS IN FINAL SERIES:
10 — **Wayne Gretzky, Edmonton,** in 1988, 4 games plus suspended game vs. Boston.
9 — Jacques Lemaire, Montreal, in 1973, 6 games vs. Chicago.
 — Wayne Gretzky, Edmonton, in 1987, 7 games vs. Philadelphia.
 — Larry Murphy, Pittsburgh, in 1991, 6 games vs. Minnesota.

MOST POINTS IN ONE SERIES (OTHER THAN FINAL):
19 — **Rick Middleton, Boston,** in 1983 DF, 7 games vs. Buffalo. 5 goals, 14 assists.
18 — Wayne Gretzky, Edmonton, in 1985 CF, 6 games vs. Chicago. 4 goals, 14 assists.
17 — Mario Lemieux, Pittsburgh, in 1992 DSF, 6 games vs. Washington. 7 goals, 10 assists.
16 — Barry Pederson, Boston, in 1983 DF, 7 games vs. Buffalo. 7 goals, 9 assists.
 — Doug Gilmour, Toronto, in 1994 CSF, 7 games vs. San Jose. 3 goals, 13 assists.
15 — Jari Kurri, Edmonton, in 1985 CF, 6 games vs. Chicago. 12 goals, 3 assists.
 — Wayne Gretzky, Edmonton, in 1987 DSF, 5 games vs. Los Angeles. 2 goals, 13 assists.
 — Tim Kerr, Philadelphia, in 1989 DF, 7 games vs. Pittsburgh. 10 goals, 5 assists.
 — Mario Lemieux, Pittsburgh, in 1991 CF, 6 games vs. Boston. 6 goals, 9 assists.

MOST GOALS IN ONE SERIES (OTHER THAN FINAL):
12 — **Jari Kurri, Edmonton,** in 1985 CF, 6 games vs. Chicago.
11 — Newsy Lalonde, Montreal, in 1919 NHL F, 5 games vs. Ottawa.
10 — Tim Kerr, Philadelphia, in 1989 DF, 7 games vs. Pittsburgh.
9 — Reggie Leach, Philadelphia, in 1976 SF, 5 games vs. Boston.
 — Bill Barber, Philadelphia, in 1980 SF, 5 games vs. Minnesota.
 — Mike Bossy, NY Islanders, in 1983 CF, 6 games vs. Boston.
 — Mario Lemieux, Pittsburgh, in 1989 DF, 7 games vs. Philadelphia.

MOST ASSISTS IN ONE SERIES (OTHER THAN FINAL):
14 — **Rick Middleton, Boston,** in 1983 DF, 7 games vs. Buffalo.
 — **Wayne Gretzky, Edmonton,** in 1985 CF, 6 games vs. Chicago.
13 — Wayne Gretzky, Edmonton, in 1987 DSF, 5 games vs. Los Angeles.
 — Doug Gilmour, Toronto, in 1994 CSF, 7 games vs. San Jose.
11 — Mark Messier, Edmonton, in 1989 DSF, 7 games vs. Los Angeles.
 — Al MacInnis, Calgary, in 1984 DF, 7 games vs. Edmonton.
 — Mike Ridley, Washington, in 1992 DSF, 7 games vs. Pittsburgh.
 — Ron Francis, Pittsburgh, in 1995 CQF, 7 games vs. Washington.
10 — Fleming Mackell, Boston, in 1958 SF, 6 games vs. NY Rangers.
 — Stan Mikita, Chicago, in 1962 SF, 6 games vs. Montreal.
 — Bob Bourne, NY Islanders, in 1983 DF, 6 games vs. NY Rangers.
 — Wayne Gretzky, Edmonton, in 1988 DSF, 5 games vs. Winnipeg.
 — Mario Lemieux, Pittsburgh, in 1992 DSF, 6 games vs. Washington.

MOST GAME-WINNING GOALS, ONE PLAYOFF SERIES:
4 — **Mike Bossy, NY Islanders,** 1983, CF vs. Boston, won by NY Islanders 4-2.

MOST OVERTIME GOALS, ONE PLAYOFF SERIES:
3 — **Mel Hill, Boston,** 1939, SF vs. NY Rangers, won by Boston 4-3. Hill scored at 59:25 overtime March 21 for a 2-1 win; at 8:24, March 23 for a 3-2 win; and at 48:00, April 2 for a 2-1 win.

MOST POWER-PLAY GOALS, ONE PLAYOFF SERIES:
6 — **Chris Kontos, Los Angeles,** 1989, DSF vs. Edmonton, won by Los Angeles 4-3.
5 — Andy Bathgate, Detroit, 1966, SF vs. Chicago, won by Detroit 4-2.
 — Denis Potvin, NY Islanders, 1981, QF vs. Edmonton, won by NY Islanders 4-2.
 — Ken Houston, Calgary, 1981, QF vs. Philadelphia, won by Calgary 4-3.
 — Rick Vaive, Chicago, 1988, DSF vs. St. Louis, won by St. Louis 4-1.
 — Tim Kerr, Philadelphia, 1989, DF vs. Pittsburgh, won by Philadelphia 4-3.
 — Mario Lemieux, Pittsburgh, 1989, DF vs. Philadelphia won by Philadelphia 4-3.
 — John Druce, Washington, 1990, DF vs. NY Rangers won by Washington 4-1.
 — Pat LaFontaine, Buffalo, 1992, DSF vs. Boston won by Boston 4-3.

MOST SHORTHAND GOALS, ONE PLAYOFF SERIES:
3 — **Bill Barber, Philadelphia,** 1980, SF vs. Minnesota, won by Philadelphia 4-1.
 — **Wayne Presley, Chicago,** 1989, DSF vs. Detroit, won by Chicago 4-2.
2 — Mac Colville, NY Rangers, 1940, SF vs. Boston, won by NY Rangers 4-2.
 — Jerry Toppazzini, Boston, 1958, SF vs. NY Rangers, won by Boston 4-2.
 — Dave Keon, Toronto, 1963, F vs. Detroit, won by Toronto 4-1.
 — Bob Pulford, Toronto, 1964, F vs. Detroit, won by Toronto 4-3.
 — Serge Savard, Montreal, 1968, F vs. St. Louis, won by Montreal 4-0.
 — Derek Sanderson, Boston, 1969, SF vs. Montreal, won by Montreal 4-2.
 — Bryan Trottier, NY Islanders, 1980, PR vs. Los Angeles, won by NY Islanders 3-1.
 — Bobby Lalonde, Boston, 1981, PR vs. Minnesota, won by Minnesota 3-0.
 — Butch Goring, NY Islanders, 1981, SF vs. NY Rangers, won by NY Islanders 4-0.
 — Wayne Gretzky, Edmonton, 1983, DSF vs. Winnipeg, won by Edmonton 3-0.
 — Mark Messier, Edmonton, 1983, DF vs. Calgary, won by Edmonton 4-1.
 — Jari Kurri, Edmonton, 1983, CF vs. Chicago, won by Edmonton 4-0.
 — Wayne Gretzky, Edmonton, 1985, DF vs. Winnipeg, won by Edmonton 4-0.
 — Kevin Lowe, Edmonton, 1987, F vs. Philadelphia, won by Edmonton 4-3.
 — Bob Gould, Washington, 1988, DSF vs. Philadelphia, won by Washington 4-3.
 — Dave Poulin, Philadelphia, 1989, DF vs. Pittsburgh, won by Philadelphia 4-3.
 — Russ Courtnall, Montreal, 1991, DF vs. Boston, won by Boston 4-3.
 — Sergei Fedorov, Detroit, 1992 DSF vs. Minnesota, won by Detroit 4-3.
 — Mark Messier, NY Rangers, 1992, DSF vs. New Jersey, won by NY Rangers 4-3.
 — Tom Fitzgerald, NY Islanders, 1993, DF vs. Pittsburgh, won by NY Islanders 4-3.
 — Mark Osborne, Toronto, 1994, CSF vs. San Jose, won by Toronto 4-3.

MOST THREE-OR-MORE-GOAL GAMES, ONE PLAYOFF SERIES:
3 — **Jari Kurri, Edmonton** 1985, CF vs. Chicago won by Edmonton 4-2. Kurri scored 3 G May 7 at Edmonton in 7-3 win, 3 G May 14 in 10-5 win and 4 G May 16 at Chicago in 8-2 win.
2 — Doug Bentley, Chicago, 1944, SF vs. Detroit, won by Chicago 4-1. Bentley scored 3 G Mar. 28 at Chicago in 7-1 win and 3 G Mar. 30 at Detroit in 5-2 win.
— Norm Ullman, Detroit, 1964, SF vs. Chicago, won by Detroit 4-3. Ullman scored 3 G Mar. 29 at Chicago in 7-1 win and 3 G April 7 at Detroit in 7-2 win.
— Mark Messier, Edmonton, 1983, DF vs. Calgary won by Edmonton 4-1. Messier scored 4 G April 14 at Edmonton in 6-3 win and 3 G April 17 at Calgary in 10-2 win.
— Mike Bossy, NY Islanders, 1983, CF vs. Boston won by NY Islanders 4-2. Bossy scored 3 G May 3 at New York in 8-3 win and 4 G on May 7 at New York in 8-4 win.

Single Playoff Game Records

MOST POINTS, ONE GAME:
8 — **Patrik Sundstrom, New Jersey,** April 22, 1988 at New Jersey during 10-4 win over Washington. Sundstrom had 3 goals, 5 assists.
— **Mario Lemieux, Pittsburgh,** April 25, 1989 at Pittsburgh during 10-7 win over Philadelphia. Lemieux had 5 goals, 3 assists.
7 — Wayne Gretzky, Edmonton, April 17, 1983 at Calgary during 10-2 win. Gretzky had 4 goals, 3 assists.
— Wayne Gretzky, Edmonton, April 25, 1985 at Winnipeg during 8-3 win. Gretzky had 3 goals, 4 assists.
— Wayne Gretzky, Edmonton, April 9, 1987, at Edmonton during 13-3 win over Los Angeles. Gretzky had 1 goal, 6 assists.
6 — Dickie Moore, Montreal, March 25, 1954, at Montreal during 8-1 win over Boston. Moore had 2 goals, 4 assists.
— Phil Esposito, Boston, April 2, 1969, at Boston during 10-0 win over Toronto. Esposito had 4 goals, 2 assists.
— Darryl Sittler, Toronto, April 22, 1976, at Toronto during 8-5 win over Philadelphia. Sittler had 5 goals, 1 assist.
— Guy Lafleur, Montreal, April 11, 1977, at Montreal during 7-2 victory vs. St. Louis. Lafleur had 3 goals, 3 assists.
— Mikko Leinonen, NY Rangers, April 8, 1982, at New York during 7-3 win over Philadelphia. Leinonen had 6 assists.
— Paul Coffey, Edmonton, May 14, 1985 at Edmonton during 10-5 win over Chicago. Coffey had 1 goal, 5 assists.
— John Anderson, Hartford, April 12, 1986 at Hartford during 9-4 win over Quebec. Anderson had 2 goals, 4 assists.
— Mario Lemieux, Pittsburgh, April 23, 1992 at Pittsburgh during 6-4 win over Washington. Lemieux had 3 goals, 3 assists.

MOST POINTS BY A DEFENSEMAN, ONE GAME:
6 — **Paul Coffey, Edmonton,** May 14, 1985 at Edmonton vs. Chicago. 1 goal, 5 assists. Edmonton won 10-5.
5 — Eddie Bush, Detroit, April 9, 1942, at Detroit vs. Toronto. 1 goal, 4 assists. Detroit won 5-2.
— Bob Dailey, Philadelphia, May 1, 1980, at Philadelphia vs. Minnesota. 1 goal, 4 assists. Philadelphia won 7-0.
— Denis Potvin, NY Islanders, April 17, 1981, at New York vs. Edmonton. 3 goals, 2 assists. NY Islanders won 6-3.
— Risto Siltanen, Quebec, April 14, 1987 at Hartford. 5 assists. Quebec won 7-5.

MOST GOALS, ONE GAME:
5 — **Newsy Lalonde, Montreal,** March 1, 1919, at Montreal. Final score: Montreal 6, Ottawa 3.
— **Maurice Richard, Montreal,** March 23, 1944, at Montreal. Final score: Montreal 5, Toronto 1.
— **Darryl Sittler, Toronto,** April 22, 1976, at Toronto. Final score: Toronto 8, Philadelphia 5.
— **Reggie Leach, Philadelphia,** May 6, 1976, at Philadelphia. Final score: Philadelphia 6, Boston 3.
— **Mario Lemieux, Pittsburgh,** April 25, 1989 at Pittsburgh. Final score: Pittsburgh 10, Philadelphia 7.

MOST GOALS BY A DEFENSEMAN, ONE GAME:
3 — **Bobby Orr, Boston,** April 11, 1971 at Montreal. Final score: Boston 5, Montreal 2.
— **Dick Redmond, Chicago,** April 4, 1973 at Chicago. Final score: Chicago 7, St. Louis 1.
— **Denis Potvin, NY Islanders,** April 17, 1981 at New York. Final score: NY Islanders 6, Edmonton 3.
— **Paul Reinhart, Calgary,** April 14, 1983 at Edmonton. Final score: Edmonton 6, Calgary 3.
— **Paul Reinhart, Calgary,** April 8, 1984 at Vancouver. Final score: Calgary 5, Vancouver 1.
— **Doug Halward, Vancouver,** April 7, 1984 at Vancouver. Final score: Vancouver 7, Calgary 0.
— **Al Iafrate, Washington,** April 26, 1993 at Washington. Final score: Washington 6, NY Islanders 4.
— **Eric Desjardins, Montreal,** June 3, 1993 at Montreal. Final score: Montreal 3, Los Angeles 2.
— **Gary Suter, Chicago,** April 24, 1994, at Chicago. Final score: Chicago 4, Toronto 3.
— **Brian Leetch, NY Rangers,** May 22, 1995 at Philadelphia. Final score: Philadelphia 4, NY Rangers 3.

MOST POWER-PLAY GOALS, ONE GAME:
3 — **Syd Howe, Detroit,** March 23, 1939, at Detroit vs. Montreal, Detroit won 7-3.
— **Sid Smith, Toronto,** April 10, 1949, at Detroit. Toronto won 3-1.
— **Phil Esposito, Boston,** April 2, 1969 vs. Toronto. Boston won 10-0.
— **John Bucyk, Boston,** April 21, 1974, at Boston vs. Chicago. Boston won 8-6.
— **Denis Potvin, NY Islanders,** April 17, 1981, at New York vs. Edmonton. NY Islanders won 6-3.
— **Tim Kerr, Philadelphia,** April 13, 1985, at NY Rangers. Philadelphia won 6-5.
— **Jari Kurri, Edmonton,** April 9, 1987, at Edmonton vs. Los Angeles. Edmonton won 13-3.
— **Mark Johnson, New Jersey,** April 22, 1988, at New Jersey vs. Washington. New Jersey won 10-4.
— **Dino Ciccarelli, Detroit,** April 29, 1993, at Toronto, in 7-3 win by Detroit.
— **Dino Ciccarelli, Detroit,** May 11, 1995, at Dallas, in 5-1 win by Detroit.

MOST SHORTHAND GOALS, ONE GAME:
2 — **Dave Keon, Toronto,** April 18, 1963, at Toronto, in 3-1 win vs. Detroit.
— **Bryan Trottier, NY Islanders,** April 8, 1980 at New York, in 8-1 win vs. Los Angeles.
— **Bobby Lalonde, Boston,** April 11, 1981 at Minnesota, in 6-3 win by Minnesota.
— **Wayne Gretzky, Edmonton,** April 6, 1983 at Edmonton, in 6-3 win vs. Winnipeg.
— **Jari Kurri, Edmonton,** April 24, 1983, at Edmonton, in 8-3 win vs. Chicago.
— **Mark Messier, NY Rangers,** April 21, 1992, at New York, in 7-3 loss vs. New Jersey.
— **Tom Fitzgerald, NY Islanders,** May 8, 1993, at Long Island, in 6-5 win vs. Pittsburgh.

MOST ASSISTS, ONE GAME:
6 — **Mikko Leinonen, NY Rangers,** April 8, 1982, at New York. Final score: NY Rangers 7, Philadelphia 3.
— **Wayne Gretzky, Edmonton,** April 9, 1987, at Edmonton. Final score: Edmonton 13, Los Angeles 3.
5 — Toe Blake, Montreal, March 23, 1944, at Montreal. Final score: Montreal 5, Toronto 1.
— Maurice Richard, Montreal, March 27, 1956, at Montreal. Final score: Montreal 7, NY Rangers 0.
— Bert Olmstead, Montreal, March 30, 1957, at Montreal. Final score: Montreal 8, NY Rangers 3.
— Don McKenney, Boston, April 5, 1958, at Boston. Final score: Boston 8, NY Rangers 2.
— Stan Mikita, Chicago, April 4, 1973, at Chicago. Final score: Chicago 7, St. Louis 1.
— Wayne Gretzky, Edmonton, April 8, 1981, at Montreal. Final score: Edmonton 6, Montreal 3.
— Paul Coffey, Edmonton, May 14, 1985, at Edmonton. Final score: Edmonton 10, Chicago 5.
— Doug Gilmour, St. Louis, April 15, 1986, at Minnesota. Final score: St. Louis 6, Minnesota 3.
— Risto Siltanen, Quebec, April 14, 1987 at Hartford. Final score: Quebec 7, Hartford 5.
— Patrik Sundstrom, New Jersey, April 22, 1988, at New Jersey. Final score: New Jersey 10, Washington 4.

MOST PENALTY MINUTES, ONE GAME:
42 — **Dave Schultz, Philadelphia,** April 22, 1976, at Toronto. One minor, 2 majors, 1 10-minute misconduct and 2 game-misconducts. Final score: Toronto 8, Philadelphia 5.

MOST PENALTIES, ONE GAME:
8 — **Forbes Kennedy, Toronto,** April 2, 1969, at Boston. Four minors, 2 majors, 1 10-minute misconduct, 1 game misconduct. Final score: Boston 10, Toronto 0.
— **Kim Clackson, Pittsburgh,** April 14, 1980, at Boston. Five minors, 2 majors, 1 10-minute misconduct. Final score: Boston 6, Pittsburgh 2

MOST POINTS, ONE PERIOD:
4 — **Maurice Richard, Montreal,** March 29, 1945, at Montreal vs. Toronto. Third period, 3 goals, 1 assist. Final score: Montreal 10, Toronto 3.
— **Dickie Moore, Montreal,** March 25, 1954, at Montreal vs. Boston. First period, 2 goals, 2 assists. Final score: Montreal 8, Boston 1.
— **Barry Pederson, Boston,** April 8, 1982, at Boston vs. Buffalo. Second period, 3 goals, 1 assist. Final score: Boston 7, Buffalo 3.
— **Peter McNab, Boston,** April 11, 1982, at Buffalo. Second period, 1 goal, 3 assists. Final score: Boston 5, Buffalo 2.
— **Tim Kerr, Philadelphia,** April 13, 1985 at New York. Second period, 4 goals. Final score: Philadelphia 6, Rangers 5.
— **Ken Linseman, Boston,** April 14, 1985 at Boston vs. Montreal. Second period, 2 goals, 2 assists. Final score: Boston 7, Montreal 6.
— **Wayne Gretzky, Edmonton,** April 12, 1987 at Los Angeles. Third period, 1 goal, 3 assists. Final score: Edmonton 6, Los Angeles 3.
— **Glenn Anderson, Edmonton,** April 6, 1988, at Edmonton vs. Winnipeg. Third period, 3 goals, 1 assist. Final score: Edmonton 7, Winnipeg 4.
— **Mario Lemieux, Pittsburgh,** April 25, 1989 at Pittsburgh vs. Philadelphia. First period, 4 goals. Final score: Pittsburgh 10, Philadelphia 7.
— **Dave Gagner, Minnesota,** April 8, 1991, at Minnesota vs. Chicago. First period, 2 goals, 2 assists. Final score: Chicago 6, Minnesota 5.
— **Mario Lemieux, Pittsburgh,** April 23, 1992, at Pittsburgh vs. Washington. Second period, 2 goals, 2 assists. Final score: Pittsburgh 6, Washington 4.

PLAYOFF INDIVIDUAL RECORDS • 119

MOST GOALS, ONE PERIOD:
4 — Tim Kerr, Philadelphia, April 13, 1985, at New York vs. NY Rangers, second period. Final score: Philadelphia 6, NY Rangers 5.
— **Mario Lemieux, Pittsburgh,** April 25, 1989, at Pittsburgh vs. Philadelphia, first period. Final score: Pittsburgh 10, Philadelphia 7.
3 — Harvey (Busher) Jackson, Toronto, April 5, 1932, at New York vs. NY Rangers, second period. Final score: Toronto 6, NY Rangers 4.
— Maurice Richard, Montreal, March 23, 1944, at Montreal vs. Toronto, second period. Final score: Montreal 5, Toronto 1.
— Maurice Richard, Montreal, March 29, 1945, at Montreal vs. Toronto, third period. Final score: Montreal 10, Toronto 3.
— Maurice Richard, Montreal, April 6, 1957 at Montreal vs. Boston, second period. Final score: Montreal 5, Boston 1.
— Ted Lindsay, Detroit, April 5, 1955, at Detroit vs. Montreal, second period. Final score: Detroit 7, Montreal 1.
— Red Berenson, St. Louis, April 15, 1969, at St. Louis vs. Los Angeles, second period. Final score: St. Louis 4, Los Angeles 0.
— Jacques Lemaire, Montreal, April 20, 1971, at Montreal vs. Minnesota, second period. Final score: Montreal 7, Minnesota 2.
— Rick MacLeish, Philadelphia, April 11, 1974, at Philadelphia vs. Atlanta, second period. Final score: Philadelphia 5, Atlanta 1.
— Tom Williams, Los Angeles, April 14, 1974, at Los Angeles vs. Chicago, third period. Final score: Los Angeles 5, Chicago 1.
— Darryl Sittler, Toronto, April 22, 1976, at Toronto vs. Philadelphia, second period. Final score: Toronto 8, Philadelphia 5.
— Reggie Leach, Philadelphia, May 6, 1976, at Philadelphia vs. Boston, second period. Final score: Philadelphia 6, Boston 3.
— Bobby Schmautz, Boston, April 11, 1977, at Boston vs. Los Angeles, first period. Final score: Boston 8, Los Angeles 3.
— George Ferguson, Toronto, April 11, 1978, at Toronto vs. Los Angeles, third period. Final score: Toronto 7, Los Angeles 3.
— Barry Pederson, Boston, April 8, 1982, at Boston vs. Buffalo, second period. Final score: Boston 7, Buffalo 3.
— Peter Stastny, Quebec, April 5, 1983, at Boston, first period. Final score: Boston 4, Quebec 3.
— Wayne Gretzky, Edmonton, April 6, 1983 at Edmonton, second period. Final score: Edmonton 6, Winnipeg 3.
— Mike Bossy, NY Islanders, May 7, 1983 at New York, second period. Final score: NY Islanders 8, Boston 4.
— Dave Andreychuk, Buffalo, April 14, 1985, at Buffalo vs. Quebec, third period. Final score: Buffalo 7, Quebec 4.
— Wayne Gretzky, Edmonton, May 25, 1985, at Edmonton vs. Philadelphia, first period. Final score: Edmonton 4, Philadelphia 3.
— Glenn Anderson, Edmonton, April 6, 1988, at Edmonton vs. Winnipeg, third period. Final score: Edmonton 7, Winnipeg 4.
— Tim Kerr, Philadelphia, April 19, 1989, at Pittsburgh vs. Penguins, first period. Final score: Philadelphia 4, Pittsburgh 2.
— Petr Klima, Edmonton, May 4, 1991, at Edmonton vs. Minnesota, first period. Final score: Edmonton 7, Minnesota 2.
— Dino Ciccarelli, Washington, April 25, 1992, at Pittsburgh, third period. Final score: Washington 7, Pittsburgh 2.
— Kevin Stevens, Pittsburgh, May 17, 1992, at Boston, first period. Final score: Pittsburgh 5, Boston 1.
— Dirk Graham, Chicago, June 1, 1992, at Chicago vs. Pittsburgh, first period. Final score: Pittsburgh 6, Chicago 5.
— Ray Ferraro, NY Islanders, April 26, 1993, at Washington, third period. Final score: Washington 6, NY Islanders 4.
— Mark Messier, NY Rangers, May 25, 1994, at New Jersey, third period. Final score: NY Rangers 4, New Jersey 2.
— Brendan Shanahan, St. Louis, May 13, 1995, at Vancouver, second period. Final score: St. Louis 5, Vancouver 4.

MOST POWER-PLAY GOALS, ONE PERIOD:
3 — Tim Kerr, Philadelphia, April 13, 1985 at New York, second period in 6-5 win vs. NY Rangers.
2 — Two power-play goals have been scored by one player in one period on 43 occasions. Charlie Conacher of Toronto was the first to score two power-play goals in one period, setting the mark on Mar. 26, 1936. Dmitri Mironov of Toronto is the most recent to equal this mark with two power-play goals in the second period at Toronto, May 18, 1994. Final score: Vancouver 4, Toronto 3.

MOST SHORTHAND GOALS, ONE PERIOD:
2 — Bryan Trottier, NY Islanders, April 8, 1980, second period at New York in 8-1 win vs. Los Angeles.
— **Bobby Lalonde, Boston,** April 11, 1981, third period at Minnesota in 6-3 win by Minnesota.
— **Jari Kurri, Edmonton,** April 24, 1983, third period at Edmonton in 8-4 win vs. Chicago.

MOST ASSISTS, ONE PERIOD:
3 — Three assists by one player in one period of a playoff game has been recorded on 62 occasions. Vyacheslav Kozlov of the Detroit Red Wings is the most recent to equal this mark with 3 assists in the third period at Detroit, May 21, 1995. Final score: Detroit 6, San Jose 0.
Wayne Gretzky has had 3 assists in one period 5 times; Ray Bourque, 3 times; Toe Blake, Jean Beliveau, Doug Harvey and Bobby Orr, twice. Nick Metz of Toronto was the first player to be credited with 3 assists in one period of a playoff game Mar. 21, 1941 at Toronto vs. Boston.

MOST PENALTIES, ONE PERIOD AND MOST PENALTY MINUTES, ONE PERIOD:
6 Penalties; 39 Minutes — Ed Hospodar, NY Rangers, April 9, 1981, at Los Angeles, first period. Two minors, 1 major, 1 10-minute misconduct, 2 game misconducts. Final score: Los Angeles 5, NY Rangers 4.

FASTEST TWO GOALS:
5 Seconds — Norm Ullman, Detroit, at Detroit, April 11, 1965, vs. Chicago and goaltender Glenn Hall. Ullman scored at 17:35 and 17:40 of second period. Detroit won 4-2.

FASTEST GOAL FROM START OF GAME:
6 Seconds — Don Kozak, Los Angeles, April 17, 1977, at Los Angeles vs. Boston and goaltender Gerry Cheevers. Los Angeles won 7-4.
7 Seconds — Bob Gainey, Montreal, May 5, 1977, at New York vs. NY Islanders and goaltender Glenn Resch. Montreal won 2-1.
— Terry Murray, Philadelphia, April 12, 1981, at Quebec vs. goaltender Dan Bouchard. Quebec won 4-3 in overtime.
8 Seconds — Stan Smyl, Vancouver, April 7, 1982, at Vancouver vs. Calgary and goaltender Pat Riggin. Vancouver won 5-3.

FASTEST GOAL FROM START OF PERIOD (OTHER THAN FIRST):
6 Seconds — Pelle Eklund, Phiadelphia, April 25, 1989, at Pittsburgh vs. goaltender Tom Barrasso, second period. Pittsburgh won 10-7.
9 Seconds — Bill Collins, Minnesota, April 9, 1968, at Minnesota vs. Los Angeles and goaltender Wayne Rutledge, third period. Minnesota won 7-5.
— Dave Balon, Minnesota, April 25, 1968, at St. Louis vs. goaltender Glenn Hall, third period. Minnesota won 5-1.
— Murray Oliver, Minnesota, April 8, 1971, at St. Louis vs. goaltender Ernie Wakely, third period. St. Louis won 4-2.
— Clark Gillies, NY Islanders, April 15, 1977, at Buffalo vs. goaltender Don Edwards, third period. NY Islanders won 4-3.
— Eric Vail, Atlanta, April 11, 1978, at Atlanta vs. Detroit and goaltender Ron Low, third period. Detroit won 5-3.
— Stan Smyl, Vancouver, April 10, 1979, at Philadelphia vs. goaltender Wayne Stephenson, third period. Vancouver won 3-2.
— Wayne Gretzky, Edmonton, April 6, 1983, at Edmonton vs. Winnipeg and goaltender Brian Hayward, second period. Edmonton won 6-3.
— Mark Messier, Edmonton, April 16, 1984, at Calgary vs. goaltender Don Edwards, third period. Edmonton won 5-3.
— Brian Skrudland, Montreal, May 18, 1986 at Calgary vs. goaltender Mike Vernon, overtime. Montreal won 3-2.

FASTEST TWO GOALS FROM START OF GAME:
1 Minute, 8 Seconds — Dick Duff, Toronto, April 9, 1963 at Toronto vs. Detroit and goaltender Terry Sawchuk. Duff scored at 49 seconds and 1:08. Final score: Toronto 4, Detroit 2.

FASTEST TWO GOALS FROM START OF PERIOD:
35 Seconds — Pat LaFontaine, NY Islanders, May 19, 1984 at Edmonton vs. goaltender Andy Moog. LaFontaine scored at 13 and 35 seconds of third period. Final score: Edmonton 5, NY Islanders 2.

Early Playoff Records
1893-1918
Team Records

MOST GOALS, BOTH TEAMS, ONE GAME:
25 — **Ottawa Silver Seven, Dawson City** at Ottawa, Jan. 16, 1905. Ottawa 23, Dawson City 2. Ottawa won best-of-three series 2-0.

MOST GOALS, ONE TEAM, ONE GAME:
23 — **Ottawa Silver Seven** at Ottawa, Jan. 16, 1905. Ottawa defeated Dawson City 23-2.

MOST GOALS, BOTH TEAMS, BEST-OF-THREE SERIES:
42 — **Ottawa Silver Seven, Queen's University** at Ottawa, 1906. Ottawa defeated Queen's 16-7, Feb. 27, and 12-7, Feb. 28.

MOST GOALS, ONE TEAM, BEST-OF-THREE SERIES:
32 — **Ottawa Silver Seven** in 1905 at Ottawa. Defeated Dawson City 9-2, Jan. 13, and 23-2, Jan. 16.

MOST GOALS, BOTH TEAMS, BEST-OF-FIVE SERIES:
39 — **Toronto Arenas, Vancouver Millionaires** at Toronto, 1918. Toronto won 5-3, Mar. 20; 6-3, Mar. 26; 2-1, Mar. 30. Vancouver won 6-4, Mar. 23, and 8-1, Mar. 28. Toronto scored 18 goals; Vancouver 21.

MOST GOALS, ONE TEAM, BEST-OF-FIVE SERIES:
26 — **Vancouver Millionaires** in 1915 at Vancouver. Defeated Ottawa Senators 6-2, Mar. 22; 8-3, Mar. 24; and 12-3 Mar. 26.

Individual Records

MOST GOALS IN PLAYOFFS:
63 — **Frank McGee, Ottawa Silver Seven,** in 22 playoff games. Seven goals in four games, 1903; 21 goals in eight games, 1904; 18 goals in four games, 1905; 17 goals in six games, 1906.

MOST GOALS, ONE PLAYOFF SERIES:
15 — **Frank McGee, Ottawa Silver Seven,** in two games in 1905 at Ottawa. Scored one goal, Jan. 13, in 9-2 victory over Dawson City and 14 goals, Jan. 16, in 23-2 victory.

MOST GOALS, ONE PLAYOFF GAME:
14 — **Frank McGee, Ottawa Silver Seven,** Jan. 16, 1905 at Ottawa in 23-2 victory over Dawson City.

FASTEST THREE GOALS:
40 Seconds — **Marty Walsh, Ottawa Senators,** at Ottawa, March 16, 1911, at 3:00, 3:10, and 3:40 of third period. Ottawa defeated Port Arthur 13-4.

Three-or-more-Goal Games, Playoffs 1918–1995

Player	Team	Date	City	Total Goals	Opposing Goaltender	Score	
Wayne Gretzky (8)	Edm.	Apr. 11/81	Edm.	3	Richard Sevigny	Edm. 6	Mtl. 2
		Apr. 19/81	Edm.	3	Billy Smith	Edm. 5	NYI 2
		Apr. 6/83	Edm.	4	Brian Hayward	Edm. 6	Wpg. 3
		Apr. 17/83	Cgy.	4	Rejean Lemelin	Edm. 10	Cgy. 2
		Apr. 25/85	Wpg.	3	Bryan Hayward (2) Marc Behrend (1)	Edm. 8	Wpg. 3
		May 25/85	Edm.	3	Pelle Lindbergh	Edm. 4	Phi. 3
		Apr. 24/86	Cgy.	3	Mike Vernon	Edm. 7	Cgy. 4
	L.A.	May 29/93	Tor.	3	Felix Potvin	L.A. 5	Tor. 4
Maurice Richard (7)	Mtl.	Mar. 23/44	Mtl.	5	Paul Bibeault	Mtl. 5	Tor. 1
		Apr. 7/44	Chi.	3	Mike Karakas	Mtl. 3	Chi. 1
		Mar. 29/45	Mtl.	4	Frank McCool	Mtl. 10	Tor. 3
		Apr. 14/53	Bos.	3	Gord Henry	Mtl. 7	Bos. 3
		Mar. 20/56	Mtl.	3	Lorne Worsley	Mtl. 7	NYR 1
		Apr. 6/57	Mtl.	4	Don Simmons	Mtl. 5	Bos. 1
		Apr. 1/58	Det.	3	Terry Sawchuk	Mtl. 4	Det. 3
Jari Kurri (7)	Edm.	Apr. 4/84	Edm.	3	Doug Soetaert (1) Mike Veisor (2)	Edm. 9	Wpg. 2
		Apr. 25/85	Wpg.	3	Bryan Hayward (2) Marc Behrend (1)	Edm. 8	Wpg. 3
		May 7/85	Edm.	3	Murray Bannerman	Edm. 7	Chi. 3
		May 14/85	Edm.	3	Murray Bannerman	Edm. 10	Chi. 5
		May 16/85	Chi.	4	Murray Bannerman	Edm. 8	Chi. 2
		Apr. 9/87	Edm.	4	Roland Melanson (2) Daren Eliot (2)	Edm. 13	L.A. 3
		May 18/90	Bos.	3	Andy Moog (2) Rejean Lemelin (1)	Edm. 7	Bos. 2
Dino Ciccarelli (6)	Min.	May 5/81	Min.	3	Pat Riggin	Min. 7	Cgy. 4
		Apr. 10/82	Min.	3	Murray Bannerman	Min. 7	Chi. 1
	Wsh.	Apr. 5/90	N.J.	3	Sean Burke	Wsh. 5	N.J. 4
		Apr. 25/92	Pit.	4	Tom Barrasso (1) Ken Wregget (3)	Wsh. 7	Pit. 2
	Det.	Apr. 29/93	Tor.	3	Felix Potvin (2) Daren Puppa (1)	Det. 7	Tor. 3
		May 11/95	Dal.	3	Andy Moog (2) Darcy Wakaluk (1)	Det. 5	Dal. 1
Mike Bossy (5)	NYI	Apr. 16/79	NYI	3	Tony Esposito	NYI 6	Chi. 2
		May 8/82	NYI	3	Richard Brodeur	NYI 6	Van. 5
		Apr. 10/83	Wsh.	3	Al Jensen	NYI 6	Wsh. 3
		May 3/83	NYI	3	Pete Peeters	NYI 8	Bos. 3
		May 7/83	NYI	4	Pete Peeters	NYI 8	Bos. 4
Phil Esposito (4)	Bos.	Apr. 2/69	Bos.	4	Bruce Gamble	Bos. 10	Tor. 0
		Apr. 8/70	Bos.	3	Ed Giacomin	Bos. 8	NYR 2
		Apr. 19/70	Chi.	3	Tony Esposito	Bos. 6	Chi. 3
		Apr. 8/75	Bos.	3	Tony Esposito (2) Michel Dumas (1)	Bos. 8	Chi. 2
Mark Messier (4)	Edm.	Apr. 14/83	Edm.	4	Rejean Lemelin	Edm. 6	Cgy. 3
		Apr. 17/83	Cgy.	3	Rejean Lemelin (1) Don Edwards (2)	Edm. 10	Cgy. 2
		Apr. 26/83	Edm.	3	Murray Bannerman	Edm. 8	Chi. 2
	NYR	May 25/94	N.J.	3	Martin Brodeur (2) ENG (1)	NYR 4	N.J. 2
Bernie Geoffrion (3)	Mtl.	Mar. 27/52	Mtl.	3	Jim Henry	Mtl. 4	Bos. 0
		Apr. 7/55	Mtl.	3	Terry Sawchuk	Mtl. 4	Det. 2
		Mar. 30/57	Mtl.	3	Lorne Worsley	Mtl. 8	NYR 3
Norm Ullman (3)	Det.	Mar. 29/64	Chi.	3	Glenn Hall	Det. 5	Chi. 4
		Apr. 7/64	Det.	3	Glenn Hall (2) Denis DeJordy (1)	Det. 7	Chi. 2
		Apr. 11/65	Det.	3	Glenn Hall	Det. 4	Chi. 2
John Bucyk (3)	Bos.	May 3/70	St. L.	3	Jacques Plante (1) Ernie Wakely (2)	Bos. 6	St. L. 1
		Apr. 20/72	Bos.	3	Jacques Caron (1) Ernie Wakely (2)	Bos. 10	St. L. 2
		Apr. 21/74	Bos.	3	Tony Esposito	Bos. 8	Chi. 6
Rick MacLeish (3)	Phil	Apr. 11/74	Phil	3	Phil Myre	Phi. 5	Atl. 1
		Apr. 13/75	Phil	3	Gord McRae	Phi. 6	Tor. 3
		May 13/75	Phil	3	Glenn Resch	Phi. 4	NYI 1
Denis Savard (3)	Chi.	Apr. 19/82	Chi.	3	Mike Liut	Chi. 7	StL. 4
		Apr. 10/86	Chi.	4	Ken Wregget	Tor. 6	Chi. 4
		Apr. 9/88	St. L.	3	Greg Millen	Chi. 6	St. L. 3
Tim Kerr (3)	Phi.	Apr. 13/85	NYR	4	Glen Hanlon	Phi. 6	NYR 5
		Apr. 20/87	Phi.	3	Kelly Hrudey	Phi. 4	NYI 2
		Apr. 19/89	Pit.	3	Tom Barrasso	Phi. 4	Pit. 2
Cam Neely (3)	Bos.	Apr. 9/87	Mtl.	3	Patrick Roy	Mtl. 4	Bos. 3
		Apr. 5/91	Bos.	3	Peter Sidorkiewicz	Bos. 4	Hfd. 3
		Apr. 25/91	Bos.	3	Patrick Roy	Bos. 4	Mtl. 1
Petr Klima (3)	Det.	Apr. 7/88	Tor.	3	Alan Bester (2) Ken Wregett (1)	Det. 6	Tor. 2
		Apr. 21/88	St. L.	3	Greg Millen	Det. 6	St. L. 0
	Edm.	May 4/91	Edm.	3	Jon Casey	Edm. 7	Min. 2
Esa Tikkanen (3)	Edm.	May 22/88	Edm.	3	Rejean Lemelin	Edm. 6	Bos. 3
		Apr. 16/91	Cgy.	3	Mike Vernon	Edm. 5	Cgy. 4
		Apr. 26/92	L.A.	3	Kelly Hrudey	Edm. 5	L.A. 2
Newsy Lalonde (2)	Mtl.	Mar. 1/19	Mtl.	5	Clint Benedict	Mtl. 6	Ott. 3
		Mar. 22/19	Sea.	4	Harry Holmes	Mtl. 4	Sea. 2
Howie Morenz (2)	Mtl.	Mar. 22/24	Mtl.	3	Charles Reid	Mtl. 6	Cgy.T. 1
		Mar. 27/25	Mtl.	3	Harry Holmes	Mtl. 4	Vic. 2
Toe Blake (2)	Mtl.	Mar. 22/38	Mtl.	3	Mike Karakas	Mtl. 6	Chi. 4
		Mar. 26/46	Chi.	3	Mike Karakas	Mtl. 7	Chi. 2
Doug Bentley (2)	Chi.	Mar. 28/44	Chi.	3	Connie Dion	Chi. 7	Det. 1
		Mar. 30/44	Det.	3	Connie Dion	Chi. 5	Det. 2

Player	Team	Date	City	Total Goals	Opposing Goaltender	Score	
Ted Kennedy (2)	Tor.	Apr. 14/45	Tor.	3	Harry Lumley	Det. 5	Tor. 3
		Mar. 27/48	Tor.	4	Frank Brimsek	Tor. 5	Bos. 3
Bobby Hull (2)	Chi.	Apr. 7/63	Det.	3	Terry Sawchuk	Det. 7	Chi. 4
		Apr. 9/72	Pitt	3	Jim Rutherford	Chi. 6	Pit. 5
F. St. Marseille (2)	St. L.	Apr. 28/70	St. L.	3	Al Smith	St. L. 5	Pit. 0
		Apr. 6/72	Min.	3	Cesare Maniago	Min. 6	St. L. 5
Pit Martin (2)	Chi.	Apr. 4/73	Chi.	3	W. Stephenson	Chi. 7	St. L. 1
		May 10/73	Chi.	3	Ken Dryden	Mtl. 6	Chi. 4
Yvan Cournoyer (2)	Mtl.	Apr. 5/73	Mtl.	3	Dave Dryden	Mtl. 7	Buf. 3
		Apr. 11/74	Mtl.	3	Ed Giacomin	Mtl. 4	NYR 1
Guy Lafleur (2)	Mtl.	May 1/75	Mtl.	3	Roger Crozier (1) Gerry Desjardins (2)	Mtl. 7	Buf. 0
		Apr. 11/77	Mtl.	3	Ed Staniowski	Mtl. 7	St. L. 2
Lanny McDonald (2)	Tor.	Apr. 9/77	Pitt	3	Denis Herron	Tor. 5	Pit. 2
		Apr. 17/77	Tor.	4	W. Stephenson	Phi. 6	Tor. 5
Butch Goring (2)	L.A.	Apr. 9/77	L.A.	3	Phil Myre	L.A. 4	Atl. 2
	NYI	May 17/81	Min.	3	Gilles Meloche	NYI 7	Min. 5
Bryan Trottier (2)	NYI	Apr. 8/80	NYI	3	Doug Keans	NYI 8	L.A. 1
		Apr. 9/81	NYI	3	Michel Larocque	NYI 5	Tor. 1
Bill Barber (2)	Phil	May 4/80	Min.	4	Gilles Meloche	Phi. 5	Min. 3
		Apr. 9/81	Phil	3	Dan Bouchard	Phi. 8	Que. 5
Brian Propp (2)	Phi.	Apr. 22/81	Phi.	3	Pat Riggin	Phi. 9	Cgy. 4
		Apr. 21/85	Phi.	3	Billy Smith	Phi. 5	NYI 2
Paul Reinhart (2)	Cgy	Apr. 14/83	Edm.	3	Andy Moog	Edm. 6	Cgy. 3
		Apr. 8/84	Van	3	Richard Brodeur	Cgy. 5	Van. 1
Peter Stastny (2)	Que.	Apr. 5/83	Bos.	3	Pete Peeters	Bos. 4	Que. 3
		Apr. 11/87	Que.	3	Mike Liut (2) Steve Weeks (1)	Que. 5	Hfd. 1
Glenn Anderson (2)	Edm.	Apr. 26/83	Edm.	4	Murray Bannerman	Edm. 8	Chi. 2
		Apr. 6/88	Wpg.	3	Daniel Berthiaume	Edm. 7	Wpg. 4
Michel Goulet (2)	Que.	Apr. 23/85	Que.	3	Steve Penney	Que. 7	Mtl. 6
		Apr. 12/87	Que.	3	Mike Liut	Que. 4	Hfd. 1
Peter Zezel (2)	Phi.	Apr. 13/86	NYR	3	J. Vanbiesbrouck	Phi. 7	NYR 1
	St. L.	Apr. 11/89	St. L.	3	Jon Casey (2) Kari Takko (1)	St. L. 6	Min. 1
Steve Yzerman (2)	Det.	Apr. 6/89	Det.	3	Alain Chevrier	Chi. 5	Det. 4
		Apr. 4/91	St. L.	3	Vincent Riendeau (2) Pat Jablonski (1)	Det. 6	St. L. 3
Mario Lemieux (2)	Pit.	Apr. 25/89	Pit.	5	Ron Hextall	Pit. 10	Phi. 7
		Apr. 23/92	Pit.	3	Don Beaupre	Pit. 6	Wsh. 4
Mike Gartner (2)	NYR	Apr. 13/90	NYR	3	Mark Fitzpatrick (2) Glenn Healy (1)	NYR 6	NYI 5
		Apr. 27/92	NYR	3	Chris Terreri	NYR 8	N.J. 5
Geoff Courtnall (2)	Van.	Apr. 4/91	L.A.	3	Kelly Hrudey	Van. 6	L.A. 5
		Apr. 30/92	Van.	3	Rick Tabaracci	Van. 5	Win. 5
Harry Meeking	Tor.	Mar. 11/18	Tor.	3	Georges Vezina	Tor. 7	Mtl. 3
Alf Skinner	Tor.	Mar. 23/18	Tor.	3	Hugh Lehman	Van.M. 6	Tor. 4
Joe Malone	Mtl.	Feb. 23/19	Mtl.	3	Clint Benedict	Mtl. 8	Ott. 4
Odie Cleghorn	Mtl.	Feb. 27/19	Ott.	3	Clint Benedict	Mtl. 5	Ott. 3
Jack Darragh	Ott.	Apr. 1/20	Tor.	3	Harry Holmes	Ott. 6	Sea. 1
George Boucher	Ott.	Mar. 10/21	Ott.	3	Jake Forbes	Ott. 5	Tor. 0
Babe Dye	Tor.	Mar. 28/22	Tor.	4	Hugh Lehman	Tor. 5	Van.M. 1
Perk Galbraith	Bos.	Mar. 31/27	Bos.	3	Hugh Lehman	Bos. 4	Chi. 4
Busher Jackson	Tor.	Apr. 5/32	NYR	3	John Ross Roach	Tor. 6	NYR 4
Frank Boucher	NYR	Apr. 9/32	Tor.	3	Lorne Chabot	Tor. 6	NYR 4
Charlie Conacher	Tor.	Mar. 26/36	Tor.	3	Tiny Thompson	Tor. 8	Bos. 3
Syd Howe	Det.	Mar. 23/39	Det.	3	Claude Bourque	Det. 7	Mtl. 3
Bryan Hextall	NYR	Apr. 3/40	NYR	3	Turk Broda	NYR 6	Tor. 2
Joe Benoit	Mtl.	Mar. 22/41	Mtl.	3	Sam LoPresti	Mtl. 4	Chi. 3
Syl Apps	Tor.	Mar. 25/41	Tor.	3	Frank Brimsek	Tor. 7	Bos. 2
Jack McGill	Bos.	Mar. 29/42	Bos.	3	Johnny Mowers	Det. 6	Bos. 4
Don Metz	Tor.	Apr. 14/42	Tor.	3	Johnny Mowers	Tor. 9	Det. 3
Mud Bruneteau	Det.	Apr. 1/43	Det.	3	Frank Brimsek	Det. 6	Bos. 2
Don Grosso	Det.	Apr. 7/43	Bos.	3	Frank Brimsek	Det. 4	Bos. 0
Carl Liscombe	Det.	Apr. 3/45	Bos.	4	Paul Bibeault	Det. 5	Bos. 3
Billy Reay	Mtl.	Apr. 1/47	Bos.	4	Frank Brimsek	Mtl. 5	Bos. 1
Gerry Plamondon	Mtl.	Mar. 24/49	Det.	3	Harry Lumley	Mtl. 4	Det. 3
Sid Smith	Tor.	Apr. 10/49	Det.	3	Harry Lumley	Tor. 3	Det. 1
Pentti Lund	NYR	Apr. 2/50	NYR	3	Bill Durnan	NYR 4	Mtl. 1
Ted Lindsay	Det.	Apr. 5/55	Det.	4	Charlie Hodge (1) Jacques Plante (3)	Det. 7	Mtl. 1
Gordie Howe	Det.	Apr. 10/55	Det.	3	Jacques Plante	Det. 5	Mtl. 1
Phil Goyette	Mtl.	Mar. 25/58	Mtl.	3	Terry Sawchuk	Mtl. 8	Det. 1
Jerry Toppazzini	Bos.	Apr. 5/58	Bos.	3	Lorne Worsley	Bos. 8	NYR 2
Bob Pulford	Tor.	Apr. 19/62	Tor.	3	Glenn Hall	Tor. 8	Chi. 4
Dave Keon	Tor.	Apr. 9/64	Mtl.	3	Charlie Hodge	Tor. 3	Mtl. 1
Henri Richard	Mtl.	Apr. 20/67	Mtl.	3	Terry Sawchuk (2) Johnny Bower (1)	Mtl. 6	Tor. 2
Rosaire Paiement	Phi.	Apr. 13/68	Phi.	3	Glenn Hall (1) Seth Martin (2)	Phi. 6	St. L. 1
Jean Beliveau	Mtl.	Apr. 20/68	Mtl.	3	Denis DeJordy	Mtl. 4	Chi. 1
Red Berenson	St. L.	Apr. 15/69	St. L.	3	Gerry Desjardins	St. L. 4	L.A. 0
Ken Schinkel	Pit.	Apr. 11/70	Oak.	3	Gary Smith	Pit. 5	Oak. 2
Jim Pappin	Chi.	Apr. 11/71	Phi.	3	Bruce Gamble	Chi. 6	Phi. 2
Bobby Orr	Bos.	Apr. 11/71	Mtl.	3	Ken Dryden	Bos. 5	Mtl. 2
Jacques Lemaire	Mtl.	Apr. 20/71	Mtl.	3	Lorne Worsley	Mtl. 7	Min. 2
Vic Hadfield	NYR	Apr. 22/71	NYR	3	Tony Esposito	NYR 4	Chi. 1
Fred Stanfield	Bos.	Apr. 18/72	Bos.	3	Jacques Caron	Bos. 6	St. L. 1
Ken Hodge	Bos.	Apr. 30/72	Bos.	3	Ed Giacomin	Bos. 6	NYR 5
Steve Vickers	NYR	Apr. 10/73	Bos.	3	Ross Brooks (2) Ed Johnston (1)	NYR 6	Bos. 3
Dick Redmond	Chi.	Apr. 4/73	Chi.	3	Wayne Stephenson	Chi. 7	St. L. 1
Tom Williams	L.A.	Apr. 14/74	L.A.	3	Mike Veisor	L.A. 5	Chi. 1

LEADING PLAYOFF SCORERS

Player	Team	Date	City	Total Goals	Opposing Goaltender	Score	
Marcel Dionne	L.A.	Apr. 15/76	L.A.	3	Gilles Gilbert	L.A. 6	Bos. 4
Don Saleski	Phi.	Apr. 20/76	Phi.	3	Wayne Thomas	Phi. 7	Tor. 1
Darryl Sittler	Tor.	Apr. 22/76	Tor.	5	Bernie Parent	Tor. 8	Phi. 5
Reggie Leach	Phi.	May 6/76	Phi.	5	Gilles Gilbert	Phi. 6	Bos. 3
Jim Lorentz	Buf.	Apr. 7/77	Min.	3	Pete LoPresti (2)		
					Gary Smith (1)	Buf. 7	Min. 1
Bobby Schmautz	Bos.	Apr. 11/77	Bos.	3	Rogatien Vachon	Bos. 8	L.A. 3
Billy Harris	NYI	Apr. 23/77	Mtl.	3	Ken Dryden	Mtl. 4	NYI 3
George Ferguson	Tor.	Apr. 11/78	Tor.	3	Rogatien Vachon	Tor. 7	L.A. 3
Jean Ratelle	Bos.	May 3/79	Bos.	3	Ken Dryden	Bos. 4	Mtl. 3
Stan Jonathan	Bos.	May 8/79	Bos.	3	Ken Dryden	Bos. 5	Mtl. 2
Ron Duguay	NYR	Apr. 20/80	NYR	3	Pete Peeters	NYR 4	Phi. 2
Steve Shutt	Mtl.	Apr. 22/80	Mtl.	3	Gilles Meloche	Mtl. 6	Min. 2
Gilbert Perreault	Buf.	May 6/80	NYI	3	Billy Smith (2)		
					ENG (1)	Buf. 7	NYI 4
Paul Holmgren	Phi.	May 15/80	Phil	3	Billy Smith	Phi. 8	NYI 3
Steve Payne	Min.	Apr. 8/81	Bos.	3	Rogatien Vachon	Min. 5	Bos. 4
Denis Potvin	NYI	Apr. 17/81	NYI	3	Andy Moog	NYI 6	Edm. 3
Barry Pederson	Bos.	Apr. 8/82	Bos.	3	Don Edwards	Bos. 7	Buf. 3
Duane Sutter	NYI	Apr. 15/83	NYI	3	Glen Hanlon	NYI 5	NYR 0
Doug Halward	Van.	Apr. 7/84	Van.	3	Rejean Lemelin (2)		
					Don Edwards (1)	Van. 7	Cgy. 0
Jorgen Pettersson	St. L.	Apr. 8/84	Det.	3	Ed Mio	St. L. 3	Det. 2
Clark Gillies	NYI	May 12/84	NYI	3	Grant Fuhr	NYI 6	Edm. 1
Ken Linseman	Bos.	Apr. 14/85	Bos.	3	Steve Penney	Bos. 7	Mtl. 6
Dave Andreychuk	Buf.	Apr. 14/85	Buf.	3	Dan Bouchard	Que. 4	Buf. 7
Greg Paslawski	StL.	Apr. 15/86	Min.	3	Don Beaupre	St. L. 6	Min. 3
Doug Risebrough	Cgy.	May 4/86	Cgy.	3	Rick Wamsley	Cgy. 8	St. L. 2
Mike McPhee	Mtl.	Apr. 11/87	Bos.	3	Doug Keans	Mtl. 5	Bos. 4
John Ogrodnick	Que.	Apr. 14/87	Hfd.	3	Mike Liut	Que. 7	Hfd. 5
Pelle Eklund	Phi.	May 10/87	Mtl.	3	Patrick Roy (1)		
					Bryan Hayward (2)	Phi. 6	Mtl. 3
John Tucker	Buf.	Apr. 9/88	Bos.	4	Andy Moog	Buf. 6	Bos. 2
Tony Hrkac	St. L.	Apr. 10/88	St. L.	3	Darren Pang	St. L. 6	Chi. 5
Hakan Loob	Cgy.	Apr. 10/88	Cgy.	3	Glenn Healy	Cgy. 7	L.A. 3
Ed Olczyk	Tor.	Apr. 12/88	Tor.	3	Greg Stefan (2)		
					Glen Hanlon (1)	Tor. 6	Det. 5
Aaron Broten	N.J.	Apr. 20/88	N.J.	3	Pete Peeters	N.J. 5	Wsh. 2
Mark Johnson	N.J.	Apr. 22/88	Wsh.	4	Pete Peeters	N.J. 10	Wsh. 4
Patrik Sundstrom	N.J.	Apr. 22/88	Wsh.	3	Pete Peeters (2)		
					Clint Malarchuk (1)	N.J. 10	Wsh. 4
Bob Brooke	Min.	Apr. 5/89	St. L.	3	Greg Millen	St. L. 4	Min. 3
Chris Kontos	L.A.	Apr. 6/89	L.A.	3	Grant Fuhr	L.A. 5	Edm. 2
Wayne Presley	Chi.	Apr. 13/89	Chi.	3	Greg Stefan (1)		
					Glen Hanlon (2)	Chi. 7	Det. 1
Tony Granato	L.A.	Apr. 10/90	L.A.	3	Mike Vernon (1)		
					Rick Wamsley (2)	L.A. 12	Cgy. 4
Tomas Sandstrom	L.A.	Apr. 10/90	L.A.	3	Mike Vernon (1)		
					Rick Wamsley (2)	L.A. 12	Cgy. 4
Dave Taylor	L.A.	Apr. 10/90	L.A.	3	Mike Vernon (1)		
					Rick Wamsley (2)	L.A. 12	Cgy. 4
Bernie Nicholls	NYR	Apr. 19/90	NYR	3	Mike Liut	NYR 7	Wsh. 3
John Druce	Wsh.	Apr. 21/90	NYR	3	John Vanbiesbrouck	Wsh. 6	NYR 3
Adam Oates	St. L.	Apr. 12/91	St. L.	3	Tim Chevaldae	St. L. 6	Det. 1
Luc Robitaille	L.A.	Apr. 26/91	L.A.	3	Grant Fuhr	L.A. 5	Edm. 2
Ron Francis	Pit.	May 9/92	Pit.	3	Mike Richter (2)		
					John V'brouck (1)	Pit. 5	NYR. 4
Dirk Graham	Chi.	June 1/92	Chi.	3	Tom Barrasso	Pit. 5	Chi. 2
Joe Murphy	Edm.	May 6/92	Edm.	3	Kirk McLean	Edm. 5	Van. 2
Ray Sheppard	Det.	Apr. 24/92	Min.	3	Jon Casey	Min. 5	Det. 2
Kevin Stevens	Pit.	May 21/92	Pit.	4	Andy Moog	Pit. 5	Bos. 2
Pavel Bure	Van.	Apr. 28/92	Wpg.	3	Rick Tabaracci	Van. 8	Wpg. 3
Brian Noonan	Chi.	Apr. 18/93	Chi.	3	Curtis Joseph	St. L. 4	Chi. 3
Dale Hunter	Wsh.	Apr. 20/93	Wsh.	3	Glenn Healy	NYI 5	Wsh. 4
Teemu Selanne	Wpg.	Apr. 23/93	Wpg.	3	Kirk McLean	Wpg. 5	Van. 4
Ray Ferraro	NYI	Apr. 26/93	Wsh.	4	Don Beaupre	Wsh. 6	NYI 4
Al Iafrate	Wsh.	Apr. 26/93	Wsh.	3	Glenn Healy (2)		
					Mark Fitzpatrick (1)	Wsh. 6	NYI 4
Paul Di Pietro	Mtl.	Apr. 28/93	Mtl.	3	Ron Hextall	Mtl. 6	Que. 2
Wendel Clark	Tor.	May 27/93	L.A.	3	Kelly Hrudey	L.A. 5	Tor. 4
Eric Desjardins	Mtl.	Jun. 3/93	Mtl.	3	Kelly Hrudey	Mtl. 3	L.A. 2
Tony Amonte	Chi.	Apr. 23/94	Chi.	4	Felix Potvin	Chi. 5	Tor. 4
Gary Suter	Chi.	Apr. 24/94	Chi.	3	Felix Potvin	Chi. 4	Tor. 3
Ulf Dahlen	S.J.	May 6/94	S.J.	3	Felix Potvin	S.J. 5	Tor. 2
Joe Sakic	Que.	May 6/95	Que.	3	Mike Richter	Que. 5	NYR 4
Mike Sullivan	Cgy.	May 11/95	S.J.	3	Arturs Irbe (2)		
					Wade Flaherty (1)	Cgy. 9	S.J. 2
Theoren Fleury	Cgy.	May 13/95	S.J.	4	Arturs Irbe (3)		
					ENG (1)	Cgy. 6	S.J. 4
Brendan Shanahan	St. L.	May 13/95	Van.	3	Kirk McLean	St. L. 5	Van. 2
John LeClair	Phi.	May 21/95	Phi.	3	Mike Richter	Phi. 5	NYR 4
Brian Leetch	NYR	May 22/95	Phi.	3	Ron Hextall	Phi. 4	NYR 3

Leading Playoff Scorers, 1918–1995

Season	Player and Club	Games Played	Goals	Assists	Points
1994-95	Sergei Fedorov, Detroit	17	7	17	24
1993-94	Brian Leetch, NY Rangers	23	11	23	34
1992-93	Wayne Gretzky, Los Angeles	24	15	25	40
1991-92	Mario Lemieux, Pittsburgh	15	16	18	34
1990-91	Mario Lemieux, Pittsburgh	23	16	28	44
1989-90	Craig Simpson, Edmonton	22	16	15	31
	Mark Messier, Edmonton	22	9	22	31
1988-89	Al MacInnis, Calgary	22	7	24	31
1987-88	Wayne Gretzky, Edmonton	19	12	31	43
1986-87	Wayne Gretzky, Edmonton	21	5	29	34
1985-86	Doug Gilmour, St. Louis	19	9	12	21
	Bernie Federko, St. Louis	19	7	14	21
1984-85	Wayne Gretzky, Edmonton	18	17	30	47
1983-84	Wayne Gretzky, Edmonton	19	13	22	35
1982-83	Wayne Gretzky, Edmonton	16	12	26	38
1981-82	Bryan Trottier, NY Islanders	19	6	23	29
1980-81	Mike Bossy, NY Islanders	18	17	18	35
1979-80	Bryan Trottier, NY Islanders	21	12	17	29
1978-79	Jacques Lemaire, Montreal	16	11	12	23
	Guy Lafleur, Montreal	16	10	13	23
1977-78	Larry Robinson, Montreal	15	4	17	21
	Guy Lafleur, Montreal	15	10	11	21
1976-77	Guy Lafleur, Montreal	14	9	17	26
1975-76	Reggie Leach, Philadelphia	16	19	5	24
1974-75	Rick MacLeish, Philadelphia	17	11	9	20
1973-74	Rick MacLeish, Philadelphia	17	13	9	22
1972-73	Yvan Cournoyer, Montreal	17	15	10	25
1971-72	Phil Esposito, Boston	15	9	15	24
	Bobby Orr, Boston	15	5	19	24
1970-71	Frank Mahovlich, Montreal	20	14	13	27
1969-70	Phil Esposito, Boston	14	13	14	27
1968-69	Phil Esposito, Boston	10	8	10	18
1967-68	Bill Goldsworthy, Minnesota	14	8	7	15
1966-67	Jim Pappin, Toronto	12	7	8	15
1965-66	Norm Ullman, Detroit	12	6	9	15
1964-65	Bobby Hull, Chicago	14	10	7	17
1963-64	Gordie Howe, Detroit	14	9	10	19
1962-63	Gordie Howe, Detroit	11	7	9	16
	Norm Ullman, Detroit	11	4	12	16
1961-62	Stan Mikita, Chicago	12	6	15	21
1960-61	Gordie Howe, Detroit	11	4	11	15
	Pierre Pilote, Chicago	12	3	12	15
1959-60	Henri Richard, Montreal	8	3	9	12
	Bernie Geoffrion, Montreal	8	2	10	12
1958-59	Dickie Moore, Montreal	11	5	12	17
1957-58	Fleming Mackell, Boston	12	5	14	19
1956-57	Bernie Geoffrion, Montreal	11	11	7	18
1955-56	Jean Béliveau, Montreal	10	12	7	19
1954-55	Gordie Howe, Detroit	11	9	11	20
1953-54	Dickie Moore, Montreal	11	5	8	13
1952-53	Ed Sanford, Boston	11	8	3	11
1951-52	Ted Lindsay, Detroit	8	5	2	7
	Floyd Curry, Montreal	11	4	3	7
	Metro Prystai, Detroit	8	2	5	7
	Gordie Howe, Detroit	8	2	5	7
1950-51	Maurice Richard, Montreal	11	9	4	13
	Max Bentley, Toronto	11	2	11	13
1949-50	Pentti Lund, NY Rangers	12	6	5	11
1948-49	Gordie Howe, Detroit	11	8	3	11
1947-48	Ted Kennedy, Toronto	9	8	6	14
1946-47	Maurice Richard, Montreal	10	6	5	11
1945-46	Elmer Lach, Montreal	9	5	12	17
1944-45	Joe Carveth, Detroit	14	5	6	11
1943-44	Toe Blake, Montreal	9	7	11	18
1942-43	Carl Liscombe, Detroit	10	6	8	14
1941-42	Don Grosso, Detroit	12	8	6	14
1940-41	Milt Schmidt, Boston	11	5	6	11
1939-40	Phil Watson, NY Rangers	12	3	6	9
	Neil Colville, NY Rangers	12	2	7	9
1938-39	Bill Cowley, Boston	12	3	11	14
1937-38	Johnny Gottselig, Chicago	10	5	3	8
1936-37	Marty Barry, Detroit	10	4	7	11
1935-36	Buzz Boll, Toronto	9	7	3	10
1934-35	Baldy Northcott, Mtl. Maroons	7	4	1	5
	Harvey Jackson, Toronto	7	3	2	5
	Marvin Wentworth, Mtl. Maroons	7	1	4	5
1933-34	Larry Aurie, Detroit	9	3	7	10
1932-33	Cecil Dillon, NY Rangers	8	8	2	10
1931-32	Frank Boucher, NY Rangers	7	3	6	9
1930-31	Cooney Weiland, Boston	5	6	3	9
1929-30	Marty Barry, Boston	6	3	3	6
	Cooney Weiland, Boston	6	1	5	6
1928-29	Andy Blair, Toronto	4	3	0	3
	Butch Keeling, NY Rangers	6	3	0	3
	Ace Bailey, Toronto	4	1	2	3
1927-28	Frank Boucher, NY Rangers	9	7	3	10
1926-27	Harry Oliver, Boston	8	4	2	6
	Perk Galbraith, Boston	8	3	3	6
	Frank Fredrickson, Boston	8	2	4	6
1925-26	Nels Stewart, Mtl. Maroons	8	6	3	9
1924-25	Howie Morenz, Montreal	6	7	2	9
1923-24	Howie Morenz, Montreal	6	7	3	9
1922-23	Punch Broadbent, Ottawa	8	6	1	7
1921-22	Babe Dye, Toronto	7	11	2	13
1920-21	Cy Denneny, Ottawa	7	4	2	6
1919-20	Frank Nighbor, Ottawa	5	6	1	7
	Jack Darragh, Ottawa	5	5	2	7
1918-19	Newsy Lalonde, Montreal	10	17	1	18
1917-18	Alf Skinner, Toronto	7	8	1	9

Overtime Games since 1918

Abbreviations: Teams/Cities: — **Atl.** - Atlanta; **Bos.** - Boston; **Buf.** - Buffalo; **Cgy.** - Calgary; **Cgy. T.** - Calgary Tigers (Western Canada Hockey League); **Chi.** - Chicago; **Col.** - Colorado; **Dal.** - Dallas; **Det.** - Detroit; **Edm.** - Edmonton; **Edm. E.** - Edmonton Eskimos (WCHL); **Hfd.** - Hartford; **K.C.** - Kansas City; **L.A.** - Los Angeles; **Min.** - Minnesota; **Mtl.** - Montreal; **Mtl.M.** - Montreal Maroons; **N.J.** - New Jersey; **NYA** - NY Americans; **NYI** - New York Islanders; **NYR** - New York Rangers; **Oak.** - Oakland; **Ott.** - Ottawa; **Phi.** - Philadelphia; **Pit.** - Pittsburgh; **Que.** - Quebec; **St. L.** - St. Louis; **Sea.** - Seattle Metropolitans (Pacific Coast Hockey Association); **S.J.** - San Jose; **Tor.** - Toronto; **Van.** - Vancouver; **Van. M** - Vancouver Millionaires (PCHA); **Vic.** - Victoria Cougars (WCHL); **Wpg.** - Winnipeg; **Wsh.** - Washington.

SERIES — **CF** - conference final; **CSF** - conference semi-final; **CQF** - conference quarter-final; **DF** - division final; **DSF** - division semi-final; **F** - final; **PR** - preliminary round; **QF** - quarter final; **SF** - semi-final.

Date	City	Series	Score		Scorer	Overtime	Series Winner
Mar. 26/19	Sea.	F	Mtl. 0	Sea. 0	no scorer	20:00	
Mar. 29/19	Sea.	F	Mtl. 4	Sea. 3	Odie Cleghorn	15:57	
Mar. 21/22	Tor.	F	Tor 2	Van.M. 1	Babe Dye	4:50	Tor.
Mar. 29/23	Van.	F	Ott. 2	Edm.E. 1	Cy Denneny	2:08	Ott.
Mar. 31/27	Mtl.	QF	Mtl. 1	Mtl. M. 0	Howie Morenz	12:05	Mtl.
Apr. 7/27	Bos.	F	Ott. 0	Bos. 0	no scorer	20:00	Ott.
Apr. 11/27	Ott.	F	Bos. 1	Ott. 1	no scorer	20:00	Ott.
Apr. 3/28	Mtl.	QF	Mtl. M. 1	Mtl. 0	Russ Oatman	8:20	Mtl. M.
Apr. 7/28	Mtl.	F	NYR 2	Mtl. M. 1	Frank Boucher	7:05	NYR
Mar. 21/29	NY	QF	NYR 1	NYA 0	Butch Keeling	29:50	NYR
Mar. 26/29	Tor.	SF	NYR 2	Tor. 1	Frank Boucher	2:03	NYR
Mar. 20/30	Mtl.	SF	Bos. 2	Mtl. M. 1	Harry Oliver	45:35	Bos.
Mar. 25/30	Bos.	SF	Mtl. M. 1	Bos. 0	Archie Wilcox	26:27	Bos.
Mar. 26/30	Mtl.	QF	Chi. 2	Mtl. 2	Howie Morenz (Mtl.)	51:43	Mtl.
Mar. 28/30	Mtl.	SF	Mtl. 2	NYR 1	Gus Rivers	68:52	Mtl.
Mar. 24/31	Bos.	SF	Bos. 5	Mtl. 4	Cooney Weiland	18:56	Mtl.
Mar. 26/31	Chi.	QF	Chi. 2	Tor. 1	Steward Adams	19:20	Chi.
Mar. 28/31	Mtl.	SF	Mtl. 4	Bos. 3	Georges Mantha	5:10	Mtl.
Apr. 1/31	Mtl.	SF	Mtl. 3	Bos. 2	Wildor Larochelle	19:00	Mtl.
Apr. 5/31	Chi.	F	Chi. 2	Mtl. 1	Johnny Gottselig	24:50	Mtl.
Apr. 9/31	Mtl.	F	Chi. 3	Mtl. 2	Cy Wentworth	53:50	Mtl.
Mar. 26/32	Mtl.	SF	NYR 4	Mtl. 3	Fred Cook	59:32	NYR
Apr. 2/32	Tor.	SF	Tor. 3	Mtl. M. 2	Bob Gracie	17:59	Tor.
Mar. 25/33	Bos.	SF	Bos. 2	Tor. 1	Marty Barry	14:14	Tor.
Mar. 28/33	Bos.	SF	Tor. 1	Bos. 0	Busher Jackson	15:03	Tor.
Mar. 30/33	Tor.	SF	Bos. 2	Tor. 1	Eddie Shore	4:23	Tor.
Apr. 3/33	Tor.	SF	Tor. 1	Bos. 0	Ken Doraty	104:46	Tor.
Apr. 13/33	Tor.	F	NYR 1	Tor. 0	Bill Cook	7:33	NYR
Mar. 22/34	Tor.	SF	Det. 2	Tor. 1	Herbie Lewis	1:33	Det.
Mar. 25/34	Chi.	QF	Chi. 1	Mtl. 1	Mush March (Chi)	11:05	Chi.
Apr. 3/34	Det.	F	Chi. 2	Det. 1	Paul Thompson	21:10	Chi.
Apr. 10/34	Chi.	F	Chi. 1	Det. 0	Mush March	30:05	Chi.
Mar. 23/35	Bos.	SF	Bos. 1	Tor. 0	Dit Clapper	33:26	Tor.
Mar. 26/35	Chi.	QF	Mtl. M. 1	Chi. 0	Baldy Northcott	4:02	Mtl. M.
Mar. 30/35	Tor.	SF	Tor. 2	Bos. 1	Pep Kelly	1:36	Tor.
Apr. 4/35	Tor.	F	Mtl. M. 3	Tor. 2	Dave Trottier	5:28	Mtl. M.
Mar. 24/36	Mtl.	SF	Det. 1	Mtl. M. 0	Mud Bruneteau	116:30	Det.
Apr. 9/36	Tor.	F	Tor. 4	Det. 3	Buzz Boll	0:31	Det.
Mar. 25/37	NY	QF	NYR 2	Tor. 1	Babe Pratt	13:05	NYR
Apr. 1/37	Mtl.	SF	Det. 2	Mtl. 1	Hec Kilrea	51:49	Det.
Mar. 22/38	NY	QF	NYA 2	NYR 1	Johnny Sorrell	21:25	NYA
Mar. 24/38	Tor.	SF	Tor. 1	Bos. 0	George Parsons	21:31	Tor.
Mar. 26/38	Mtl.	QF	Chi. 3	Mtl. 2	Paul Thompson	11:49	Chi.
Mar. 27/38	NY	QF	NYA 3	NYR 2	Lorne Carr	60:40	NYA
Mar. 29/38	Bos.	SF	Tor. 3	Bos. 2	Gord Drillon	10:04	Tor.
Mar. 31/38	Chi.	SF	Chi. 1	NYA 0	Cully Dahlstrom	33:01	Chi.
Mar. 21/39	NY	SF	Bos. 2	NYR 1	Mel Hill	59:25	Bos.
Mar. 23/39	Bos.	SF	Bos. 3	NYR 2	Mel Hill	8:24	Bos.
Mar. 26/39	Det.	QF	Det. 1	Mtl. 0	Marty Barry	7:47	Det.
Mar. 30/39	Bos.	SF	NYR 2	Bos. 1	Clint Smith	17:19	Bos.
Apr. 1/39	Tor.	SF	Tor. 5	Det. 4	Gord Drillon	5:42	Tor.
Apr. 2/39	Bos.	SF	Bos. 2	NYR 1	Mel Hill	48:00	Bos.
Apr. 9/39	Bos.	F	Tor. 3	Bos. 2	Doc Romnes	10:38	Bos.
Mar. 19/40	Det.	QF	Det. 2	NYA 1	Syd Howe	0:25	Det.
Mar. 19/40	Tor.	QF	Tor. 3	Chi. 2	Syl Apps	6:35	Tor.
Apr. 2/40	NY	F	NYR 2	Tor. 1	Alf Pike	15:30	NYR
Apr. 11/40	Tor.	F	NYR 2	Tor. 1	Muzz Patrick	31:43	NYR
Apr. 13/40	Tor.	F	NYR 3	Tor. 2	Bryan Hextall	2:07	NYR
Mar. 20/41	Det.	QF	Det. 2	NYR 1	Gus Giesebrecht	12:01	Det.
Mar. 22/41	Mtl.	QF	Mtl. 4	Chi. 3	Charlie Sands	34:04	Chi.
Mar. 29/41	Bos.	SF	Tor. 2	Bos. 1	Pete Langelle	17:31	Bos.
Mar. 30/41	Chi.	SF	Det. 2	Chi. 1	Gus Giesebrecht	9:15	Det.
Mar. 22/42	Chi.	QF	Bos. 2	Chi. 1	Des Smith	6:51	Bos.
Mar. 21/43	Bos.	SF	Bos. 5	Mtl. 4	Don Gallinger	12:30	Bos.
Mar. 23/43	Det.	SF	Tor. 3	Det. 2	Jack McLean	70:18	Det.
Mar. 25/43	Mtl.	SF	Bos. 3	Mtl. 2	Harvey Jackson	3:20	Bos.
Mar. 30/43	Tor.	SF	Det. 3	Tor. 2	Adam Brown	9:21	Det.
Mar. 30/43	Bos.	SF	Bos. 5	Mtl. 4	Ab DeMarco	3:41	Bos.
Apr. 13/44	Mtl.	F	Mtl. 5	Chi. 4	Toe Blake	9:12	Mtl.
Mar. 27/45	Tor.	SF	Tor. 4	Mtl. 3	Gus Bodnar	12:36	Tor.
Mar. 29/45	Det.	SF	Det. 3	Bos. 2	Mud Bruneteau	17:12	Det.
Apr. 21/45	Tor.	F	Det. 1	Tor. 0	Ed Bruneteau	14:16	Tor.
Mar. 28/46	Bos.	SF	Bos. 4	Det. 3	Don Gallinger	9:51	Bos.
Mar. 30/46	Mtl.	F	Mtl. 4	Bos. 3	Maurice Richard	9:08	Mtl.
Apr. 2/46	Mtl.	F	Mtl. 3	Bos. 2	Jim Peters	16:55	Mtl.
Apr. 7/46	Bos.	F	Bos. 3	Mtl. 2	Terry Reardon	15:13	Mtl.
Mar. 26/47	Tor.	SF	Tor. 3	Det. 2	Howie Meeker	3:05	Tor.
Mar. 27/47	Mtl.	SF	Mtl. 2	Bos. 1	Ken Mosdell	5:38	Mtl.
Apr. 3/47	Mtl.	SF	Mtl. 4	Bos. 3	John Quilty	36:40	Mtl.
Apr. 15/47	Tor.	F	Tor. 2	Mtl. 1	Syl Apps	16:36	Tor.
Mar. 24/48	Tor.	SF	Tor. 5	Bos. 4	Nick Metz	17:03	Tor.
Mar. 22/49	Det.	SF	Det. 2	Mtl. 1	Max McNab	44:52	Det.
Mar. 24/49	Det.	SF	Mtl. 4	Det. 3	Gerry Plamondon	2:59	Det.
Mar. 26/49	Tor.	SF	Bos. 5	Tor. 4	Woody Dumart	16:14	Tor.
Apr. 8/49	Det.	F	Tor. 3	Det. 2	Joe Klukay	17:31	Tor.
Apr. 4/50	Tor.	SF	Det. 2	Tor. 1	Leo Reise	20:38	Det.
Apr. 4/50	Mtl.	SF	Mtl. 3	NYR 2	Elmer Lach	15:19	Mtl.
Apr. 9/50	Det.	SF	Det. 1	Tor. 0	Leo Reise	8:39	Det.
Apr. 18/50	Det.	F	NYR 4	Det. 3	Don Raleigh	8:34	Det.
Apr. 20/50	Det.	F	NYR 2	Det. 1	Don Raleigh	1:38	Det.
Apr. 23/50	Det.	F	Det. 4	NYR 3	Pete Babando	28:31	Det.
Mar. 27/51	Det.	SF	Mtl. 3	Det. 2	Maurice Richard	61:09	Mtl.
Mar. 29/51	Det.	SF	Mtl. 1	Det. 0	Maurice Richard	42:20	Mtl.
Mar. 31/51	Tor.	SF	Bos. 1	Tor. 1	no scorer	20:00	Tor.
Apr. 11/51	Tor.	F	Tor. 3	Mtl. 2	Sid Smith	5:51	Tor.
Apr. 14/51	Tor.	F	Mtl. 3	Tor. 2	Maurice Richard	2:55	Tor.
Apr. 17/51	Mtl.	F	Tor. 2	Mtl. 1	Ted Kennedy	4:47	Tor.
Apr. 19/51	Mtl.	F	Tor. 3	Mtl. 2	Harry Watson	5:15	Tor.
Apr. 21/51	Tor.	F	Tor. 3	Mtl. 2	Bill Barilko	2:53	Tor.
Apr. 6/52	Bos.	SF	Mtl. 3	Bos. 2	Paul Masnick	27:49	Mtl.
Mar. 29/53	Bos.	SF	Bos. 2	Det. 1	Jack McIntyre	12:29	Bos.
Mar. 29/53	Chi.	SF	Chi. 2	Mtl. 1	Al Dewsbury	5:18	Mtl.
Apr. 16/53	Mtl.	F	Mtl. 1	Bos. 0	Elmer Lach	1:22	Mtl.
Apr. 1/54	Det.	SF	Det. 4	Tor. 3	Ted Lindsay	21:01	Det.
Apr. 11/54	Det.	F	Mtl. 1	Det. 0	Ken Mosdell	5:45	Det.
Apr. 16/54	Det.	F	Det. 2	Mtl. 1	Tony Leswick	4:29	Det.
Mar. 29/55	Bos.	SF	Mtl. 4	Bos. 3	Don Marshall	3:05	Mtl.
Mar. 24/56	Tor.	SF	Det. 5	Tor. 4	Ted Lindsay	4:22	Det.
Mar. 28/57	NY	SF	NYR 4	Mtl. 3	Andy Hebenton	13:38	Mtl.
Apr. 4/57	Mtl.	SF	Mtl. 4	NYR 3	Maurice Richard	1:11	Mtl.
Mar. 27/58	NY	SF	Bos. 4	NYR 3	Jerry Toppazzini	4:46	Bos.
Mar. 30/58	Det.	SF	Mtl. 2	Det. 1	André Pronovost	11:52	Mtl.
Apr. 17/58	Mtl.	F	Mtl. 3	Bos. 2	Maurice Richard	5:45	Mtl.
Mar. 28/59	Tor.	SF	Tor. 3	Bos. 2	Gerry Ehman	5:02	Tor.
Mar. 31/59	Tor.	SF	Tor. 3	Bos. 2	Frank Mahovlich	11:21	Tor.
Apr. 14/59	Tor.	F	Tor. 3	Mtl. 2	Dick Duff	10:06	Mtl.
Mar. 26/60	Mtl.	SF	Mtl. 4	Chi. 3	Doug Harvey	8:38	Mtl.
Mar. 27/60	Det.	SF	Tor. 5	Det. 4	Frank Mahovlich	43:00	Tor.
Mar. 29/60	Det.	SF	Det. 2	Tor. 1	Gerry Melnyk	1:54	Tor.
Mar. 22/61	Tor.	SF	Tor. 3	Det. 2	George Armstrong	24:51	Det.
Mar. 26/61	Chi.	SF	Chi. 2	Mtl. 1	Murray Balfour	52:12	Chi.
Apr. 5/62	Tor.	SF	Tor. 3	NYR 2	Red Kelly	24:23	Tor.
Apr. 2/64	Det.	SF	Chi. 3	Det. 2	Murray Balfour	8:21	Det.
Apr. 14/64	Tor.	F	Det. 4	Tor. 3	Larry Jeffrey	7:52	Tor.
Apr. 23/64	Det.	F	Tor. 4	Det. 3	Bobby Baun	1:43	Tor.
Apr. 6/65	Tor.	SF	Tor. 3	Mtl. 2	Dave Keon	4:17	Mtl.
Apr. 13/65	Tor.	SF	Mtl. 4	Tor. 3	Claude Provost	16:33	Mtl.
May 5/66	Det.	F	Mtl. 3	Det. 2	Henri Richard	2:20	Mtl.
Apr. 13/67	NY	SF	Mtl. 2	NYR 1	John Ferguson	6:28	Mtl.
Apr. 25/67	Tor.	F	Tor. 3	Mtl. 2	Bob Pulford	28:26	Tor.
Apr. 10/68	St. L.	QF	St. L. 3	Phi. 2	Larry Keenan	24:10	St. L.
Apr. 16/68	St. L.	QF	Phi. 2	St. L. 1	Don Blackburn	31:18	St. L.
Apr. 16/68	Min.	QF	Min. 4	L.A. 3	Milan Marcetta	9:11	Min.
Apr. 22/68	Min.	SF	Min. 3	St. L. 2	Parker MacDonald	3:41	St. L.
Apr. 27/68	St. L.	SF	St. L. 4	Min. 3	Gary Sabourin	1:32	St. L.
Apr. 28/68	Mtl.	SF	Mtl. 4	Chi. 3	Jacques Lemaire	2:14	Mtl.
Apr. 29/68	St. L.	SF	St. L. 3	Min. 2	Bill McCreary	17:27	St. L.
May 3/68	St. L.	SF	St. L. 2	Min. 1	Ron Schock	22:50	St. L.
May 5/68	St. L.	F	Mtl. 3	St. L. 2	Jacques Lemaire	1:41	Mtl.
May 9/68	Mtl.	F	Mtl. 4	St. L. 3	Bobby Rousseau	1:13	Mtl.
Apr. 2/69	Oak.	QF	L.A. 5	Oak. 4	Ted Irvine	0:19	L.A.
Apr. 10/69	Mtl.	SF	Mtl. 3	Bos. 2	Ralph Backstrom	0:42	Mtl.
Apr. 13/69	Mtl.	SF	Mtl. 4	Bos. 3	Mickey Redmond	4:55	Mtl.
Apr. 24/69	Bos.	SF	Mtl. 2	Bos. 1	Jean Béliveau	31:28	Mtl.
Apr. 12/70	Oak.	QF	Pit. 3	Oak. 2	Michel Briere	8:28	Pit.
May 10/70	Bos.	F	Bos. 4	St. L. 3	Bobby Orr	0:40	Bos.
Apr. 15/71	Tor.	QF	NYR 2	Tor. 1	Bob Nevin	9:07	NYR
Apr. 18/71	Chi.	SF	NYR 2	Chi. 1	Pete Stemkowski	1:37	Chi.
Apr. 27/71	Chi.	SF	Chi. 3	NYR 2	Bobby Hull	6:35	Chi.
Apr. 29/71	NY	SF	NYR 3	Chi. 2	Pete Stemkowski	41:29	Chi.
May 4/71	Chi.	F	Chi. 2	Mtl. 1	Jim Pappin	21:11	Mtl.
Apr. 6/72	Bos.	QF	Tor. 4	Bos. 3	Jim Harrison	2:58	Bos.
Apr. 6/72	Min.	QF	Min. 6	St. L. 5	Bill Goldsworthy	1:36	St. L.
Apr. 9/72	Pit.	QF	Chi. 6	Pit. 5	Pit Martin	0:12	Chi.
Apr. 16/72	Min.	QF	St. L. 2	Min. 1	Kevin O'Shea	10:07	St. L.
Apr. 1/73	Mtl.	QF	Buf. 3	Mtl. 2	René Robert	9:18	Mtl.
Apr. 10/73	Phi.	QF	Phi. 3	Min. 2	Gary Dornhoefer	8:35	Phi.
Apr. 14/73	Mtl.	SF	Phi. 5	Mtl. 4	Rick MacLeish	2:56	Mtl.
Apr. 17/73	Mtl.	SF	Mtl. 4	Phi. 3	Larry Robinson	6:45	Mtl.
Apr. 14/74	Tor.	QF	Bos. 4	Tor. 3	Ken Hodge	1:27	Bos.
Apr. 14/74	Atl.	QF	Phi. 4	Atl. 3	Dave Schultz	5:40	Phi.
Apr. 16/74	Mtl.	QF	NYR 3	Mtl. 2	Ron Harris	4:07	NYR
Apr. 23/74	Chi.	SF	Chi. 4	Bos. 3	Jim Pappin	3:48	Bos.
Apr. 28/74	NY	SF	NYR 2	Phi. 1	Rod Gilbert	4:20	Phi.
May 9/74	Bos.	F	Phi. 3	Bos. 2	Bobby Clarke	12:01	Phi.
Apr. 8/75	L.A.	PR	L.A. 3	Tor. 2	Mike Murphy	8:53	Tor.
Apr. 10/75	Tor.	PR	Tor. 3	L.A. 2	Blaine Stoughton	10:19	Tor.
Apr. 10/75	Chi.	PR	Chi. 4	Bos. 3	Ivan Boldirev	7:33	Chi.
Apr. 11/75	NY	PR	NYI 4	NYR 3	Jean-Paul Parise	0:11	NYI
Apr. 19/75	Tor.	QF	Phi. 4	Tor. 3	André Dupont	1:45	Phi.
Apr. 17/75	Chi.	QF	Chi. 5	Buf. 4	Stan Mikita	2:31	Buf.
Apr. 22/75	Mtl.	QF	Mtl. 5	Van. 4	Guy Lafleur	17:06	Mtl.
May 1/75	Phi.	SF	Phi. 5	NYI 4	Bobby Clarke	2:56	Phi.
May 7/75	NYI	SF	NYI 4	Phi. 3	Jude Drouin	1:53	Phi.
Apr. 27/75	Buf.	SF	Buf. 6	Mtl. 5	Danny Gare	4:42	Buf.
May 6/75	Buf.	SF	Buf. 5	Mtl. 4	René Robert	5:56	Buf.
May 20/75	Buf.	F	Buf. 5	Phi. 4	René Robert	18:29	Phi.
Apr. 8/76	Buf.	PR	Buf. 3	St. L. 2	Danny Gare	11:43	Buf.
Apr. 9/76	Buf.	PR	Buf. 2	St. L. 1	Don Luce	14:27	Buf.
Apr. 13/76	Bos.	QF	L.A. 3	Bos. 2	Butch Goring	0:27	Bos.
Apr. 13/76	Buf.	QF	Buf. 3	NYI 2	Danny Gare	14:04	NYI
Apr. 22/76	L.A.	QF	L.A. 4	Bos. 3	Butch Goring	18:28	Bos.
Apr. 29/76	Phi.	SF	Phi. 2	Bos. 1	Reggie Leach	13:38	Phi.
Apr. 15/77	Tor.	QF	Phi. 4	Tor. 3	Rick MacLeish	2:55	Phi.
Apr. 17/77	Tor.	QF	Phi. 6	Tor. 5	Reggie Leach	19:10	Phi.
Apr. 24/77	Phi.	SF	Bos. 4	Phi. 3	Rick Middleton	2:57	Bos.
Apr. 26/77	Phi.	SF	Bos. 5	Phi. 4	Terry O'Reilly	30:07	Bos.
May 3/77	Mtl.	SF	NYI 4	Mtl. 3	Billy Harris	3:58	Mtl.
May 14/77	Bos.	F	Mtl. 2	Bos. 1	Jacques Lemaire	4:32	Mtl.

124 • OVERTIME

Date	City	Series	Score		Scorer	Overtime	Series Winner	Date	City	Series	Score		Scorer	Overtime	Series Winner
Apr. 11/78	Phi.	PR	Phi. 3	Col. 2	Mel Bridgman	0:23	Phi.	Apr. 14/81	St. L.	PR	St. L. 4	Pit. 3	Mike Crombeen	25:16	St. L.
Apr. 13/78	NY	PR	NYR 4	Buf. 3	Don Murdoch	1:37	Buf.	Apr. 16/81	Buf.	QF	Min. 4	Buf. 3	Steve Payne	0:22	Min.
Apr. 19/78	Bos.	QF	Bos. 4	Chi. 3	Terry O'Reilly	1:50	Bos.	Apr. 20/81	Min.	QF	Buf. 5	Min. 4	Craig Ramsay	16:32	Min.
Apr. 19/78	NYI	QF	NYI 3	Tor. 2	Mike Bossy	2:50	Tor.	Apr. 20/81	Edm.	QF	NYI 5	Edm. 4	Ken Morrow	5:41	NYI
Apr. 21/78	Chi.	QF	Bos. 4	Chi. 3	Peter McNab	10:17	Bos.	Apr. 7/82	Min.	DSF	Chi. 3	Min. 2	Greg Fox	3:34	Chi.
Apr. 25/78	NYI	QF	NYI 2	Tor. 1	Bob Nystrom	8:02	Tor.	Apr. 8/82	Edm.	DSF	Edm. 3	L.A. 2	Wayne Gretzky	6:20	L.A.
Apr. 29/78	NYI	QF	Tor. 2	NYI 1	Lanny McDonald	4:13	Tor.	Apr. 8/82	Van.	DSF	Van. 2	Cgy. 1	Dave Williams	14:20	Van.
May 2/78	Bos.	SF	Bos. 3	Phi. 2	Rick Middleton	1:43	Bos.	Apr. 10/82	Pit.	DSF	Pit. 2	NYI 1	Rick Kehoe	4:14	NYI
May 16/78	Mtl.	F	Mtl. 3	Bos. 2	Guy Lafleur	13:09	Mtl.	Apr. 10/82	L.A.	DSF	L.A. 6	Edm. 5	Daryl Evans	2:35	L.A.
May 21/78	Bos.	F	Bos. 4	Mtl. 3	Bobby Schmautz	6:22	Mtl.	Apr. 13/82	Mtl.	DSF	Que. 3	Mtl. 2	Dale Hunter	0:22	Que.
Apr. 12/79	L.A.	PR	NYR 2	L.A. 1	Phil Esposito	6:11	NYR	Apr. 13/82	NY	DSF	NYI 4	Pit. 3	John Tonelli	6:19	NYI
Apr. 14/79	Buf.	PR	Pit. 4	Buf. 3	George Ferguson	0:47	Pit.	Apr. 16/82	Van.	DF	L.A. 3	Van. 2	Steve Bozek	4:33	Van.
Apr. 16/79	Phi.	QF	Phi. 3	NYR 2	Ken Linseman	0:44	NYR	Apr. 18/82	Que.	DF	Que. 3	Bos. 2	Wilf Paiement	11:44	Que.
Apr. 18/79	NYI	QF	NYI 1	Chi. 0	Mike Bossy	2:31	NYI	Apr. 18/82	NY	DF	NYI 4	NYR 3	Bryan Trottier	3:00	NYI
Apr. 21/79	Tor.	QF	Mtl. 4	Tor. 3	Cam Connor	25:25	Mtl.	Apr. 18/82	L.A.	DF	Van. 4	L.A. 3	Colin Campbell	1:23	Van.
Apr. 22/79	Tor.	QF	Mtl. 5	Tor. 4	Larry Robinson	4:14	Mtl.	Apr. 21/82	St. L.	DF	St. L. 3	Chi. 2	Bernie Federko	3:28	Chi.
Apr. 28/79	NYI	SF	NYI 4	NYR 3	Denis Potvin	8:02	NYR	Apr. 23/82	Que.	DF	Bos. 6	Que. 5	Peter McNab	10:54	Que.
May 3/79	NY	SF	NYI 3	NYR 2	Bob Nystrom	3:40	NYR	Apr. 27/82	Chi.	CF	Van. 2	Chi. 1	Jim Nill	28:58	Van.
May 3/79	Bos.	SF	Bos. 4	Mtl. 3	Jean Ratelle	3:46	Mtl.	May 1/82	Que.	CF	NYI 5	Que. 4	Wayne Merrick	16:52	NYI
May 10/79	Mtl.	SF	Mtl. 5	Bos. 4	Yvon Lambert	9:33	Mtl.	May 8/82	NYI	F	NYI 6	Van. 5	Mike Bossy	19:58	NYI
May 19/79	NY	F	Mtl. 4	NYR 3	Serge Savard	7:25	Mtl.	Apr. 5/83	Bos.	DSF	Bos. 4	Que. 3	Barry Pederson	1:46	Bos.
Apr. 8/80	NY	PR	NYR 2	Atl. 1	Steve Vickers	0:33	NYR	Apr. 6/83	Cgy.	DSF	Cgy. 4	Van. 3	Eddy Beers	12:27	Cgy.
Apr. 8/80	Phi.	PR	Phi. 4	Edm. 3	Bobby Clarke	8:06	Phi.	Apr. 7/83	Min.	DSF	Min. 5	Tor. 4	Bobby Smith	5:03	Min.
Apr. 8/80	Chi.	PR	Chi. 3	St. L. 2	Doug Lecuyer	12:34	Chi.	Apr. 10/83	Tor.	DSF	Min. 5	Tor. 4	Dino Ciccarelli	8:05	Min.
Apr. 11/80	Hfd.	PR	Mtl. 4	Hfd. 3	Yvon Lambert	0:29	Mtl.	Apr. 10/83	Van.	DSF	Cgy. 4	Van. 3	Greg Meredith	1:06	Cgy.
Apr. 11/80	Tor.	PR	Min. 4	Tor. 3	Al MacAdam	0:32	Min.	Apr. 18/83	Min.	DF	Chi. 4	Min. 3	Rich Preston	10:34	Chi.
Apr. 11/80	L.A.	PR	NYI 4	L.A. 3	Ken Morrow	6:55	NYI	Apr. 24/83	Bos.	DF	Bos. 3	Buf. 2	Brad Park	1:52	Bos.
Apr. 11/80	Edm.	PR	Phi. 3	Edm. 2	Ken Linseman	23:56	Phi.	Apr. 5/84	Edm.	DSF	Edm. 5	Wpg. 4	Randy Gregg	0:21	Edm.
Apr. 16/80	Bos.	QF	NYI 2	Bos. 1	Clark Gillies	1:02	NYI	Apr. 7/84	Det.	DSF	St. L. 4	Det. 3	Mark Reeds	37:07	St. L.
Apr. 17/80	Bos.	QF	NYI 5	Bos. 4	Bob Bourne	1:24	NYI	Apr. 8/84	Det.	DSF	St. L. 3	Det. 2	Jorgen Pettersson	2:42	St. L.
Apr. 21/80	NYI	QF	Bos. 4	NYI 3	Terry O'Reilly	17:13	NYI	Apr. 10/84	NYI	DSF	NYI 3	NYR 2	Ken Morrow	8:56	NYI
May 1/80	Buf.	SF	NYI 2	Buf. 1	Bob Nystrom	21:20	NYI	Apr. 13/84	Min.	DF	St. L. 4	Min. 3	Doug Gilmour	16:16	Min.
May 13/80	Phi.	F	NYI 4	Phi. 3	Denis Potvin	4:07	NYI	Apr. 13/84	Edm.	DF	Cgy. 6	Edm. 5	Carey Wilson	3:42	Edm.
May 24/80	NYI	F	NYI 5	Phi. 4	Bob Nystrom	7:11	NYI	Apr. 13/84	NYI	DF	NYI 5	Wsh. 4	Anders Kallur	7:35	NYI
Apr. 8/81	Buf.	PR	Buf. 3	Van. 2	Alan Haworth	5:00	Buf.	Apr. 16/84	Mtl.	DF	Que. 4	Mtl. 3	Bo Berglund	3:00	Mtl.
Apr. 8/81	Bos.	PR	Min. 5	Bos. 4	Steve Payne	3:34	Min.	Apr. 20/84	Cgy.	DF	Cgy. 5	Edm. 4	Lanny McDonald	1:04	Edm.
Apr. 11/81	Chi.	PR	Cgy. 5	Chi. 4	Willi Plett	35:17	Cgy.	Apr. 22/84	Min.	DF	Min. 4	St. L. 3	Steve Payne	6:00	Min.
Apr. 12/81	Que.	PR	Que. 4	Phi. 3	Dale Hunter	0:37	Phi.	Apr. 10/85	Phi.	DSF	Phi. 5	NYR 4	Mark Howe	8:01	Phi.

Maurice Richard, seen here scoring his 542nd career goal, scored the last overtime goal of his career on April 17, 1958 giving the Montreal Canadiens a 3-2 final series win over the Boston Bruins.

Date	City	Series	Score		Scorer	Overtime	Series Winner
Apr. 10/85	Wsh.	DSF	Wsh. 4	NYI 3	Alan Haworth	2:28	NYI
Apr. 10/85	Edm.	DSF	Edm. 3	L.A. 2	Lee Fogolin	3:01	Edm.
Apr. 10/85	Wpg.	DSF	Wpg. 5	Cgy. 4	Brian Mullen	7:56	Wpg.
Apr. 11/85	Wsh.	DSF	Wsh. 2	NYI 1	Mike Gartner	21:23	NYI
Apr. 13/85	L.A.	DSF	Edm. 4	L.A. 3	Glenn Anderson	0:46	Edm.
Apr. 18/85	Mtl.	DF	Que. 2	Mtl. 1	Mark Kumpel	12:23	Que.
Apr. 23/85	Que.	DF	Que. 7	Mtl. 6	Dale Hunter	18:36	Que.
May 2/85	Mtl.	DF	Que. 3	Mtl. 2	Peter Stastny	2:22	Que.
Apr. 25/85	Min.	DF	Chi. 7	Min. 6	Darryl Sutter	21:57	Chi.
Apr. 28/85	Chi.	DF	Min. 5	Chi. 4	Dennis Maruk	1:14	Chi.
Apr. 30/85	Min.	DF	Chi. 6	Min. 5	Darryl Sutter	15:41	Chi.
May 5/85	Que.	CF	Que. 2	Phi. 1	Peter Stastny	6:20	Phi.
Apr. 9/86	Que.	DSF	Hfd. 3	Que. 2	Sylvain Turgeon	2:36	Hfd.
Apr. 12/86	Wpg.	DSF	Cgy. 4	Wpg. 3	Lanny McDonald	8:25	Cgy.
Apr. 17/86	Wsh.	DF	NYR 4	Wsh. 3	Brian MacLellan	1:16	NYR
Apr. 20/86	Edm.	DF	Edm. 6	Cgy. 5	Glenn Anderson	1:04	Cgy.
Apr. 23/86	Hfd.	DF	Hfd. 2	Mtl. 1	Kevin Dineen	1:07	Mtl.
Apr. 23/86	NYR	DF	NYR 6	Wsh. 5	Bob Brooke	2:40	NYR
Apr. 26/86	St L.	DF	St L. 4	Tor. 3	Mark Reeds	7:11	St L.
Apr. 29/86	Mtl.	DF	Mtl. 2	Hfd. 1	Claude Lemieux	5:55	Mtl.
May 5/86	NYR	CF	Mtl. 4	NYR 3	Claude Lemieux	9:41	Mtl.
May 12/86	St L.	CF	St L. 6	Cgy. 5	Doug Wickenheiser	7:30	Cgy.
May 18/86	Cgy.	F	Mtl. 3	Cgy. 2	Brian Skrudland	0:09	Mtl.
Apr. 8/87	Hfd.	DSF	Hfd. 3	Que. 2	Paul MacDermid	2:20	Que.
Apr. 9/87	Mtl.	DSF	Mtl. 4	Bos. 3	Mats Naslund	2:38	Mtl.
Apr. 9/87	St. L.	DSF	Tor. 3	St. L. 2	Rick Lanz	10:17	Tor.
Apr. 11/87	Wpg.	DSF	Cgy. 3	Wpg. 2	Mike Bullard	3:53	Wpg.
Apr. 11/87	Chi.	DSF	Det. 4	Chi. 3	Shawn Burr	4:51	Det.
Apr. 16/87	Que.	DSF	Que. 5	Hfd. 4	Peter Stastny	6:05	Que.
Apr. 18/87	Wsh.	DSF	NYI 3	Wsh. 2	Pat LaFontaine	68:47	NYI
Apr. 21/87	Edm.	DF	Edm. 3	Wpg. 2	Glenn Anderson	0:36	Edm.
Apr. 26/87	Que.	DF	Mtl. 3	Que. 2	Mats Naslund	5:30	Mtl.
Apr. 27/87	Tor.	DF	Tor. 3	Det. 2	Mike Allison	9:31	Det.
May 4/87	Phi.	CF	Phi. 4	Mtl. 3	Ilkka Sinislao	9:11	Phi.
May 20/87	Edm.	F	Edm. 3	Phi. 2	Jari Kurri	6:50	Edm.
Apr. 6/88	NYI	DSF	NYI 4	N.J. 3	Pat LaFontaine	6:11	N.J.
Apr. 10/88	Phi.	DSF	Phi. 5	Wsh. 4	Murray Craven	1:18	Wsh.
Apr. 10/88	N.J.	DSF	NYI 5	N.J. 4	Brent Sutter	15:07	N.J.
Apr. 10/88	Buf.	DSF	Buf. 6	Bos. 5	John Tucker	5:32	Bos.
Apr. 12/88	Det.	DSF	Tor. 6	Det. 5	Ed Olczyk	0:34	Det.
Apr. 16/88	Wsh.	DSF	Wsh. 5	Phi. 4	Dale Hunter	5:57	Wsh.
Apr. 21/88	Cgy.	DF	Edm. 5	Cgy. 4	Wayne Gretzky	7:54	Edm.
May 4/88	Bos.	CF	N.J. 3	Bos. 2	Doug Brown	17:46	Bos.
May 9/88	Det.	CF	Edm. 4	Det. 3	Jari Kurri	11:02	Edm.
Apr. 5/89	St. L.	DSF	St. L. 4	Min. 3	Brett Hull	11:55	St. L.
Apr. 5/89	Cgy.	DSF	Van. 4	Cgy. 3	Paul Reinhart	2:47	Cgy.
Apr. 6/89	St. L.	DSF	St. L. 4	Min. 3	Rick Meagher	5:30	St. L.
Apr. 6/89	Det.	DSF	Chi. 5	Det. 4	Duane Sutter	14:36	Chi.
Apr. 8/89	Hfd.	DSF	Mtl. 5	Hfd. 4	Stephane Richer	5:01	Mtl.
Apr. 8/89	Phi.	DSF	Wsh. 4	Phi. 3	Kelly Miller	0:51	Phi.
Apr. 9/89	Hfd.	DSF	Mtl. 4	Hfd. 3	Russ Courtnall	15:12	Mtl.
Apr. 15/89	Cgy.	DSF	Cgy. 4	Van. 3	Joel Otto	19:21	Cgy.
Apr. 18/89	Cgy.	DF	Cgy. 4	L.A. 3	Doug Gilmour	7:47	Cgy.
Apr. 19/89	Mtl.	DF	Mtl. 3	Bos. 2	Bobby Smith	12:24	Mtl.
Apr. 20/89	St. L.	DF	St. L. 5	Chi. 4	Tony Hrkac	33:49	Chi.
Apr. 21/89	Phi.	DF	Pit. 4	Phi. 3	Phil Bourque	12:08	Phi.
May 8/89	Chi.	CF	Cgy. 2	Chi. 1	Al MacInnis	15:05	Cgy.
May 9/89	Mtl.	CF	Phi. 2	Mtl. 1	Dave Poulin	5:02	Mtl.
May 19/89	Mtl.	F	Mtl. 4	Cgy. 3	Ryan Walter	38:08	Cgy.
Apr. 5/90	N.J.	DSF	Wsh. 5	N.J. 4	Dino Ciccarelli	5:34	Wsh.
Apr. 6/90	Edm.	DSF	Edm. 3	Wpg. 2	Mark Lamb	4:21	Edm.
Apr. 8/90	Tor.	DSF	St. L. 6	Tor. 5	Sergio Momesso	6:04	St. L.
Apr. 8/90	L.A.	DSF	L.A. 2	Cgy. 1	Tony Granato	8:37	L.A.
Apr. 9/90	Mtl.	DSF	Mtl. 2	Buf. 1	Brian Skrudland	12:35	Mtl.
Apr. 9/90	NYI	DSF	NYI 4	NYR 3	Brent Sutter	20:59	NYR
Apr. 10/90	Wpg.	DSF	Wpg. 4	Edm. 3	Dave Ellett	21:08	Edm.
Apr. 14/90	L.A.	DSF	L.A. 4	Cgy. 3	Mike Krushelnyski	23:14	L.A.
Apr. 15/90	Hfd.	DSF	Hfd. 3	Bos. 2	Kevin Dineen	12:30	Bos.
Apr. 21/90	Bos.	DF	Bos. 5	Mtl. 4	Garry Galley	3:42	Bos.
Apr. 24/90	L.A.	DF	Edm. 6	L.A. 5	Joe Murphy	4:42	Edm.
Apr. 25/90	Wsh.	DF	Wsh. 4	NYR 3	Rod Langway	0:34	Wsh.
Apr. 27/90	NYR	DF	Wsh. 2	NYR 1	John Druce	6:48	Wsh.
May 15/90	Bos.	F	Edm. 3	Bos. 2	Petr Klima	55:13	Edm.
Apr. 4/91	Chi.	DSF	Min. 4	Chi. 3	Brian Propp	4:14	Min.
Apr. 5/91	Pit.	DSF	Pit. 5	N.J. 4	Jaromir Jagr	8:52	Pit.
Apr. 6/91	L.A.	DSF	L.A. 3	Van. 2	Wayne Gretzky	11:08	L.A.
Apr. 8/91	Van.	DSF	Van. 2	L.A. 1	Cliff Ronning	3:12	L.A.
Apr. 11/91	NYR	DSF	Wsh. 5	NYR 4	Dino Ciccarelli	6:44	Wsh.
Apr. 11/91	Mtl.	DSF	Mtl. 4	Buf. 3	Russ Courtnall	5:56	Mtl.
Apr. 14/91	Edm.	DSF	Cgy. 2	Edm. 1	Theo Fleury	4:40	Edm.
Apr. 16/91	Cgy.	DSF	Edm. 5	Cgy. 4	Esa Tikkanen	6:58	Edm.
Apr. 18/91	L.A.	DF	L.A. 4	Edm. 3	Luc Robitaille	2:13	Edm.
Apr. 19/91	Bos.	DF	Mtl. 4	Bos. 3	Stephane Richer	0:27	Bos.
Apr. 19/91	Pit.	DF	Pit. 7	Wsh. 6	Kevin Stevens	8:10	Pit.
Apr. 20/91	L.A.	DF	Edm. 4	L.A. 3	Petr Klima	24:48	Edm.
Apr. 22/91	Edm.	DF	Edm. 4	L.A. 3	Esa Tikkanen	20:48	Edm.
Apr. 27/91	Mtl.	DF	Mtl. 3	Bos. 2	Shayne Corson	17:47	Bos.
Apr. 28/91	Edm.	DF	Edm. 4	L.A. 3	Craig MacTavish	16:57	Edm.
May 3/91	Bos.	CF	Bos. 5	Pit. 4	Vladimir Ruzicka	8:14	Pit.
Apr. 21/92	Bos.	DSF	Bos. 3	Buf. 2	Adam Oates	11:14	Bos.
Apr. 22/92	Min.	DSF	Det. 5	Min. 4	Yves Racine	1:15	Det.
Apr. 22/92	St. L.	DSF	St. L. 5	Chi. 4	Brett Hull	23:33	Chi.
Apr. 25/92	Buf.	DSF	Bos. 5	Buf. 4	Ted Donato	2:08	Bos.
Apr. 28/92	Min.	DSF	Det. 1	Min. 0	Sergei Fedorov	16:13	Det.
Apr. 29/92	Hfd.	DSF	Hfd. 2	Mon. 1	Yvon Corriveau	0:24	Mtl.
May 1/92	Mtl.	DSF	Mtl. 3	Hfd. 2	Russ Courtnall	25:26	Mtl.
May 3/92	Van.	DF	Edm. 4	Van. 3	Joe Murphy	8:36	Edm.
May 5/92	Mtl.	DF	Bos. 3	Mtl. 2	Peter Douris	3:12	Bos.
May 7/92	Pit.	DF	NYR 6	Pit. 5	Kris King	1:29	Pit.
May 9/92	Pit.	DF	Pit. 5	NYR 4	Ron Francis	2:47	Pit.
May 17/92	Pit.	CF	Pit. 4	Bos. 3	Jaromir Jagr	9:44	Pit.
May 20/92	Edm.	CF	Chi. 4	Edm. 3	Jeremy Roenick	2:45	Chi.
Apr. 18/93	Bos.	DSF	Buf. 5	Bos. 4	Bob Sweeney	11:03	Buf.

Date	City	Series	Score		Scorer	Overtime	Series Winner
Apr. 18/93	Que.	DSF	Que. 3	Mtl. 2	Scott Young	16:49	Mtl.
Apr. 20/93	Wsh.	DSF	NYI 5	Wsh. 4	Brian Mullen	34:50	NYI
Apr. 22/93	Mtl.	DSF	Mtl. 2	Que. 1	Vincent Damphousse	10:30	Mtl.
Apr. 22/93	Buf.	DSF	Buf. 4	Bos. 3	Yuri Khmylev	1:05	Buf.
Apr. 22/93	NYI	DSF	NYI 4	Wsh. 3	Ray Ferraro	4:46	NYI
Apr. 24/93	Buf.	DSF	Buf. 6	Bos. 5	Brad May	4:48	Buf.
Apr. 24/93	NYI	DSF	NYI 4	Wsh. 3	Ray Ferraro	25:40	NYI
Apr. 25/93	St. L.	DSF	St. L. 4	Chi. 3	Craig Janney	10:43	St. L.
Apr. 26/93	Que.	DSF	Mtl. 5	Que. 4	Kirk Muller	8:17	Mtl.
Apr. 27/93	Det.	DSF	Tor. 5	Det. 4	Mike Foligno	2:05	Tor.
Apr. 27/93	Van.	DSF	Wpg. 4	Van. 3	Teemu Selanne	6:18	Van.
Apr. 29/93	Wpg.	DSF	Van. 4	Wpg. 3	Greg Adams	4:30	Van.
May 1/93	Det.	DSF	Tor. 4	Det. 3	Nikolai Borschevsky	2:35	Tor.
May 3/93	Tor.	DF	Tor. 2	St. L. 1	Doug Gilmour	23:16	Tor.
May 4/93	Mtl.	DF	Mtl. 4	Buf. 3	Guy Carbonneau	2:50	Mtl.
May 5/93	Tor.	DF	St. L. 2	Tor. 1	Jeff Brown	23:03	Tor.
May 6/93	Buf.	DF	Mtl. 4	Buf. 3	Gilbert Dionne	8:28	Mtl.
May 8/93	Buf.	DF	Mtl. 4	Buf. 3	Kirk Muller	11:37	Mtl.
May 11/93	Van.	DF	L.A. 4	Van. 3	Gary Shuchuk	26:31	L.A.
May 14/93	Pit.	DF	NYI 4	Pit. 3	Dave Volek	5:16	NYI
May 18/93	Mtl.	CF	Mtl. 4	NYI 3	Stephan Lebeau	26:21	Mtl.
May 20/93	NYI	CF	Mtl. 2	NYI 1	Guy Carbonneau	12:34	Mtl.
May 25/93	Tor.	CF	Tor. 3	L.A. 2	Glenn Anderson	19:20	L.A.
May 27/93	L.A.	CF	L.A. 5	Tor. 4	Wayne Gretzky	1:41	L.A.
Jun. 3/93	Mtl.	F	Mtl. 3	L.A. 2	Eric Desjardins	0:51	Mtl.
Jun. 5/93	L.A.	F	Mtl. 4	L.A. 3	John LeClair	0:34	Mtl.
Jun. 7/93	L.A.	F	Mtl. 3	L.A. 2	John LeClair	14:37	Mtl.
Apr. 20/94	Tor.	CQF	Tor. 1	Chi. 0	Todd Gill	2:15	Tor.
Apr. 22/94	St. L.	CQF	Dal. 5	St. L. 4	Paul Cavallini	8:34	Dal.
Apr. 24/94	Chi.	CQF	Chi. 4	Tor. 3	Jeremy Roenick	1:23	Tor.
Apr. 25/94	Bos.	CQF	Mtl. 2	Bos. 1	Kirk Muller	17:18	Bos.
Apr. 26/94	Cgy.	CQF	Van. 2	Cgy. 1	Geoff Courtnall	7:15	Van.
Apr. 27/94	Buf.	CQF	Buf. 1	N.J. 0	Dave Hannan	65:43	N.J.
Apr. 28/94	Van.	CQF	Van. 3	Cgy. 2	Trevor Linden	16:43	Van.
Apr. 30/94	Cgy.	CQF	Van. 4	Cgy. 3	Pavel Bure	22:20	Van.
May 3/94	N.J.	CSF	Bos. 6	N.J. 5	Don Sweeney	9:08	N.J.
May 7/94	Bos.	CSF	N.J. 5	Bos. 4	Stephane Richer	14:19	N.J.
May 8/94	Van.	CSF	Van. 2	Dal. 1	Sergio Momesso	11:01	Van.
May 12/94	Tor.	CSF	Tor. 3	S.J. 2	Mike Gartner	8:53	Tor.
May 15/94	NYR	CF	N.J. 4	NYR 3	Stephane Richer	35:23	NYR
May 16/94	Tor.	CF	Tor. 3	Van. 2	Peter Zezel	16:55	Van.
May 19/94	N.J.	CF	NYR 3	N.J. 2	Stephane Matteau	26:13	NYR
May 24/94	Van.	CF	Van. 4	Tor. 3	Greg Adams	20:14	Van.
May 27/94	NYR	CF	NYR 2	N.J. 1	Stephane Matteau	24:24	NYR
May 31/94	NYR	F	Van. 3	NYR 2	Greg Adams	19:26	NYR
May 7/95	Phi.	CQF	Phi. 4	Buf. 3	Karl Dykhuis	10:06	Phi.
May 9/95	Cgy.	CQF	S.J. 5	Cgy. 4	Ulf Dahlen	12:21	S.J.
May 12/95	NYR	CQF	NYR 3	Que. 2	Steve Larmer	8:09	NYR
May 12/95	N.J.	CQF	N.J. 1	Bos. 0	Randy McKay	8:51	N.J.
May 14/95	Pit.	CQF	Pit. 6	Wsh. 5	Luc Robitaille	4:30	Pit.
May 15/95	St. L.	CQF	Van. 6	St. L. 5	Cliff Ronning	1:48	Van.
May 17/95	Tor.	CQF	Tor. 5	Chi. 4	Randy Wood	10:00	Chi.
May 19/95	Cgy.	CQF	S.J. 5	Cgy. 4	Ray Whitney	21:54	S.J.
May 21/95	Phi.	CSF	Phi. 5	NYR 4	Eric Desjardins	7:03	Phi.
May 21/95	Chi.	CSF	Chi. 2	Van. 1	Joe Murphy	9:04	Chi.
May 22/95	Phi.	CSF	Phi. 4	NYR 3	Kevin Haller	0:25	Phi.
May 25/95	Van.	CSF	Chi. 3	Van. 2	Chris Chelios	6:22	Chi.
May 26/95	N.J.	CSF	N.J. 2	Pit. 1	Neal Broten	18:36	N.J.
May 27/95	Van.	CSF	Chi. 4	Van. 3	Chris Chelios	5:35	Chi.
Jun. 1/95	Det.	CF	Det. 2	Chi. 1	Nicklas Lidstrom	1:01	Det.
Jun. 6/95	Chi.	CF	Det. 4	Chi. 3	Vladimir Konstantinov	29:25	Det.
Jun. 7/95	N.J.	CF	Phi. 3	N.J. 2	Eric Lindros	4:19	N.J.
Jun. 11/95	Det.	CF	Det. 2	Chi. 1	Vyacheslav Kozlov	22:25	Det.

Left: Ray Whitney scored at 1:54 of the second overtime period in game seven of the Western Conference Quarter-Finals to give the San Jose Sharks a 5-4 victory over the Calgary Flames. Right: Karl Dykhuis scored the first overtime goal of the 1994-95 playoffs, sneaking a shot past Buffalo's Dominik Hasek to give the Philadelphia Flyers a 4-3 win over the Sabres in game one of the Eastern Conference Quarter-Finals.

Jacques Lemaire, left, Frank Boucher, center, and Toe Blake have scored a Stanley Cup-winning goal and coached a Stanley Cup-winning team.

Stanley Cup Coaching Records

Coaches listed in order of total games coached in playoffs. Minimum: 65 games.

Coach	Team	Years	Series	Series W	Series L	G	Games W	Games L	T	Cups	%
Bowman, Scott	St. Louis	4	10	6	4	52	26	26	0	0	.500
	Montreal	8	19	16	3	98	70	28	0	5	.714
	Buffalo	5	8	3	5	36	18	18	0	0	.500
	Pittsburgh	2	6	5	1	33	23	10	0	1	.696
	Detroit	2	5	3	2	25	15	10	0	0	.600
	Total	21	48	33	15	244	152	92	0	6	.623
Arbour, Al	St. Louis	1	2	1	1	11	4	7	0	0	.364
	NY Islanders	15	40	29	11	198	119	79	0	4	.601
	Total	16	42	30	12	209	123	86	0	4	.589
Irvin, Dick	Chicago	1	3	2	1	9	5	3	1	0	.611
	Toronto	9	20	12	8	66	33	32	1	1	.508
	Montreal	14	22	11	11	115	62	53	0	3	.539
	Total	24	45	25	20	190	100	88	2	4	.532
Keenan, Mike	Philadelphia	4	10	6	4	57	32	25	0	0	.561
	Chicago	4	11	7	4	60	33	27	0	0	.550
	NY Rangers	1	4	4	0	23	16	7	0	1	.695
	St. Louis	1	1	0	1	7	3	4	0	0	.428
	Total	10	26	17	9	147	84	63	0	1	.571
Sather, Glen	Edmonton	10	27	21	6	*126	89	37	0	4	.706
Blake, Toe	Montreal	13	23	18	5	119	82	37	0	8	.689
Reay, Billy	Chicago	12	22	10	12	117	57	60	0	0	.487
Shero, Fred	Philadelphia	6	16	12	4	83	48	35	0	2	.578
	NY Rangers	2	5	3	2	25	13	12	0	0	.520
	Total	8	21	15	6	108	61	47	0	2	.565
Adams, Jack	Detroit	15	27	15	12	105	52	52	1	3	.500
Demers, Jacques	St. Louis	3	6	3	3	33	16	17	0	0	.485
	Detroit	3	7	4	3	38	20	18	0	0	.526
	Montreal	2	5	4	1	27	19	8	0	1	.704
	Total	8	18	11	7	98	55	43	0	1	.561
Quinn, Pat	Philadelphia	3	8	5	3	39	22	17	0	0	.564
	Los Angeles	1	1	0	1	3	0	3	0	0	.000
	Vancouver	4	9	5	4	55	29	26	0	0	.527
	Total	8	18	10	8	97	51	46	0	0	.525
Burns, Pat	Montreal	4	10	6	4	56	30	26	0	0	.535
	Toronto	3	7	4	3	46	23	23	0	0	.500
	Total	7	17	10	7	102	53	49	0	0	.519
Francis, Emile	NY Rangers	9	14	5	9	75	34	41	0	0	.453
	St. Louis	3	4	1	3	18	6	12	0	0	.333
	Total	12	18	6	12	93	40	53	0	0	.430
Imlach, Punch	Toronto	11	17	10	7	92	44	48	0	4	.478
Day, Hap	Toronto	9	14	10	4	80	49	31	0	5	.613
Murray, Bryan	Washington	7	10	3	7	53	24	29	0	0	.452
	Detroit	3	4	1	3	25	10	15	0	0	.400
	Total	10	14	4	10	78	34	44	0	0	.435
Johnson, Bob	Calgary	5	10	5	5	52	25	27	0	0	.481
	Pittsburgh	1	4	4	0	24	16	8	0	1	.666
	Total	6	14	9	5	76	41	35	0	1	.539
Abel, Sid	Chicago	1	1	0	1	7	3	4	0	0	.429
	Detroit	8	12	4	8	69	29	40	0	0	.420
	Total	9	13	4	9	76	32	44	0	0	.421
Ross, Art	Boston	12	19	9	10	70	32	33	5	1	.493
Bergeron, Michel	Quebec	7	13	6	7	68	31	37	0	0	.456
Lemaire, Jacques	Montreal	2	5	3	2	27	15	12	0	0	.555
	New Jersey	2	7	6	1	40	27	13	0	1	.675
	Total	4	12	9	3	67	42	25	0	1	.626
Muckler, John	Edmonton	2	7	6	1	40	25	15	0	1	.625
	Buffalo	4	5	1	4	27	11	16	0	0	.407
	Total	6	12	7	5	67	36	31	0	1	.537
Ivan, Tommy	Detroit	7	12	8	4	67	36	31	0	3	.537
Neilson, Roger	Toronto	2	5	3	2	19	8	11	0	0	.421
	Buffalo	1	2	1	1	8	4	4	0	0	.500
	Vancouver	2	5	3	2	21	12	9	0	0	.571
	NY Rangers	2	3	1	2	19	8	11	0	0	.421
	Total	7	15	8	7	67	32	35	0	0	.473
Pulford, Bob	Los Angeles	4	6	2	4	26	11	15	0	0	.423
	Chicago	5	9	4	5	41	17	24	0	0	.415
	Total	9	15	6	9	67	28	39	0	0	.418
Patrick, Lester	NY Rangers	12	24	14	10	65	31	26	8	2	.538

* Does not include suspended game, May 24, 1988.

Penalty Shots in Stanley Cup Playoff Games

Date	Player	Goaltender	Scored	Final Score				Series
Mar. 25/37	Lionel Conacher, Mtl. Maroons	Tiny Thompson, Boston	No	Mtl. M.	0	at Bos.	4	QF
Apr. 15/37	Alex Shibicky, NY Rangers	Earl Robertson, Detroit	No	NYR	0	at Det.	3	F
Apr. 13/44	Virgil Johnson, Chicago	Bill Durnan, Montreal	No	Chi.	4	at Mtl.	5*	F
Apr. 9/68	Wayne Connelly, Minnesota	Terry Sawchuk, Los Angeles	Yes	L.A.	5	at Min.	7	QF
Apr. 27/68	Jim Roberts, St. Louis	Cesare Maniago, Minnesota	No	St. L.	4	at Min.	3	SF
May 16/71	Frank Mahovlich, Montreal	Tony Esposito, Chicago	No	Chi.	3	at Mtl.	4	F
May 7/75	Bill Barber, Philadelphia	Glenn Resch, NY Islanders	No	Phi.	3	at NYI	4*	SF
Apr. 20/79	Mike Walton, Chicago	Glenn Resch, NY Islanders	No	NYI	4	at Chi.	0	QF
Apr. 9/81	Peter McNab, Boston	Don Beaupre, Minnesota	No	Min.	5	at Bos.	4*	PR
Apr. 17/81	Anders Hedberg, NY Rangers	Mike Liut, St. Louis	Yes	NYR	6	at St. L.	4	QF
Apr. 9/83	Denis Potvin, NY Islanders	Pat Riggin, Washington	No	NYI	6	at Wsh.	2	DSF
Apr. 28/84	Wayne Gretzky, Edmonton	Don Beaupre, Minnesota	Yes	Edm.	8	at Min.	5	CF
May 1/84	Mats Naslund, Montreal	Bill Smith, NY Islanders	No	Mtl.	1	at NYI	3	CF
Apr. 14/85	Bob Carpenter, Washington	Bill Smith, NY Islanders	No	Wsh.	4	at NYI.	6	DF
May 28/85	Ron Sutter, Philadelphia	Grant Fuhr, Edmonton	No	Phi.	3	at Edm.	5	F
May 30/85	Dave Poulin, Philadelphia	Grant Fuhr, Edmonton	No	Phi.	3	at Edm.	8	F
Apr. 9/88	John Tucker, Buffalo	Andy Moog, Boston	Yes	Bos.	2	at Buf.	6	DSF
Apr. 9/88	Petr Klima, Detroit	Allan Bester, Toronto	Yes	Det.	6	at Tor.	3	DSF
Apr. 8/89	Neal Broten, Minnesota	Greg Millen, St. Louis	Yes	St. L.	5	at Min.	3	DSF
Apr. 4/90	Al MacInnis, Calgary	Kelly Hrudey, Los Angeles	Yes	L.A.	5	at Cgy.	3	DSF
Apr. 5/90	Randy Wood, NY Islanders	Mike Richter, NY Rangers	No	NYI	1	at NYR	2	DSF
May 3/90	Kelly Miller, Washington	Andy Moog, Boston	No	Wsh.	3	at Bos.	5	CF
May 18/90	Petr Klima, Edmonton	Rejean Lemelin, Boston	No	Edm.	7	at Bos.	2	F
Apr. 6/91	Basil McRae, Minnesota	Ed Belfour, Chicago	Yes	Min.	2	at Chi.	5	DSF
Apr. 10/91	Steve Duchesne, Los Angeles	Kirk McLean, Vancouver	Yes	L.A.	6	at Van.	1	DSF
May 11/92	Jaromir Jagr, Pittsburgh	John Vanbiesbrouck, NYR	Yes	Pit.	3	at NYR	2	DF
May 13/92	Shawn McEachern, Pittsburgh	John Vanbiesbrouck, NYR	No	NYR	1	at Pit.	5	DF
June 7/94	Pavel Bure, Vancouver	Mike Richter, NYR	Yes	NYR	4	at Van.	2	F
May 9/95	Patrick Poulin, Chicago	Felix Potvin, Toronto	No	Tor.	3	at Chi.	0	CQF
May 10/95	Michal Pivonka, Washington	Tom Barrasso, Pittsburgh	No	Pit.	2	at Wsh.	6	CQF

* Game was decided in overtime, but shot taken during regulation time.

Ten Longest Overtime Games

Date	City	Series	Score		Scorer	Overtime	Series Winner
Mar. 24/36	Mtl.	SF	Det. 1	Mtl. M. 0	Mud Bruneteau	116:30	Det.
Apr. 3/33	Tor.	SF	Tor. 1	Bos. 0	Ken Doraty	104:46	Tor.
Mar. 23/43	Det.	SF	Tor. 3	Det. 2	Jack McLean	70:18	Det.
Mar. 28/30	Mtl.	SF	Mtl. 2	NYR 1	Gus Rivers	68:52	Mtl.
Apr. 18/87	Wsh.	DSF	NYI 3	Wsh. 2	Pat LaFontaine	68:47	NYI
Apr. 27/94	Buf.	CQF	Buf. 1	N.J. 0	Dave Hannan	65:43	N.J.
Mar. 27/51	Det.	SF	Mtl. 3	Det. 2	Maurice Richard	61:09	Mtl.
Mar. 27/38	NY	QF	NYA 3	NYR 2	Lorne Carr	60:40	NYA
Mar. 26/32	Mtl.	SF	NYR 4	Mtl. 3	Fred Cook	59:32	NYR
Mar. 21/39	NY	SF	Bos. 2	NYR 1	Mel Hill	59:25	Bos.

Two penalty shots were taken in the 1995 playoffs. Although Michal Pivonka, above, was stopped by Pittsburgh's Tom Barrasso, the Capitals held on for a 6–2 victory in game three of the Penguins-Capitals Eastern Conference Quarter-Final series. Felix Potvin, below, stopped Chicago's Patrick Poulin on a penalty shot in game two of the Western Quarter-Finals, preserving his shutout in a 3–0 victory for the Leafs.

Overtime Record of Current Teams

(Listed by number of OT games played)

	Overall			Home				Road				
Team	GP	W	L	T	GP	W	L	T	Last OT Game	GP	W	L	T	Last OT Game
Montreal	115	66	47	2	53	35	17	1	Jun. 3/93	62	31	30	1	Apr. 25/94
Boston	93	36	54	3	43	20	22	1	May 9/94	50	16	32	2	May 12/94
Toronto	87	44	42	1	55	28	26	1	May 17/95	32	16	16	0	May 24/94
NY Rangers	59	27	32	0	25	11	14	0	May 12/95	34	16	18	0	May 22/95
Chicago	56	26	28	2	26	14	11	1	Jun. 6/95	30	12	17	1	Jun. 11/95
Detroit	54	25	29	0	33	12	21	0	Jun. 11/95	21	13	8	0	Jun. 6/95
NY Islanders	38	29	9	0	17	14	3	0	May 20/93	21	15	6	0	May 18/93
Philadelphia	38	22	16	0	16	11	5	0	May 22/95	22	11	11	0	Jun. 7/95
St. Louis	33	19	14	0	17	13	4	0	May 15/95	16	6	10	0	May 5/93
Los Angeles	30	12	18	0	16	8	8	0	Jun. 7/93	14	4	10	0	Jun. 3/93
* Calgary	29	11	18	0	13	4	9	0	May 19/95	16	7	9	0	Apr. 28/94
Buffalo	28	14	14	0	17	11	6	0	Apr. 27/94	11	3	8	0	May 7/95
Vancouver	28	13	15	0	12	5	7	0	May 27/95	16	8	8	0	May 21/95
** Dallas	28	12	16	0	14	5	9	0	Apr. 28/92	14	7	7	0	May 8/94
Edmonton	27	17	10	0	14	9	5	0	May 20/92	13	8	5	0	May 3/92
*** Colorado	19	10	9	0	11	6	5	0	Apr. 26/93	8	4	4	0	May 12/95
Washington	18	8	10	0	7	4	3	0	Apr. 20/93	11	4	7	0	May 14/95
Pittsburgh	16	9	7	0	9	6	3	0	May 14/95	7	3	4	0	May 26/95
**** New Jersey	15	5	10	0	7	2	5	0	Jun. 7/95	8	3	5	0	May 27/94
Hartford	11	5	6	0	7	4	3	0	Apr. 29/92	4	1	3	0	May 1/92
Winnipeg	9	4	5	0	5	2	3	0	Apr. 29/93	4	2	2	0	Apr. 27/93
San Jose	3	2	1	0	0	0	0	0		3	2	1	0	May 19/95

*Totals include those of Atlanta 1972-80.
**Totals include those of Minnesota 1967-93.
***Totals include those of Quebec 1979-95.
****Totals include those of Kansas City and Colorado 1974-82.

This Date in... Stanley Cup Playoff History

Dec. 27, 1897 • In the only Stanley Cup challenge of the season, the defending champion Montreal Victorias turned back the Ottawa Capitals 15-2 to retain their champion status.

Dec. 27, 1906 • Riley Hern, "Pud" Glass, "Hod" Stuart, Ernie Johnson and Jack Marshall of the Montreal Wanderers became the first professionals to compete for the Stanley Cup. Glass scored four goals as the defending champion Montreal club downed the challenging New Glasgow Cubs 10-3 in the first game of a two-game, total-goal series.

Dec. 30, 1896 • Ernie McLea notched the first hat-trick in Stanley Cup history as the Montreal Victorias regained possession of the coveted trophy with a 6-5 win versus the defending champion Winnipeg Victorias. Winnipeg had won the Cup earlier in the year, on February 14, 1896, from Montreal.

Dec. 30, 1904 • In the first game of a best-of-three challenge between the Winnipeg Rowing Club and the defending champion Ottawa Silver Seven, a red line was drawn between each set of goalposts to aid the referee in awarding goals. These lines became the first known "Goal Lines" in hockey history.

Jan. 16, 1905 • "One-Eyed" Frank McGee netted an all-time Stanley Cup record 14 goals in the Ottawa Silver Seven's 23-2 win over the Dawson City Nuggets, who had trekked over 4,000 miles by dogsled, boat and train to challenge for the Cup.

Feb. 14, 1896 • Winnipeg Victorias' goaltender G.H. Merritt, credited as the first netminder to wear goalie pads, posted a 2-0 shutout to capture the Stanley Cup from the reigning champion Montreal Victorias. The game marked the first successful challenge in Stanley Cup history.

Feb. 25, 1904 • Ottawa Silver Seven sniper Frank McGee registered the first five-goal performance in Stanley Cup history in an 11-2 win over the challenging Toronto Marlboros.

Mar. 5, 1900 • Defending champion Montreal Shamrocks' forward Arthur Farrell led his club to a 10-2 victory against the challenging Halifax Crescents with an unprecedented four-goal Stanley Cup performance.

Mar. 9, 1893 • Upon defeating the Montreal Crystals 2-1, the Montreal Amateur Athletic Association (MAAA) captured the 1893 Amateur Hockey Association (AHA) title and the first Stanley Cup championship. The MAAA lineup consisted of nine players: Billy Barlow (forward), Allan Cameron (defense), Archie Hodgson (forward), Alex Irving (forward), A. Kingan (forward), J. Lowe (forward), T. Paton (goaltender), Harvie Routh (forward) and James Stewart (defense).

Mar. 9, 1895 • In the first official challenge for the Stanley Cup, the defending champion Montreal AAA team retained possession of the trophy with a 5-1 triumph over the Queen's University Golden Gaels.

Mar. 11, 1914 • The Toronto Blueshirts (later renamed the Maple Leafs) captured their first Stanley Cup title with a 6-0 home-ice shutout against the Montreal Canadiens, who were making their championship series debut. The game marked the first Stanley Cup contest ever played on an artificial ice surface.

Mar. 14, 1908 • Making his Stanley Cup debut, "Newsy" Lalonde scored twice to lead the Montreal Wanderers to a 6-4 win and a successful defense of their championship title against the Toronto Trolley Leaguers.

Mar. 16, 1911 • Ottawa Senators' forward Marty Walsh scored 10 goals — second in Stanley Cup history only to Frank McGee's 14-goal total (January 16, 1905) — en route to a 14-4 win over the Port Arthur Bearcats.

Mar. 16, 1923 • For the first time in Stanley Cup history, two brothers opposed each other in the Finals. In fact, two sets of brothers — Cy and Corb Denneny, and George and Frank Boucher — lined up on opposite sides of the ice. Cy and George skated for the Ottawa Senators, while Corb and Frank played for Vancouver Maroons. None of the four scored in this opening game, won by Ottawa 1-0.

Mar. 18, 1992 • At a dinner of the Ottawa Amateur Athletic Association, Lord Kilcoursie, a player on the Ottawa Rebels hockey club, read the following message on behalf of Lord Stanley of Preston, the Governor-General of Canada,: "It would be a good thing if there were a challenge cup which should be held from year to year by the champion hockey team in the Dominion (of Canada)....I am willing to give a cup which shall be held...by the winning team." That cup eventually became the Stanley Cup, which has been presented annually since 1893.

Mar. 21, 1921 • More than 11,000 fans jammed the Vancouver Arena for the first game of this best-of-five Stanley Cup series between the hometown Millionaires and the visiting Ottawa Senators. It marked the largest crowd ever to witness a hockey game anywhere in the world up until this date. Vancouver downed Ottawa 2-1.

Mar. 22, 1894 • Forward Billy Barlow netted two goals as the Montreal AAA downed the Ottawa Generals 3-1 in this one-game battle for the 1894 Stanley Cup.

Mar. 22, 1919 • Montreal center "Newsy" Lalonde became the first NHL player ever to score four goals in one Finals game, spurring the Canadiens to a 4-2 win against the PCHA's Seattle Metropolitans. Only Detroit's Ted Lindsay (April 5, 1955) and Montreal's Maurice "Rocket" Richard (April 6, 1957) have since matched Lalonde's four-goal feat.

Mar. 22, 1924 • In the first Stanley Cup game of his career, 21-year-old, 160-pound rookie center Howie Morenz recorded a hat-trick as the Montreal Canadiens defeated the WCHL's Calgary Tigers 6-1. The game also marked the Stanley Cup debuts for two other Montreal rookies, Aurel Joliat and Sylvio Mantha.

Mar. 23, 1918 • Alf Skinner of the Toronto Arenas registered the first hat-trick by an NHL player in a Stanley Cup Finals game. The PCHA's Vancouver Millionaires downed Toronto 6-4 in Game Two of the 1918 Finals, the first Stanley Cup series involving an NHL franchise.

Mar. 25, 1917 • The Seattle Metropolitans of the Pacific Coast Hockey Association (PCHA) distinguished themselves as the first United States team to win the Stanley Cup. Seattle's Bernie Morris scored six times en route to a 9-1 triumph over the Montreal Canadiens.

Mar. 25, 1922 • Toronto goaltender John Roach blanked the Vancouver Millionaires 6-0, recording the first Stanley Cup shutout by an NHL rookie.

Mar. 26, 1919 • In the longest game in Finals history, the Montreal Canadiens and Seattle Metropolitans (PCHA) played for 60 minutes of regulation time and 100 minutes of overtime without scoring a goal. Georges Vezina and Harry Holmes dominated the marathon contest with their superior goaltending.

Mar. 27, 1925 • Howie Morenz led the Montreal Canadiens to a 4-2 win over the PCHA's Victoria Cougars with his record-setting second three-goal output of his Stanley Cup Finals career. Maurice "Rocket" Richard later surpassed Morenz's mark with three hat-tricks, including one four-goal and two three-goal performances.

Mar. 28, 1929 • For the first time in history, two American teams — the Boston Bruins and New York Rangers — clashed in the Finals. The Bruins' "Dit" Clapper and "Dutch" Gainor scored goals, and "Tiny" Thompson posted the third Stanley Cup shutout ever by an NHL rookie to give Boston a 2-0 win in Game One. The Bruins won 2-1 the following night to capture their first championship title.

Mar. 29, 1929 • Harry Oliver scored a goal and an assist, and Bill Carson netted the game-winning tally as the Boston Bruins earned their first Stanley Cup title with a 2-1 win versus the New York Rangers. The victory completed a two-game sweep by Boston in the best-of-three Finals.

Mar. 30, 1916 • In the fifth and final game for the 1916 Stanley Cup title, the Montreal Canadiens downed the PCHA's Portland Rosebuds 2-1 on goals by Skene Ronan and Goldie Prodgers, who netted the winning tally. The victory marked the first of Montreal's 23 championships, a record unsurpassed by any other team in professional sports history.

Mar. 30, 1918 • In the fifth and final game of the 1918 Finals, Alf Skinner and Odie Cleghorn engineered a successful comeback with unanswered goals in a 2-1 win over the PCHA's Vancouver Millionaires. Cleghorn notched the game-winner as the Toronto Arenas became the first NHL team to capture Lord Stanley's Cup.

Mar. 30, 1919 • Montreal Canadiens' right-winger Odie Cleghorn scored the first overtime goal by an NHL player in the Finals, snapping a 3-3 tie at 15.57 of the overtime period. The game knotted the 1919 Finals between Montreal and the Seattle Metropolitans at 2-2-1 after five outings. However, the series never resumed because players from both squads suffered the consequences of a raging flu epidemic. Montreal's Joe Hall, who had been become ill during this fifth game, later died as a result of the sickness.

Mar. 30, 1925 • The Victoria Cougars of the Western Canada Hockey League downed the Montreal Canadiens 6-1 to become the last non-NHL team to capture the Stanley Cup. The win gave Victoria a 3-1 margin over Montreal in the best-of-five championship series.

Mar. 30, 1946 • In Game One, right-winger Maurice "Rocket" Richard registered the first of his record three overtime goals in Finals action, snapping a 3-3 tie at 9.08 of the extra period. The goal gave the Montreal Canadiens the first of their four victories versus the Boston Bruins en route to the 1946 Stanley Cup.

April 3, 1930 • The Montreal Canadiens downed the Boston Bruins 4-3 to complete a two-game sweep of the 1930 Finals. For the defending Stanley Cup champion Boston Bruins, who had posted the NHL's best regular-season record in 1929-30 with a 38-5-1 mark, the games marked their first back-to-back losses of the year.

April 4, 1921 • The Ottawa Senators defeated the Vancouver Millionaires 2-1 in the decisive fifth game of the 1921 Stanley Cup series. Jack Darragh scored both goals for the Senators, who became the first NHL team to capture back-to-back Stanley Cup titles.

April 4, 1944 • Montreal Canadiens' rookie right-winger Maurice "Rocket" Richard made his Stanley Cup debut, tallying an assist on linemate "Toe" Blake's game-winning goal in this 5-1 victory against the Chicago Blackhawks in Game One of the 1944 Finals. Richard continued to play a key role in Montreal's drive towards the title, scoring four more goals in the remaining three games of the Canadiens' four-game sweep against Chicago.

April 5, 1931 • Over 18,000 fans jammed Chicago Stadium for Game Two of the 1931 championship series, setting a new record for the largest attendance for one game in hockey history. Blackhawks' left-winger Johnny Gottselig thrilled the hometown fans with the game-winning goal in double overtime as Chicago downed the Montreal Canadiens 2-1. The Canadiens later won the Stanley Cup series three games to two.

April 5, 1955 • Detroit Red Wings' left-winger Ted Lindsay became the second player in NHL history to score four goals in one Stanley Cup game and tied a Finals record with three goals in one period. Joining "Newsy" Lalonde (March 22, 1919) in achieving the four-goal feat, Lindsay scored the game-winning tally as Detroit downed Montreal 7-1.

April 6, 1926 • Goaltender Clint Benedict backstopped the Montreal Maroons to their first Stanley Cup title, blanking the Victoria Cougars 2-0 to win the best-of-five confrontation 3-1. The shutout was Benedict's third of the series, establishing a new Stanley Cup record for one year.

April 6, 1937 • When regular netminder Normie Smith left Game One of the Finals with an elbow injury, the Detroit Red Wings placed minor leaguer Earl Robertson of the International League's Pittsburgh Hornets into the nets to finish the series. After this 5-1 loss to the New York Rangers in the opener, Robertson, who had never before played an NHL game, backstopped the Red Wings to three wins in their next four outings to capture the 1937 Stanley Cup.

April 6, 1944 • Rookie right-winger Maurice "Rocket" Richard registered the first of his NHL record three Stanley Cup hat-tricks as Montreal won Game Two 3-1 over Chicago. The victory was the second of four straight by the Canadiens versus the Blackhawks en route to the 1944 title.

April 6, 1945 • For the first time in Stanley Cup history, two rookie goaltenders — Toronto's Frank McCool and Detroit's Harry Lumley — opposed each other in the Finals. On the strength of Dave "Sweeney" Schriner's first-period goal, McCool and the Leafs blanked the Wings 1-0 to open the best-of-seven series. For McCool, it was the first of a record three straight Stanley Cup shutouts and four victories en route to winning the 1945 title.

April 6, 1954 • Dickie Moore and Maurice "Rocket" Richard of the Montreal Canadiens combined for the fastest three goals by an NHL team in Finals history, scoring three times within 56 seconds. Moore scored at 15.03 of the first period, followed by Richard at 15.28 and 15.59. The Canadiens downed the Red Wings 3-2 in Detroit.

April 6, 1957 • Right-winger Maurice "Rocket" Richard tied "Newsy" Lalonde and Ted Lindsay for the NHL record with four goals in one Stanley Cup game, leading Montreal to a 5-1 triumph over the Boston Bruins in Game One of the 1957 Finals. The four-goal effort also distinguished Richard as the only NHL player ever to record three hat-tricks in a Stanley Cup career. Montreal went on to win the best-of-seven series four games to one.

April 6, 1961 • In their Stanley Cup debuts, Bobby Hull (2-0-2) and Stan Mikita (0-2-2) led the Chicago Blackhawks to a 3-2 win against the Detroit Red Wings in Game One of the 1961 Finals. Hull netted the winning tally at 13.15 of the first period. Chicago went on to defeat Detroit four games to two in the best-of-seven series.

April 7, 1927 • The American Division champion Boston Bruins battled the Canadian Division champion Ottawa Senators to a 0-0 overtime tie in the first all-NHL Stanley Cup game. The best-of-five series, eventually won by Ottawa 2-0-2 over Boston, marked the dawn of the modern Stanley Cup era.

April 7, 1928 • After losing starting goaltender Lorne Chabot to an eye injury midway through Game Two, 45-year-old New York Rangers' coach and former defenseman Lester Patrick took over between the pipes and inspired his club to a 2-1 overtime victory in Game Two of the 1928 Finals. After signing New York Americans' rookie netminder Joe Miller the following day, the Rangers skated to two wins in their next three outings to win the best-of-five championship series 3-2.

April 7, 1948 • 20-year-old right-winger Gordie Howe of Detroit made his Stanley Cup debut in Game One of the 1948 Finals but failed to register a point as the Toronto Maple Leafs downed the Red Wings 5-3. The Leafs later went on to sweep Detroit in four straight games to capture the best-of-seven series. Howe did not score at all in the series.

April 7, 1960 • In Game One of the 1960 Finals, Montreal right-winger Maurice "Rocket" Richard extended his all-time record of Stanley Cup series appearances to 12, while Toronto's Bert Olmstead and Montreal's Doug Harvey, Bernie "Boom Boom" Geoffrion and Tom Johnson extended their records for consecutive Finals appearances to 10. Montreal defeated Toronto 4-2.

April 7, 1982 • The Edmonton Oilers and Los Angeles Kings combined for 18 goals, setting an NHL record for the highest scoring playoff game ever. Edmonton won the game 10-8 in Game #1 of their best-of-five Smythe DSF. Los Angeles won the series 3-2.

April 8, 1934 • Detroit Red Wings' goaltender Wilf Cude suffered a broken nose midway through Game Three but remained in nets until the final buzzer sounded, inspiring his team to a 5-2 upset win against the Blackhawks in Chicago. It was Detroit's only victory during the best-of-five Finals won by Chicago, three games to one.

April 8, 1937 • Referee Clarence Campbell officiated his first Stanley Cup contest in Game Two of the 1937 Finals, a 4-2 win for the Detroit Red Wings over the New York Rangers. Campbell, who later became the third League President in NHL history in 1946, doled out three penalties during the affair.

April 8, 1943 • After blanking Boston 4-0 the previous night, Detroit goalie Johnny Mowers shut out the Bruins 2-0, completing a four-game sweep in the 1943 Finals. Joe Carveth of the Red Wings registered the winning tally at 12.09 of the first period, and teammate Carl Liscombe added an insurance marker to lock up the title.

April 8, 1980 • Gordie Howe established an NHL record for most years in the playoffs (20) by appearing for the Hartford Whalers in Game #1 of their best-of-three Preliminary round series against Montreal. Howe, making his first NHL playoff appearance since the 1969-70 season, passed former Detroit and Toronto defenseman Red Kelly, who had played in 19 playoff seasons.

April 8, 1982 • Mikko Leinonen of the New York Rangers became the first NHL player to record six assists in a playoff game, helping his club to a 7-3 win over Philadelphia in Game #2 of their Patrick DF. Leinonen's mark was equalled by Edmonton's Wayne Gretzky during the 1987 playoffs

April 9, 1932 • The Toronto Maple Leafs defeated the New York Rangers 6-4 to complete a three-game sweep of the 1932 Finals. The series marked the Stanley Cup debut of the Leafs' famed "Kid Line" of Harvey "Busher" Jackson, Charlie Conacher and Joe Primeau, who combined for eight goals in Toronto's three victories.

April 9, 1935 • After winning the first two games of the 1935 Finals in Toronto, the Montreal Maroons completed a three-game sweep of the Maple Leafs with a 4-1 win in the best-of-five Stanley Cup series.

April 9, 1942 • Eddie Bush of the Detroit Red Wings established a new NHL record with five points (1-4-5) by a defenseman in one Stanley Cup Finals game. Bush, who never scored another point in his NHL career, led Detroit to a 5-2 victory over the Toronto Maple Leafs.

April 9, 1946 • In Game Five of the 1946 Finals, Montreal center Elmer Lach scored a goal and two assists in a 6-3 win against the Boston Bruins. The victory gave the Canadiens their second Stanley Cup in three years.

April 9, 1987 • The Edmonton Oilers established an NHL record for most goals in a playoff game, recording a 13-3 win over Los Angeles in Game #2 of their Smythe DSF. Edmonton went on to win the best-of- seven series 4-1.

April 10, 1934 • The Chicago Blackhawks earned their first Stanley Cup title with a 1-0 overtime victory versus the Detroit Red Wings in Game Four of the best-of-five championship. Harold "Mush" March potted the series-winner at 10.05 of the second overtime period.

April 10, 1949 • Toronto left-winger Sid Smith set a new NHL record with three power-play goals in one Finals game. Toronto defeated Detroit 3-1.

April 10, 1956 • Center Jean Beliveau notched a goal and two assists as the Montreal Canadiens took Game Five (3-1) and the 1956 Stanley Cup title from the Detroit Red Wings. The goal gave Beliveau seven versus Detroit, establishing the record for one Final series. New York Islanders' right-winger Mike Bossy (1982) and Edmonton Oilers' center Wayne Gretzky (1985) have since tied Beliveau's all-time Stanley Cup mark.

April 10, 1982 • The Los Angeles Kings scored five third-period goals and added the game-winner in overtime to defeat the Edmonton Oilers 6-5 in Game #3 of the 1982 Smythe Division DSF in one of the greatest comebacks in NHL playoff history. Trailing 5-0 entering the third period, Los Angeles forward Steve Bozek scored the tying goal with just five seconds remaining and Daryl Evans capped the furious Kings' rally by adding the overtime winner at 2:35. Los Angeles went on to win the best-of-five series 3-2.

April 10, 1985 • Detroit Red Wings' defenseman Brad Park set an NHL record by appearing in post-season play for the 17th consecutive season. Park, marking his second playoff year in a Red Wings uniform, played in all three games of Detroit's Norris DSF series against Chicago, which the Blackhawks won 3-0. He had previously made playoff appearances for the NY Rangers (seven seasons) and Boston Bruins (eight seasons).

April 11, 1936 • Detroit coach Jack Adams steered the Red Wings to their first Stanley Cup championship with a 3-2 victory over the Toronto Maple Leafs in Game Four of the best-of-five Stanley Cup confrontation. The Wings, who had entered the NHL in 1926-27, became the last of the League's "Original Six" teams to win the Cup.

April 11, 1965 • Detroit Red Wings' center Norm Ullman set NHL individual and team playoff records by scoring two goals just five seconds apart in Game #5 of their Semi-Final series against Chicago. Ullman scored at 17:35 and 17:40 of the second period. Chicago won the best-of-seven series 4-3.

April 11, 1971 • Boston Bruins' defenseman Bobby Orr became the first defenseman ever to score three goals in a playoff game during a 5-2 win over the Montreal Canadiens. Since then, four other defensemen have equalled Orr's mark; Dick Redmond (1973), Denis Potvin (1981), Paul Reinhart (1983 and 1984), Doug Halward (1984) and Eric Desjardins (1993).

April 11, 1980 • Montreal's Yvon Lambert scored at 0:29 of overtime to give the Canadiens a 4-3 victory over Hartford and a sweep of the best-of-five series. The game marked the final NHL appearance of two Hall-of-Famers, as Hartford's Gordie Howe and Bobby Hull retired following the Whalers' elimination from the playoffs.

April 11, 1981 • The Boston Bruins set a new playoff record by scoring three shorthanded goals against the Minnesota North Stars in Game #3 of their QF series. The three shorthanded goals were not enough as Minnesota won the game 6-3 and swept the best-of-five series.

April 12, 1938 • The Chicago Blackhawks captured the 1938 Stanley Cup title with a 4-1 victory against the Toronto Maple Leafs in Game Four of the best-of-five title series. Eight American-born players — Carl Dahlstrom, Roger Jenkins, Virgil Johnson, Mike Karakas, Alex Levinsky, Elwin "Doc" Romnes, Louis Trudel and Carl Voss — skated for Chicago in the Finals to set a new Stanley Cup record for United States talent on a championship team.

April 12, 1941 • For the first time since the NHL adopted the best-of-seven Finals format in 1939, a team won the Stanley Cup in straight games. The Boston Bruins topped the Detroit Red Wings 3-1 to complete their four-game sweep of the 1941 series.

April 12, 1945 • Maple Leafs' rookie netminder Frank McCool set a new record with his third consecutive Stanley Cup shutout, 1-0 against the Red Wings, as Toronto moved to within one game of sweeping Detroit in the Finals. The Leafs later won the championship series in seven games.

April 12, 1960 • Right-winger Maurice "Rocket" Richard scored his all-time record 34th and final Stanley Cup goal, helping the Montreal Canadiens to a 5-2 win over the Toronto Maple Leafs in Game Three of the 1960 Finals. The Canadiens' victory was the third in a four-game sweep against the Leafs.

April 12, 1979 • The Toronto Maple Leafs set a playoff record for the fastest three goals by one team during a 7-4 victory over the Atlanta Flames in Game #2 of their Preliminary round series. Darryl Sittler scored at 4:04 and 4:16 and Ron Ellis at 4:27 of the first period. Toronto went on to win the best-of-three series 2-0.

April 13, 1985 • Philadelphia Flyers' center Tim Kerr set a new playoff record by scoring four goals in one period, eclipsing the mark of three held by many players. Kerr scored the four goals in the second period of a 6-5 win over the New York Rangers. Three of Kerr's goals were scored on the power-play, also setting a new record.

April 13, 1933 • Bill Cook snapped a scoreless tie at 7.33 of overtime to give the New York Rangers a 1-0 victory against the Toronto Maple Leafs. Rangers' rookie goaltender Andy Aitkenhead posted the shutout as New York captured the best-of-five series in four games.

April 13, 1940 • Frank Boucher, who played on New York's first two Stanley Cup championship teams in 1928 and 1933, coached the Rangers to a third title with a 3-2 overtime win in Game Six of the best-of-seven series. Among Boucher's players on the team were brothers Lynn and "Muzz" Patrick, the third and fourth members of the legendary Patrick family (including their father Lester and uncle Frank) to have their names engraved on the Cup.

April 13, 1944 • Montreal's famed "Punch Line" — left-winger "Toe" Blake, center Elmer Lach and right-winger Maurice "Rocket" Richard — powered the Canadiens to a 5-4 series-clinching comeback victory versus the Chicago Blackhawks in Game Four of the 1944 Finals. After Chicago had taken a 4-1 lead through two periods, Lach scored at 10.02 of the third, followed by Richard's back-to-back tallies at 16.05 and 17.20 to tie the game at four goals apiece after regulation time. Blake then ended the game and the season with a blast past netminder Mike Karakas at 9.12 of overtime. The win gave the Canadiens their first Stanley Cup title in 14 years, ending their longest period without a championship from their first season in the National Hockey Association (NHA), 1909-1910, to the present.

April 13, 1952 • Right-winger Gordie Howe registered his first two Stanley Cup goals and goaltender Terry Sawchuk posted a shutout to lead the Detroit Red Wings past the Montreal Canadiens 3-0 in the Game Three of the 1952 Finals. The win was Detroit's third straight en route to a four-game sweep of Montreal in the best-of-seven season finale.

April 14, 1928 • In only their second season as an NHL franchise, the New York Rangers captured the 1928 Stanley Cup with a 2-1 triumph over the Montreal Maroons in final game of the best-of-five title series. The Rangers became only the second American team in history to win the Stanley Cup, joining the 1917 champion Seattle Metropolitans of the Pacific Coast Hockey Association.

April 14, 1931 • Goaltender George Hainsworth blanked the Chicago Blackhawks 2-0 as the Montreal Canadiens became the second NHL team to win Stanley Cup championships in two consecutive seasons. The Ottawa Senators first accomplished the feat in 1920 and 1921.

April 14, 1942 • Brothers Don Metz (3-2-5) and Nick Metz (1-2-3) led the Toronto Maple Leafs to a record-tying 9-3 victory against the Detroit Red Wings in the 1942 Finals. The Leafs' nine-goal outburst matched the Finals scoring mark for an NHL team set by Detroit on April 7, 1936, in a 9-4 win against Toronto.

April 14, 1948 • The Toronto Maple Leafs repeated as Stanley Cup champions with a 7-2 win against the Detroit Red Wings, thus completing a four-game sweep of the 1948 Finals. The game spelled the end of a career for Toronto captain Syl Apps, who punctuated his stint in the NHL with a goal in this series-ending victory.

April 14, 1953 • Maurice "Rocket" Richard became the second NHL player to register two hat-tricks in Finals history, joining Howie Morenz in achieving the feat. Richard, who led Montreal to a 7-3 win against Boston, later added a four-goal performance to his record, April 6, 1957.

April 14, 1955 • Right-winger Gordie Howe scored the winning goal in Game Seven of the 1955 Stanley Cup Finals to lead the Detroit Red Wings past the Montreal Canadiens 3-1. The goal gave Howe a 5-7-12 scoring mark in the series, setting a new individual mark for Finals competition.

April 14, 1960 • Goaltender Jacques Plante blanked the Toronto Maple Leafs 4-0 as the Montreal Canadiens captured their record-setting fifth straight Stanley Cup championship. The victory marked the end of a career for Maurice "Rocket" Richard, the NHL's all-time leader with 34 goals in Stanley Cup play.

April 15, 1937 • In Game Five of the 1937 Stanley Cup series, referee Mickey Ion awarded Rangers' right-winger Alex Shibicky the first penalty shot in Finals history. Red Wings' rookie goaltender Earl Robertson stopped Shibicky's shot and posted his second straight shutout, 3-0 against New York, as Detroit became the first American team to repeat as Cup champions.

April 15, 1952 • In his fourth shutout in eight post-season games, Detroit Red Wings' goalie Terry Sawchuk blanked the Montreal Canadiens 3-0 to complete a four-game sweep of the 1952 Finals. The Wings, who had also swept the Toronto Maple Leafs in the Semi-Finals, distinguished themselves as the first NHL team to win every post-season game in one year.

April 16, 1939 • Goaltender Frank Brimsek, alias "Mr. Zero", allowed only one goal, his sixth in five Stanley Cup games against Toronto, to lead the Boston Bruins past the Maple Leafs 3-1 to win the 1939 championship.

April 16, 1949 • The Toronto Maple Leafs swept the Detroit Red Wings to become the first NHL team ever to win three consecutive Stanley Cups (1947-49). The 3-1 series-ending victory also marked the Leafs' ninth straight win in Finals action.

April 16, 1953 • Assisted by linemate Maurice "Rocket" Richard, Elmer Lach scored the only goal in Game Five at 1.22 of overtime, and goalie Gerry McNeil blanked the Boston Bruins for the second time in three outings as the Montreal Canadiens earned the 1953 Stanley Cup championship.

April 16, 1954 • Tony Leswick's Stanley Cup-winning tally was the second overtime goal ever scored in the seventh game of a Final series. Leswick, who notched the decisive goal at 4.29 of overtime in Detroit's 2-1 victory over Montreal in Game Seven, matched the feat first accomplished by former Red Wings' left-winger Pete Babando in 1950.

April 16, 1961 • The Chicago Blackhawks earned their first Stanley Cup championship since 1938 and their third title since joining the NHL in 1926-27. The Blackhawks downed Detroit 5-1 to take the best-of-seven Finals four games to two.

April 16, 1994 • The Boston Bruins opened their Eastern Conference Quarterfinal series against the Montreal Canadiens, extending their NHL record for most consecutive playoff appearances to 27 years.

April 17, 1958 • Right-winger Maurice "Rocket" Richard led the Montreal Canadiens to a 3-2 win against the Boston Bruins in Game Five with a goal at 5.45 of overtime. The goal was Richard's third in a Stanley Cup game and sixth in a playoff game, extending his record in each category. The Canadiens went on to win the best-of-seven series in six games.

April 17, 1977 • Don Kozak of the Los Angeles Kings scored the fastest goal from the start of an NHL playoff game, tallying just six seconds into his club's 7-4 win over the Boston Bruins in Game #4 of their Quarter-Final series.

April 18, 1942 • The Toronto Maple Leafs completed the greatest comeback in Stanley Cup history with their fourth straight victory after losing the first three games of the Finals to the Detroit Red Wings. Leafs' goaltender Turk Broda provided the heroics, allowing the Red Wings only seven goals in the last four games, including this 3-1 series-ending victory.

April 18, 1959 • Montreal Canadiens' left-winger Marcel Bonin scored the Stanley Cup-winning goal at 9.55 of the second period en route to a 5-3 win over the Toronto Maple Leafs in Game Six. This series-ending win gave Montreal its fourth of its record five straight Stanley Cup titles.

April 18, 1963 • In Game Five of the 1963 Finals, Toronto Maple Leafs' center Dave Keon scored two short-handed goals against the Detorit Red Wings, setting an overall playoff record for one game. Keon's heroics led Toronto to a 3-1 Cup-winning triumph over Detroit. It marked the second of three straight Stanley Cups for the Leafs.

April 18, 1987 • Pat LaFontaine scored the dramatic game-winning goal at 8:42 of the fourth overtime period in Game #7 of the Patrick DF vs. Washington.

April 18, 1994 • The San Jose Sharks defeated the Detroit Red Wings 5-4 at Joe Louis Arena in Detroit in Game One of their Western Conference Quarterfinal series to become the first club since the 1975 New York Islanders to win the first Stanley Cup playoff game in franchise history. Since the Islanders defeated the New York Rangers 3-2 on April 8, 1975, seven clubs had lost their playoff debuts prior to San Jose's win.

April 18, 1994 • The New York Rangers posted their second consecutive 6-0 shutout to open the Stanley Cup playoffs against the New York Islanders. The Rangers became the first club to open the post-season with consecutive shutouts since the Buffalo Sabres defeated Montreal 1-0 and 3-0 in 1983.

April 19, 1947 • After assisting defenseman Vic Lynn's goal at 5.39 of the second period to tie the game at one goal apiece, Toronto Maple Leafs' center Ted "Teeder" Kennedy scored the Cup-winner at 14.39 of the third period to defeat the Montreal Canadiens 2-1 in Game Six. The series-ending victory earned Toronto its third Stanley Cup title in six seasons.

April 20, 1950 • New York center Don Raleigh set a Stanley Cup record with his second overtime goal in as many games as the Rangers downed the Detroit Red Wings 4-3 in Game Five of the 1950 Finals. The win proved to be the Rangers' last of the series as Detroit went on to win the final two games and the Stanley Cup.

April 20, 1967 • In Game One of the 1967 Finals, a 6-2 win for the Montreal Canadiens, defenseman Leonard "Red" Kelly skated in the 12th Stanley Cup series of his career, tying Maurice "Rocket" Richard (12) for the all-time record. Montreal's Henri Richard and Jean Beliveau, both of whom played in the game, would later tie the mark as well.

April 20, 1993 • The Pittsburgh Penguins set an NHL playoff record with their 13th consecutive post-season win, a 7-0 decision over the New Jersey Devils in Game #2 of their Patrick Division Semi-Final. The Penguins passed the previous mark of 12, set by the Edmonton Oilers in the 1984 and 1985 playoff seasons. The Penguins extended their record to 14 games before dropping Game #4 to the Devils, ending the streak.

April 21, 1951 • Toronto Maple Leafs' defenseman Bill Barilko scored the Cup-winning goal at 2.53 of overtime to defeat the Montreal Canadiens 3-2 in Game Five of the 1951 Finals. It was the only Stanley Cup series in which every game had ended in overtime. Toronto's Sid Smith, Ted Kennedy, Harry Watson, Barilko and Montreal's Maurice "Rocket" Richard each netted overtime winners during the five-game matchup. Barilko, who later died in an off-season plane crash, never played another NHL game.

April 22, 1945 • At 12.14 of the third period, Maple Leafs' defenseman Walter "Babe" Pratt scored the Cup-winning goal to give Toronto a 2-1 victory over the Detroit Red Wings in Game Seven. Leafs' rookie goaltender Frank McCool, who allowed only nine goals in seven starts, limited the Wings to one goal or less for the fifth time in the series.

April 22, 1962 • Toronto's Bob Nevin and Dick Duff notched third-period goals to defeat the Chicago Blackhawks 2-1 in Game Six of the 1962 Finals. The win propelled the Maple Leafs to their first of three straight Stanley Cup championships.

April 22, 1976 • Toronto center Darryl Sittler equalled Maurice Richard's 32-year-old record for most goals in one playoff game by scoring five goals in the Maple Leafs' 8-5 Quarter-Final series win over the Philadelphia Flyers. Philadelphia's Reg Leach joined Richard and Sittler just days later, as Leach scored five of his playoff-record 19 goals on May 6, 1976, in a 6-3 win over the Boston Bruins.

April 22, 1988 • Patrik Sundstrom set an NHL record by recording eight points (3-5-8) in New Jersey's 10-4 win over Washington in Game #3 of the Patrick DF.

April 23, 1950 • In the first Game Seven overtime in Finals history, left-winger Pete Babando, assisted by center George Gee at 8.31 of the second overtime period, gave the Detroit Red Wings a 4-3 win and the 1950 Stanley Cup title. Four years later, another Detroit left-winger, Tony Leswick, repeated Babando's overtime feat in Game Seven of the 1954 Finals. Since then, no player has scored the Cup-winning goal in overtime in the seventh and deciding game of the Finals.

April 24, 1994 • Chicago Blackhawks defenseman Gary Suter tallied three goals in a 4-3 overtime win over the Toronto Maple Leafs in Game Four of their Western Conference Quarterfinal series. Suter became the eighth defenseman in Stanley Cup playoffs history to a post a hat-trick, joining Bobby Orr, Dick Redmond, Denis Potvin, Doug Halward, Paul Reinhart (twice), Al Iafrate and Eric Desjardins.

April 25, 1964 • Toronto goalie Johnny Bower blanked the Detroit Red Wings 4-0 to propel the Maple Leafs to their third straight Stanley Cup title. Four different scorers provided the offensive support for Bower.

April 26, 1975 • Goaltender Glenn Resch and the New York Islanders blanked the Pittsburgh Penguins 1-0 to win Game #7 and capture their 1975 QF series. The Islanders became just the second team in NHL history to win a best-of-seven series after losing the first three games, joining the 1942 Toronto Maple Leafs. The Islanders nearly repeated the feat in the Semi-Finals against Philadelphia. The Islanders again lost the first three games of the series only to bounce back and win the next three. Their bid for an unprecedented second straight 0-3 comeback was stopped as they lost Game #7 at Philadelphia, 4-1.

April 27, 1980 • Minnesota's Al MacAdam scored the series-winning goal late in the third period to give the visiting North Stars a 3-2 win over the Montreal Canadiens in Game #7 of the 1980 QF series. The Minnesota win stopped the Canadiens' bid for a record-tying fifth consecutive Stanley Cup, a mark set by Montreal from 1956-60.

April 27, 1994 • Buffalo Sabres center Dave Hannan scored at 5:43 of the fourth overtime period in a 1-0 home win over the New Jersey Devils in Game Six of their Eastern Conference Quarterfinal series. This game was the sixth longest in NHL history, beginning at 7:39 p.m. and concluding at 1:51 a.m. – six hours and 12 minutes later. Sabres goaltender Dominik Hasek turned aside all 70 shots he faced, which New Jersey netminder Martin Brodeur made 49 saves on 50 shots.

April 29, 1973 • Tony Esposito of the Chicago Blackhawks and Ken Dryden of the Montreal Canadiens, who had been Team Canada's goaltending duo in the 1972 Summit Series versus the Soviet Union, faced each other on opposite sides of the ice in Game One of the 1973 Finals. Dryden and the Canadiens won the contest 8-3 and went on to win the title series in six games. Montreal's Henri Richard tied brother Maurice and Leonard "Red" Kelly for the all-time record for Finals appearances with the 12th of his career.

April 30, 1972 • The New York Rangers made their first appearance in a Stanley Cup finals series game since 1950, losing to the Boston Bruins 6-5 in the opening contest. The 1972 championship clash between New York and Boston marked the first time in 43 years that the two had met in the Finals. Boston won the best-of-seven series in six games.

May 1, 1965 • Montreal captain Jean Beliveau notched the game-winning goal and added one assist to lead the Canadiens past the Chicago Blackhawks in Game Seven of the 1965 Finals. Beliveau, who posted a 5-5-10 scoring total in the seven-game Stanley Cup series, received the Conn Smythe Trophy as the most valuable player to his team in the playoffs.

May 2, 1967 • With the oldest lineup in Finals history, the Toronto Maple Leafs defeated the Montreal Canadiens 3-1 in Game Six to win the 1967 Stanley Cup. The Leafs' roster included 42-year-old goalie Johnny Bower and 41-year-old defenseman Allan Stanley as well as seven others at least 30 years old. Toronto defenseman Leonard "Red" Kelly played his 65th game in Finals competition, setting a Stanley Cup record later tied by Montreal's Henri Richard.

May 4, 1969 • With a 2-1 win in Game Four of the 1969 Stanley Cup, the Montreal Canadiens swept the St. Louis Blues in the Finals for the second straight season. The Conn Smythe Trophy was presented to Serge Savard, the first defenseman to receive the award.

May 4, 1972 • New York Rangers' defenseman Brad Park registered two power-play goals in the first period of a 5-2 win against the Boston Bruins to tie a Stanley Cup Finals record for one period. Park joined Sid Smith (April 10, 1949) of Toronto and Maurice "Rocket" Richard (April 6, 1954) and Bernie "Boom Boom" Geoffrion (April 7, 1955) in accomplishing this power-play feat.

May 5, 1966 • At 2.30 of overtime in Game Six, Montreal Canadiens' center Henri Richard became the ninth player in NHL history to record a Stanley Cup-winning goal in sudden-death. Richard's overtime goal gave Montreal a 3-2 win versus the Detroit Red Wings. Detroit goaltender Roger Crozier, who amassed a 2.17 goals-against-average and one shutout in 12 playoff games, earned the Conn Smythe Trophy as the most valuable player to his team in post-season competition.

May 7, 1995 • The Boston Bruins made their 1995 Stanley Cup Playoffs debut, dropping a 5-0 home decision to the New Jersey Devils. The Bruins extended their NHL record by appearing in the playoffs for the 28th consecutive year.

May 8, 1973 • The Chicago Blackhawks and Montreal Canadiens combined to set an NHL record with 15 goals in one Finals game. Led by Stan Mikita's two-goal, two-assist performance, the Blackhawks edged the Canadiens 8-7 in Game Five at the Montreal Forum. Montreal went on to win the series four games to two.

May 8, 1982 • The Vancouver Canucks became the team since the 1924 Vancouver Maroons of the Western Canada Hockey League (WCHL) to represent that city in the Stanley Cup Finals. The Canucks lost this opening game 6-5 in overtime to the New York Islanders, who went on to take the series in four straight games.

May 8, 1995 • New York Rangers center Mark Messier scored the 100th goal of his playoff career in an 8-3 win over the Quebec Nordiques in Game Two of their Eastern Conference Quarterfinal. He become just the third player in NHL history to reach the milestone, joining Wayne Gretzky (110 career playoff goals) and Jari Kurri (102).

May 10, 1970 • Bobby Orr, who had distinguished himself in 1969-70 as the first defenseman in NHL history to record 100 points (33-87-120) in a season, scored just 40 seconds into overtime to give the Boston Bruins a 4-3 win and a four-game sweep versus the St. Louis Blues in the 1970 Finals. For Orr, the Conn Smythe Trophy winner, the goal was his first of the series.

May 10, 1973 • In Montreal's 6-4 series-ending victory in Game Six, Yvan Cournoyer (6-6-12) and Jacques Lemaire (5-7-12) tallied 1-2-3 and 0-2-2 scoring totals, respectively, to tie Gordie Howe's

THIS DATE IN STANLEY CUP HISTORY • 135

record of 12 points in one Final series. Meanwhile, Montreal's Henri Richard tied Leonard "Red" Kelly's all-time record for Stanley Cup games with the 65th of his career.

May 11, 1968 • The Montreal Canadiens swept the St. Louis Blues in straight games with a 3-2 win in Game Four of the 1968 Finals. For Montreal coach "Toe" Blake, it was his 11th Stanley Cup title, setting an all-time record for one individual. Blake, who had won three championships as a player and eight as a coach, retired following the series. Canadiens' center Henri Richard later tied Blake's mark with his 11th Stanley Cup in 1973.

May 11, 1972 • For the second time in three seasons, defenseman Bobby Orr scored the Stanley Cup-winning goal as the Boston Bruins blanked the New York Rangers 3-0 in Game Six. The goal gave Orr, who won the Conn Smythe Trophy, a 5-19-24 scoring total in 15 playoff games.

May 11, 1995 • Detroit Red Wings right wing Dino Ciccarelli tallied three power play goals in a 5-1 win over the Dallas Stars in Game Three of their Western Conference Quarterfinal to tie an NHL playoff record for most power play goals in one game. Nine players, including Ciccarelli, had previously shared the record. Ciccarelli was the last player to accomplish the feat, on April 29, 1993 versus Toronto, and became the first player in NHL history to post three power play goals in a playoff game on separate occasions.

May 12, 1995 • New Jersey Devils goaltender Martin Brodeur became just the fifth goaltender since the NHL introduced the best-of-seven format in 1939 to register three shutouts in one playoff series, following a 1-0 overtime win over the Boston Bruins in Game Three of their Conference Quarterfinal series. Brodeur joined Dave Kerr of the New York Rangers (1940), and three Toronto Maple Leafs goaltenders — Frank McCool (1945), Turk Broda (1950) and Felix Potvin (1994).

May 14, 1977 • Montreal Canadiens' center Jacques Lemaire scored his third game-winning goal of the 1977 Finals and his second career overtime tally in a Stanley Cup game, leading the Montreal Canadiens to a 2-1 series-clinching win against the Boston Bruins. Only Maurice "Rocket" Richard (3) and Don Raleigh (2) have ever posted more than one career overtime goal in Finals history.

May 14, 1993 • The New York Islanders defeated the Pittsburgh Penguins 4-3 in overtime to win their Patrick Division Final in seven games. For Islanders' coach Al Arbour, it represented his 30th career playoff series win as a coach, moving him into a tie for the all-time lead with Penguins' coach Scott Bowman. The win was also Arbour's 200th in the post-season, joining Bowman as the only coaches to reach the milestone.

May 15, 1990 • Edmonton's Petr Klima scored 15.13 into the third overtime period to lead the Oilers to a 3-2 triumph over the Boston Bruins in Game #1 of the 1990 Finals at Boston Garden. The 55.13 overtime was the longest in Finals history, 1.23 longer than the 53.50 of overtime played in Game #3 of the 1931 Finals between Chicago and Montreal.

May 15, 1995 • The Vancouver Canucks tallied two shorthanded goals in 0:17 during the second period of their 6-5 win over the St. Louis Blues in Game Five of their Conference Quarterfinal series to set an NHL playoff record for the fastest two shorthanded goals by one team. The Canucks passed the old mark of 0:24 set by the 1978 Montreal Canadiens versus Detroit on April 23, 1978. Christian Ruuttu scored for Vancouver at 4:31 of the second period, followed by Geoff Courtnall at 4:48.

May 16, 1971 • Center Jean Beliveau tallied two assists, the final two points of his NHL career, as the Montreal Canadiens downed the Chicago Blackhawks 4-3 in Game Six of the 1971 Finals. Beliveau, the all-time leader in Finals history with a 30-31-61 scoring total, helped his club win the Stanley Cup two days later in Game Seven.

May 16, 1976 • In Game Four of the 1976 Finals, Philadelphia Flyers' right-winger Reggie Leach scored his 19th goal of the playoffs, extending his NHL record in that category. Although the Flyers lost the game 5-3 and the series 4-0 to the Montreal Canadiens, Leach won the Conn Smythe Trophy as the most valuable player to his team in the playoffs.

May 16, 1982 • Right-winger Mike Bossy scored twice, including the series-winning goal, to lead the New York Islanders to their third straight Stanley Cup championship. The 3-1 victory gave New York a four-game sweep against the Vancouver Canucks.

May 16, 1993 • Montreal Canadiens' goaltender Patrick Roy recorded his 60th career playoff win in the Canadiens' 4-1 win in Game #1 of the Wales Conference Final, becoming just the fifth goaltender in NHL history to reach the plateau. Other goaltenders with 60-or-more post-season wins are Billy Smith (88), Ken Dryden (80), Grant Fuhr (77) and Jacques Plante (71).

May 17, 1981 • In Game Three of the 1981 Finals, Minnesota North Stars' right wing Dino Ciccarelli broke Don Maloney's one-year rookie playoff scoring record (20 points in 1979) with his 21st point, a goal against the New York Islanders. The Islanders won the game 7-5 and later took the series 4-1.

May 17, 1983 • The New York Islanders beat the Edmonton Oilers 4-2 to complete a four-game sweep of the 1983 Finals. It was the Islanders' fourth straight Stanley Cup, one short of the NHL record for consecutive championships set by the Montreal Canadiens (1956 - 1960).

May 18, 1971 • The Montreal Canadiens, who had missed the playoffs in 1970, won the 1971 Stanley Cup with a 3-2 triumph over the Chicago Blackhawks in Game Seven. 23-year-old rookie goalie Ken Dryden took the Conn Smythe Trophy with a 12-8 record and a 3.00 average in the playoffs.

May 18, 1986 • Montreal center Brian Skrudland notched the fastest overtime goal in playoff history, scoring just nine seconds into overtime to give the Canadiens a 3-2 victory over the Calgary Flames in Game Two of the 1986 Finals. The win was the first of four straight for Montreal en route to the team's 23rd Stanley Cup title.

May 19, 1974 • The Philadelphia Flyers, who had entered the NHL in 1967-68, became the first expansion team to win the Stanley Cup, downing the Boston Bruins 1-0 in Game Six of the 1974 Finals. Left-winger Rick MacLeish scored the game's only goal, while goaltender Bernie Parent, who won the Conn Smythe Trophy, recorded the shutout.

May 19, 1984 • The Edmonton Oilers, one of four former WHA teams which joined the League in 1979-80, won their first Stanley Cup title. Oilers' center Mark Messier, who registered an 8-18-26 scoring mark in 19 playoff games, won the Conn Smythe Trophy.

May 20, 1986 • In the first period of Game Three, Montreal and Calgary combined for the fastest four goals by two teams in a Finals game. Calgary's Joel Otto (17.59) and Montreal's Bobby Smith (18.25), Mats Naslund (19.17) and Bob Gainey (19.33) posted goals within one minute and 34 seconds to set the mark. The Canadiens defeated the Flames 5-3.

May 20, 1993 • The Montreal Canadiens won their seventh overtime game in the post-season, a 2-1 win over the New York Islanders, to set a new playoff record. The Canadiens passed the previous mark of six, set by the Islanders in 1980.

May 21, 1979 • Center Jacques Lemaire scored twice, including his second career Stanley Cup-winning goal, to power the Montreal Canadiens past the New York Rangers 4-1 in Game Five. The win gave Montreal its fourth straight Stanley Cup, one short of the record (5) set by the same team, 1956-60.

May 21, 1981 • New York Islanders' center Butch Goring notched two goals to help defeat the Minnesota North Stars 5-1 in the fifth and final game of the 1981 Finals. Goring, who assisted the winning goal in Game Two and scored the winner in Game Three, earned the Conn Smythe Trophy.

May 22, 1987 • In Game Three of the 1987 Finals, Edmonton Oilers' center Mark Messier set a new playoff record with his eighth career short-handed goal. Edmonton lost the game 5-3 loss to the Philadelphia Flyers but went on to win the series in seven games.

May 24, 1980 • Right-winger Bob Nystrom scored at 7.11 of the overtime period as the New York Islanders defeated the Philadelphia Flyers 5-4 and captured the 1980 Stanley Cup in six games. Nystrom's goal was the fourth and final overtime tally of his playoff career and moved him into second place on the all-time list behind Maurice "Rocket" Richard (6).

May 24, 1986 • The Montreal Canadiens defeated the Calgary Flames 4-3 in Game Five en route to their 23rd Stanley Cup title, a new professional record for the most championship seasons. Montreal had been tied with Major League Baseball's New York Yankees, winners of 22 World Series.

May 24, 1990 • The Edmonton Oilers won their fifth Stanley Cup in seven years with a 4-1 win over the Boston Bruins in Game #5 of the 1990 Finals at Boston Garden. Edmonton goaltender Bill Ranford, who registered all 16 wins for the Oilers in the post-season, captured the Conn Smythe Trophy as playoff MVP. Seven Oilers' players - Glenn Anderson, Grant Fuhr, Randy Gregg, Charlie Huddy, Jari Kurri, Kevin Lowe and Mark Messier - were members of all five championship clubs.

May 24, 1994 • Greg Adams of the Vancouver Canucks scored at fourteen seconds of the second overtime period to give his team a 4-3 win over the Toronto Maple Leafs in Game Five of the Western Conference Final at Pacific Coliseum. The win clinched the series for the Canucks and earned them a berth in the Stanley Cup Championship for the first time since 1982.

May 24, 1995 • New York Rangers center Mark Messier's goal in the second period of a 5-2 loss to the Philadelphia Flyers in Game Three of their Conference Semifinal was the 102nd of his playoff career, tying Jari Kurri for second place on the all-time list.

May 25, 1978 • Conn Smythe Trophy winner Larry Robinson assisted Mario Tremblay's Stanley Cup-winning goal to lead the Montreal Canadiens past the Boston Bruins 4-1 in Game Six. Robinson was one of three Canadiens, including Doug Jarvis and Steve Shutt, who appeared in all 95 games during the 1977-78 season.

May 25, 1985 • Edmonton Oilers' center Wayne Gretzky notched three goals in the first period of a 4-3 win against the Philadelphia Flyers to tie a an NHL record for one Finals period. Three players — Toronto's Harvey "Busher" Jackson (April 5, 1932), Detroit's Ted Lindsay (April 5, 1955) and Montreal's Maurice "Rocket" Richard (April 6, 1957) — previously shared the mark.

May 25, 1989 • The Calgary Flames captured their first-ever Stanley Cup with a 4-2 win over the Montreal Canadiens in Game #6 of the 1989 Stanley Cup Championship. Goaltender Mike Vernon recorded his 16th victory of the post-season, tying an NHL playoff record set by Edmonton's Grant Fuhr the previous year, and defenseman Al MacInnis won the Conn Smythe Trophy after leading all playoff scorers with totals of 7-24-31 in 22 games.

May 27, 1975 • Philadelphia goaltender Bernie Parent blanked the Buffalo Sabres 2-0 in Game Six en route to the Flyers' second straight Stanley Cup title. Parent earned the Conn Smythe Trophy to become the first back-to-back winner of the award and the second player, after Bobby Orr, to win it twice. Edmonton's Wayne Gretzky collected his second career Conn Smythe Trophy in 1988, becoming the third player to do so.

May 27, 1994 • Stephane Matteau of the New York Rangers scored at 4:24 of the second overtime period to give his team a 2-1 win over the New Jersey Devils in the seventh and deciding game of the Eastern Conference Final at Madison Square Garden. A record three games in the series were decided in double overtime, with Matteau scoring the winner in two of them. The win earned the Rangers a berth in the Stanley Cup Championship for the first time since 1979.

May 27, 1995 • Detroit Red Wings defenseman Paul Coffey became the all-time leading scorer for defensemen in Stanley Cup playoff history, tallying two points (1-1-2) in Detroit's 6-2 win over the San Jose Sharks in Game Four of their Conference Semifinal. The Red Wings clinched the series in four straight games. Coffey's first-period goal was the 165th point in the postseason (51-114-165 in 146 games), moving him past former New York Islanders rearguard and Hockey Hall of Famer Denis Potvin. Potvin registered 164 points (56-108-164) in 185 career playoff games.

May 30, 1985 • The Edmonton Oilers downed the Philadelphia Flyers 8-3 in Game Five to take the 1985 Stanley Cup and their second straight championship title. Conn Smythe Trophy winner Wayne Gretzky scored a goal and assisted three others to set one-year playoff records for assists (30) and points (47), and Jari Kurri tied Reg Leach's record with his 19th goal of the playoffs.

May 31, 1987 • Right-winger Jari Kurri scored the Stanley Cup-winning goal at 14.59 of the second period as the Edmonton Oilers beat the Philadelphia Flyers 3-1 in Game Seven of the 1987 Finals. It marked the third time in four seasons that Edmonton had won the Cup.

June 1, 1992 • In the first NHL game ever played in the month of June, the Pittsburgh Penguins captured their second consecutive Stanley Cup championship with a 6-5 win over the Chicago Blackhawks at Chicago Stadium. The Penguins, who won the best-of-seven series 4-0, tied an NHL playoff record by winning their 11th straight game in the post-season. Mario Lemieux led all playoff scorers and became just the second player ever to earn back-to-back Conn Smythe Trophy honors.

June 3, 1993 • Montreal Canadiens' defenseman Eric Desjardins became the first defenseman in NHL history to record a hat-trick in the Stanley Cup Finals. Desjardins tallied a game-tying power-play goal late in the third period and added the overtime winner in a 4-3 win. The tying goal came as a result of a stick measurement requested by Canadiens' coach Jacques Demers. The stick used by Los Angeles defenseman Marty McSorley was found to have a curve that exceeded the allowable limit, resulting in a two-minute penalty to McSorely at 18:15 of the third period. Desjardins scored 32 seconds later. His winning goal was scored after just 51 seconds of overtime.

June 7, 1993 • John LeClair posted his second overtime goal in as many games to lead the Canadiens to a 3-2 win at Los Angeles to take a 3-1 series lead in the Finals. LeClair became the second player in NHL history, after Don Raleigh of the New York Rangers in 1950 versus Detroit, to tally overtime goals in consecutive games in the Finals.

June 9, 1993 • The Montreal Canadiens captured their 24th Stanley Cup championship, defeating the Los Angeles Kings 4-1 to win the Stanley Cup Final series in five games. Canadiens goaltender Patrick Roy was awarded the Conn Smythe Trophy as playoff MVP, posting a 16-4 record and 2.13 record in 20 games.

June 14, 1994 • The New York Rangers defeated the Vancouver Canucks 3-2 at Madison Square Garden in Game Seven of the Stanley Cup Finals. This was the first seven-game Final series since 1987 and just the third since 1967. Rangers defenseman Brian Leetch captured the Conn Smythe Trophy as playoff MVP, leading all post-season scorers with 34 points (11-23-34) in 23 games.

June 17, 1995 • The 1995 Stanley Cup Championship series opened at Joe Louis Arena and the New Jersey Devils captured Game One with a 2-1 win. Right wing Claude Lemieux scored the game-winning goal early in the third period, his third game-winner of the playoffs and 14th of his career in the postseason. The Devils improved their road record in the playoffs to 9-1, setting a new NHL record for most road wins by one team in the playoffs.

June 20, 1995 • The New Jersey Devils defeated the Detroit Red Wings 4-2 at Joe Louis Arena to take a two games to none series lead in the Stanley Cup Championship. New Jersey extended its playoff record by winning its 10th game on the road and tied another playoff record by winning their seventh straight road game.

PENALTY SHOTS IN THE FINALS

A total of seven penalty shots have been awarded to players in Stanley Cup Finals history. None of the seven has been successful:

Date	Shooter	Goalie
4/15/37	Alex Shibicky (NYR)	Earl Robertson (Det)
4/13/44	Virgil Johnson (Chi)	Bill Durnan (Mtl)
5/16/71	Frank Mahovlich (Mtl)	Tony Esposito (Chi)
5/28/85	Ron Sutter (Phi)	Grant Fuhr (Edm)
5/30/85	Dave Poulin (Phi)	Grant Fuhr (Edm)
5/18/90	Petr Klima (Edm)	Rejean Lemelin (Bos)
6/7/94	Pavel Bure (Van)	Mike Richter (NYR)

SUB-.500 TEAMS IN THE FINALS

A total of 15 teams have reached the Finals after posting regular-season records below the .500-mark, including the 1938 Stanley Cup champion Chicago Blackhawks and the 1949 champion Toronto Maple Leafs:

Year	Team	Record
1937	New York Rangers	19-20- 9
1938	Chicago Blackhawks	14-25- 9
1939	Toronto Maple Leafs	19-20- 9
1942	Detroit Red Wings	19-25- 4
1944	Chicago Blackhawks	22-23- 5
1949	Toronto Maple Leafs	22-25-13
1950	New York Rangers	28-31-11
1951	Montreal Canadiens	25-30-15
1953	Boston Bruins	28-29-13
1958	Boston Bruins	27-28-15
1959	Toronto Maple Leafs	27-32-11
1961	Detroit Red Wings	25-29-16
1968	St. Louis Blues	27-31-16
1982	Vancouver Canucks	30-33-17
1991	Minnesota North Stars	27-39-14

National Hockey League
Stanley Cup Playoffs
Fact Guide
1996

Section IV

•

Stanley Cup Championship

Final Series Results, Top Five Scorers, Team-by-Team ....page **140**
Final Series Record Book **143**
Final Series Scoring, Year-by-Year **153**
Players on Stanley Cup Championship teams, 1893-1995 **169**
Final Series Coaching Register **180**
Final Series Player Register **180**
Final Series Goaltending Register **182**

Final Series Results, Team by Team

OVERALL FINAL SERIES RECORD
1918-95

TEAM	SERIES	W	L	GP	W	L	GF	GA
Anaheim	—	—	—	—	—	—	—	—
Boston	17	5	12	77	28	47	168	219
Buffalo	1	0	1	6	2	4	12	19
Calgary	2	1	1	11	5	6	32	31
Chicago	10	3	7	53	22	31	132	158
Dallas	2	0	2	11	3	8	32	54
Detroit	19	7	12	101	42	59	239	270
Edmonton	6	5	1	30	20	10	108	78
Florida	—	—	—	—	—	—	—	—
Hartford	—	—	—	—	—	—	—	—
Los Angeles	1	0	1	5	1	4	12	15
Montreal	*32	23	8	163	105	57	481	381
New Jersey	1	1	0	4	4	0	16	7
Ottawa	—	—	—	—	—	—	—	—
NY Islanders	5	4	1	24	17	7	99	78
NY Rangers	10	4	6	50	22	28	115	130
Philadelphia	6	2	4	34	14	20	100	108
Pittsburgh	2	2	0	10	8	2	43	26
Quebec	—	—	—	—	—	—	—	—
St. Louis	3	0	3	12	0	12	24	63
San Jose	—	—	—	—	—	—	—	—
Tampa Bay	—	—	—	—	—	—	—	—
Toronto	21	13	8	105	56	49	278	269
Vancouver	2	0	2	11	3	8	29	39
Washington	—	—	—	—	—	—	—	—
Winnipeg	—	—	—	—	—	—	—	—

* No decision in 1919 Finals, interrupted by flu epidemic. Seattle and Montreal had each won two games. One game was tied.

BOSTON 1925-95
ALL-TIME FINAL SERIES RECORD

Versus	Series	W	L	GP	W	L	GF	GA
Detroit	2	1	1	8	4	4	17	22
Edmonton	2	0	2	9	1	8	17	38
Montreal	7	0	7	33	7	26	64	107
NY Rangers	2	2	0	8	6	2	22	17
Philadelphia	1	0	1	6	2	4	13	15
St. Louis	1	1	0	4	4	0	20	7
Toronto	1	1	0	5	4	1	12	6
Defunct Teams*	1	0	1	4	0	2	3	7
TOTALS	17	5	12	77	28	47	168	219

FINAL SERIES APPEARANCES

Versus	Year	Winner	W	L	GF	GA
Ottawa*	1927	Ottawa	0	2	3	7
NY Rangers	1929	Boston	2	0	4	1
Montreal	1930	Montreal	0	2	3	7
Toronto	1939	Boston	4	1	12	6
Detroit	1941	Boston	4	0	12	6
Detroit	1943	Detroit	0	4	5	16
Montreal	1946	Montreal	1	4	13	19
Montreal	1953	Montreal	1	4	9	16
Montreal	1957	Montreal	1	4	6	15
Montreal	1958	Montreal	2	4	14	16
St. Louis	1970	Boston	4	0	20	7
NY Rangers	1972	Boston	4	2	18	16
Philadelphia	1974	Philadelphia	2	4	13	15
Montreal	1977	Montreal	0	4	6	16
Montreal	1978	Montreal	2	4	13	18
Edmonton	1988	Edmonton	0	4	9	18
Edmonton	1990	Edmonton	1	4	8	20

* includes two ties

TOP FIVE FINAL SERIES SCORERS

Player	GP	G	A	TP	PIM
Bobby Orr	16	8	12	20	31
Phil Esposito	16	4	15	19	28
Ken Hodge	16	6	10	16	27
Milt Schmidt	18	6	8	14	4
John Bucyk	16	8	5	13	4

BUFFALO 1971-95
ALL-TIME FINAL SERIES RECORD

Versus	Series	W	L	GP	W	L	GF	GA
Philadelphia	1	0	1	6	2	4	12	19
TOTALS	1	0	1	6	2	4	12	19

FINAL SERIES APPEARANCES

Versus	Year	Winner	W	L	GF	GA
Philadelphia	1975	Philadelphia	2	4	12	19

TOP FIVE FINAL SERIES SCORERS

Player	GP	G	A	TP	PIM
Rick Martin	6	2	4	6	6
Don Luce	6	2	3	5	12
Danny Gare	6	2	1	3	4
Jerry Korab	6	2	1	3	6
Jim Lorentz	6	1	2	3	2

CALGARY 1973-95
ALL-TIME FINAL SERIES RECORD

Versus	Series	W	L	GP	W	L	GF	GA
Montreal	2	1	1	11	5	6	32	31
TOTALS	2	1	1	11	5	6	32	31

FINAL SERIES APPEARANCES

Versus	Year	Winner	W	L	GF	GA
Montreal	1986	Montreal	1	4	13	15
Montreal	1989	Calgary	4	2	19	16

TOP FIVE FINAL SERIES SCORERS

Player	GP	G	A	TP	PIM
Al MacInnis	11	5	8	13	26
Joe Mullen	10	7	4	11	8
Joel Otto	11	3	8	11	14
Doug Gilmour	6	4	3	7	6
Jim Peplinski	9	1	5	6	47

CHICAGO 1927-95
ALL-TIME FINAL SERIES RECORD

Versus	Series	W	L	GP	W	L	GF	GA
Detroit	2	2	0	10	7	3	28	19
Montreal	5	0	5	29	10	19	69	98
Pittsburgh	1	0	1	4	0	4	10	15
Toronto	2	1	1	10	5	5	25	26
TOTALS	10	3	7	53	22	31	132	158

FINAL SERIES APPEARANCES

Versus	Year	Winner	W	L	GF	GA
Montreal	1931	Montreal	2	3	8	11
Detroit	1934	Chicago	3	1	9	7
Toronto	1938	Chicago	3	1	10	8
Montreal	1944	Montreal	0	4	8	16
Detroit	1961	Chicago	4	2	19	12
Toronto	1962	Toronto	2	4	15	18
Montreal	1965	Montreal	3	4	12	18
Montreal	1971	Montreal	3	4	18	20
Montreal	1973	Montreal	2	4	23	33
Pittsburgh	1992	Pittsburgh	0	4	10	15

TOP FIVE FINAL SERIES SCORERS

Player	GP	G	A	TP	PIM
Stan Mikita	31	10	21	31	58
Bobby Hull	26	11	17	28	26
Pierre Pilote	17	2	13	15	22
Jim Pappin	13	7	4	11	18
Johnny Gottselig	13	6	5	11	6

DALLAS 1968-95
ALL-TIME FINAL SERIES RECORD*

Versus	Series	W	L	GP	W	L	GF	GA
NY Islanders	1	0	1	5	1	4	16	26
Pittsburgh	1	0	1	6	2	4	16	28
TOTALS	2	0	2	11	3	8	32	54

* Includes final series appearances by Minnesota North Stars in 1981 and 1991.

FINAL SERIES APPEARANCES

Versus	Year	Winner	W	L	GF	GA
NY Islanders	1981	NY Islanders	1	4	16	26
Pittsburgh	1991	Pittsburgh	2	4	16	28

TOP FIVE FINAL SERIES SCORERS

Player	GP	G	A	TP	PIM
Bobby Smith	11	4	5	9	8
Steve Payne	5	5	2	7	2
Dave Gagner	6	4	2	6	14
Dino Ciccarelli	5	3	2	5	19
Neal Broten	11	3	2	5	4

DETROIT 1927-95
ALL-TIME FINAL SERIES RECORD

Versus	Series	W	L	GP	W	L	GF	GA
Boston	2	1	1	8	4	4	22	17
Chicago	2	0	2	10	3	7	19	28
Montreal	5	3	2	29	15	14	75	70
New Jersey	1	0	1	4	0	4	7	16
NY Rangers	2	2	0	12	7	5	31	25
Toronto	7	1	6	38	13	25	85	114
TOTALS	19	7	12	101	42	59	239	270

FINAL SERIES APPEARANCES

Versus	Year	Winner	W	L	GF	GA
Chicago	1934	Chicago	1	3	7	9
Toronto	1936	Detroit	3	1	18	11
NY Rangers	1937	Detroit	3	2	9	8
Boston	1941	Boston	0	4	6	12
Toronto	1942	Toronto	3	4	19	25
Boston	1943	Detroit	4	0	16	5
Toronto	1945	Toronto	3	4	9	9
Toronto	1948	Toronto	0	4	7	18
Toronto	1949	Toronto	0	4	5	12
NY Rangers	1950	Detroit	4	3	22	17
Montreal	1952	Detroit	4	0	11	2
Montreal	1954	Detroit	4	3	14	12
Montreal	1955	Detroit	4	3	27	20
Montreal	1956	Montreal	1	4	9	18
Chicago	1961	Chicago	2	4	12	19
Toronto	1963	Toronto	1	4	10	17
Toronto	1964	Toronto	3	4	17	22
Montreal	1966	Montreal	2	4	14	18
New Jersey	1995	New Jersey	0	4	7	16

TOP FIVE FINAL SERIES SCORERS

Player	GP	G	A	TP	PIM
Gordie Howe	55	18	32	50	94
Alex Delvecchio	47	16	22	38	2
Ted Lindsay	44	19	15	34	48
Sid Abel	34	9	11	20	25
Syd Howe	28	8	12	20	4

EDMONTON 1980-95
ALL-TIME FINAL SERIES RECORD

Versus	Series	W	L	GP	W	L	GF	GA
Boston	2	2	0	9	8	1	38	17
NY Islanders	2	1	1	9	4	5	27	29
Philadelphia	2	2	0	12	8	4	43	32
TOTALS	6	5	1	30	20	10	108	78

FINAL SERIES APPEARANCES

Versus	Year	Winner	W	L	GF	GA
NY Islanders	1983	NY Islanders	0	4	6	17
NY Islanders	1984	Edmonton	4	1	21	12
Philadelphia	1985	Edmonton	4	1	21	14
Philadelphia	1987	Edmonton	4	3	22	18
Boston	1988	Edmonton	4	0	19	9
Boston	1990	Edmonton	4	1	20	8

TOP FIVE FINAL SERIES SCORERS

Player	GP	G	A	TP	PIM
Wayne Gretzky	26	16	30	46	6
Jari Kurri	31	14	24	38	14
Glenn Anderson	31	14	12	26	55
Mark Messier	31	9	15	24	35
Paul Coffey	21	7	15	22	24

LOS ANGELES 1968-95
ALL-TIME FINAL SERIES RECORD

Versus	Series	W	L	GP	W	L	GF	GA
Montreal	1	0	1	5	1	4	12	15
TOTALS	1	0	1	5	1	4	12	15

FINAL SERIES APPEARANCES

Versus	Year	Winner	W	L	GF	GA
Montreal	1993	Montreal	1	4	12	15

TOP FIVE FINAL SERIES SCORERS

Player	GP	G	A	TP	PIM
Wayne Gretzky	5	2	5	7	2
Luc Robitaille	5	3	2	5	4
Tony Granato	5	1	3	4	10
Marty McSorley	5	2	0	2	16
Dave Taylor	3	1	1	2	6

MONTREAL 1918-95
ALL-TIME FINAL SERIES RECORD

Versus	Series	W	L	GP	W	L	GF	GA
Boston	7	7	0	33	26	7	107	64
Calgary	2	1	1	11	6	5	31	32
Chicago	5	5	0	29	19	10	98	69
Detroit	5	2	3	29	14	15	70	75
Los Angeles	1	1	0	5	4	1	15	12
NY Rangers	1	1	0	5	4	1	19	11
Philadelphia	1	1	0	4	4	0	14	9
St. Louis	2	2	0	8	8	0	23	10
Toronto	5	2	3	26	13	13	72	60
Defunct Clubs	*3	1	1	13	7	5	32	39
TOTALS	32	23	8	163	105	57	481	381

* No decision in 1919 Finals, interrupted by flu epidemic. Seattle and Montreal had each won two games. One game was tied.

FINAL SERIES APPEARANCES

Versus	Year	Winner	W	L	GF	GA
Seattle	1919	no decision	2	2	10	19
Van/Cgy	1924	Montreal	4	0	14	4
Victoria	1925	Victoria	1	3	8	16
Boston	1930	Montreal	2	0	7	3
Chicago	1931	Montreal	3	2	11	8
Chicago	1944	Montreal	4	0	16	8
Boston	1946	Montreal	4	1	19	13
Toronto	1947	Toronto	2	4	13	13
Toronto	1951	Toronto	1	4	10	13
Detroit	1952	Detroit	0	4	2	11
Boston	1953	Montreal	4	1	16	9
Detroit	1954	Detroit	3	4	12	14
Detroit	1955	Detroit	3	4	20	27
Detroit	1956	Montreal	4	1	18	9
Boston	1957	Montreal	4	1	15	6
Boston	1958	Montreal	4	2	16	14
Toronto	1959	Montreal	4	1	18	12
Toronto	1960	Montreal	4	0	15	5
Chicago	1965	Montreal	4	3	18	12
Detroit	1966	Montreal	4	2	18	14
Toronto	1967	Toronto	2	4	16	17
St. Louis	1968	Montreal	4	0	11	7
St. Louis	1969	Montreal	4	0	12	3
Chicago	1971	Montreal	4	3	20	18
Chicago	1973	Montreal	4	2	33	23
Philadelphia	1976	Montreal	4	0	14	9
Boston	1977	Montreal	4	0	16	6
Boston	1978	Montreal	4	2	18	13
NY Rangers	1979	Montreal	4	1	19	11
Calgary	1986	Montreal	4	1	15	13
Calgary	1989	Calgary	2	4	16	19
Los Angeles	1993	Montreal	4	1	15	12

TOP FIVE FINAL SERIES SCORERS

Player	GP	G	A	TP	PIM
Jean Beliveau	64	30	32	62	78
Henri Richard	65	21	26	47	68
Maurice Richard	59	34	12	46	83
Bernie Geoffrion	53	24	22	46	32
Yvan Cournoyer	50	21	19	40	18

NEW JERSEY DEVILS 1975-95
ALL-TIME FINAL SERIES RECORD

Versus	Series	W	L	GP	W	L	GF	GA
Detroit	1	1	0	4	4	0	16	7
TOTALS	1	1	0	4	4	0	16	7

FINAL SERIES APPEARANCES

Versus	Year	Winner	W	L	GF	GA
Detroit	1995	New Jersey	4	0	16	7

TOP FIVE FINAL SERIES SCORERS

Player	GP	G	A	TP	PIM
Neal Broten	4	3	3	6	4
John MacLean	4	1	4	5	0
Stephane Richer	4	2	2	4	0
Scott Niedermayer	4	1	3	4	0
Bill Guerin	4	0	4	4	12

142 • FINAL SERIES RESULTS, Team by Team

NEW YORK ISLANDERS
1973-95
ALL-TIME FINAL SERIES RECORD

Versus	Series	W	L	GP	W	L	GF	GA
Edmonton	2	1	1	9	5	4	29	27
Minnesota	1	1	0	5	4	1	26	16
Philadelphia	1	1	0	6	4	2	26	25
Vancouver	1	1	0	4	4	0	18	10
TOTALS	5	4	1	24	17	7	99	78

FINAL SERIES APPEARANCES

Versus	Year	Winner	W	L	GF	GA
Philadelphia	1980	NY Islanders	4	2	26	25
Minnesota	1981	NY Islanders	4	1	26	16
Vancouver	1982	NY Islanders	4	0	18	10
Edmonton	1983	NY Islanders	4	0	17	6
Edmonton	1984	Edmonton	1	4	12	21

TOP FIVE FINAL SERIES SCORERS

Player	GP	G	A	TP	PIM
Mike Bossy	23	17	17	34	4
Bryan Trottier	24	10	20	30	30
Denis Potvin	24	8	18	26	28
Clark Gillies	24	9	14	23	35
Butch Goring	24	9	7	16	2

NEW YORK RANGERS 1927-95
ALL-TIME FINAL SERIES RECORD

Versus	Series	W	L	GP	W	L	GF	GA
Boston	2	0	2	8	2	6	17	22
Detroit	2	0	2	12	5	7	25	31
Montreal	1	0	1	5	1	4	11	19
Toronto	3	2	1	13	7	6	35	34
Vancouver	1	1	0	7	4	3	21	19
Defunct Teams	1	1	0	5	3	2	6	5
TOTALS	10	4	6	50	22	28	115	130

FINAL SERIES APPEARANCES

Versus	Year	Winner	W	L	GF	GA
Mtl Maroons	1928	NY Rangers	3	2	6	5
Boston	1929	Boston	0	2	1	4
Toronto	1932	Toronto	0	3	10	18
Toronto	1933	NY Rangers	3	1	11	5
Detroit	1937	Detroit	2	3	8	9
Toronto	1940	NY Rangers	4	2	14	11
Detroit	1950	Detroit	3	4	17	22
Boston	1972	Boston	2	4	16	18
Montreal	1979	Montreal	1	4	11	19
Vancouver	1994	NY Rangers	4	3	21	19

TOP FIVE FINAL SERIES SCORERS

Player	GP	G	A	TP	PIM
Frank Boucher	19	8	6	14	6
Brian Leetch	7	5	6	11	4
Bill Cook	14	3	5	8	24
Fred "Bun" Cook	14	5	2	7	18
Rod Gilbert	6	4	3	7	11

PHILADELPHIA 1968-95
ALL-TIME FINAL SERIES RECORD

Versus	Series	W	L	GP	W	L	GF	GA
Boston	1	1	0	6	4	2	15	13
Buffalo	1	1	0	6	4	2	19	12
Edmonton	2	0	2	12	4	8	32	43
Montreal	1	0	1	4	0	4	9	14
NY Islanders	1	0	1	6	2	4	25	26
TOTALS	6	2	4	34	14	20	100	108

FINAL SERIES APPEARANCES

Versus	Year	Winner	W	L	GF	GA
Boston	1974	Philadelphia	4	2	15	13
Buffalo	1975	Philadelphia	4	2	19	12
Montreal	1976	Montreal	0	4	9	14
NY Islanders	1980	NY Islanders	2	4	25	26
Edmonton	1985	Edmonton	1	4	14	21
Edmonton	1987	Edmonton	3	4	18	22

TOP FIVE FINAL SERIES SCORERS

Player	GP	G	A	TP	PIM
Bobby Clarke	22	9	12	21	22
Brian Propp	18	9	9	18	4
Rick MacLeish	18	6	9	15	8
Bill Barber	22	5	10	15	17
Reg Leach	16	8	5	13	0

PITTSBURGH 1968-95
ALL-TIME FINAL SERIES RECORD

Versus	Series	W	L	GP	W	L	GF	GA
Chicago	1	1	0	4	4	0	15	10
Minnesota	1	1	0	6	4	2	18	16
TOTALS	2	2	0	10	8	2	43	26

FINAL SERIES APPEARANCES

Versus	Year	Winner	W	L	GF	GA
Minnesota	1991	Pittsburgh	4	2	28	16
Chicago	1992	Pittsburgh	4	0	15	10

TOP FIVE FINAL SERIES SCORERS

Player	GP	G	A	TP	PIM
Mario Lemieux	9	10	9	19	6
Larry Murphy	10	2	11	13	8
Kevin Stevens	10	6	6	12	27
Ron Francis	10	4	5	9	6
Joe Mullen	6	3	5	8	0

ST. LOUIS 1968-95
ALL-TIME FINAL SERIES RECORD

Versus	Series	W	L	GP	W	L	GF	GA
Boston	1	0	1	4	0	4	7	20
Montreal	2	0	2	8	0	8	17	43
TOTALS	3	0	3	12	0	12	24	63

FINAL SERIES APPEARANCES

Versus	Year	Winner	W	L	GF	GA
Montreal	1968	Montreal	0	4	7	11
Montreal	1969	Montreal	0	4	3	12
Boston	1970	Boston	0	4	7	20

TOP FIVE FINAL SERIES SCORERS

Player	GP	G	A	TP	PIM
Frank St. Marseille	12	4	3	7	4
G. 'Red' Berenson	12	3	1	4	15
Barclay Plager	9	1	2	3	6
Jim Roberts	12	1	2	3	10
Noel Picard	12	0	3	3	28

TORONTO 1918-95
ALL-TIME FINAL SERIES RECORD

Versus	Series	W	L	GP	W	L	GF	GA
Boston	1	0	1	5	1	4	6	12
Chicago	2	1	1	10	5	5	26	25
Detroit	7	6	1	38	25	13	114	85
Montreal	5	3	2	26	13	13	60	72
NY Rangers	3	1	2	13	6	7	34	35
Defunct Teams	3	2	1	13	6	7	38	40
TOTALS	21	13	8	105	56	49	278	269

FINAL SERIES APPEARANCES

Versus	Year	Winner	W	L	GF	GA
Vancouver	1918	Toronto	3	2	18	21
Vancouver	1921	Toronto	3	2	16	9
NY Rangers	1932	Toronto	3	0	18	10
NY Rangers	1933	NY Rangers	1	3	5	11
Mtl Maroons	1935	Maroons	0	3	4	10
Detroit	1936	Detroit	1	3	11	18
Chicago	1938	Chicago	1	3	8	10
Boston	1939	Boston	1	4	6	12
NY Rangers	1940	NY Rangers	2	4	11	14
Detroit	1942	Toronto	4	3	25	19
Detroit	1945	Toronto	4	3	9	9
Montreal	1947	Toronto	4	2	13	13
Detroit	1948	Toronto	4	0	18	7
Detroit	1949	Toronto	4	0	12	5
Montreal	1951	Toronto	4	1	13	10
Montreal	1959	Montreal	1	4	12	18
Montreal	1960	Montreal	0	4	5	15
Chicago	1962	Toronto	4	2	18	15
Detroit	1963	Toronto	4	1	17	10
Detroit	1964	Toronto	4	3	22	17
Montreal	1967	Toronto	4	2	17	16

TOP FIVE FINAL SERIES SCORERS

Player	GP	G	A	TP	PIM
Ted Kennedy	26	12	11	23	8
George Armstrong	33	9	13	22	22
Frank Mahovlich	32	7	15	22	39
Syl Apps	32	10	11	21	6
Bob Pulford	33	8	13	21	44

VANCOUVER 1971-95
ALL-TIME FINAL SERIES RECORD
Versus	Series	W	L	GP	W	L	GF	GA
NY Islanders	1	0	1	4	0	4	10	18
NY Rangers	1	0	1	7	3	4	19	21
TOTALS	2	0	2	11	3	8	29	39

FINAL SERIES APPEARANCES
Versus	Year	Winner	W	L	GF	GA
NY Islanders	1982	NY Islanders	0	4	10	18
NY Rangers	1994	NY Rangers	3	4	19	21

TOP FIVE FINAL SERIES SCORERS
Player	GP	G	A	TP	PIM
Pavel Bure	7	3	5	8	15
Cliff Ronning	7	1	6	7	6
Geoff Courtnall	7	4	1	5	11
Thomas Gradin	4	3	2	5	2
Trevor Linden	7	3	2	5	6

These NHL clubs have not appeared in the Stanley Cup Championship

MIGHTY DUCKS OF ANAHEIM
FLORIDA PANTHERS
HARTFORD WHALERS
OTTAWA SENATORS
QUEBEC NORDIQUES
TAMPA BAY LIGHTNING
SAN JOSE SHARKS
WASHINGTON CAPITALS
WINNIPEG JETS

Stanley Cup Final Series Records, 1918-95

TEAM RECORDS

Note: Statistics from the suspended game in 1988 Final have not been included in the compilation of categories in the Team Records section, but are included in the Individual Records section.

MOST STANLEY CUP CHAMPIONSHIPS (1893-1995)
- 24 – **Montreal Canadiens** (1916-24-30-31-44-46-53-56-57-58-59-60-65-66-68-69-71-73-76-77-78-79-86-93)
- 14 – Toronto Maple Leafs (1914-18-22-32-42-45-47-48-49-51-62-63-64-67)
- 7 – Detroit Red Wings (1936-37-43-50-52-54-55)

MOST CONSECUTIVE STANLEY CUP CHAMPIONSHIPS
- 5 – **Montreal Canadiens** (1956-57-58-59-60)
- 4 – New York Islanders (1980-81-82-83)
- – Montreal Canadiens (1976-77-78-79)

MOST YEARS IN THE FINALS (1893-1995)
- 35 – Montreal Canadiens
- 22 – Toronto Maple Leafs
- 19 – Detroit Red Wings

MOST CONSECUTIVE YEARS IN THE FINALS
- 10 – **Montreal Canadiens** (1951-60, inclusive)
- 5 – Montreal Canadiens (1965-69, inclusive)
- – New York Islanders (1980-84, inclusive)

MOST GOALS, BOTH TEAMS, ONE SERIES
- 56 – **Montreal Canadiens, Chicago Black Hawks** in 1973. Montreal won series 4-2, outscoring Chicago 33-23.
- 51 – NY Islanders, Philadelphia Flyers in 1980. New York won series 4-2, outscoring Philadelphia 26-25.

MOST GOALS, ONE TEAM, ONE SERIES
- 33 – **Montreal Canadiens** in 1973. Montreal won best-of-seven series 4-2, outscoring Chicago 33-23.
- 28 – Pittsburgh Penguins in 1991. Pittsburgh won best-of-seven series 4-2, outscoring Minnesota 28-16.

MOST GOALS, BOTH TEAMS, FOUR-GAME SERIES
- 29 – **Detroit Red Wings, Toronto Maple Leafs** in 1936. Detroit won series 3-1, outscoring Toronto 18-11.
- 28 – NY Islanders, Vancouver Canucks in 1982. New York won series 4-0, outscoring Vancouver 18-10.

MOST GOALS, ONE TEAM, FOUR-GAME SERIES
- 20 – **Boston Bruins** in 1970. Boston won best-of-seven series 4-0, outscoring St. Louis 20-7.
- 18 – Detroit Red Wings in 1936. Detroit won best-of-five series 3-1, outscoring Toronto 18-11.
- – Toronto Maple Leafs in 1948. Toronto won best-of-seven series 4-0, outscoring Detroit 18-7.
- – New York Islanders in 1982. New York won best-of-seven series 4-0, outscoring Vancouver 18-10.
- – Edmonton Oilers in 1988. Edmonton won best-of-seven series 4-0, outscoring Boston 18-9.

MOST GOALS, BOTH TEAMS, FIVE-GAME SERIES
- 42 – **NY Islanders, Minnesota North Stars** in 1981. New York won series 4-1, outscoring Minnesota 26-16.
- 35 – Edmonton Oilers, Philadelphia Flyers in 1985. Edmonton won series 4-1, outscoring Philadelphia 21-14.

MOST GOALS, ONE TEAM, FIVE-GAME SERIES
- 26 – **New York Islanders** in 1981. New York won best-of-seven series 4-1, outscoring Minnesota 26-16.
- 21 – Edmonton Oilers in 1984. Edmonton won best-of-seven series 4-1, outscoring NY Islanders 21-12.
- – Edmonton Oilers in 1985. Edmonton won best-of-seven series 4-1, outscoring Philadelphia 21-14.

MOST GOALS, BOTH TEAMS, SIX-GAME SERIES
- 56 – **Montreal Canadiens, Chicago Black Hawks** in 1973. Montreal won series 4-2, outscoring Chicago 33-23.
- 51 – New York Islanders, Philadelphia Flyers in 1980. New York won series 4-2, outscoring Philadelphia. 26-25.

MOST GOALS, ONE TEAM, SIX-GAME SERIES
- 33 – **Montreal Canadiens** in 1973. Montreal won best-of-seven series 4-2, outscoring Chicago 33-23.
- 28 – Pittsburgh Penguins in 1991. Pittsburgh won best-of-seven series 4-2, outscoring Minnesota 28-16.

MOST GOALS, BOTH TEAMS, SEVEN-GAME SERIES
- 47 — **Detroit Red Wings, Montreal Canadiens** in 1955. Detroit won series 4-3, outscoring Montreal 27-20.
- 44 — Toronto Maple Leafs, Detroit Red Wings in 1942. Toronto won series 4-3, outscoring Detroit 25-19.

MOST GOALS, ONE TEAM, SEVEN-GAME SERIES
- 27 — **Detroit Red Wings** in 1955. Detroit won best-of-seven series 4-3, outscoring Montreal 27-20.
- 25 — Toronto Maple Leafs in 1942. Toronto won best-of-seven series 4-3, outscoring Detroit 25-19.

FEWEST GOALS, BOTH TEAMS, FOUR-GAME SERIES
- 9 — **Ottawa Senators, Boston Bruins** in 1927. Ottawa won best-of-five 2-0-2, outscoring Boston 7-2.
- 13 — Detroit Red Wings, Montreal Canadiens in 1952. Detroit won series 4-0, outscoring Montreal 11-2.

FEWEST GOALS, ONE TEAM, FOUR-GAME SERIES
- 2 — **Boston Bruins** in 1927. Ottawa Senators won best-of-five series 2-0-2, outscoring Boston 7-2.
- — Montreal Canadiens in 1952. Detroit won best-of-seven series 4-0, outscoring Montreal 11-2.
- 3 — St. Louis Blues in 1969. Montreal won best-of-seven series 4-0, outscoring St. Louis 12-3.

FEWEST GOALS, BOTH TEAMS, FIVE-GAME SERIES
- 11 — **NY Rangers, Montreal Maroons** in 1928. New York won best-of-five 3-2, outscoring Montreal 6-5.
- 17 — Detroit Red Wings, NY Rangers in 1937. Detroit won best-of-five 3-2, outscoring New York 9-8.

FEWEST GOALS, ONE TEAM, FIVE-GAME SERIES
- 5 — **Montreal Maroons** in 1928. New York Rangers won best-of-five series 3-2, outscoring Montreal 6-5.
- 6 — New York Rangers in 1928. New York won best-of-five series 3-2, outscoring Montreal 6-5.
- — Toronto Maple Leafs in 1939. Boston won best-of-seven series 4-1, outscoring Toronto 12-6.
- — Boston Bruins in 1957. Montreal won best-of-seven series 4-1, outscoring Boston 15-6.

FEWEST GOALS, BOTH TEAMS, SIX-GAME SERIES
- 25 — **NY Rangers, Toronto Maple Leafs** in 1940. New York won best-of-seven 4-2, outscoring Toronto 14-11.
- 26 — Toronto Maple Leafs, Montreal Canadiens in 1947. Toronto won series 4-2, tied in scoring 13-13.

FEWEST GOALS, ONE TEAM, SIX-GAME SERIES
- 11 — **Toronto Maple Leafs** in 1940. NY Rangers won best-of-seven series 4-2, outscoring Toronto 14-11.
- 12 — Detroit Red Wings in 1961. Chicago won best-of-seven series 4-2, outscoring Detroit 19-12.
- — Buffalo Sabres in 1975. Philadelphia won best-of-seven series 4-2, outscoring Buffalo 19-12.

FEWEST GOALS, BOTH TEAMS, SEVEN-GAME SERIES
- 18 — **Toronto Maple Leafs, Detroit Red Wings** in 1945. Toronto won series 4-3, teams even in scoring 9-9.
- 26 — Detroit Red Wings, Montreal Canadiens in 1954. Detroit won series 4-3, outscoring Montreal 14-12.

FEWEST GOALS, ONE TEAM, SEVEN-GAME SERIES
- 9 — **Detroit Red Wings** in 1945. Toronto won best-of-seven series 4-3, teams even in scoring 9-9.
- — Toronto Maple Leafs in 1945. Toronto won best-of-seven series 4-3, teams even in scoring 9-9.
- 12 — Montreal Canadiens in 1954. Detroit won best-of-seven series 4-3, outscoring Montreal 14-12.
- — Chicago Black Hawks in 1965. Montreal won best-of-seven series 4-3, outscoring Chicago 18-12.

MOST GOALS, BOTH TEAMS, ONE GAME
- 15 — **Chicago Black Hawks 8 at Montreal Canadiens 7,** in Game #5, May 8, 1973. Montreal won series 4-2.
- 13 — Toronto Maple Leafs 4 at Detroit Red Wings 9, in Game #2, April 7, 1936. Detroit won series 3-1.

MOST GOALS, ONE TEAM, ONE GAME
- 9 — **Detroit Red Wings,** in Game #2, April 7, 1936. Toronto 4 at Detroit 9. Detroit won series 3-1.
- — Toronto Maple Leafs in Game #5, April 14, 1942. Detroit 3 at Toronto 9. Toronto won series 4-3.

MOST GOALS, BOTH TEAMS, ONE PERIOD
- 8 — **Chicago Black Hawks (5), Montreal Canadiens (3)** in 2nd period of Game #5, May 8, 1973. Chicago 8 at Montreal 7. Montreal won best-of-seven series 4-2.
  Vancouver Canucks (5), NY Rangers (3) in 3rd period of Game #5, June 9, 1994. Vancouver 6 at NY Rangers 3. NY Rangers won best-of-seven series 4-3.
- 6 — Toronto Maple Leafs (3), New York Rangers (3) in 3rd period of Game #3, April 9, 1932. New York 4 at Toronto 6. Toronto won best-of-five series 3-0.
- — Montreal Canadiens (4), Calgary Flames (2) in 1st period of Game #3, May 20, 1986. Calgary 3 at Montreal 5. Montreal won best-of-seven series 4-1.
- — Pittsburgh Penguins (3), Chicago Blackhawks (3) in 1st period of Game #4, June 1, 1992. Pittsburgh 6 at Chicago 5. Pittsburgh won best-of-seven series 4-0.

MOST GOALS, ONE TEAM, ONE PERIOD
- 5 — **Toronto Maple Leafs,** in 2nd period of Game #5, April 14, 1942. Detroit 3 at Toronto 9. Toronto won best-of-seven series 4-3.
- — **Chicago Black Hawks,** in 2nd period of Game #5, May 8, 1973. Chicago 8 at Montreal 7. Montreal won best-of-seven series 4-2.
- — **Vancouver Canucks,** in 3rd period of Game #5, June 9, 1994. Vancouver 6 at NY Rangers 3. Rangers won best-of-seven series 4-3.

LONGEST OVERTIME
- 55.13 — **Edmonton Oilers 3 at Boston Bruins 2** in Game #1, May 15, 1990. Edmonton's Petr Klima, assisted by Jari Kurri and Craig MacTavish, scored at 15.13 of the 3rd overtime period, 115.13 from start of game. Edmonton won best-of-seven series 4-1.
- 53.50 — Chicago Black Hawks 3 at Montreal Canadiens 2 in Game #3, April 9, 1931. Chicago's Marvin "Cy" Wentworth, assisted by Stewart Adams, scored at 13.50 of the 3rd overtime period, 113.50 from start of game. Montreal won best-of-five series 3-2.
- 38.08 — Calgary Flames 3 at Montreal Canadiens 4 in Game #3, May 19, 1989. Montreal's Ryan Walter, assisted by Stephane Richer, scored at 18.08 of the 2nd overtime period, 78.08 from start of game. Calgary won best-of-seven series 4-2.

SHORTEST OVERTIME
- 0.09 — **Montreal Canadiens 3 at Calgary Flames 2** in Game #2, May 18, 1986. Montreal's Brian Skrudland, assisted by Mike McPhee and Claude Lemieux, scored nine seconds into overtime. Montreal won best-of-seven series 4-1.
- 0.31 — Detroit Red Wings 3 at Toronto Maple Leafs 4, April 9, 1936. Toronto's Frank "Buzz" Boll, assisted by Reg "Red" Horner and Art Jackson, scored 31 seconds into overtime. Detroit won best-of-five series 3-1.

MOST OVERTIME GAMES, ONE SERIES
- 5 — **1951.** Of the five games played in the series, all went into overtime. Toronto Maple Leafs won four of the five games to defeat Montreal Canadiens 4-1 in best-of-seven series. Sid Smith, Ted "Teeder" Kennedy, Harry Watson and Bill Barilko scored the overtime winners for Toronto, while Maurice Richard replied for Montreal.

STANLEY CUP FINALS RECORD BOOK, 1918-1995 • 145

MOST OVERTIME VICTORIES, ONE TEAM, ONE SERIES
4 – **Toronto Maple Leafs** in 1951. Sid Smith, Ted "Teeder" Kennedy, Harry Watson and Bill Barilko scored the overtime winners in Games #1,3,4,5, respectively, for Toronto, who defeated Montreal 4-1 in best-of-seven series.

MOST HOME VICTORIES, BOTH TEAMS, ONE SERIES
7 – **Detroit Red Wings (4), Montreal Canadiens (3)** in 1955. Detroit won Games #1,2,5,7 at home and Montreal won Games #3,4,6 at home. Detroit won best-of-seven series 4-3.
– **Montreal Canadiens (4), Chicago Black Hawks (3)** in 1965. Montreal won Games #1,2,5,7 at home and Chicago won Games #3,4,6 at home. Montreal won best-of-seven series 4-3.

MOST HOME VICTORIES, ONE TEAM, ONE SERIES
4 – **Detroit Red Wings** in 1955. Detroit defeated Montreal Canadiens 4-3 in best-of-seven series, winning Games #1,2,5,7 in Detroit.
– **Montreal Canadiens** in 1965. Montreal defeated Chicago Black Hawks 4-3 in best-of-seven series, winning Games #1,2,5,7 in Montreal.

MOST ROAD VICTORIES, BOTH TEAMS, ONE SERIES
5 – **Toronto Maple Leafs (3), Detroit Red Wings (2)** in 1945. Toronto won Games #1,2,7 in Detroit and Detroit won Games #4,6 in Toronto. Toronto won best-of-seven series 4-3.
– **Montreal Canadiens (3), Detroit Red Wings (2)** in 1966. Montreal won Games #3,4,6 in Detroit and Detroit won Games #1,2 in Montreal. Montreal won best-of-seven series 4-2.

MOST ROAD VICTORIES, ONE TEAM, ONE SERIES
3 – **NY Rangers** in 1928. New York defeated Montreal Maroons 3-2 in best-of-five, winning Games #2,4,5 in Montreal. All five games were played in Montreal as the circus occupied Madison Square Garden.
– **Toronto Maple Leafs** in 1945. Toronto defeated Detroit Red Wings 4-3 in best-of-seven, winning Games #1,2,7 in Detroit.
– **Montreal Canadiens** in 1966. Montreal defeated Detroit Red Wings 4-2 in best-of-seven, winning Games #3,4,6 in Detroit.
– **Edmonton Oilers** in 1990. Edmonton defeated Boston Bruins 4-1 in best-of-seven, winning Games #1,2,5 in Boston.

MOST CONSECUTIVE FINAL SERIES GAME VICTORIES
10 – **Montreal Canadiens.** Streak began May 9, 1976, at Montreal with a 4-3 win over Philadelphia in Game #1 and ended May 18, 1978, at Boston with a 4-0 loss in Game #3. Included in the streak were 4 wins over Philadelphia in 1976, 4 over Boston in 1977 and 2 more over Boston in 1978.
9 – **Toronto Maple Leafs.** Streak began April 19, 1947, at Toronto with a 2-1 win over Montreal in Game #6 and ended when the team failed to advance to 1950 Finals. Included in the streak were 1 win over Montreal in 1947, 4 over Detroit in 1948 and 4 more over Detroit in 1949.
– **New York Islanders.** Streak began May 21, 1981, at New York with a 5-1 win over Minnesota in Game #5 and ended May 10, 1984, at New York with a 1-0 loss to Edmonton in Game #1. Included in the streak were 1 win over Minnesota in 1981, 4 over Vancouver in 1982 and 4 over Edmonton in 1983.

MOST SHUTOUTS, BOTH TEAMS, ONE SERIES
5 – **Toronto Maple Leafs (3), Detroit Red Wings (2)** in 1945. Toronto won best-of-seven series 4-3.
3 – Montreal Maroons (2), New York Rangers (1) in 1928. New York won best-of-five 3-2.
– Detroit Red Wings (2), New York Rangers (1) in 1937. Detroit won best-of-five series 3-2.
– Montreal Canadiens (3), Chicago Black Hawks (0) in 1965. Montreal won best-of-seven series 4-3.

MOST SHUTOUTS, ONE TEAM, ONE SERIES
3 – **Toronto Maple Leafs** in 1945. Toronto defeated Detroit 4-3 in best-of-seven series.
– **Montreal Canadiens** in 1965. Montreal defeated Chicago 4-3 in best-of-seven series.

MOST PENALTIES, BOTH TEAMS, ONE SERIES
142 – **Philadelphia Flyers (75), Boston Bruins (67)** in 1974. Philadelphia defeated Boston in series 4-2.
128 – Philadelphia Flyers (72), NY Islanders (56) in 1980. NY Islanders won best-of-seven series 4-2.

MOST PENALTIES, ONE TEAM, ONE SERIES
75 – **Philadelphia Flyers** in 1974. Philadelphia defeated Boston in best-of-seven series 4-2.
– **Philadelphia Flyers** in 1980. New York Islanders won best-of-seven series 4-2.

MOST PENALTY MINUTES, BOTH TEAMS, ONE SERIES
511 – **Calgary Flames (256), Montreal Canadiens (255)** in 1986. Montreal won best-of-seven series 4-1.
395 – Philadelphia Flyers (219), NY Islanders (176) in 1980. New York won best-of-seven series 4-2.

MOST PENALTY MINUTES, ONE TEAM, ONE SERIES
256 – **Calgary Flames** in 1986. Montreal won best-of-seven series 4-1.
255 – Montreal Canadiens in 1986. Montreal defeated Calgary in best-of-seven series 4-1.

MOST PENALTIES, BOTH TEAMS, ONE GAME
43 – **Philadelphia Flyers (22) at Boston Bruins (21)** in Game #5, May 16, 1974. Boston 5, Philadelphia 1. Philadelphia won best-of-seven series 4-2.
37 – Boston Bruins (22) at Montreal Canadiens (15) in Game #5, May 23, 1978. Montreal 4, Boston 1. Montreal won best-of-seven series 4-2.

MOST PENALTIES, ONE TEAM, ONE GAME
22 – **Philadelphia Flyers** in Game #5, May 16, 1974. Boston 5, Philadelphia 1. Philadelphia won best-of-seven series 4-2.
21 – Boston Bruins in Game #5, May 16, 1974. Philadelphia 1 at Boston 5. Philadelphia won series 4-2.

MOST PENALTY MINUTES, BOTH TEAMS, ONE GAME
176 – **Calgary Flames (86) at Montreal Canadiens (90)** in Game #4, May 22, 1986. Montreal 1, Calgary 0. Montreal won series 4-1.
135 – Philadelphia Flyers (67) at Boston Bruins (68) in Game #5, May 16, 1974. Boston 5, Philadelphia 1. Philadelphia won best-of-seven series 4-2.

MOST PENALTY MINUTES, ONE TEAM, ONE GAME
90 – **Montreal Canadiens** in Game #4, May 22, 1986. Calgary 0 at Montreal 1. Montreal won series 4-1.
86 – Calgary Flames in Game #4, May 22, 1986. Calgary 0 at Montreal 1. Montreal won series 4-1.

MOST PENALTIES, BOTH TEAMS, ONE PERIOD
21 – **Philadelphia Flyers (10) at Boston Bruins (11)** in 1st period of Game #4, May 14, 1974. Philadelphia 4, Boston 2. Philadelphia won series 4-2.
20 – Philadelphia Flyers (10) at NY Islanders (10) in 2nd period of Game #3, May 17, 1980. NY Islanders 6, Philadelphia 2. NY Islanders won series 4-2.
– Calgary Flames (10) at Montreal Canadiens (10) in 3rd period of Game #4, May 22, 1986. Montreal 1, Calgary 0. Montreal won series 4-1.

MOST PENALTIES, ONE TEAM, ONE PERIOD
11 – **Boston Bruins** in 1st period of Game #4, May 14, 1974. Philadelphia 4 at Boston 2. Philadelphia won series 4-2.
10 – several teams tied.

MOST PENALTY MINUTES, BOTH TEAMS, ONE PERIOD
- **152** – Calgary Flames (72) at Montreal Canadiens (80) in 3rd period of Game #4, May 22, 1986. Montreal 1, Calgary 0. Montreal won series 4-1.
- **104** – Vancouver Canucks (52) at NY Islanders (52) in 2nd period of Game #1, May 8, 1982. NY Islanders 6, Vancouver 5 (OT). NY Islanders won series 4-0.

MOST PENALTY MINUTES, ONE TEAM, ONE PERIOD
- **80** – Montreal Canadiens in 3rd period of Game #4, May 22, 1986. Montreal 1, Calgary 0. Montreal won series 4-1.
- **72** – Calgary Flames in 3rd period of Game #4, May 22, 1986. Montreal 1, Calgary 0. Montreal won series 4-1.

FEWEST PENALTIES, BOTH TEAMS, ONE SERIES
- **19** – Detroit Red Wings (10), Toronto Maple Leafs (9) in 1945. Toronto won best-of-seven series 4-3.

FEWEST PENALTIES, ONE TEAM, ONE SERIES
- **9** – Toronto Maple Leafs in 1945. Toronto defeated Detroit in best-of-seven series 4-3.
- **10** – Detroit Red Wings in 1945. Toronto defeated Detroit in best-of-seven series 4-3.

FEWEST PENALTY MINUTES, BOTH TEAMS, ONE SERIES
- **41** – Toronto Maple Leafs (21), Detroit Red Wings (20) in 1945. Toronto won best-of-seven series 4-3.

FEWEST PENALTY MINUTES, ONE TEAM, ONE SERIES
- **21** – Toronto Maple Leafs in 1945. Toronto defeated Detroit in best-of-seven series 4-3.
- **20** – Detroit Red Wings in 1945. Toronto defeated Detroit in best-of-seven series 4-3.

FEWEST PENALTIES AND PENALTY MINUTES, BOTH TEAMS, ONE GAME
- **0** – Toronto Maple Leafs 1 at Detroit Red Wings 0 in Game #6, April 16, 1942. Toronto won series 4-3.

FEWEST PENALTIES AND PENALTY MINUTES, ONE TEAM, ONE GAME
- **0** – Toronto Maple Leafs in Game #6, April 16, 1942. Toronto 1 at Detroit 0. Toronto won series 4-3.
- – Detroit Red Wings in Game #6, April 16, 1942. Toronto 1 at Detroit 0. Toronto won series 4-3.
- – Detroit Red Wings in Game #2, April 8, 1945. Detroit 0 at Toronto 2. Toronto won series 4-3.
- – Toronto Maple Leafs in Game #3, April 12, 1945. Detroit 0 at Toronto 1. Toronto won series 4-3.
- – New York Rangers in Game #2, April 13, 1950. NY Rangers 3, Detroit 1 (at Toronto). Detroit won series 4-3.
- – Boston Bruins in Game #5, April 16, 1953. Boston 0 at Montreal 1 (OT). Montreal won series 4-1.

MOST POWER-PLAY GOALS, BOTH TEAMS, ONE SERIES
- **21** – New York Islanders (15), Philadelphia Flyers (6) in 1980. New York won best-of-seven series 4-2.
- **14** – Montreal Canadiens (10), Chicago Black Hawks (4) in 1965. Montreal won best-of-seven series 4-3.

MOST POWER-PLAY GOALS, ONE TEAM, ONE SERIES
- **15** – New York Islanders in 1980. New York defeated Philadelphia in best-of-seven series 4-2.
- **10** – Montreal Canadiens in 1965. Montreal defeated Chicago in best-of-seven series 4-3.

MOST POWER-PLAY GOALS, BOTH TEAMS, ONE GAME
- **5** – six times.

MOST POWER-PLAY GOALS, ONE TEAM, ONE GAME
- **5** – New York Islanders, May 17, 1980, in Game #3 at New York. NY Islanders 6, Philadelphia 2. New York won best-of-seven series 4-2.
- **4** – Toronto Maple Leafs, April 10, 1947, in Game #2 at Montreal. Toronto 4, Montreal 0. Toronto won best-of-seven series 4-2.
- – Montreal Canadiens, April 27, 1965, in Game #5 at Montreal. Montreal 6, Chicago 0. Montreal won best-of-seven series 4-3.
- – Edmonton Oilers, May 28, 1985, in Game #4 at Edmonton. Edmonton 5, Philadelphia 3. Edmonton won best-of-seven series 4-1.

MOST POWER-PLAY GOALS, BOTH TEAMS, ONE PERIOD
- **3** – 16 times.

MOST POWER-PLAY GOALS, ONE TEAM, ONE PERIOD
- **3** – Montreal Canadiens, April 6, 1954, in 1st period of Game #2 at Detroit. Montreal 3, Detroit 1. Detroit won best-of-seven series 4-3.
- – NY Rangers, May 4, 1972, in 1st period of Game #3 at New York. NY Rangers 5, Boston 2. Boston won best-of-seven series 4-2.
- – Montreal Canadiens, May 12, 1977, in 1st period of Game #3 at Boston. Montreal 4, Boston 2. Montreal won best-of-seven series 4-0.
- – NY Islanders, May 17, 1980, in 1st period of Game #3 at New York. NY Islanders 7, Philadelphia 5. NY Islanders won best-of-seven 4-2.

MOST SHORTHANDED GOALS, BOTH TEAMS, ONE SERIES
- **6** – Pittsburgh Penguins (3), Minnesota North Stars (3) in 1991. Pittsburgh won best-of-seven series 4-2.
- **4** – New York Rangers (4), Toronto Maple Leafs (0) in 1933. NY Rangers won best-of-five series 3-1.

MOST SHORTHANDED GOALS, ONE TEAM, ONE SERIES
- **4** – New York Rangers in 1933. NY Rangers defeated Toronto in best-of-five series 3-1.
- **3** – Detroit Red Wings in 1955. Detroit defeated Montreal in best-of-seven series 4-3.
- – Toronto Maple Leafs in 1963. Toronto defeated Detroit in best-of-seven series 4-1.
- – Boston Bruins in 1972. Boston defeated NY Rangers in best-of-seven series 4-2.
- – Edmonton Oilers in 1987. Edmonton defeated Philadelphia in best-of-seven series 4-3.
- – Pittsburgh Penguins in 1991. Pittsburgh defeated Minnesota in best-of-seven series 4-2.
- – Minnesota North Stars in 1991. Pittsburgh defeated Minnesota in best-of-seven series 4-2.

MOST SHORTHANDED GOALS, BOTH TEAMS, ONE GAME
- **2** – nine times.

MOST SHORTHANDED GOALS, ONE TEAM, ONE GAME
- **2** – seven times.

MOST SHORTHANDED GOALS, BOTH TEAMS, ONE PERIOD
- **2** – NY Rangers (0) at Boston Bruins (2), in 1st per. of Game #1, April 30, 1972. Boston 6, NY Rangers 5. Boston won best-of-seven series 4-2.
- – Montreal Canadiens (0) at Chicago Black Hawks (2), in 1st period of Game #3, May 3, 1973. Chicago 7, Montreal 4. Montreal won series 4-2.
- – Minnesota North Stars (0), NY Islanders (2), in 1st period of Game #1, May 12, 1981. NY Islanders 6, Minnesota 3. Islanders won series 4-1.
- – Minnesota North Stars (1), Pittsburgh Penguins (1), in 2nd period of Game #1, May 15, 1991. Minnesota 5, Pittsburgh 4. Pittsburgh won series 4-2.

MOST SHORTHANDED GOALS, ONE TEAM, ONE PERIOD
2 – **Boston Bruins** in 1st period of Game #1, April 30, 1972. Boston 6, NY Rangers 5. Boston won best-of-seven series 4-2.
  – **Chicago Black Hawks** in 1st period of Game #3, May 3, 1973. Chicago 7, Montreal 4. Montreal won best-of-seven series 4-2.
  – **NY Islanders** in 1st period of Game #1, May 12, 1981. NY Islanders 6, Minnesota 3. NY Islanders won series 4-1.

FASTEST TWO GOALS, BOTH TEAMS
0.10 – **Toronto Maple Leafs at Detroit Red Wings** in Game #1, April 5, 1936. Detroit's Wally Kilrea and Toronto's Frank "Buzz" Boll scored at 12.05 and 12.15 of 1st period, respectively. Detroit 3, Toronto 1. Detroit won best-of-five series 3-1.
  – **Montreal Canadiens at Toronto Maple Leafs** in Game #3, April 12, 1947. Toronto's Vic Lynn and Montreal's Leo Gravelle scored at 12.23 and 12.33 of 2nd period, respectively. Toronto 4, Montreal 2. Toronto won best-of-seven series 4-2.
0.13 – Detroit Red Wings at Toronto Maple Leafs in Game #1, April 11, 1964. Detroit's Bruce MacGregor and Toronto's George Armstrong scored at 4.31 and 4.44 of 1st period, respectively. Toronto 3, Detroit 2. Toronto won best-of-seven series 4-3.

FASTEST TWO GOALS, ONE TEAM
0.12 – **Montreal Maroons**, April 9, 1935, in Game #3 at Montreal. Montreal 4, Toronto 1. Lawrence "Baldy" Northcott and Marvin "Cy" Wentworth scored at 16.18 and 16.30 of 2nd period, respectively. Montreal won best-of-five series 3-0.
  – **Montreal Canadiens**, April 7, 1955 in Game #3 at Montreal. Montreal 4, Detroit 2. Bernie "Boom Boom" Geoffrion scored at 8.30 and 8.42 of first period. Detroit won best-of-seven series 4-3.
0.15 – Edmonton Oilers, May 25, 1985, in Game #3 at Edmonton. Edmonton 4, Philadelphia 3. Wayne Gretzky scored at 1.10 and 1.25 of 1st period. Edmonton won best-of-seven series 4-1.

FASTEST THREE GOALS, BOTH TEAMS
0.30 – **Pittsburgh Penguins 6 at Chicago Blackhawks 5** in Game #4, June 1, 1992. Chicago's Dirk Graham scored at 6:21 of 1st period, Pittsburgh's Kevin Stevens scored at 6:33 and Graham scored at 6:51. Pittsburgh won best-of-seven series 4-0.
0.31 – Philadelphia Flyers 3 at Edmonton Oilers 4 in Game #3, May 25, 1985. Edmonton's Wayne Gretzky scored at 1.10 and 1.25 of first period and Philadelphia's Derrick Smith scored at 1.41. Edmonton won series 4-1.
1.18 – Calgary Flames 3 at Montreal Canadiens 5 in Game #3, May 20, 1986. Calgary's Joel Otto scored at 17.59 of first period, and Montreal's Bobby Smith at 18.25 and Mats Naslund at 19.17. Montreal won best-of-seven series 4-1.

FASTEST THREE GOALS, ONE TEAM
0.56 – **Montreal Canadiens**, April 6, 1954, in Game #2 at Detroit. Montreal 3, Detroit 1. Dickie Moore scored at 15.03 of first period, and Maurice "Rocket" Richard scored at 15.28 and again at 15.59. Detroit won best-of-seven series 4-3.
1.08 – Montreal Canadiens, May 20, 1986, in Game #3 at Montreal. Montreal 5, Calgary 3. Bobby Smith scored at 18.25, Mats Naslund at 19.17 and Bob Gainey at 19.33 of 1st period. Montreal won series 4-1.

FASTEST FOUR GOALS, BOTH TEAMS
1.34 – **Calgary Flames 3 at Montreal Canadiens 5** in Game #3, May 20, 1986. Calgary's Joel Otto scored at 17.59 of 1st period, followed by Montreal's Bobby Smith at 18.25, Mats Naslund at 19.17 and Bob Gainey at 19.33. Montreal won best-of-seven series 4-1.
2.54 – New York Rangers 4 at Toronto Maple Leafs 6 in Game #3, April 9, 1932. New York's Fred "Bun" Cook scored at 16.32 of 3rd period, followed by Toronto's Bob Gracie at 17.36 and New York's Frank Boucher at 18.26 and again at 19.26. Toronto won best-of-five series 3-0.

FASTEST FOUR GOALS, ONE TEAM
5.29 – **Montreal Canadiens**, March 31, 1956, in Game #1 at Montreal. Montreal 6, Detroit 4. Jack LeClair, Bernie "Boom Boom" Geoffrion, Jean Beliveau and Claude Provost scored at 5.20, 6.20, 7.31 and 10.49 of 3rd period, respectively. Montreal won best-of-seven series 4-1.
5.57 – Montreal Canadiens, April 29, 1973, in Game #1 at Montreal. Montreal 8, Chicago 3. Jacques Lemaire, Peter Mahovlich, Frank Mahovlich and Chuck Lefley scored at 8.38, 12.36, 13.34 and 14.35 of 3rd period, respectively. Montreal won best-of-seven series 4-2.

FASTEST FIVE GOALS, BOTH TEAMS
4.20 – **New York Rangers 4 at Toronto Maple Leafs 6** in Game #3, April 9, 1932. Toronto's Irvine "Ace" Bailey scored at 15.07 of 1st period, followed by New York's Fred "Bun" Cook at 16.34, Toronto's Bob Gracie at 17.36 and New York's Frank Boucher at 18.24 and again at 19.27. Toronto won best-of-five series 3-0.
6.32 – Chicago Black Hawks 8 at Montreal Canadiens 7 in Game #5, May 8, 1973. Montreal's Claude Larose scored at 0.37 of the 2nd period, followed by Chicago's Dave Kryskow at 3.10, Larose again at 4.23, Chicago's Stan Mikita at 6.21 and Montreal's Yvan Cournoyer at 7.09. Montreal won best-of-seven series 4-2.

FASTEST FIVE GOALS, ONE TEAM
10.29 – **Edmonton Oilers**, May 15, 1984, in Game #3 at Edmonton. Edmonton 7, NY Islanders 2. Glenn Anderson scored at 19.12 of 2nd period, followed by Paul Coffey at 19.29, Mark Messier at 5.32 of 3rd period and Dave Semenko at 5.52. Edmonton won series 4-1.
14.20 – New York Islanders, May 12, 1983, in Game #2 at Edmonton. NY Islanders 6, Edmonton 3. Tomas Jonsson scored at 14.21 of 2nd period, followed by Bob Nystrom at 17.55, Mike Bossy at 19.17, Bob Bourne at 8.03 of 3rd period, and Brent Sutter at 8.41. NY Islanders won series 4-0.

Individual Records

Note: Statistics from the suspended game in 1988 Final have not been included in the compilation of categories in the Team Records section, but are included in the Individual Records section.

MOST YEARS IN FINALS
12 – **Maurice Richard,** Montreal (1944-46-47-51-52-53-54-56-57-58-59-60)
  – Leonard "Red" Kelly, Detroit (1948-49-50-52-54-55-56) and Toronto (1960-62-63-64-67)
  – Jean Beliveau, Montreal (1954-55-56-57-58-60-65-66-67-68-69-71)
  – Henri Richard, Montreal (1956-57-58-59-60-65-66-67-68-69-71-73)
11 – Bert Olmstead, Montreal (1951-52-53-54-55-56-57-58) and Toronto (1959-60-62)
  – Doug Harvey, Montreal (1951-52-53-54-55-56-57-58-59-60) and St. Louis (1968)
  – Jean-Guy Talbot, Montreal (1956-57-58-59-60-65-66-67) and St. Louis (1968-69-70)
10 – Gordie Howe, Detroit (1948-49-52-54-55-56-61-63-64-66)
  – Yvan Cournoyer, Montreal (1965-66-67-68-69-71-73-76-77-78)
  – Claude Provost, Montreal (1956-57-58-59-60-65-66-67-68-69)

MOST CONSECUTIVE YEARS IN FINALS
10 – **Bernie Geoffrion,** Montreal (1951-60 inclusive)
  – **Doug Harvey,** Montreal (1951-60 inclusive)
  – **Tom Johnson,** Montreal (1951-60 inclusive)
  – **Bert Olmstead,** Montreal (1951-58, inclusive) and Toronto (1959-60)
9 – Dickie Moore, Montreal (1952-60 inclusive)
8 – Floyd Curry, Montreal (1951-58 inclusive)
7 – Dollard St. Laurent, Montreal (1952-58 inclusive)

MOST GAMES PLAYED IN FINALS
- **65 – Leonard "Red" Kelly,** Detroit (37) and Toronto (28)
  - – Henri Richard, Montreal
- 64 – Jean Beliveau, Montreal
- 59 – Maurice Richard, Montreal
- 56 – Bert Olmstead, Montreal (43) and Toronto (13)
- 55 – Gordie Howe, Detroit
  - – Jean-Guy Talbot, Montreal (43) and St. Louis (12)
- 54 – Emile "Butch" Bouchard, Montreal
  - – Yvan Cournoyer, Montreal
  - – Doug Harvey, Montreal (52) and St. Louis (2).

MOST CONSECUTIVE GAMES IN FINALS
- **53 – Bernie Geoffrion,** Montreal (Game #1 in 1951 through Game #4 in 1960)
- 48 – Dickie Moore, Montreal (Game #1 in 1952 through Game #4 in 1960)
- 41 – Floyd Curry, Montreal (Game #1 in 1951 through Game #3 in 1958)
- 40 – Bert Olmstead, Montreal (Game #1 in 1951 through Game #2 in 1958)
- 38 – Tom Johnson, Montreal (Game #1 in 1951 through Game #5 in 1957)
- 36 – Doug Harvey, Montreal (Game #4 in 1954 through Game #4 in 1960)

MOST CAREER POINTS IN FINALS
- **62 – Jean Beliveau,** Montreal (30-32-62 in 64 games)
- 53 – Wayne Gretzky, Edmonton, Los Angeles (18-35-53 in 31 games)
- 50 – Gordie Howe, Detroit (18-32-50 in 55 games)
- 47 – Henri Richard, Montreal (21-26-47 in 65 games)
- 46 – Maurice Richard, Montreal (34-12-46 in 59 games)
  - – Bernie Geoffrion, Montreal (24-22-46 in 53 games)
- 41 – Frank Mahovlich, Toronto (7-15-22 in 32 games) and Montreal (9-10-19 in 13 games) (16-25-41 in 45 games overall)
- 40 – Yvan Cournoyer, Montreal (21-19-40 in 50 games)
- 39 – Jari Kurri, Edmonton, Los Angeles (15-24-39 in 36 games)
- 38 – Alex Delvecchio, Detroit (16-22-38 in 47 games)
- 37 – Jacques Lemaire, Montreal (19-18-37 in 40 games)
- 35 – Dick Duff, Toronto (5-7-12 in 20 games) and Montreal (10-13-23 in 27 games) (15-20-35 in 47 games overall)
  - – Doug Harvey, Montreal (4-30-34 in 52 games) and St.Louis (0-1-1 in 2 games) (4-31-35 in 54 games overall)

MOST CAREER GOALS IN FINALS
- **34 – Maurice Richard,** Montreal (34-12-46 in 59 games)
- 30 – Jean Beliveau, Montreal (30-32-62 in 65 games)
- 24 – Bernie Geoffrion, Montreal (24-22-46 in 53 games)
- 21 – Yvan Cournoyer, Montreal (21-19-40 in 50 games)
  - – Henri Richard, Montreal (21-26-47 in 65 games)
- 19 – Jacques Lemaire, Montreal (19-18-37 in 40 games)
- 18 – Gordie Howe, Detroit (18-32-50 in 55 games)
  - – Ted Lindsay, Detroit (19-14-34 in 44 games)
  - – Wayne Gretzky, Edmonton, Los Angeles (18-35-53 in 31 games)
- 17 – Mike Bossy, NY Islanders (17-17-34 in 23 games)
- 16 – Frank Mahovlich, Toronto (7-15-22 in 32 games) and Montreal (9-10-19 in 13 games) (16-25-41 in 45 games overall)
  - – Glenn Anderson, Edmonton (14-12-26 in 31 games) and NY Rangers (2-1-3 in 7 games) (16-13-29 in 38 games overall)

MOST CAREER ASSISTS IN FINALS
- **35 – Wayne Gretzky,** Edmonton, Los Angeles (18-35-53 in 31 games)
- 32 – Jean Beliveau, Montreal (30-32-62 in 64 games)
  - – Gordie Howe, Detroit (18-32-50 in 55 games)
- 31 – Doug Harvey, Montreal (4-30-34 in 52 games) and St.Louis (0-1-1 in 2 games) (4-31-35 in 54 games overall)
- 26 – Henri Richard, Montreal (21-26-47 in 65 games)
- 25 – Frank Mahovlich, Toronto (7-15-22 in 32 games) and Montreal (9-10-19 in 13 games) (16-25-41 in 45 games overall)
- 24 – Jari Kurri, Edmonton, Los Angeles (15-24-39 in 36 games)
- 22 – Bernie Geoffrion, Montreal (24-22-46 in 53 games)
  - – Alex Delvecchio, Detroit (16-22-38 in 47 games)
- 20 – Dick Duff, Toronto (5-7-12 in 20 games) and Montreal (10-13-23 in 27 games) (15-20-35 in 47 games)
  - – Leonard "Red" Kelly, Detroit (6-7-13 in 37 games) and Toronto (5-13-18 in 28 games) (11-20-31 in 65 games)
  - – Mark Messier, Edmonton (9-15-24 in 31 games) and NY Rangers (2-5-7 in 7 games) (11-20-31 in 38 games overall)

MOST CAREER GAME-WINNING GOALS IN FINALS
- **9 – Jean Beliveau,** Montreal
- 8 – Maurice Richard, Montreal
- 6 – Yvan Cournoyer, Montreal
  - – Bernie Geoffrion, Montreal

MOST CAREER OVERTIME GOALS IN FINALS
- **3 – Maurice Richard,** Montreal (1 in 1946, 1 in 1951, 1 in 1958)
- 2 – Don Raleigh, New York Rangers (2 in 1950)
  - – Jacques Lemaire, Montreal (1 in 1968; 1 in 1977)
  - – John LeClair, Montreal (2 in 1993)

MOST CAREER OVERTIME ASSISTS IN FINALS
- **2 – Elwin "Doc" Romnes,** Chicago (2 in 1934)
  - – Emile "Butch" Bouchard, Montreal (1 in 1944, 1 in 1946)
  - – Ed Slowinski, New York Rangers (2 in 1950)
  - – Tod Sloan, Toronto (2 in 1951)
  - – Guy Lafleur, Montreal (1 in 1977, 1 in 1979)
  - – John Tonelli, New York Islanders (2 in 1980)
  - – Harry Watson, Toronto Maple Leafs (1 in 1947, 1 in 1951)

MOST CAREER OVERTIME POINTS IN FINALS
- **4 – Maurice Richard,** Montreal (3-1-4)
- 3 – Elwin "Doc" Romnes, Chicago (0-2-2) and Toronto (1-0-1) (1-2-3 overall)
  - – Guy Lafleur, Montreal (1-2-3)
  - – Harry Watson, Toronto (1-2-3)

MOST CAREER POWER-PLAY GOALS IN FINALS
- **11 – Jean Beliveau,** Montreal
- 10 – Bernie Geoffrion, Montreal
- 8 – Mike Bossy, New York Islanders
  - – Yvan Cournoyer, Montreal
- 7 – Alex Delvecchio, Detroit

MOST CAREER POWER-PLAY ASSISTS IN FINALS
- **16 – Jean Beliveau,** Montreal
- 14 – Gordie Howe, Detroit
  - – Wayne Gretzky, Edmonton, Los Angeles
- 12 – Doug Harvey, Montreal (11) and St. Louis (1)
  - – Denis Potvin, New York Islanders
- 11 – Mike Bossy, New York Islanders

MOST CAREER POWER-PLAY POINTS IN FINALS
- **27 – Jean Beliveau,** Montreal (11-16-27)
- 19 – Mike Bossy, New York Islanders (8-11-19)
  - – Wayne Gretzky, Edmonton, Los Angeles (5-14-19)
- 18 – Bernie Geoffrion, Montreal (10-8-18)
  - – Yvan Cournoyer, Montreal (8-10-18)
  - – Denis Potvin, New York Islanders (6-12-18)
  - – Gordie Howe, Detroit (4-14-18)
- 16 – Alex Delvecchio, Detroit (7-9-16)
- 15 – Bryan Trottier, New York Islanders (4-11-15)

MOST CAREER SHORTHANDED GOALS IN FINALS
- 2 – **Cecil Dillion,** New York Rangers (2 in 1933)
  – Dave Keon, Toronto (2 in 1963)
  – Bob Pulford, Toronto (2 in 1964)
  – Marcel Pronovost, Detroit (1 in 1955) and Toronto (1 in 1967)
  – Serge Savard, Montreal (2 in 1968)
  – Derek Sanderson, Boston (1 in 1970, 1 in 1972)
  – Peter Mahovlich, Montreal (1 in 1971, 1 in 1973)
  – Kevin Lowe, Edmonton (2 in 1987)
  – Mario Lemieux, Pittsburgh (2 in 1991)

MOST CAREER SHORTHANDED ASSISTS IN FINALS
- 4 – **Bobby Orr,** Boston (2 in 1970, 1 in 1972, 1 in 1974)
- 2 – George Armstrong, Toronto (2 in 1963)
  – Allan Stanley, Toronto (1 in 1963, 1 in 1964)
  – Claude Provost, Montreal (1 in 1968, 1 in 1969)
  – Bob Bourne, New York Islanders (1 in 1980, 1 in 1982)
  – Wayne Gretzky, Edmonton (2 in 1987)

MOST CAREER SHORTHANDED POINTS IN FINALS
- 4 – **Bobby Orr,** Boston (0-4-4)
- 2 – several players tied.

MOST CAREER PENALTY MINUTES IN FINALS
- 94 – **Gordie Howe,** Detroit (in 55 games)
- 87 – Kevin McClelland, Edmonton (in 22 games)
- 86 – Duane Sutter, New York Islanders (in 24 games)
- 83 – Maurice Richard, Montreal (in 59 games)
- 79 – Wayne Cashman, Boston (in 26 games)
- 78 – Jean Beliveau, Montreal (in 64 games)

MOST PENALTY MINUTES, ONE GAME
- 29 – **Kevin McClelland,** Edmonton, in Game #5, May 30, 1985. Philadelphia 3 at Edmonton 8. McClelland was assessed 2 minors, 1 major, 1 misconduct and 1 game misconduct.
- 27 – Claude Lemieux, Montreal, in Game #4, May 22, 1986. Calgary 0 at Montreal 1. Lemieux was assessed 1 minor, 1 major, 1 misconduct and 1 game misconduct.

MOST PENALTY MINUTES, ONE PERIOD
- 25 – **Kevin McClelland,** Edmonton, in third period of Game #5, May 30, 1985. Philadelphia 3 at Edmonton 8. McClelland was assessed 1 major, 1 misconduct and 1 game misconduct.
  – Claude Lemieux, Montreal, in third period of Game #4, May 22, 1986. Calgary 0 at Montreal 1. Lemieux was assessed 1 major, 1 misconduct and 1 game misconduct.

MOST CAREER SHUTOUTS IN FINALS
- 4 – **Walter "Turk" Broda,** Toronto (1 in 1940, 1 in 1942, 1 in 1947, 1 in 1948)
  – Jacques Plante, Montreal (1 in 1956, 1 in 1957, 1 in 1958, 1 in 1960)
- 3 – Harry Lumley, Detroit (2 in 1945, 1 in 1950)
  – Frank McCool, Toronto (3 in 1945)
  – Gerry McNeil, Montreal (2 in 1953, 1 in 1954)
  – Terry Sawchuk, Detroit (2 in 1952, 1 in 1954)
  – Lorne "Gump" Worsley, Montreal (2 in 1965, 1 in 1968)

MOST CAREER GAMES PLAYED BY A GOALTENDER IN FINALS
- 41 – **Jacques Plante,** Montreal (38) and St.Louis (3)
- 38 – Walter "Turk" Broda, Toronto
- 37 – Terry Sawchuk, Detroit (33) and Toronto (4)
- 32 – Ken Dryden, Montreal
- 32 – Glenn Hall, Chicago (19), St.Louis (8) and Detroit (5)

MOST CAREER MINUTES PLAYED BY A GOALTENDER IN FINALS
- 2,423 – **Jacques Plante,** Montreal (2,279) and St.Louis (164)
- 2,369 – Walter "Turk" Broda, Toronto
- 2,185 – Terry Sawchuk, Detroit (1,960) and Toronto (225)
- 1,947 – Ken Dryden, Montreal
- 1,844 – Glenn Hall, Detroit (300), Chicago (1,060), St.Louis (484)

MOST YEARS BY A GOALTENDER IN FINALS
- 10 – **Jacques Plante,** Montreal (8) and St.Louis (2)
- 8 – Walter "Turk" Broda, Toronto
- 7 – Terry Sawchuk, Detroit (6) and Toronto (1)
  – Glenn Hall Chicago (3), St. Louis (3) and Detroit (1)
- 6 – Johnny Bower, Toronto
  – Ken Dryden, Montreal

MOST CONSECUTIVE YEARS BY A GOALTENDER IN FINALS
- 8 – **Jacques Plante,** Montreal (1953-60, inclusive)
- 5 – Billy Smith, New York Islanders (1980-84, inclusive)

MOST CAREER WINS BY A GOALTENDER IN FINALS
- 25 – **Jacques Plante,** Montreal
- 24 – Ken Dryden, Montreal
- 21 – Walter "Turk" Broda, Toronto
- 19 – Terry Sawchuk, Detroit (17) and Toronto (2)
- 17 – Billy Smith, New York Islanders

MOST CONSECUTIVE WINS BY A GOALTENDER IN FINALS
- 10 – **Ken Dryden,** Montreal. Streak began May 9, 1976, at Montreal with a 4-3 win over Philadelphia in Game #1 and ended May 18, 1978, at Boston with a 4-0 loss in Game #3. Included were four wins over Philadelphia in 1976, four over Boston in 1977 and two more over Boston in 1978.
- 9 – Walter "Turk" Broda, Toronto. Streak began April 19, 1947, at Toronto with a 2-1 win over Montreal in Game #6 and ended when the team failed to advance to the 1950 Finals. Included were one win over Montreal in 1947, four over Detroit in 1948 and four more over Detroit in 1949.
  – Billy Smith, New York Islanders. Streak began May 21, 1981, at New York with a 5-1 win over Minnesota in Game #5 and ended May 10, 1984, at New York with a 1-0 loss to Edmonton in Game #1. Included were one win over Minnesota in 1981, four over Vancouver in 1982 and four over Edmonton in 1983.

LOWEST CAREER GOALS-AGAINST AVERAGE
(MINIMUM 15 GAMES PLAYED)
- 1.82 – **Lorne "Gump" Worsley,** Montreal (in 16 games)
- 1.86 – Gerry McNeil, Montreal (15 games)
- 2.11 – Bill Durnan, Montreal (in 15 games)
- 2.15 – Walter "Turk" Broda, Toronto (in 38 games)
- 2.28 – Jacques Plante, Montreal and St. Louis (in 41 games)

HIGHEST CAREER WINNING PERCENTAGE,
(MINIMUM 15 GAMES PLAYED)
- .750 – **Ken Dryden,** Montreal (24-8)
- .739 – Billy Smith, New York Islanders (17-6)
- .737 – Grant Fuhr, Edmonton (14-5)
- .733 – Lorne "Gump" Worsley, Montreal (11-4)
- .667 – Bill Durnan, Montreal (10-5)
- .641 – Jacques Plante, Montreal (25-12) and St. Louis (0-2) (25-14 overall).

MOST POINTS, ONE SERIES
- 13 – **Wayne Gretzky,** Edmonton (3-10-13 in 4 games plus suspended game), in 1988.
- 12 – Yvan Cournoyer, Montreal (6-6-12 in 6 games), in 1973.
  – Mario Lemieux, Pittsburgh (6-6-12 in 6 games), in 1991.
  – Gordie Howe, Detroit, (5-7-12 in 7 games), in 1955.
  – Jacques Lemaire, Montreal (3-9-12 in 6 games) in 1973.
- 11 – Wayne Gretzky, Edmonton (7-4-11 in 5 games), in 1985.
  – Ted Lindsay, Detroit (5-6-11 in 7 games), in 1955.
  – Frank Mahovlich, Montreal (5-6-11 in 6 games), in 1973.
  – Mike Bossy, New York Islanders (4-7-11 in 6 games), in 1980.
  – Paul Coffey, Edmonton (3-8-11 in 5 games), in 1985.
  – Wayne Gretzky, Edmonton (2-9-11 in 7 games), in 1987.
  – Brian Leetch, NY Rangers (5-6-11 in 7 games), in 1994.

MOST POINTS, FOUR-GAME SERIES
- 13 – **Wayne Gretzky,** Edmonton (3-10-13), in 1988.
- 9 – Guy Lafleur, Montreal (2-7-9), in 1977.
  - Denis Potvin, New York Islanders (2-7-9), in 1982.
- 8 – Mike Bossy, New York Islanders (7-1-8), in 1982.
  - Hector "Toe" Blake, Montreal (3-5-8), in 1944.
  - Henri Richard, Montreal, (3-5-8), in 1960.
  - Phil Esposito, Boston (2-6-8), in 1970.
  - Rick Tocchet, Pittsburgh (2-6-8), in 1992.

MOST POINTS, FIVE-GAME SERIES
- 11 – **Wayne Gretzky,** Edmonton (7-4-11), in 1985.
  - **Paul Coffey,** Edmonton (3-8-11), in 1985.
- 10 – Jean Beliveau, Montreal (7-3-10), in 1956.

MOST POINTS, SIX-GAME SERIES
- 12 – **Yvan Cournoyer,** Montreal (6-6-12), in 1973.
  - **Mario Lemieux,** Pittsburgh (5-7-12), in 1991.
  - **Jacques Lemaire,** Montreal (3-9-12) in 1973.
- 11 – Frank Mahovlich, Montreal (5-6-11), in 1973.
  - Mike Bossy, New York Islanders (4-7-11), in 1980.

MOST POINTS, SEVEN-GAME SERIES
- 12 – **Gordie Howe,** Detroit, (5-7-12 in 7 games), in 1955.
- 11 – Ted Lindsay, Detroit (5-6-11 in 7 games), in 1955.
  - Wayne Gretzky, Edmonton (2-9-11 in 7 games), in 1987.
  - Brian Leetch, NY Rangers (5-6-11 in 7 games), in 1994.

MOST POINTS BY A DEFENSEMAN, ONE SERIES
- 11 – **Paul Coffey,** (3-8-11 in 5 games), Edmonton, in 1985.
  - **Brian Leetch,** NY Rangers (5-6-11 in 7 games), in 1994.
- 10 – Larry Murphy, (1-9-10 in 6 games), Pittsburgh, in 1991.
- 9 – Denis Potvin, (5-4-9 in 6 games), New York Islanders, in 1980.
  - Al MacInnis, (5-4-9 in 6 games), Calgary Flames, 1989.
  - Denis Potvin, (2-7-9 in 4 games), New York Islanders, in 1982.
- 8 – Bobby Orr, (4-4-8 in 6 games), Boston, in 1972.
  - Pierre Pilote, (2-6-8 in 6 games), Chicago, in 1961.
  - Pat Stapleton, (0-8-8 in 6 games), Chicago, in 1973.

MOST POINTS BY A ROOKIE, ONE SERIES
- 7 – **Roy Conacher** (5-2-7 in 5 games), Boston, in 1939.
  - Ralph Backstrom (3-4-7 in 5 games), Montreal, in 1959.
- 6 – Johnny Gagnon (4-2-6 in 5 games), Montreal, in 1931.
  - Brian Propp (3-3-6 in 6 games), Philadelphia, in 1980.

MOST GOALS, ONE SERIES
- 7 – **Mike Bossy,** New York Islanders (in 4 games), in 1982.
  - Jean Beliveau, Montreal (in 5 games), in 1956.
  - Wayne Gretzky, Edmonton (in 5 games), in 1985.
- 6 – John Bucyk, Boston (in 4 games), in 1970.
  - Yvan Cournoyer, Montreal (in 6 games), in 1973.
  - Alex Delvecchio, Detroit (in 7 games), in 1955.
  - Bernie Geoffrion, Montreal (in 7 games), in 1955.
  - Esa Tikkanen, Edmonton (in 4 games plus suspended game), in 1988.

MOST GOALS, FOUR-GAME SERIES
- 7 – **Mike Bossy,** New York Islanders, in 1982.
- 6 – John Bucyk, Boston, in 1970.
  - Esa Tikkanen, Edmonton, in 1988.

MOST GOALS, FIVE-GAME SERIES
- 7 – **Jean Beliveau,** Montreal, in 1956.
  - **Wayne Gretzky,** Edmonton, in 1985.
- 5 – six players tied.

MOST GOALS, SIX-GAME SERIES
- 6 – **Yvan Cournoyer,** Montreal, in 1973.
- 5 – Bernie Geoffrion, Montreal, in 1958.
  - Ken Hodge, Boston, in 1972.
  - Pit Martin, Chicago, in 1973.
  - Frank Mahovlich, Montreal, in 1973.
  - Denis Potvin, New York Islanders, in 1980.
  - Al MacInnis, Calgary, in 1989.
  - Joe Mullen, Calgary, in 1989.

MOST GOALS, SEVEN-GAME SERIES
- 6 – **Alex Delvecchio,** Detroit, in 1955.
  - **Bernie Geoffrion,** Montreal, in 1955.
- 5 – 9 players tied.

MOST GOALS BY A DEFENSEMAN, ONE SERIES
- 5 – **Denis Potvin** (in 6 games), New York Islanders, in 1980.
  - **Al MacInnis** (in 6 games), Calgary, in 1989.
  - **Brian Leetch** (in 7 games), NY Rangers, in 1994.
- 4 – Bobby Orr (in 6 games), Boston, in 1972.
  - Brad Park (in 6 games), Boston, in 1978.

MOST GOALS BY A ROOKIE, ONE SERIES
- 5 – **Roy Conacher** (in 5 games), Boston, in 1939.
- 4 – Johnny Gagnon (in 5 games), Montreal, in 1931.

MOST ASSISTS, ONE SERIES
- 10 – **Wayne Gretzky,** Edmonton (in 4 games plus suspended game), in 1988.
- 9 – Jacques Lemaire, Montreal (in 6 games), in 1973.
  - Larry Murphy, Pittsburgh (in 6 games), in 1991.
  - Wayne Gretzky, Edmonton (in 7 games), in 1987.
- 8 – Billy Taylor, Toronto (in 7 games), in 1942.
  - Bert Olmstead, Montreal (in 5 games), in 1956.
  - Phil Esposito, Boston (in 6 games), in 1972.
  - Pat Stapleton, Chicago (in 6 games), in 1973.
  - Paul Coffey, Edmonton (in 5 games), in 1985.

MOST ASSISTS, FOUR-GAME SERIES
- 10 – **Wayne Gretzky,** Edmonton, in 1988.
- 7 – Guy Lafleur, Montreal, in 1977.
  - Denis Potvin, New York Islanders, in 1982.
- 6 – Bernie Geoffrion, Montreal, in 1960.
  - Phil Esposito, Boston, in 1970.
  - Rick Tocchet, Pittsburgh, in 1992.

MOST ASSISTS, FIVE-GAME SERIES
- 8 – **Bert Olmstead,** Montreal, in 1956.
  - **Paul Coffey,** Edmonton, in 1985.
- 7 – Bill Cowley, Boston, in 1939.

MOST ASSISTS, SIX-GAME SERIES
- 9 – **Jacques Lemaire,** Montreal (in 6 games), in 1973.
  - **Larry Murphy,** Pittsburgh (in 6 games), in 1991.
- 8 – Phil Esposito, Boston (in 6 games), in 1972.
  - Pat Stapleton, Chicago (in 6 games), in 1973.

MOST ASSISTS, SEVEN-GAME SERIES
- 9 – **Wayne Gretzky,** Edmonton (in 7 games), in 1987.
- 8 – Billy Taylor, Toronto (in 7 games), in 1942.

MOST ASSISTS BY A DEFENSEMAN, ONE SERIES
- 9 – **Larry Murphy** (in 6 games), Pittsburgh, in 1991.
- 8 – Pat Stapleton (in 6 games), Chicago, in 1973.
  - Paul Coffey (in 5 games), Edmonton, in 1985.
- 7 – Denis Potvin (in 4 games), New York Islanders, in 1982.

MOST ASSISTS BY A ROOKIE, ONE SERIES
5 – **Jaromir Jagr** (in 6 games), Pittsburgh, in 1991.
4 – Ralph Backstrom (in 5 games), Montreal, in 1959.
 – Lars Molin (in 4 games), Vancouver, in 1982.
 – Derrick Smith (in 5 games), Philadelphia, in 1985.
3 – Brian Propp (in 6 games), Philadelphia, in 1980.
 – Dino Ciccarelli (in 5 games), Minnesota, in 1981.
 – Billy Carroll (in 5 games), New York Islanders, in 1981.
 – Patrick Flatley (in 5 games), New York Islanders, in 1984.

MOST OVERTIME GOALS, ONE SERIES
2 – **Don Raleigh,** New York Rangers (in 7 games), in 1950.
 – John LeClair, Montreal Canadiens (in 5 games), in 1993.

MOST POWER-PLAY GOALS, ONE SERIES
4 – **Jean Beliveau,** Montreal Canadiens (in 7 games), in 1965.
 – Mike Bossy, New York Islanders (in 6 games), in 1980.
3 – Bernie Geoffrion, Montreal (in 7 games), in 1955.
 – Dick Duff, Montreal (in 4 games), in 1969.
 – Steve Shutt, Montreal (in 4 games), in 1976.
 – Denis Potvin, New York Islanders (in 6 games), in 1980.
 – Mike Bossy, New York Islanders (in 4 games), in 1982.
 – Clark Gillies, New York Islanders (in 5 games), in 1984.
 – Joe Mullen, Calgary (in 6 games), in 1989.

MOST POWER-PLAY ASSISTS, ONE SERIES
6 – **Mike Bossy,** New York Islanders (in 6 games), in 1980.
 – Wayne Gretzky, Edmonton (in 4 games plus suspended game), in 1988.
4 – eight players tied.

MOST SHORTHANDED GOALS, ONE SERIES
2 – **Cecil Dillon,** New York Rangers (in 4 games), in 1933.
 – Dave Keon, Toronto (in 5 games), in 1963.
 – Bob Pulford, Toronto (in 7 games), in 1964.
 – Serge Savard, Montreal (in 4 games), in 1968.
 – Kevin Lowe, Edmonton Oilers (in 7 games), in 1987.

MOST PENALTY MINUTES, ONE SERIES
53 – **Mel Bridgman,** Philadelphia (in 6 games), in 1980.
49 – Chris Nilan, Montreal (in 3 games), in 1986.
43 – Tim Hunter, Calgary (in 5 games), in 1986.
 – Brad Marsh, Philadelphia (in 5 games), in 1985.
41 – Jimmy Orlando, Detroit (in 7 games), in 1942.
 – Wayne Cashman, Boston (in 6 games), in 1974.

MOST SHUTOUTS BY A GOALTENDER, ONE SERIES
3 – **Frank McCool,** Toronto (in 7 games), in 1945.
2 – seven goaltenders tied.

MOST MINUTES PLAYED BY A GOALTENDER, ONE SERIES
459 – **Harry Lumley,** Detroit (in 7 games), in 1950.
 – Chuck Rayner, New York Rangers (in 7 games), in 1950.
441 – Ken Dryden, Montreal (in 7 games), in 1971.
 – Tony Esposito, Chicago (in 7 games), in 1971.

LONGEST SHUTOUT SEQUENCE BY A GOALTENDER
188.35 – **Frank McCool,** Toronto, in 1945. McCool posted shutouts in each of the first three games against Detroit and did not allow a goal until 8.35 of the first period in Game #4.
161.23 – Terry Sawchuk, Detroit, in 1952. Sawchuk did not allow a Montreal goal from 18.37 of the first period in Game #2 through the end of Game #4, the concluding match of the series.

FEWEST GOALS ALLOWED BY A GOALTENDER, ONE SERIES (MINIMUM 4 GAMES PLAYED)
2 – **Alex Connell,** Ottawa Senators (in 4 games), in 1927.
 – Terry Sawchuk, Detroit (in 4 games), in 1952.
3 – Rogie Vachon, Montreal (in 4 games), in 1969.

MOST GOALS ALLOWED BY A GOALTENDER, ONE SERIES
32 – **Tony Esposito,** Chicago (in 6 games), in 1973.
25 – Johnny Mowers, Detroit (in 7 games), in 1942.

MOST GOALS, ONE GAME
4 – **Ted Lindsay,** Detroit, in Game #2, April 5, 1955. Montreal 1 at Detroit 7.
 – Maurice Richard, Montreal, in Game #1, April 6, 1957. Boston 1 at Montreal 5.
3 – 25 players tied.

MOST ASSISTS, ONE GAME
4 – **Eddie Bush,** Detroit, in Game #3, April 9, 1942. Toronto 2 at Detroit 5.
 – Sid Abel, Detroit, in Game #1, April 1, 1943. Boston 2 at Detroit 6.
 – Hector "Toe" Blake, Montreal, in Game #4, April 13, 1944. Chicago 4 at Montreal 5.
 – Earl "Dutch" Reibel, Detroit, in Game #2, April 5, 1955. Montreal 1 at Detroit 7.
 – Brad Maxwell, Minnesota, in Game #4, May 19, 1981. New York Islanders 2 at Minnesota 4.
 – Brian Propp, Philadelphia, in Game #5, May 26, 1987. Philadelphia 4 at Edmonton 3.
 – Wayne Gretzky, Edmonton, in Game #3, May 22, 1988. Edmonton 6 at Boston 3.
 – Larry Murphy, Pittsburgh, in Game #5, May 23, 1991. Minnesota 4 at Pittsburgh 6.

MOST POINTS, ONE GAME
5 – **Eddie Bush** (1-4-5), Detroit, in Game #3, April 9, 1942. Toronto 2 at Detroit 5.
 – Syl Apps (2-3-5), Toronto, in Game #5, April 14, 1942. Detroit 3 at Toronto 9.
 – Don Metz (3-2-5), Toronto, in Game #5, April 14, 1942. Detroit 3 at Toronto 9.
 – Sid Abel (1-4-5), Detroit, in Game #1, April 1, 1943. Boston 2 at Detroit 6.
 – Hector "Toe" Blake (1-4-5), Montreal, in Game #4, April 13, 1944. Chicago 4 at Montreal 5.
 – Jari Kurri (3-2-5), Edmonton, in Game #2, May 17, 1990. Edmonton 7 at Boston 2.

MOST POWER-PLAY GOALS, ONE GAME
3 – **Sid Smith,** Toronto, in Game #2, April 10, 1949. Detroit 1 at Toronto 3.
2 – several players tied.

MOST GOALS, ONE PERIOD
3 – **Harvey "Busher" Jackson,** Toronto, in 2nd period of Game #1, April 5, 1932. Toronto 6 at New York Rangers 4.
 – Ted Lindsay, Detroit, in 2nd period of Game #2, April 5, 1955. Montreal 4 at Detroit 7.
 – Maurice Richard, Montreal, in 2nd period of Game #1, April 6, 1957. Boston 1 at Montreal 5.
 – Wayne Gretzky, Edmonton, in 1st period of Game #3, May 25, 1985. Philadelphia 3 at Edmonton 4.
 – Dirk Graham, Chicago, in 1st period of Game #4, June 1, 1992. Pittsburgh 6 at Chicago 5.

MOST ASSISTS, ONE PERIOD
3 – **Joe Primeau,** Toronto, in 3rd period of Game #2, April 7, 1932. Toronto 6 at New York Rangers 2.
 – Hector "Toe" Blake, Montreal, in 3rd period of Game #4, April 13, 1944. Chicago 4 at Montreal 5 (OT).
 – Doug Harvey, Montreal, in 2nd period of Game #1, April 6, 1957. Boston 1 at Montreal 5.
 – Henri Richard, Montreal, in 1st period of Game #1, April 7, 1960. Toronto 2 at Montreal 4.
 – Bobby Rousseau, Montreal, in 1st period of Game #7, May 1, 1965. Chicago 0 at Montreal 4.
 – Pat Stapleton, Chicago, in 1st period of Game #1, April 29, 1973. Chicago 3 at Montreal 8.
 – Paul Coffey, Edmonton, in 1st period of Game #3, May 25, 1985. Philadelphia 3 at Edmonton 4.
 – Larry Murphy, Pittsburgh, in 1st period of Game #5, May 23, 1991. Minnesota 4 at Pittsburgh 6.

152 • STANLEY CUP FINALS RECORD BOOK, 1918-1995

MOST POINTS, ONE PERIOD
3 – 32 players tied.

MOST POWER-PLAY GOALS, ONE PERIOD
2 – **Sid Smith,** Toronto, in 1st period of Game #2, April 10, 1949. Detroit 1 at Toronto 3.
– **Maurice Richard,** Montreal, in 1st of Game #2, April 6, 1954. Montreal 3 at Detroit 1.
– **Bernie Geoffrion,** Montreal, in 1st period of Game #3, April 7, 1955. Detroit 2 at Montreal 4.
– **Brad Park,** New York Rangers, in 1st period of Game #3, May 4, 1972. Boston 2 at New York Rangers 5.

MOST SHORTHAND GOALS, ONE PERIOD
1 – several players tied.

FASTEST TWO GOALS
0.12 – **Bernie Geoffrion,** Montreal, in Game #3, April 7, 1955. Detroit 2 at Montreal 5. Geoffrion scored at 8.30 and 8.42 of 1st period.
0.15 – **Wayne Gretzky,** Edmonton, in Game #3, May 25, 1985. Philadelphia 3 at Edmonton 4. Gretzky scored at 1.10 and 1.25 of 1st period.

FASTEST GOAL FROM START OF A GAME
0.10 – **John Byce,** Boston, in Game #3, May 20, 1990. Boston 2 at Edmonton 1.
0.10 – **Glenn Anderson,** Edmonton, in suspended game, May 24, 1988. Edmonton 3 at Boston 3.

FASTEST GOAL FROM START OF PERIOD
0.09 – **Brian Skrudland,** Montreal, in 1st overtime of Game #2, May 18, 1986. Montreal 3 at Calgary 2 (OT).
0.10 – **Glenn Anderson,** Edmonton, in 1st period of suspended game, May 24, 1988. Edmonton 3 at Boston 3.
– **John Byce,** Boston, in 1st period of Game #3, May 20, 1990. Boston 2 at Edmonton 1.

FASTEST OVERTIME GOAL
0.09 – **Brian Skrudland,** Montreal, in Game #2, May 18, 1986. Montreal 3 at Calgary 2 (OT).
0.31 – **Frank "Buzz" Boll,** Toronto, in Game #3, April 9, 1936. Detroit 3 at Toronto 4 (OT).

FASTEST TWO GOALS FROM START OF GAME
1.08 – **Dick Duff,** Toronto, in Game #1, April 9, 1963. Detroit 2 at Toronto 4. Duff scored at 0.49 and 1.08 of 1st period.

FASTEST TWO GOALS FROM START OF PERIOD
0.35 – **Pat LaFontaine,** New York Islanders, in Game #5, May 19, 1984. New York Islanders 2 at Edmonton 5. LaFontaine scored at 0.13 and 0.35 of 3rd period.

Coaching

MOST STANLEY CUP CHAMPIONSHIPS BY A COACH
8 – **Hector "Toe" Blake,** Montreal (1956-57-58-59-60-65-66-68)
7 – Scott Bowman, Montreal (1973-76-77-78-79), Pittsburgh (1992) and Detroit (1995)
5 – Clarence "Hap" Day, Toronto (1942-45-47-48-49)
4 – Dick Irvin, Toronto (1932) and Montreal (1944-46-53)
– George "Punch" Imlach, Toronto (1962-63-64-67)
– Al Arbour, New York Islanders (1980-81-82-83)
– Glen Sather, Edmonton (1984-85-87-88)
3 – Jack Adams, Detroit (1936-37-43)
– Tommy Ivan, Detroit (1950-52-54)

MOST YEARS IN THE FINALS BY A COACH
16 – **Dick Irvin,** Chicago (1931), Toronto (1932-33-35-36-38-39-40) and Montreal (1944-46-47-51-52-53-54-55)
10 – Scott Bowman, St. Louis (1968-69-70), Montreal (1973-76-77-78-79), Pittsburgh (1992) and Detroit (1995)
9 – Hector "Toe" Blake, Montreal (1956-57-58-59-60-65-66-67-68)
6 – George "Punch" Imlach, Toronto (1959-60-62-63-64-67)
5 – Lester Patrick, New York Rangers (1928-29-32-33-37)
– Jack Adams, Detroit (1936-37-42-43-45)
– Tommy Ivan, Detroit (1948-49-50-52-54)
– Al Arbour, New York Islanders (1980-81-82-83-84)
– Clarence "Hap" Day, Toronto (1942-45-47-48-49)
– Glen Sather, Edmonton (1983-84-85-87-88)

MOST GAMES BY A COACH
77 – **Dick Irvin,** Chicago (5), Toronto (29) and Montreal (43)
48 – Hector "Toe" Blake, Montreal
45 – Scott Bowman, St. Louis (12), Montreal (25), Pittsburgh (4) and Detroit (4)
33 – George "Punch" Imlach, Toronto
28 – Clarence "Hap" Day, Toronto
26 – Tommy Ivan, Detroit

MOST WINS BY A COACH
32 – **Dick Irvin,** Chicago (2), Toronto (9) and Montreal (21)
– **Hector "Toe" Blake,** Montreal
24 – Scott Bowman, St. Louis (0), Montreal (20) and Pittsburgh (4)
20 – Clarence "Hap" Day, Toronto
17 – George "Punch" Imlach, Toronto
– Al Arbour, New York Islanders
16 – Glen Sather, Edmonton

BEST WINNING PERCENTAGE BY A COACH (MINIMUM 15 GAMES)
.714 – **Clarence "Hap" Day,** Toronto (20-8 in 28 games)
.708 – Al Arbour, New York Islanders (17-7 in 24 games)
.667 – Hector "Toe" Blake, Montreal (32-16 in 48 games)
.640 – Glen Sather, Edmonton (16-9 in 25 games)
.533 – Scott Bowman, St. Louis (0-12 in 12 games), Montreal (20-5 in 25 games), Pittsburgh (4-0 in 4 games) and Detroit (0-4 in 4 games); 24-21 in 45 games overall)
.522 – Jack Adams, Detroit (12-11 in 23 games)
.515 – George "Punch" Imlach, Toronto (17-16 in 33 games)

Officiating

MOST GAMES OFFICIATED BY A REFEREE
42 – **Bill Chadwick** (1941 through 1955)
34 – Andy vanHellemond (1977 through 1994)
24 – Frank Udvari (1956 through 1966)
20 – Frank "King" Clancy (1940 through 1949)
17 – Art Skov (1964 through 1975)
15 – Eddie Powers (1957 through 1962)
14 – John Ashley (1964 through 1972)
– Ag Smith (1933 through 1940)
13 – Bobby Hewitson (1929 through 1934)

MOST GAMES OFFICIATED BY A LINESMAN
56 – **Matt Pavelich** (1957 through 1979)
54 – George Hayes (1948 through 1964)
52 – John D'Amico (1965 through 1987)
48 – Neil Armstrong (1960 through 1977)
40 – Sam Babcock (1942 through 1956)
38 – Ray Scapinello (1980 through 1995)
34 – Bill Morrison (1951 through 1965)
– Ron Finn (1979 through 1990)
27 – Claude Bechard (1969 through 1979)
21 – Kevin Collins (1987 through 1995)
15 – Leon Stickle (1977 through 1985)

Final Series Scoring 1927-1995

1927

OTTAWA
	GP	G	A	PTS	PIM
Cy Denneny	4	4	0	4	0
Frank Finnigan	4	2	0	2	0
F.'King' Clancy	4	1	1	2	4
Frank Nighbor	4	0	1	1	0
Hec Kilrea	4	0	1	1	2
R.'Hooley' Smith	4	0	1	1	12
Milt Halliday	4	0	0	0	0
Ed Gorman	4	0	0	0	0
Jack Adams	4	0	0	0	2
Alex Smith	4	0	0	0	8
George Boucher	4	0	0	0	27

GOALTENDERS	GP	W	L	T	MIN	GA	SO	AVG
Alex Connell	4	2	0	2	240	3	1	0.75

BOSTON
	GP	G	A	PTS	PIM
Harry Oliver	4	2	1	3	2
Jimmy Herberts	4	1	0	1	18
Harry Meeking	4	0	0	0	0
Percy Galbraith	4	0	0	0	0
Bill Stuart	4	0	0	0	0
Billy Boucher	4	0	0	0	0
Billy Couture	4	0	0	0	2
Sprague Cleghorn	4	0	0	0	4
Frank Fredrickson	4	0	0	0	16
Lionel Hitchman	4	0	0	0	17
Eddie Shore	4	0	0	0	20

GOALTENDERS	GP	W	L	T	MIN	GA	SO	AVG
Hal Winkler	4	0	2	2	240	7	1	1.75

1928

MTL MAROONS
	GP	G	A	PTS	PIM
Bill Phillips	5	2	0	2	2
Nels Stewart	5	2	0	2	8
A.'Babe' Siebert	4	1	1	2	10
M.'Red' Dutton	5	1	1	2	13
R.'Hooley' Smith	5	0	2	2	13
Dunc Munro	5	0	1	1	2
Joe Lamb	4	0	0	0	21
Frank Carson	5	0	0	0	0
Fred Brown	5	0	0	0	0
Jimmy Ward	5	0	0	0	2
Russell Oatman	5	0	0	0	12

GOALTENDER	GP	W	L	MIN	GA	SO	AVG
Clint Benedict	5	2	3	307	5	1	0.98

NY RANGERS
	GP	G	A	PTS	PIM
Frank Boucher	5	4	0	4	2
Bill Cook	5	1	2	3	16
I.'Ching' Johnson	5	0	2	2	26
F.'Bun' Cook	5	0	1	1	4
C.'Taffy' Abel	5	0	1	1	10
Paul Thompson	3	0	0	0	19
Pat Callighen	5	0	0	0	0
Alex Gray	5	0	0	0	0
Bill Boyd	5	0	0	0	2
Leo Bourgeault	5	0	0	0	6
Murray Murdoch	5	0	0	0	10

GOALTENDERS	GP	W	L	MIN	GA	SO	AVG
Joe Miller	3	2	1	180	3	1	1.00
Lester Patrick	1	1	0	47	1	0	1.28
Lorne Chabot	2	0	1	80	2	0	1.50

1929

NY RANGERS
	GP	G	A	PTS	PIM
M.'Butch' Keeling	2	1	0	1	0
Russell Oatman	1	0	0	0	0
Gerald Carson	1	0	0	0	0
Bill Boyd	1	0	0	0	0
Leroy Goldsworthy	1	0	0	0	0
Ralph Taylor	1	0	0	0	0
Frank Boucher	2	0	0	0	0
Murray Murdoch	2	0	0	0	0
M.'Sparky' Vail	2	0	0	0	0
Leo Bourgeault	2	0	0	0	0
I.'Ching' Johnson	2	0	0	0	2
Bill Cook	2	0	0	0	4
F.'Bun' Cook	2	0	0	0	4
Paul Thompson	2	0	0	0	4
C.'Taffy' Abel	2	0	0	0	4

GOALTENDER	GP	W	L	MIN	GA	SO	AVG
John Roach	2	0	2	120	4	0	2.00

BOSTON
	GP	G	A	PTS	PIM
Harry Oliver	2	1	1	2	2
A.'Dit' Clapper	2	1	0	1	0
N.'Dutch' Gainor	2	1	0	1	0
Bill Carson	2	1	0	1	2
Red Green	1	0	0	0	0
Frank Fredrickson	1	0	0	0	0
Ernie Rodden	1	0	0	0	0
Cy Denneny	1	0	0	0	0
Lloyd Klein	1	0	0	0	0
R.'Cooney' Weiland	2	0	0	0	0
Mickey MacKay	2	0	0	0	0
George Owen	2	0	0	0	0
Miles Lane	2	0	0	0	0
Percy Galbraith	2	0	0	0	2
Eddie Shore	2	0	0	0	8
Lionel Hitchman	2	0	0	0	10

GOALTENDER	GP	W	L	MIN	GA	SO	AVG
'Tiny' Thompson	2	2	0	120	1	1	0.50

1930

MONTREAL
	GP	G	A	PTS	PIM
Albert Leduc	2	1	2	3	0
Sylvio Mantha	2	2	0	2	2
A.'Pit' Lepine	2	1	1	2	0
Nick Wasnie	2	1	1	2	6
Bert McCaffrey	2	1	0	1	0
Howie Morenz	2	1	0	1	6
Marty Burke	2	0	1	1	0
Aurel Joliat	2	0	1	1	0
Georges Mantha	2	0	0	0	0
Gerald Carson	2	0	0	0	0
Gus Rivers	2	0	0	0	0
Armand Mondou	2	0	0	0	2
Wildor Larochelle	2	0	0	0	8

GOALTENDER	GP	W	L	MIN	GA	SO	AVG
Geo. Hainsworth	2	2	0	120	3	1	1.50

BOSTON
	GP	G	A	PTS	PIM
A.'Dit' Clapper	2	1	0	1	0
Percy Galbraith	2	1	0	1	2
Eddie Shore	2	1	0	1	8
R.'Cooney' Weiland	2	0	1	1	0
Harry Oliver	2	0	1	1	2
N.'Dutch' Gainor	1	0	0	0	0
Bill Carson	2	0	0	0	0
Harry Connor	2	0	0	0	0
Miles Lane	2	0	0	0	0
Mickey MacKay	2	0	0	0	2
George Owen	2	0	0	0	2
Lionel Hitchman	2	0	0	0	4
Marty Barry	2	0	0	0	6

GOALTENDER	GP	W	L	MIN	GA	SO	AVG
'Tiny' Thompson	2	0	2	120	7	0	3.50

1931

MONTREAL
	GP	G	A	PTS	PIM
Johnny Gagnon	5	4	2	6	2
A.'Pit' Lepine	5	3	1	4	4
Georges Mantha	5	2	1	3	4
Aurel Joliat	5	0	2	2	2
Nick Wasnie	5	1	1	2	2
Howie Morenz	5	1	0	1	6
Albert Leduc	2	0	1	1	0
Marty Burke	5	0	1	1	2
Wildor Larochelle	5	0	1	1	6
Armand Mondou	3	0	0	0	0
Jean Pusie	3	0	0	0	0
Gus Rivers	5	0	0	0	0
Art Lesieur	5	0	0	0	4
Sylvio Mantha	5	0	0	0	16

GOALTENDER	GP	W	L	MIN	GA	SO	AVG
Geo. Hainsworth	5	3	2	379	8	1	1.27

CHICAGO
	GP	G	A	PTS	PIM
Johnny Gottselig	5	2	2	4	2
Stewart Adams	5	2	1	3	2
Vic Ripley	5	1	1	2	2
E.'Ty' Arbour	5	1	0	1	0
H.'Mush' March	5	1	0	1	6
M.'Cy' Wentworth	5	1	0	1	8
R.'Lolo' Couture	5	0	1	1	2
Frank Ingram	5	0	1	1	2
Tom Cook	5	0	1	1	7
Art Somers	5	0	0	0	0
Vic Desjardins	5	0	0	0	0
E.'Doc' Romnes	5	0	0	0	2
C.'Taffy' Abel	5	0	0	0	6
Helge Bostrum	5	0	0	0	8
Ted Graham	5	0	0	0	10

GOALTENDER	GP	W	L	MIN	GA	SO	AVG
Chuck Gardiner	5	2	3	379	11	0	1.74

1932

TORONTO	GP	G	A	PTS	PIM
H.'Busher' Jackson	3	5	2	7	9
Charlie Conacher	3	3	2	5	2
C.'Happy' Day	3	1	3	4	4
Joe Primeau	3	0	4	4	0
Andy Blair	3	2	0	2	2
F.'King' Clancy	3	2	0	2	8
Bob Gracie	3	1	1	2	0
R.'Red' Horner	3	1	1	2	6
Frank Finnigan	3	1	1	2	8
H.'Baldy' Cotton	3	1	1	2	10
I.'Ace' Bailey	3	1	0	1	0
Earl Miller	2	0	0	0	0
Harry Darragh	3	0	0	0	0
Fred Robertson	3	0	0	0	0
Alex Levinsky	3	0	0	0	2

GOALTENDER	GP	W	L	MIN	GA	SO	AVG
Lorne Chabot	3	3	0	180	10	0	3.33

NY RANGERS	GP	G	A	PTS	PIM
Frank Boucher	3	3	3	6	0
F.'Bun' Cook	3	4	1	5	6
Bill Cook	3	0	2	2	0
Cecil Dillon	3	1	0	1	4
Doug Brennan	3	1	0	1	4
I.'Ching' Johnson	3	1	0	1	10
Murray Murdoch	3	0	1	1	0
Ott Heller	3	0	1	1	2
Hib Milks	3	0	0	0	0
Vic Desjardins	3	0	0	0	0
N.'Dutch' Gainor	3	0	0	0	2
Art Somers	3	0	0	0	4
Earl Seibert	3	0	0	0	6
M.'Butch' Keeling	3	0	0	0	10

GOALTENDER	GP	W	L	MIN	GA	SO	AVG
John Roach	3	0	3	180	18	0	6.00

1933

NY RANGERS	GP	G	A	PTS	PIM
Cecil Dillon	4	3	1	4	4
Bill Cook	4	2	1	3	4
Art Somers	4	0	3	3	4
Ott Heller	4	2	0	2	4
Murray Murdoch	4	1	1	2	2
M.'Butch' Keeling	4	1	1	2	6
Earl Seibert	4	1	0	1	2
Fred 'Bun' Cook	4	1	0	1	4
Ossie Asmundson	4	0	1	1	2
Frank Boucher	4	0	1	1	4
Gord Pettinger	4	0	0	0	0
Doug Brennan	4	0	0	0	2
I.'Ching' Johnson	4	0	0	0	8
A.'Babe' Siebert	4	0	0	0	10

GOALTENDER	GP	W	L	MIN	GA	SO	AVG
Andy Aitkenhead	4	3	1	248	5	1	1.21

TORONTO	GP	G	A	PTS	PIM
Ken Doraty	4	3	0	3	2
F.'King' Clancy	4	0	2	2	6
Alex Levinsky	4	1	0	1	6
R.'Red' Horner	4	1	0	1	8
Charlie Sands	4	0	1	1	0
Bob Gracie	4	0	1	1	0
H.'Baldy' Cotton	4	0	1	1	2
Joe Primeau	4	0	1	1	4
F.'Buzz' Boll	1	0	0	0	0
Andy Blair	4	0	0	0	0
I.'Ace' Bailey	4	0	0	0	2
H.'Busher' Jackson	4	0	0	0	2
Bill Thoms	4	0	0	0	2
Charlie Conacher	4	0	0	0	6
C.'Happy' Day	4	0	0	0	6

GOALTENDER	GP	W	L	MIN	GA	SO	AVG
Lorne Chabot	4	1	3	248	11	0	2.66

1934

CHICAGO	GP	G	A	PTS	PIM
E.'Doc' Romnes	4	1	3	4	0
Paul Thompson	4	2	1	3	0
Johnny Gottselig	4	2	1	3	4
H.'Mush' March	4	1	1	2	2
R.'Lolo' Couture	4	1	1	2	2
Lionel Conacher	4	1	0	1	2
Art Coulter	4	1	0	1	4
Don McFayden	4	0	1	1	2
Bill Kendall	1	0	0	0	0
John Sheppard	3	0	0	0	0
Roger Jenkins	4	0	0	0	0
Leroy Goldsworthy	4	0	0	0	0
Tom Cook	4	0	0	0	0
Louis Trudel	4	0	0	0	0
C.'Taffy' Abel	4	0	0	0	2

GOALTENDER	GP	W	L	MIN	GA	SO	AVG
Chuck Gardiner	4	3	1	291	7	1	1.44

DETROIT	GP	G	A	PTS	PIM
Larry Aurie	4	2	2	4	0
Herbie Lewis	4	2	1	3	2
R.'Cooney' Weiland	4	1	1	2	2
Gord Pettinger	3	1	0	1	0
Doug Young	4	1	0	1	2
Frank Carson	2	0	1	1	0
Wilf Starr	3	0	1	1	2
Walter Buswell	4	0	1	1	2
Ted Graham	4	0	1	1	4
Ron Moffatt	2	0	0	0	0
Burr Williams	2	0	0	0	0
Eddie Wiseman	3	0	0	0	0
Gene Carrigan	3	0	0	0	0
Leighton Emms	3	0	0	0	2
Gus Marker	3	0	0	0	2
John Sorrell	4	0	0	0	0
Ebbie Goodfellow	4	0	0	0	6

GOALTENDER	GP	W	L	MIN	GA	SO	AVG
Wilf Cude	4	1	3	291	9	0	1.86

1935

MTL MAROONS	GP	G	A	PTS	PIM
M.'Cy' Wentworth	3	2	2	4	0
Earl Robinson	3	2	1	3	0
L.'Baldy' Northcott	3	2	1	3	0
Jimmy Ward	3	1	1	2	0
Russ Blinco	3	1	1	2	0
Gus Marker	3	1	0	1	0
Dave Trottier	3	1	0	1	4
Allan Shields	3	0	1	1	2
Herb Cain	3	0	0	0	0
Bob Gracie	3	0	0	0	0
Bill Miller	3	0	0	0	0
Stewart Evans	3	0	0	0	4
R.'Hooley' Smith	3	0	0	0	4
Lionel Conacher	3	0	0	0	8

GOALTENDER	GP	W	L	MIN	GA	SO	AVG
Alex Connell	3	3	0	185	4	0	1.30

TORONTO	GP	G	A	PTS	PIM
Frank Finnigan	3	1	1	2	0
H.'Busher' Jackson	3	1	0	1	0
Bill Thoms	3	1	0	1	0
F.'King' Clancy	3	1	0	1	4
Nick Metz	3	0	1	1	0
Ken Doraty	1	0	0	0	0
Andy Blair	1	0	0	0	2
Frank 'Buzz' Boll	2	0	0	0	0
Hec Kilrea	2	0	0	0	2
B.'Flash' Hollett	3	0	0	0	0
C.'Happy' Day	3	0	0	0	0
H.'Baldy' Cotton	3	0	0	0	0
Joe Primeau	3	0	0	0	0
R.'Pep' Kelly	3	0	0	0	0
Charlie Conacher	3	0	0	0	4
R.'Red' Horner	3	0	0	0	4

GOALTENDER	GP	W	L	MIN	GA	SO	AVG
Geo. Hainsworth	3	0	3	185	10	0	3.24

1936

DETROIT	GP	G	A	PTS	PIM
John Sorrell	4	2	3	5	0
Syd Howe	4	2	3	5	2
Gord Pettinger	4	2	2	4	0
Marty Barry	4	2	2	4	2
W.'Bucko' McDonald	4	3	0	3	4
Wally Kilrea	4	2	1	3	0
M.'Mud' Bruneteau	4	1	2	3	0
Herbie Lewis	4	1	2	3	0
Pete Kelly	4	1	1	2	0
R.'Scotty' Bowman	4	1	1	2	2
Doug Young	4	0	2	2	0
Hec Kilrea	4	0	2	2	0
Ebbie Goodfellow	4	0	1	1	2
Larry Aurie	4	0	1	1	2

GOALTENDER	GP	W	L	MIN	GA	SO	AVG
Normie Smith	4	3	1	241	11	0	2.74

TORONTO	GP	G	A	PTS	PIM
Frank 'Buzz' Boll	4	3	1	4	0
Joe Primeau	4	3	1	4	0
Bill Thoms	4	2	2	4	0
Bob Davidson	4	1	2	3	2
Reg 'Pep' Kelly	4	2	0	2	0
Frank Finnigan	4	0	2	2	0
H.'Busher' Jackson	4	0	2	2	2
R.'Red' Horner	4	0	2	2	8
Art Jackson	4	0	1	1	0
Charlie Conacher	4	0	1	1	2
Jack Shill	4	0	1	1	4
Andy Blair	4	0	0	0	2
F.'King' Clancy	4	0	0	0	0
C.'Happy' Day	4	0	0	0	4

GOALTENDER	GP	W	L	MIN	GA	SO	AVG
Geo. Hainsworth	4	1	3	241	18	0	4.48

FINAL SERIES SCORING, 1927-1995 • 155

1937

NY RANGERS

	GP	G	A	PTS	PIM
M.'Butch' Keeling	5	2	1	3	0
Frank Boucher	5	1	2	3	0
Joe Cooper	5	1	2	3	12
Lynn Patrick	5	2	0	2	2
Neil Colville	5	1	1	2	0
W.'Babe' Pratt	5	1	1	2	9
Cecil Dillon	5	0	2	2	0
Art Coulter	5	0	2	2	6
Murray Murdoch	5	0	1	1	0
Mac Colville	5	0	1	1	0
Alex Shibicky	5	0	0	0	0
I.'Ching' Johnson	5	0	0	0	2
Phil Watson	5	0	0	0	4
Ott Heller	5	0	0	0	5

GOALTENDER	GP	W	L	MIN	GA	SO	AVG
Dave Kerr	5	2	3	300	9	1	1.80

DETROIT

	GP	G	A	PTS	PIM
Syd Howe	5	1	4	5	0
Marty Barry	5	3	1	4	0
John Sorrell	5	2	2	4	2
Ebbie Goodfellow	4	0	2	2	12
M.'Mud' Bruneteau	5	1	0	1	2
Herbie Lewis	5	1	0	1	4
John Gallagher	5	1	0	1	8
Hec Kilrea	5	0	1	1	0
Gord Pettinger	5	0	1	1	2
John Sherf	5	0	1	1	2
Wally Kilrea	5	0	1	1	4
Pete Kelly	3	0	0	0	0
Howie Mackie	3	0	0	0	0
W.'Bucko' McDonald	5	0	0	0	0
R.'Scotty' Bowman	5	0	0	0	2

GOALTENDERS	GP	W	L	MIN	GA	SO	AVG
Earl Robertson	5	2	2	280	8	2	1.71
Normie Smith	1	1	0	20	0	0	0.00

1938

CHICAGO

	GP	G	A	PTS	PIM
Johnny Gottselig	4	2	2	4	0
Paul Thompson	4	1	2	3	2
Elwin 'Doc' Romnes	4	1	2	3	2
Carl Voss	4	2	0	2	0
H.'Mush' March	3	1	1	2	6
C.'Cully' Dahlstrom	4	1	1	2	0
Jack Shill	4	1	1	2	4
Earl Seibert	4	1	1	2	8
Roger Jenkins	4	0	2	2	6
Louis Trudel	4	0	1	1	0
Virgil Johnson	2	0	0	0	0
Pete Palangio	3	0	0	0	0
Alex Levinsky	4	0	0	0	0
Art Wiebe	4	0	0	0	2
Bill McKenzie	4	0	0	0	9

GOALTENDERS	GP	W	L	MIN	GA	SO	AVG
Mike Karakas	2	2	0	120	2	0	1.00
Alfie Moore	1	1	0	60	1	0	1.00
Paul Goodman	1	0	1	60	5	0	5.00

TORONTO

	GP	G	A	PTS	PIM
Gordie Drillon	4	4	1	5	2
Syl Apps	4	1	2	3	0
George Parsons	3	2	0	2	11
Jimmy Fowler	4	0	2	2	0
R.'Pep' Kelly	4	0	2	2	0
Bill Thoms	4	0	2	2	0
Bob Davidson	4	0	2	2	4
H.'Busher' Jackson	4	1	0	1	8
Reg Hamilton	4	0	1	1	2
R.'Red' Horner	4	0	1	1	8
Murray Armstrong	2	0	0	0	0
E.'Murph' Chamberlain	2	0	0	0	2
Nick Metz	4	0	0	0	0
Frank 'Buzz' Boll	4	0	0	0	2
R.'Bingo' Kampman	4	0	0	0	6

GOALTENDER	GP	W	L	MIN	GA	SO	AVG
W.'Turk' Broda	4	1	3	240	10	0	2.50

1939

BOSTON

	GP	G	A	PTS	PIM
Roy Conacher	5	5	2	7	6
Bill Cowley	5	0	7	7	2
Mel Hill	5	2	2	4	4
Bobby Bauer	5	2	1	3	0
Eddie Shore	5	0	3	3	6
Jack Crawford	5	1	1	2	4
Milt Schmidt	5	0	2	2	0
B.'Flash' Hollett	5	1	0	1	0
Woody Dumart	5	1	0	1	2
A.'Dit' Clapper	5	0	0	0	0
R.'Cooney' Weiland	5	0	0	0	0
Gord Pettinger	5	0	0	0	0
Ray Getliffe	5	0	0	0	2
R.'Red' Hamill	5	0	0	0	2
Jack Portland	5	0	0	0	2

GOALTENDER	GP	W	L	MIN	GA	SO	AVG
Frank Brimsek	5	4	1	311	6	1	1.16

TORONTO

	GP	G	A	PTS	PIM
E.'Doc' Romnes	5	1	3	4	0
Gus Marker	5	1	2	3	0
R.'Bingo' Kampman	5	1	1	2	12
Gordie Drillon	5	0	2	2	4
E.'Murph' Chamberlain	5	1	0	1	0
Syl Apps	5	1	0	1	2
R.'Red' Horner	5	1	0	1	6
H.'Busher' Jackson	3	0	1	1	2
Nick Metz	5	0	1	1	2
Jack Church	1	0	0	0	0
Don Metz	2	0	0	0	0
Robert 'Red' Heron	2	0	0	0	4
Jimmy Fowler	4	0	0	0	0
Pete Langelle	4	0	0	0	0
R.'Pep' Kelly	4	0	0	0	0
Bob Davidson	5	0	0	0	0
W.'Bucko' McDonald	5	0	0	0	0
Reg Hamilton	5	0	0	0	4

GOALTENDER	GP	W	L	MIN	GA	SO	AVG
W.'Turk' Broda	5	1	4	311	12	0	2.32

1940

NY RANGERS

	GP	G	A	PTS	PIM
Bryan Hextall	6	4	1	5	7
Neil Colville	6	2	3	5	12
Phil Watson	6	1	4	5	8
W.'Dutch' Hiller	6	1	2	3	0
Alf Pike	6	2	0	2	4
Lynn Patrick	6	1	1	2	0
W.'Babe' Pratt	6	1	1	2	6
Alex Shibicky	5	0	2	2	2
Ott Heller	6	0	2	2	8
M.'Muzz' Patrick	6	1	0	1	6
Art Coulter	6	1	0	1	8
Clint Smith	6	0	1	1	2
Mac Colville	6	0	1	1	6
Stan Smith	1	0	0	0	0
Bert Gardiner	2	0	0	0	0
Kilby MacDonald	6	0	0	0	4

GOALTENDER	GP	W	L	MIN	GA	SO	AVG
Dave Kerr	6	4	2	394	11	0	1.68

TORONTO

	GP	G	A	PTS	PIM
Syl Apps	6	2	2	4	2
Hank Goldup	6	2	1	3	0
D.'Sweeney' Schriner	5	0	3	3	2
Gordie Drillon	6	2	0	2	0
Nick Metz	5	1	1	2	9
Gus Marker	6	1	1	2	0
R.'Red' Horner	5	0	2	2	14
Pete Langelle	6	0	2	2	0
Billy Taylor	2	1	0	1	0
R.'Red' Heron	6	1	0	1	0
Wally Stanowski	6	1	0	1	2
Jack Church	2	0	1	1	2
Bob Davidson	6	0	1	1	11
Reg Hamilton	1	0	0	0	0
W.'Bucko' McDonald	1	0	0	0	0
R.'Pep' Kelly	2	0	0	0	0
Don Metz	2	0	0	0	0
E.'Murph' Chamberlain	3	0	0	0	2
R.'Bingo' Kampman	6	0	0	0	19

GOALTENDER	GP	W	L	MIN	GA	SO	AVG
W.'Turk' Broda	6	2	4	394	14	1	2.13

1941

BOSTON

	GP	G	A	PTS	PIM
Milt Schmidt	4	3	4	7	0
Eddie Wiseman	4	3	0	3	0
Roy Conacher	4	1	2	3	0
Woody Dumart	4	0	3	3	2
Bobby Bauer	4	1	1	2	0
Terry Reardon	4	1	1	2	2
B.'Flash' Hollett	4	1	1	2	4
Pat McReavy	4	1	1	2	5
Jack Crawford	4	0	2	2	0
A.'Dit' Clapper	4	0	2	2	2
Des Smith	4	0	2	2	2
Art Jackson	4	1	0	1	0
Herb Cain	4	0	1	1	0
Mel Hill	4	0	0	0	0

GOALTENDER	GP	W	L	MIN	GA	SO	AVG
Frank Brimsek	4	4	0	240	6	0	1.50

DETROIT

	GP	G	A	PTS	PIM
Carl Liscombe	4	2	1	3	5
Syd Howe	4	1	2	3	0
Bill Jennings	4	1	1	2	0
Sid Abel	4	1	1	2	2
Connie Brown	3	0	2	2	0
M.'Mud' Bruneteau	4	1	0	1	0
R.'Gus' Giesebrecht	4	0	1	1	0
Don Grosso	4	0	1	1	0
J.'Black Jack' Stewart	4	0	1	1	2
Jimmy Orlando	4	0	1	1	6
Eddie Bruneteau	2	0	0	0	0

156 • FINAL SERIES SCORING, 1927-1995

Ken Kilrea	2	0	0	0	0
Eddie Wares	3	0	0	0	0
Hal Jackson	4	0	0	0	0
Bob Whitelaw	4	0	0	0	0
Alex Motter	4	0	0	0	2

GOALTENDER	GP	W	L	MIN	GA	SO	AVG
Johnny Mowers	4	0	4	240	12	0	3.00

1942

TORONTO	GP	G	A	PTS	PIM
Billy Taylor	7	1	8	9	2
D.'Sweeney' Schriner	7	5	3	8	4
Don Metz	4	4	3	7	0
Syl Apps	7	3	4	7	2
Wally Stanowski	7	2	5	7	0
Lorne Carr	7	3	2	5	6
Nick Metz	7	2	3	5	4
Bob Goldham	7	2	2	4	22
John McCreedy	7	1	2	3	6
Pete Langelle	7	1	1	2	0
Bob Davidson	7	1	1	2	14
R.'Bingo' Kampman	7	0	2	2	8
Hank Goldup	3	0	0	0	0
W.'Bucko' McDonald	3	0	0	0	0
Gordie Drillon	3	0	0	0	0
Gaye Stewart	3	0	0	0	0
Ernie Dickens	5	0	0	0	4

GOALTENDER	GP	W	L	MIN	GA	SO	AVG
W.'Turk' Broda	7	4	3	420	19	1	2.71

DETROIT	GP	G	A	PTS	PIM
Don Grosso	7	4	4	8	14
Syd Howe	7	3	3	6	0
Carl Liscombe	7	2	4	6	2
Eddie Bush	6	1	5	6	16
M.'Mud' Bruneteau	7	2	1	3	4
Sid Abel	7	2	1	3	4
Eddie Wares	7	0	3	3	20
Jerry Brown	7	2	0	2	4
Pat McReavy	6	1	1	2	2
Alex Motter	7	1	1	2	6
Jimmy Orlando	7	0	2	2	41
Joe Carveth	7	1	0	1	0
Adam Brown	5	0	1	1	4
J.'Black Jack' Stewart	7	0	1	1	6
R.'Gus' Giesebrecht	2	0	0	0	0
Doug McCaig	2	0	0	0	6

GOALTENDER	GP	W	L	MIN	GA	SO	AVG
Johnny Mowers	7	3	4	420	25	0	3.57

1943

DETROIT	GP	G	A	PTS	PIM
Sid Abel	4	1	5	6	2
Carl Liscombe	4	2	3	5	2
M.'Mud' Bruneteau	3	3	0	3	0
Joe Carveth	4	3	0	3	2
Don Grosso	4	3	0	3	4
Les Douglas	4	2	1	3	2
Eddie Wares	4	0	3	3	2
J.'Black Jack' Stewart	4	1	1	2	8
Jimmy Orlando	4	0	2	2	6
Syd Howe	3	1	0	1	0
Alex Motter	1	0	1	1	0
Hal Jackson	4	0	1	1	4
Harry Watson	1	0	0	0	0

Joe Fisher	1	0	0	0	0
John Simon	3	0	0	0	0
Adam Brown	4	0	0	0	2

GOALTENDER	GP	W	L	MIN	GA	SO	AVG
Johnny Mowers	4	4	0	240	5	2	1.25

BOSTON	GP	G	A	PTS	PIM
Art Jackson	4	3	0	3	7
Herb Cain	2	0	2	2	0
Bill Cowley	4	0	2	2	2
Jack Crawford	3	1	0	1	2
Ab DeMarco	4	1	0	1	0
B.'Flash' Hollett	4	0	1	1	0
Don Gallinger	4	0	1	1	4
E.'Murph' Chamberlain	4	0	1	1	6
A.'Bep' Guidolin	4	0	1	1	8
Ossie Aubuchon	1	0	0	0	0
Jackie Schmidt	2	0	0	0	0
A.'Dit' Clapper	4	0	0	0	0
I.'Yank' Boyd	4	0	0	0	2
H.'Busher' Jackson	4	0	0	0	2
Jack Shewchuk	4	0	0	0	4

GOALTENDER	GP	W	L	MIN	GA	SO	AVG
Frank Brimsek	4	0	4	240	16	0	4.00

1944

MONTREAL	GP	G	A	PTS	PIM
H.'Toe' Blake	4	3	5	8	2
Maurice Richard	4	5	2	7	4
Elmer Lach	4	2	3	5	0
Ray Getliffe	4	2	1	3	4
Phil Watson	4	2	1	3	6
E.'Butch' Bouchard	4	0	3	3	0
E.'Murph' Chamberlain	4	1	0	1	2
Mike McMahon	4	1	0	1	12
Jerry Heffernan	2	0	1	1	0
H.'Buddy' O'Connor	3	0	1	1	2
Leo Lamoureux	4	0	1	1	2
Fern Majeau	1	0	0	0	0
Bob Fillion	2	0	0	0	2
Glen Harmon	4	0	0	0	0

GOALTENDER	GP	W	L	MIN	GA	SO	AVG
Bill Durnan	4	4	0	249	8	0	1.93

CHICAGO	GP	G	A	PTS	PIM
George Allen	4	3	2	5	4
Clint Smith	4	1	3	4	0
John Harms	4	3	0	3	2
Doug Bentley	4	1	2	3	2
C.'Cully' Dahlstrom	4	0	2	2	2
Virgil Johnson	4	0	1	1	2
Bill Mosienko	4	0	1	1	2
Art Wiebe	4	0	1	1	4
George Gregor	1	0	0	0	0
Jack Toupin	1	0	0	0	0
Johnny Gottselig	2	0	0	0	0
Earl Seibert	4	0	0	0	0
Cliff Purpur	4	0	0	0	0
Joe Cooper	4	0	0	0	6

GOALTENDER	GP	W	L	MIN	GA	SO	AVG
Mike Karakas	4	0	4	249	16	0	3.86

1945

TORONTO	GP	G	A	PTS	PIM
T.'Teeder' Kennedy	7	4	1	5	2
Mel Hill	7	1	2	3	4
W.'Babe' Pratt	7	1	1	2	4
Gus Bodnar	7	1	0	1	2
E.'Moe' Morris	7	1	0	1	2
D.'Sweeney' Schriner	7	1	0	1	2
Nick Metz	3	0	1	1	0
Wally Stanowski	7	0	1	1	0
Bob Davidson	7	0	1	1	0
John McCreedy	4	0	0	0	0
Reg Hamilton	7	0	0	0	0
Art Jackson	7	0	0	0	0
Don Metz	7	0	0	0	0
Lorne Carr	7	0	0	0	5

GOALTENDER	GP	W	L	MIN	GA	SO	AVG
Frank McCool	7	4	3	434	9	3	1.24

DETROIT	GP	G	A	PTS	PIM
B.'Flash' Hollett	7	2	2	4	0
Joe Carveth	7	2	1	3	0
Eddie Bruneteau	7	2	1	3	0
Murray Armstrong	7	2	0	2	0
Ted Lindsay	7	1	0	1	4
M.'Mud' Bruneteau	7	0	1	1	2
Bill Quackenbush	7	0	1	1	2
Tony Bukovich	1	0	0	0	0
Steve Wochy	2	0	0	0	0
Cliff Purpur	4	0	0	0	4
Syd Howe	5	0	0	0	2
Carl Liscombe	7	0	0	0	0
J.'Jud' McAtee	7	0	0	0	0
Earl Seibert	7	0	0	0	2
Hal Jackson	7	0	0	0	4

GOALTENDER	GP	W	L	MIN	GA	SO	AVG
Harry Lumley	7	3	4	434	9	2	1.24

1946

MONTREAL	GP	G	A	PTS	PIM
Elmer Lach	5	3	4	7	0
Maurice Richard	5	3	2	5	0
E.'Murph' Chamberlain	5	2	1	3	0
W.'Dutch' Hiller	5	2	1	3	0
E.'Butch' Bouchard	5	2	1	3	4
Glen Harmon	5	1	2	3	0
Bob Fillion	5	2	0	2	2
Ken Mosdell	5	2	0	2	2
Frank Eddolls	4	0	1	1	0
Jim Peters	5	1	0	1	4
H.'Toe' Blake	5	0	1	1	5
Gerry Plamondon	1	0	0	0	0
H.'Buddy' O'Connor	5	0	0	0	0
Leo Lamoureux	5	0	0	0	2
Billy Reay	5	0	0	0	2
Kenny Reardon	5	0	0	0	4

GOALTENDER	GP	W	L	MIN	GA	SO	AVG
Bill Durnan	5	4	1	341	13	0	2.29

BOSTON	GP	G	A	PTS	PIM
A.'Bep' Guidolin	5	2	1	3	9
Don Gallinger	5	1	2	3	0
Bill Cowley	5	1	2	3	2
Milt Schmidt	5	1	2	3	2
Bobby Bauer	5	2	0	2	2

	GP	G	A	PTS	PIM
Terry Reardon	5	2	0	2	2
Woody Dumart	5	1	1	2	0
Ken Smith	5	0	2	2	0
Herb Cain	5	0	2	2	2
Murray Henderson	5	1	0	1	0
Jack Crawford	5	1	0	1	0
Pat Egan	5	1	0	1	4
Bill Shill	3	0	1	1	2
Roy Conacher	1	0	0	0	0
A.'Dit' Clapper	1	0	0	0	0
Jack McGill	5	0	0	0	0
Jack Church	5	0	0	0	2

GOALTENDER	GP	W	L	MIN	GA	SO	AVG
Frank Brimsek	5	1	4	341	19	0	3.34

1947

TORONTO	GP	G	A	PTS	PIM
T.'Teeder' Kennedy	6	3	2	5	2
Vic Lynn	6	3	1	4	12
Harry Watson	6	2	1	3	0
Gaye Stewart	6	1	2	3	6
Howie Meeker	6	0	3	3	6
N.'Bud' Poile	5	2	0	2	2
Syl Apps	6	1	1	2	0
Gus Mortson	6	1	1	2	6
Don Metz	6	0	2	2	4
Bill Barilko	6	0	2	2	6
Gus Bodnar	1	0	0	0	0
Nick Metz	1	0	0	0	0
Wally Stanowski	5	0	0	0	0
Joe Klukay	6	0	0	0	0
Garth Boesch	6	0	0	0	6
Jimmy Thomson	6	0	0	0	12
Bill Ezinicki	6	0	0	0	16

GOALTENDER	GP	W	L	MIN	GA	SO	AVG
W.'Turk' Broda	6	4	2	377	13	1	2.07

MONTREAL	GP	G	A	PTS	PIM
H.'Buddy' O'Connor	6	3	3	6	0
H.'Toe' Blake	6	0	4	4	0
Maurice Richard	5	3	0	3	25
E.'Butch' Bouchard	6	0	3	3	14
Leo Gravelle	4	2	0	2	2
Billy Reay	6	2	0	2	2
Glen Harmon	6	1	1	2	0
George Allen	6	1	1	2	6
Roger Leger	6	0	2	2	6
E.'Murph' Chamberlain	6	1	0	1	6
John Quilty	2	0	1	1	2
Jim Peters	6	0	1	1	4
Leo Lamoureux	2	0	0	0	4
Hub Macey	3	0	0	0	0
Kenny Reardon	4	0	0	0	16
Bob Fillion	5	0	0	0	0
Frank Eddolls	5	0	0	0	2
Murdo McKay	6	0	0	0	0

GOALTENDER	GP	W	L	MIN	GA	SO	AVG
Bill Durnan	6	2	4	377	13	1	2.07

1948

TORONTO	GP	G	A	PTS	PIM
Harry Watson	4	5	1	6	4
Max Bentley	4	2	4	6	0
T.'Teeder' Kennedy	4	2	2	4	0
Syl Apps	4	2	2	4	0
Les Costello	4	1	2	3	0
Gus Mortson	1	1	1	2	0
Joe Klukay	4	1	1	2	2
Bill Ezinicki	4	1	1	2	4
Vic Lynn	4	1	1	2	18
Garth Boesch	4	1	0	1	0
Howie Meeker	4	1	0	1	7
Phil Samis	3	0	1	1	2
Wally Stanowski	4	0	1	1	0
Jim Thomson	4	0	1	1	5
Nick Metz	4	0	0	0	2
Bill Barilko	4	0	0	0	13

GOALTENDER	GP	W	L	MIN	GA	SO	AVG
W.'Turk' Broda	4	4	0	240	7	1	1.75

DETROIT	GP	G	A	PTS	PIM
Pete Horeck	4	2	2	4	8
Jim McFadden	4	1	1	2	0
Jim Conacher	4	1	0	1	0
Ted Lindsay	4	1	0	1	2
Leo Reise	4	1	0	1	4
Fern Gauthier	4	1	0	1	5
Pat Lundy	1	0	1	1	0
Lee Fogolin Sr.	2	0	1	1	6
Bill Quackenbush	4	0	1	1	0
Marty Pavelich	4	0	1	1	2
Sid Abel	4	0	1	1	9
Enio Sclisizzi	1	0	0	0	0
Al Dewsbury	1	0	0	0	0
Rod Morrison	1	0	0	0	0
A.'Bep' Guidolin	1	0	0	0	2
J.'Black Jack' Stewart	3	0	0	0	0
Eddie Bruneteau	3	0	0	0	0
Max McNab	3	0	0	0	2
L.'Red' Kelly	4	0	0	0	0
Gordie Howe	4	0	0	0	9

GOALTENDER	GP	W	L	MIN	GA	SO	AVG
Harry Lumley	4	0	4	240	18	0	4.50

1949

TORONTO	GP	G	A	PTS	PIM
Sid Smith	4	3	1	4	0
Max Bentley	4	2	2	4	0
Ray Timgren	4	1	3	4	0
Jim Thomson	4	1	3	4	4
Joe Klukay	4	1	2	3	2
T.'Teeder' Kennedy	4	1	2	3	2
Fleming Mackell	4	0	3	3	2
Cal Gardner	4	1	1	2	0
Bill Ezinicki	4	1	1	2	10
Gus Mortson	4	1	0	1	2
Harry Watson	4	0	1	1	2
Garth Boesch	4	0	1	1	4
Bill Barilko	4	0	1	1	8
Vic Lynn	4	0	0	0	0
Bob Dawes	4	0	0	0	2
Bill Juzda	4	0	0	0	4

GOALTENDER	GP	W	L	MIN	GA	SO	AVG
W.'Turk' Broda	4	4	0	258	5	0	1.16

DETROIT	GP	G	A	PTS	PIM
Ted Lindsay	4	1	2	3	6
George Gee	4	1	2	3	14
Pete Horeck	4	1	1	2	4
J.'Black Jack' Stewart	4	1	1	2	8
Gordie Howe	4	0	2	2	2
Bill Quackenbush	4	1	0	1	0
Jim McFadden	4	0	1	1	4
Fred Glover	2	0	0	0	0
Jerry Reid	2	0	0	0	2
Marty Pavelich	2	0	0	0	4
Gerry Couture	3	0	0	0	0
N.'Bud' Poile	3	0	0	0	0
Lee Fogolin Sr.	3	0	0	0	0
Nels Podolsky	3	0	0	0	0
Enio Sclisizzi	3	0	0	0	2
Max McNab	3	0	0	0	2
L.'Red' Kelly	4	0	0	0	0
Leo Reise	4	0	0	0	2
Sid Abel	4	0	0	0	4

GOALTENDER	GP	W	L	MIN	GA	SO	AVG
Harry Lumley	4	0	4	258	12	0	2.79

1950

DETROIT	GP	G	A	PTS	PIM
Sid Abel	7	5	2	7	2
Ted Lindsay	6	4	2	6	6
Gerry Couture	7	4	2	6	0
George Gee	7	2	3	5	0
Pete Babando	5	2	2	4	2
Joe Carveth	7	1	3	4	4
Jim McFadden	7	2	1	3	2
Marty Pavelich	7	2	1	3	6
Al Dewsbury	5	0	3	3	8
L.'Red' Kelly	7	0	3	3	2
J.'Black Jack' Stewart	7	0	3	3	10
Jim Peters	5	0	2	2	0
Johnny Wilson	5	0	1	1	0
Marcel Pronovost	6	0	1	1	4
Doug McKay	1	0	0	0	0
Larry Wilson	2	0	0	0	0
Clare Martin	3	0	0	0	0
Max McNab	4	0	0	0	0
Lee Fogolin Sr.	4	0	0	0	2
Steve Black	6	0	0	0	0
Leo Reise	7	0	0	0	8

GOALTENDER	GP	W	L	MIN	GA	SO	AVG
Harry Lumley	7	4	3	459	17	1	2.22

NY RANGERS	GP	G	A	PTS	PIM
Edgar Laprade	7	3	3	6	2
Tony Leswick	7	2	4	6	2
H.'Buddy' O'Connor	7	3	1	4	2
Dunc Fisher	7	2	2	4	12
Nick Mickoski	7	0	4	4	0
Allan Stanley	7	2	1	3	6
Alex Kaleta	7	0	3	3	0
Ed Slowinski	7	0	3	3	4
Don Raleigh	7	2	0	2	0
Pentti Lund	7	1	1	2	0
Pat Egan	7	1	1	2	4
Gus Kyle	7	1	0	1	14
Jack Gordon	4	0	1	1	2
Jack Lancien	2	0	0	0	0
Fred Shero	4	0	0	0	0
Jack McLeod	5	0	0	0	0
Frank Eddolls	7	0	0	0	2

GOALTENDER	GP	W	L	MIN	GA	SO	AVG
Chuck Rayner	7	3	4	459	22	0	2.88

1951

TORONTO
	GP	G	A	PTS	PIM
Tod Sloan	5	3	4	7	7
Sid Smith	5	5	1	6	0
T.'Teeder' Kennedy	5	2	4	6	2
Max Bentley	5	0	4	4	2
Harry Watson	5	1	2	3	4
Howie Meeker	5	1	1	2	10
Bill Barilko	5	1	0	1	6
Gus Mortson	5	0	1	1	0
Danny Lewicki	3	0	0	0	0
Fern Flaman	3	0	0	0	6
Ray Timgren	5	0	0	0	0
Joe Klukay	5	0	0	0	0
Cal Gardner	5	0	0	0	0
Bill Juzda	5	0	0	0	2
Fleming Mackell	5	0	0	0	2
Jim Thomson	5	0	0	0	4

GOALTENDERS	GP	W	L	MIN	GA	SO	AVG
Al Rollins	3	3	0	193	5	0	1.55
W.'Turk' Broda	2	1	1	129	5	0	2.33

MONTREAL
	GP	G	A	PTS	PIM
Maurice Richard	5	5	2	7	4
Billy Reay	5	1	2	3	10
Doug Harvey	5	0	3	3	2
Paul Masnick	5	2	0	2	4
Paul Meger	5	1	1	2	2
Bert Olmstead	5	0	2	2	7
Elmer Lach	5	1	0	1	2
E.'Butch' Bouchard	5	0	1	1	0
J.'Bud' MacPherson	5	0	1	1	4
Ross Lowe	1	0	0	0	0
Bob Dawes	1	0	0	0	2
Eddie Mazur	2	0	0	0	0
Calum MacKay	5	0	0	0	0
Tom Johnson	5	0	0	0	2
Kenny Mosdell	5	0	0	0	2
Floyd Curry	5	0	0	0	2
Bernie Geoffrion	5	0	0	0	4

GOALTENDER	GP	W	L	MIN	GA	SO	AVG
Gerry McNeil	5	1	4	322	13	0	2.42

1952

DETROIT
	GP	G	A	PTS	PIM
Ted Lindsay	4	3	0	3	4
Metro Prystai	4	2	1	3	0
Gordie Howe	4	2	1	3	2
Tony Leswick	4	2	1	3	14
Marty Pavelich	4	1	2	3	2
Glen Skov	4	1	2	3	12
Vic Stasiuk	3	0	1	1	0
Johnny Wilson	4	0	1	1	0
Alex Delvecchio	4	0	1	1	2
Sid Abel	4	0	1	1	2
Leo Reise	2	0	0	0	0
L.'Red' Kelly	3	0	0	0	0
Larry Zeidel	3	0	0	0	0
Benny Woit	4	0	0	0	2
Marcel Pronovost	4	0	0	0	2
Bob Goldham	4	0	0	0	4

GOALTENDER	GP	W	L	MIN	GA	SO	AVG
Terry Sawchuk	4	4	0	240	2	2	0.50

MONTREAL
	GP	G	A	PTS	PIM
Tom Johnson	4	1	0	1	0
Elmer Lach	4	1	0	1	4
Bernie Geoffrion	4	0	1	1	0
Floyd Curry	4	0	1	1	0
Bert Olmstead	4	0	1	1	2
Stan Long	2	0	0	0	0
Dollard St. Laurent	2	0	0	0	0
Dick Gamble	2	0	0	0	0
Billy Reay	3	0	0	0	0
Eddie Mazur	3	0	0	0	4
Paul Meger	4	0	0	0	0
J.'Bud' MacPherson	4	0	0	0	0
Maurice Richard	4	0	0	0	4
E.'Butch' Bouchard	4	0	0	0	6
Doug Harvey	4	0	0	0	6
Paul Masnick	4	0	0	0	6
Dickie Moore	4	0	0	0	12

GOALTENDER	GP	W	L	MIN	GA	SO	AVG
Gerry McNeil	4	0	4	240	10	0	2.50

1953

MONTREAL
	GP	G	A	PTS	PIM
Maurice Richard	5	4	1	5	0
Kenny Mosdell	5	2	2	4	4
Calum MacKay	5	1	2	3	6
Dickie Moore	5	2	0	2	9
Floyd Curry	5	1	1	2	0
Elmer Lach	5	1	1	2	0
Bert Olmstead	5	1	1	2	2
Dollard St. Laurent	5	0	2	2	2
Doug Harvey	5	0	2	2	4
Paul Masnick	3	1	0	1	0
Bernie Geoffrion	5	1	0	1	0
Lorne Davis	5	1	0	1	2
Tom Johnson	5	1	0	1	4
E.'Butch' Bouchard	5	0	1	1	2
Eddie Mazur	5	0	1	1	11
Paul Meger	1	0	0	0	0
John McCormack	2	0	0	0	0
Billy Reay	4	0	0	0	0

GOALTENDERS	GP	W	L	MIN	GA	SO	AVG
Gerry McNeil	3	3	0	181	3	2	0.99
Jacques Plante	2	1	1	120	6	0	3.00

BOSTON
	GP	G	A	PTS	PIM
Ed Sandford	5	2	1	3	5
Fleming Mackell	5	0	3	3	2
Milt Schmidt	4	2	0	2	2
Dave Creighton	5	1	1	2	0
Leo Labine	5	1	1	2	4
Woody Dumart	5	0	2	2	0
Jack McIntyre	4	1	0	1	0
John Peirson	5	1	0	1	2
Bob Armstrong	5	0	1	1	6
Bill Quackenbush	5	0	1	1	2
Frank Martin	5	0	1	1	2
Real Chevrefils	5	0	1	1	6
Joe Klukay	5	0	1	1	7
Hal Laycoe	5	0	1	1	10
Warren Godfrey	5	0	0	0	0
Jerry Toppazzini	5	0	0	0	4

GOALTENDERS	GP	W	L	MIN	GA	SO	AVG
Gordie Henry	3	1	2	163	10	0	3.68
'Sugar' Jim Henry	3	0	2	138	5	0	2.17

1954

DETROIT
	GP	G	A	PTS	PIM
Alex Delvecchio	7	2	4	6	0
L.'Red' Kelly	7	3	1	4	0
Metro Prystai	7	2	2	4	0
Ted Lindsay	7	2	2	4	14
Gordie Howe	7	1	2	3	23
Johnny Wilson	7	2	0	2	0
Earl Reibel	4	1	1	2	0
Tony Leswick	7	1	1	2	8
Bob Goldham	7	0	1	1	0
Benny Woit	7	0	1	1	4
Marty Pavelich	7	0	1	1	4
Marcel Pronovost	7	0	0	0	8
Glen Skov	7	0	1	1	10
Gilles Dube	2	0	0	0	0
Keith Allen	3	0	0	0	0
Jim Peters	6	0	0	0	0
Bill Dineen	7	0	0	0	0

GOALTENDER	GP	W	L	MIN	GA	SO	AVG
Terry Sawchuk	7	4	3	430	12	1	1.67

MONTREAL
	GP	G	A	PTS	PIM
Floyd Curry	7	3	0	3	2
Maurice Richard	7	3	0	3	20
Bernie Geoffrion	7	2	1	3	16
Dickie Moore	7	1	2	3	8
Paul Masnick	6	0	3	3	4
Elmer Lach	4	0	2	2	0
Jean Beliveau	6	0	2	2	2
Dollard St. Laurent	6	1	0	1	6
Kenny Mosdell	7	1	0	1	2
Tom Johnson	7	1	0	1	8
Calum MacKay	3	0	1	1	0
Doug Harvey	6	0	1	1	4
Eddie Mazur	7	0	1	1	0
Bert Olmstead	7	0	1	1	8
Paul Meger	2	0	0	0	2
J.'Bud' MacPherson	2	0	0	0	4
Gaye Stewart	3	0	0	0	0
John McCormack	4	0	0	0	0
E.'Butch' Bouchard	7	0	0	0	4
Lorne Davis	7	0	0	0	6

GOALTENDERS	GP	W	L	MIN	GA	SO	AVG
Gerry McNeil	3	2	1	190	3	1	0.95
Jacques Plante	4	1	3	240	10	0	2.50

1955

DETROIT
	GP	G	A	PTS	PIM
Gordie Howe	7	5	7	12	24
Ted Lindsay	7	5	6	11	6
Alex Delvecchio	7	6	4	10	0
Earl Reibel	7	2	5	7	2
Vic Stasiuk	7	3	3	6	2
L.'Red' Kelly	7	2	3	5	17
Marcel Pronovost	7	1	2	3	2
Marty Pavelich	7	1	2	3	12
Bob Goldham	7	0	2	2	2
Jim Hay	5	1	0	1	0
Glen Skov	7	0	1	1	4
Marcel Bonin	7	0	1	1	4
Tony Leswick	7	0	1	1	10
Johnny Wilson	7	0	0	0	0
Bill Dineen	7	0	0	0	2
Benny Woit	7	0	0	0	4

GOALTENDER	GP	W	L	MIN	GA	SO	AVG
Terry Sawchuk	7	4	3	420	20	0	2.86

FINAL SERIES SCORING, 1927-1995 • 159

MONTREAL	GP	G	A	PTS	PIM
Bernie Geoffrion	7	6	2	8	2
Jean Beliveau	7	3	5	8	12
Floyd Curry	7	5	1	6	2
Calum MacKay	7	2	4	6	2
Kenny Mosdell	7	1	4	5	6
Doug Harvey	7	0	5	5	4
Jack LeClair	7	2	0	2	2
Dickie Moore	7	0	2	2	16
Tom Johnson	7	1	0	1	16
Dollard St. Laurent	7	0	1	1	10
Bert Olmstead	7	0	1	1	14
E.'Butch' Bouchard	7	0	1	1	31
Jim Bartlett	2	0	0	0	0
Paul Ronty	2	0	0	0	2
Dick Gamble	2	0	0	0	2
George McAvoy	3	0	0	0	0
Don Marshall	7	0	0	0	2

GOALTENDER	GP	W	L	MIN	GA	SO	AVG
Jacques Plante	7	3	3	403	24	0	3.57
Charlie Hodge	1	0	1	17	3	0	10.59

1956

MONTREAL	GP	G	A	PTS	PIM
Jean Beliveau	5	7	3	10	8
Bert Olmstead	5	0	8	8	4
Bernie Geoffrion	5	3	3	6	2
Maurice Richard	5	2	2	4	12
Floyd Curry	5	1	3	4	4
Henri Richard	5	2	1	3	11
Claude Provost	5	1	2	3	2
Dickie Moore	5	0	3	3	6
Doug Harvey	5	0	3	3	6
Jack LeClair	5	1	1	2	4
Don Marshall	5	1	0	1	0
Kenny Mosdell	4	0	1	1	0
Jean-Guy Talbot	4	0	1	1	2
E.'Butch' Bouchard	1	0	0	0	0
Dollard St. Laurent	3	0	0	0	2
Bob Turner	5	0	0	0	4
Tom Johnson	5	0	0	0	8

GOALTENDER	GP	W	L	MIN	GA	SO	AVG
Jacques Plante	5	4	1	300	9	1	1.80

DETROIT	GP	G	A	PTS	PIM
Gordie Howe	5	1	5	6	4
Ted Lindsay	5	2	3	5	6
Alex Delvecchio	5	3	1	4	0
Norm Ullman	5	1	1	2	11
L.'Red' Kelly	5	1	0	1	2
Bill Dineen	5	1	0	1	4
Al Arbour	4	0	1	1	0
Earl Reibel	5	0	1	1	2
John Bucyk	5	0	1	1	4
Lorne Ferguson	5	0	1	1	8
Marty Pavelich	5	0	1	1	8
Cummy Burton	1	0	0	0	0
Murray Costello	2	0	0	0	0
Gord Hollingworth	2	0	0	0	2
Gerry Melnyk	4	0	0	0	0
Metro Prystai	4	0	0	0	4
Bob Goldham	5	0	0	0	2
Marcel Pronovost	5	0	0	0	2
Larry Hillman	5	0	0	0	2

GOALTENDER	GP	W	L	MIN	GA	SO	AVG
Glenn Hall	5	1	4	300	18	0	3.60

1957

MONTREAL	GP	G	A	PTS	PIM
Bernie Geoffrion	5	4	2	6	2
Doug Harvey	5	0	5	5	6
Maurice Richard	5	4	0	4	2
Floyd Curry	5	2	2	4	0
Dickie Moore	5	1	3	4	2
Don Marshall	5	1	2	3	2
Phil Goyette	5	1	1	2	2
Jean Beliveau	5	1	1	2	6
Tom Johnson	5	0	2	2	2
Henri Richard	5	0	2	2	8
Bert Olmstead	5	0	2	2	9
Andre Pronovost	3	1	0	1	0
Connie Braden	4	0	1	1	0
Claude Provost	5	0	1	1	2
Dollard St. Laurent	5	0	1	1	9
Bob Turner	2	0	0	0	0
Jean-Guy Talbot	5	0	0	0	6

GOALTENDER	GP	W	L	MIN	GA	SO	AVG
Jacques Plante	5	4	1	300	5	1	1.00

BOSTON	GP	G	A	PTS	PIM
Fleming Mackell	5	4	0	4	2
Don McKenney	5	1	1	2	0
Leo Labine	5	1	1	2	12
Larry Regan	5	0	2	2	4
Doug Mohns	5	0	1	1	0
Bob Armstrong	5	0	1	1	2
Jerry Toppazzini	5	0	1	1	2
Leo Boivin	5	0	1	1	4
Fern Flaman	5	0	1	1	13
Cal Gardner	5	0	0	0	0
Jack Caffery	5	0	0	0	0
Vic Stasiuk	5	0	0	0	2
Real Chevrefils	5	0	0	0	2
Jack Bionda	5	0	0	0	6
Carl Boone	5	0	0	0	10
John Peirson	5	0	0	0	12

GOALTENDER	GP	W	L	MIN	GA	SO	AVG
Don Simmons	5	1	4	300	15	1	3.00

1958

MONTREAL	GP	G	A	PTS	PIM
Bernie Geoffrion	6	5	3	8	0
Doug Harvey	6	2	5	7	8
Jean Beliveau	6	2	4	6	8
Dickie Moore	6	1	5	6	2
Maurice Richard	6	4	1	5	8
Henri Richard	6	1	2	3	9
Claude Provost	6	1	0	1	2
Bert Olmstead	5	0	1	1	0
Marcel Bonin	5	0	1	1	10
Don Marshall	6	0	1	1	0
Connie Braden	1	0	0	0	0
Ab McDonald	1	0	0	0	2
Tom Johnson	2	0	0	0	0
Al Langlois	3	0	0	0	0
Floyd Curry	3	0	0	0	0
Dollard St. Laurent	4	0	0	0	8
Bob Turner	6	0	0	0	2
Phil Goyette	6	0	0	0	2
Jean-Guy Talbot	6	0	0	0	6
Andre Pronovost	6	0	0	0	10

GOALTENDER	GP	W	L	MIN	GA	SO	AVG
Jacques Plante	6	4	2	366	14	1	2.30

BOSTON	GP	G	A	PTS	PIM
Larry Regan	6	2	4	6	2
Don McKenney	6	4	1	5	0
Fleming Mackell	6	1	4	5	6
Bronco Horvath	6	3	1	4	4
Allan Stanley	6	1	2	3	4
Vic Stasiuk	6	0	3	3	0
Norm Johnson	6	2	0	2	4
Jerry Toppazzini	6	1	1	2	2
Doug Mohns	6	0	2	2	8
Leo Labine	6	0	2	2	8
Carl Boone	6	0	1	1	4
Fern Flaman	6	0	1	1	4
Leo Boivin	6	0	1	1	9
John Peirson	2	0	0	0	0
Larry Hillman	5	0	0	0	2
John Bucyk	6	0	0	0	6

GOALTENDER	GP	W	L	MIN	GA	SO	AVG
Don Simmons	6	2	4	366	15	0	2.46

1959

MONTREAL	GP	G	A	PTS	PIM
Bernie Geoffrion	5	3	4	7	6
Ralph Backstrom	5	3	4	7	8
Henri Richard	5	1	5	6	5
Doug Harvey	5	0	6	6	10
Marcel Bonin	5	3	2	5	2
Dickie Moore	5	2	3	5	8
Claude Provost	5	2	2	4	2
Tom Johnson	5	2	1	3	2
Ab McDonald	5	1	1	2	0
Phil Goyette	5	0	2	2	0
Andre Pronovost	5	1	0	1	0
Don Marshall	5	0	1	1	0
Jean-Guy Talbot	5	0	1	1	6
Bob Turner	5	0	1	1	8
Bill Hicke	1	0	0	0	0
Al Langlois	4	0	0	0	2
Maurice Richard	4	0	0	0	2

GOALTENDER	GP	W	L	MIN	GA	SO	AVG
Jacques Plante	5	4	1	310	12	0	2.32

TORONTO	GP	G	A	PTS	PIM
Billy Harris	5	3	1	4	14
Frank Mahovlich	5	2	2	4	6
Gerry Ehman	5	0	4	4	4
Ron Stewart	5	2	1	3	2
Dick Duff	5	2	1	3	4
Bert Olmstead	5	1	3	3	6
Bob Pulford	5	1	2	3	4
George Armstrong	5	0	2	2	6
Carl Brewer	5	0	2	2	18
Dave Creighton	5	0	1	1	0
Tim Horton	5	0	1	1	2
Allan Stanley	5	0	1	1	2
Barry Cullen	1	0	0	0	0
Noel Price	2	0	0	0	2
Larry Regan	3	0	0	0	0
Brian Cullen	3	0	0	0	0
Marc Reaume	4	0	0	0	0
Bob Baun	5	0	0	0	11

GOALTENDER	GP	W	L	MIN	GA	SO	AVG
Johnny Bower	5	1	4	310	18	0	3.48

FINAL SERIES SCORING, 1927-1995

1960

MONTREAL
	GP	G	A	PTS	PIM
Henri Richard	4	3	5	8	9
Bernie Geoffrion	4	0	6	6	0
Dickie Moore	4	2	3	5	2
Jean Beliveau	4	4	0	4	4
Maurice Richard	4	1	2	3	2
Phil Goyette	4	2	0	2	2
Doug Harvey	4	2	0	2	6
Marcel Bonin	4	0	2	2	6
Al Langlois	4	0	2	2	12
Don Marshall	4	1	0	1	0
Bill Hicke	4	0	1	1	0
Jean-Guy Talbot	4	0	1	1	4
Claude Provost	4	0	1	1	0
Andre Pronovost	4	0	1	1	0
Bob Turner	4	0	0	0	0
Ralph Backstrom	4	0	0	0	2
Tom Johnson	4	0	0	0	2

GOALTENDER	GP	W	L	MIN	GA	SO	AVG
Jacques Plante	4	4	0	240	5	1	1.25

TORONTO
	GP	G	A	PTS	PIM
Bert Olmstead	4	2	0	2	0
Larry Regan	4	1	1	2	0
L.'Red' Kelly	4	0	2	2	2
George Armstrong	4	0	2	2	2
Johnny Wilson	4	1	0	1	2
Bob Baun	4	1	0	1	17
Billy Harris	3	0	1	1	0
Tim Horton	4	0	1	1	0
Dick Duff	4	0	1	1	2
Gary Edmundson	4	0	1	1	2
Carl Brewer	4	0	1	1	6
Gerry Ehman	3	0	0	0	2
Allan Stanley	4	0	0	0	0
Jerry James	4	0	0	0	0
Ron Stewart	4	0	0	0	0
Frank Mahovlich	4	0	0	0	0
Bob Pulford	4	0	0	0	8

GOALTENDER	GP	W	L	MIN	GA	SO	AVG
Johnny Bower	4	0	4	240	15	0	3.75

1961

CHICAGO
	GP	G	A	PTS	PIM
Pierre Pilote	6	2	6	8	2
Stan Mikita	6	3	4	7	2
Bobby Hull	6	2	5	7	2
Murray Balfour	5	3	3	6	4
Bill Hay	6	1	3	4	8
Ron Murphy	6	2	1	3	0
Ken Wharram	6	2	1	3	10
Ab McDonald	6	1	1	2	0
Eric Nesterenko	6	1	1	2	2
Reg Fleming	6	1	0	1	2
Jack Evans	6	1	0	1	10
Ed Litzenberger	4	0	1	1	0
Dollard St. Laurent	5	0	1	1	2
Tod Sloan	6	0	1	1	6
Elmer Vasko	6	0	1	1	6
Chico Maki	1	0	0	0	0
Wayne Hillman	1	0	0	0	0
Wayne Hicks	1	0	0	0	2
Al Arbour	3	0	0	0	2
Earl Balfour	6	0	0	0	0

GOALTENDER	GP	W	L	MIN	GA	SO	AVG
Glenn Hall	6	4	2	360	12	0	2.00

DETROIT
	GP	G	A	PTS	PIM
Gordie Howe	6	1	7	8	8
Alex Delvecchio	6	3	3	6	0
Allan Johnson	6	1	2	3	0
Vic Stasiuk	6	1	2	3	4
Bruce MacGregor	6	1	2	3	6
Howie Young	6	1	1	2	18
Norm Ullman	5	0	2	2	2
Val Fonteyne	6	0	2	2	0
Len Lunde	5	1	0	1	0
Parker MacDonald	6	1	0	1	0
Leo Labine	6	1	0	1	0
Marcel Pronovost	4	0	1	1	0
Warren Godfrey	6	0	1	1	10
Gerry Melnyk	6	0	0	0	0
Gerry Odrowski	6	0	0	0	4
Pete Goegan	6	0	0	0	14

GOALTENDERS	GP	W	L	MIN	GA	SO	AVG
Hank Bassen	4	1	2	220	9	0	2.45
Terry Sawchuk	3	1	2	140	10	0	4.29

1962

TORONTO
	GP	G	A	PTS	PIM
Frank Mahovlich	6	4	3	7	21
George Armstrong	6	3	4	7	0
Tim Horton	6	1	6	7	12
Dick Duff	6	1	4	5	16
Ron Stewart	6	0	5	5	2
Bob Pulford	6	3	0	3	14
Billy Harris	6	2	1	3	0
Dave Keon	6	2	1	3	0
L.'Red' Kelly	6	1	2	3	0
Bob Baun	6	0	3	3	15
Bob Nevin	6	1	1	2	4
Bert Olmstead	4	1	0	1	0
Allan Stanley	6	0	1	1	2
Carl Brewer	6	0	1	1	18
Al Arbour	2	0	0	0	0
Ed Litzenberger	4	0	0	0	2
Eddie Shack	5	0	0	0	12

GOALTENDERS	GP	W	L	MIN	GA	SO	AVG
Johnny Bower	4	2	1	195	7	0	2.15
Don Simmons	3	2	1	165	8	0	2.91

CHICAGO
	GP	G	A	PTS	PIM
Bobby Hull	6	4	4	8	6
Stan Mikita	6	3	5	8	15
Ab McDonald	6	3	2	5	0
Bill Hay	6	0	4	4	4
Pierre Pilote	6	0	4	4	6
Eric Nesterenko	6	0	4	4	14
Reg Fleming	6	2	0	2	18
Bronco Horvath	6	1	1	2	2
Murray Balfour	6	1	1	2	11
Bob Turner	6	0	1	1	0
Ken Wharram	6	0	1	1	4
Dollard St. Laurent	6	0	1	1	8
Merv Kuryluk	2	0	0	0	0
Gerry Melnyk	5	0	0	0	2
Elmer Vasko	6	0	0	0	0
Jack Evans	6	0	0	0	12

GOALTENDER	GP	W	L	MIN	GA	SO	AVG
Glenn Hall	6	2	4	360	18	1	3.00

1963

TORONTO
	GP	G	A	PTS	PIM
Dave Keon	5	4	2	6	0
L.'Red' Kelly	5	2	2	4	2
Tim Horton	5	1	3	4	4
Allan Stanley	5	0	4	4	4
Bob Nevin	5	3	0	3	0
Dick Duff	5	2	1	3	2
George Armstrong	5	1	2	3	0
Ed Litzenberger	5	1	2	3	4
Bob Pulford	5	0	3	3	8
Ron Stewart	5	2	0	2	2
Eddie Shack	5	1	1	2	4
Frank Mahovlich	4	0	1	1	4
Billy Harris	5	1	0	1	0
Kent Douglas	5	0	1	1	2
Carl Brewer	5	0	1	1	4
Bob Baun	5	0	1	1	6
John MacMillan	1	0	0	0	0

GOALTENDER	GP	W	L	MIN	GA	SO	AVG
Johnny Bower	5	4	1	300	10	0	2.00

DETROIT
	GP	G	A	PTS	PIM
Gordie Howe	5	3	3	6	8
Marcel Pronovost	5	0	4	4	0
Norm Ullman	5	0	4	4	2
Larry Jeffrey	5	2	1	3	4
Alex Delvecchio	5	1	2	3	0
Alex Faulkner	5	2	0	2	2
Floyd Smith	5	0	2	2	4
Vic Stasiuk	4	1	0	1	0
Eddie Joyal	5	1	0	1	0
Bruce MacGregor	5	0	1	1	0
Andre Pronovost	5	0	1	1	0
Parker MacDonald	5	0	1	1	2
Bob Dillabough	1	0	0	0	0
Howie Young	2	0	0	0	0
Gerry Odrowski	2	0	0	0	2
Val Fonteyne	5	0	0	0	0
Pete Goegan	5	0	0	0	2
Doug Barkley	5	0	0	0	6
Bill Gadsby	5	0	0	0	12

GOALTENDER	GP	W	L	MIN	GA	SO	AVG
Terry Sawchuk	5	1	4	300	17	0	3.40

1964

TORONTO
	GP	G	A	PTS	PIM
Frank Mahovlich	7	1	7	8	0
George Armstrong	7	4	3	7	10
L.'Red' Kelly	7	2	4	6	2
Don McKenney	5	1	5	6	0
Dave Keon	7	4	1	5	0
Bob Pulford	7	3	2	5	10
Andy Bathgate	7	3	2	5	12
Allan Stanley	7	1	3	4	12
Bob Baun	7	1	2	3	16
Ron Stewart	7	0	3	3	2
Billy Harris	7	1	1	2	4
Tim Horton	7	0	2	2	12
Gerry Ehman	7	1	0	1	2
Carl Brewer	5	0	1	1	10
Al Arbour	1	0	0	0	0
Ed Litzenberger	1	0	0	0	10
Larry Hillman	6	0	0	0	2
Jim Pappin	7	0	0	0	0
Eddie Shack	7	0	0	0	4

GOALTENDER	GP	W	L	MIN	GA	SO	AVG
Johnny Bower	7	4	3	430	17	1	2.37

FINAL SERIES SCORING, 1927-1995 • 161

DETROIT

	GP	G	A	PTS	PIM
Gordie Howe	7	4	4	8	8
Alex Delvecchio	7	1	4	5	0
Norm Ullman	7	1	3	4	2
Floyd Smith	7	3	0	3	0
Bruce MacGregor	7	3	0	3	4
Doug Barkley	7	0	3	3	8
Eddie Joyal	7	2	1	3	6
Larry Jeffrey	7	1	2	3	4
Pit Martin	7	1	2	3	10
Andre Pronovost	7	0	2	2	8
Bill Gadsby	7	0	2	2	14
Paul Henderson	7	1	0	1	4
John MacMillan	4	0	1	1	2
Parker MacDonald	7	0	1	1	0
Alex Faulkner	1	0	0	0	0
Bob Dillabough	1	0	0	0	0
Irv Spencer	7	0	0	0	0
Al Langlois	7	0	0	0	8
Marcel Pronovost	7	0	0	0	8

GOALTENDER	GP	W	L	MIN	GA	SO	AVG
Terry Sawchuk	7	3	4	430	22	0	3.07

1965

MONTREAL

	GP	G	A	PTS	PIM
Jean Beliveau	7	5	5	10	18
Dick Duff	7	3	5	8	5
Bobby Rousseau	7	1	5	6	4
J.C. Tremblay	7	1	5	6	14
Henri Richard	7	3	0	3	20
John Ferguson	7	2	1	3	13
Ted Harris	7	0	3	3	34
Yvan Cournoyer	7	2	0	2	0
Ralph Backstrom	7	1	1	2	4
Claude Provost	7	0	2	2	12
Noel Picard	3	0	1	1	0
G.'Red' Berenson	7	0	1	1	2
Jean Lanthier	2	0	0	0	4
Dave Balon	5	0	0	0	0
Claude Larose	7	0	0	0	4
Jim Roberts	7	0	0	0	14
Jean-Guy Talbot	7	0	0	0	18
Terry Harper	7	0	0	0	19

GOALTENDERS	GP	W	L	MIN	GA	SO	AVG
L.'Gump' Worsley	4	3	1	240	5	2	1.25
Charlie Hodge	3	1	2	180	7	1	2.33

CHICAGO

	GP	G	A	PTS	PIM
Bobby Hull	7	2	2	4	10
Chico Maki	7	1	3	4	8
Pierre Pilote	5	0	3	3	14
Stan Mikita	7	0	3	3	35
Fred Stanfield	7	1	1	2	0
Matt Ravlich	7	1	1	2	8
Phil Esposito	7	1	1	2	8
Elmer Vasko	7	1	1	2	12
Doug Mohns	7	1	1	2	15
Ken Wharram	5	1	0	1	2
Bill Hay	7	1	0	1	0
Camille Henry	7	1	0	1	2
Doug Jarrett	7	1	0	1	10
Dennis Hull	1	0	0	0	0
John McKenzie	4	0	0	0	0
Gerry Melnyk	6	0	0	0	0
Eric Nesterenko	7	0	0	0	6
Al MacNeil	7	0	0	0	12

GOALTENDERS	GP	W	L	MIN	GA	SO	AVG
Glenn Hall	7	3	4	400	15	0	2.25
Denis DeJordy	1	0	0	20	3	0	9.00

1966

MONTREAL

	GP	G	A	PTS	PIM
J.C. Tremblay	6	1	5	6	0
Jean Beliveau	6	3	2	5	0
Henri Richard	6	1	4	5	2
Gilles Tremblay	6	2	2	4	0
Ralph Backstrom	6	2	2	4	2
Dave Balon	6	2	2	4	16
Dick Duff	6	1	3	4	2
Yvan Cournoyer	6	2	1	3	0
Bobby Rousseau	6	1	2	3	4
Terry Harper	6	1	2	3	4
Leon Rochefort	4	1	1	2	4
Claude Provost	6	1	1	2	2
Noel Price	1	0	1	1	0
Jean-Guy Talbot	6	0	1	1	8
Jim Roberts	6	0	1	1	10
Claude Larose	2	0	0	0	0
Ted Harris	6	0	0	0	4
John Ferguson	6	0	0	0	8

GOALTENDER	GP	W	L	MIN	GA	SO	AVG
L.'Gump' Worsley	6	4	2	362	14	0	2.32

DETROIT

	GP	G	A	PTS	PIM
Norm Ullman	6	4	2	6	6
Floyd Smith	6	3	1	4	0
Paul Henderson	6	1	3	4	4
Andy Bathgate	6	1	3	4	4
Ab McDonald	4	1	2	3	2
Alex Delvecchio	6	0	3	3	0
Dean Prentice	6	1	1	2	2
Bill Gadsby	6	1	1	2	2
Bruce MacGregor	6	1	1	2	2
Gordie Howe	6	1	1	2	6
Bert Marshall	6	0	2	2	8
Gary Bergman	6	0	1	1	4
Warren Godfrey	1	0	0	0	0
Irv Spencer	1	0	0	0	0
Murray Hall	1	0	0	0	0
Bob Wall	4	0	0	0	2
Val Fonteyne	6	0	0	0	0
Parker MacDonald	6	0	0	0	2
Leo Boivin	6	0	0	0	6
Bryan Watson	6	0	0	0	12

GOALTENDERS	GP	W	L	MIN	GA	SO	AVG
Roger Crozier	6	2	3	308	16	0	3.12
Hank Bassen	1	0	1	54	2	0	2.22

1967

TORONTO

	GP	G	A	PTS	PIM
Jim Pappin	6	4	4	8	6
Bob Pulford	6	1	6	7	0
Pete Stemkowski	6	2	4	6	4
Tim Horton	6	2	3	5	8
Mike Walton	6	2	1	3	0
L.'Red' Kelly	6	0	3	3	2
Larry Hillman	6	1	1	2	0
Dave Keon	6	1	1	2	0
Ron Ellis	6	1	1	2	4
Brian Conacher	6	1	1	2	19
Frank Mahovlich	6	0	2	2	8
Marcel Pronovost	6	1	0	1	4
George Armstrong	6	1	0	1	4
Allan Stanley	6	0	1	1	6
Aut Erickson	1	0	0	0	2
Milan Marcetta	2	0	0	0	0
Eddie Shack	4	0	0	0	8
Bob Baun	5	0	0	0	2

GOALTENDERS	GP	W	L	MIN	GA	SO	AVG
Johnny Bower	3	2	0	163	3	1	1.10
Terry Sawchuk	4	2	2	225	12	0	3.20

MONTREAL

	GP	G	A	PTS	PIM
Henri Richard	6	4	3	7	0
Jean Beliveau	6	4	2	6	10
Yvan Cournoyer	6	2	2	4	4
Bobby Rousseau	6	0	4	4	2
Dick Duff	6	1	2	3	4
Ralph Backstrom	6	2	0	2	2
Leon Rochefort	6	1	1	2	2
John Ferguson	6	1	1	2	16
Dave Balon	5	0	2	2	2
J.C. Tremblay	6	0	2	2	0
Jim Roberts	3	1	0	1	0
Gilles Tremblay	6	0	1	1	0
Ted Harris	6	0	1	1	12
Claude Larose	6	0	1	1	15
Claude Provost	4	0	0	0	0
Jean-Guy Talbot	6	0	0	0	0
Jacques Laperriere	6	0	0	0	2
Terry Harper	6	0	0	0	6

GOALTENDERS	GP	W	L	MIN	GA	SO	AVG
Rogie Vachon	5	2	3	308	14	0	2.73
L.'Gump' Worsley	2	0	1	80	2	0	1.50

1968

MONTREAL

	GP	G	A	PTS	PIM
Yvan Cournoyer	4	2	2	4	2
Henri Richard	4	2	1	3	0
John Ferguson	4	0	3	3	4
Serge Savard	4	2	0	2	0
J.C. Tremblay	4	1	1	2	0
Ralph Backstrom	4	1	1	2	0
Dick Duff	4	1	1	2	2
Jacques Lemaire	4	1	1	2	4
Bobby Rousseau	4	1	0	1	6
Claude Larose	4	0	1	1	0
Claude Provost	4	0	1	1	2
Ted Harris	4	0	1	1	6
Jean Beliveau	1	0	0	0	0
Carol Vadnais	1	0	0	0	2
Mickey Redmond	2	0	0	0	0
Danny Grant	4	0	0	0	0
Terry Harper	4	0	0	0	4
Jacques Laperriere	4	0	0	0	6

GOALTENDER	GP	W	L	MIN	GA	SO	AVG
L.'Gump' Worsley	4	4	0	243	7	1	1.73

162 • FINAL SERIES SCORING, 1927-1995

ST. LOUIS

	GP	G	A	PTS	PIM
G.'Red' Berenson	4	2	1	3	7
Frank St. Marseille	4	1	1	2	0
Barclay Plager	4	1	1	2	6
Craig Cameron	1	1	0	1	0
Gary Sabourin	4	1	0	1	2
Dickie Moore	4	1	0	1	4
Doug Harvey	2	0	1	1	4
Gary Veneruzzo	3	0	1	1	0
Al Arbour	4	0	1	1	0
Tim Ecclestone	4	0	1	1	2
Jean-Guy Talbot	4	0	1	1	4
Noel Picard	4	0	1	1	6
Bill McCreary	3	0	0	0	0
Gerry Melnyk	3	0	0	0	0
Ron Schock	4	0	0	0	0
Larry Keenan	4	0	0	0	0
Terry Crisp	4	0	0	0	0
Jim Roberts	4	0	0	0	2
Bob Plager	4	0	0	0	20

GOALTENDER	GP	W	L	MIN	GA	SO	AVG
Glenn Hall	4	0	4	243	11	0	2.72

1969

MONTREAL

	GP	G	A	PTS	PIM
Dick Duff	4	4	2	6	2
Jean Beliveau	4	0	5	5	4
Yvan Cournoyer	4	1	3	4	0
John Ferguson	4	2	0	2	20
Ralph Backstrom	4	1	1	2	4
Serge Savard	4	1	1	2	8
J.C. Tremblay	4	0	2	2	6
Bobby Rousseau	4	1	0	1	2
Jacques Lemaire	4	1	0	1	4
Ted Harris	4	1	0	1	6
Claude Provost	3	0	1	1	0
Mickey Redmond	4	0	1	1	0
Henri Richard	4	0	1	1	2
Christian Bordeleau	3	0	0	0	0
Terry Harper	4	0	0	0	4
Jacques Laperriere	4	0	0	0	22

GOALTENDER	GP	W	L	MIN	GA	SO	AVG
Rogie Vachon	4	4	0	240	3	1	0.75

ST. LOUIS

	GP	G	A	PTS	PIM
Frank St. Marseille	4	1	1	2	2
Terry Gray	3	1	0	1	8
Larry Keenan	4	1	0	1	8
Barclay Plager	4	0	1	1	0
Terry Crisp	4	0	1	1	2
Jim Roberts	4	0	1	1	4
Bill McCreary	4	0	1	1	4
Noel Picard	4	0	1	1	8
Camille Henry	2	0	0	0	0
Craig Cameron	2	0	0	0	0
Bob Plager	2	0	0	0	2
Bill Plager	3	0	0	0	4
Jean-Guy Talbot	4	0	0	0	2
Ron Schock	4	0	0	0	4
Al Arbour	4	0	0	0	4
G.'Red' Berenson	4	0	0	0	4
Gary Sabourin	4	0	0	0	4
Ab McDonald	4	0	0	0	4
Tim Ecclestone	4	0	0	0	10

GOALTENDERS	GP	W	L	MIN	GA	SO	AVG
Glenn Hall	2	0	2	120	5	0	2.50
Jacques Plante	2	0	2	120	6	0	3.00

1970

BOSTON

	GP	G	A	PTS	PIM
Phil Esposito	4	2	6	8	4
John Bucyk	4	6	0	6	0
Derek Sanderson	4	3	3	6	8
Bobby Orr	4	1	4	5	6
John McKenzie	4	1	4	5	14
Ed Westfall	4	2	1	3	0
Rick Smith	4	1	3	4	2
Fred Stanfield	4	1	3	4	4
Ken Hodge	4	0	3	3	2
Wayne Cashman	4	2	0	2	8
Wayne Carleton	4	1	1	2	0
Dallas Smith	4	0	1	1	6
Don Awrey	4	0	1	1	12
Bill Speer	1	0	0	0	0
Bill Lesuk	2	0	0	0	0
Jim Lorentz	4	0	0	0	0
Don Marcotte	4	0	0	0	0
Gary Doak	4	0	0	0	2

GOALTENDER	GP	W	L	MIN	GA	SO	AVG
Gerry Cheevers	4	4	0	241	7	0	1.74

ST. LOUIS

	GP	G	A	PTS	PIM
Frank St. Marseille	4	2	1	3	2
Jim Roberts	4	1	1	2	4
Phil Goyette	4	0	2	2	2
Gary Sabourin	4	1	0	1	0
Terry Gray	4	1	0	1	0
Larry Keenan	4	1	0	1	0
G.'Red' Berenson	4	0	1	1	4
Bill McCreary	3	0	1	1	0
Ab McDonald	4	0	1	1	0
Tim Ecclestone	4	0	1	1	6
Bob Plager	4	0	1	1	6
Noel Picard	4	0	1	1	14
Barclay Plager	1	0	0	0	0
Ron Anderson	1	0	0	0	2
Norm Dennis	1	0	0	0	2
Bill Plager	2	0	0	0	0
Al Arbour	2	0	0	0	0
Andre Boudrias	3	0	0	0	2
Ray Fortin	3	0	0	0	6
Jean-Guy Talbot	4	0	0	0	0
Terry Crisp	4	0	0	0	0

GOALTENDERS	GP	W	L	MIN	GA	SO	AVG
Jacques Plante	1	0	0	24	1	0	2.50
Glenn Hall	2	0	2	121	8	0	3.97
Ernie Wakely	2	0	2	96	11	0	6.87

1971

MONTREAL

	GP	G	A	PTS	PIM
Frank Mahovlich	7	4	4	8	4
Pete Mahovlich	7	5	2	7	16
Yvan Cournoyer	7	4	2	6	6
Jacques Lemaire	7	3	1	4	11
Jean Beliveau	7	1	3	4	6
Henri Richard	7	2	1	3	2
Guy Lapointe	7	1	2	3	19
Jacques Laperriere	7	0	3	3	2
J.C. Tremblay	7	0	3	3	7
Rejean Houle	7	0	3	3	10
Terry Harper	7	0	2	2	10
John Ferguson	6	0	1	1	8
Claude Larose	2	0	0	0	0
Bob Murdoch	2	0	0	0	0
Pierre Bouchard	3	0	0	0	2
Phil Roberto	5	0	0	0	12
Leon Rochefort	6	0	0	0	6
Marc Tardif	7	0	0	0	19

GOALTENDER	GP	W	L	MIN	GA	SO	AVG
Ken Dryden	7	4	3	441	18	0	2.45

CHICAGO

	GP	G	A	PTS	PIM
Bobby Hull	7	3	6	9	8
Jim Pappin	7	4	2	6	8
Cliff Koroll	7	2	3	5	4
Stan Mikita	7	1	4	5	6
Dennis Hull	7	3	1	4	2
Lou Angotti	7	2	2	4	9
Chico Maki	7	2	1	3	4
Danny O'Shea	7	1	1	2	12
Pit Martin	6	0	2	2	4
Pat Stapleton	7	0	2	2	0
Bill White	7	0	2	2	10
Rick Foley	4	0	1	1	4
Doug Jarrett	7	0	1	1	2
Dan Maloney	2	0	0	0	4
Jerry Korab	2	0	0	0	14
Paul Shmyr	3	0	0	0	17
Gerry Pinder	5	0	0	0	2
Eric Nesterenko	7	0	0	0	8
Keith Magnuson	7	0	0	0	36

GOALTENDER	GP	W	L	MIN	GA	SO	AVG
Tony Esposito	7	3	4	441	20	1	2.72

1972

BOSTON

	GP	G	A	PTS	PIM
Ken Hodge	6	5	3	8	19
Bobby Orr	6	4	4	8	17
Phil Esposito	6	0	8	8	14
Mike Walton	6	1	4	5	6
Wayne Cashman	6	3	1	4	15
Fred Stanfield	6	1	2	3	0
John Bucyk	6	1	2	3	2
Ed Westfall	6	0	2	2	10
John McKenzie	6	0	2	2	25
Don Marcotte	5	0	1	1	6
Garnet 'Ace' Bailey	6	1	0	1	14
Derek Sanderson	6	1	0	1	26
Dallas Smith	6	0	1	1	10
Carol Vadnais	6	0	1	1	13
Ted Green	4	0	0	0	0
Don Awrey	6	0	0	0	21

GOALTENDERS	GP	W	L	MIN	GA	SO	AVG
Ed Johnston	3	2	1	180	6	0	2.00
Gerry Cheevers	3	2	1	180	10	1	3.33

NY RANGERS

	GP	G	A	PTS	PIM
Rod Gilbert	6	4	3	7	11
Brad Park	6	2	4	6	11
Ted Irvine	6	1	4	5	10
Bobby Rousseau	6	2	2	4	5
Pete Stemkowski	6	1	3	4	8
Vic Hadfield	6	1	3	4	16
Bruce MacGregor	6	1	2	3	2
Walt Tkaczuk	6	1	2	3	17
Dale Rolfe	6	0	2	2	10
Rod Seiling	6	1	1	2	6
Bill Fairbairn	6	0	2	2	0
Jim Neilson	3	0	1	1	2
Jean Ratelle	6	0	1	1	0

Ron Stewart	1	0	0	0	0
Jim Dorey	1	0	0	0	0
Ab DeMarco	1	0	0	0	0
Phil Goyette	3	0	0	0	0
Gary Doak	5	0	0	0	34
Gene Carr	6	0	0	0	9
Glen Sather	6	0	0	0	11

GOALTENDERS	GP	W	L	MIN	GA	SO	AVG
Gilles Villemure	3	1	2	180	7	0	2.33
Ed Giacomin	3	1	2	180	11	0	3.67

1973

MONTREAL	GP	G	A	PTS	PIM
Yvan Cournoyer	6	6	6	12	0
Jacques Lemaire	6	3	9	12	0
Frank Mahovlich	6	5	6	11	0
Pete Mahovlich	6	3	5	8	12
Claude Larose	6	3	4	7	2
Chuck Lefley	6	3	3	6	2
Marc Tardif	6	3	3	6	4
Guy Lapointe	6	1	3	4	8
Henri Richard	6	2	1	3	0
Rejean Houle	6	1	2	3	0
Jacques Laperriere	2	1	1	2	0
Guy Lafleur	6	0	2	2	0
Larry Robinson	6	0	2	2	2
Murray Wilson	6	0	2	2	2
Pierre Bouchard	6	1	0	1	4
Serge Savard	6	1	0	1	6
Bob Murdoch	4	0	0	0	2
Jim Roberts	6	0	0	0	6

GOALTENDER	GP	W	L	MIN	GA	SO	AVG
Ken Dryden	6	4	2	360	21	1	3.50

CHICAGO	GP	G	A	PTS	PIM
Stan Mikita	5	3	5	8	0
Pat Stapleton	6	0	8	8	4
Dennis Hull	6	3	4	7	4
Pit Martin	6	5	0	5	4
Jim Pappin	6	3	2	5	10
Ralph Backstrom	6	1	3	4	0
Bill White	6	1	3	4	2
Cliff Koroll	6	1	2	3	2
Dave Kryskow	3	2	0	2	0
Len Frig	4	1	1	2	0
Lou Angotti	6	1	1	2	0
John Marks	6	1	1	2	2
Chico Maki	6	0	2	2	0
J.P. Bordeleau	6	1	0	1	4
Dick Redmond	4	0	1	1	0
Doug Jarrett	6	0	1	1	0
Phil Russell	6	0	1	1	16
Jerry Korab	5	0	0	0	6

GOALTENDERS	GP	W	L	MIN	GA	SO	AVG
Tony Esposito	6	2	4	355	32	0	5.41
Gary Smith	1	0	0	5	0	0	0.00

1974

PHILADELPHIA	GP	G	A	PTS	PIM
Bobby Clarke	6	3	3	6	14
Rick MacLeish	6	2	3	5	4
Andre Dupont	6	2	1	3	33
Dave Schultz	6	1	2	3	38
Bill Flett	6	0	3	3	4
Don Saleski	6	0	3	3	6
Orest Kindrachuk	6	2	0	2	11
Bill Barber	6	1	1	2	2
Ross Lonsberry	6	1	1	2	2
Terry Crisp	6	1	1	2	2
Tom Bladon	6	1	1	2	21
Ed Van Impe	6	0	2	2	13
Joe Watson	6	0	2	2	16
Bill Clement	3	1	0	1	2
Simon Nolet	6	0	1	1	0
Jimmy Watson	6	0	1	1	30
Gary Dornhoefer	3	0	0	0	0
Bruce Cowick	6	0	0	0	7

GOALTENDER	GP	W	L	MIN	GA	SO	AVG
Bernie Parent	6	4	2	372	13	1	2.10

BOSTON	GP	G	A	PTS	PIM
Bobby Orr	6	3	4	7	8
Gregg Sheppard	6	2	3	5	2
Ken Hodge	6	1	4	5	6
Wayne Cashman	6	2	2	4	41
John Bucyk	6	1	3	4	2
Phil Esposito	6	2	1	3	10
Carol Vadnais	6	0	3	3	22
Andre Savard	6	1	1	2	20
Dallas Smith	6	0	2	2	8
Don Marcotte	6	1	0	1	2
Dave Forbes	6	0	1	1	2
Terry O'Reilly	6	0	1	1	25
Rich Leduc	5	0	0	0	9
Darryl Edestrand	6	0	0	0	0
Al Sims	6	0	0	0	4
Bobby Schmautz	6	0	0	0	18

GOALTENDER	GP	W	L	MIN	GA	SO	AVG
Gilles Gilbert	6	2	4	372	15	0	2.42

1975

PHILADELPHIA	GP	G	A	PTS	PIM
Bill Barber	6	2	4	6	0
Bobby Clarke	6	2	3	5	2
Reggie Leach	6	3	1	4	0
Bob Kelly	5	2	2	4	7
Rick MacLeish	6	1	3	4	2
Terry Crisp	4	0	4	4	0
Ross Lonsberry	6	2	1	3	2
Dave Schultz	6	2	0	2	13
Gary Dornhoefer	6	2	0	2	14
Don Saleski	6	1	1	2	8
Larry Goodenough	2	0	2	2	2
Orest Kindrachuk	5	0	2	2	2
Jimmy Watson	6	0	2	2	0
Ted Harris	6	0	2	2	2
Ed Van Impe	6	0	2	2	8
Bill Clement	5	1	0	1	2
Andre Dupont	6	1	0	1	10
Tom Bladon	4	0	1	1	8
Joe Watson	6	0	0	0	2

GOALTENDER	GP	W	L	MIN	GA	SO	AVG
Bernie Parent	6	4	2	378	20	1	3.17

BUFFALO	GP	G	A	PTS	PIM
Rick Martin	6	2	4	6	6
Don Luce	6	2	3	5	12
Danny Gare	6	2	1	3	4
Jerry Korab	6	2	1	3	6
Jim Lorentz	6	1	2	3	2
Rene Robert	6	1	2	3	6
Gilbert Perreault	6	1	1	2	6
Craig Ramsay	6	0	2	2	0
Jim Schoenfeld	6	0	2	2	11
Bill Hajt	6	1	0	1	2
Rick Dudley	4	0	1	1	9
Brian Spencer	6	0	1	1	4
Jocelyn Guevremont	6	0	1	1	8
Lee Fogolin Jr.	4	0	0	0	0
Peter McNab	6	0	0	0	0
Fred Stanfield	6	0	0	0	0
Larry Carriere	6	0	0	0	4

GOALTENDER	GP	W	L	MIN	GA	SO	AVG
Roger Crozier	2	1	1	118	3	0	1.53
Gerry Desjardins	5	1	3	260	16	0	3.69

1976

MONTREAL	GP	G	A	PTS	PIM
Guy Lafleur	4	2	5	7	2
Steve Shutt	4	3	3	6	0
Pete Mahovlich	4	1	4	5	4
Pierre Bouchard	4	2	0	2	2
Jacques Lemaire	4	2	0	2	2
Yvan Cournoyer	4	1	1	2	0
Larry Robinson	4	1	1	2	4
Doug Risebrough	4	0	2	2	2
Jim Roberts	4	1	0	1	0
Guy Lapointe	4	1	0	1	8
Murray Wilson	3	0	1	1	0
Bill Nyrop	4	0	1	1	2
Bob Gainey	4	0	1	1	12
Rick Chartraw	2	0	0	0	0
Mario Tremblay	2	0	0	0	7
Yvon Lambert	3	0	0	0	4
Doug Jarvis	4	0	0	0	0
Serge Savard	4	0	0	0	2

GOALTENDER	GP	W	L	MIN	GA	SO	AVG
Ken Dryden	4	4	0	240	9	0	2.25

PHILADELPHIA	GP	G	A	PTS	PIM
Reggie Leach	4	4	0	4	0
Tom Bladon	4	0	3	3	2
Bobby Clarke	4	0	3	3	4
Larry Goodenough	4	1	1	2	2
Bill Barber	4	1	1	2	6
Andre Dupont	4	1	1	2	7
Mel Bridgman	4	0	2	2	4
Ross Lonsberry	4	1	0	1	0
Dave Schultz	4	1	0	1	10
Jack McIlhargey	4	0	1	1	4
Gary Dornhoefer	4	0	1	1	6
Terry Crisp	1	0	0	0	0
Terry Murray	2	0	0	0	0
Orest Kindrachuk	4	0	0	0	0
Bob Kelly	4	0	0	0	2
Joe Watson	4	0	0	0	2
Don Saleski	4	0	0	0	4
Jimmy Watson	4	0	0	0	4

GOALTENDER	GP	W	L	MIN	GA	SO	AVG
Wayne Stephenson	4	0	4	240	14	0	3.50

1977

MONTREAL
	GP	G	A	PTS	PIM
Guy Lafleur	4	2	7	9	4
Jacques Lemaire	4	4	2	6	2
Steve Shutt	4	2	3	5	0
Yvon Lambert	4	2	2	4	6
Pete Mahovlich	4	1	3	4	4
Guy Lapointe	4	0	4	4	0
Doug Risebrough	2	2	1	3	2
Larry Robinson	4	0	3	3	6
Mario Tremblay	4	2	0	2	5
Serge Savard	4	0	2	2	0
Rick Chartraw	4	1	0	1	4
Doug Jarvis	4	0	1	1	0
Murray Wilson	4	0	1	1	6
Pierre Bouchard	4	0	1	1	6
Bill Nyrop	1	0	0	0	0
Mike Polich	1	0	0	0	0
Pierre Mondou	2	0	0	0	0
Jim Roberts	4	0	0	0	4
Bob Gainey	4	0	0	0	12

GOALTENDER	GP	W	L	MIN	GA	SO	AVG
Ken Dryden	4	4	0	240	6	1	1.50

BOSTON
	GP	G	A	PTS	PIM
Brad Park	4	1	4	5	2
Bobby Schmautz	4	2	0	2	0
Rick Middleton	4	0	2	2	0
Peter McNab	4	1	0	1	2
Gregg Sheppard	4	1	0	1	6
Terry O'Reilly	4	1	0	1	8
Jean Ratelle	4	0	1	1	0
Wayne Cashman	4	0	1	1	13
Matti Hagman	1	0	0	0	0
Earl Anderson	2	0	0	0	0
Darryl Edestrand	2	0	0	0	0
John Bucyk	2	0	0	0	0
Al Sims	2	0	0	0	0
John Wensink	3	0	0	0	4
Mike Milbury	3	0	0	0	20
Dave Forbes	4	0	0	0	0
Gary Doak	4	0	0	0	4
Stan Jonathan	4	0	0	0	4
Don Marcotte	4	0	0	0	4
Rick Smith	4	0	0	0	6

GOALTENDER	GP	W	L	MIN	GA	SO	AVG
Gerry Cheevers	4	0	4	240	16	0	4.00

1978

MONTREAL
	GP	G	A	PTS	PIM
Larry Robinson	6	2	4	6	4
Guy Lafleur	6	3	2	5	8
Steve Shutt	6	3	1	4	2
Pierre Mondou	6	1	3	4	4
Mario Tremblay	3	2	1	3	14
Yvon Lambert	6	1	2	3	2
Yvan Cournoyer	6	1	2	3	6
Jacques Lemaire	6	1	2	3	6
Serge Savard	6	0	3	3	4
Doug Jarvis	6	0	3	3	10
Rejean Houle	6	1	1	2	4
Bob Gainey	6	1	1	2	10
Bill Nyrop	5	0	2	2	6
Guy Lapointe	6	0	2	2	5
Pierre Larouche	2	1	0	1	0
Doug Risebrough	6	1	0	1	7
Brian Englbom	1	0	0	0	0
Gilles Lupien	2	0	0	0	17
Rick Chartraw	3	0	0	0	0
Pierre Bouchard	4	0	0	0	5

GOALTENDER	GP	W	L	MIN	GA	SO	AVG
Ken Dryden	6	4	2	379	13	0	2.06

BOSTON
	GP	G	A	PTS	PIM
Brad Park	6	4	1	5	8
Peter McNab	6	2	3	5	2
Gregg Sheppard	6	1	3	4	2
Don Marcotte	6	1	2	3	4
Bobby Schmautz	6	1	2	3	11
Terry O'Reilly	6	1	2	3	16
Jean Ratelle	6	0	3	3	0
Mike Milbury	6	0	3	3	10
Wayne Cashman	6	0	2	2	2
Rick Middleton	6	1	0	1	0
Gary Doak	6	1	0	1	4
Rick Smith	6	1	0	1	10
Bob Miller	6	0	1	1	9
Al Sims	3	0	0	0	0
Dennis O'Brien	5	0	0	0	6
Stan Jonathan	6	0	0	0	20
John Wensink	6	0	0	0	24

GOALTENDERS	GP	W	L	MIN	GA	SO	AVG
Gerry Cheevers	6	2	4	359	18	1	3.01
Ron Grahame	1	0	0	20	0	0	0.00

1979

MONTREAL
	GP	G	A	PTS	PIM
Jacques Lemaire	5	4	3	7	2
Steve Shutt	5	2	4	6	2
Yvon Lambert	5	2	4	6	4
Bob Gainey	5	3	2	5	6
Rejean Houle	5	1	4	5	2
Guy Lafleur	5	2	1	3	0
Serge Savard	5	1	2	3	2
Doug Risebrough	5	1	2	3	12
Mario Tremblay	5	1	1	2	4
Rick Chartraw	5	1	1	2	12
Doug Jarvis	5	0	2	2	2
Mark Napier	5	1	0	1	2
Larry Robinson	5	0	1	1	0
Pierre Larouche	1	0	0	0	0
Gilles Lupien	4	0	0	0	2
Brian Engblom	5	0	0	0	0
Pierre Mondou	5	0	0	0	2
Rod Langway	5	0	0	0	12

GOALTENDERS	GP	W	L	MIN	GA	SO	AVG
Ken Dryden	5	4	1	287	11	0	2.30
Michel Larocque	1	0	0	20	0	0	0.00

NY RANGERS
	GP	G	A	PTS	PIM
Phil Esposito	5	2	1	3	10
Pat Hickey	5	1	2	3	0
Anders Hedberg	5	1	2	3	2
Dave Maloney	5	1	2	3	10
Ron Duguay	5	2	0	2	4
Steve Vickers	5	1	1	2	0
Don Murdoch	5	1	1	2	2
Mike McEwen	5	0	2	2	4
Carol Vadnais	5	1	0	1	0
Ron Greschner	5	0	1	1	8
Bobby Sheehan	5	0	1	1	0
Walt Tkaczuk	5	0	1	1	4
Don Maloney	5	0	1	1	6
Dave Farrish	1	0	0	0	0
Lucien DeBlois	2	0	0	0	0
Ulf Nilsson	2	0	0	0	2
Pierre Plante	5	0	0	0	0
Ed Johnstone	5	0	0	0	2
Mario Marois	5	0	0	0	4

GOALTENDER	GP	W	L	MIN	GA	SO	AVG
John Davidson	5	1	4	307	19	0	3.17

1980

NY ISLANDERS
	GP	G	A	PTS	PIM
Mike Bossy	6	4	7	11	4
Denis Potvin	6	5	4	9	6
Bryan Trottier	6	4	4	8	0
Clark Gillies	6	2	6	8	13
Stefan Persson	6	3	4	7	10
Butch Goring	6	3	3	6	0
Bob Nystrom	6	3	1	4	30
Duane Sutter	6	1	3	4	28
Bob Bourne	6	0	4	4	2
John Tonelli	6	0	3	3	4
Lorne Henning	6	1	1	2	0
Garry Howatt	6	0	1	1	21
Wayne Merrick	6	0	0	0	0
Bob Lorimer	6	0	0	0	6
Ken Morrow	6	0	0	0	6
Dave Langevin	6	0	0	0	9
Gord Lane	6	0	0	0	28

GOALTENDERS	GP	W	L	MIN	GA	SO	AVG
Billy Smith	6	4	2	351	23	0	3.93
G.'Chico' Resch	1	0	0	20	2	0	6.00

PHILADELPHIA
	GP	G	A	PTS	PIM
Paul Holmgren	5	4	4	8	15
Ken Linseman	6	1	7	8	16
Bobby Clarke	6	4	3	7	2
Rick MacLeish	6	3	3	6	2
Brian Propp	6	3	3	6	4
Reggie Leach	6	1	4	5	0
Bill Barber	6	1	4	5	9
Bob Dailey	6	1	3	4	4
Mel Bridgman	6	1	3	4	53
Behn Wilson	6	0	4	4	28
Mike Busniuk	6	2	1	3	7
Tom Gorence	5	1	1	2	16
John Paddock	2	0	2	2	0
Bob Kelly	6	1	0	1	9
Jimmy Watson	5	0	1	1	9
Andre Dupont	6	0	1	1	14
Norm Barnes	1	0	0	0	4
Al Hill	6	0	0	0	2
Jack McIlhargey	6	0	0	0	25

GOALTENDERS	GP	W	L	MIN	GA	SO	AVG
Pete Peeters	5	2	3	311	20	0	3.86
Phil Myre	1	0	1	60	6	0	6.00

1981

NY ISLANDERS
	GP	G	A	PTS	PIM
Mike Bossy	5	4	4	8	0
Wayne Merrick	5	3	5	8	0
Butch Goring	5	5	2	7	0
Bryan Trottier	5	2	5	7	14
Denis Potvin	5	2	4	6	8
John Tonelli	5	0	5	5	8

	GP	G	A	PTS	PIM
Anders Kallur	5	2	2	4	4
Bob Nystrom	5	2	2	4	10
Billy Carroll	5	1	3	4	0
Mike McEwen	5	2	1	3	2
Bob Bourne	5	1	2	3	12
Clark Gillies	5	0	3	3	8
Dave Langevin	5	0	2	2	10
Ken Morrow	5	1	0	1	2
Gord Lane	5	1	0	1	18
Duane Sutter	5	0	1	1	0
Bob Lorimer	5	0	0	0	9

GOALTENDER	GP	W	L	MIN	GA	SO	AVG
Billy Smith	5	4	1	300	16	0	3.20

MINNESOTA

	GP	G	A	PTS	PIM
Steve Payne	5	5	2	7	2
Dino Ciccarelli	5	3	2	5	19
Bobby Smith	5	2	3	5	2
Craig Hartsburg	5	1	4	5	2
Steve Christoff	5	2	2	4	0
Al MacAdam	5	1	3	4	2
Brad Maxwell	4	0	4	4	9
Tim Young	2	0	3	3	0
Tom McCarthy	3	0	3	3	2
Kent-Erik Andersson	5	1	0	1	0
Brad Palmer	5	1	0	1	4
Neal Broten	5	0	1	1	2
Gordie Roberts	5	0	1	1	2
Greg Smith	5	0	1	1	6
Ken Solheim	1	0	0	0	0
Jack Carlson	2	0	0	0	0
Paul Shmyr	2	0	0	0	2
Kevin Maxwell	2	0	0	0	4
Mike Polich	3	0	0	0	0
Tom Younghans	3	0	0	0	4
Fred Barrett	3	0	0	0	6
Curt Giles	5	0	0	0	2

GOALTENDERS	GP	W	L	MIN	GA	SO	AVG
Don Beaupre	3	1	2	180	13	0	4.33
Gilles Meloche	2	0	2	120	12	0	6.00

1982

NY ISLANDERS

	GP	G	A	PTS	PIM
Denis Potvin	4	2	7	9	4
Mike Bossy	4	7	1	8	0
Bryan Trottier	4	1	6	7	10
Stefan Persson	4	0	5	5	4
Clark Gillies	4	2	1	3	8
Butch Goring	4	1	2	3	2
Bob Nystrom	4	2	0	2	21
Billy Carroll	4	1	1	2	2
Bob Bourne	4	1	1	2	17
Brent Sutter	4	0	2	2	0
John Tonelli	4	0	2	2	4
Duane Sutter	4	1	0	1	32
Tomas Jonsson	2	0	1	1	2
Wayne Merrick	4	0	1	1	0
Mike McEwen	2	0	0	0	0
Anders Kallur	4	0	0	0	0
Ken Morrow	4	0	0	0	0
Dave Langevin	4	0	0	0	0
Gord Lane	4	0	0	0	22

GOALTENDER	GP	W	L	MIN	GA	SO	AVG
Billy Smith	4	4	0	260	10	1	2.31

VANCOUVER

	GP	G	A	PTS	PIM
Thomas Gradin	4	3	2	5	2
Lars Molin	4	0	4	4	0
Gerry Minor	4	1	2	3	0
Dave Williams	4	0	3	3	14
Curt Fraser	4	0	3	3	28
Ivan Boldirev	4	2	0	2	2
Stan Smyl	4	2	0	2	19
Lars Lindgren	4	1	0	1	2
Jim Nill	3	1	0	1	6
Doug Halward	4	0	1	1	4
Colin Campbell	4	0	1	1	26
Per-Olov Brasar	1	0	0	0	0
Garth Butcher	1	0	0	0	0
Blair MacDonald	1	0	0	0	0
Ivan Hlinka	2	0	0	0	0
Gary Lupul	2	0	0	0	0
Marc Crawford	3	0	0	0	0
Anders Eldebrink	3	0	0	0	2
Ron Delorme	4	0	0	0	4
Neil Belland	4	0	0	0	4
Harold Snepsts	4	0	0	0	16
Darcy Rota	4	0	0	0	19

GOALTENDER	GP	W	L	MIN	GA	SO	AVG
Richard Brodeur	4	0	4	260	17	0	3.92

1983

NY ISLANDERS

	GP	G	A	PTS	PIM
Duane Sutter	4	2	5	7	0
Ken Morrow	4	3	2	5	2
Brent Sutter	4	3	2	5	10
Mike Bossy	3	2	2	4	0
Bob Bourne	4	2	2	4	6
Bryan Trottier	4	1	3	4	4
Denis Potvin	4	0	3	3	4
Bob Nystrom	4	1	1	2	2
Anders Kallur	4	1	1	2	4
Tomas Jonsson	4	1	1	2	8
Stefan Persson	4	0	2	2	4
John Tonelli	4	1	0	1	0
Dave Langevin	4	0	1	1	0
Clark Gillies	4	0	1	1	6
Greg Gilbert	1	0	0	0	0
Butch Goring	4	0	0	0	0
Billy Carroll	4	0	0	0	0
Wayne Merrick	4	0	0	0	0
Gord Lane	4	0	0	0	2

GOALTENDER	GP	W	L	MIN	GA	SO	AVG
Billy Smith	4	4	0	240	6	1	1.50

EDMONTON

	GP	G	A	PTS	PIM
Wayne Gretzky	4	0	4	4	0
Jari Kurri	4	3	0	3	2
Glenn Anderson	4	1	1	2	11
Lee Fogolin Jr.	4	0	2	2	0
Mark Messier	4	1	0	1	2
Dave Semenko	4	1	0	1	0
Charlie Huddy	4	0	1	1	0
Tom Roulston	4	0	1	1	0
Paul Coffey	4	0	1	1	4
Ray Cote	4	0	0	0	0
Willy Lindstrom	4	0	0	0	0
Randy Gregg	4	0	0	0	0
Pat Hughes	4	0	0	0	2
Kevin Lowe	4	0	0	0	2
Don Jackson	4	0	0	0	4
Ken Linseman	4	0	0	0	4
Dave Hunter	4	0	0	0	8
Dave Lumley	4	0	0	0	9

GOALTENDER	GP	W	L	MIN	GA	SO	AVG
Andy Moog	4	0	4	240	15	0	3.75

1984

EDMONTON

	GP	G	A	PTS	PIM
Wayne Gretzky	5	4	3	7	4
Jari Kurri	5	1	5	6	2
Mark Messier	5	3	1	4	7
Paul Coffey	5	2	2	4	0
Kevin McClelland	5	2	2	4	16
Glenn Anderson	5	1	3	4	8
Willy Lindstrom	5	2	1	3	0
Dave Semenko	5	1	2	3	4
Charlie Huddy	5	0	3	3	4
Pat Hughes	5	0	3	3	4
Dave Lumley	5	1	1	2	17
Ken Linseman	5	1	1	2	26
Pat Conacher	2	1	0	1	0
Randy Gregg	5	1	0	1	2
Kevin Lowe	5	1	0	1	4
Dave Hunter	3	0	1	1	6
Lee Fogolin Jr.	5	0	1	1	6
Jaroslav Pouzar	5	0	0	0	6
Don Jackson	5	0	0	0	13

GOALTENDERS	GP	W	L	MIN	GA	SO	AVG
Andy Moog	3	2	0	128	4	0	1.88
Grant Fuhr	3	2	1	172	8	1	2.79

NY ISLANDERS

	GP	G	A	PTS	PIM
Clark Gillies	5	5	3	8	0
Pat Flatley	5	1	3	4	8
Bryan Trottier	5	2	2	4	2
Pat LaFontaine	5	2	1	3	0
Brent Sutter	5	1	2	3	6
Mike Bossy	5	0	3	3	0
Greg Gilbert	5	1	1	2	26
Stefan Persson	4	0	2	2	2
Paul Boutilier	5	0	2	2	0
Anders Kallur	5	0	1	1	0
Ken Morrow	5	0	1	1	4
Denis Potvin	5	0	1	1	6
Billy Carroll	1	0	0	0	0
Mats Hallin	2	0	0	0	0
Bob Nystrom	2	0	0	0	4
Dave Langevin	2	0	0	0	5
Gord Dineen	3	0	0	0	24
Butch Goring	5	0	0	0	0
John Tonelli	5	0	0	0	4
Tomas Jonsson	5	0	0	0	8
Duane Sutter	5	0	0	0	26

GOALTENDERS	GP	W	L	MIN	GA	SO	AVG
Billy Smith	5	1	3	245	17	0	4.16
Roland Melanson	3	0	1	55	3	0	3.27

1985

EDMONTON

	GP	G	A	PTS	PIM
Wayne Gretzky	5	7	4	11	0
Paul Coffey	5	3	8	11	6
Jari Kurri	5	1	6	7	0
Mark Messier	5	2	4	6	6
Charlie Huddy	5	1	5	6	6
Mike Krushelnyski	5	2	2	4	4
Willy Lindstrom	5	3	0	3	2
Glenn Anderson	5	1	1	2	12
Dave Hunter	5	1	0	1	25
Randy Gregg	4	0	1	1	2

166 • FINAL SERIES SCORING, 1927-1995

	GP	G	A	PTS	PIM
Kevin McClelland	5	0	1	1	41
Jaroslav Pouzar	1	0	0	0	0
Larry Melnyk	1	0	0	0	0
Dave Lumley	1	0	0	0	2
Billy Carroll	2	0	0	0	0
Esa Tikkanen	3	0	0	0	4
Pat Hughes	4	0	0	0	2
Dave Semenko	4	0	0	0	14
Mark Napier	5	0	0	0	0
Kevin Lowe	5	0	0	0	4
Lee Fogolin Jr.	5	0	0	0	8
Don Jackson	5	0	0	0	35

GOALTENDER	GP	W	L	MIN	GA	SO	AVG
Grant Fuhr	5	4	1	300	13	0	2.60

PHILADELPHIA

	GP	G	A	PTS	PIM
Derrick Smith	5	1	4	5	0
Dave Poulin	5	1	3	4	4
Rich Sutter	3	3	0	3	4
Brian Propp	5	2	1	3	0
Tim Kerr	3	2	1	3	9
Murray Craven	5	1	2	3	4
Ron Sutter	5	1	2	3	6
Todd Bergen	4	1	1	2	0
Mark Howe	5	1	1	2	0
Lindsay Carson	3	0	2	2	2
Doug Crossman	5	0	2	2	12
Rick Tocchet	5	0	2	2	14
Ilkka Sinisalo	5	1	0	1	0
Peter Zezel	5	0	1	1	4
Brad Marsh	5	0	1	1	43
Len Hachborn	1	0	0	0	0
Ray Allison	1	0	0	0	2
Dave Brown	1	0	0	0	19
Thomas Eriksson	4	0	0	0	0
Miroslav Dvorak	5	0	0	0	2
Joe Paterson	5	0	0	0	19
Ed Hospodar	5	0	0	0	34

GOALTENDERS	GP	W	L	MIN	GA	SO	AVG
Pelle Lindbergh	4	1	3	185	11	0	3.57
Bob Froese	3	0	1	115	9	0	4.70

1986

MONTREAL

	GP	G	A	PTS	PIM
Mats Naslund	5	3	4	7	0
Bobby Smith	5	2	2	4	8
Chris Chelios	5	1	3	4	19
Gaston Gingras	4	2	1	3	0
David Maley	5	1	2	3	2
Claude Lemieux	5	1	2	3	31
Larry Robinson	5	0	3	3	15
Guy Carbonneau	5	0	3	3	23
Brian Skrudland	5	2	0	2	32
Mike Lalor	5	0	2	2	19
Mike McPhee	5	0	2	2	24
Kjell Dahlin	4	1	0	1	0
Rick Green	5	1	0	1	0
Bob Gainey	5	1	0	1	2
Ryan Walter	5	0	1	1	2
Stephane Richer	1	0	0	0	0
Steve Rooney	1	0	0	0	0
Serge Boisvert	2	0	0	0	0
Chris Nilan	3	0	0	0	49
Craig Ludwig	5	0	0	0	14
John Kordic	5	0	0	0	15

GOALTENDER	GP	W	L	MIN	GA	SO	AVG
Patrick Roy	5	4	1	301	12	1	2.39

CALGARY

	GP	G	A	PTS	PIM
Dan Quinn	5	1	4	5	4
Jim Peplinski	5	1	3	4	37
Al MacInnis	5	0	4	4	8
Joe Mullen	4	2	1	3	4
Lanny McDonald	5	2	1	3	6
Joel Otto	5	1	2	3	12
Steve Bozek	4	2	0	2	19
John Tonelli	5	2	0	2	15
Paul Reinhart	5	1	1	2	2
Hakan Loob	5	0	2	2	2
Doug Risebrough	5	1	0	1	12
Nick Fotiu	2	0	1	1	10
Paul Baxter	4	0	1	1	17
Jamie Macoun	5	0	1	1	4
Tim Hunter	5	0	1	1	43
Brian Bradley	1	0	0	0	0
Yves Courteau	1	0	0	0	0
Brett Hull	2	0	0	0	0
Colin Patterson	2	0	0	0	0
Mike Eaves	2	0	0	0	2
Perry Berezan	2	0	0	0	4
Terry Johnson	2	0	0	0	12
Robin Bartel	4	0	0	0	12
Neil Sheehy	5	0	0	0	31

GOALTENDERS	GP	W	L	MIN	GA	SO	AVG
Mike Vernon	5	1	4	260	14	0	3.23
Rejean Lemelin	1	0	0	41	1	0	1.46

1987

EDMONTON

	GP	G	A	PTS	PIM
Wayne Gretzky	7	2	9	11	2
Jari Kurri	7	5	4	9	4
Paul Coffey	7	2	4	6	14
Glenn Anderson	7	4	1	5	14
Mark Mesier	7	2	3	5	10
Kevin Lowe	7	2	1	3	4
Randy Gregg	7	1	2	3	0
Mike Krushelnyski	7	1	1	2	6
Craig MacTavish	7	0	2	2	6
Charlie Huddy	7	0	2	2	10
Kevin McClelland	7	1	0	1	4
Marty McSorley	7	1	0	1	10
Jaroslav Pouzar	3	0	1	1	2
Craig Muni	5	0	1	1	0
Kent Nilsson	7	0	1	1	0
Dave Hunter	7	0	1	1	4
Kelly Buchberger	3	0	0	0	5
Steve Smith	3	0	0	0	0
Reijo Ruotsalainen	7	0	0	0	4
Esa Tikkanen	7	0	0	0	6

GOALTENDER	GP	W	L	MIN	GA	SO	AVG
Grant Fuhr	7	4	3	427	17	0	2.39

PHILADELPHIA

	GP	G	A	PTS	PIM
Brian Propp	7	4	5	9	0
Pelle Eklund	7	1	7	8	0
Rick Tocchet	7	3	4	7	24
Ron Sutter	7	0	4	4	6
Brad McCrimmon	7	2	1	3	10
Scott Mellanby	7	1	2	3	4
Doug Crossman	7	1	2	3	6
Murray Craven	6	2	0	2	2
Peter Zezel	7	1	1	2	2
Brad Marsh	7	0	2	2	2
J.J. Daigneault	5	1	0	1	0
Lindsay Carson	6	1	0	1	0
Derrick Smith	7	1	0	1	10
Mark Howe	7	0	1	1	0
Kjell Samuelsson	7	0	1	1	10
Dave Brown	7	0	1	1	11
Tim Tookey	1	0	0	0	0
Don Nachbaur	1	0	0	0	0
Daryl Stanley	4	0	0	0	2
Ilkka Sinisalo	5	0	0	0	2
Dave Poulin	7	0	0	0	8

GOALTENDER	GP	W	L	MIN	GA	SO	AVG
Ron Hextall	7	3	4	427	22	0	3.09

1988 includes suspended game, May 24, 1988

EDMONTON

	GP	G	A	PTS	PIM
Wayne Gretzky	5	3	10	13	0
Esa Tikkanen	5	6	3	9	18
Glenn Anderson	5	3	3	6	4
Jari Kurri	5	1	4	5	4
Craig Simpson	5	3	1	4	10
Steve Smith	5	0	4	4	2
Mike Krushelnyski	5	1	2	3	6
Kevin McClelland	5	1	2	3	26
Mark Messier	5	1	2	3	4
Randy Gregg	5	0	3	3	4
Kevin Lowe	5	0	2	2	4
Craig Muni	5	0	2	2	0
Keith Acton	5	1	0	1	0
Normand Lacombe	5	1	0	1	4
Charlie Huddy	1	0	0	0	0
Jeff Beukeboom	4	0	0	0	0
Geoff Courtnall	5	0	0	0	0
Craig MacTavish	5	0	0	0	2
Marty McSorley	5	0	0	0	4

GOALTENDER	GP	W	L	MIN	GA	SO	AVG
Grant Fuhr	5	4	0	277	12	0	2.60

BOSTON

	GP	G	A	PTS	PIM
Ken Linseman	5	2	2	4	6
Glen Wesley	5	2	2	4	0
Cam Neely	5	2	1	3	4
Ray Bourque	5	0	3	3	6
Steve Kasper	5	2	0	2	2
Randy Burridge	5	1	1	2	2
Bob Joyce	5	1	1	2	0
Moe Lemay	5	1	1	2	6
Craig Janney	5	0	2	2	0
Bob Sweeney	5	0	2	2	2
Greg Hawgood	2	1	0	1	0
Greg Johnston	1	0	1	1	0
Keith Crowder	5	0	1	1	10
Gord Kluzak	5	0	1	1	4
Rick Middleton	5	0	1	1	0
Nevin Markwart	1	0	0	0	2
Tom McCarthy	1	0	0	0	0
Willi Plett	2	0	0	0	4
Reed Larson	2	0	0	0	2
Jay Miller	3	0	0	0	24
Allen Pedersen	4	0	0	0	6
Michael Thelven	4	0	0	0	6
Bill O'Dwyer	5	0	0	0	0

GOALTENDERS	GP	W	L	MIN	GA	SO	AVG
Andy Moog	3	0	2	157	11	0	4.20
Rejean Lemelin	2	0	2	120	8	0	4.00

1989

CALGARY	GP	G	A	PTS	PIM
Al MacInnis	6	5	4	9	18
Joe Mullen	6	5	3	8	4
Joel Otto	6	2	6	8	2
Doug Gilmour	6	4	3	7	6
Theoren Fleury	6	1	1	2	2
Joe Nieuwendyk	6	1	1	2	2
Colin Patterson	6	1	1	2	16
Tim Hunter	4	0	2	2	6
Jim Peplinski	4	0	2	2	10
Jamie Macoun	6	0	2	2	8
Rob Ramage	6	0	2	2	10
Lanny McDonald	3	1	0	1	2
Mark Hunter	4	0	1	1	12
Hakan Loob	6	0	1	1	0
Brian MacLellan	6	0	1	1	4
Brad McCrimmon	6	0	1	1	6
Dana Murzyn	6	0	1	1	8
Jiri Hrdina	3	0	0	0	0
Ric Nattress	6	0	0	0	12
Gary Roberts	6	0	0	0	8

GOALTENDER	GP	W	L	MIN	GA	SO	AVG
Mike Vernon	6	4	2	397	16	0	2.42

MONTREAL	GP	G	A	PTS	PIM
Chris Chelios	6	1	6	7	10
Bobby Smith	6	3	2	5	20
Mike McPhee	6	1	3	4	4
Claude Lemieux	4	2	1	3	18
Larry Robinson	6	2	1	3	4
Mike Keane	6	1	2	3	4
Mats Naslund	6	1	2	3	4
Brian Skrudland	6	0	3	3	18
Petr Svoboda	6	0	3	3	8
Russ Courtnall	6	2	0	2	12
Stephane Richer	6	1	1	2	10
Rick Green	6	1	0	1	2
Ryan Walter	6	1	0	1	4
Shayne Corson	6	0	1	1	18
Bob Gainey	6	0	1	1	4
Brent Gilchrist	2	0	0	0	4
Guy Carbonneau	6	0	0	0	6
Eric Desjardins	6	0	0	0	2
Craig Ludwig	6	0	0	0	8

GOALTENDER	GP	W	L	MIN	GA	SO	AVG
Patrick Roy	6	2	4	395	17	0	2.58

1990

EDMONTON	GP	G	A	PTS	PIM
Craig Simpson	5	4	4	8	6
Jari Kurri	5	3	5	8	2
Glenn Anderson	5	4	3	7	6
Esa Tikkanen	5	3	2	5	10
Mark Messier	5	0	5	5	6
Joe Murphy	5	2	2	4	4
Steve Smith	5	1	2	3	13
Mark Lamb	5	0	3	3	2
Adam Graves	5	2	0	2	0
Craig MacTavish	5	0	2	2	2
Reijo Ruotsalainen	5	0	2	2	2
Petr Klima	5	1	0	1	2
Martin Gelinas	5	0	1	1	2
Randy Gregg	5	0	1	1	0
Kelly Buchberger	5	0	0	0	2
Charlie Huddy	5	0	0	0	4
Kevin Lowe	5	0	0	0	0
Craig Muni	5	0	0	0	2

GOALTENDER	GP	W	L	MIN	GA	SO	AVG
Bill Ranford	5	4	1	355	8	0	1.35

BOSTON	GP	G	A	PTS	PIM
Ray Bourque	5	3	2	5	6
Cam Neely	5	0	4	4	10
Greg Hawgood	5	1	2	3	4
Randy Burridge	5	0	2	2	2
Lyndon Byers	2	1	0	1	0
John Byce	3	1	0	1	0
Greg Johnston	4	0	1	1	4
John Carter	5	1	0	1	19
Bob Sweeney	5	0	1	1	7
Don Sweeney	5	0	1	1	6
Peter Douris	1	0	0	0	0
Andy Brickley	2	0	0	0	0
Dave Poulin	2	0	0	0	0
Jim Wiemer	2	0	0	0	0
Bob Gould	4	0	0	0	0
Bob Carpenter	5	0	0	0	2
Dave Christian	5	0	0	0	0
Garry Galley	5	0	0	0	4
Craig Janney	5	0	0	0	0
Allen Pedersen	5	0	0	0	2
Brian Propp	5	0	0	0	0
Glen Wesley	5	0	0	0	2

GOALTENDER	GP	W	L	MIN	GA	SO	AVG
Andy Moog	5	1	4	319	16	0	3.01
Rejean Lemelin	1	0	0	36	4	0	6.67

1991

PITTSBURGH	GP	G	A	PTS	PIM
Mario Lemieux	5	5	7	12	6
Larry Murphy	6	1	9	10	6
Joe Mullen	6	3	5	8	0
Kevin Stevens	6	4	3	7	27
Ron Francis	6	3	3	6	6
Jaromir Jagr	6	0	5	5	0
Phil Bourque	6	2	2	4	4
Bob Errey	6	2	1	3	8
Mark Recchi	6	2	1	3	8
Ulf Samuelsson	6	2	1	3	12
Bryan Trottier	6	1	2	3	14
Peter Taglianetti	5	0	3	3	8
Scott Young	1	1	1	2	0
Paul Coffey	5	0	2	2	0
Jim Paek	5	1	0	1	2
Troy Loney	6	1	0	1	26
Jiri Hrdina	2	0	0	0	0
Grant Jennings	2	0	0	0	2
Randy Gilhen	5	0	0	0	12
Gordie Roberts	6	0	0	0	23
Paul Stanton	6	0	0	0	8

GOALTENDER	GP	W	L	MIN	GA	SO	AVG
Tom Barrasso	6	3	2	319	13	1	2.45
Frank Pietrangelo	1	1	0	40	3	0	4.50

MINNESOTA	GP	G	A	PTS	PIM
Dave Gagner	6	4	2	6	14
Neal Broten	6	3	1	4	2
Ulf Dahlen	6	2	2	4	0
Mike Modano	6	2	2	4	6
Bobby Smith	6	1	3	4	4
Brian Propp	6	1	3	4	4
Stewart Gavin	6	0	3	3	2
Gaetan Duchesne	6	1	1	2	6
Brian Bellows	6	0	2	2	16
Shawn Chambers	6	0	2	2	6
Marc Bureau	6	1	0	1	8
Chris Dahlquist	6	0	1	1	4
Jim Johnson	6	0	1	1	10
Mark Tinordi	6	0	1	1	15
Perry Berezan	1	0	0	0	0
Doug Smail	1	0	0	0	0
Shane Churla	5	0	0	0	4
Basil McRae	5	0	0	0	26
Brian Glynn	6	0	0	0	6
Neil Wilkinson	6	0	0	0	2

GOALTENDER	GP	W	L	MIN	GA	SO	AVG
Jon Casey	6	2	3	290	21	0	4.34
Brian Hayward	2	0	1	67	6	0	5.37

1992

PITTSBURGH	GP	G	A	PTS	PIM
Rick Tocchet	4	2	6	8	2
Mario Lemieux	4	5	2	7	0
Kevin Stevens	4	2	3	5	0
Ron Francis	4	1	2	3	0
Larry Murphy	4	1	2	3	2
Jim Paek	4	0	3	3	2
Jaromir Jagr	4	2	0	2	2
Shawn McEachern	4	0	2	2	0
Bob Errey	3	1	0	1	0
Phil Bourque	4	0	1	1	0
Troy Loney	4	0	1	1	0
Kjell Samuelsson	4	0	1	1	2
Paul Stanton	4	0	1	1	20
Dave Michayluk	1	0	0	0	0
Jiri Hrdina	3	0	0	0	0
Jock Callender	4	0	0	0	0
Gordie Roberts	4	0	0	0	8
Ulf Samuelsson	4	0	0	0	2
Bryan Trottier	4	0	0	0	2

GOALTENDER	GP	W	L	MIN	GA	SO	AVG
Tom Barrasso	4	4	0	240	10	1	2.50

CHICAGO	GP	G	A	PTS	PIM
Chris Chelios	4	1	4	5	19
Dirk Graham	4	4	0	4	0
Brian Noonan	4	0	3	3	2
Jeremy Roenick	4	2	0	2	0
Brent Sutter	4	1	1	2	0
Greg Gilbert	3	0	2	2	10
Michel Goulet	4	1	0	1	2
Bryan Marchment	4	1	0	1	2
Stu Grimson	2	1	0	1	0
Rod Buskas	3	0	1	1	0
Steve Larmer	4	0	1	1	2
Jocelyn Lemieux	4	0	1	1	0
Stephane Matteau	4	0	1	1	0
Cam Russell	1	0	0	0	0
Rob Brown	3	0	0	0	2
Mike Peluso	3	0	0	0	4
Mike Hudson	4	0	0	0	2
Frantisek Kucera	4	0	0	0	0
Steve Smith	4	0	0	0	4
Igor Kravchuk	4	0	0	0	2

GOALTENDER	GP	W	L	MIN	GA	SO	AVG
Ed Belfour	4	0	3	187	11	0	3.53
Dominik Hasek	1	0	1	53	4	0	4.53

FINAL SERIES SCORING, 1927-1995

1993

MONTREAL

	GP	G	A	PTS	PIM
Eric Desjardins	5	3	1	4	6
John LeClair	5	2	2	4	0
Kirk Muller	5	2	2	4	6
Vincent Damphousse	5	1	3	4	8
Stephan Lebeau	5	1	2	3	4
Mike Keane	4	0	3	3	2
Paul DiPietro	5	2	0	2	0
Gilbert Dionne	5	1	1	2	4
Brian Bellows	5	1	1	2	4
Ed Ronan	5	1	1	2	6
Mathieu Schneider	5	1	1	2	8
Lyle Odelein	5	0	2	2	6
Kevin Haller	3	0	1	1	0
Benoit Brunet	5	0	1	1	2
Guy Carbonneau	5	0	1	1	0
Gary Leeman	5	0	1	1	2
Donald Dufresne	1	0	0	0	0
Sean Hill	1	0	0	0	0
Denis Savard	1	0	0	0	0
Patrice Brisebois	5	0	0	0	8
J.J. Daigneault	5	0	0	0	6

GOALTENDER	GP	W	L	MIN	GA	SO	AVG
Patrick Roy	5	4	1	315	11	0	2.10

LOS ANGELES

	GP	G	A	PTS	PIM
Wayne Gretzky	5	2	5	7	2
Luc Robitaille	5	3	2	5	4
Tony Granato	5	1	3	4	10
Marty McSorley	5	2	0	2	16
Dave Taylor	3	1	1	2	6
Mike Donnelly	5	1	1	2	0
Tomas Sandstrom	5	0	2	2	4
Pat Conacher	5	1	0	1	2
Jari Kurri	5	1	0	1	2
Jimmy Carson	2	0	1	1	0
Mark Hardy	4	0	1	1	4
Rob Blake	5	0	1	1	18
Alexei Zhitnik	5	0	1	1	4
Lonnie Loach	1	0	0	0	0
Charlie Huddy	4	0	0	0	4
Corey Millen	5	0	0	0	2
Warren Rychel	5	0	0	0	2
Gary Shuchuk	5	0	0	0	0
Darryl Sydor	5	0	0	0	4
Tim Watters	5	0	0	0	4

GOALTENDER	GP	W	L	MIN	GA	SO	GAA
Kelly Hrudey	5	1	4	316	15	0	2.85

1994

NY RANGERS

	GP	G	A	PTS	PIM
Brian Leetch	7	5	6	11	.4
Alexei Kovalev	7	4	3	7	2
Mark Messier	7	2	5	7	17
Sergei Zubov	6	1	5	6	0
Steve Larmer	7	4	0	4	2
Adam Graves	7	1	3	4	4
Glenn Anderson	7	2	1	3	4
Doug Lidster	7	2	0	2	10
Jeff Beukeboom	7	0	2	2	25
Sergei Nemchinov	7	0	2	2	2
Greg Gilbert	7	0	1	1	2
Craig MacTavish	7	0	1	1	6
Stephane Matteau	7	0	1	1	6
Brian Noonan	7	0	1	1	0
Esa Tikkanen	7	0	1	1	12
Nick Kypreos	1	0	0	0	0
Alex. Karpovtsev	2	0	0	0	0
Joe Kocur	6	0	0	0	2
Kevin Lowe	6	0	0	0	6
Jay Wells	7	0	0	0	8

GOALTENDER	GP	W	L	MIN	GA	SO	AVG
Mike Richter	7	4	3	439	19	0	2.60

VANCOUVER

	GP	G	A	PTS	PIM
Pavel Bure	7	3	5	8	15
Cliff Ronning	7	1	6	7	6
Geoff Courtnall	7	4	1	5	11
Trevor Linden	7	3	2	5	6
Jeff Brown	7	3	1	4	8
Bret Hedican	7	1	3	4	4
Jyrki Lumme	7	0	4	4	6
Greg Adams	7	1	2	3	2
Nathan Lafayette	7	0	3	3	0
Sergio Momesso	7	1	1	2	17
Murray Craven	7	0	2	2	4
Dave Babych	7	1	0	1	2
Martin Gelinas	7	1	0	1	4
Shawn Antoski	7	0	1	1	8
Gerald Diduck	7	0	1	1	6
Brian Glynn	7	0	1	1	0
Tim Hunter	7	0	0	0	18
John McIntyre	7	0	0	0	6

GOALTENDER	GP	W	L	MIN	GA	SO	AVG
Kirk McLean	7	3	4	437	20	0	2.75

1995

NEW JERSEY

	GP	G	A	PTS	PIM
Neal Broten	4	3	3	6	4
John MacLean	4	1	4	5	0
Stephane Richer	4	2	2	4	0
Scott Niedermayer	4	1	3	4	0
Bill Guerin	4	0	4	4	12
Shawn Chambers	4	2	1	3	0
Bruce Driver	4	1	2	3	0
Claude Lemieux	4	2	0	2	4
Jim Dowd	1	1	1	2	2
Sergei Brylin	3	1	1	2	4
Bobby Holik	4	1	1	2	8
Tom Chorske	3	0	2	2	0
Tommy Albelin	4	0	2	2	2
Scott Stevens	4	0	2	2	4
Randy McKay	4	1	0	1	0
Brian Rolston	2	0	1	1	0
Bob Carpenter	4	0	1	1	2
Valeri Zelepukin	3	0	0	0	4
Mike Peluso	4	0	0	0	0
Ken Daneyko	4	0	0	0	6

GOALTENDER	GP	W	L	MIN	GA	SO	AVG
Martin Brodeur	4	4	0	206	7	0	1.75

DETROIT

	GP	G	A	PTS	PIM
Sergei Fedorov	4	3	2	5	0
Doug Brown	4	0	3	3	2
Viacheslav Fetisov	4	0	3	3	0
Dino Ciccarelli	4	1	1	2	6
Paul Coffey	4	1	1	2	0
Nicklas Lidstrom	4	0	2	2	0
Steve Yzerman	4	1	0	1	0
Vyacheslav Kozlov	4	1	0	1	0
Martin Lapointe	2	0	1	1	8
Ray Sheppard	3	0	1	1	0
Kris Draper	4	0	0	0	4
Bob Errey	4	0	0	0	4
Bob Rouse	4	0	0	0	0
Vlad. Konstantinov	4	0	0	0	8
Darren McCarty	4	0	0	0	4
Keith Primeau	3	0	0	0	8
Shawn Burr	2	0	0	0	0
Stu Grimson	2	0	0	0	2
Mark Howe	2	0	0	0	0
Mike Krushelnyski	2	0	0	0	0
Mike Ramsey	2	0	0	0	0
Tim Taylor	2	0	0	0	2

GOALTENDER	GP	W	L	MIN	GA	SO	AVG
Mike Vernon	4	0	4	240	14	0	4.08
Chris Osgood	1	0	0	32	1	0	1.88

PLAYERS ON STANLEY CUP CHAMPIONSHIP TEAMS, 1893-1995

A TOTAL OF 914 PLAYERS HAVE SKATED FOR STANLEY CUP CHAMPIONSHIP TEAMS since the trophy was first awarded to the Montreal Amateur Athletic Association (MAAA) hockey club in 1893. Of the 914, 494 players (54.0%) have won only one Cup in each of their careers, while 420 (46.0%) have won on two or more occasions.

Stanley Cups	1	2	3	4	5	6	7	8	9	10	11
Players	494	227	68	71	30	15	2	3	1	2	1
Pct.	54.0	24.8	7.4	7.8	3.3	1.6					

Henri Richard holds the record for playing on the largest number of Stanley Cup-winning teams at 11. During Richard's 20-year NHL career with the Montreal Canadiens from 1955-56 to 1974-75, "The Pocket Rocket" never played more than four consecutive seasons without earning a new Stanley Cup ring.

Jean Beliveau and Yvan Cournoyer of the Canadiens share second place behind Richard with 10 Cups apiece, and Montreal's Claude Provost ranks third with nine. Red Kelly, Maurice Richard and Jacques Lemaire are tied with eight, while Serge Savard and Jean-Guy Talbot have seven each.

Kelly, Dick Duff, Frank Mahovlich and Bryan Trottier are the only four players in history to win multiple Stanley Cups with two different teams. Duff won four times with Montreal and twice with Toronto, Mahovlich won four with Toronto and two with Montreal, while Trottier won four with the New York Islanders and two with Pittsburgh. Of the 420 players to win more than one Stanley Cup, 335 won with the same team every time. 79 players won with two teams, while five won with three and one won with four.

Jack Marshall owns the record for playing with four different teams to win the Stanley Cup. Marshall played on championship teams with the 1901 Winnipeg Vics, 1902 Montreal Maroons, 1907 and 1910 Montreal Wanderers and 1914 Toronto Blueshirts.

Five players skated for three different Stanley Cup winning franchises in their careers. Frank Foyston and Jack Walker won three Cups in their careers with three different clubs, while Larry Hillman, Harry Holmes and Gordon Pettinger won four Cups with three separate teams.

A

Abel, Clarence 'Taffy' — NY Rangers 28; Chicago 34
Abel, Sid — Detroit 43,50,52
Acton, Keith — Edmonton 88
Adams, Jack — Toronto 18; Ottawa 27
Aitkenhead, Andy — NY Rangers 33
Albelin, Tommy — New Jersey 95
Allen, 'Bones' — Ottawa 05
Allen, Keith — Detroit 54
Anderson, Doug — Montreal 53
Anderson, Glenn — Edmonton 84,85,87,88,90; NY Rangers 94
Anderson, Jocko — Victoria 25
Andrews, Lloyd — Toronto 22
Apps, Syl — Toronto 42,47,48
Arbour, Al — Chicago 61; Toronto 62,64
Arbour, Amos — Montreal 16
Armitage, J.C. — Winnipeg Vics 1896
Armstrong, George — Toronto 62,63,64,67
Arnold, Josh — Mtl Wanderers 06
Ashbee, Barry — Philadelphia 74
Asmundson, Ossie — NY Rangers 33
Aurie, Larry — Detroit 36,37
Awrey, Don — Boston 70,72

B

Babando, Pete — Detroit 50
Backor, Peter — Toronto 45
Backstrom, Ralph — Montreal 59,60,65,66,68,69
Bailey, Garnet 'Ace' — Boston 72
Bailey, Irvine 'Ace' — Toronto 32
Bain, Dan — Winnipeg Vics 1896, 01
Balfour, Earl — Chicago 61
Balfour, Murray — Chicago 61
Balon, Dave — Montreal 65,66
Barber, Bill — Philadelphia 74,75
Barilko, Bill — Toronto 47,48,49,51
Barlow, Billy — Mtl AAA 1893,94
Barrasso, Tom — Pittsburgh 91,92
Barry, Marty — Detroit 36,37
Bathgate, Andy — Toronto 64
Bauer, Bobby — Boston 39,41
Baun, Bob — Toronto 62,63,64,67
Beaudro, Roxy — Kenora 07
Beliveau, Jean — Montreal 56,57,58,59,60,65, 66,68,69,71

170 • PLAYERS ON STANLEY CUP CHAMPIONSHIP TEAMS

Name	Team(s)
Bell, Billy	Montreal 24
Bellingham, Billy	Mtl AAA 02
Bellows, Brian	Montreal 93
Benedict, Clint	Ottawa 20,21,23; Mtl Maroons 26
Benoit, Joe	Montreal 46
Bentley, Max	Toronto 48,49,51
Berenson, Gordon 'Red'	Montreal 65,66
Berlinquette, Louis	Montreal 16
Beukeboom, Jeff	Edmonton 87,88,90; NY Rangers 94
Blachford, Cecil	Mtl Wanderers 06,07,08,10
Black, Steve	Detroit 50
Bladon, Tom	Philadelphia 74,75
Blair, Andy	Toronto 32
Blake, Hector 'Toe'	Mtl Maroons 35; Montreal 44,46
Blinco, Russ	Mtl Maroons 35
Bodnar, Gus	Toronto 45,47
Boesch, Garth	Toronto 47,48,49
Boisvert, Serge	Montreal 86
Bonin, Marcel	Detroit 55; Montreal 58,59,60
Boon, Dick	Mtl AAA 02
Bordeleau, Christian	Montreal 69
Bossy, Mike	NY Islanders 80,81,82,83
Bouchard, Emile 'Butch'	Montreal 44,46,53,56
Bouchard, Pierre	Montreal 71,73,76,77,78
Boucher, Billy	Montreal 24
Boucher, Bobby	Montreal 24
Boucher, Frank	NY Rangers 28,33
Boucher, George	Ottawa 20,21,23,27
Bourgeault, Leo	NY Rangers 28
Bourque, Phil	Pittsburgh 91,92
Bourne, Bob	NY Islanders 80,81,82,83
Boutilier, Paul	NY Islanders 83
Bower, Johnny	Toronto 62,63,64,67
Bowman, Ralph 'Scotty'	Detroit 36,37
Boyd, Bill	NY Rangers 28
Brannen, Jack	Mtl Shamrocks 1899,1900
Brennan, Doug	NY Rangers 33
Brewer, Carl	Toronto 62,63,64
Brimsek, Frank	Boston 31,41
Brisebois, Patrice	Montreal 93
Broadbent, Harry	Ottawa 20,21,23; Mtl Maroons 26
Broda, Walter 'Turk'	Toronto 42,47,48,49,51
Broden, Connie	Montreal 57,58
Brodeur, Martin	New Jersey 95
Brophy, Bernie	Mtl Maroons 26
Broten, Neal	New Jersey 95
Brown, A.	Winnipeg Vics 01
Brown, Adam	Detroit 43
Brown, Dave	Edmonton 90
Brown, Pat	Detroit 43
Bruce, Morley	Ottawa 20,21
Brunet, Benoit	Montreal 93
Bruneteau, Moderre 'Mud'	Detroit 36,37,43
Brylin, Sergei	New Jersey 95
Buchberger, Kelly	Edmonton 87,90
Bucyk, Johnny	Boston 70,72
Burke, Marty	Montreal 30,31

C

Name	Team(s)
Cain, Herb	Mtl Maroons 35; Boston 41
Cain, J.	Mtl Maroons 26
Callender, Jock	Pittsburgh 92
Callighen, Pat	NY Rangers 28
Cameron, Allan	Mtl AAA 1893,94
Cameron, Billy	Montreal 24
Cameron, Harry	Toronto 14,18,22
Campbell, C.J.	Winnipeg Vics 1896
Carbonneau, Guy	Montreal 86, 93
Carleton, Wayne	Boston 70
Carpenter, Bob	New Jersey 95
Carpenter, Ed	Seattle 17
Carr, Lorne	Toronto 42,45
Carroll, Billy	NY Islanders 81,82,83; Edmonton 85
Carson, Bill	Boston 29
Carson, Frank	Mtl Maroons 26
Carson, Gerald	Montreal 30
Carveth, Joe	Detroit 43,50
Cashman, Wayne	Boston 70,72
Caufield, Jay	Pittsburgh 91,92
Chabot, Lorne	NY Rangers 28; Toronto 32
Chamberlain, Erwin 'Murph'	Montreal 44,46
Chambers, Shawn	New Jersey 95
Chartraw, Rick	Montreal 76,77,78,79
Cheevers, Gerry	Boston 70,72
Chelios, Chris	Montreal 86
Chorske, Tom	New Jersey 95
Chychrun, Jeff	Pittsburgh 92
Clancy, Frank 'King'	Ottawa 23,27; Toronto 32
Clapper, Aubrey 'Dit'	Boston 29,39,41
Clarke, Bobby	Philadelphia 74,75
Cleghorn, Odie	Montreal 24
Cleghorn, Sprague	Ottawa 20,21; Montreal 24
Clement, Bill	Philadelphia 74,75
Coffey, Paul	Edmonton 84,85,87; Pittsburgh 91
Cole, Danton	New Jersey 95
Collins, Herb	Mtl AAA 1894
Colville, Mac	NY Rangers 40
Colville, Neil	NY Rangers 40
Conacher, Brian	Toronto 67
Conacher, Charlie	Toronto 32
Conacher, Lionel	Chicago 34; Mtl Maroons 35
Conacher, Pat	Edmonton 84
Conacher, Roy	Boston 39,41
Connell, Alex	Ottawa 27; Mtl Maroons 35
Connolly, Bert	Chicago 38
Connor, Cam	Montreal 79
Cook, Bill	NY Rangers 28,33
Cook, Fred 'Bun'	NY Rangers 28,33
Cook, Lloyd	Vancouver 15
Cook, Tom	Chicago 34
Corbeau, Bert	Montreal 16
Corbeau, Con	Toronto 14
Costello, Les	Toronto 48
Cotton, Harold 'Baldy'	Toronto 32
Coughlin, Jack	Toronto 18
Coulter, Art	Chicago 34; NY Rangers 40
Cournoyer, Yvan	Montreal 65,66,68,69,71,73, 76,77,78,79
Courtnall, Geoff	Edmonton 88
Couture, Billy 'Coutu'	Montreal 24
Couture, Gerald 'Doc'	Detroit 50
Cowick, Bruce	Philadelphia 74
Cowley, Bill	Boston 39,41
Crawford, Jack	Boston 31,41
Crawford, Russell 'Rusty'	Quebec 13; Toronto 18
Creighton, Billy	Quebec 13
Crisp, Terry	Philadelphia 74,75
Currie, Alex	Ottawa 11
Curry, Floyd	Montreal 53,56,57,58

D

Name	Team(s)
Dahlin, Kjell	Montreal 86
Dahlstrom, Carl 'Cully'	Chicago 38
Daigneault, J.J.	Montreal 93
Dalby	Mtl Shamrocks 1899
Damphousse, Vincent	Montreal 93
Daneyko, Ken	New Jersey 95
Daniels, Jeff	Pittsburgh 92
Darragh, Harold	Toronto 32
Darragh, Jack	Ottawa 11,20,21,23
Davidson, Bob	Toronto 42,45
Davidson, Cam	Mtl Victorias 1896,97,98
Davidson, Shirley	Mtl Victorias 1895,96,97
Davis, Lorne	Montreal 53
Dawes, Robert	Toronto 49
Day, Clarence 'Hap'	Toronto 32
Dean, Kevin	New Jersey 95
DeBlois, Lucien	Montreal 86
Delvecchio, Alex	Detroit 52,54,55
Denneny, Corb	Toronto 18,22
Denneny, Cy	Ottawa 20,21,23,27; Boston 29
Desjardins, Eric	Montreal 93
Dewsbury, Al	Detroit 50
Dey, Edgar	Ottawa 09
Dickens, Ernie	Toronto 42
Dillon, Cecil	NY Rangers 33
Dineen, Bill	Detroit 54,55
Dinsmore, Chuck	Mtl Maroons 26
Dionne, Gilbert	Montreal 93
DiPietro, Paul	Montreal 93
Doak, Gary	Boston 70
Dornhoefer, Gary	Philadelphia 74,75
Douglas, Kent	Toronto 63
Douglas, Les	Detroit 43
Dowd, Jim	New Jersey 95
Drillon, Gordie	Toronto 42
Drinkwater, Graham	Mtl Victorias 1895,96,97,98
Driver, Bruce	New Jersey 95
Dryden, Ken	Montreal 71,73,76,77,78,79
Dube, Gilles	Detroit 54
Dufresne, Donald	Montreal 93
Duff, Dick	Toronto 62,63; Montreal 65,66,68,69
Dumart, Woody	Boston 31, 41
Dupont, Andre 'Moose'	Philadelphia 74,75
Durnan, Bill	Montreal 44,46
Dye, Cecil 'Babe'	Toronto 22

E

Name	Team(s)
Eddolls, Frank	Montreal 46
Ehman, Gerry	Toronto 64
Elliot, Roland	Mtl Victorias 1895; Mtl AAA 02
Ellis, Ron	Toronto 67
Elmer, Wally	Victoria 25
Engblom, Brian	Montreal 77,78,79
Erickson, Aut	Toronto 67
Errey, Bob	Pittsburgh 91,92
Esposito, Phil	Boston 70,72
Esposito, Tony	Montreal 69
Evans, Jack	Chicago 61
Evans, Stewart	Mtl Maroons 35
Ewen, Todd	Montreal 93
Ewing, Jack	Mtl Victorias 1897,98
Ezinicki, Bill	Toronto 47,48,49

F

Name	Team(s)
Farrell, Art	Mtl Shamrocks 1899,1900
Fenwick, Art	Mtl Victorias 1895
Ferguson, John	Montreal 65,66,68,69,71
Fillion, Bob	Montreal 44,46
Finnie, Dave	Ottawa 05
Finnigan, Frank	Ottawa 27; Toronto 32
Fisher, Joe	Detroit 43
Flaman, Fern	Toronto 51
Fleming, Reg	Chicago 61
Flett, Bill	Philadelphia 74

Flett, Magnus	Winnipeg Vics 01	Griffis, Si	Kenora 07; Vancouver 15	Hughes, Pat	Montreal 79; Edmonton 84,85
Flett, Rod	Winnipeg Vics 1896, 01	Grosso, Don	Detroit 43	Hull, Bobby	Chicago 61
Fleury, Theoren	Calgary 89	Guerin, Bill	New Jersey 95	Hunter, Dave	Edmonton 84,85,87
Fogolin, Lee, Sr.	Detroit 50			Hunter, Mark	Calgary 89
Fogolin, Lee, Jr.	Edmonton 84,85	## H		Hunter, Tim	Calgary 89
Fortier, Charles	Montreal 24			Hutton, Bouse	Ottawa 03,04
Fournier, Jack	Montreal 16	Haidy, Gordon	Detroit 50	Hyland, Harry	Mtl Wanderers 10
Foyston, Frank	Toronto 14; Seattle 17; Victoria 25	Hainsworth, George	Montreal 30,31		
		Halderson, Harold 'Slim'	Victoria 25	## I–J	
Francis, Ron	Pittsburgh 91,92	Hall, Glenn	Chicago 61		
Franks, Jim	Detroit 37	Hall, Joe	Quebec 12,13	Irving, Alex	Mtl AAA 1893,1894
Fraser	Ottawa 03	Haller, Kevin	Montreal 93	Jackson, Art	Boston 41; Toronto 45
Fraser, Gordon	Victoria 25	Halliday, Milt	Ottawa 27	Jackson, Don	Edmonton 84,85
Fredrickson, Frank	Victoria 25, Boston 29	Hallin, Mats	NY Islanders 83	Jackson, Harold	Chicago 38; Detroit 43
Fuhr, Grant	Edmonton 84,85,87,88,90	Hamill, Robert 'Red'	Boston 39	Jackson, Harvey 'Busher'	Toronto 32
		Hamilton, Reg	Toronto 42,45	Jackson, Stan	Toronto 22
## G		Hannan, Dave	Edmonton 88	Jagr, Jaromir	Pittsburgh 91,92
		Harmon, Glen	Montreal 44,46	James, G.	Mtl AAA 1894
Gagnon, Johnny	Montreal 31	Harper, Terry	Montreal 65,66,68,69,71	Jarvis, Doug	Montreal 76,77,78,79
Gainey, Bob	Montreal 76,77,78,79,86	Harris, Ted	Montreal 65,66,68,69; Philadelphia 75	Jeffrey, Larry	Toronto 67
Gainor, Norman 'Dutch'	Boston 29; Montreal 44			Jenkins, Roger	Chicago 34,38
Galbraith, Percy 'Perk'	Boston 29	Harris, Billy	Toronto 62,63,64	Jennings, Grant	Pittsburgh 91,92
Gallagher, John	Detroit 37	Harriston	Toronto 14	Johnson, Ernie	Mtl Wanderers 06,07,08,10
Gamble, Dick	Montreal 53,56	Hart, Harold 'Gizzy'	Victoria 25	Johnson, Ivan 'Ching'	NY Rangers 28,33
Gardiner, Chuck	Chicago 34	Hartman, Mike	NY Rangers 94	Johnson, Tom	Montreal 53,56,57,58,59,60
Gardner, Cal	Toronto 49,51	Harvey, Doug	Montreal 53,56,57,58,59,60	Johnson, Virgil	Chicago 38
Gardner, Jimmy	Mtl AAA 02; Mtl Wanderers 10	Hay, Jim	Detroit 55	Johnston, Ed	Boston 70,72
		Hay, Bill	Chicago 61	Johnstone, Charles	Winnipeg Vics 1896, 01
Gaul, Horace	Ottawa 05,11	Hayes, Chris	Boston 72	Johnstone, Ross	Toronto 45
Gauthier, Jean	Montreal 65	Healy, Glenn	NY Rangers 94	Joliat, Aurel	Montreal 24,30,31
Gee, George	Detroit 50	Hebert, Sammy	Toronto 18	Jones, Robert	Mtl Victorias 1895,96
Gelinas, Martin	Edmonton 90	Heffernan, Gerry	Montreal 44	Jonsson, Tomas	NY Islanders 82,83
Geoffrion, Bernie	Montreal 53,56,57,58,59,60	Heller, Ott	NY Rangers 33,40	Juzda, Bill	Toronto 51
Gerard, Eddie	Ottawa 20,21,23; Toronto 22	Helman, Harry	Ottawa 23		
Geroux, Eddie	Kenora 07	Henderson, Harold	Mtl Victorias 1895,96,97	## K	
Getliffe, Ray	Boston 39; Montreal 44	Henning, Lorne	NY Islanders 80,81		
Gilbert, Greg	NY Islanders 82,83; NY Rangers 94	Hern, Riley	Mtl Wanderers 07,08,10	Kallur, Anders	NY Islanders 80,81,82,83
		Hextall, Bryan Sr.	NY Rangers 40	Kampman, Rudolph 'Bingo'	Toronto 42
Gillelan, D.	Mtl Victorias 1896,1897	Hicke, Bill	Montreal 59,60	Karakas, Mike	Chicago 38
Gillies, Clark	NY Islanders 80,81,82,83	Hicks, Wayne	Chicago 61	Karpovtsev, Alexander	NY Rangers 94
Gilhen, Randy	Pittsburgh 91	Higginbotham	Winnipeg Vics 1896	Keane, Mike	Montreal 93
Gilmour, Billy	Ottawa 03,04,05,09	Hill, Mel	Boston 39,41; Toronto 45	Keeling, Mel 'Butch'	NY Rangers 33
Gilmour, Dave	Ottawa 03	Hill, Sean	Montreal 93	Kelly, Bob	Philadelphia 74,75
Gilmour, Doug	Calgary 89	Hiller, Wilbert 'Dutch'	NY Rangers 40; Montreal 46	Kelly, Leonard 'Red'	Detroit 50,52,54,55; Toronto 62,63,64,67
Gilmour, Larry	Mtl Wanderers 08	Hillier, Randy	Pittsburgh 91		
Gilmour, Suddy	Ottawa 03,04	Hillman, Larry	Detroit 55; Toronto 64,67; Montreal 69	Kelly, Pete	Detroit 36,37
Gingras, Gaston	Montreal 86			Kendall, Bill	Chicago 34
Gingras, Tony	Winnipeg Vics 01	Hillman, Wayne	Chicago 61	Kennedy, Rod	Mtl Wanderers 06,07
Glass, Frank 'Pud'	Mtl Wanderers 06,07,08,10	Hitchman, Lionel	Ottawa 23; Boston 29	Kennedy, Ted 'Teeder'	Toronto 45, 47,48,49,51
Goldham, Bob	Toronto 42, 47; Detroit 52,54,55	Hodge, Charlie	Montreal 65	Keon, Dave	Toronto 62,63,64,67
		Hodge, Ken	Boston 70,72	Kerr, Albert 'Dubbie'	Ottawa 09,11
Goldsworthy, Leroy	Chicago 34	Hodge, Tom	Mtl AAA 02	Kerr, Dave	NY Rangers 40
Goldup, Hank	Toronto 42	Hodgson, Archie	Mtl AAA 1893,94	Kilrea, Hec	Ottawa 27; Detroit 36,37
Goodenough, Larry	Philadelphia 75	Hoerner	Mtl Shamrocks 1899	Kindrachuk, Orest	Philadelphia 74,75
Goodfellow, Ebbie	Detroit 36,37,43	Holik, Bobby	New Jersey 95	Kingan, A.	Mtl AAA 1893,94
Goodman, Paul	Chicage 38	Hollett, Bill 'Flash'	Boston 39, 41	Kitchen, Chapman 'Hobey'	Mtl Maroons 26
Goring, Butch	NY Islanders 80,81,82,83	Holmes, Harry	Toronto 14,18; Seattle 17; Victoria 25	Klein, Lloyd	Boston 29
Gorman, Ed	Ottawa 27			Klima, Petr	Edmonton 90
Gottselig, Johnny	Chicago 34,38	Holway, Albert 'Toots'	Mtl Maroons 26	Klukay, Joe	Toronto 47,48,49,51
Goyette, Phil	Montreal 57,58,59,60	Hooper, Art	Mtl AAA 02	Kocur, Joe	NY Rangers 94
Gracie, Bob	Toronto 32; Mtl Maroons 35	Hooper, Tom	Kenora 07; Mtl Wanderers 08	Kordic, John	Montreal 86
Graham, Leth	Ottawa 21			Kovalev, Alexei	NY Rangers 94
Grant, Danny	Montreal 68	Horne, George 'Shorty'	Mtl Maroons 26	Krushelnyski, Mike	Edmonton 85,87,88
Grant, Mike	Mtl Victorias 1895,96,97,98	Horner, Reginald 'Red'	Toronto 32	Kurri, Jari	Edmonton 84,85,87,88,90
Graves, Adam	Edmonton 90; NY Rangers 94	Horton, Tim	Toronto 62,63,64,67	Kurvers, Tom	Montreal 86
		Houle, Rejean	Montreal 71,73,77,78,79	Kypreos	NY Rangers 94
Gray, Alex	NY Rangers 28	Howard, H.	Winnipeg Vics 1896		
Green, Red	Boston 29	Howatt, Garry	NY Islanders 80,81	## L	
Green, Rick	Montreal 86	Howe, Gordie	Detroit 50,52,54,55		
Green, Ted	Boston 72	Howe, Syd	Detroit 36,37,43	Lach, Elmer	Montreal 44,46,53
Gregg, Randy	Edmonton 84,85,87,88,90	Hrdina, Jiri	Calgary 89, Pittsburgh 91,92	Lacombe, Normand	Edmonton 88
Grenier, Lucien	Montreal 69	Huddy, Charlie	Edmonton 84,85,87,88,90	Lafleur, Guy	Montreal 73,76,77,78,79
Gretzky, Wayne	Edmonton 84,85,87,88	Hudson, Mike	NY Rangers 94		

172 • PLAYERS ON STANLEY CUP CHAMPIONSHIP TEAMS

Lake, Fred	Ottawa 09,11
Lalonde, Edouard 'Newsy'	Montreal 16
Lalor, Mike	Montreal 86
Lamb, Mark	Edmonton 90
Lambert, Yvon	Montreal 76,77,78,79
Lamoureux, Leo	Montreal 44,46
Lane, Gord	NY Islanders 80,81,82,83
Lane, Myles	Boston 29
Langelle, Pete	Toronto 42
Langevin, Dave	NY Islanders 80,81,82,83
Langlois, Al	Montreal 58,59,60
Langway, Rod	Montreal 79
Laperriere, Jacques	Montreal 65,66,68,69,71,73
Lapointe, Guy	Montreal 71,73,76,77,78,79
Larmer, Steve	NY Rangers 94
Larochelle, Wildor	Montreal 30,31
Larocque, Michel 'Bunny'	Montreal 76,77,78,79
Larose, Claude	Montreal 65,66,68,71,73
Larouche, Pierre	Montreal 78, 79
Laviolette, Jack	Montreal 16
Leach, Jamie	Pittsburgh 92
Leach, Reg	Philadelphia 75
Lebeau, Stephan	Montreal 93
LeClair, Jack	Montreal 56
LeClair, John	Montreal 93
Leduc, Albert	Montreal 30,31
Leetch, Brian	NY Rangers 94
Leeman, Gary	Montreal 93
Lefley, Chuck	Montreal 71,73
Lehman, Hugh	Vancouver 15
Lemaire, Jacques	Montreal 68,69,71,73,76, 77,78,79
Lemay, Moe	Edmonton 87
Lemieux, Claude	Montreal 86; New Jersey 95
Lemieux, Mario	Pittsburgh 91,92
Leonard	Quebec 12
Lepine, Alfred 'Pit'	Montreal 30,31
Lesieur, Art	Montreal 31
LeSueur, Percy	Ottawa 09,11
Lesuk, Bill	Boston 70
Leswick, Jack	Chicago 34
Leswick, Tony	Detroit 52, 54,55
Levinsky, Alex	Toronto 32; Chicago 38
Lewicki, Dan	Toronto 51
Lewis, Gordon	Mtl Victorias 1896,97,98
Lewis, Herbie	Detroit 36,37
Lidster, Doug	NY Rangers 94
Liffiton, Charles	Mtl AAA 02; Mtl Wanderers 08
Lindsay, Ted	Detroit 50,52,54,55
Lindstrom, Willy	Edmonton 84,85
Linseman, Ken	Edmonton 84
Liscombe, Carl	Detroit 43
Litzenberger, Eddie	Chicago 61; Toronto 62,63,64
Loney, Troy	Pittsburgh 91,92
Lonsberry, Ross	Philadelphia 74,75
Loob, Hakan	Calgary 89
Lorentz, Jim	Boston 70
Lorimer, Bob	NY Islanders 80,81
Loughlin, Clem	Victoria 25
Lowe, Jim	Mtl AAA 1893
Lowe, Kevin	Edmonton 84,85,87,88,90; NY Rangers 94
Lowery, Fred 'Frock'	Mtl Maroons 26
Ludwig, Craig	Montreal 86
Lumley, Dave	Edmonton 84,85
Lumley, Harry	Detroit 50
Lupien, Gilles	Montreal 78,79
Lynn, Vic	Toronto 47,48,49

M

MacAdam, Al	Philadelphia 74
MacDonald, Kilby	NY Rangers 40
MacInnis, Al	Calgary 89
MacKay, Calum 'Baldy'	Montreal 53
MacKay, Mickey	Vancouver 15; Boston 29
Mackie, Howie	Detroit 37
Mackell, Fleming	Toronto 49,51
MacLean, John	New Jersey 95
MacLeish, Rick	Philadelphia 74,75
MacLellan, Brian	Calgary 89
MacMillan, John	Toronto 62,63
Macoun, Jamie	Calgary 89
MacPherson, James 'Bud'	Montreal 53
MacTavish, Craig	Edmonton 87,88,90; NY Rangers 94
Mahovlich, Frank	Toronto 62,63,64,67; Montreal 71,73
Mahovlich, Peter	Montreal 71,73,76,77
Majeau, Fern	Montreal 44
Maki, Ronald 'Chico'	Chicago 61
Maley, David	Montreal 86
Mallen, Ken	Vancouver 15
Malone, Jeff	Quebec 13
Malone, Joe	Quebec 12,13; Montreal 24
Mantha, Georges	Montreal 30,31
Mantha, Sylvio	Montreal 24,30,31
Marcetta, Milan	Toronto 67
March, Harold 'Mush'	Chicago 34,38
Marcotte, Don	Boston 70,72
Marini, Hector	NY Islanders 81,82
Marker, Gus	Mtl Maroons 35
Marks, Jack	Quebec 12,13; Toronto 18
Marshall, Don	Montreal 56,57,58,59,60
Marshall, Jack	Winnipeg Vics 01; Mtl Maroons 02; Mtl Wanderers 07,10; Toronto 14
Martin, Clare	Detroit 50
Masnick, Paul	Montreal 53
Matteau, Stephane	NY Rangers 94
Matz, Johnny	Vancouver 15
Mazur, Eddie	Montreal 53
McAlpine, Chris	New Jersey 95
McCaffrey, Bert	Montreal 30,31
McClelland, Kevin	Edmonton 84,85,87,88
McCool, Frank	Toronto 45
McCormack, John	Toronto 51; Montreal 53
McCreedy, John	Toronto 42,45
McCrimmon, Brad	Calgary 89
McDonald	Ottawa 05
McDonald, Ab	Montreal 58,59,60; Chicago 61
McDonald, Jack	Quebec 12
McDonald, Lanny	Calgary 89
McDonald, Wilfrid 'Bucko'	Detroit 36,37; Toronto 42
McDougall, A.	Mtl Victorias 1895
McDougall, Bob	Mtl Victorias 1895,96,97,98
McDougall, Hartland	Mtl Victorias 1895,96,97,98
McEachern, Shawn	Pittsburgh 92
McEwen, Mike	NY Islanders 81,82,83
McFadden, Jim	Detroit 50
McFadyen, Don	Chicago 34
McGee, Frank	Ottawa 03,04,05
McGee, Jim	Ottawa 04
McGiffen, Roy 'Minnie'	Toronto 14
McGimsie, Billy	Kenora 07
McKay, Doug	Detroit 50
McKay, Randy	New Jersey 95
McKell, Jack	Ottawa 21
McKendry, Alex	NY Islanders 80
McKenna, Joe	Mtl Shamrocks 1899,1900
McKenney, Don	Toronto 64
McKenzie, Bill	Chicago 38
McKenzie, John	Boston 70,72
McLea, Ernest	Mtl Victorias 1896,97,98
McLean, Jack	Toronto 45
McLellan	Mtl Victorias 1897
McMahon, Mike	Montreal 44
McManus, Sam	Mtl Maroons 35
McNab, Max	Detroit 50
McNamara, George	Toronto 14
McNamara, Howard	Montreal 16
McNeil, Gerry	Montreal 53
McPhee, Mike	Montreal 86
McReavy, Pat	Boston 41
McSorley, Marty	Edmonton 87,88
Meeker, Howie	Toronto 47,48,51
Meeking, Harry	Toronto 18; Victoria 25
Meger, Paul	Montreal 53
Melanson, Roland	NY Islanders 81,82,83
Melnyk, Larry	Edmonton 85
Menard, H.	Mtl Wanderers 06
Merrick, Wayne	NY Islanders 80,81,82,83
Merrill, Horace	Ottawa 20
Merritt, G.H.	Winnipeg Vics 1896
Messier, Mark	Edmonton 84,85,87,88,90; NY Rangers 94
Metz, Don	Toronto 42,45,47,48,49
Metz, Nick	Toronto 42,45,47,48
Michayluk, Dave	Pittsburgh 92
Mikita, Stan	Chicago 61
Miller, Bill	Mtl Maroons 35
Miller, Earl	Toronto 32
Mitchell, Ivan	Toronto 22
Molson, Percy	Mtl Victorias 1897
Mondou, Armand	Montreal 30,31
Mondou, Pierre	Montreal 77,78,79
Moog, Andy	Edmonton 84,85,87
Moore, Alfie	Chicago 38
Moore, Art	Ottawa 03,04,05
Moore, Dickie	Montreal 53,56,57,58,59,60
Moran, Paddy	Quebec 12,13
Morenz, Howie	Montreal 24,30,31
Morris, Bernie	Seattle 17
Morris, Elwin 'Moe'	Toronto 45
Morrow, Ken	NY Islanders 80,81,82,83
Mortson, Gus	Toronto 47,48,49,51
Mosdell, Kenny	Montreal 46,53,56,59
Motter, Alex	Detroit 43
Mowers, Johnny	Detroit 43
Mullen, Joe	Calgary 89, Pittsburgh 91,92
Muller, Kirk	Montreal 93
Mummery, Harry	Quebec 13; Toronto 18
Muni, Craig	Edmonton 87,88,90
Munro, Dunc	Mtl Maroons 26
Murdoch, Bob	Montreal 71,73
Murdoch, Murray	NY Rangers 28,33
Murphy, Joe	Edmonton 90
Murphy, Larry	Pittsburgh 91,92
Murphy, Ron	Chicago 61
Murzyn, Dana	Calgary 89
Mussen, Clare	Mtl AAA 1894

N

Napier, Mark	Montreal 79; Edmonton 85
Naslund, Mats	Montreal 86
Nattress, Ric	Calgary 89
Needham, Mike	Pittsburgh 92
Nemchinove, Sergei	NY Rangers 94
Nesterenko, Eric	Chicago 61
Neville, Mike	Toronto 18
Nevin, Bob	Toronto 62,63
Nicholson, Billy	Mtl AAA 02
Niedermayer, Scott	New Jersey 95
Nieuwendyk, Joe	Calgary 89
Nighbor, Frank	Vancouver 15; Ottawa 20,21,23,27

PLAYERS ON STANLEY CUP CHAMPIONSHIP TEAMS • 173

Nilan, Chris	Montreal 86	Pronovost, Andre	Montreal 57,58,59,60	Samis, Phil	Toronto 48
Nilsson, Kent	Edmonton 87	Pronovost, Marcel	Detroit 50,52,54,55;	Samuelsson, Kjell	Pittsburgh 92
Noble, Reg	Toronto 18,22;		Toronto 67	Samuelsson, Ulf	Pittsburgh 91,92
	Mtl Maroons 26	Provost, Claude	Montreal 56,57,58,59,60,65,	Sanderson, Derek	Boston 70,72
Nolan, Pat	Toronto 22		66,68,69	Sands, Charlie	Boston 39
Nolet, Simon	Philadelphia 74	Prystai, Metro	Detroit 52,54	Savard, Denis	Montreal 93
Noonan, Brian	NY Rangers 94	Pulford, Bob	Toronto 62,63,64,67	Savard, Serge	Montreal 68,69,73,76,
Northcott, Lawrence 'Baldy'	Mtl Maroons 35	Pulford, Harvey	Ottawa 03,04,05		77,78,79
Nyrop, Bill	Montreal 76,77,78	Pullan	Mtl Victorias 1895	Sawchuk, Terry	Detroit 52,54,55; Toronto 67
Nystrom, Bob	NY Islanders 80,81,82,83	Pusie, Jean	Montreal 31	Scanlon, Fred	Mtl Shamrocks 1899, 1900
				Schmidt, Milt	Boston 39,41
O		**R**		Schneider, Mathieu	Montreal 93
Oatman, Eddie	Quebec 12	Racicot, Andre	Montreal 93	Schriner, David	Toronto 42,45
O'Brien, E.	Mtl AAA 1894	Ramage, Rob	Calgary 89, Montreal 93	Schultz, Dave	Philadelphia 74,75
O'Connor, Herbert 'Buddy'	Montreal 44,46	Randall, Ken	Toronto 18,22	Scott	Ottawa 04
Odelein, Lyle	Montreal 93	Ranford, Bill	Edmonton 88,90	Scott, Laurie	NY Rangers 28
Olczyk, Ed	NY Rangers 94	Rankin, N.	Mtl Victorias 1895	Seaborn, Jimmy	Vancouver 15
Oliver, Harry	Boston 29	Reardon, Kenny	Montreal 46	Seibert, Earl	NY Rangers 33; Chicago 38
Olmstead, Bert	Montreal 53,56,57,58;	Reardon, Terry	Boston 41	Semenko, Dave	Edmonton 84,85
	Toronto 62	Reay, Billy	Montreal 46,53	Sevigny, Richard	Montreal 79
O'Neill, Tom	Toronto 45	Recchi, Mark	Pittsburgh 91	Shack, Edward	Toronto 62,63,64, 67
Orlando, Jimmy	Detroit 43	Reddick, Eldon	Edmonton 90	Sheehan, Bobby	Montreal 71
Orr, Bobby	Boston 70,72	Redmond, Mickey	Montreal 68,69	Sheppard, John	Chicago 34
Otto, Joel	Calgary 89	Reibel, Earl 'Dutch'	Detroit 54,55	Sherf, John	Detroit 37
Owen, George	Boston 29	Reise, Leo Jr.	Detroit 50, 52	Shewchuk, Jack	Boston 41
		Resch, Glenn 'Chico'	NY Islanders 80	Shibicky, Alex	NY Rangers 40
P		Richard, Henri	Montreal 56,57,58,59,60,65,	Shields, Allan	Mtl Maroons 35
Paek, Jim	Pittsburgh 91,92		66,68,69,71,73	Shill, Jack	Chicago 38
Palangio, Pete	Chicago 38	Richard, Maurice 'Rocket'	Montreal 44,46,53,56,57,	Schock, Dan	Boston 70
Pappin, Jim	Toronto 64,67		58,59,60	Shore, Eddie	Boston 29,39
Parent, Bernie	Philadelphia 74,75	Richardson, Frank	Mtl Victorias 1898	Shore, Hamby	Ottawa 05,11
Paton, Tom	Mtl AAA 1893	Richer, Stephane	Montreal 86; New Jersey 95	Shutt, Steve	Montreal 73,76,77,78,79
Patrick, Frank	Vancouver 15	Richter, Mike	NY Rangers 94	Siebert, Albert 'Babe'	Mtl Maroons 26;
Patrick, Lester	Mtl Wanderers 06,07;	Rickey, Roy	Seattle 17		NY Rangers 33
	NY Rangers 28	Ridpath, Bruce	Ottawa 11	Simmons, Donald	Toronto 62
Patrick, Lynn	NY Rangers 40	Riley, Jim	Seattle 17	Simms, Percy	Ottawa 03
Patrick, Murray 'Muzz'	NY Rangers 40	Risebrough, Doug	Montreal 76,77,78,79	Simon, John	Detroit 43
Patterson, Colin	Calgary 89	Rivers, Gus	Montreal 30,31	Simpson, Craig	Edmonton 88,90
Pavelich, Marty	Detroit 50,52,54,55	Roach, John	Toronto 22	Skinner, Alf	Toronto 18
Pederson, Barry	Pittsburgh 91	Roberge, Mario	Montreal 93	Skov, Glen	Detroit 52,54,55
Peluso, Mike	New Jersey 95	Roberto, Phil	Montreal 71	Skrudland, Brian	Montreal 86
Peplinski, Jim	Calgary 89	Roberts, Gary	Calgary 89	Sloan, Tod	Toronto 51; Chicago 61
Persson, Stefan	NY Islanders 80,81,82,83	Roberts, Gord	Pittsburgh 91,92	Smail, Wally	Mtl Wanderers 08
Peters, Garry	Boston 72	Roberts, Jimmy	Montreal 65,66,73,76,77	Smith, Alex	Ottawa 27
Peters, Jim	Montreal 46; Detroit 50,54	Robertson, Earl	Detroit 37	Smith, Alf	Ottawa 04,05
Pettinger, Gordon	NY Rangers 33;	Robertson, Fred	Toronto 32	Smith, Billy	NY Islanders 80,81,82,83
	Detroit 36,37; Boston 39	Robinson, Earl	Mtl Maroons 35	Smith, Bobby	Montreal 86
Phillips, Bill	Mtl Maroons 26	Robinson, Larry	Montreal 73,76,77,78,79,86	Smith, Clint	NY Rangers 40
Phillips, Tom	Kenora 07	Rochefort, Leon	Montreal 66,71	Smith, Dallas	Boston 70,72
Picard, Noel	Montreal 65	Rodden, Eddie	Boston 29	Smith, Des	Boston 41
Pietrangelo, Frank	Pittsburgh 91	Rollins, Al	Toronto 51	Smith, Geoff	Edmonton 90
Pike, Alf	NY Rangers 40	Rolston, Brian	New Jersey 95	Smith, Normie	Detroit 36,37
Pilote, Pierre	Chicago 61	Romnes, Elwin 'Doc'	Chicago 34,38	Smith, Reginald 'Hooley'	Ottawa 27; Mtl Maroons 35
Pitre, Didier 'Pit'	Montreal 16	Ronan, Ed	Montreal 93	Smith, Rick	Boston 70
Plamondon, Gerry	Montreal 46	Ronan, Skene	Montreal 16	Smith, Sid	Toronto 48,49,51
Plante, Jacques	Montreal 53,56,57,58,59,60	Rooney, Steve	Montreal 86	Smith, Stan	NY Rangers 40
Plasse, Michel	Montreal 73	Rooney, Walter	Quebec 12	Smith, Steve	Edmonton 87,88,90
Poile, Norman 'Bud'	Toronto 47	Ross, Art	Kenora 07; Mtl Wanderers 08	Smylie, Rod	Toronto 22
Polich, Mike	Montreal 77	Rothchild, Sam	Mtl Maroons 26	Soetaert, Doug	Montreal 86
Portland, Jack	Boston 39	Roulston, William 'Rolly'	Detroit 37	Somers, Art	NY Rangers 33
Potvin, Denis	NY Islanders 80,81,82,83	Rousseau, Bobby	Montreal 65,66,68,69	Sorrell, John	Detroit 36,37
Potvin, Jean	NY Islanders 80	Routh, Harvie	Mtl AAA 83,94	Speer, Bill	Boston 70
Poulin, 'Skinner'	Montreal 16	Rowe, Bob	Seattle 17	Spittal, Charles	Ottawa 23
Pouzar, Jaroslav	Edmonton 84,85,87	Roy, Patrick	Montreal 86, 93	Stackhouse, Ted	Toronto 22
Power, 'Rocket'	Quebec 13	Ruotsalainen, Reijo	Edmonton 87,90	Stanfield, Fred	Boston 70,72
Pratt, Walter 'Babe'	NY Rangers 40; Toronto 45	Russell, Ernie	Mtl Wanderers 06,07,08, 10	Stanley, Allan	Toronto 62,63,64,67
Price	Ottawa 20			Stanley, Barney	Vancouver 15
Price, Noel	Montreal 66	**S**		Stanowski, Wally	Toronto 42,45,47,48
Priestlay, Ken	Pittsburgh 92	St. Laurent, Dollard	Montreal 53,56,57,58;	Stanton, Paul	Pittsburgh 91,92
Primeau, Joe	Toronto 32		Chicago 61	Starr, Wilf	Detroit 36
Prodgers, George 'Goldie'	Quebec 12; Montreal 16	Saleski, Don	Philadelphia 74,75	Stasiuk, Vic	Detroit 52,55
				Stemkowski, Peter	Toronto 67

Stephenson, Wayne	Philadelphia 75
Stevens, Kevin	Pittsburgh 91,92
Stevens, Scott	New Jersey 95
Stewart, Gaye	Toronto 42,47
Stewart, John "Black Jack"	Detroit 43,50
Stewart, James	Mtl AAA 1893,94
Stewart, Nels	Mtl Maroons 26
Stewart, Ron	Toronto 62,63,64
Strachan, Billy	Mtl Wanderers 06,07
Stuart, Bill	Toronto 22
Stuart, Bruce	Mtl Wanderers 08; Ottawa 09,11
Stuart, Hod	Mtl Wanderers 07
Suter, Gary	Calgary 89
Sutter, Brent	NY Islanders 82,83
Sutter, Duane	NY Islanders 80,81,82,83
Svoboda, Petr	Montreal 86

T

Talbot, Jean,Guy	Montreal 56,57,58,59, 60,65,66
Taglianetti, Peter	Pittsburgh 91,92
Tambellini, Steve	NY Islanders 80
Tansey, Frank	Mtl Shamrocks 1899, 00
Tardif, Marc	Montreal 71,73
Taylor, Billy	Toronto 42
Taylor, Bobby	Philadelphia 74
Taylor, Fred 'Cyclone'	Ottawa 09; Vancouver 15
Taylor, Harry	Toronto 49
Terreri, Chris	New Jersey 95
Thompson, Cecil 'Tiny'	Boston 29
Thompson, Paul	NY Rangers 28; Chicago 34,38
Thomson, Jimmy	Toronto 47,48,49,51
Tikkanen, Esa	Edmonton 85,87,88,90; NY Rangers 94
Timgren, Ray	Toronto 49,51
Tocchet, Rick	Pittsburgh 92
Tonelli, John	NY Islanders 80,81,82,83
Tremblay, Gilles	Montreal 66,68
Tremblay, J.C.	Montreal 65,66,68,69,71
Tremblay, Mario	Montreal 76,77,78,79,86
Trihey, Harry	Mtl Shamrocks 1899, 00
Trottier, Bryan	NY Islanders 80,81,82,83 Pittsburgh 91,92
Trottier, Dave	Mtl Maroons 35
Trudel, Louis	Chicago 34,38
Turner, Bob	Montreal 56,57,58,59,60

V

Vachon, Rogie	Montreal 68,69,71
Vadnais, Carol	Montreal 68; Boston 72
Van Impe, Ed	Philadelphia 74,75
Vasko, Elmer	Chicago 61
Vernon, Mike	Calgary 89
Vezina, Georges	Montreal 16,24
Voss, Carl	Chicago 38

W

Walker, Jack	Toronto 14; Seattle 17; Victoria 25
Wall, Frank	Mtl Shamrocks 1899, 00
Wallace, W.	Mtl Victorias 1896
Walsh, Marty	Ottawa 09,11
Walter, Ryan	Montreal 86
Walton, Mike	Toronto 67; Boston 72
Wamsley, Rick	Calgary 89
Ward, Jimmy	Mtl Maroons 35
Wares, Eddie	Detroit 43
Wasnie, Nick	Montreal 30,31
Watson, Harry	Detroit 43; Toronto 47,48,49,51
Watson, Jimmy	Philadelphia 74,75
Watson, Joe	Philadelphia 74,75
Watson, Phil	NY Rangers 40; Montreal 44
Waud, A.	Mtl AAA 1894
Weiland, Ralph 'Cooney'	Boston 29,39
Wells, Jay	NY Rangers 94
Wentworth, Marvin 'Cy'	Mtl Maroons 35
Westfall, Ed	Boston 70,72
Westwick, Harry	Ottawa 03,04,05
Wharram, Ken	Chicago 61
White, Frank	Ottawa 05
Wiebe, Art	Chicago 38
Willett, S.	Mtl Victorias 1896
Wilson, Carol 'Cully'	Toronto 14; Seattle 17
Wilson, Johnny	Detroit 50,52,54,55
Wilson, Larry	Detroit 50
Wilson, Murray	Montreal 73,76,77
Wiseman, Eddie	Boston 41
Woit, Benny	Detroit 52,54,55
Wood, Burke	Winnipeg Vics 01
Wood, F.	Ottawa 03
Worsley, Lorne 'Gump'	Montreal 65,66,68,69
Wregget, Ken	Pittsburgh 92

Y-Z

Young, Doug	Detroit 36,37
Young, Scott	Pittsburgh 91
Young, Wendell	Pittsburgh 91,92
Zelepukin, Valeri	New Jersey 95
Zeidel, Larry	Detroit 52
Zubov, Sergei	NY Rangers 94

Final Series Coaching Register 1927-1995

COACH	YRS	CUPS	GC	W	L	PCT
Sid Abel	4	0	24	8	16	.333
Jack Adams	5	3	23	12	11	.522
Al Arbour	5	4	24	17	7	.708
Toe Blake	9	8	48	32	16	.667
Frank Boucher	1	1	6	4	2	.667
Scotty Bowman	10	6	45	24	21	.533
Pat Burns	1	0	6	2	4	.333
Don Cherry	2	0	10	2	8	.200
Dit Clapper	1	0	5	1	4	.200
Terry Crisp	1	1	6	4	2	.667
Hap Day	5	5	28	20	8	.714
Jacques Demers	1	1	5	4	1	.800
Cy Denneny	1	1	2	2	0	1.000
Emile Francis	1	0	6	2	4	.333
Bob Gainey	1	0	6	2	4	.333
Eddie Gerard	1	0	5	2	3	.400
Dave Gill*	1	1	4	2	0	.750
Ebbie Goodfellow	1	0	4	0	4	.000
Tommy Gorman	2	2	7	6	1	.857
Bep Guidolin	1	0	6	2	4	.333
Cecil Hart	2	2	7	5	2	.714
Punch Imlach	6	4	33	17	16	.515
Dick Irvin	16	4	77	32	45	.416
Tommy Ivan	5	3	26	12	14	.462
Bob Johnson	2	1	11	5	6	.455
Tom Johnson	1	1	6	4	2	.667
Mike Keenan	4	1	23	8	15	.348
Jacques Lemaire	1	1	4	4	0	1.000
Herbie Lewis	1	0	4	1	3	.250
Al MacNeil	1	1	7	4	3	.571
Barry Melrose	1	0	4	1	4	.200
Mike Milbury	1	0	5	1	4	.200
John Muckler	1	1	5	4	1	.800
Roger Neilson	1	0	4	0	4	.000
Terry O'Reilly	1	0	4	0	4	.000
Lester Patrick	5	2	19	8	11	.421
Lynn Patrick	2	0	12	4	8	.333
Jean Perron	1	1	5	4	1	.800
Rudy Pilous	2	1	12	6	6	.500
Joe Primeau	1	1	5	4	1	.800
Pat Quinn	2	0	13	5	8	.385
Billy Reay	3	0	20	8	12	.400
Art Ross*	4	1	15	4	9	.333
Claude Ruel	1	1	4	4	0	1.000
Glen Sather	5	4	25	16	9	.640
Fred Shero	4	2	21	9	12	.429
Jimmy Skinner	2	1	12	5	7	.417
Milt Schmidt	2	0	11	3	8	.273
Harry Sinden	1	1	4	4	0	1.000
Floyd Smith	1	0	6	2	4	.333
Glen Sonmor	1	0	5	1	4	.200
Bill Stewart	1	1	4	3	1	.750
Paul Thompson	1	0	4	0	4	.000
Cooney Weiland	1	1	4	4	0	1.000

also recorded two ties in the 1927 Finals

Final Series Player Register 1927-1995

A

PLAYER	YRS	GP	G	A	TP	PIM
'Taffy' Abel	4	16	0	1	1	22
Sid Abel	7	34	9	11	20	25
Keith Acton	1	5	1	0	1	0
Greg Adams	1	7	1	2	3	2
Jack Adams	1	4	0	0	0	2
Stewart Adams	1	5	2	1	3	2
Tommy Albelin	1	4	0	2	2	2
George Allen	2	10	4	3	7	10
Keith Allen	1	3	0	0	0	2
Ray Allison	1	1	0	0	0	2
Earl Anderson	1	2	0	0	0	0
Glenn Anderson	7	38	16	13	29	59
Ron Anderson	1	1	0	0	0	2
Kent-Erik Andersson	1	5	1	0	1	0
Lou Angotti	2	13	3	3	6	9
Shawn Antoski	1	7	0	1	1	8
Syl Apps	6	32	10	11	21	6
Al Arbour	7	20	0	2	2	6
Ernest 'Ty' Arbour	1	5	1	0	1	0
Bob Armstrong	2	10	1	1	2	8
George Armstrong	6	33	9	13	22	22
Murray Armstrong	2	9	2	0	2	0
Ossie Asmundson	1	4	0	1	1	2
Ossie Aubuchon	1	1	0	0	0	0
Larry Aurie	2	8	2	3	5	2
Don Awrey	2	10	0	1	1	33

B

PLAYER	YRS	GP	G	A	TP	PIM
Pete Babando	1	5	2	2	4	2
Dave Babych	1	7	1	0	1	2
Ralph Backstrom	8	42	11	12	23	22
Garnet 'Ace' Bailey	1	6	1	0	1	14
Irvine 'Ace' Bailey	1	7	1	0	1	2
Earl Balfour	1	6	0	0	0	0
Murray Balfour	2	11	4	4	8	15
Dave Balon	3	16	2	4	6	18
Bill Barber	4	22	5	10	15	17
Bill Barilko	4	19	1	3	4	33
Doug Barkley	2	12	0	3	3	14
Norm Barnes	1	1	0	0	0	4
Fred Barrett	1	3	0	0	0	6
Marty Barry	3	11	5	3	8	8
Robin Bartel	1	4	0	0	0	12
Jim Bartlett	1	2	0	0	0	0
Andy Bathgate	2	13	4	5	9	16
Bobby Bauer	3	19	5	2	7	2
Bob Baun	6	32	2	6	8	67
Paul Baxter	1	4	0	1	1	17
Jean Beliveau	12	64	30	32	62	78
Neil Belland	1	4	0	0	0	4
Brian Bellows	2	11	1	3	4	20
Doug Bentley	1	4	1	2	3	2
Max Bentley	3	13	4	10	14	2
Gordon 'Red' Berenson	4	19	3	2	5	17
Perry Berezan	2	3	0	0	0	4
Todd Bergen	1	4	1	1	2	0
Gary Bergman	1	6	0	1	1	4
Jeff Beukeboom	2	11	0	2	2	25
Jack Bionda	1	5	0	0	0	6
Steve Black	1	6	0	0	0	0
Tom Bladon	3	14	1	5	6	31
Andy Blair	4	12	2	0	2	6
Hector 'Toe' Blake	3	15	4	9	13	7
Rob Blake	1	5	0	1	1	18
Russ Blinco	1	3	1	1	2	0
Gus Bodnar	2	8	1	0	1	2
Garth Boesch	3	14	1	0	1	10
Serge Boisvert	1	2	0	0	0	0
Leo Boivin	3	17	0	2	2	19
Ivan Boldirev	1	4	2	0	2	2
Frank 'Buzz' Boll	4	11	3	1	4	2
Marcel Bonin	4	21	3	6	9	22
Carl Boone	2	11	0	1	1	14
Christian Bordeleau	1	3	0	0	0	0
J.P. Bordeleau	1	6	1	0	1	4
Mike Bossy	5	23	17	17	34	4
Helge Bostrum	1	5	0	0	0	8
Emile 'Butch' Bouchard	9	44	2	10	12	61
Pierre Bouchard	5	21	3	1	4	19
Billy Boucher	1	4	0	0	0	0
Frank Boucher	5	19	8	6	14	6
George Boucher	1	4	0	0	0	27
Andre Boudrias	1	3	0	0	0	2
Leo Bourgeault	2	7	0	0	0	6
Bob Bourne	4	19	4	9	13	37
Phil Bourque	2	10	3	2	5	4
Raymond Bourque	2	10	3	5	8	12
Paul Boutilier	1	5	0	2	2	0
Ralph 'Scotty' Bowman	2	9	1	1	2	4
Bill Boyd	2	6	0	0	0	2
Irwin 'Yank' Boyd	1	4	0	0	0	2
Steve Bozek	1	4	2	0	2	19
Connie Braden	2	5	0	1	1	0
Brian Bradley	1	1	0	0	0	0
Per-Olov Brasar	1	1	0	0	0	0
Doug Brennan	2	7	1	0	1	6
Carl Brewer	5	25	0	6	6	56
Andy Brickley	1	2	0	0	0	0
Mel Bridgman	2	10	1	5	6	57
Patrice Brisebois	1	5	0	0	0	8
Neal Broten	3	15	6	5	11	4
Adam Brown	2	9	0	1	1	6
Connie Brown	1	3	0	2	2	0
Dave Brown	2	8	0	1	1	30
Doug Brown	1	4	0	3	3	2
Fred Brown	1	5	0	0	0	0
Jeff Brown	1	7	3	1	4	8
Jerry Brown	1	7	2	0	2	4
Rob Brown	1	3	0	0	0	2
Eddie Bruneteau	3	12	2	1	3	0
Benoit Brunet	1	5	0	1	1	2
Moderre 'Mud' Bruneteau	6	30	8	4	12	8
Sergei Brylin	1	3	1	1	2	4
Kelly Buchberger	2	8	0	0	0	7
John Bucyk	6	29	8	6	14	14
Tony Bukovich	1	1	0	0	0	0
Pavel Bure	1	7	3	5	8	15
Marc Bureau	1	6	1	0	1	8
Marty Burke	2	7	0	2	2	2
Shawn Burr	1	2	0	0	0	0
Randy Burridge	2	10	1	3	4	2
Cummy Burton	1	1	0	0	0	0
Eddie Bush	1	6	1	5	6	16
Rod Buskas	1	3	0	1	1	0
Mike Busniuk	1	6	2	1	3	7
Walter Buswell	1	4	0	1	1	2
Garth Butcher	1	1	0	0	0	0
John Byce	1	3	1	0	1	0
Lyndon Byers	1	2	1	0	1	0

• 175

176 • FINAL SERIES SCORING REGISTER

C

PLAYER	YRS	GP	G	A	TP	PIM
Jack Caffery	1	5	0	0	0	0
Herb Cain	4	14	0	5	5	2
Jock Callender	1	4	0	0	0	0
Pat Callighen	1	5	0	0	0	0
Craig Cameron	2	3	1	0	1	0
Colin Campbell	1	4	0	1	1	26
Guy Carbonneau	3	16	0	4	4	29
Wayne Carleton	1	4	1	1	2	0
Jack Carlson	1	2	0	0	0	0
Bob Carpenter	2	9	0	1	1	4
Gene Carr	1	6	0	0	0	9
Lorne Carr	2	14	3	2	5	11
Larry Carriere	1	6	0	0	0	4
Gene Carrigan	1	3	0	0	0	0
Billy Carroll	5	16	2	4	6	2
Bill Carson	2	4	1	0	1	2
Frank Carson	2	7	0	1	1	0
Gerald Carson	2	3	0	0	0	0
Jimmy Carson	1	2	0	1	1	0
Lindsay Carson	2	9	1	2	3	2
John Carter	1	5	1	0	1	19
Joe Carveth	4	25	7	4	11	6
Wayne Cashman	5	26	7	6	13	79
E. 'Murph' Chamberlain	7	29	5	2	7	18
Shawn Chambers	2	10	2	3	5	6
Rick Chartraw	4	14	2	1	3	16
Chris Chelios	3	15	3	13	16	48
Real Chevrefils	2	10	0	1	1	8
Tom Chorske	1	3	0	2	2	0
Dave Christian	1	5	0	0	0	0
Steve Christoff	1	5	2	2	4	0
Jack Church	3	8	0	1	1	4
Shane Churla	1	5	0	0	0	4
Dino Ciccarelli	2	9	4	3	7	25
Frank 'King' Clancy	5	18	4	3	7	24
Aubrey 'Dit' Clapper	6	18	2	2	4	2
Bobby Clarke	4	22	9	12	21	22
Sprague Cleghorn	1	4	0	0	0	4
Bill Clement	2	8	2	0	2	4
Paul Coffey	6	31	8	18	26	24
Mac Colville	2	11	0	2	2	6
Neil Colville	2	11	3	4	7	12
Brian Conacher	1	6	1	1	2	19
Charlie Conacher	4	14	3	3	6	14
Jim Conacher	4	4	1	0	1	0
Lionel Conacher	2	7	1	0	1	10
Pat Conacher	2	7	2	0	2	2
Roy Conacher	3	10	6	4	10	6
Harry Connor	1	2	0	0	0	0
Bill Cook	4	14	3	5	8	24
Fred 'Bun' Cook	4	14	5	2	7	18
Tom Cook	2	9	0	1	1	7
Joe Cooper	2	9	1	2	3	18
Shayne Corson	1	6	0	1	1	18
Les Costello	1	4	1	2	3	0
Murray Costello	1	2	0	0	0	0
Ray Cote	1	4	0	0	0	0
Harold 'Baldy' Cotton	3	10	1	2	3	12
Art Coulter	3	15	2	2	4	18
Yvan Cournoyer	9	50	21	19	40	18
Yves Courteau	1	1	0	0	0	0
Geoff Courtnall	2	12	4	1	5	11
Russ Courtnall	1	6	2	0	2	12
Billy Couture	1	4	0	0	0	2
Gerry Couture	2	10	4	2	6	0
Rosie 'Lolo' Couture	2	9	1	2	3	4
Bruce Cowick	1	6	0	0	0	7
Bill Cowley	3	14	1	11	12	6
Murray Craven	3	18	3	4	7	10
Jack Crawford	4	17	3	3	6	6
Marc Crawford	1	3	0	0	0	0
Dave Creighton	2	10	1	2	3	0
Terry Crisp	6	23	1	6	7	4
Doug Crossman	2	12	1	4	5	18
Keith Crowder	1	5	0	1	1	10
Barry Cullen	1	1	0	0	0	0
Brian Cullen	1	3	0	0	0	0
Floyd Curry	8	41	12	8	20	10

D

PLAYER	YRS	GP	G	A	TP	PIM
Ulf Dahlen	1	6	2	2	4	0
Kjell Dahlin	1	4	1	0	1	0
Chris Dahlquist	1	6	0	1	1	4
Carl 'Cully' Dahlstrom	2	8	1	3	4	2
J.J. Daigneault	2	10	1	0	1	6
Bob Dailey	1	6	1	3	4	4
Vincent Damphousse	1	5	1	3	4	8
Ken Daneyko	1	4	0	0	0	6
Harry Darragh	1	3	0	0	0	0
Bob Davidson	6	33	2	7	9	31
Lorne Davis	2	12	1	0	1	8
Bob Dawes	2	5	0	0	0	4
Clarence 'Hap' Day	4	14	1	3	4	14
Lucien DeBlois	1	2	0	0	0	0
Ron Delorme	1	4	0	0	0	4
Alex Delvecchio	8	47	16	22	38	2
Ab DeMarco	2	5	1	0	1	0
Cy Denneny	2	5	4	0	4	0
Norm Dennis	1	1	0	0	0	2
Eric Desjardins	2	11	3	1	4	8
Vic Desjardins	2	8	0	0	0	0
Al Dewsbury	2	6	0	3	3	8
Ernie Dickens	1	5	0	0	0	4
Gerald Diduck	1	7	0	1	1	6
Bob Dillabough	2	2	0	0	0	0
Cecil Dillon	3	12	4	3	7	8
Bill Dineen	3	19	1	0	1	6
Gord Dineen	1	3	0	0	0	24
Gilbert Dionne	1	5	1	1	2	4
Paul DiPietro	1	5	2	0	2	0
Gary Doak	4	19	1	0	1	44
Mike Donnelly	1	5	1	1	2	0
Ken Doraty	2	5	3	0	3	2
Jim Dorey	1	1	0	0	0	0
Gary Dornhoefer	3	13	2	1	3	20
Kent Douglas	1	5	0	1	1	2
Les Douglas	1	4	2	1	3	2
Peter Douris	1	1	0	0	0	0
Jim Dowd	1	1	1	1	2	2
Kris Draper	1	4	0	0	0	4
Gordie Drillon	4	20	6	3	9	6
Bruce Driver	1	4	1	2	3	0
Gilles Dube	1	2	0	0	0	0
Gaetan Duchesne	1	6	1	1	2	6
Rick Dudley	1	4	0	1	1	9
Dick Duff	9	47	15	20	35	39
Donald Dufresne	1	1	0	0	0	0
Ron Duguay	1	5	2	0	2	4
Woody Dumart	4	19	2	6	8	4
Andre 'Moose' Dupont	4	22	4	3	7	64
Mervyn 'Red' Dutton	1	5	1	1	2	13
Miroslav Dvorak	1	5	0	0	0	2

E

PLAYER	YRS	GP	G	A	TP	PIM
Mike Eaves	1	2	0	0	0	2
Tim Ecclestone	3	12	0	2	2	18
Frank Eddolls	3	16	0	1	1	4
Darryl Edestrand	2	8	0	0	0	2
Gary Edmundson	1	4	0	1	1	2
Pat Egan	2	12	2	1	3	8
Gerry Ehman	3	15	1	4	5	8
Pelle Eklund	1	7	1	7	8	0
Anders Eldebrink	1	3	0	0	0	2
Ron Ellis	1	6	1	1	2	4
Leighton 'Hap' Emms	1	3	0	0	0	2
Brian Englblom	2	6	0	0	0	0
Aut Erickson	1	1	0	0	0	2
Thomas Eriksson	1	4	0	0	0	0
Bob Errey	3	13	3	1	4	12
Phil Esposito	5	28	7	17	24	46
Jack Evans	2	12	1	0	1	22
Stewart Evans	1	3	0	0	0	4
Bill Ezinicki	3	14	2	2	4	30

F

PLAYER	YRS	GP	G	A	TP	PIM
Bill Fairbairn	1	6	0	2	2	0
Dave Farrish	1	1	0	0	0	0
Alex Faulkner	2	6	2	0	2	2
Sergei Fedorov	1	4	3	2	5	0
John Ferguson	6	33	5	6	11	69
Lorne Ferguson	1	5	0	1	1	8
Viacheslav Fetisov	1	4	0	3	3	0
Bob Fillion	3	12	0	2	2	4
Frank Finnigan	4	14	4	4	8	8
Dunc Fisher	1	7	2	2	4	12
Joe Fisher	1	1	0	0	0	0
Fern Flaman	3	14	0	2	2	23
Patrick Flatley	1	5	1	3	4	8
Reg Fleming	2	12	3	0	3	20
Bill Flett	1	6	0	3	3	4
Theoren Fleury	1	6	1	1	2	2
Lee Fogolin, Jr.	4	18	0	3	3	14
Lee Fogolin, Sr.	3	9	0	1	1	8
Rick Foley	1	4	0	1	1	4
Val Fonteyne	3	17	0	2	2	0
Dave Forbes	2	10	0	1	1	2
Ray Fortin	1	3	0	0	0	6
Nick Fotiu	1	2	0	1	1	10
Jimmy Fowler	2	8	0	2	2	0
Ron Francis	2	10	4	5	9	6
Curt Fraser	1	4	0	3	3	28
Frank Fredrickson	2	5	0	0	0	16
Len Frig	1	4	1	1	2	0

G

PLAYER	YRS	GP	G	A	TP	PIM
Bill Gadsby	3	18	1	3	4	28
Dave Gagner	1	6	4	2	6	14
Johnny Gagnon	1	5	4	2	6	2
Bob Gainey	6	30	5	5	10	46
Norman 'Dutch' Gainor	3	6	1	0	1	2
Percy Galbraith	3	8	1	0	1	4
John Gallagher	1	5	1	0	1	8
Don Gallinger	2	9	1	3	4	4
Garry Galley	1	5	0	0	0	4
Dick Gamble	2	4	0	0	0	2
Bert Gardiner	1	2	0	0	0	0
Cal Gardner	3	14	1	1	2	0
Danny Gare	1	6	2	1	3	4
Fern Gauthier	1	4	1	0	1	5
Stewart Gavin	1	6	0	3	3	2
George Gee	2	11	3	5	8	14
Martin Gelinas	2	12	1	1	2	6
Bernie Geoffrion	10	53	24	22	46	32
Ray Getliffe	2	9	2	1	3	6
Roy 'Gus' Giesebrecht	2	6	0	1	1	0
Greg Gilbert	4	16	1	4	5	38
Rod Gilbert	1	6	4	3	7	11
Brent Gilchrist	1	2	0	0	0	4

PLAYER	YRS	GP	G	A	TP	PIM
Curt Giles	1	5	0	0	0	2
Randy Gilhen	1	5	0	0	0	12
Clark Gillies	5	24	9	14	23	35
Doug Gilmour	1	6	4	3	7	6
Gaston Gingras	1	4	2	1	3	0
Fred Glover	1	2	0	0	0	0
Howie Glover	1	6	1	0	1	0
Brian Glynn	2	13	9	1	1	6
Warren Godfrey	3	12	0	1	1	10
Pete Goegan	2	11	0	0	0	16
Bob Goldham	5	30	2	5	7	30
Leroy Goldsworthy	2	5	0	0	0	0
Hank Goldup	2	9	2	1	3	0
Larry Goodenough	2	6	1	3	4	4
Ebbie Goodfellow	3	12	1	2	3	20
Jack Gordon	1	4	0	1	1	2
Tom Gorence	1	5	1	1	2	16
Butch Goring	5	24	9	7	16	2
Ed Gorman	1	4	0	0	0	0
Johnny Gottselig	4	15	6	5	11	6
Bob Gould	1	4	0	0	0	0
Michel Goulet	1	4	1	0	1	2
Phil Goyette	6	27	3	5	8	8
Bob Gracie	3	10	1	2	3	0
Thomas Gradin	1	4	3	2	5	2
Dirk Graham	1	4	4	0	4	0
Ted Graham	2	9	0	1	1	14
Tony Granato	1	5	1	3	4	10
Danny Grant	1	4	0	0	0	0
Leo Gravelle	1	4	2	0	2	2
Adam Graves	2	12	3	3	6	4
Alex Gray	1	5	0	0	0	0
Terry Gray	2	7	2	0	2	8
Red Green	1	1	0	0	0	0
Rick Green	2	11	2	0	2	2
Ted Green	1	4	0	0	0	0
Randy Gregg	6	31	2	7	9	8
George Gregor	1	1	0	0	0	0
Ron Greschner	1	5	1	0	1	8
Wayne Gretzky	6	31	18	35	53	8
Stu Grimson	2	4	0	1	1	2
Don Grosso	3	15	7	5	12	14
Bill Guerin	1	4	0	4	4	12
Jocelyn Guevremont	1	6	0	1	1	8
Armand 'Bep' Guidolin	3	10	2	2	4	19

H

PLAYER	YRS	GP	G	A	TP	PIM
Len Hachborn	1	1	0	0	0	0
Vic Hadfield	1	6	1	3	4	16
Matti Hagman	1	1	0	0	0	0
Bill Hajt	1	6	1	0	1	2
Murray Hall	1	1	0	0	0	0
Kevin Haller	1	3	0	1	1	0
Milt Halliday	1	4	0	0	0	0
Mats Hallin	1	2	0	0	0	0
Doug Halward	1	4	0	1	1	4
Robert 'Red' Hamill	1	5	0	0	0	2
Reg Hamilton	4	17	0	1	1	6
Mark Hardy	1	4	0	1	1	4
Glen Harmon	3	15	2	3	5	0
John Harms	1	4	3	0	3	2
Terry Harper	6	34	1	4	5	47
Billy Harris	5	26	6	5	11	18
Ted Harris	6	33	1	7	8	64
Craig Hartsburg	1	5	1	4	5	2
Doug Harvey	11	54	4	31	35	60
Greg Hawgood	2	7	2	2	4	4
Bill Hay	3	19	2	7	9	12
Jim Hay	1	5	1	0	1	4
Anders Hedberg	1	5	1	2	3	2
Bret Hedican	1	7	1	3	4	4

PLAYER	YRS	GP	G	A	TP	PIM
Jerry Heffernan	1	2	0	1	1	0
Ott Heller	4	18	2	3	5	19
Murray Henderson	1	5	1	0	1	0
Paul Henderson	2	13	2	3	5	8
Lorne Henning	1	6	1	1	2	0
Camille Henry	2	9	1	0	1	2
Jimmy Herberts	1	4	1	0	1	18
Robert 'Red' Heron	2	8	1	0	1	4
Bryan Hextall	1	6	4	1	5	7
Bill Hicke	2	5	0	1	1	0
Pat Hickey	1	5	1	2	3	0
Wayne Hicks	1	1	0	0	0	2
Al Hill	1	6	0	0	0	2
Mel Hill	3	16	3	4	7	8
Sean Hill	1	1	0	0	0	0
Wilbert 'Dutch' Hiller	2	11	3	3	6	0
Larry Hillman	4	22	1	1	2	6
Wayne Hillman	1	1	0	0	0	0
Lionel Hitchman	3	8	0	0	0	31
Ivan Hlinka	1	2	0	0	0	0
Ken Hodge	3	16	6	10	16	27
Bobby Holik	1	4	1	1	2	8
Bill 'Flash' Hollett	5	23	4	4	8	4
Gord Hollingworth	1	2	0	0	0	2
Paul Holmgren	1	5	4	4	8	15
Pete Horeck	2	8	3	3	6	12
Reginald 'Red' Horner	7	28	3	6	9	54
Tim Horton	6	33	4	16	20	38
Bronco Horvath	2	12	4	2	6	6
Ed Hospodar	1	5	0	0	0	34
Rejean Houle	4	24	3	10	13	16
Garry Howatt	1	6	0	1	1	21
Gordie Howe	10	55	18	32	50	94
Mark Howe	3	14	1	2	3	0
Syd Howe	6	28	8	12	20	4
Jiri Hrdina	3	8	0	0	0	0
Charlie Huddy	7	31	1	11	12	28
Mike Hudson	1	4	0	0	0	2
Pat Hughes	3	13	0	3	3	8
Bobby Hull	4	26	11	17	28	26
Brett Hull	1	2	0	0	0	0
Dennis Hull	3	14	6	5	11	6
Dave Hunter	4	19	1	2	3	43
Mark Hunter	1	4	0	1	1	12
Tim Hunter	3	16	0	3	3	67

I-J

PLAYER	YRS	GP	G	A	TP	PIM
Frank Ingram	1	5	0	1	1	2
Ted Irvine	1	6	1	4	5	10
Art Jackson	4	19	4	1	5	7
Don Jackson	3	14	0	0	0	52
Hal Jackson	3	15	0	1	1	8
Harvey 'Busher' Jackson	7	25	7	5	12	25
Jaromir Jagr	2	10	2	5	7	2
Jerry James	1	4	0	0	0	0
Craig Janney	2	10	0	2	2	0
Doug Jarrett	3	20	1	2	3	12
Doug Jarvis	4	19	0	6	6	12
Larry Jeffrey	2	12	3	3	6	8
Roger Jenkins	2	8	0	2	2	6
Bill Jennings	1	4	1	1	2	0
Grant Jennings	1	2	0	0	0	2
Allan Johnson	1	6	1	2	3	0
Ivan 'Ching' Johnson	5	19	1	2	3	48
Jim Johnson	1	6	0	1	1	10
Norm Johnson	1	6	2	0	2	4
Terry Johnson	1	6	0	0	0	12
Tom Johnson	10	49	6	3	9	44
Virgil Johnson	2	6	0	1	1	2
Greg Johnston	2	5	1	2	3	4
Ed Johnstone	1	5	0	0	0	2

PLAYER	YRS	GP	G	A	TP	PIM
Aurel Joliat	2	7	0	3	3	2
Stan Jonathan	2	10	0	0	0	24
Tomas Jonsson	3	11	1	2	3	18
Eddie Joyal	2	12	3	1	4	6
Bob Joyce	1	5	1	1	2	0
Bill Juzda	2	9	0	0	0	6

K

PLAYER	YRS	GP	G	A	TP	PIM
Alex Kaleta	1	7	0	3	3	0
Anders Kallur	4	18	3	4	7	8
Rudolph 'Bingo' Kampman	4	22	1	3	4	45
Alexander Karpovtsev	1	2	0	0	0	0
Steve Kasper	1	5	2	0	2	2
Mike Keane	2	10	1	5	6	6
Mel 'Butch' Keeling	4	14	4	2	6	16
Larry Keenan	3	12	2	0	2	8
Bob Kelly	3	15	3	2	5	18
Leonard 'Red' Kelly	12	65	11	20	31	29
Pete Kelly	2	7	1	1	2	0
Reginald 'Pep' Kelly	5	17	2	2	4	0
Bill Kendall	1	1	0	0	0	0
Ted 'Teeder' Kennedy	5	26	12	11	23	8
Dave Keon	4	24	11	5	16	0
Tim Kerr	1	3	2	1	3	9
Hec Kilrea	4	15	0	4	4	4
Ken Kilrea	1	2	0	0	0	0
Wally Kilrea	2	9	2	2	4	4
Orest Kindrachuk	3	15	2	2	4	13
Lloyd Klein	1	1	0	0	0	0
Petr Klima	1	5	1	0	1	0
Joe Klukay	5	24	2	4	6	11
Gord Kluzak	1	5	0	1	1	4
Joe Kocur	1	6	0	0	0	2
Vlad. Konstantinov	1	4	0	0	0	8
Jerry Korab	3	11	2	1	3	26
John Kordic	1	5	0	0	0	15
Cliff Koroll	2	13	3	5	8	6
Alexei Kovalev	1	7	4	3	7	2
Vyacheslav Kozlov	1	4	1	0	1	0
Igor Kravchuk	1	4	0	0	0	2
Mike Krushelnyski	4	19	4	5	9	16
Dave Kryskow	1	3	2	0	2	0
Frantisek Kucera	1	4	0	0	0	0
Jari Kurri	7	36	15	24	39	16
Merv Kuryluk	1	2	0	0	0	0
Gus Kyle	1	7	1	0	1	14
Nick Kypreos	1	1	0	0	0	0

L

PLAYER	YRS	GP	G	A	TP	PIM
Leo Labine	4	22	3	4	7	24
Elmer Lach	6	27	8	10	18	6
Normand Lacombe	1	5	1	0	1	4
Nathan Lafayette	1	7	0	3	3	0
Guy Lafleur	5	25	9	17	26	14
Pat LaFontaine	1	5	2	1	3	0
Mike Lalor	1	5	0	2	2	19
Joe Lamb	1	4	0	0	0	21
Mark Lamb	1	5	0	3	3	2
Yvon Lambert	4	18	5	8	13	16
Leo Lamoureux	3	11	0	1	1	8
Jack Lancien	1	2	0	0	0	0
Gord Lane	4	19	1	0	1	70
Miles Lane	2	4	0	0	0	0
Pete Langelle	3	17	1	3	4	0
Dave Langevin	5	21	0	3	3	26
Al Langlois	4	18	0	2	2	22
Rod Langway	1	5	0	0	0	12

PLAYER	YRS	GP	G	A	TP	PIM
Jean Lanthier	1	2	0	0	0	4
Jacques Laperriere	5	23	1	4	5	32
Guy Lapointe	5	27	3	11	14	40
Martin Lapointe	1	2	0	1	1	8
Edgar Laprade	1	7	3	3	6	2
Steve Larmer	2	11	4	1	5	4
Wildor Larochelle	2	7	0	1	1	14
Claude Larose	6	27	3	6	9	21
Pierre Larouche	2	3	1	0	1	0
Reed Larson	1	2	0	0	0	2
Hal Laycoe	1	5	0	1	1	10
Reggie Leach	3	16	8	5	13	0
Stephan Lebeau	1	5	1	2	3	4
Jack LeClair	2	12	3	1	4	6
John LeClair	1	5	2	2	4	0
Albert Leduc	2	4	1	3	4	2
Richie Leduc	1	5	0	0	0	9
Brian Leetch	1	7	5	6	11	4
Gary Leeman	1	5	0	1	1	2
Chuck Lefley	1	6	3	3	6	2
Roger Leger	1	6	0	2	2	6
Jacques Lemaire	8	40	19	18	37	31
Moe Lemay	1	5	1	1	2	6
Claude Lemieux	3	13	5	3	8	53
Jocelyn Lemieux	1	4	0	1	1	0
Mario Lemieux	2	9	10	9	19	6
Alfred 'Pit' Lepine	2	7	4	2	6	4
Art Lesieur	1	5	0	0	0	4
Bill Lesuk	1	2	0	0	0	0
Tony Leswick	4	25	5	7	12	34
Alex Levinsky	3	11	1	0	1	8
Danny Lewicki	1	3	0	0	0	0
Herbie Lewis	3	13	4	3	7	6
Doug Lidster	1	7	2	0	2	10
Nicklas Lidstrom	1	4	0	2	2	0
Trevor Linden	1	7	3	2	5	6
Lars Lindgren	1	4	1	0	1	2
Ted Lindsay	8	44	19	15	34	48
Willy Lindstrom	3	14	5	1	6	2
Ken Linseman	4	20	4	10	14	52
Carl Liscombe	4	22	6	8	14	9
Ed Litzenberger	4	14	1	3	4	16
Lonnie Loach	1	1	0	0	0	0
Troy Loney	2	10	1	1	2	26
Stan Long	1	2	0	0	0	0
Ross Lonsberry	3	16	4	2	6	4
Hakan Loob	2	11	0	3	3	2
Jim Lorentz	2	10	1	2	3	2
Bob Lorimer	2	11	0	0	0	15
Kevin Lowe	7	37	3	3	6	24
Ross Lowe	1	1	0	0	0	0
Don Luce	1	6	2	3	5	12
Craig Ludwig	2	11	0	0	0	22
Dave Lumley	3	10	1	1	2	28
Jyrki Lumme	1	7	0	4	4	6
Pentti Lund	1	7	1	1	2	0
Len Lunde	1	5	1	0	1	0
Pat Lundy	1	1	0	1	1	0
Gilles Lupien	2	6	0	0	0	19
Gary Lupul	1	2	0	0	0	0
Vic Lynn	3	14	4	2	6	30

M

PLAYER	YRS	GP	G	A	TP	PIM
Al MacAdam	1	5	1	3	4	2
Blair MacDonald	1	1	0	0	0	0
Kilby MacDonald	1	6	0	0	0	4
Parker MacDonald	4	24	3	1	4	14
Hub Macey	1	3	0	0	0	0
Bruce MacGregor	5	30	6	6	12	14
Al MacInnis	2	11	5	8	13	26
Calum MacKay	4	20	3	7	10	8
Mickey MacKay	2	4	0	0	0	2
Fleming Mackell	5	25	5	10	15	14
Howie Mackie	1	3	0	0	0	0
John MacLean	1	4	1	4	5	0
Rick MacLeish	3	18	6	9	15	8
Brian MacLellan	1	6	0	1	1	4
John MacMillan	2	5	0	1	1	2
Al MacNeil	1	7	0	0	0	12
Jamie Macoun	2	11	0	3	3	12
James 'Bud' MacPherson	3	11	0	1	1	8
Craig MacTavish	4	24	0	5	5	16
Keith Magnuson	1	7	0	0	0	36
Frank Mahovlich	8	45	16	25	41	43
Peter Mahovlich	4	21	10	14	24	36
Fern Majeau	1	1	0	0	0	0
Chico Maki	4	21	3	6	9	12
David Maley	1	5	1	2	3	2
Dan Maloney	1	2	0	0	0	4
Dave Maloney	1	5	1	2	3	10
Don Maloney	1	5	0	1	1	6
Georges Mantha	2	7	2	1	3	4
Sylvio Mantha	2	7	2	0	2	18
Milan Marcetta	1	2	0	0	0	0
Harold 'Mush' March	3	12	3	2	5	14
Bryan Marchment	1	4	1	0	1	2
Don Marcotte	5	25	3	2	5	16
Gus Marker	4	17	3	3	6	4
John Marks	1	6	1	1	2	2
Nevin Markwart	1	1	0	0	0	2
Mario Marois	1	5	0	0	0	4
Brad Marsh	2	12	0	3	3	45
Bert Marshall	1	6	0	2	2	8
Don Marshall	6	32	3	4	7	4
Clare Martin	1	3	0	0	0	0
Frank Martin	1	5	0	1	1	2
Hubert 'Pit' Martin	3	19	6	4	10	18
Rick Martin	1	6	2	4	6	6
Paul Masnick	4	18	3	3	6	14
Stephane Matteau	2	11	0	2	2	6
Brad Maxwell	1	4	0	4	4	9
Kevin Maxwell	1	2	0	0	0	4
Eddie Mazur	4	17	0	2	2	15
Jerome 'Jud' McAtee	1	7	0	0	0	0
George McAvoy	1	3	0	0	0	0
Bert McCaffrey	1	2	1	0	1	0
Doug McCaig	1	2	0	0	0	6
Darren McCarty	1	4	0	0	0	0
Tom McCarthy	2	4	0	3	3	2
Kevin McClelland	4	22	4	5	9	87
John McCormack	2	6	0	0	0	0
Bill McCreary	3	10	0	2	2	4
John McCreedy	2	11	1	2	3	6
Brad McCrimmon	2	13	2	2	4	16
Ab McDonald	7	30	6	7	13	8
Lanny McDonald	2	8	3	1	4	8
Wilfrid 'Bucko' McDonald	5	18	3	0	3	4
Shawn McEachern	1	4	0	2	2	0
Mike McEwen	3	12	2	3	5	6
Jim McFadden	3	15	3	3	6	6
Don McFayden	1	4	0	1	1	2
Jack McGill	1	5	0	0	0	0
Jack McIlhargey	2	10	0	1	1	29
Jack McIntyre	1	4	1	0	1	0
Doug McKay	1	1	0	0	0	0
Murdo McKay	1	6	0	0	0	0
Randy McKay	1	4	1	0	1	0
Don McKenney	3	16	6	7	13	0
Bill McKenzie	1	4	0	0	0	9
John McKenzie	3	14	1	6	7	39
Jack McLeod	1	5	0	0	0	0
Mike McMahon	1	4	1	0	1	12
Max McNab	3	10	0	0	0	4
Peter McNab	3	16	3	3	6	4
Mike McPhee	2	11	1	5	6	28
Basil McRae	1	5	0	0	0	26
Pat McReavy	2	10	2	2	4	7
Marty McSorley	3	17	3	0	3	30
Howie Meeker	3	15	2	4	6	23
Harry Meeking	1	4	0	0	0	0
Paul Meger	4	12	1	1	2	4
Scott Mellanby	1	7	1	2	3	4
Gerry Melnyk	5	24	0	0	0	2
Larry Melnyk	1	1	0	0	0	0
Wayne Merrick	4	19	3	6	9	0
Mark Messier	7	38	11	20	31	52
Don Metz	5	21	4	5	9	4
Nick Metz	8	32	3	7	10	17
Dave Michayluk	1	1	0	0	0	0
Nick Mickoski	1	7	0	4	4	0
Rick Middleton	3	15	1	3	4	0
Stan Mikita	5	31	10	21	31	58
Mike Milbury	2	9	0	3	3	30
Hib Milks	1	3	0	0	0	0
Corey Millen	1	5	0	0	0	2
Bill Miller	1	3	0	0	0	0
Bob Miller	1	6	0	1	1	9
Earl Miller	1	2	0	0	0	0
Jay Miller	1	3	0	0	0	24
Gerry Minor	1	4	1	2	3	0
Mike Modano	1	6	2	2	4	6
Ron Moffatt	1	2	0	0	0	0
Doug Mohns	3	18	1	4	5	23
Lars Molin	1	4	0	4	4	0
Sergio Momesso	1	7	1	1	2	17
Armand Mondou	2	5	0	0	0	2
Pierre Mondou	3	13	1	3	4	6
Dickie Moore	10	52	10	21	31	69
Howie Morenz	2	7	2	0	2	12
Elwin 'Moe' Morris	1	7	1	0	1	2
Rod Morrison	1	1	0	0	0	0
Ken Morrow	5	24	4	3	7	14
Gus Mortson	4	16	3	3	6	8
Kenny Mosdell	6	33	6	7	13	16
Bill Mosienko	1	4	0	1	1	2
Alex Motter	3	12	1	2	3	8
Joe Mullen	3	16	10	9	19	8
Kirk Muller	1	5	2	2	4	6
Craig Muni	3	15	0	3	3	2
Dunc Munro	1	5	0	1	1	2
Bob Murdoch	2	6	0	0	0	0
Don Murdoch	1	5	1	1	2	2
Murray Murdoch	5	19	1	3	4	12
Joe Murphy	1	5	2	2	4	4
Larry Murphy	2	10	2	11	13	8
Ron Murphy	1	6	2	1	3	0
Terry Murray	1	2	0	0	0	0
Dana Murzyn	1	6	0	1	1	8

N

PLAYER	YRS	GP	G	A	TP	PIM
Don Nachbaur	1	1	0	0	0	0
Mark Napier	2	10	1	0	1	2
Mats Naslund	2	11	4	6	10	4
Ric Nattress	1	6	0	0	0	12
Cam Neely	2	10	2	5	7	14
Jim Neilson	1	3	0	1	1	2
Sergei Nemchinov	1	7	0	2	2	2
Eric Nesterenko	4	26	1	5	6	30
Bob Nevin	2	11	4	1	5	4
Scott Niedermayer	1	4	1	3	4	0
Joe Nieuwendyk	1	6	1	1	2	0
Frank Nighbor	1	4	0	1	1	0
Chris Nilan	1	3	0	0	0	49
Jim Nill	1	3	0	1	1	6
Kent Nilsson	1	7	0	1	1	0

Player	YRS	GP	G	A	TP	PIM
Ulf Nilsson	1	2	0	0	0	2
Simon Nolet	1	6	0	1	1	0
Brian Noonan	2	11	0	4	4	2
Larry 'Baldy' Northcott	1	3	2	1	3	0
Bill Nyrop	3	10	0	3	3	8
Bob Nystrom	5	21	8	4	12	67

O

PLAYER	YRS	GP	G	A	TP	PIM
Russell Oatman	2	6	0	0	0	12
Dennis O'Brien	1	5	0	0	0	6
Herbert 'Buddy' O'Connor	4	21	6	5	11	4
Lyle Odelein	1	5	0	2	2	6
Gerry Odrowski	2	8	0	0	0	6
Bill O'Dwyer	1	5	0	0	0	0
Harry Oliver	3	8	3	3	6	6
Bert Olmstead	11	56	5	19	24	52
Terry O'Reilly	3	16	2	3	5	49
Jimmy Orlando	3	15	0	5	5	53
Bobby Orr	3	16	8	12	20	31
Danny O'Shea	1	7	1	1	2	12
Joel Otto	2	11	3	8	11	14
George Owen	2	4	0	0	0	2

P-Q

PLAYER	YRS	GP	G	A	TP	PIM
John Paddock	1	2	0	2	2	0
Jim Paek	2	9	1	3	4	4
Pete Palangio	1	3	0	0	0	0
Brad Palmer	1	5	1	0	1	4
Jim Pappin	4	26	11	8	19	24
Brad Park	3	16	7	9	16	21
George Parsons	1	3	2	0	2	11
Joe Paterson	1	5	0	0	0	19
Lynn Patrick	2	11	3	1	4	2
Murray 'Muzz' Patrick	1	6	1	0	1	6
Colin Patterson	2	8	1	1	2	16
Marty Pavelich	7	36	4	8	12	38
Steve Payne	1	5	5	2	7	2
Allen Pedersen	2	9	0	0	0	8
John Peirson	3	12	1	0	1	14
Mike Peluso	2	7	0	0	0	4
Jim Peplinski	2	9	1	5	6	47
Gilbert Perreault	1	6	1	1	2	6
Stefan Persson	4	18	3	13	16	20
Jim Peters	4	22	1	3	4	8
Gord Pettinger	5	21	3	3	6	2
Bill Phillips	1	5	2	0	2	2
Noel Picard	4	15	0	4	4	28
Alf Pike	1	6	2	0	2	4
Pierre Pilote	3	17	2	13	15	22
Gerry Pinder	1	5	0	0	0	2
Barclay Plager	3	9	1	2	3	6
Bill Plager	2	5	0	0	0	4
Bob Plager	3	10	0	1	1	28
Gerry Plamondon	1	1	0	0	0	0
Pierre Plante	1	5	0	0	0	0
Willi Plett	1	2	0	0	0	4
Nels Podolsky	1	3	0	0	0	0
Norman 'Bud' Poile	2	8	2	0	2	2
Mike Polich	2	4	0	0	0	0
Jack Portland	1	5	0	0	0	2
Denis Potvin	5	24	9	19	28	28
Dave Poulin	3	14	1	3	4	12
Jaroslav Pouzar	3	9	0	1	1	8
Walter 'Babe' Pratt	3	18	3	3	6	19
Dean Prentice	1	6	1	1	2	2
Noel Price	2	3	0	1	1	2
Keith Primeau	1	3	0	0	0	8
Joe Primeau	4	14	3	6	9	4
Andre Pronovost	6	30	2	4	6	18
Marcel Pronovost	9	51	2	8	10	30
Brian Propp	5	29	10	12	22	8
Claude Provost	10	49	5	11	16	24
Metro Prystai	3	15	4	3	7	4
Bob Pulford	6	33	8	13	21	44
Cliff Purpur	2	8	0	0	0	4
Jean Pusie	1	3	0	0	0	0
Bill Quackenbush	4	20	1	3	4	4
John Quilty	1	2	0	1	1	2
Dan Quinn	1	5	1	4	5	4

R

PLAYER	YRS	GP	G	A	TP	PIM
Don Raleigh	1	7	2	0	2	0
Rob Ramage	1	6	0	2	2	10
Craig Ramsay	1	6	0	2	2	0
Mike Ramsey	1	2	0	0	0	0
Jean Ratelle	3	16	0	5	5	0
Matt Ravlich	1	7	1	1	2	8
Kenny Reardon	2	9	0	0	0	20
Terry Reardon	2	9	3	1	4	4
Marc Reaume	1	4	0	0	0	0
Billy Reay	5	23	3	2	5	14
Mark Recchi	1	6	2	1	3	8
Dick Redmond	1	4	0	1	1	0
Mickey Redmond	2	6	0	1	1	0
Larry Regan	4	18	3	7	10	6
Earl Reibel	3	16	3	7	10	4
Jerry Reid	1	2	0	0	0	2
Leo Reise	4	17	1	0	1	14
Paul Reinhart	1	5	1	1	2	2
Henri Richard	12	65	21	26	47	68
Maurice 'Rocket' Richard	12	59	34	12	46	83
Vic Ripley	1	5	1	1	2	2
Doug Risebrough	5	22	5	5	10	35
Gus Rivers	2	7	0	0	0	0
Rene Robert	1	6	1	2	3	6
Phil Roberto	1	5	0	0	0	12
Gary Roberts	1	6	0	0	0	8
Gordie Roberts	3	15	0	1	1	33
Jim Roberts	9	42	3	3	6	44
Fred Robertson	1	3	0	0	0	0
Earl Robinson	1	3	2	1	3	0
Larry Robinson	7	36	5	15	20	35
Luc Robitaille	1	5	3	2	5	4
Leon Rochefort	3	16	2	2	4	12
Ernie Rodden	1	1	0	0	0	0
Jeremy Roenick	1	4	0	2	2	0
Dale Rolfe	1	6	2	0	2	10
Brian Rolston	1	2	0	1	1	0
Elwin 'Doc' Romnes	4	18	3	8	11	4
Ed Ronan	1	5	1	1	2	6
Paul Ronty	1	2	0	0	0	2
Steve Rooney	1	1	0	0	0	0
Darcy Rota	1	4	0	0	0	19
Tom Roulston	1	4	0	1	1	0
Bob Rouse	1	4	0	0	0	0
Bobby Rousseau	6	33	6	13	19	23
Reijo Ruotsalainen	2	12	0	2	2	6
Cam Russell	1	1	0	0	0	0
Phil Russell	1	6	0	1	1	16
Warren Rychel	1	5	0	0	0	2

S

PLAYER	YRS	GP	G	A	TP	PIM
Gary Sabourin	3	12	2	0	2	6
Dollard St. Laurent	9	43	1	6	7	47
Frank St. Marseille	3	12	4	3	7	4
Don Saleski	3	16	1	4	5	18
Kjell Samuelsson	2	11	0	2	2	12
Ulf Samuelsson	2	10	1	2	3	14
Phil Samis	1	3	0	1	1	2
Derek Sanderson	2	10	4	3	7	34
Ed Sandford	1	5	2	1	3	5
Charlie Sands	1	4	0	1	1	0
Tomas Sandstrom	1	5	0	2	2	4
Glen Sather	1	6	0	0	0	11
Andre Savard	1	6	1	1	2	20
Denis Savard	1	1	0	0	0	0
Serge Savard	7	33	5	8	13	22
Bobby Schmautz	3	16	3	2	5	29
Jackie Schmidt	1	2	0	0	0	0
Milt Schmidt	4	18	6	8	14	4
Mathieu Schneider	1	5	1	1	2	8
Ron Schock	2	8	0	0	0	2
Jim Schoenfeld	1	6	0	2	2	11
Dave 'Sweeney' Schriner	3	19	6	6	12	8
Dave Schultz	3	16	4	2	6	61
Enio Sclisizzi	2	4	0	0	0	2
Earl Seibert	5	22	2	1	3	18
Rod Seiling	1	6	1	1	2	6
Dave Semenko	3	13	2	2	4	18
Eddie Shack	4	21	1	1	2	28
Bobby Sheehan	1	5	0	1	1	0
Neil Sheehy	1	5	0	0	0	31
Gregg Sheppard	3	16	4	6	10	10
John Sheppard	1	3	0	0	0	0
Ray Sheppard	1	3	0	1	1	0
John Sherf	1	5	0	1	1	2
Fred Shero	1	4	0	0	0	0
Jack Shewchuk	1	4	0	0	0	4
Alex Shibicky	2	10	0	2	2	2
Allan Shields	1	3	0	1	1	2
Bill Shill	1	3	0	1	1	2
Jack Shill	2	8	1	2	3	8
Paul Shmyr	2	5	0	0	0	19
Eddie Shore	4	13	1	3	4	42
Gary Shuchuk	1	5	0	0	0	0
Steve Shutt	4	19	10	11	21	4
Albert 'Babe' Siebert	2	8	1	1	2	20
John Simon	1	3	0	0	0	0
Craig Simpson	2	10	7	5	12	16
Al Sims	3	11	0	0	0	4
Ilkka Sinisalo	2	10	1	0	1	2
Glen Skov	3	18	2	3	5	26
Brian Skrudland	2	11	3	2	5	50
Tod Sloan	2	11	3	5	8	13
Ed Slowinski	1	7	0	3	3	4
Doug Smail	1	1	0	0	0	0
Alex Smith	1	4	0	0	0	8
Bobby Smith	4	22	8	10	18	34
Clint Smith	2	10	1	4	5	2
Dallas Smith	3	16	0	4	4	24
Derrick Smith	2	12	2	4	6	10
Des Smith	1	4	0	2	2	2
Floyd Smith	3	18	6	3	9	4
Greg Smith	1	5	0	1	1	6
Ken Smith	1	5	0	2	2	0
Reginald 'Hooley' Smith	3	12	0	3	3	29
Rick Smith	3	14	2	3	5	18
Sid Smith	2	9	8	2	10	0
Stan Smith	1	1	0	0	0	0
Steve Smith	4	17	1	6	7	25
Stan Smyl	1	4	2	0	2	19
Harold Snepsts	1	4	0	0	0	16
Ken Solheim	1	1	0	0	0	0
Art Somers	3	12	0	3	3	8
John Sorrell	3	13	4	5	9	2
Bill Speer	1	1	0	0	0	0
Brian Spencer	1	6	0	1	1	4
Irv Spencer	2	8	0	0	0	0
Fred Stanfield	4	23	3	6	9	4
Allan Stanley	8	46	4	13	17	36
Daryl Stanley	1	4	0	0	0	2

PLAYER	YRS	GP	G	A	TP	PIM
Wally Stanowski	5	29	3	7	10	2
Paul Stanton	2	10	0	1	1	28
Pat Stapleton	2	13	0	10	10	4
Wilf Starr	1	3	0	1	1	2
Vic Stasiuk	6	31	5	9	14	8
Peter Stemkowski	2	12	3	7	10	12
Kevin Stevens	2	10	6	6	12	27
Scott Stevens	1	4	0	2	2	4
Gaye Stewart	3	12	1	2	3	6
John 'Black Jack' Stewart	6	29	2	7	9	34
Nels Stewart	1	5	2	0	2	4
Ron Stewart	6	28	4	9	13	8
Bill Stuart	1	4	0	0	0	0
Brent Sutter	4	17	5	7	12	16
Duane Sutter	5	24	4	9	13	86
Rich Sutter	1	3	3	0	3	4
Ron Sutter	2	12	1	6	7	12
Petr Svoboda	1	6	0	3	3	8
Bob Sweeney	2	10	0	3	3	9
Don Sweeney	1	5	0	1	1	6
Darryl Sydor	1	5	0	0	0	4

T

PLAYER	YRS	GP	G	A	TP	PIM
Peter Taglianetti	1	5	0	3	3	8
Jean-Guy Talbot	11	55	0	5	5	56
Marc Tardif	2	13	3	3	6	23
Billy Taylor	2	9	2	8	10	2
Dave Taylor	1	3	1	1	2	6
Ralph Taylor	1	1	0	0	0	0
Tim Taylor	1	2	0	0	0	2
Michael Thelven	1	4	0	0	0	6
Jimmy Thomson	1	6	0	0	0	12
Paul Thompson	4	13	3	3	6	25
Bill Thoms	4	15	3	4	7	2
Jim Thomson	3	13	1	4	5	13
Esa Tikkanen	5	27	9	6	15	50
Ray Timgren	2	9	1	3	4	21
Mark Tinordi	1	6	0	1	1	15
Walt Tkaczuk	2	11	1	3	4	0
Rick Tocchet	3	16	5	12	17	40
John Tonelli	6	29	3	10	13	35
Tim Tookey	1	1	0	0	0	0
Jerry Toppazzini	3	16	1	2	3	8
Jack Toupin	1	1	0	0	0	0
Gilles Tremblay	2	12	2	3	5	0
J.C. Tremblay	6	34	3	18	21	27
Mario Tremblay	4	14	5	2	7	30
Dave Trottier	1	3	1	0	1	4
Bryan Trottier	7	34	11	22	33	46
Louis Trudel	2	8	0	1	1	0
Bob Turner	6	28	1	1	2	14

U-V

PLAYER	YRS	GP	G	A	TP	PIM
Norm Ullman	5	28	6	12	18	23
Carol Vadnais	4	18	1	4	5	37
Mel 'Sparky' Vail	1	2	0	0	0	0
Ed Van Impe	2	12	0	4	4	21
Elmer Vasko	3	19	1	2	3	18
Gary Veneruzzo	1	3	0	1	1	0
Steve Vickers	1	5	1	1	2	0
Carl Voss	1	4	2	0	2	0

W

PLAYER	YRS	GP	G	A	TP	PIM
Bob Wall	1	4	0	0	0	2
Ryan Walter	2	11	1	1	2	6
Mike Walton	2	12	3	5	8	6
Jimmy Ward	2	8	1	1	2	2
Eddie Wares	3	14	0	6	6	22
Nick Wasnie	2	7	2	2	4	8
Bryan Watson	1	6	0	0	0	12
Harry Watson	5	20	8	5	13	10
Jimmy Watson	4	21	0	4	4	43
Joe Watson	3	16	0	2	2	20
Phil Watson	3	15	3	5	8	18
Tim Watters	1	5	0	0	0	4
Ralph 'Cooney' Weiland	4	13	1	2	3	2
Jay Wells	1	7	0	0	0	8
John Wensink	2	9	0	0	0	28
Marvin 'Cy' Wentworth	2	8	3	2	5	8
Glen Wesley	2	10	2	2	4	2
Ed Westfall	2	10	2	3	5	10
Ken Wharram	3	17	3	2	5	16
Bill White	2	13	1	5	6	12
Bob Whitelaw	1	4	0	0	0	0
Art Wiebe	2	8	0	1	1	6
Jim Wiemer	1	2	0	0	0	0
Neil Wilkinson	1	6	0	0	0	2
Burr Williams	1	2	0	0	0	0
Dave 'Tiger' Williams	1	4	0	3	3	14
Behn Wilson	1	6	0	4	4	28
Johnny Wilson	5	27	3	2	5	2
Larry Wilson	1	2	0	0	0	0
Murray Wilson	3	13	0	4	4	8
Eddie Wiseman	2	7	3	0	3	0
Steve Wochy	1	2	0	0	0	0
Benny Woit	3	18	0	1	1	10

Y-Z

PLAYER	YRS	GP	G	A	TP	PIM
Doug Young	2	8	1	2	3	2
Howie Young	2	8	1	1	2	18
Scott Young	1	1	1	1	2	0
Tim Young	1	2	0	3	3	0
Tom Younghans	1	3	0	0	0	4
Steve Yzerman	1	4	1	0	1	0
Larry Zeidel	1	3	0	0	0	0
Valeri Zelepukin	1	3	0	0	0	4
Peter Zezel	2	12	1	2	3	6
Alexei Zhitnik	1	5	0	1	1	4
Sergei Zubov	1	6	1	5	6	0

Final Series Goaltending Register 1927-1995

GOALTENDER	YRS	GP	W	L	MIN	GA	SO	AVG
Andy Aitkenhead	1	4	3	1	248	5	1	1.21
Tom Barrasso	2	10	7	2	559	23	2	2.47
Hank Bassen	2	5	1	3	274	11	0	2.41
Don Beaupre	1	3	1	2	180	13	0	4.33
Ed Belfour	1	4	0	3	187	11	0	3.53
Clint Benedict	1	5	2	3	307	5	1	0.98
Johnny Bower	6	28	13	13	1638	70	2	2.56
Frank Brimsek	4	18	9	9	1132	47	1	2.49
Walter 'Turk' Broda	8	38	21	17	2369	85	4	2.15
Martin Brodeur	1	4	4	0	206	7	0	1.75
Richard Brodeur	1	4	0	4	260	17	0	3.92
Jon Casey	1	6	2	3	290	21	0	4.34
Lorne Chabot	3	9	4	4	508	23	0	2.72
Gerry Cheevers	4	17	8	9	1020	51	2	3.00
Alex Connell*	2	7	5	0	425	7	1	0.99
Roger Crozier	2	8	3	4	426	19	0	2.68
Wilf Cude	1	4	1	3	291	9	0	1.86
John Davidson	1	5	1	4	307	19	0	3.17
Denis DeJordy	1	1	0	0	20	3	0	9.00
Gerry Desjardins	1	5	1	3	260	16	0	3.69
Ken Dryden	6	32	24	8	1947	78	2	2.40
Bill Durnan	3	15	10	5	967	34	1	2.11
Tony Esposito	2	13	5	8	796	52	1	3.92
Bob Froese	1	3	0	1	115	9	0	4.70
Grant Fuhr	4	20	14	5	1176	50	1	2.55
Chuck Gardiner	2	9	5	4	670	18	1	1.61
Ed Giacomin	1	3	1	2	180	11	0	3.67
Gilles Gilbert	1	6	2	4	372	15	0	2.42
Paul Goodman	1	1	0	1	60	5	0	5.00
Ron Grahame	1	1	0	0	20	0	0	0.00
George Hainsworth	4	14	6	8	925	39	2	2.53
Glenn Hall	7	32	10	22	1904	87	1	2.74
Dominik Hasek	1	1	0	1	53	4	0	4.53
Brian Hayward	1	2	0	1	67	6	0	5.37
Gordie Henry	1	3	1	2	163	10	0	3.68
'Sugar' Jim Henry	1	3	0	2	138	5	0	2.17
Ron Hextall	1	7	3	4	427	22	0	3.09
Charlie Hodge	2	4	1	3	197	10	1	3.05
Kelly Hrudey	1	5	1	4	316	15	0	2.85
Ed Johnston	1	3	2	1	180	6	0	2.00
Mike Karakas	2	6	2	4	369	18	0	2.93
Dave Kerr	2	11	6	5	694	20	1	1.73
Michel Larocque	1	1	0	0	20	0	0	0.00
Rejean Lemelin	3	4	0	2	197	13	0	3.96
Pelle Lindbergh	1	4	1	3	185	11	0	3.57
Harry Lumley	4	22	7	15	1391	56	3	2.42
Frank McCool	1	7	4	3	434	9	3	1.24
Kirk McLean	1	7	3	4	437	20	0	2.75
Gerry McNeil	4	15	6	9	933	29	3	1.86
Roland Melanson	1	3	0	1	55	3	0	3.27
Gilles Meloche	1	2	0	2	120	12	0	6.00
Joe Miller	1	3	2	1	180	3	1	1.00
Andy Moog	4	15	3	10	844	46	0	3.27
Alfie Moore	1	1	1	0	60	1	0	1.00
Johnny Mowers	3	15	7	8	900	42	2	2.80
Phil Myre	1	1	0	1	60	6	0	6.00
Chris Osgood	1	1	0	0	32	1	0	1.88
Bernie Parent	2	12	8	4	750	33	2	2.64
Lester Patrick	1	1	1	0	47	1	0	1.28
Pete Peeters	1	5	2	3	311	20	0	3.86
Frank Pietrangelo	1	1	1	0	40	3	0	4.50
Jacques Plante	10	41	25	14	2423	92	4	2.28
Bill Ranford	1	5	4	1	355	8	0	1.35
Chuck Rayner	1	7	3	4	459	22	0	2.88
Glenn 'Chico' Resch	1	1	0	0	20	2	0	6.00
Mike Richter	1	7	4	3	439	19	0	2.60
John Roach	2	5	0	5	300	22	0	4.40
Earl Robertson	1	5	2	2	280	8	2	1.71
Al Rollins	1	3	3	0	193	5	0	1.55
Patrick Roy	3	16	10	6	1011	40	1	2.37
Terry Sawchuk	7	37	19	18	2185	95	3	2.61
Don Simmons	3	14	5	9	831	38	1	2.74
Billy Smith	5	24	17	6	1396	72	2	3.09
Gary Smith	1	1	0	0	5	0	0	0.00
Normie Smith	2	5	4	1	261	11	0	2.53
Wayne Stephenson	1	4	0	4	240	14	0	3.50
Cecil 'Tiny' Thompson	2	4	2	2	240	8	1	2.00
Rogie Vachon	2	9	6	3	548	17	1	1.86
Mike Vernon	3	15	5	10	897	44	0	2.94
Gilles Villemure	1	3	1	2	180	7	0	2.33
Ernie Wakely	1	2	0	2	96	11	0	6.87
Hal Winkler*	1	4	0	2	240	7	1	1.75
Lorne 'Gump' Worsley	4	16	11	5	925	28	3	1.82

* also recorded two ties in the 1927 Finals.

National Hockey League
**Stanley Cup Playoffs
Fact Guide
1996**

Section V

•

Final Series Game Summaries 1980 – 1995

Game Summaries.. page **183**

FIRST-GAME WINNERS
HOLD DECISIVE EDGE

Since the National Hockey League implemented the best-of-seven Finals format in 1939, the following winning trends have developed:

- Teams winning Game #1 have won the Cup 45 of 56 times or 80.3%.
- Teams winning both Games #1 and #2 have won the Cup 34 of 37 times or 91.9%.
- Teams winning Games #1, #2 and #3 have won the Cup 21 of 22 times or 95.5%.
- Teams winning Game #3 after splitting the first two games have won the Cup 17 of 20 times or 85%.
- Teams holding a 2-1 series lead have won the Cup 30 of 35 times or 85.7%.
- Teams winning Game #5 after splitting the first four games have won the Cup 12 of 15 times or 80%.
- Teams holding a 3-2 series lead have won the Cup 21 of 25 times or 84%.

U.S.-BASED TEAMS IN THE FINALS

The 1916 Portland Rosebuds were the first team based in the United States to participate in a Stanley Cup championship, while the 1917 Seattle Metropolitans were the first to win the Cup.

The Detroit Red Wings have won seven Stanley Cups, more than any other American team, and were the first to win back-to-back titles (1936 and 1937).

Game Summaries Stanley Cup Finals, 1980-1995

1980
NEW YORK ISLANDERS - PHILADELPHIA FLYERS

GAME #1 - May 13, 1980 - The Spectrum - NY Islanders 4, Philadelphia 3 (OT)

NY ISLANDERS: Mike Bossy, Bob Bourne, Clark Gillies, Butch Goring, Lorne Henning, Garry Howatt, Gord Lane, Dave Langevin, Bob Lorimer, Wayne Merrick, Ken Morrow, Bob Nystrom, Stefan Persson, Denis Potvin, Glenn "Chico" Resch, Billy Smith, Duane Sutter, John Tonelli, Bryan Trottier.

PHILADELPHIA: Bill Barber, Mel Bridgman, Mike Busniuk, Bobby Clarke, Bob Dailey, Andre Dupont, Tom Gorence, Al Hill, Paul Holmgren, Bob Kelly, Reg Leach, Ken Linseman, Rick MacLeish, Jack McIlhargey, Phil Myre, Pete Peeters, Brian Propp, Jimmy Watson, Behn Wilson.

First Period
1. PHILADELPHIA   BRIDGMAN (unassisted)   10.31
2. NY ISLANDERS   BOSSY (TROTTIER)   12.02   (PPG)

Penalties: Sutter (NYI) (elbowing) 9.36; Wilson (Phi) (highsticking) 9.36; Dailey (Phi) (tripping) 11.51.

Second Period
3. NY ISLANDERS   POTVIN (GILLIES, GORING)   2.20
4. PHILADELPHIA   CLARKE (BARBER, LEACH)   17.08   (PPG)

Penalties: Sutter (NYI) (fighting) 2.56; Watson (Phi) (fighting) 2.56; Linseman (Phi) (hooking) 12.00; Lorimer (NYI) (hooking) 16.08.

Third Period
5. PHILADELPHIA   MacLEISH (HOLMGREN)   13.10
6. NY ISLANDERS   PERSSON (BOSSY, POTVIN)   16.18   (PPG)

Penalties: Clarke (Phi) (tripping) 2.33; Persson (NYI) (holding) 10.49; Hill (Phi) (hooking) 14.35.

Overtime
7. NY ISLANDERS   POTVIN (TONELLI, NYSTROM)   4.07   (PPG, GWG)

Penalties: Watson (Phi) (holding) 2.08.

Goalies: Smith (NYI), Peeters (Phi)
Shots: NYI 15 - 9 - 11 - 1   36
       Phi 9 - 12 - 11 - 1 33
Referee: Andy vanHellemond
Linesmen: John D'Amico, Ray Scapinello

GAME #2 - May 15, 1980 - The Spectrum - Philadelphia 8, NY Islanders 3

NY ISLANDERS: Mike Bossy, Bob Bourne, Clark Gillies, Butch Goring, Lorne Henning, Garry Howatt, Gord Lane, Dave Langevin, Bob Lorimer, Wayne Merrick, Ken Morrow, Bob Nystrom, Stefan Persson, Denis Potvin, Glenn Resch, Billy Smith, Duane Sutter, John Tonelli, Bryan Trottier.

PHILADELPHIA: Bill Barber, Mel Bridgman, Mike Busniuk, Bobby Clarke, Bob Dailey, Andre Dupont, Tom Gorence, Al Hill, Paul Holmgren, Bob Kelly, Reg Leach, Ken Linseman, Rick MacLeish, Jack McIlhargey, Phil Myre, Pete Peeters, Brian Propp, Jim Watson, Behn Wilson.

First Period
1. NY ISLANDERS   GORING (GILLIES, SUTTER)   3.23
2. PHILADELPHIA   HOLMGREN (BRIDGMAN, DAILEY)   7.22   (PPG)
3. PHILADELPHIA   KELLY (CLARKE, WILSON)   8.37
4. PHILADELPHIA   CLARKE (WATSON, BARBER)   17.23

Penalties: Gorence (Phi) (hooking) 4.09; Persson (NYI) (tripping) 5.37; Linseman (Phi) (elbowing) 9.31; Wilson (Phi) (holding) 12.10.

Second Period
5. PHILADELPHIA   BARBER (LEACH, CLARKE)   1.06   (GWG)
6. NY ISLANDERS   TROTTIER (BOSSY)   3.28   (PPG)
7. PHILADELPHIA   HOLMGREN (LINSEMAN, BARBER)   4.13   (PPG)
8. PHILADELPHIA   PROPP (DAILEY, CLARKE)   15.47   (PPG)

Penalties: Dupont (Phi) (hooking) 3.03; Morrow (NYI) (interference) 4.02; Wilson (Phi) (roughing) 5.27; Lorimer (NYI) (highsticking) 12.54; Propp (Phi) (highsticking) 12.54; Howatt (NYI) (tripping) 13.58; Smith (NYI) (slashing) 14.12; Lane (NYI) (slashing) 14.12; Barber (Phi) (highsticking) 14.12.

Third Period
9. PHILADELPHIA   GORENCE (DAILEY, BRIDGMAN)   1.40
10. PHILADELPHIA   HOLMGREN (LINSEMEN, WILSON)   4.19
11. NY ISLANDERS   GORING (BOURNE, PERSSON)   15.00   (PPG)

Penalties: McIlhargey (Phi) (tripping) 1.55; Sutter (NYI) (slashing, fighting, misconduct) 7.01; Bridgman (Phi) (fighting, misconduct) 7.01; Wilson (Phi) (crosschecking, double roughing, game misconduct) 14.13; Lane (NYI) (slashing) 19.10.

Goalies: Peeters (Phi); Smith (NYI), Resch (NYI) (entered at 0.00 3rd);
Shots: NYI 10 - 5 - 8   23
       Phi 10 - 16 - 5 31
Referee: Wally Harris
Linesmen: Ron Finn, Leon Stickle

GAME #3 - May 17, 1980 - Nassau Coliseum - NY Islanders 6, Philadelphia 2

NY ISLANDERS: Mike Bossy, Bob Bourne, Clark Gillies, Butch Goring, Lorne Henning, Garry Howatt, Gord Lane, Dave Langevin, Bob Lorimer, Wayne Merrick, Ken Morrow, Bob Nystrom, Stefan Persson, Denis Potvin, Glenn "Chico" Resch, Billy Smith, Duane Sutter, John Tonelli, Bryan Trottier.

PHILADELPHIA: Bill Barber, Mel Bridgman, Mike Busniuk, Bobby Clarke, Bob Dailey, Andre Dupont, Tom Gorence, Al Hill, Paul Holmgren, Bob Kelly, Reg Leach, Ken Linseman, Rick MacLeish, Jack McIlhargey, Phil Myre, Pete Peeters, Brian Propp, Jimmy Watson, Behn Wilson.

First Period
1. NY ISLANDERS   HENNING (BOURNE)   2.38   (SHG)
2. NY ISLANDERS   POTVIN (unassisted)   7.43   (PPG)
3. NY ISLANDERS   TROTTIER (BOSSY, POTVIN)   13.04   (PPG, GWG)
4. NY ISLANDERS   BOSSY (GILLIES, POTVIN)   14.29   (PPG)

Penalties: Sutter (NYI) (hooking) 1.01; Langevin (NYI) (interference) 4.11; Kelly (Phi) (tripping) 6.54; Gillies (NYI) (tripping) 9.32; MacLeish (Phi) (slashing) 12.24; Dailey (Phi) (holding) 12.56; Tonelli (NYI) (hooking) 16.46.

Second Period
5. NY ISLANDERS   GILLIES (PERSSON)   15.41   (PPG)
6. NY ISLANDERS   POTVIN (PERSSON, BOSSY)   17.25   (PPG)

Penalties: Henning (NYI) (slashing) 1.21; Busniuk (Phi) (fighting) 10.45; Wilson (Phi) (roughing) 10.45; Nystrom (NYI) (fighting) 10.45; Persson (NYI) (roughing) 10.45; Wilson (Phi) (highsticking) 13.32; Gillies (NYI) (roughing) 13.32; Linseman (Phi) (slashing) 14.15; McIlhargey (Phi) (fighting, misconduct) 16.43; Gorence (Phi) (roughing, misconduct) 16.43; Lane (NYI) (fighting, misconduct) 16.43; Howatt (NYI) (roughing, misconduct) 16.43; Barber (Phi) (highsticking) 17.18; Linseman (Phi) (roughing) 19.23; Nystrom (NYI) (roughing, highsticking) 19.23.

Third Period
7. PHILADELPHIA   CLARKE (LEACH, BUSNIUK)   9.48
8. PHILADELPHIA   BUSNIUK (BRIDGMAN)   11.32

Penalties: Wilson (Phi) (roughing) 19.31; Sutter (NYI) (roughing) 19.31.

Goalies: Smith (NYI), Myre (Phi)
Shots: Phi 9 - 8 - 15   32
       NYI 12 - 21 - 7   40
Referee: Bob Myers
Linesmen: John D'Amico, Ray Scapinello

GAME #4 - May 19, 1980 - Nassau Coliseum - NY Islanders 5, Philadelphia 2

NY ISLANDERS: Mike Bossy, Bob Bourne, Clark Gillies, Butch Goring, Lorne Henning, Garry Howatt, Gord Lane, Dave Langevin, Bob Lorimer, Wayne Merrick, Ken Morrow, Bob Nystrom, Stefan Persson, Denis Potvin, Glenn "Chico" Resch, Billy Smith, Duane Sutter, John Tonelli, Bryan Trottier.

PHILADELPHIA: Bill Barber, Norm Barnes, Mel Bridgman, Mike Busniuk, Bobby Clarke, Bob Dailey, Andre Dupont, Tom Gorence, Al Hill, Bob Kelly, Reg Leach, Ken Linseman, Rick MacLeish, Jack McIlhargey, Phil Myre, John Paddock, Pete Peeters, Brian Propp, Behn Wilson.

First Period
1.	NY ISLANDERS	BOSSY (GILLIES, TROTTIER)	7.23	(PPG)
2.	NY ISLANDERS	GORING (GILLIES, SUTTER)	13.06	

Penalties: Smith (NYI) (slashing) 3.47; Gorence (Phi) (interference) 5.56; Bossy (NYI) (tripping) 16.50.

Second Period
3.	PHILADELPHIA	PADDOCK (MacLEISH, WILSON)	1.35	

Penalties: McIlhargey (Phi) (interference) 1.48; Potvin (NYI) (highsticking) 2.36; Bridgman (Phi) (fighting) 3.06; Langevin (NYI) (fighting) 3.06; Langevin (NYI) (holding) 13.45; Dupont (Phi) (tripping) 16.19; Persson (NYI) (hooking) 17.55.

Third Period
4.	NY ISLANDERS	TROTTIER (HOWATT)	6.06	(GWG)
5.	PHILADELPHIA	LINSEMAN (PROPP, GORENCE)	11.53	
6.	NY ISLANDERS	NYSTROM (BOURNE)	12.35	
7.	NY ISLANDERS	GILLIES (SUTTER)	14.08	

Penalties: Barnes (Phi) (holding) 0.44; McIlhargey (Phi) (holding) 9.16; Barnes (Phi) (hooking) 17.42.

Goalies: Smith (NYI), Peeters (Phi)
Shots: Phi 13 - 11 - 12 36
       NYI   9 - 8 - 10 27

Referee: Andy vanHellemond
Linesmen: Ron Finn, Leon Stickle

GAME #5 - May 22, 1980 - The Spectrum - Philadelphia 6, NY Islanders 3

NY ISLANDERS: Mike Bossy, Bob Bourne, Clark Gillies, Butch Goring, Lorne Henning, Garry Howatt, Gord Lane, Dave Langevin, Bob Lorimer, Wayne Merrick, Ken Morrow, Bob Nystrom, Stefan Persson, Denis Potvin, Glenn "Chico" Resch, Billy Smith, Duane Sutter, John Tonelli, Bryan Trottier.

PHILADELPHIA: Bill Barber, Mel Bridgman, Mike Busniuk, Bobby Clarke, Bob Dailey, Andre Dupont, Tom Gorence, Al Hill, Paul Holmgren, Bob Kelly, Reg Leach, Ken Linseman, Rick MacLeish, Jack McIlhargey, Phil Myre, Pete Peeters, Brian Propp, Jimmy Watson, Behn Wilson.

First Period
1.	NY ISLANDERS	PERSSON (BOSSY)	10.58	(PPG)

Penalties: Holmgren (Phi) (highsticking) 2.48; Gillies (NYI) (interference) 3.44; Holmgren (Phi) (slashing) 9.03; Dupont (Phi) (holding) 10.40; Propp (Phi) (slashing) 15.24.

Second Period
2.	PHILADELPHIA	CLARKE (LEACH, WILSON)	1.45	
3.	PHILADELPHIA	MacLEISH (unassisted)	5.55	
4.	NY ISLANDERS	TROTTIER (PERSSON, BOSSY)	16.16	
5.	PHILADELPHIA	BUSNIUK (PROPP, LINSEMAN)	17.04	

Penalties: Persson (NYI) (interference) 9.26.

Third Period
6.	PHILADELPHIA	MacLEISH (BRIDGMAN)	9.43	(GWG)
7.	PHILADELPHIA	PROPP (LINSEMAN, HOLMGREN)	12.33	(PPG)
8.	NY ISLANDERS	PERSSON (GORING, POTVIN)	14.57	(PPG)
9.	PHILADELPHIA	HOLMGREN (LINSEMAN)	17.26	

Penalties: McIlhargey (Phi) (highsticking) 2.48; Lorimer (NYI) (hooking) 6.43; Kelly (Phi) (interference) 10.03; Morrow (NYI) (slashing, unsportsmanlike conduct) 12.03; Linseman (Phi) (highsticking) 13.00; Bridgman (Phi) (elbowing, roughing, fighting, misconduct) 19.52; Howatt (NYI) (fighting) 19.52; Smith (NYI) (slashing) 19.52; Philadelphia (bench minor, too many men on the ice, served by Propp) 19.52.

Goalies: Smith (NYI), Peeters (Phi)
Shots: NYI 10 - 15 - 13 38
       Phi   6 - 13 - 12 31

Referee: Wally Harris
Linesmen: John D'Amico, Ray Scapinello

GAME #6 - May 24, 1980 - Nassau Coliseum - NY Islanders 5, Philadelphia 4 (OT)

NY ISLANDERS: Mike Bossy, Bob Bourne, Clark Gillies, Butch Goring, Lorne Henning, Garry Howatt, Gord Lane, Dave Langevin, Bob Lorimer, Wayne Merrick, Ken Morrow, Bob Nystrom, Stefan Persson, Denis Potvin, Glenn Resch, Billy Smith, Duane Sutter, John Tonelli, Bryan Trottier.

PHILADELPHIA: Bill Barber, Mel Bridgman, Mike Busniuk, Bob Clarke, Bob Dailey, Andre Dupont, Al Hill, Paul Holmgren, Bob Kelly, Reg Leach, Ken Linseman, Rick MacLeish, Jack McIlhargey, Phil Myre, John Paddock, Pete Peeters, Brian Propp, Jim Watson, Behn Wilson.

First Period
1.	PHILADELPHIA	LEACH (MacLEISH, BARBER)	7.21	(PPG)
2.	NY ISLANDERS	POTVIN (BOSSY, TROTTIER)	11.56	(PPG)
3.	NY ISLANDERS	SUTTER (GILLIES, GORING)	14.08	
4.	PHILADELPHIA	PROPP (HOLMGREN, LINSEMAN)	18.58	

Penalties: Holmgren (Phi) (highsticking) 1.00; Lane (NYI) (highsticking) 1.00; Dupont (Phi) (highsticking) 2.24; Kelly (Phi) (fighting) 5.55; Nystrom (NYI) (roughing, fighting) 5.55; Potvin (NYI) (crosschecking) 6.29; Holmgren (Phi) (hooking) 7.42; Linseman (Phi) (delay of game) 7.42; Bourne (NYI) (delay of game) 7.42; Busniuk (Phi) (holding) 10.15; Bridgman (Phi) (roughing, misconduct) 15.18; Nystrom (NYI) (roughing, misconduct) 15.18; Dupont (Phi) (holding) 16.25.

Second Period
5.	NY ISLANDERS	BOSSY (BOURNE, TROTTIER)	7.34	(PPG)
6.	NY ISLANDERS	NYSTROM (TONELLI)	19.46	

Penalties: Watson (Phi) (roughing) 3.15; Howatt (NYI) (roughing) 3.15; Wilson (Phi) (holding) 6.39; McIlhargey (Phi) (hooking) 8.46; Bridgman (Phi) (roughing) 11.10; Bossy (NYI) (highsticking) 11.10; Dupont (Phi) (roughing, interference) 14.22; Tonelli (NYI) (slashing) 14.22; Linseman (Phi) (charging) 15.09; Potvin (NYI) (charging) 15.09.

Third Period
7.	PHILADELPHIA	DAILEY (LINSEMAN, HOLMGREN)	1.47	
8.	PHILADELPHIA	PADDOCK (DUPONT, MacLEISH)	6.02	

Penalties: Nystrom (NYI) (holding) 3.20; Holmgren (Phi) (crosschecking, fighting) 8.09; Gillies (NYI) (slashing, fighting) 8.09; Linseman (Phi) (roughing) 9.21.

Overtime
9.	NY ISLANDERS	NYSTROM (HENNING, TONELLI)	7.11	(GWG)

Penalties: none.

Goalies: Smith (NYI), Peeters (Phi)
Shots: Phi   6 - 6 - 11 - 2 25
       NYI 13 - 12 - 5 - 3 33

Referee: Bob Myers
Linesmen: Ron Finn, Leon Stickle

1981

NEW YORK ISLANDERS - MINNESOTA NORTH STARS

GAME #1 - May 12, 1981 - Nassau Coliseum - NY Islanders 6, Minnesota 3

NY ISLANDERS: Mike Bossy, Bob Bourne, Billy Carroll, Clark Gillies, Butch Goring, Anders Kallur, Gord Lane, Dave Langevin, Bob Lorimer, Mike McEwen, Roland Melanson, Wayne Merrick, Ken Morrow, Bob Nystrom, Denis Potvin, Billy Smith, Duane Sutter, John Tonelli, Bryan Trottier.

MINNESOTA: Kent-Erik Andersson, Fred Barrett, Don Beaupre, Neal Broten, Jack Carlson, Steve Christoff, Dino Ciccarelli, Curt Giles, Craig Hartsburg, Al MacAdam, Brad Maxwell, Tom McCarthy, Gilles Meloche, Brad Palmer, Steve Payne, Gordie Roberts, Bobby Smith, Greg Smith, Ken Solheim.

First Period
1. NY ISLANDERS   KALLUR (LANGEVIN, GORING)   2.54
2. NY ISLANDERS   TROTTIER (CARROLL)   14.38   (SHG)
3. NY ISLANDERS   KALLUR (TROTTIER)   15.25   (SHG)

Penalties: Maxwell (Min) (highsticking) 6.44; Bourne (NYI) (spearing major) 11.12; McCarthy (Min) (slashing) 19.45.

Second Period
4. NY ISLANDERS   CARROLL (SUTTER, NYSTROM)   9.58   (GWG)
5. MINNESOTA   ANDERSSON (CICCARELLI)   13.04

Penalties: G. Smith (Min) (interference) 6.06; Tonelli (NYI) (highsticking) 14.13; Trottier (NYI) (tripping) 17.29.

Third Period
6. NY ISLANDERS   MERRICK (unassisted)   0.58
7. MINNESOTA   PAYNE (HARTSBURG, B. SMITH)   3.08   (PPG)
8. NY ISLANDERS   MERRICK (LANGEVIN, TONELLI)   13.15
9. MINNESOTA   CICCARELLI (McCARTHY)   15.14

Penalties: Lane (NYI) (crosschecking) 2.39; Trottier (NYI) (roughing) 18.09.

Goalies: Smith (NYI), Meloche (Min)
Shots: Min   8 - 8 - 10   26
         NYI 10 - 10 - 3   23
Referee: Andy vanHellemond
Linesmen: John D'Amico, Ron Finn

GAME #2 - May 14, 1981 - Nassau Coliseum - NY Islanders 6, Minnesota 3

NY ISLANDERS: Mike Bossy, Bob Bourne, Billy Carroll, Clark Gillies, Butch Goring, Anders Kallur, Gord Lane, Dave Langevin, Bob Lorimer, Mike McEwen, Roland Melanson, Wayne Merrick, Ken Morrow, Bob Nystrom, Denis Potvin, Billy Smith, Duane Sutter, John Tonelli, Bryan Trottier.

MINNESOTA: Kent-Erik Andersson, Fred Barrett, Don Beaupre, Neal Broten, Jack Carlson, Steve Christoff, Dino Ciccarelli, Curt Giles, Craig Hartsburg, Al MacAdam, Brad Maxwell, Tom McCarthy, Gilles Meloche, Brad Palmer, Steve Payne, Gordie Roberts, Bobby Smith, Greg Smith, Tim Young.

First Period
1. MINNESOTA   CICCARELLI (HARTSBURG, CHRISTOFF)   3.38   (PPG)
2. NY ISLANDERS   BOSSY (McEWEN, POTVIN)   4.38   (PPG)
3. NY ISLANDERS   NYSTROM (MERRICK, TROTTIER)   14.39
4. NY ISLANDERS   POTVIN (MERRICK)   17.48

Penalties: Kallur (NYI) (holding) 1.31; Trottier (NYI) (hooking) 2.15; Barrett (Min) (holding) 4.08; Langevin (NYI) (holding) 4.53; Morrow (NYI) (highsticking) 5.04; MacAdam (Min) (highsticking) 5.04; Langevin (NYI) (elbowing) 11.01; Barrett (Min) (roughing) 19.15; Bourne (NYI) (roughing) 19.15.

Second Period
5. MINNESOTA   PALMER (BROTEN, G. SMITH)   9.15

Penalties: Tonelli (NYI) (roughing) 10.26.

Third Period
6. MINNESOTA   PAYNE (ROBERTS, YOUNG)   0.30
7. NY ISLANDERS   POTVIN (GORING)   8.00   (PPG, GWG)
8. NY ISLANDERS   MORROW (POTVIN, MERRICK)   11.57
9. NY ISLANDERS   BOSSY (TROTTIER, BOURNE)   16.22

Penalties: Potvin (NYI) (tripping) 3.39; Broten (Min) (hooking) 6.22; Barrett (Min) (highsticking) 7.01; Trottier (NYI) (highsticking) 7.01; Trottier (NYI) (tripping) 12.58; Potvin (NYI) (closing hand on puck) 13.31; Maxwell (Min) (fighting) 16.44; Bourne (NYI) (fighting) 16.44; Ciccarelli (Min) (minor, misconduct) 16.44; Lane (NYI) (minor, misconduct) 16.44.

Goalies: Smith (NYI), Beaupre (Min)
Shots: Min   9 - 11 - 8   28
         NYI 11 - 11 - 16 38
Referee: Bryan Lewis
Linesmen: Leon Stickle, Ron Finn

GAME #3 - May 17, 1981 - Met Center - NY Islanders 7, Minnesota 5

NY ISLANDERS: Mike Bossy, Bob Bourne, Billy Carroll, Clark Gillies, Butch Goring, Anders Kallur, Gord Lane, Dave Langevin, Bob Lorimer, Mike McEwen, Roland Melanson, Wayne Merrick, Ken Morrow, Bob Nystrom, Denis Potvin, Billy Smith, Duane Sutter, John Tonelli, Bryan Trottier.

MINNESOTA: Kent-Erik Andersson, Fred Barrett, Don Beaupre, Neal Broten, Steve Christoff, Dino Ciccarelli, Curt Giles, Craig Hartsburg, Al MacAdam, Tom McCarthy, Gilles Meloche, Brad Palmer, Steve Payne, Mike Polich, Gordie Roberts, Bobby Smith, Greg Smith, Tim Young, Tom Younghans.

First Period
1. MINNESOTA   CHRISTOFF (HARTSBURG, CICCARELLI)   3.25   (PPG)
2. MINNESOTA   PAYNE (MacADAM, YOUNG)   14.09
3. NY ISLANDERS   BOSSY (GILLIES)   14.47
4. MINNESOTA   B. SMITH (HARTSBURG, PAYNE)   16.30   (PPG)

Penalties: Nystrom (NYI) (interference) 2.10; Younghans (Min) (interference) 3.55; Payne (Min) (holding) 6.37; Nystrom (NYI) (roughing) 7.05; Younghans (Min) (roughing) 7.05; Trottier (NYI) (hooking) 7.19; Langevin (NYI) (boarding) 11.26; Nystrom (NYI) (interference) 15.20.

Second Period
5. NY ISLANDERS   NYSTROM (TONELLI, MERRICK)   4.10
6. NY ISLANDERS   GORING (POTVIN, BOSSY)   7.16   (PPG)
7. NY ISLANDERS   GORING (GILLIES)   11.57

Penalties: B. Smith (Min) (tripping) 5.39; Gillies (NYI) (highsticking) 5.56; G. Smith (Min) (interference) 5.56; Gillies (NYI) (interference) 9.40; Trottier (NYI) (tripping) 16.00; McEwen (NYI) (hooking) 18.25.

Third Period
8. MINNESOTA   PAYNE (CHRISTOFF, YOUNG)   1.11
9. NY ISLANDERS   BOSSY (TROTTIER)   2.05
10. NY ISLANDERS   GORING (POTVIN, CARROLL)   6.34   (GWG)
11. MINNESOTA   CICCARELLI (B. SMITH)   13.35
12. NY ISLANDERS   TROTTIER (BOSSY, MERRICK)   19.16   (ENG)

Penalties: Tonelli (NYI) (tripping) 4.15.

Goalies: Smith (NYI), Meloche (Min)
Shots: NYI 11 - 8 - 10   29
         Min   8 - 7 - 13   28
Referee: Bruce Hood
Linesmen: John D'Amico, Ron Finn

GAME #4 - May 19, 1981 - Met Center - Minnesota 4, NY Islanders 2

NY ISLANDERS: Mike Bossy, Bob Bourne, Billy Carroll, Clark Gillies, Butch Goring, Anders Kallur, Gord Lane, Dave Langevin, Bob Lorimer, Mike McEwen, Roland Melanson, Wayne Merrick, Ken Morrow, Bob Nystrom, Denis Potvin, Billy Smith, Duane Sutter, John Tonelli, Bryan Trottier.

MINNESOTA: Kent-Erik Andersson, Don Beaupre, Neal Broten, Steve Christoff, Dino Ciccarelli, Curt Giles, Craig Hartsburg, Al MacAdam, Brad Maxwell, Kevin Maxwell, Gilles Meloche, Brad Palmer, Steve Payne, Mike Polich, Gordie Roberts, Paul Shmyr, Bobby Smith, Greg Smith, Tom Younghans.

First Period
1. NY ISLANDERS   LANE (BOSSY, TROTTIER)   3.47
2. MINNESOTA   HARTSBURG (B. SMITH, B. MAXWELL)   11.34   (PPG)

Penalties: Gillies (NYI) (slashing) 1.00; Hartsburg (Min) (slashing) 4.00; Langevin (NYI) (crosschecking) 10.03; Roberts (Min) (hooking) 12.23; Gillies (NYI) (roughing) 13.44; Giles (Min) (tripping) 16.21.

Second Period
3. MINNESOTA MacADAM (PAYNE, B. MAXWELL) 5.15
4. NY ISLANDERS McEWEN (TONELLI, KALLUR) 7.37 (PPG)

Penalties: Nystrom (NYI) (charging) 3.12; Palmer (Min) (crosschecking) 5.47; Potvin (NYI) (elbowing) 9.13; Lorimer (NYI) (fighting) 11.30; Ciccarelli (Min) (crosschecking, fighting) 11.30; Langevin (NYI) (tripping) 14.54.

Third Period
5. MINNESOTA PAYNE (B. MAXWELL, MacADAM) 12.26 (GWG)
6. MINNESOTA B. SMITH (B. MAXWELL, MacADAM) 18.12 (PPG)

Penalties: Kallur (NYI) (tripping) 6.17; Potvin (NYI) (holding) 16.39.

Goalies: Smith (NYI), Beaupre (Min)
Shots: NYI 12 - 12 - 11 35
        Min 13 - 10 - 11 34

Referee: Andy vanHellemond
Linesmen: Leon Stickle, Ray Scapinello

GAME #5 - May 21, 1981 - Nassau Coliseum - NY Islanders 5, Minnesota 1

NY ISLANDERS: Mike Bossy, Bob Bourne, Billy Carroll, Clark Gillies, Butch Goring, Anders Kallur, Gord Lane, Dave Langevin, Bob Lorimer, Mike McEwen, Roland Melanson, Wayne Merrick, Ken Morrow, Bob Nystrom, Denis Potvin, Billy Smith, Duane Sutter, John Tonelli, Bryan Trottier.

MINNESOTA: Kent-Erik Andersson, Don Beaupre, Neal Broten, Steve Christoff, Dino Ciccarelli, Curt Giles, Craig Hartsburg, Al MacAdam, Brad Maxwell, Kevin Maxwell, Gilles Meloche, Brad Palmer, Steve Payne, Mike Polich, Gordie Roberts, Paul Shmyr, Bobby Smith, Greg Smith, Tom Younghans.

First Period
1. NY ISLANDERS GORING (BOURNE) 5.12 (PPG)
2. NY ISLANDERS MERRICK (TONELLI, NYSTROM) 5.37 (GWG)
3. NY ISLANDERS GORING (GILLIES, BOSSY) 10.03
4. MINNESOTA CHRISTOFF (unassisted) 16.06

Penalties: Nystrom (NYI) (holding) 0.56; Palmer (Min) (holding) 3.52; Lorimer (NYI) (slashing) 19.00.

Second Period
5. NY ISLANDERS BOURNE (CARROLL, KALLUR) 19.21

Penalties: Shmyr (Min) (elbowing) 7.33; B. Smith (Min) (crosschecking) 14.43; K. Maxwell (Min) (roughing) 19.55; Lane (NYI) (slashing) 19.55.

Third Period
6. NY ISLANDERS McEWEN (TROTTIER) 17.06

Penalties: Lorimer (NYI) (holding) 3.47; B. Maxwell (Min) (slashing) 7.57; Tonelli (NYI) (slashing) 7.57; Lane (NYI) (highsticking) 11.48; K. Maxwell (Min) (slashing) 16.42; Smith (NYI) (slashing) 16.42.

Goalies: Smith (NYI), Beaupre (Min)
Shots: Min 15 - 4 - 6 25
        NYI 10 - 16 - 7 33

Referee: Bryan Lewis
Linesmen: John D'Amico, Ron Finn

1982
NEW YORK ISLANDERS - VANCOUVER CANUCKS

GAME #1 - May 8, 1982 - Nassau Coliseum - NY Islanders 6, Vancouver 5 (OT)

NY ISLANDERS: Mike Bossy, Bob Bourne, Billy Carroll, Clark Gillies, Butch Goring, Tomas Jonsson, Anders Kallur, Gord Lane, Dave Langevin, Roland Melanson, Wayne Merrick, Ken Morrow, Bob Nystrom, Stefan Persson, Denis Potvin, Billy Smith, Brent Sutter, Duane Sutter, John Tonelli, Bryan Trottier.

VANCOUVER: Neil Belland, Ivan Boldirev, Per-Olav Brasar, Richard Brodeur, Colin Campbell, Marc Crawford, Ron Delorme, Anders Eldebrink, Curt Fraser, Thomas Gradin, Doug Halward, Rick Heinz, Lars Lindgren, Gerry Minor, Lars Molin, Jim Nill, Darcy Rota, Stan Smyl, Harold Snepsts, Dave Williams.

First Period
1. VANCOUVER GRADIN (MOLIN) 1.29
2. NY ISLANDERS GILLIES (POTVIN, TROTTIER) 11.35 (PPG)
3. NY ISLANDERS BOSSY (GILLIES, CARROLL) 15.52
4. VANCOUVER GRADIN (MOLIN, FRASER) 17.40 (PPG)
5. NY ISLANDERS POTVIN (GORING) 19.51 (PPG)

Penalties: Snepsts (Van) (holding) 10.51; Gillies (NYI) (slashing) 13.36; Williams (Van) (roughing) 16.37; Langevin (NYI) (roughing) 16.37; Lane (NYI) (highsticking) 17.25; Belland (Van) (interference) 18.00.

Second Period
6. NY ISLANDERS POTVIN (TROTTIER, PERSSON) 3.15 (PPG)
7. VANCOUVER SMYL (GRADIN, FRASER) 5.06 (PPG)
8. VANCOUVER BOLDIREV (WILLIAMS) 9.27

Penalties: Eldebrink (Van) (holding) 2.52; Lane (NYI) (tripping) 4.07; Campbell (Van) (double fighting, misconduct) 10.19; Rota (Van) (fighting, misconduct) 10.19; D. Sutter (NYI) (double fighting, misconduct) 10.19; Bourne (NYI) (fighting, misconduct) 10.19; Smyl (Van) (fighting, misconduct) 17.20; Nystrom (NYI) (fighting, misconduct) 17.20.

Third Period
9. VANCOUVER NILL (MINOR, WILLIAMS) 13.06
10. NY ISLANDERS BOSSY (TONELLI, TROTTIER) 15.14

Penalties: none.

Overtime
11. NY ISLANDERS BOSSY (unassisted) 19.58 (GWG)

Penalties: Halward (Van) (roughing) 16.11; Nystrom (NYI) (roughing) 16.11.

Goalies: Smith (NYI), Brodeur (Van)
Shots: Van 12 - 9 - 8 - 6 35
        NYI 12 - 6 - 12 - 6 36

Referee: Wally Harris
Linesmen: Ron Finn, Bob Hodges

GAME #2 - May 11, 1982 - Nassau Coliseum - NY Islanders 6, Vancouver 4

NY ISLANDERS: Mike Bossy, Bob Bourne, Billy Carroll, Clark Gillies, Butch Goring, Tomas Jonsson, Anders Kallur, Gord Lane, Dave Langevin, Roland Melanson, Wayne Merrick, Ken Morrow, Bob Nystrom, Stefan Persson, Denis Potvin, Billy Smith, Brent Sutter, Duane Sutter, John Tonelli, Bryan Trottier.

VANCOUVER: Neil Belland, Ivan Boldirev, Richard Brodeur, Colin Campbell, Marc Crawford, Ron Delorme, Anders Eldebrink, Curt Fraser, Thomas Gradin, Doug Halward, Rick Heinz, Lars Lindgren, Gary Lupul, Blair MacDonald, Gerry Minor, Lars Molin, Darcy Rota, Stan Smyl, Harold Snepsts, Dave Williams.

First Period
1. NY ISLANDERS CARROLL (BOURNE) 15.55 (SHG)

Penalties: Williams (Van) (roughing) 4.09; Trottier (NYI) (roughing) 4.09; Lane (NYI) (crosschecking) 5.16; Potvin (NYI) (tripping) 8.46; Delorme (Van) (crosschecking) 11.27; Lindgren (Van) (hooking) 12.45; Potvin (NYI) (tripping) 14.38; Boldirev (Van) (crosschecking) 16.35; Persson (NYI) (interference) 18.48; Fraser (Van) (hooking) 19.05.

Second Period
2. VANCOUVER GRADIN (MOLIN, FRASER) 8.28 (PPG)
3. VANCOUVER BOLDIREV (MOLIN, HALWARD) 13.12 (PPG)
4. NY ISLANDERS BOSSY (PERSSON, POTVIN) 17.06 (PPG)
5. VANCOUVER LINDGREN (GRADIN) 19.42

Penalties: Delorme (Van) (slashing) 6.02; Lane (NYI) (slashing) 6.02; Trottier (NYI) (hooking) 7.20; Campbell (Van) (slashing) 10.03; Tonelli (NYI) (interference, highsticking) 10.03; Fraser (Van) (charging) 16.03; Jonsson (NYI) (hooking) 18.13; Smyl (Van) (roughing) 18.49; Fraser (Van) (roughing, misconduct) 18.49; Trottier (NYI) (roughing) 18.49; Lane (NYI) (misconduct) 18.49.

Third Period
6. NY ISLANDERS BOURNE (PERSSON, BOSSY) 0.32 (PPG)
7. NY ISLANDERS D. SUTTER (B. SUTTER, POTVIN) 1.19
8. VANCOUVER MINOR (WILLIAMS) 2.27
9. NY ISLANDERS TROTTIER (JONSSON, POTVIN) 7.18 (PPG, GWG)
10. NY ISLANDERS NYSTROM (TONELLI, MERRICK) 14.10

Penalties: Nystrom (NYI) (crosschecking) 6.02; Williams (Van) (slashing, roughing) 4.37; Smith (NYI) (slashing) 4.37; Snepsts (Van) (misconduct) 8.15; D. Sutter (NYI) (misconduct) 8.15; Gillies (NYI) (roughing) 11.17; Williams (Van) (interference) 11.35; Smith (NYI) (slashing) 11.35.

Goalies: Smith (NYI), Brodeur (Van)
    Shots: Van   6 - 14 - 10   30
              NYI   15 - 9 - 12   36
Referee: Ron Wicks
Linesmen: John D'Amico, Gerard Gauthier

GAME #3 - May 13, 1982 - Pacific Coliseum - NY Islanders 3, Vancouver 0

NY ISLANDERS: Mike Bossy, Bob Bourne, Billy Carroll, Clark Gillies, Butch Goring, Anders Kallur, Gord Lane, Dave Langevin, Roland Melanson, Mike McEwen, Wayne Merrick, Ken Morrow, Bob Nystrom, Stefan Persson, Denis Potvin, Billy Smith, Brent Sutter, Duane Sutter, John Tonelli, Bryan Trottier.

VANCOUVER: Neil Belland, Ivan Boldirev, Richard Brodeur, Colin Campbell, Ron Delorme, Anders Eldebrink, Curt Fraser, Thomas Gradin, Doug Halward, Rick Heinz, Ivan Hlinka, Lars Lindgren, Gary Lupul, Gerry Minor, Lars Molin, Jim Nill, Darcy Rota, Stan Smyl, Harold Snepsts, Dave Williams.

First Period
No scoring.
Penalties: Gillies (NYI) (highsticking) 1.06; Williams (Van) (highsticking) 1.06; Goring (NYI) (unsportsmanlike conduct) 8.41; Gradin (Van) (holding) 9.00; Lane (NYI) (hooking) 13.03; Carroll (NYI) (holding) 14.03; Campbell (Van) (holding) 17.37.

Second Period
1. NY ISLANDERS   GILLIES (B. SUTTER)   2.56   (GWG)
2. NY ISLANDERS   BOSSY (PERSSON, TROTTIER)   12.30
Penalties: Trottier (NYI) (slashing) 6.48; Williams (Van) (slashing) 6.48; Halward (Van) (holding) 10.29; Morrow (NYI) (interference) 12.41.

Third Period
3. NY ISLANDERS   NYSTROM (GORING, POTVIN)   18.40
Penalties: Bourne (NYI) (roughing) 0.12; Nill (Van) (highsticking, roughing) 0.12; D. Sutter (NYI) (roughing) 4.06; Snepsts (Van) (roughing) 4.06.

Goalies: Smith (NYI), Brodeur (Van)
    Shots: NYI   9 - 18 - 5   32
              Van   8 - 8 - 7   23
Referee: Andy vanHellemond
Linesmen: Ron Finn, Bob Hodges

GAME #4 - May 16, 1982 - Pacific Coliseum - NY Islanders 3, Vancouver 1

NY ISLANDERS: Mike Bossy, Bob Bourne, Billy Carroll, Clark Gillies, Butch Goring, Anders Kallur, Gord Lane, Dave Langevin, Roland Melanson, Mike McEwen, Wayne Merrick, Ken Morrow, Bob Nystrom, Stefan Persson, Denis Potvin, Billy Smith, Brent Sutter, Duane Sutter, John Tonelli, Bryan Trottier.

VANCOUVER: Neil Belland, Ivan Boldirev, Richard Brodeur, Garth Butcher, Colin Campbell, Marc Crawford, Ron Delorme, Curt Fraser, Thomas Gradin, Doug Halward, Rick Heinz, Ivan Hlinka, Lars Lindgren, Gerry Minor, Lars Molin, Jim Nill, Darcy Rota, Stan Smyl, Harold Snepsts, Dave Williams.

First Period
1. NY ISLANDERS   GORING (POTVIN)   11.38
2. VANCOUVER   SMYL (MINOR, CAMPBELL)   18.09
Penalties: Campbell (Van) (hooking) 2.29; Gillies (NYI) (hooking) 5.53; Trottier (NYI) (holding) 8.25; Fraser (Van) (hooking) 9.31; Lane (NYI) (slashing) 13.03; Nill (Van) (slashing) 13.03; Rota (Van) (roughing) 15.40; Nystrom (NYI) (boarding) 16.53; Snepsts (Van) (elbowing) 16.53.

Second Period
3. NY ISLANDERS   BOSSY (POTVIN, TROTTIER)   5.00   (PPG,GWG)
4. NY ISLANDERS   BOSSY (PERSSON, TROTTIER)   8.00   (PPG)
Penalties: Persson (NYI) (holding) 1.21; Rota (Van) (crosschecking) 3.02; Smyl (Van) (highsticking) 6.08; Belland (Van) (tripping) 14.53.

Third Period
No scoring.

Penalties: none.

Goalies: Smith (NYI), Brodeur (Van)
    Shots: NYI   9 - 12 - 7   28
              Van   10 - 5 - 9   24
Referee: Wally Harris
Linesmen: John D'Amico, Gerard Gauthier

1983
NEW YORK ISLANDERS - EDMONTON OILERS

GAME #1 - May 10, 1983 - Northlands Coliseum - NY Islanders 2, Edmonton 0

EDMONTON: Glenn Anderson, Paul Coffey, Ray Cote, Lee Fogolin Jr., Grant Fuhr, Randy Gregg, Wayne Gretzky, Charlie Huddy, Pat Hughes, Dave Hunter, Don Jackson, Jari Kurri, Willy Lindstrom, Ken Linseman, Kevin Lowe, Dave Lumley, Mark Messier, Andy Moog, Tom Roulston, Dave Semenko.

NY ISLANDERS: Bob Bourne, Billy Carroll, Greg Gilbert, Clark Gillies, Butch Goring, Tomas Jonsson, Anders Kallur, Gord Lane, Dave Langevin, Roland Melanson, Wayne Merrick, Ken Morrow, Bob Nystrom, Stefan Persson, Denis Potvin, Billy Smith, Brent Sutter, Duane Sutter, John Tonelli, Bryan Trottier.

First Period
1. NY ISLANDERS   D. SUTTER (BOURNE, PERSSON)   5.36   (GWG)
Penalties: Morrow (NYI) (hooking) 1.15; Hunter (Edm) (elbowing) 3.21; Persson (NYI) (tripping) 9.44; Smith (NYI) (slashing) 11.10; Anderson (Edm) (interference) 11.19; Hunter (Edm) (elbowing) 14.57; Potvin (NYI) (hooking) 15.07; Linseman (Edm) (hooking) 15.34.

Second Period
No scoring.
Penalties: Jonsson (NYI) (holding) 0.39; Nystrom (NYI) (charging) 9.27.

Third Period
2. NY ISLANDERS   MORROW (POTVIN)   19.48   (ENG)
Penalties: Jonsson (NYI) (hooking) 0.51; Gillies (NYI) (slashing) 3.18; Lumley (Edm) (slashing) 3.18; B. Sutter (NYI) (hooking) 4.27; Anderson (Edm) (elbowing) 4.27.

Goalies: Moog (Edm), Smith (NYI)
    Shots: NYI   13 - 5 - 6   24
              Edm   14 - 12 - 9   35

Referee: Andy vanHellemond
Linesmen: Ron Finn, Ray Scapinello

GAME #2 - May 12, 1983 - Northlands Coliseum - NY Islanders 6, Edmonton 3

EDMONTON: Glenn Anderson, Paul Coffey, Ray Cote, Lee Fogolin Jr., Grant Fuhr, Randy Gregg, Wayne Gretzky, Charlie Huddy, Pat Hughes, Dave Hunter, Don Jackson, Jari Kurri, Willy Lindstrom, Ken Linseman, Kevin Lowe, Dave Lumley, Mark Messier, Andy Moog, Tom Roulston, Dave Semenko.

NY ISLANDERS: Mike Bossy, Bob Bourne, Billy Carroll, Clark Gillies, Butch Goring, Tomas Jonsson, Anders Kallur, Gord Lane, Dave Langevin, Roland Melanson, Wayne Merrick, Ken Morrow, Bob Nystrom, Stefan Persson, Denis Potvin, Billy Smith, Brent Sutter, Duane Sutter, John Tonelli, Bryan Trottier.

First Period
1. EDMONTON   SEMENKO (ROULSTON, HUDDY)   8.39
2. NY ISLANDERS   JONSSON (D. SUTTER, B. SUTTER) 14.21
3. NY ISLANDERS   NYSTROM (TROTTIER)   17.55
4. NY ISLANDERS   BOSSY (POTVIN)   19.17
Penalties: B. Sutter (NYI) (tripping) 2.36; Linseman (Edm) (interference) 4.44; Hughes (Edm) (crosschecking) 5.17; Kallur (NYI) (holding) 5.17.

Second Period
5. EDMONTON   KURRI (ANDERSON, GRETZKY)   5.07
6. NY ISLANDERS   BOURNE (D. SUTTER)   8.03   (GWG)
7. NY ISLANDERS   B. SUTTER (MORROW)   8.41
Penalties: Jonsson (NYI) (interference) 14.50.

Third Period
8. EDMONTON   ANDERSON (FOGOLIN, GRETZKY)   4.48
9. NY ISLANDERS   B. SUTTER (D. SUTTER, JONSSON)   14.11

Penalties: Persson (NYI) (holding) 11.22; Kurri (Edm) (slashing) 13.14; Trottier (NYI) (hooking) 13.27; Smith (NYI) (slashing major) 17.56; Lumley (Edm) (spearing major) 19.24.

Goalies: Moog (Edm), Smith (NYI)
  Shots: NYI   9 - 11 -   5   25
            Edm 10 -   9 - 14   33

Referee: Wally Harris
Linesmen: John D'Amico, Swede Knox

GAME #3 - May 14, 1983 - Nassau Coliseum - NY Islanders 5, Edmonton 1

EDMONTON: Glenn Anderson, Paul Coffey, Ray Cote, Lee Fogolin Jr., Grant Fuhr, Randy Gregg, Wayne Gretzky, Charlie Huddy, Pat Hughes, Dave Hunter, Don Jackson, Jari Kurri, Willy Lindstrom, Ken Linseman, Kevin Lowe, Dave Lumley, Mark Messier, Andy Moog, Tom Roulston, Dave Semenko.

NY ISLANDERS: Mike Bossy, Bob Bourne, Billy Carroll, Clark Gillies, Butch Goring, Tomas Jonsson, Anders Kallur, Gord Lane, Dave Langevin, Roland Melanson, Wayne Merrick, Ken Morrow, Bob Nystrom, Stefan Persson, Denis Potvin, Billy Smith, Brent Sutter, Duane Sutter, John Tonelli, Bryan Trottier.

First Period
1. NY ISLANDERS   KALLUR (BOSSY, MORROW)   19.41

Penalties: Messier (Edm) (elbowing) 4.01; B. Sutter (NYI) (highsticking) 4.01; Anderson (Edm) (holding) 5.10.

Second Period
2. EDMONTON   KURRI (GRETZKY)   1.05 (PPG)

Penalties: Bourne (NYI) (hooking) 0.54; Potvin (NYI) (holding) 3.42; Lane (NYI) (elbowing) 7.31; Hunter (Edm) (elbowing) 10.32.

Third Period
3. NY ISLANDERS   BOURNE (PERSSON, LANGEVIN)   5.11 (GWG)
4. NY ISLANDERS   MORROW (TROTTIER, KALLUR)   6.21
5. NY ISLANDERS   D. SUTTER (B. SUTTER, BOURNE) 16.43
6. NY ISLANDERS   B. SUTTER (D. SUTTER, POTVIN) 19.02 (PPG)

Penalties: Bourne (NYI) (tripping) 8.39; Hunter (Edm) (holding) 18.33.

Goalies: Moog (Edm), Smith (NYI)
  Shots: Edm 11 - 15 -   8   34
            NYI 10 -   5 - 13   28

Referee: Bryan Lewis
Linesmen: Ron Finn, Ray Scapinello

GAME #4 - May 17, 1983 - Nassau Coliseum - NY Islanders 4, Edmonton 2

EDMONTON: Glenn Anderson, Paul Coffey, Ray Cote, Lee Fogolin Jr., Grant Fuhr, Randy Gregg, Wayne Gretzky, Charlie Huddy, Pat Hughes, Dave Hunter, Don Jackson, Jari Kurri, Willy Lindstrom, Ken Linseman, Kevin Lowe, Dave Lumley, Mark Messier, Andy Moog, Tom Roulston, Dave Semenko.

NY ISLANDERS: Mike Bossy, Bob Bourne, Billy Carroll, Clark Gillies, Butch Goring, Tomas Jonsson, Anders Kallur, Gord Lane, Dave Langevin, Roland Melanson, Wayne Merrick, Ken Morrow, Bob Nystrom, Stefan Persson, Denis Potvin, Billy Smith, Brent Sutter, Duane Sutter, John Tonelli, Bryan Trottier.

First Period
1. NY ISLANDERS   TROTTIER (BOSSY, GILLIES)   11.02 (PPG)
2. NY ISLANDERS   TONELLI (NYSTROM)   11.45
3. NY ISLANDERS   BOSSY (TROTTIER)   12.39 (GWG)

Penalties: Coffey (Edm) (double roughing) 2.16; B. Sutter (NYI) (double roughing) 2.16; Gillies (NYI) (tripping) 7.40; Lumley (Edm) (interference) 9.54.

Second Period
4. EDMONTON   KURRI (GRETZKY)   0.35
5. EDMONTON   MESSIER (FOGOLIN, COFFEY)   19.39

Penalties: Bourne (NYI) (interference) 2.44; Lowe (Edm) (interference) 11.34; Jackson (Edm) (highsticking) 11.41; Gillies (NYI) (highsticking) 11.41; Kallur (NYI) (highsticking) 12.19.

Third Period
6. NY ISLANDERS   MORROW (unassisted)   18.51 (ENG)

Penalties: Jackson (Edm) (roughing) 5.10; Jonsson (NYI) (holding) 8.16; Anderson (Edm) (slashing) 8.26; Trottier (NYI) (interference) 10.18.

Goalies: Moog (Edm), Smith (NYI)
  Shots: Edm   5 - 14 -   7   26
            NYI   8 - 12 -   6   26

Referee: Andy vanHellemond
Linesmen: John D'Amico, Swede Knox

1984

EDMONTON OILERS - NEW YORK ISLANDERS

GAME #1 - May 10, 1984 - Nassau Coliseum - Edmonton 1, NY Islanders 0

EDMONTON: Glenn Anderson, Paul Coffey, Lee Fogolin Jr., Grant Fuhr, Randy Gregg, Wayne Gretzky, Charlie Huddy, Dave Hunter, Don Jackson, Mike Krushelnyski, Jari Kurri, Willy Lindstrom, Ken Linseman, Kevin Lowe, Dave Lumley, Kevin McClelland, Mark Messier, Andy Moog, Jaroslav Pouzar, Dave Semenko.

NY ISLANDERS: Mike Bossy, Paul Boutilier, Billy Carroll, Gord Dineen, Pat Flatley, Greg Gilbert, Clark Gillies, Butch Goring, Tomas Jonsson, Anders Kallur, Pat LaFontaine, Gord Lane, Roland Melanson, Ken Morrow, Denis Potvin, Billy Smith, Brent Sutter, Duane Sutter, John Tonelli, Bryan Trottier.

First Period
No scoring.
Penalties: Lowe (Edm) (tripping) 8.40; Potvin (NYI) (hooking) 11.34; Hunter (Edm) (elbowing) 14.09; Potvin (NYI) (tripping) 14.51; Jackson (Edm) (roughing) 15.47.

Second Period
No scoring.
Penalties: Dineen (NYI) (holding) 11.52; Jackson (Edm) (crosschecking) 14.37.

Third Period
1. EDMONTON   McCLELLAND (HUGHES, HUNTER)   1.55 (GWG)

Penalties: Hunter (Edm) (holding) 9.06; Jonsson (NYI) (hooking) 15.52.

Goalies: Fuhr (Edm); Smith (NYI), Melanson (NYI) (entered at 19:07 3rd)
  Shots: Edm 10 - 12 - 16   38
            NYI 14 - 12 -   8   34

Referee: Andy vanHellemond
Linesmen: John D'Amico, Ray Scapinello

GAME #2 - May 12, 1984 - Nassau Coliseum - NY Islanders 6, Edmonton 1

EDMONTON: Glenn Anderson, Paul Coffey, Lee Fogolin Jr., Grant Fuhr, Randy Gregg, Wayne Gretzky, Charlie Huddy, Dave Hunter, Don Jackson, Mike Krushelnyski, Jari Kurri, Willy Lindstrom, Ken Linseman, Kevin Lowe, Dave Lumley, Kevin McClelland, Mark Messier, Andy Moog, Jaroslav Pouzar, Dave Semenko.

NY ISLANDERS: Mike Bossy, Paul Boutilier, Gord Dineen, Pat Flatley, Greg Gilbert, Clark Gillies, Butch Goring, Mats Hallin, Tomas Jonsson, Anders Kallur, Pat LaFontaine, Roland Melanson, Ken Morrow, Stefan Persson, Denis Potvin, Billy Smith, Brent Sutter, Duane Sutter, John Tonelli, Bryan Trottier.

First Period
1. NY ISLANDERS   TROTTIER (BOSSY, BOUTILIER)   0.53
2. NY ISLANDERS   GILBERT (LaFONTAINE, PERSSON) 5.48 (PPG, GWG)
3. EDMONTON   GREGG (McCLELLAND)   15.06
4. NY ISLANDERS   GILLIES (KALLUR)   18.31

Penalties: Anderson (Edm) (slashing) 0.09; Tonelli (NYI) (slashing) 0.09; Huddy (Edm) (hooking) 4.14; Hughes (Edm) (slashing) 6.29; D. Sutter (NYI) (slashing) 6.29; Jackson (Edm) (roughing) 6.29; Hughes (Edm) (highsticking) 8.51; B. Sutter (NYI) (holding) 9.12; Jackson (Edm) (highsticking) 12.11; Gilbert (NYI) (highsticking) 12.11; Jonsson (NYI) (hooking) 12.52; McClelland (Edm) (crosschecking, fighting) 15.42; D. Sutter (NYI) (elbowing, fighting) 15.42.

Second Period
5. NY ISLANDERS   TROTTIER (B. SUTTER, FLATLEY)   4.52
6. NY ISLANDERS   GILLIES (POTVIN, BOSSY)   16.48   (PPG)

Penalties: Jonsson (NYI) (hooking) 5.37; Anderson (Edm) (highsticking) 16.05.

Third Period
7. NY ISLANDERS   GILLIES (TROTTIER, BOUTILIER)   17.04   (PPG)

Penalties: Messier (Edm) (highsticking, fighting) 6.52; Dineen (NYI) (charging, fighting) 6.52; Gretzky (Edm) (hooking) 8.30; Semenko (Edm) (roughing) 15.16; Linseman (Edm) (roughing, fighting, misconduct) 17.25; Lumley (Edm) (fighting, game misconduct) 17.25; Dineen (NYI) (fighting, game misconduct) 17.25; Gilbert (NYI) (double roughing, fighting, misconduct).

Goalies: Fuhr (Edm), Smith (NYI)
Shots: Edm   12 - 6 - 5   23
           NYI   12 - 9 - 5   26

Referee: Bryan Lewis
Linesmen: Ron Finn, Leon Stickle

GAME #3 - May 15, 1984 - Northlands Coliseum - Edmonton 7, NY Islanders 2

EDMONTON: Glenn Anderson, Paul Coffey, Lee Fogolin Jr., Grant Fuhr, Randy Gregg, Wayne Gretzky, Charlie Huddy, Dave Hunter, Don Jackson, Mike Krushelnyski, Jari Kurri, Willy Lindstrom, Ken Linseman, Kevin Lowe, Dave Lumley, Kevin McClelland, Mark Messier, Andy Moog, Jaroslav Pouzar, Dave Semenko.

NY ISLANDERS: Mike Bossy, Paul Boutilier, Gord Dineen, Pat Flatley, Greg Gilbert, Clark Gillies, Butch Goring, Mats Hallin, Tomas Jonsson, Anders Kallur, Pat LaFontaine, Roland Melanson, Ken Morrow, Stefan Persson, Denis Potvin, Billy Smith, Brent Sutter, Duane Sutter, John Tonelli, Bryan Trottier.

First Period
1. NY ISLANDERS   GILLIES (FLATLEY, B. SUTTER)   1.32
2. EDMONTON   LOWE (ANDERSON, LINDSTROM)   13.49

Penalties: D. Sutter (NYI) (highsticking) 2.27; Linseman (Edm) (highsticking) 2.27; B. Sutter (NYI) (hooking) 6.30; McClelland (Edm) (interference) 8.49; Jonsson (NYI) (interference) 10.59; Fogolin (Edm) (holding) 14.32; Flatley (NYI) (double roughing) 15.16; Gilbert (NYI) (fighting) 15.16; Gregg (Edm) (roughing) 15.16; Jackson (Edm) (fighting) 15.16; Tonelli (NYI) (highsticking) 17.53; Linseman (Edm) (highsticking) 17.53.

Second Period
3. NY ISLANDERS   GILLIES (TROTTIER, BOSSY)   2.54   (PPG)
4. EDMONTON   MESSIER (FOGOLIN)   8.38
5. EDMONTON   ANDERSON (HUDDY, GRETZKY)   19.12   (GWG)
6. EDMONTON   COFFEY (HUGHES, LINSEMAN)   19.29

Penalties: Hunter (Edm) (elbowing) 1.55; B. Sutter (NYI) (holding) 3.34; Pouzar (Edm) (tripping) 10.00; Trottier (NYI) (roughing) 14.22; Pouzar (Edm) (roughing) 14.22; D. Sutter (NYI) (highsticking, roughing) 17.53; Fogolin (Edm) (highsticking, roughing) 17.53.

Third Period
7. EDMONTON   MESSIER (McCLELLAND, HUDDY)   5.32
8. EDMONTON   McCLELLAND (LUMLEY)   5.52
9. EDMONTON   SEMENKO (KURRI, GRETZKY)   9.41

Penalties: Pouzar (Edm) (highsticking) 6.16; Anderson (Edm) (tripping) 6.56; Morrow (NYI) (highsticking) 14.19; Anderson (Edm) (highsticking) 14.19; Melanson (NYI) (highsticking) 19.37; McClelland (Edm) (highsticking) 19.37.

Goalies: Fuhr (Edm), Moog (Edm) (entered at 12.26 3rd);
          Smith (NYI), Melanson (NYI) (entered at 6.16 3rd)
Shots: NYI   10 - 8 - 7   25
           Edm   11 - 12 - 17   40

Referee: Dave Newell
Linesmen: John D'Amico, Ray Scapinello

GAME #4 - May 17, 1984 - Northlands Coliseum - Edmonton 7, NY Islanders 2

EDMONTON: Glenn Anderson, Paul Coffey, Pat Conacher, Lee Fogolin Jr., Randy Gregg, Wayne Gretzky, Charlie Huddy, Dave Hunter, Don Jackson, Jari Kurri, Willy Lindstrom, Ken Linseman, Kevin Lowe, Dave Lumley, Kevin McClelland, Mark Messier, Andy Moog, Jaroslav Pouzar, Dave Semenko, Mike Zanier.

NY ISLANDERS: Mike Bossy, Paul Boutilier, Pat Flatley, Greg Gilbert, Clark Gillies, Butch Goring, Tomas Jonsson, Anders Kallur, Pat LaFontaine, Dave Langevin, Roland Melanson, Ken Morrow, Bob Nystrom, Stefan Persson, Denis Potvin, Billy Smith, Brent Sutter, Duane Sutter, John Tonelli, Bryan Trottier.

First Period
1. EDMONTON   GRETZKY (SEMENKO, KURRI)   1.53
2. EDMONTON   LINDSTROM (ANDERSON)   3.22
3. NY ISLANDERS   B. SUTTER (GILBERT, MORROW)   14.03
4. EDMONTON   MESSIER (unassisted)   17.54   (GWG)

Penalties: Nystrom (NYI) (highsticking) 4.41; Potvin (NYI) (roughing) 13.40; Lumley (Edm) (roughing) 13.40; Langevin (NYI) (highsticking) 15.43; Morrow (NYI) (crosschecking) 17.31; Kurri (Edm) (highsticking) 17.31; Gretzky (Edm) (unsportsmanlike conduct) 17.31; Lowe (Edm) (holding) 18.25; Linseman (Edm) (highsticking) 18.51.

Second Period
5. EDMONTON   LINDSTROM (COFFEY, MESSIER)   5.21   (PPG)
6. EDMONTON   CONACHER (HUGHES)   6.58
7. EDMONTON   COFFEY (KURRI, SEMENKO)   10.52
8. NY ISLANDERS   FLATLEY (GILLIES, PERSSON)   19.44

Penalties: Nystrom (NYI) (hooking) 4.47; D. Sutter (NYI) (roughing, fighting) 13.47; McClelland (Edm) (fighting) 13.47.

Third Period
9. EDMONTON   GRETZKY (unassisted)   14.01

Penalties: Huddy (Edm) (slashing) 6.36.

Goalies: Moog (Edm), Smith (NYI)
Shots: NYI   7 - 7 - 7   21
           Edm   16 - 10 - 12   38

Referee: Andy vanHellemond
Linesmen: Ron Finn, Leon Stickle

GAME #5 - May 19, 1984 - Northlands Coliseum - Edmonton 5, NY Islanders 2

EDMONTON: Glenn Anderson, Paul Coffey, Pat Conacher, Lee Fogolin Jr., Randy Gregg, Wayne Gretzky, Charlie Huddy, Dave Hunter, Don Jackson, Jari Kurri, Willy Lindstrom, Ken Linseman, Kevin Lowe, Dave Lumley, Kevin McClelland, Mark Messier, Andy Moog, Jaroslav Pouzar, Dave Semenko, Mike Zanier.

NY ISLANDERS: Mike Bossy, Paul Boutilier, Pat Flatley, Greg Gilbert, Clark Gillies, Butch Goring, Tomas Jonsson, Anders Kallur, Pat LaFontaine, Dave Langevin, Roland Melanson, Ken Morrow, Bob Nystrom, Stefan Persson, Denis Potvin, Billy Smith, Brent Sutter, Duane Sutter, John Tonelli, Bryan Trottier.

First Period
1. EDMONTON   GRETZKY (KURRI)   12.08
2. EDMONTON   GRETZKY (KURRI)   17.26

Penalties: Edmonton (bench minor, too many men on the ice, served by Lindstrom) 0.47; Flatley (NYI) (elbowing) 4.09; Persson (NYI) (highsticking) 7.43; D. Sutter (NYI) (roughing) 18.47.

Second Period
3. EDMONTON   LINSEMAN (GRETZKY, HUDDY)   0.38   (PPG, GWG)
4. EDMONTON   KURRI (COFFEY, ANDERSON)   4.59   (PPG)

Penalties: D. Sutter (NYI) (hooking) 4.19; Semenko (Edm) (highsticking) 10.22.

Third Period
5. NY ISLANDERS   LaFONTAINE (FLATLEY, GILLIES)   0.13
6. NY ISLANDERS   LaFONTAINE (GILLIES)   0.35
7. EDMONTON   LUMLEY (unassisted)   19.47   (ENG)

Penalties: Flatley (NYI) (interference) 16.45.

Goalies: Moog (Edm); Smith (NYI), Melanson (NYI) (entered at 0.00 2nd)
Shots: NYI   8 - 6 - 11   25
           Edm   9 - 5 - 9   23

Referee: Bryan Lewis
Linesmen: John D'Amico, Ray Scapinello

1985

EDMONTON OILERS - PHILADELPHIA FLYERS

GAME #1 - May 21, 1985 - The Spectrum - Philadelphia 4, Edmonton 1

EDMONTON: Glenn Anderson, Billy Carroll, Paul Coffey, Lee Fogolin Jr., Grant Fuhr, Randy Gregg, Wayne Gretzky, Charlie Huddy, Dave Hunter, Don Jackson, Mike Krushelnyski, Jari Kurri, Willy Lindstrom, Kevin Lowe, Dave Lumley, Kevin McClelland, Mark Messier, Andy Moog, Mark Napier, Jaroslav Pouzar.

PHILADELPHIA: Todd Bergen, Lindsay Carson, Murray Craven, Doug Crossman, Miroslav Dvorak, Thomas Eriksson, Bob Froese, Ed Hospodar, Mark Howe, Tim Kerr, Pelle Lindbergh, Brad Marsh, Joe Paterson, Dave Poulin, Brian Propp, Ilkka Sinisalo, Derrick Smith, Ron Sutter, Rick Tocchet, Peter Zezel.

First Period
1. PHILADELPHIA   SINISALO (KERR, BERGEN)   15.05   (PPG)
Penalties: Poulin (Phi) (elbowing) 5.08; Coffey (Edm) (interference) 5.49; McClelland (Edm) (fighting) 11.15; Hospodar (Phi) (fighting) 11.15; Lindstrom (Edm) (crosschecking) 13.59; Huddy (Edm) (hooking) 14.13; Lumley (Edm) (hooking) 17.42.

Second Period
No scoring.
Penalties: Jackson (Edm) (elbowing) 1.59; Hospodar (Phi) (interference) 1.59; McClelland (Edm) (fighting) 1.59; Paterson (Phi) (fighting) 1.59; Anderson (Edm) (holding) 6.23; Crossman (Phi) (roughing) 6.23; Gregg (Edm) (holding) 9.51; Marsh (Phi) (holding) 12.13; Hospodar (Phi) (highsticking) 16.30.

Third Period
2. PHILADELPHIA   RON SUTTER (unassisted)   5.56   (GWG)
3. PHILADELPHIA   KERR (POULIN)   8.07
4. EDMONTON   LINDSTROM (MESSIER, GREGG)   16.52
5. PHILADELPHIA   POULIN (CARSON, RON SUTTER)   19.39   (ENG)
Penalties: Jackson (Edm) (roughing) 4.29; Tocchet (Phi) (slashing) 4.29; Jackson (Edm) (hooking) 13.47.

Goalies: Lindbergh (Phi), Fuhr (Edm)
Shots: Edm 8 - 4 - 14 26
        Phi 17 - 12 - 12 41
Referee: Andy vanHellemond
Linesmen: Ron Finn, Leon Stickle

GAME #2 - May 23, 1985 - The Spectrum - Edmonton 3, Philadelphia 1

EDMONTON: Glenn Anderson, Paul Coffey, Lee Fogolin Jr., Grant Fuhr, Randy Gregg, Wayne Gretzky, Charlie Huddy, Pat Hughes, Dave Hunter, Don Jackson, Mike Krushelnyski, Jari Kurri, Willy Lindstrom, Kevin Lowe, Kevin McClelland, Mark Messier, Andy Moog, Mark Napier, Dave Semenko, Esa Tikkanen.

PHILADELPHIA: Todd Bergen, Lindsay Carson, Murray Craven, Doug Crossman, Miroslav Dvorak, Thomas Eriksson, Bob Froese, Ed Hospodar, Mark Howe, Tim Kerr, Pelle Lindbergh, Brad Marsh, Joe Paterson, Dave Poulin, Brian Propp, Ilkka Sinisalo, Derrick Smith, Ron Sutter, Rick Tocchet, Peter Zezel.

First Period
1. EDMONTON   GRETZKY (COFFEY)   10.29
Penalties: Coffey (Edm) (tripping) 4.17; Fogolin (Edm) (highsticking) 6.03; Hunter (Edm) (roughing) 9.22; Marsh (Phi) (roughing) 9.22; Kerr (Phi) (holding) 15.16; Tikkanen (Edm) (slashing) 19.21; Tocchet (Phi) (crosschecking) 19.21.

Second Period
2. PHILADELPHIA   KERR (POULIN, CARSON)   10.22
3. EDMONTON   LINDSTROM (KRUSHELNYSKI, McCLELLAND)   16.08   (GWG)
Penalties: Hunter (Edm) (fighting) 2.39; Kerr (Phi) (fighting) 2.39; Tocchet (Phi) (highsticking) 4.54; Krushelnyski (Edm) (roughing) 7.22; Hospodar (Phi) (roughing) 7.22; Marsh (Phi) (highsticking) 12.11; Anderson (Edm) (interference) 13.35; Fogolin (Edm) (crosschecking) 17.58; Dvorak (Phi) (highsticking) 17.58; Huddy (Edm) (tripping) 18.53; Kerr (Phi) (crosschecking) 19.51.

Third Period
4. EDMONTON   HUNTER (ANDERSON)   19.33   (ENG)
Penalties: none.

Goalies: Lindbergh (Phi), Fuhr (Edm)
Shots: Edm 8 - 14 - 8 30
        Phi 6 - 8 - 4 18
Referee: Kerry Fraser
Linesmen: John D'Amico, Ray Scapinello

GAME #3 - May 25, 1985 - Northlands Coliseum - Edmonton 4, Philadelphia 3

EDMONTON: Glenn Anderson, Paul Coffey, Lee Fogolin Jr., Grant Fuhr, Wayne Gretzky, Charlie Huddy, Pat Hughes, Dave Hunter, Don Jackson, Mike Krushelnyski, Jari Kurri, Willy Lindstrom, Kevin Lowe, Kevin McClelland, Larry Melnyk, Mark Messier, Andy Moog, Mark Napier, Dave Semenko, Esa Tikkanen.

PHILADELPHIA: Lindsay Carson, Murray Craven, Doug Crossman, Miroslav Dvorak, Tomas Eriksson, Bob Froese, Ed Hospodar, Mark Howe, Tim Kerr, Pelle Lindbergh, Brad Marsh, Joe Paterson, Dave Poulin, Brian Propp, Ilkka Sinisalo, Derrick Smith, Rich Sutter, Ron Sutter, Rick Tocchet, Peter Zezel.

First Period
1. EDMONTON   GRETZKY (COFFEY, KURRI)   1.10
2. EDMONTON   GRETZKY (COFFEY, HUDDY)   1.25
3. PHILADELPHIA   SMITH (CROSSMAN, CRAVEN)   1.41
4. EDMONTON   GRETZKY (COFFEY, MESSIER)   13.32
Penalties: Ron Sutter (Phi) (hooking) 0.10; Anderson (Edm) (highsticking) 0.56; Tocchet (Phi) (roughing) 3.32; Hospodar (Phi) (roughing) 3.32; Jackson (Edm) (roughing) 3.32; Krushelnyski (Edm) (roughing) 3.32; Craven (Phi) (interference) 6.08; McClelland (Edm) (highsticking) 9.58; Marsh (Phi) (highsticking) 9.58; Anderson (Edm) (highsticking) 11.08; Anderson (Edm) (roughing) 13.20; Carson (Phi) (roughing) 13.20; Jackson (Edm) (crosschecking) 14.55; Hospodar (Phi) (roughing) 17.19; Ron Sutter (Phi) (elbowing) 17.55.

Second Period
5. EDMONTON   KRUSHELNYSKI (COFFEY, GRETZKY)   6.58   (PPG)
Penalties: Hospodar (Phi) (misconduct) 3.27; Semenko (Edm) (misconduct) 3.27; Crossman (Phi) (hooking) 6.01; Hunter (Edm) (holding) 7.45; Fogolin (Edm) (charging) 12.02; Edmonton (bench minor, too many men on the ice, served by Tikkanen) 19.19; Zezel (Phi) (interference) 19.53.

Third Period
6. PHILADELPHIA   HOWE (TOCCHET, PROPP)   9.08
7. PHILADELPHIA   PROPP (TOCCHET, CRAVEN)   14.26
Penalties: Semenko (Edm) (double roughing) 2.48; Huddy (Edm) (slashing) 10.03; Rich Sutter (Phi) (crosschecking) 10.03; Ron Sutter (Phi) (crosschecking) 11.23; Paterson (Phi) (misconduct) 14.05; Hunter (Edm) (misconduct) 14.05.

Goalies: Fuhr (Edm); Lindbergh (Phi) (started, re-entered at 0.00 2nd),
         Froese (Phi) (entered at 17.55 1st, re-entered at 6.58 2nd)
Shots: Phi 12 - 9 - 9 30
        Edm 20 - 4 - 2 26
Referee: Bryan Lewis
Linesmen: Ron Finn, Leon Stickle

GAME #4 - May 28, 1985 - Northlands Coliseum - Edmonton 5, Philadelphia 3

EDMONTON: Glenn Anderson, Paul Coffey, Lee Fogolin Jr., Grant Fuhr, Randy Gregg, Wayne Gretzky, Charlie Huddy, Pat Hughes, Dave Hunter, Don Jackson, Mike Krushelnyski, Jari Kurri, Willy Lindstrom, Kevin Lowe, Kevin McClelland, Mark Messier, Andy Moog, Mark Napier, Dave Semenko, Esa Tikkanen.

PHILADELPHIA: Ray Allison, Todd Bergen, Murray Craven, Doug Crossman, Miroslav Dvorak, Bob Froese, Len Hachborn, Ed Hospodar, Mark Howe, Pelle Lindbergh, Brad Marsh, Joe Paterson, Dave Poulin, Brian Propp, Ilkka Sinisalo, Derrick Smith, Rich Sutter, Ron Sutter, Rick Tocchet, Peter Zezel.

First Period
1. PHILADELPHIA   RICH SUTTER (RON SUTTER, SMITH)   0.46
2. EDMONTON   COFFEY (KURRI, HUDDY)   4.22   (PPG)
3. PHILADELPHIA   BERGEN (ZEZEL, CROSSMAN)   6.38   (PPG)
4. PHILADELPHIA   CRAVEN (SMITH, MARSH)   11.32   (SHG)
5. EDMONTON   HUDDY (COFFEY, KURRI)   18.23   (PPG)
Penalties: Poulin (Phi) (highsticking) 3.31; Hughes (Edm) (highsticking) 5.17; Messier (Edm) (slashing) 5.59; Crossman (Phi) (holding, unsportsmanlike conduct) 8.32; Hospodar (Phi) (slashing) 16.38.

Second Period
6. EDMONTON   ANDERSON (unassisted)   0.21
7. EDMONTON   GRETZKY (COFFEY, HUDDY)   12.53   (PPG, GWG)

Penalties: Tocchet (Phi) (roughing) 0.48; Fogolin (Edm) (roughing) 0.48; Paterson (Phi) (hooking) 12.11; Hunter (Edm) (roughing) 17.39; Allison (Phi) (slashing) 17.39; Lowe (Edm) (holding) 18.02; Crossman (Phi) (holding) 19.07; Hunter (Edm) (holding) 20.00.

Third Period
8. EDMONTON   GRETZKY (MESSIER, ANDERSON)   3.42   (PPG)

Penalties: Hospodar (Phi) (hooking) 2.46; Hunter (Edm) (kneeing) 7.58.

Goalies: Fuhr (Edm); Lindbergh (Phi), Froese (Phi) (entered at 0.00 3rd)
Shots: Phi 10 - 6 - 7   23
          Edm 10 - 12 - 10   32

Referee: Kerry Fraser
Linesmen: John D'Amico, Ray Scapinello

(NOTE: Philadelphia's Ron Sutter was awarded a penalty shot at 8.47 of the first period. Edmonton's Grant Fuhr stopped the shot).

GAME #5 - May 30, 1985 - Northlands Coliseum - Edmonton 8, Philadelphia 3

EDMONTON: Glenn Anderson, Billy Carroll, Paul Coffey, Lee Fogolin Jr., Grant Fuhr, Randy Gregg, Wayne Gretzky, Charlie Huddy, Pat Hughes, Dave Hunter, Don Jackson, Mike Krushelnyski, Jari Kurri, Willy Lindstrom, Kevin Lowe, Kevin McClelland, Mark Messier, Andy Moog, Mark Napier, Dave Semenko.

PHILADELPHIA: Todd Bergen, Dave Brown, Murray Craven, Doug Crossman, Miroslav Dvorak, Tomas Eriksson, Bob Froese, Ed Hospodar, Mark Howe, David Jensen, Brad Marsh, Joe Paterson, Dave Poulin, Brian Propp, Ilkka Sinisalo, Derrick Smith, Rich Sutter, Ron Sutter, Rick Tocchet, Peter Zezel.

First Period
1. EDMONTON   KURRI (GRETZKY, HUDDY)   4.54
2. EDMONTON   LINDSTROM (MESSIER)   5.31
3. PHILADELPHIA   RICH SUTTER (SMITH)   7.23
4. EDMONTON   COFFEY (GRETZKY)   15.31
5. EDMONTON   COFFEY (HUDDY, KURRI)   17.57   (PPG)

Penalties: Brown (Phi) (slashing) 1.03; Jackson (Edm) (slashing) 1.03; Hospodar (Phi) (holding) 8.45; Jackson (Edm) (roughing) 15.40; Crossman (Phi) (hooking) 16.47.

Second Period
6. EDMONTON   MESSIER (unassisted)   9.18
7. EDMONTON   GRETZKY (COFFEY, HUDDY)   10.20
8. EDMONTON   GRETZKY (COFFEY, HUDDY)   16.49

Penalties: Tocchet (Phi) (slashing) 3.43; Tocchet (Phi) (holding) 6.44; Messier (Edm) (hooking) 7.05; Rich Sutter (Phi) (crosschecking) 12.23; McClelland (Edm) (roughing) 12.23; Anderson (Edm) (roughing) 15.36; Paterson (Phi) (roughing) 15.36; McClelland (Edm) (roughing) 19.55; Brown (Phi) (roughing) 19.55.

Third Period
9. PHILADELPHIA   PROPP (HOWE, POULIN)   1.59   (PPG)
10. EDMONTON   MESSIER (unassisted)   3.39
11. PHILADELPHIA   RICH SUTTER (SMITH)   7.05

Penalties: Messier (Edm) (hooking) 0.38; Coffey (Edm) (roughing) 1.55; Zezel (Phi) (roughing) 1.55; Jackson (Edm) (tripping) 3.57; Lowe (Edm) (highsticking) 8.23; Craven (Phi) (hooking) 12.28; Froese (Phi) (slashing) 12.38; Brown (Phi) (fighting, misconduct) 15.22; Jackson (Edm) (roughing, unsportsmanlike conduct) 15.22; Marsh (Phi) (fighting, misconduct, game misconduct) 15.22; McClelland (Edm) (fighting, misconduct, game misconduct) 15.22.

Goalies: Fuhr (Edm), Froese (Phi)
Shots: Phi 7 - 8 - 7   22
          Edm 12 - 17 - 12   41

Referee: Bryan Lewis
Linesmen: Ron Finn, Leon Stickle

(NOTE: Philadelphia's Dave Poulin was awarded a penalty shot at 12.51 of the third period. Edmonton's Grant Fuhr stopped the shot.)

1986
MONTREAL CANADIENS - CALGARY FLAMES

GAME #1 - May 16, 1986 - Olympic Saddledome - Calgary 5, Montreal 2

MONTREAL: Guy Carbonneau, Chris Chelios, Kjell Dahlin, Bob Gainey, Rick Green, John Kordic, Mike Lalor, Claude Lemieux, Craig Ludwig, David Maley, Mike McPhee, Mats Naslund, Chris Nilan, Stephane Richer, Larry Robinson, Patrick Roy, Brian Skrudland, Bobby Smith, Doug Soetart, Ryan Walter.

CALGARY: Robin Bartel, Paul Baxter, Steve Bozek, Nick Fotiu, Tim Hunter, Rejean Lemelin, Hakan Loob, Al MacInnis, Jamie Macoun, Lanny McDonald, Joe Mullen, Joel Otto, Colin Patterson, Jim Peplinski, Dan Quinn, Paul Reinhart, Doug Risebrough, Neil Sheehy, John Tonelli, Mike Vernon.

First Period
1. MONTREAL   NASLUND (SMITH, ROBINSON)   6.04   (PPG)
2. CALGARY   TONELLI (MacINNIS, QUINN)   12.08
3. CALGARY   PEPLINSKI (BAXTER, OTTO)   19.11

Penalties: McPhee (Mtl) (hooking) 3.35; Bartel (Cgy) (misconduct) 3.35; Mullen (Cgy) (interference) 4.14; Baxter (Cgy) (charging) 10.16; Robinson (Mtl) (holding) 11.57; Ludwig (Mtl) (elbowing) 15.10; McDonald (Cgy) (roughing) 15.10; Nilan (Mtl) (roughing) 17.36; Hunter (Cgy) (roughing) 17.36; Roy (Mtl) (misconduct) 19.11.

Second Period
No scoring.

Penalties: Smith (Mtl) (roughing) 2.51; Loob (Cgy) (roughing) 2.51; Hunter (Cgy) (highsticking) 4.57; Fotiu (Cgy) (interference) 9.54; Maley (Mtl) (roughing) 18.03; Macoun (Cgy) (roughing) 18.03; Ludwig (Mtl) (roughing) 20.00; Nilan (Mtl) (fighting, misconduct) 20.00; Peplinski (Cgy) (roughing) 20.00; Hunter (Cgy) (fighting, misconduct) 20.00.

Third Period
4. CALGARY   QUINN (unassisted)   2.14   (SHG, GWG)
5. CALGARY   McDONALD (FOTIU, PEPLINSKI)   3.33
6. MONTREAL   CHELIOS (MALEY, NASLUND)   17.56
7. CALGARY   RISEBROUGH (PEPLINSKI)   19.35

Penalties: Bozek (Cgy) (crosschecking) 1.04; Carbonneau (Mtl) (roughing) 3.43; Reinhart (Cgy) (roughing) 3.43; Peplinski (Cgy) (holding) 6.16; Skrudland (Mtl) (tripping) 14.33.

Goalies: Roy (Mtl), Vernon (Cgy)
Shots: Mtl 10 - 9 - 5   24
          Cgy 13 - 7 - 10   30

Referee: Kerry Fraser
Linesmen: Ray Scapinello, Ron Finn

GAME #2 - May 18, 1986 - Olympic Saddledome - Montreal 3, Calgary 2 (OT)

MONTREAL: Guy Carbonneau, Chris Chelios, Kjell Dahlin, Bob Gainey, Gaston Gingras, Rick Green, John Kordic, Mike Lalor, Claude Lemieux, Craig Ludwig, David Maley, Mike McPhee, Mats Naslund, Chris Nilan, Larry Robinson, Patrick Roy, Brian Skrudland, Bobby Smith, Doug Soetart, Ryan Walter.

CALGARY: Robin Bartel, Paul Baxter, Steve Bozek, Mike Eaves, Tim Hunter, Rejean Lemelin, Hakan Loob, Al MacInnis, Jamie Macoun, Lanny McDonald, Joe Mullen, Joel Otto, Colin Patterson, Jim Peplinski, Dan Quinn, Paul Reinhart, Doug Risebrough, Neil Sheehy, John Tonelli, Mike Vernon.

First Period
1. CALGARY   TONELLI (MULLEN, QUINN)   9.06

Penalties: MacInnis (Cgy) (holding) 2.22; McPhee (Mtl) (misconduct) 6.08; Skrudland (Mtl) (elbowing) 9.19; Macoun (Cgy) (roughing) 9.19; Gainey (Mtl) (roughing) 10.25; Nilan (Mtl) (fighting) 10.25; Peplinski (Cgy) (roughing) 10.25; Hunter (Cgy) (fighting) 10.25; Skrudland (Mtl) (highsticking) 15.47; Carbonneau (Mtl) (roughing) 16.12; Smith (Mtl) (interference) 19.21.

Second Period
2. CALGARY   REINHART (McDONALD, LOOB)   0.15   (PPG)
3. MONTREAL   GINGRAS (unassisted)   3.45

Penalties: Otto (Cgy) (interference) 1.07; Ludwig (Mtl) (holding) 4.41; Sheehy (Cgy) (crosschecking) 11.31; MacInnis (Cgy) (hooking) 17.01.

Third Period
4. MONTREAL   MALEY (CARBONNEAU, CHELIOS)   3.30
Penalties: Ludwig (Mtl) (interference) 1.11; Mullen (Cgy) (tripping) 8.24; Kordic (Mtl) (misconduct) 10.50; Sheehy (Cgy) (misconduct) 10.50; Carbonneau (Mtl) (roughing) 18.30; Peplinski (Cgy) (roughing) 18.30.

Overtime
5. MONTREAL   SKRUDLAND (McPHEE, LEMIEUX)   0.09   (GWG)
Penalties: none.

Goalies: Roy (Mtl), Vernon (Cgy)
    Shots: Mtl   14 - 12 - 8 - 1   35
              Cgy   8 - 9 - 5 - 0   22

Referee: Andy vanHellemond
Linesmen: Bob Hodges, John D'Amico

GAME #3 - May 20, 1986 - Montreal Forum - Montreal 5, Calgary 3

MONTREAL: Guy Carbonneau, Chris Chelios, Kjell Dahlin, Bob Gainey, Gaston Gingras, Rick Green, John Kordic, Mike Lalor, Claude Lemieux, Craig Ludwig, David Maley, Mike McPhee, Mats Naslund, Chris Nilan, Larry Robinson, Patrick Roy, Brian Skrudland, Bobby Smith, Doug Soetart, Ryan Walter.

CALGARY: Robin Bartel, Perry Berezan, Yves Courteau, Brett Hull, Tim Hunter, Terry Johnson, Rejean Lemelin, Hakan Loob, Al MacInnis, Jamie Macoun, Lanny McDonald, Joe Mullen, Joel Otto, Jim Peplinski, Dan Quinn, Paul Reinhart, Doug Risebrough, Neil Sheehy, John Tonelli, Mike Vernon.

First Period
1. CALGARY   MULLEN (OTTO, LOOB)   5.45   (PPG)
2. MONTREAL   NASLUND (ROBINSON, SMITH)   6.50
3. CALGARY   OTTO (MacINNIS, REINHART)   17.59   (PPG)
4. MONTREAL   SMITH (ROBINSON, NASLUND)   18.25
5. MONTREAL   NASLUND (WALTER, CHELIOS)   19.17   (PPG)
6. MONTREAL   GAINEY (CARBONNEAU, CHELIOS) 19.33 (GWG)
Penalties: Ludwig (Mtl) (highsticking) 2.18; Lalor (Mtl) (roughing) 4.21; Johnson (Cgy) (misconduct) 6.32; Quinn (Cgy) (hooking) 7.30; Carbonneau (Mtl) (roughing) 11.20; Skrudland (Mtl) (roughing) 13.04; Quinn (Cgy) (roughing) 13.04; Lemieux (Mtl) (roughing) 16.41; Bartel (Cgy) (holding) 19.09; Sheehy (Cgy) (fighting, misconduct) 19.39; Nilan (fighting, misconduct) 19.39; Ludwig (Mtl) (highsticking) 19.39; Lanny McDonald (Cgy) (highsticking) 19.39; Peplinski (Cgy) (charging) 19.39.

Second Period
7. CALGARY   McDONALD (QUINN, MacINNIS)   7.13   (PPG)
8. MONTREAL   DAHLIN (GINGRAS, CARBONNEAU) 19.22
Penalties: Skrudland (Mtl) (hooking) 5.35; Kordic (Mtl) (fighting) 8.02; Hunter (Cgy) (fighting) 8.02; Peplinski (Cgy) (highsticking) 9.04; Walter (Mtl) (roughing) 17.53; MacInnis (Cgy) (roughing) 17.53; Nilan (Mtl) (roughing) 18.32; Hunter (Cgy) (roughing, misconduct) 18.32; Skrudland (Mtl) (misconduct) 18.32; Otto (Cgy) (misconduct) 18.32.

Third Period
No scoring.
Penalties: MacInnis (Cgy) (highsticking) 17.11.

Goalies: Roy (Mtl); Vernon (Cgy); Lemelin (Cgy) (entered at 18.39 1st)
    Shots: Cgy   10 - 9 - 7   26
              Mtl   16 - 8 - 5   29

Referee: Don Koharski
Linesmen: Ray Scapinello, Ron Finn

GAME #4 - May 22, 1986 - Montreal Forum - Montreal 1, Calgary 0

MONTREAL: Serge Boisvert, Guy Carbonneau, Chris Chelios, Kjell Dahlin, Bob Gainey, Gaston Gingras, Rick Green, John Kordic, Mike Lalor, Claude Lemieux, Craig Ludwig, David Maley, Mike McPhee, Mats Naslund, Larry Robinson, Patrick Roy, Brian Skrudland, Bobby Smith, Doug Soetart, Ryan Walter.

CALGARY: Paul Baxter, Perry Berezan, Steve Bozek, Mike Eaves, Brett Hull, Tim Hunter, Terry Johnson, Rejean Lemelin, Hakan Loob, Al MacInnis, Jamie Macoun, Lanny McDonald, Joel Otto, Jim Peplinski, Dan Quinn, Paul Reinhart, Doug Risebrough, Neil Sheehy, John Tonelli, Mike Vernon.

First Period
No scoring.
Penalties: Johnson (Cgy) (roughing) 1.31; McPhee (Mtl) (roughing) 1.31; Chelios (Mtl) (charging) 1.31; Berezan (Cgy) (hooking) 6.13; Smith (Mtl) (double roughing) 8.25; Sheehy (Cgy) (double roughing) 8.25; Lemieux (Mtl) (slashing) 19.34; Berezan (Cgy) (slashing) 19.34.

Second Period
No scoring.
Penalties: Bozek (Cgy) (holding) 7.55; Eaves (Cgy) (holding) 15.23.

Third Period
1. MONTREAL   LEMIEUX (unassisted)   11.10   (GWG)
Penalties: McPhee (Mtl) (misconduct) 17.38; Risebrough (Cgy) (highsticking) 20.00; Peplinski (Cgy) (fighting, misconduct, game misconduct) 20.00; Baxter (Cgy) (fighting, game misconduct) 20.00; Bozek (Cgy) (fighting, game misconduct) 20.00; Tonelli (Cgy) (fighting, game misconduct) 20.00; Lemieux (Mtl) (fighting, misconduct, game misconduct) 20.00; Carbonneau (Mtl) (fighting, game misconduct) 20.00; Chelios (Mtl) (fighting, game misconduct) 20.00; Lalor (Mtl) (fighting, game misconduct) 20.00

Goalies: Roy (Mtl), Vernon (Cgy)
    Shots: Cgy   7 - 2 - 6   15
              Mtl   6 - 8 - 10   24

Referee: Andy vanHellemond
Linesmen: John D'Amico, Bob Hodges

GAME #5 - May 24, 1986 - Olympic Saddledome - Montreal 4, Calgary 3

MONTREAL: Serge Boisvert, Guy Carbonneau, Chris Chelios, Bob Gainey, Gaston Gingras, Rick Green, John Kordic, Mike Lalor, Claude Lemieux, Craig Ludwig, David Maley, Mike McPhee, Mats Naslund, Larry Robinson, Steve Rooney, Patrick Roy, Brian Skrudland, Bobby Smith, Doug Soetart, Ryan Walter.

CALGARY: Robin Bartel, Paul Baxter, Steve Bozek, Brian Bradley, Nick Fotiu, Tim Hunter, Rejean Lemelin, Hakan Loob, Al MacInnis, Jamie Macoun, Lanny McDonald, Joe Mullen, Joel Otto, Jim Peplinski, Dan Quinn, Paul Reinhart, Doug Risebrough, Neil Sheehy, John Tonelli, Mike Vernon.

First Period
1. MONTREAL   GINGRAS (LEMIEUX, NASLUND)   6.53   (PPG)
Penalties: Fotiu (Cgy) (roughing) 2.43; McDonald (Cgy) (hooking) 5.53; Skrudland (Mtl) (misconduct) 15.21; Risebrough (Cgy) (misconduct) 15.21; Fotiu (Cgy) (slashing) 18.26.

Second Period
2. CALGARY   BOZEK (HUNTER, PEPLINSKI)   7.17
3. MONTREAL   SKRUDLAND (McPHEE, LEMIEUX)   10.49
Penalties: Lalor (Mtl) (roughing) 1.28; Chelios (Mtl) (slashing) 3.26; Fotiu (Cgy) (highsticking) 14.40.

Third Period
4. MONTREAL   GREEN (MALEY, LALOR)   10.11
5. MONTREAL   SMITH (NASLUND)   10.30   (GWG)
6. CALGARY   BOZEK (MACOUN)   16.46
7. CALGARY   MULLEN (QUINN, MacINNIS)   19.14
Penalties: Ludwig (Mtl) (roughing) 6.31; Fotiu (Cgy) (roughing) 6.31; Lemieux (Mtl) (interference) 13.01; Hunter (Cgy) (highsticking) 13.01.

Goalies: Roy (Mtl), Vernon (Cgy)
    Shots: Mtl   12 - 10 - 11   33
              Cgy   7 - 12 - 14   33

Referee: Don Koharski
Linesmen: Ray Scapinello, Ron Finn

1987

EDMONTON OILERS - PHILADELPHIA FLYERS

GAME #1 - May 17, 1987 - Northlands Coliseum - Edmonton 4, Philadelphia 2

EDMONTON: Glenn Anderson, Kelly Buchberger, Paul Coffey, Grant Fuhr, Randy Gregg, Wayne Gretzky, Charlie Huddy, Dave Hunter, Mike Krushelnyski, Jari Kurri, Kevin Lowe, Craig MacTavish, Kevin McClelland, Marty McSorley, Mark Messier, Andy Moog, Kent Nilsson, Reijo Ruotsalainen, Steve Smith, Esa Tikkanen.

PHILADELPHIA: Dave Brown, Doug Crossman, Pelle Eklund, Ron Hextall, Mark Howe, Brad Marsh, Brad McCrimmon, Scott Mellanby, Don Nachbaur, Dave Poulin, Brian Propp, Chico Resch, Kjell Samuelsson, Ilkka Sinisalo, Derrick Smith, Daryl Stanley, Ron Sutter, Rick Tocchet, Tim Tookey, Peter Zezel.

First Period
1. EDMONTON   GRETZKY (KURRI, LOWE)   15.06

Penalties: Philadelphia (bench minor, too many men on the ice, served by Nachbaur) 4.21; Brown (Phi) (fighting major) 17.42; Buchberger (Edm) (fighting major) 17.42.

Second Period
2. PHILADELPHIA   PROPP (TOCCHET, EKLUND)   16.08

Penalties: Krushelnyski (Edm) (interference) 3.57; McCrimmon (Phi) (interference) 17.56.

Third Period
3. EDMONTON   ANDERSON (MESSIER)   0.48
4. EDMONTON   COFFEY (GRETZKY, HUNTER)   7.09   (GWG)
5. EDMONTON   KURRI (MESSIER, COFFEY)   9.11
6. PHILADELPHIA   TOCCHET (MARSH, EKLUND)   10.18

Penalties: Tocchet (Phi) (slashing) 13.21; Lowe (Edm) (slashing) 13.21.

Goalies: Hextall (Phi), Fuhr (Edm)
Shots: Phi 10 - 10 - 11   31
       Edm 10 - 8 - 8   26

Referee: Dave Newell
Linesmen: Kevin Collins, Ron Finn

GAME #2 - May 20, 1987 - Northlands Coliseum - Edmonton 3, Philadelphia 2 (OT)

EDMONTON: Glenn Anderson, Kelly Buchberger, Paul Coffey, Grant Fuhr, Randy Gregg, Wayne Gretzky, Charlie Huddy, Dave Hunter, Mike Krushelnyski, Jari Kurri, Kevin Lowe, Craig MacTavish, Kevin McClelland, Marty McSorley, Mark Messier, Andy Moog, Kent Nilsson, Reijo Ruotsalainen, Steve Smith, Esa Tikkanen.

PHILADELPHIA: Dave Brown, Lindsay Carson, Murray Craven, Doug Crossman, Pelle Eklund, Ron Hextall, Mark Howe, Brad Marsh, Brad McCrimmon, Scott Mellanby, Dave Poulin, Brian Propp, Chico Resch, Kjell Samuelsson, Ilkka Sinisalo, Derrick Smith, Daryl Stanley, Ron Sutter, Rick Tocchet, Peter Zezel.

First Period
No scoring.
Penalties: Brown (Phi) (holding) 2.38; Coffey (Edm) (holding) 8.38; Smith (Phi) (crosschecking) 16.58; Philadelphia (bench minor, too many men on the ice, served by Carson) 19.52; McCrimmon (Phi) (holding) 20.00.

Second Period
1. EDMONTON   GRETZKY (KURRI, COFFEY)   0.45   (PPG)
2. PHILADELPHIA   SMITH (MELLANBY, SUTTER)   13.20
3. PHILADELPHIA   PROPP (TOCCHET, McCRIMMON)   16.23

Penalties: MacTavish (Edm) (interference) 2.59; Samuelsson (Phi) (slashing) 6.21; Smith (Edm) (roughing) 6.21; Mellanby (Phi) (roughing) 9.08; Coffey (Edm) (roughing) 9.08; Smith (Edm) (holding) 10.37; Tocchet (Phi) (roughing) 19.25; McSorley (Edm) (roughing) 19.25.

Third Period
4. EDMONTON   ANDERSON (GREGG)   11.40

Penalties: Crossman (Phi) (holding) 12.17; Kurri (Edm) (holding) 16.30.

Overtime
5. EDMONTON   KURRI (COFFEY, GRETZKY)   6.50   (GWG)

Penalties: Craven (Phi) (holding) 3.16; Anderson (Edm) (slashing) 3.16.

Goalies: Hextall (Phi), Fuhr (Edm)
Shots: Phi 15 - 12 - 5 - 2   34
       Edm   9 - 7 - 15 - 3   34

Referee: Andy vanHellemond
Linesmen: John D'Amico, Bob Hodges

GAME #3 - May 22, 1987 - The Spectrum - Philadelphia 5, Edmonton 3

EDMONTON: Glenn Anderson, Kelly Buchberger, Paul Coffey, Grant Fuhr, Randy Gregg, Wayne Gretzky, Charlie Huddy, Dave Hunter, Mike Krushelnyski, Jari Kurri, Kevin Lowe, Craig MacTavish, Kevin McClelland, Marty McSorley, Mark Messier, Andy Moog, Craig Muni, Kent Nilsson, Reijo Ruotsalainen, Esa Tikkanen.

PHILADELPHIA: Dave Brown, Lindsay Carson, Murray Craven, Doug Crossman, J.J. Daigneault, Pelle Eklund, Ron Hextall, Mark Howe, Brad Marsh, Brad McCrimmon, Scott Mellanby, Dave Poulin, Brian Propp, Chico Resch, Kjell Samuelsson, Derrick Smith, Daryl Stanley, Ron Sutter, Rick Tocchet, Peter Zezel.

First Period
1. EDMONTON   MESSIER (MacTAVISH)   4.14   (SHG)
2. EDMONTON   COFFEY (GRETZKY, KURRI)   19.51

Penalties: Hunter (Edm) (roughing) 2.36; Stanley (Phi) (slashing) 9.47; Krushelnyski (Edm) (holding) 14.04; Smith (Edm) (roughing) 17.36.

Second Period
3. EDMONTON   ANDERSON (MESSIER, COFFEY)   1.49   (PPG)
4. PHILADELPHIA   CRAVEN (TOCCHET, SUTTER)   9.04   (PPG)
5. PHILADELPHIA   ZEZEL (unassisted)   15.20   (PPG)

Penalties: Hextall (Phi) (interference) 1.12; Edmonton (bench minor, too many men on the ice, served by Tikkanen) 7.58; Ruotsalainen (Edm) (holding) 11.23; Tikkanen (Edm) (slashing) 14.52; Sutter (Phi) (highsticking) 17.49.

Third Period
6. PHILADELPHIA   MELLANBY (HOWE, SUTTER)   4.37
7. PHILADELPHIA   McCRIMMON (MELLANBY, SUTTER)   4.54   (GWG)
8. PHILADELPHIA   PROPP (SAMUELSSON, ZEZEL)   19.26   (ENG)

Penalties: McSorley (Edm) (roughing) 19.59; Brown (Phi) (roughing) 19.59; Sutter (Phi) (slashing) 19.59.

Goalies: Hextall (Phi), Fuhr (Edm)
Shots: Edm   8 - 10 - 10   28
       Phi 11 - 14 - 11   36

Referee: Don Koharski
Linesmen: Kevin Collins, Ron Finn

GAME #4 - May 24, 1987 - The Spectrum - Edmonton 4, Philadelphia 1

EDMONTON: Glenn Anderson, Paul Coffey, Grant Fuhr, Randy Gregg, Wayne Gretzky, Charlie Huddy, Dave Hunter, Mike Krushelnyski, Jari Kurri, Kevin Lowe, Craig MacTavish, Kevin McClelland, Marty McSorley, Mark Messier, Andy Moog, Craig Muni, Kent Nilsson, Jaroslav Pouzar, Reijo Ruotsalainen, Esa Tikkanen.

PHILADELPHIA: Dave Brown, Lindsay Carson, Murray Craven, Doug Crossman, J.J. Daigneault, Pelle Eklund, Ron Hextall, Mark Howe, Brad Marsh, Brad McCrimmon, Scott Mellanby, Dave Poulin, Brian Propp, Chico Resch, Kjell Samuelsson, Derrick Smith, Daryl Stanley, Ron Sutter, Rick Tocchet, Peter Zezel.

First Period
1. EDMONTON   KURRI (GRETZKY)   5.53
2. EDMONTON   LOWE (GRETZKY)   18.44   (SHG, GWG)

Penalties: Tikkanen (Edm) (roughing) 1.16; Smith (Phi) (roughing) 1.16; Lowe (Edm) (highsticking) 3.32; McCrimmon (Phi) (hooking) 9.35; MacTavish (Edm) (holding) 12.42; Messier (Edm) (crosschecking) 17.28.

Second Period
3. PHILADELPHIA   McCRIMMON (EKLUND, PROPP)   8.17   (PPG)
4. EDMONTON   GREGG (GRETZKY)   12.31   (PPG)

Penalties: Gretzky (Edm) (hooking) 6.34; Samuelsson (Phi) (interference) 10.38; Zezel (Phi) (tripping) 13.59; Coffey (Edm) (roughing) 19.45; Tocchet (Phi) (roughing) 19.45.

Third Period
5. EDMONTON   KRUSHELNYSKI (unassisted)   4.17

Penalties: Anderson (Edm) (crosschecking) 1.01; Hextall (Phi) (misconduct) 4.31; Huddy (Edm) (misconduct) 7.39; Tocchet (Phi) (misconduct) 7.39; Hextall (Phi) (slashing major) 8.50.

Goalies: Hextall (Phi), Fuhr (Edm)
Shots: Edm   8 - 10 - 11   29
       Phi   8 - 11 - 9   28

Referee: Andy vanHellemond
Linesmen: John D'Amico, Bob Hodges

GAME #5 - May 26, 1987 - Northlands Coliseum - Philadelphia 4, Edmonton 3

EDMONTON: Glenn Anderson, Paul Coffey, Grant Fuhr, Randy Gregg, Wayne Gretzky, Charlie Huddy, Dave Hunter, Mike Krushelnyski, Jari Kurri, Kevin Lowe, Craig MacTavish, Kevin McClelland, Marty McSorley, Mark Messier, Andy Moog, Craig Muni, Kent Nilsson, Jaroslav Pouzar, Reijo Ruotsalainen, Esa Tikkanen.

PHILADELPHIA: Dave Brown, Lindsay Carson, Murray Craven, Doug Crossman, J.J. Daigneault, Pelle Eklund, Ron Hextall, Mark Howe, Brad Marsh, Brad McCrimmon, Scott Mellanby, Dave Poulin, Brian Propp, Chico Resch, Kjell Samuelsson, Ilkka Sinisalo, Derrick Smith, Ron Sutter, Rick Tocchet, Peter Zezel.

First Period
1. EDMONTON   KURRI (GRETZKY, KRUSHELNYSKI)   2.58   (PPG)
2. EDMONTON   McSORLEY (GRETZKY)   6.35
3. PHILADELPHIA TOCCHET (PROPP, EKLUND)   19.10

Penalties: Tocchet (Phi) (roughing) 2.23; Coffey (Edm) (roughing) 2.23; Brown (Phi) (holding) 2.49; Samuelsson (Phi) (holding) 10.52; Pouzar (Edm) (hooking) 15.10.

Second Period
4. EDMONTON   McSORLEY (HUDDY, POUZAR)   1.32
5. PHILADELPHIA CROSSMAN (PROPP, EKLUND)   8.08
6. PHILADELPHIA EKLUND (PROPP, TOCCHET)   12.40 (PPG)

Penalties: Messier (Edm) (tripping) 12.10; Sutter (Phi) (roughing) 12.48; Krushelnyski (Edm) (roughing) 12.48; Smith (Phi) (slashing) 18.39; Kurri (Edm) (slashing) 18.39.

Third Period
7. PHILADELPHIA TOCCHET (PROPP)   5.26   (GWG)

Penalties: Smith (Phi) (roughing) 6.11; Ruotsalainen (Edm) (roughing) 6.11.

Goalies: Hextall (Phi), Fuhr (Edm)
Shots: Phi 16 - 6 - 13   35
       Edm 16 - 10 - 8   34

Referee: Don Koharski
Linesmen: Kevin Collins, Ron Finn

GAME #6 - May 28, 1987 - The Spectrum - Philadelphia 3, Edmonton 2

EDMONTON: Glenn Anderson, Paul Coffey, Grant Fuhr, Randy Gregg, Wayne Gretzky, Charlie Huddy, Dave Hunter, Mike Krushelnyski, Jari Kurri, Kevin Lowe, Craig MacTavish, Kevin McClelland, Marty McSorley, Mark Messier, Andy Moog, Craig Muni, Kent Nilsson, Jaroslav Pouzar, Reijo Ruotsalainen, Esa Tikkanen.

PHILADELPHIA: Dave Brown, Lindsay Carson, Murray Craven, Doug Crossman, J.J. Daigneault, Pelle Eklund, Ron Hextall, Mark Howe, Brad Marsh, Brad McCrimmon, Scott Mellanby, Dave Poulin, Brian Propp, Chico Resch, Kjell Samuelsson, Ilkka Sinisalo, Derrick Smith, Ron Sutter, Rick Tocchet, Peter Zezel.

First Period
1. EDMONTON   LOWE (GRETZKY, KURRI)   5.02   (SHG)
2. EDMONTON   McCLELLAND (MacTAVISH, MUNI)   15.16

Penalties: McSorley (Edm) (highsticking) 2.15; Tocchet (Phi) (roughing) 2.15; Hunter (Edm) (holding) 3.22; Poulin (Phi) (highsticking) 6.04; Coffey (Edm) (highsticking) 6.04; McClelland (Edm) (double roughing) 8.45; Tocchet (Phi) (roughing) 8.45; Anderson (Edm) (roughing) 12.39; Samuelsson (Phi) (roughing) 12.39; Poulin (Phi) (interference) 13.09; Poulin (Phi) (highsticking) 15.19; Anderson (Edm) (highsticking) 20.00; Samuelsson (Phi) (highsticking) 20.00.

Second Period
3. PHILADELPHIA CARSON (BROWN, MARSH)   7.12

Penalties: Coffey (Edm) (tripping) 1.41; McCrimmon (Phi) (highsticking, unsportsmanlike conduct) 9.06; Anderson (Edm) (roughing, highsticking) 9.06; Crossman (Phi) (tripping) 9.48; McSorley (Edm) (holding) 15.12.

Third Period
4. PHILADELPHIA PROPP (EKLUND, CROSSMAN)   13.04 (PPG)
5. PHILADELPHIA DAIGNEAULT (unassisted)   14.28 (GWG)

Penalties: Messier (Edm) (hooking) 0.09; Anderson (Edm) (highsticking) 12.21.

Goalies: Hextall (Phi), Fuhr (Edm)
Shots: Edm 15 - 9 - 8   32
       Phi   5 - 8 - 10   23

Referee: Dave Newell
Linesmen: John D'Amico, Bob Hodges

GAME #7 - May 31, 1987 - Northlands Coliseum - Edmonton 3, Philadelphia 1

EDMONTON: Glenn Anderson, Paul Coffey, Grant Fuhr, Randy Gregg, Wayne Gretzky, Charlie Huddy, Dave Hunter, Mike Krushelnyski, Jari Kurri, Kevin Lowe, Craig MacTavish, Kevin McClelland, Marty McSorley, Mark Messier, Andy Moog, Craig Muni, Kent Nilsson, Reijo Ruotsalainen, Steve Smith, Esa Tikkanen.

PHILADELPHIA: Dave Brown, Lindsay Carson, Murray Craven, Doug Crossman, J.J. Daigneault, Pelle Eklund, Ron Hextall, Mark Howe, Brad Marsh, Brad McCrimmon, Scott Mellanby, Dave Poulin, Brian Propp, Chico Resch, Kjell Samuelsson, Ilkka Sinisalo, Derrick Smith, Ron Sutter, Rick Tocchet, Peter Zezel.

First Period
1. PHILADELPHIA CRAVEN (EKLUND, CROSSMAN)   1.41   (PPG)
2. EDMONTON   MESSIER (NILSSON, ANDERSON)   7.45

Penalties: Messier (Edm) (crosschecking) 0.34; Coffey (Edm) (holding) 1.13; Poulin (Phi) (hooking) 4.22.

Second Period
3. EDMONTON   KURRI (GRETZKY)   14.59 (GWG)

Penalties: Sinisalo (Phi) (hooking) 3.39; Marsh (Phi) (tripping) 12.15; Mellanby (Phi) (roughing) 15.27; Smith (Edm) (roughing) 15.27; Messier (Edm) (charging) 16.02.

Third Period
4. EDMONTON   ANDERSON (HUDDY)   17.36

Penalties: Crossman (Phi) (holding) 14.16; Tikkanen (Edm) (roughing) 14.16.

Goalies: Hextall (Phi), Fuhr (Edm)
Shots: Phi 12 - 6 - 2   20
       Edm 18 - 13 - 12 43

Referee: Andy vanHellemond
Linesmen: John D'Amico, Ron Finn

1988

EDMONTON OILERS - BOSTON BRUINS

Game #1 - May 18, 1988 - Northlands Coliseum - Edmonton 2, Boston 1

EDMONTON: Keith Acton, Glenn Anderson, Jeff Beukeboom, Geoff Courtnall, Grant Fuhr, Randy Gregg, Wayne Gretzky, Mike Krushelnyski, Jari Kurri, Normand Lacombe, Kevin Lowe, Craig MacTavish, Kevin McClelland, Marty McSorley, Mark Messier, Craig Muni, Bill Ranford, Craig Simpson, Steve Smith, Esa Tikkanen.

BOSTON: Raymond Bourque, Randy Burridge, Keith Crowder, Craig Janney, Bob Joyce, Steve Kasper, Gord Kluzak, Moe Lemay, Rejean Lemelin, Ken Linseman, Rick Middleton, Jay Miller, Andy Moog, Cam Neely, Bill O'Dwyer, Allen Pedersen, Willi Plett, Bob Sweeney, Michael Thelven, Glen Wesley.

First Period
No scoring.

Penalties: Neely (Bos) (tripping) 1.01; Tikkanen (Edm) (holding) 2.10; Edmonton (bench minor, too many men on the ice, served by Tikkanen) 4.20; Pedersen (Bos) (holding) 9.17; Plett (Bos) (crosschecking) 12.17; Simpson (Edm) (crosschecking) 12.17; Linseman (Bos) (highsticking) 14.13; Kurri (Edm) (double minor, roughing) 14.13.

Second Period
1. EDMONTON   GRETZKY (SMITH, KURRI)   1.56   (PPG)
2. BOSTON   NEELY (JANNEY, KLUZAK)   13.15

Penalties: Boston (bench minor, too many men on the ice, served by Crowder) 1.08; Tikkanen (Edm) (elbowing) 4.29; Plett (Bos) (holding) 16.08.

Third Period
3. EDMONTON   ACTON (SMITH, McCLELLAND)   1.15   (GWG)

Penalties: Tikkanen (Edm) (tripping) 2.26; Gregg (Edm) (highsticking) 6.21.

Goalies: Fuhr (Edm), Moog (Bos)
Shots: Bos 5 - 4 - 5   14
       Edm 6 - 8 - 8   22

Referee: Denis Morel
Linesmen: Ron Finn, Ray Scapinello

Game #2 - May 20, 1988 - Northlands Coliseum - Edmonton 4, Boston 2

EDMONTON: Keith Acton, Glenn Anderson, Jeff Beukeboom, Geoff Courtnall, Grant Fuhr, Randy Gregg, Wayne Gretzky, Mike Krushelnyski, Jari Kurri, Normand Lacombe, Kevin Lowe, Craig MacTavish, Kevin McClelland, Marty McSorley, Mark Messier, Craig Muni, Bill Ranford, Craig Simpson, Steve Smith, Esa Tikkanen.

BOSTON: Raymond Bourque, Randy Burridge, Keith Crowder, Craig Janney, Bob Joyce, Steve Kasper, Gord Kluzak, Moe Lemay, Rejean Lemelin, Ken Linseman, Rick Middleton, Jay Miller, Andy Moog, Cam Neely, Bill O'Dwyer, Allen Pedersen, Willi Plett, Bob Sweeney, Michael Thelven, Glen Wesley.

First Period
1. EDMONTON   ANDERSON (GRETZKY, TIKKANEN)   15.57   (PPG)
2. EDMONTON   MESSIER (GRETZKY, KURRI)   19.30   (PPG)

Penalties: Thelven (Bos) (highsticking) 0.43; Miller (Bos) (fighting) 3.09; McClelland (Edm) (fighting) 3.09; Lemay (Bos) (slashing) 3.57; Gregg (Edm) (hooking) 5.59; Simpson (Edm) (elbowing) 10.20; Crowder (Bos) (roughing) 10.23; Kluzak (Bos) (highsticking) 14.28; Bourque (Bos) (highsticking) 15.48; Lemelin (Bos) (delay of game) 18.41; Burridge (Bos) (highsticking) 19.06.

Second Period
No scoring.

Penalties: McClelland (Edm) (holding) 2.05; Crowder (Bos) (roughing) 6.15; Krushelnyski (Edm) (roughing) 6.15; Miller (Bos) (roughing, misconduct) 10.57; McClelland (Edm) (roughing, misconduct) 10.57; Crowder (Bos) (crosschecking) 15.22; Linseman (Bos) (slashing) 16.53.

Third Period
3. BOSTON   JOYCE (JANNEY, NEELY)   0.45
4. BOSTON   LINSEMAN (LEMAY, CROWDER)   3.16
5. EDMONTON   GRETZKY (TIKKANEN)   11.21   (GWG)
6. EDMONTON   KURRI (KRUSHELNYSKI)   19.53   (ENG)

Penalties: Kluzak (Bos) (roughing) 19.21; Tikkanen (Edm) (roughing) 19.21.

Goalies: Fuhr (Edm), Lemelin (Bos)
Shots: Bos 5 - 2 - 5   12
        Edm 13 - 8 - 11   32

Referee: Don Koharski
Linesmen: Kevin Collins, Swede Knox

Game #3 - May 22, 1988 - Boston Garden - Edmonton 6, Boston 3

EDMONTON: Keith Acton, Glenn Anderson, Jeff Beukeboom, Geoff Courtnall, Grant Fuhr, Randy Gregg, Wayne Gretzky, Mike Krushelnyski, Jari Kurri, Normand Lacombe, Kevin Lowe, Craig MacTavish, Kevin McClelland, Marty McSorley, Mark Messier, Craig Muni, Bill Ranford, Craig Simpson, Steve Smith, Esa Tikkanen.

BOSTON: Raymond Bourque, Randy Burridge, Keith Crowder, Craig Janney, Bob Joyce, Steve Kasper, Gord Kluzak, Moe Lemay, Rejean Lemelin, Ken Linseman, Tom McCarthy, Rick Middleton, Jay Miller, Andy Moog, Cam Neely, Bill O'Dwyer, Allen Pedersen, Bob Sweeney, Michael Thelven, Glen Wesley.

First Period
1. BOSTON   BURRIDGE (SWEENEY)   2.46
2. EDMONTON   McCLELLAND (GRETZKY, KRUSHELNYSKI)   16.18

Penalties: Thelven (Bos) (holding) 5.31; McClelland (Edm) (tripping) 8.45; Neely (Bos) (boarding) 9.59.

Second Period
3. EDMONTON   TIKKANEN (GRETZKY, ANDERSON)   10.25   (PPG)
4. EDMONTON   ANDERSON (SIMPSON)   12.57

Penalties: MacTavish (Edm) (roughing) 4.56; Pedersen (Bos) (roughing) 4.56; McClelland (Edm) (fighting) 8.41; Miller (Bos) (roughing, fighting) 8.41; Tikkanen (Edm) (holding) 14.42; Simpson (Edm) (holding) 18.25.

Third Period
5. EDMONTON   TIKKANEN (GRETZKY, GREGG)   1.32   (GWG)
6. BOSTON   LEMAY (LINSEMAN, BOURQUE)   4.19
7. EDMONTON   SIMPSON (ANDERSON, MESSIER)   10.28
8. BOSTON   NEELY (JOYCE, WESLEY)   14.02   (PPG)
9. EDMONTON   TIKKANEN (GRETZKY, ANDERSON)   19.40   (ENG)

Penalties: McSorley (Edm) (hooking) 13.51; Edmonton (bench minor, too many men on the ice, served by Tikkanen) 15.42.

Goalies: Fuhr (Edm), Lemelin (Bos)
Shots: Edm: 11 - 6 - 8   25
        Bos: 10 - 8 - 10   28

Referee: Andy vanHellemond
Linesmen: Ron Finn, Ray Scapinello

Suspended Game - May 24, 1988 - Boston Garden - Edmonton 3, Boston 3

EDMONTON: Keith Acton, Glenn Anderson, Jeff Beukeboom, Geoff Courtnall, Grant Fuhr, Randy Gregg, Wayne Gretzky, Mike Krushelnyski, Jari Kurri, Normand Lacombe, Kevin Lowe, Craig MacTavish, Kevin McClelland, Marty McSorley, Mark Messier, Craig Muni, Bill Ranford, Craig Simpson, Steve Smith, Esa Tikkanen.

BOSTON: Raymond Bourque, Randy Burridge, Keith Crowder, Greg Hawgood, Craig Janney, Bob Joyce, Steve Kasper, Gord Kluzak, Reed Larson, Moe Lemay, Rejean Lemelin, Ken Linseman, Nevin Markwart, Rick Middleton, Andy Moog, Cam Neely, Bill O'Dwyer, Allen Pedersen, Bob Sweeney, Glen Wesley.

First Period
1. EDMONTON   ANDERSON (MESSIER, MUNI)   0.10
2. EDMONTON   TIKKANEN (GRETZKY)   15.33   (PPG)
3. BOSTON   HAWGOOD (MIDDLETON, SWEENEY)   16.56

Penalties: Kasper (Bos) (highsticking) 1.59; Lacombe (Edm) (highsticking) 1.59; McSorley (Edm) (tripping) 5.30; Messier (Edm) (tripping) 8.01; Pedersen (Bos) (holding) 14.22; Bourque (Bos) (roughing) 14.30; Tikkanen (Edm) (tripping) 19.25.

Second Period
4. BOSTON   WESLEY (unassisted)   6.12   (SHG)
5. BOSTON   WESLEY (LINSEMAN)   7.37   (PPG)
6. EDMONTON   SIMPSON (SMITH, GRETZKY)   16.37   (PPG)

Penalties: Edmonton (bench minor, too many men on the ice, served by Simpson) 0.44; Lemay (Bos) (tripping) 4.46; Lowe (Edm) (holding) 7.34; Markwart (Bos) (roughing) 10.28; Anderson (Edm) (tripping) 10.28; Sweeney (Bos) (roughing) 13.05; Smith (Edm) (roughing) 13.05; Simpson (Edm) (holding) 14.15; Crowder (Bos) (holding) 15.10.

Goalies: Fuhr (Edm), Moog (Bos)

Referee: Denis Morel
Linesmen: Kevin Collins, Swede Knox

PLAY SUSPENDED AT 16.37 OF SECOND PERIOD DUE TO POWER FAILURE

Game #4 - May 26, 1988 - Northlands Coliseum - Edmonton 6, Boston 3

EDMONTON: Keith Acton, Glenn Anderson, Geoff Courtnall, Grant Fuhr, Randy Gregg, Wayne Gretzky, Charlie Huddy, Mike Krushelnyski, Jari Kurri, Normand Lacombe, Kevin Lowe, Craig MacTavish, Kevin McClelland, Marty McSorley, Mark Messier, Craig Muni, Bill Ranford, Craig Simpson, Steve Smith, Esa Tikkanen.

BOSTON: Raymond Bourque, Randy Burridge, Keith Crowder, Greg Hawgood, Craig Janney, Greg Johnston, Bob Joyce, Steve Kasper, Gord Kluzak, Reed Larson, Moe Lemay, Rejean Lemelin, Ken Linseman, Rick Middleton, Andy Moog, Cam Neely, Bill O'Dwyer, Bob Sweeney, Michael Thelven, Glen Wesley.

First Period
1. BOSTON   KASPER (BURRIDGE, BOURQUE)   0.43
2. EDMONTON   LACOMBE (MUNI, LOWE)   6.07
3. BOSTON   LINSEMAN (BOURQUE)   9.44   (PPG)
4. EDMONTON   TIKKANEN (KURRI, GRETZKY)   15.03   (PPG)

Penalties: Bourque (Bos) (highsticking) 3.55; Tikkanen (Edm) (hooking) 8.30; Messier (Edm) (slashing) 9.16; Crowder (Bos) (hooking) 13.29.

Second Period
5. EDMONTON   KRUSHELNYSKI (McCLELLAND, LOWE)   6.38
6. EDMONTON   GRETZKY (TIKKANEN, SMITH)   9.44   (PPG, GWG)
7. EDMONTON   SIMPSON (GRETZKY, GREGG)   19.58

Penalties: Simpson (Edm) (unsportsmanlike conduct) 0.52; Larson (Bos) (tripping) 3.31; Lemay (Bos) (roughing) 7.08; Lacombe (Edm) (roughing) 7.08; Thelven (Bos) (holding) 8.00; Boston (bench minor, too many men on the ice, served by Joyce) 10.42; Anderson (Edm) (hooking) 11.55.

Third Period
8. EDMONTON   TIKKANEN (KURRI, GREGG)   1.21
9. BOSTON   KASPER (JOHNSTON, WESLEY)   6.35

Penalties: Krushelnyski (Edm) (holding) 12.09; Tikkanen (Edm) (double minor, highsticking) 14.38; Linseman (Bos) (highsticking) 14.38; Krushelnyski (Edm) (hooking) 18.48.

Goalies: Fuhr (Edm), Moog (Bos)
Shots: Bos 8 - 6 - 5   19
Edm 8 - 10 - 8   26

Referee: Andy vanHellemond
Linesmen: Ron Finn, Ray Scapinello

1989
CALGARY FLAMES - MONTREAL CANADIENS

GAME #1 - May 14, 1989 - Olympic Saddledome - Calgary 3, Montreal 2

CALGARY: Theoren Fleury, Doug Gilmour, Tim Hunter, Hakan Loob, Al MacInnis, Jamie Macoun, Brian MacLellan, Brad McCrimmon, Lanny McDonald, Joe Mullen, Dana Murzyn, Ric Nattress, Joe Nieuwendyk, Joel Otto, Colin Patterson, Jim Peplinski, Rob Ramage, Gary Roberts, Mike Vernon, Rick Wamsley.

MONTREAL: Guy Carbonneau, Chris Chelios, Shayne Corson, Russ Courtnall, Eric Desjardins, Bob Gainey, Rick Green, Brian Hayward, Mike Keane, Claude Lemieux, Craig Ludwig, Mike McPhee, Mats Naslund, Larry Robinson, Patrick Roy, Stephane Richer, Brian Skrudland, Bobby Smith, Petr Svoboda, Ryan Walter.

First Period
1. MONTREAL   RICHER (CORSON, CHELIOS)   2.43   (PPG)
2. CALGARY   MacINNIS (OTTO, MULLEN)   6.51   (PPG)
3. CALGARY   MacINNIS (OTTO, PEPLINSKI) 8.33
4. MONTREAL   ROBINSON (SMITH, KEANE)   10.02
Penalties: Peplinski (Cgy) (hooking) 0.49; Robinson (Mtl) (hooking) 6.33; Roy (Mtl) (delay of game) 10.29; Carbonneau (Mtl) (interference) 18.51; Gilmour (Cgy) (slashing) 18.51; Skrudland (Mtl) (elbowing) 19.22.

Second Period
5. CALGARY   FLEURY (MACOUN, T. HUNTER) 11.45 (GWG)
Penalties: Peplinski (Cgy) (crosschecking) 6.07; Smith (Mtl) (interference) 6.15; Macoun (Cgy) (tripping) 7.32; McCrimmon (Cgy) (tripping) 14.20.

Third Period
No scoring.
Penalties: Ludwig (Mtl) (tripping) 1.36; Smith (Mtl) (misconduct) 19.39.

Goalies: Roy (Mtl); Vernon (Cgy)
Shots: Mtl 6 - 16 - 9   31
Cgy 13 - 12 - 10   35

Referee: Andy vanHellemond
Linesmen: Kevin Collins, Ray Scapinello

GAME #2 - May 17, 1989 - Olympic Saddledome - Montreal 4, Calgary 2

CALGARY: Theoren Fleury, Doug Gilmour, Tim Hunter, Hakan Loob, Al MacInnis, Jamie Macoun, Brian MacLellan, Brad McCrimmon, Lanny McDonald, Joe Mullen, Dana Murzyn, Ric Nattress, Joe Nieuwendyk, Joel Otto, Colin Patterson, Jim Peplinski, Rob Ramage, Gary Roberts, Mike Vernon, Rick Wamsley.

MONTREAL: Guy Carbonneau, Chris Chelios, Shayne Corson, Russ Courtnall, Eric Desjardins, Bob Gainey, Brent Gilchrist, Rick Green, Brian Hayward, Mike Keane, Craig Ludwig, Mike McPhee, Mats Naslund, Larry Robinson, Patrick Roy, Stephane Richer, Brian Skrudland, Bobby Smith, Petr Svoboda, Ryan Walter.

First Period
1. MONTREAL   ROBINSON (McPHEE, SKRUDLAND)   4.18
Penalties: McCrimmon (Cgy) (holding) 2.14; Gilchrist (Mtl) (crosschecking) 5.31; Chelios (Mtl) (roughing) 7.15; Corson (Mtl) (roughing) 10.48; Peplinski (Cgy) (roughing) 10.48; McPhee (Mtl) (unsportsmanlike conduct) 16.35; T. Hunter (Cgy) (unsportsmanlike conduct) 16.35; Corson (Mtl) (roughing) 20.00; Roberts (Cgy) (roughing) 20.00.

Second Period
2. MONTREAL   SMITH (KEANE, CHELIOS)   1.55   (PPG)
3. CALGARY   NIEUWENDYK (MacLELLAN)   5.14
4. CALGARY   OTTO (MULLEN, MacINNIS)   13.49 (PPG)
Penalties: Murzyn (Cgy) (roughing) 1.23; Gilchrist (Mtl) (hooking) 2.58; Svoboda (Mtl) (elbowing) 7.56; Skrudland (Mtl) (elbowing) 13.32; Murzyn (Cgy) (tripping) 16.07; Chelios (Mtl) (crosschecking) 18.18; McPhee (Mtl) (unsportsmanlike conduct) 19.48; MacLellan (Cgy) (unsportsmanlike conduct) 19.48.

Third Period
5. MONTREAL   CHELIOS (SKRUDLAND, SVOBODA) 8.01   (GWG)
6. MONTREAL   COURTNALL (CHELIOS, SVOBODA) 9.35   (PPG)
Penalties: T. Hunter (Cgy) (holding) 2.31; Keane (Mtl) (holding) 3.11; Roberts (Cgy) (holding) 8.13; Naslund (Mtl) (elbowing) 11.21; Chelios (Mtl) (roughing) 13.19; Nieuwendyk (Cgy) (roughing) 13.19.

Goalies: Roy (Mtl); Vernon (Cgy)
Shots: Mtl 11 - 4 - 8   23
Cgy 8 - 16 - 8   32

Referee: Denis Morel
Linesmen: Swede Knox, Ron Finn

GAME #3 - May 19, 1989 - Montreal Forum - Montreal 4, Calgary 3 (2 OT)

CALGARY: Theoren Fleury, Doug Gilmour, Mark Hunter, Tim Hunter, Hakan Loob, Al MacInnis, Jamie Macoun, Brian MacLellan, Brad McCrimmon, Joe Mullen, Dana Murzyn, Ric Nattress, Joe Nieuwendyk, Joel Otto, Colin Patterson, Jim Peplinski, Rob Ramage, Gary Roberts, Mike Vernon, Rick Wamsley.

MONTREAL: Guy Carbonneau, Chris Chelios, Shayne Corson, Russ Courtnall, Eric Desjardins, Bob Gainey, Brent Gilchrist, Rick Green, Brian Hayward, Mike Keane, Craig Ludwig, Mike McPhee, Mats Naslund, Larry Robinson, Patrick Roy, Stephane Richer, Brian Skrudland, Bobby Smith, Petr Svoboda, Ryan Walter.

First Period
1. MONTREAL   McPHEE (unassisted)   1.32
2. CALGARY   MULLEN (McCRIMMON, GILMOUR) 17.15
Penalties: Chelios (Mtl) (highsticking) 0.34; Gilmour (Cgy) (hooking) 0.34; Ramage (Cgy) (highsticking) 2.57; Ludwig (Mtl) (roughing) 6.42; M. Hunter (Cgy) (roughing) 6.42; Fleury (Cgy) (crosschecking) 7.10; Svoboda (Mtl) (roughing) 11.06; MacInnis (Cgy) (crosschecking) 11.39; Ludwig (Mtl) (elbowing) 12.07; Smith (Mtl) (slashing) 14.25; Patterson (Cgy) (roughing) 17.15; Desjardins (Mtl) (roughing) 17.15; MacInnis (Cgy) (unsportsmanlike conduct) 20.00; Skrudland (Mtl) (unsportsmanlike conduct) 20.00.

Second Period
3. CALGARY   MULLEN (MacINNIS, FLEURY)   15.35 (PPG)
Penalties: Carbonneau (Mtl) (hooking) 0.49; Macoun (Cgy) (holding) 4.04; McCrimmon (Cgy) (highsticking) 6.15; Macoun (Cgy) (roughing) 6.58; Skrudland (Mtl) (roughing) 6.58; Skrudland (Mtl) (roughing) 14.25; Ramage (Cgy) (holding) 16.08; Skrudland (Mtl) (unsportsmanlike conduct) 19.00; Murzyn (Cgy) (unsportsmanlike conduct) 19.00.

Third Period
4. MONTREAL   SMITH (NASLUND, SVOBODA)   1.36
5. CALGARY   GILMOUR (T. HUNTER)   13.02
6. MONTREAL   NASLUND (unassisted)   19.19
Penalties: MacInnis (Cgy) (highsticking) 10.11; Corson (Mtl) (crosschecking) 10.11.

First Overtime
No scoring.
Penalties: T. Hunter (Cgy) (roughing) 11.38; Corson (Mtl) (highsticking) 11.38; MacInnis (Cgy) (roughing) 16.09; Smith (Mtl) (roughing) 16.09; M. Hunter (Cgy) (unsportsmanlike conduct) 17.34; Skrudland (Mtl) (unsportsmanlike conduct) 17.34; Ramage (Cgy) (roughing) 17.59; Corson (Mtl) (roughing) 17.59.

Second Overtime
7. MONTREAL   WALTER (RICHER)   18.08 (GWG)
Penalties: MacInnis (Cgy) (highsticking) 9.25; Gainey (Mtl) (highsticking) 9.25; M. Hunter (Cgy) (boarding) 16.08.

Goalies: Roy (Mtl); Vernon (Cgy)
Shots: Cgy 13 - 7 - 8 - 5 - 4 37
       Mtl 4 - 7 - 6 - 12 - 6 35

Referee: Kerry Fraser
Linesmen: Ray Scapinello, Kevin Collins

GAME #4 - May 21, 1989 - Montreal Forum - Calgary 4, Montreal 2

CALGARY: Theoren Fleury, Doug Gilmour, Jiri Hrdina, Mark Hunter, Tim Hunter, Hakan Loob, Al MacInnis, Jamie Macoun, Brian MacLellan, Brad McCrimmon, Joe Mullen, Dana Murzyn, Ric Nattress, Joe Nieuwendyk, Joel Otto, Colin Patterson, Rob Ramage, Gary Roberts, Mike Vernon, Rick Wamsley.

MONTREAL: Guy Carbonneau, Chris Chelios, Shayne Corson, Russ Courtnall, Eric Desjardins, Bob Gainey, Rick Green, Brian Hayward, Mike Keane, Claude Lemieux, Craig Ludwig, Mike McPhee, Mats Naslund, Larry Robinson, Patrick Roy, Stephane Richer, Brian Skrudland, Bobby Smith, Petr Svoboda, Ryan Walter.

First Period
No scoring.
Penalties: Svoboda (Mtl) (highsticking) 5.44; MacInnis (Cgy) (roughing) 9.46; Keane (Mtl) (interference) 11.07; Ramage (Cgy) (roughing) 15.19; Carbonneau (Mtl) (hooking) 18.03; Gainey (Mtl) (slashing) 18.19.

Second Period
1. CALGARY   GILMOUR (unassisted)   11.56
2. CALGARY   MULLEN (MacINNIS, OTTO)   18.43 (PPG)

Penalties: MacInnis (Cgy) (slashing) 7.03; Gilmour (Cgy) (holding) 9.47; Svoboda (Mtl) (highsticking) 13.22; Patterson (Cgy) (crosschecking) 15.38; Robinson (Mtl) (crosschecking) 18.18; Otto (Cgy) (holding) 19.56.

Third Period
3. MONTREAL   COURTNALL (McPHEE, CHELIOS)   10.59
4. CALGARY   MacINNIS (OTTO)   18.22 (GWG)
5. MONTREAL   LEMIEUX (ROBINSON)   19.33
6. CALGARY   MULLEN (GILMOUR, PATTERSON)   19.49 (PPG,ENG)

Penalties: Bench minor (Mtl) (too many men on the ice, served by Lemieux) 5.57; Macoun (Cgy) (highsticking) 12.47; Nattress (Cgy) (misconduct) 12.47; Lemieux (Mtl) (slashing) 19.33; Patterson (Cgy) (highsticking, misconduct) 19.49; Richer (Mtl) (misconduct) 19.49; Courtnall (Mtl) (misconduct) 19.49.

Goalies: Roy (Mtl); Vernon (Cgy)
Shots: Cgy 13 - 9 - 13 35
       Mtl 3 - 10 - 6 19

Referee: Andy vanHellemond
Linesmen: Ron Finn, Swede Knox

GAME #5 - May 23, 1989 - Olympic Saddledome - Calgary 3, Montreal 2

CALGARY: Theoren Fleury, Doug Gilmour, Jiri Hrdina, Mark Hunter, Hakan Loob, Al MacInnis, Jamie Macoun, Brian MacLellan, Brad McCrimmon, Joe Mullen, Dana Murzyn, Ric Nattress, Joe Nieuwendyk, Joel Otto, Colin Patterson, Jim Peplinski, Rob Ramage, Gary Roberts, Mike Vernon, Rick Wamsley.

MONTREAL: Guy Carbonneau, Chris Chelios, Shayne Corson, Russ Courtnall, Eric Desjardins, Bob Gainey, Rick Green, Brian Hayward, Mike Keane, Claude Lemieux, Craig Ludwig, Mike McPhee, Mats Naslund, Larry Robinson, Patrick Roy, Stephane Richer, Brian Skrudland, Bobby Smith, Petr Svoboda, Ryan Walter.

First Period
1. CALGARY   OTTO (PEPLINSKI, M. HUNTER)   0.28
2. CALGARY   MULLEN (GILMOUR, RAMAGE)   8.15
3. MONTREAL   SMITH (CHELIOS, NASLUND)   13.24 (PPG)
4. CALGARY   MacINNIS (RAMAGE, OTTO)   19.31 (PPG,GWG)

Penalties: Corson (Mtl) (elbowing) 2.31; Walter (Mtl) (roughing) 6.10; Mullen (Cgy) (slashing) 9.14; Peplinski (Cgy) (holding) 11.57; Peplinski (Cgy) (boarding) 13.50; Green (Mtl) (interference) 19.18.

Second Period
5. MONTREAL   KEANE (SMITH, GAINEY)   14.17

Penalties: Lemieux (Mtl) (highsticking) 18.20.

Third Period
No scoring.
Penalties: MacInnis (Cgy) (holding) 8.40; Smith (Mtl) (interference) 9.32; Lemieux (Mtl) (unsportsmanlike conduct) 10.06; Vernon (Cgy) (unsportsmanlike conduct, served by Roberts) 10.06; Corson (Mtl) (roughing) 16.28; MacLellan (Cgy) (roughing) 16.28.

Goalies: Roy (Mtl); Vernon (Cgy)
Shots: Mtl 10 - 7 - 11 28
       Cgy 10 - 13 - 5 28

Referee: Kerry Fraser
Linesmen: Kevin Collins, Ray Scapinello

GAME #6 - May 25, 1989 - Montreal Forum - Calgary 4, Montreal 2

CALGARY: Theoren Fleury, Doug Gilmour, Jiri Hrdina, Mark Hunter, Hakan Loob, Al MacInnis, Jamie Macoun, Brian MacLellan, Brad McCrimmon, Lanny McDonald, Joe Mullen, Dana Murzyn, Ric Nattress, Joe Nieuwendyk, Joel Otto, Colin Patterson, Rob Ramage, Gary Roberts, Mike Vernon, Rick Wamsley.

MONTREAL: Guy Carbonneau, Chris Chelios, Shayne Corson, Russ Courtnall, Eric Desjardins, Bob Gainey, Rick Green, Brian Hayward, Mike Keane, Claude Lemieux, Craig Ludwig, Mike McPhee, Mats Naslund, Larry Robinson, Patrick Roy, Stephane Richer, Brian Skrudland, Bobby Smith, Petr Svoboda, Ryan Walter.

First Period
1. CALGARY   PATTERSON (MURZYN, MacINNIS) 18.51

Penalties: Mullen (Cgy) (hooking) 0.54; Chelios (Mtl) (elbowing) 5.09; Naslund (Mtl) (interference) 8.20; M. Hunter (Cgy) (roughing) 9.53; Skrudland (Mtl) (roughing) 9.53; Murzyn (Cgy) (tripping) 10.26; Roberts (Cgy) (roughing) 18.30; Ramage (Cgy) (roughing) 18.30; Corson (Mtl) (roughing) 18.30; Smith (Mtl) (roughing) 18.30.

Second Period
2. MONTREAL   LEMIEUX (SKRUDLAND, CHELIOS) 1.23
3. CALGARY   McDONALD (NIEUWENDYK, LOOB)   4.24

Penalties: McDonald (Cgy) (holding) 2.13; M. Hunter (Cgy) (roughing) 4.53; Walter (Mtl) (roughing) 4.53; Vernon (Cgy) (roughing) 6.37; Roberts (Cgy) (roughing) 6.37; Corson (Mtl) (roughing) 6.37; Ludwig (Mtl) (slashing) 11.08; Nattress (Cgy) (hooking) 16.36.

Third Period
4. CALGARY   GILMOUR (OTTO, MacINNIS)   11.02 (PPG,GWG)
5. MONTREAL   GREEN (McPHEE, LEMIEUX)   11.53
6. CALGARY   GILMOUR (MULLEN, MACOUN)   18.57 (ENG)

Penalties: M. Hunter (Cgy) (holding) 2.17; Skrudland (Mtl) (roughing) 2.17; Courtnall (Mtl) (boarding) 10.46; MacInnis (Cgy) (roughing) 18.34; Lemieux (Mtl) (roughing, misconduct) 18.34.

Goalies: Roy (Mtl); Vernon (Cgy)
Shots: Cgy 4 - 8 - 7 19
       Mtl 9 - 7 - 6 22

Referee: Denis Morel
Linesmen: Ron Finn, Swede Knox

1990
EDMONTON OILERS - BOSTON BRUINS

Game #1 - May 15, 1990 - Boston Garden - Edmonton 3, Boston 2 (3 OT)

EDMONTON: Glenn Anderson, Kelly Buchberger, Martin Gelinas, Adam Graves, Randy Gregg, Charlie Huddy, Petr Klima, Jari Kurri, Mark Lamb, Kevin Lowe, Craig MacTavish, Mark Messier, Craig Muni, Joe Murphy, Bill Ranford, Eldon Reddick, Reijo Ruotsalainen, Craig Simpson, Steve Smith, Esa Tikkanen.

BOSTON: Raymond Bourque, Randy Burridge, Lyndon Byers, Bob Carpenter, John Carter, Dave Christian, Garry Galley, Bob Gould, Greg Hawgood, Craig Janney, Rejean Lemelin, Andy Moog, Cam Neely, Allen Pedersen, Dave Poulin, Brian Propp, Bob Sweeney, Don Sweeney, Glen Wesley, Jim Wiemer.

First Period
1. EDMONTON   GRAVES (MURPHY, SIMPSON)   9.46
Penalties: Anderson (Edm) (crosschecking) 3.05; Neely (Bos) (interference) 4.41; Messier (Edm) (tripping) 12.24; Carter (Bos) (roughing) 15.53.

Second Period
2. EDMONTON   ANDERSON (MESSIER, RUOTSALAINEN)   13.00
Penalties: Tikkanen (Edm) (holding) 9.44; Huddy (Edm) (hooking) 14.38.

Third Period
3. BOSTON   BOURQUE (HAWGOOD, NEELY)   3.43
4. BOSTON   BOURQUE (NEELY, HAWGOOD)   18.31
Penalties: None.

First Overtime
No scoring.
Penalties: None.

Second Overtime
No scoring.
Penalties: None.

Third Overtime
5. EDMONTON   KLIMA (KURRI, MacTAVISH)   15.13 (GWG)
Penalties: Neely (Bos) (roughing) 2.41; Smith (Edm) (roughing) 2.41; Moog (Bos) (slashing) 13.48; Tikkanen (Edm) (slashing) 13.48.

Goalies: Ranford (Edm), Moog (Bos)
    Shots: Edm   6 - 4 - 6 - 7 - 5 - 3   31
              Bos   10 - 6 - 15 - 6 - 7 - 8   52

Referee: Don Koharski
Linesmen: Ray Scapinello, Swede Knox

Game #2 - May 18, 1990 - Boston Garden - Edmonton 7, Boston 2

EDMONTON: Glenn Anderson, Kelly Buchberger, Martin Gelinas, Adam Graves, Randy Gregg, Charlie Huddy, Petr Klima, Jari Kurri, Mark Lamb, Kevin Lowe, Craig MacTavish, Mark Messier, Craig Muni, Joe Murphy, Bill Ranford, Eldon Reddick, Reijo Ruotsalainen, Craig Simpson, Steve Smith, Esa Tikkanen.

BOSTON: Raymond Bourque, Randy Burridge, Bob Carpenter, John Carter, Dave Christian, Garry Galley, Bob Gould, Greg Hawgood, Craig Janney, Greg Johnston, Rejean Lemelin, Andy Moog, Cam Neely, Allen Pedersen, Dave Poulin, Brian Propp, Bob Sweeney, Don Sweeney, Glen Wesley, Jim Wiemer.

First Period
1. EDMONTON   GRAVES (MURPHY, GREGG)   8.38
2. EDMONTON   KURRI (TIKKANEN)   10.53 (PPG)
3. BOSTON   BOURQUE (NEELY)   19.07
Penalties: Messier (Edm) (roughing) 0.49; Anderson (Edm) (tripping) 4.45; Carter (Bos) (highsticking major, game misconduct) 6.20; Smith (Edm) (hooking) 6.45; D. Sweeney (Bos) (elbowing) 12.55; Buchberger (Edm) (unsportsmanlike conduct) 12.55; Lamb (Edm) (tripping) 14.56.

Second Period
4. BOSTON   HAWGOOD (BOURQUE, BURRIDGE)   2.56 (PPG)
5. EDMONTON   KURRI (TIKKANEN)   4.21
6. EDMONTON   SIMPSON (KURRI)   15.28
7. EDMONTON   TIKKANEN (KURRI)   17.10
8. EDMONTON   MURPHY (SMITH)   19.12
Penalties: Tikkanen (Edm) (holding) 1.14; Neely (Bos) (roughing) 2.27; Smith (Edm) (roughing) 2.27; Tikkanen (Edm) (roughing) 11.00; Hawgood (Bos) (roughing) 11.00; Ranford (Edm) (delay of game) 11.14.

Third Period
9. EDMONTON   KURRI (RUOTSALAINEN, LAMB)   7.27
Penalties: B. Sweeney (Bos) (holding) 5.30; Johnston (Bos) (double minor, roughing) 12.50; Murphy (roughing, unsportsmanlike conduct) 12.50.

Goalies: Ranford (Edm), Moog, Lemelin (Bos),
    Shots: Edm   2 - 9 - 11   22
              Bos   10 - 12 - 5   27

Referee: Kerry Fraser
Linesmen: Ron Finn, Wayne Bonney

(NOTE: Edmonton's Petr Klima was awarded a penalty shot at 19.00 of the second period. He was unsuccessful against Boston's Rejean Lemelin).

Game #3 - May 20, 1990 - Northlands Coliseum - Boston 2, Edmonton 1

EDMONTON: Glenn Anderson, Kelly Buchberger, Martin Gelinas, Adam Graves, Randy Gregg, Charlie Huddy, Petr Klima, Jari Kurri, Mark Lamb, Kevin Lowe, Craig MacTavish, Mark Messier, Craig Muni, Joe Murphy, Bill Ranford, Eldon Reddick, Reijo Ruotsalainen, Craig Simpson, Steve Smith, Esa Tikkanen.

BOSTON: Raymond Bourque, Andy Brickley, Randy Burridge, John Byce, Bob Carpenter, John Carter, Dave Christian, Garry Galley, Bob Gould, Greg Hawgood, Craig Janney, Greg Johnston, Rejean Lemelin, Andy Moog, Cam Neely, Allen Pedersen, Brian Propp, Bob Sweeney, Don Sweeney, Glen Wesley.

First Period
1. BOSTON   BYCE (NEELY)   0.10
2. BOSTON   JOHNSTON (BURRIDGE, B. SWEENEY)   16.18
Penalties: D. Sweeney (Bos) (holding) 3.16; Gelinas (Edm) (hooking) 6.32; MacTavish (Edm) (tripping) 12.18; Kurri (Edm) (interference) 17.17.

Second Period
No scoring.
Penalties: Simpson (Edm) (interference) 12.28; Pedersen (Bos) (holding) 15.37.

Third Period
3. EDMONTON   TIKKANEN (KURRI, SMITH)   5.54 (PPG)
Penalties: D. Sweeney (Bos) (holding) 1.30; Galley (Bos) (holding) 5.32; Bourque (Bos) (holding) 6.01; Smith (Edm) (interference) 6.33.

Goalies: Ranford (Edm), Moog (Bos)
    Shots: Bos   13 - 7 - 2   22
              Edm   11 - 4 - 14   29

Referee: Andy vanHellemond
Linesmen: Ray Scapinello, Swede Knox

Game #4 - May 22, 1990 - Northlands Coliseum - Edmonton 5, Boston 1

EDMONTON: Glenn Anderson, Kelly Buchberger, Martin Gelinas, Adam Graves, Randy Gregg, Charlie Huddy, Petr Klima, Jari Kurri, Mark Lamb, Kevin Lowe, Craig MacTavish, Mark Messier, Craig Muni, Joe Murphy, Bill Ranford, Eldon Reddick, Reijo Ruotsalainen, Craig Simpson, Steve Smith, Esa Tikkanen.

BOSTON: Raymond Bourque, Andy Brickley, Randy Burridge, John Byce, Bob Carpenter, John Carter, Dave Christian, Peter Douris, Garry Galley, Greg Hawgood, Craig Janney, Greg Johnston, Rejean Lemelin, Andy Moog, Cam Neely, Allen Pedersen, Brian Propp, Bob Sweeney, Don Sweeney, Glen Wesley.

First Period
1. EDMONTON   ANDERSON (SIMPSON, LAMB)   2.13 (PPG)
2. EDMONTON   ANDERSON (MESSIER, SIMPSON)   16.27
Penalties: Carpenter (Bos) (interference) 0.24; Neely (Bos) (roughing) 3.16; Muni (Edm) (roughing) 3.16; Messier (Edm) (boarding) 13.33; Carter (Bos) (unsportsmanlike conduct) 16.11; Ruotsalainen (Edm) (unsportsmanlike conduct) 16.11; Hawgood (Bos) (slashing) 18.52.

Second Period
3. EDMONTON   SIMPSON (MESSIER, ANDERSON)   1.00
4. EDMONTON   TIKKANEN (KURRI, MacTAVISH)   19.15
Penalties: Wesley (Bos) (hooking) 6.20; Simpson (Edm) (tripping) 12.39; Anderson (Edm) (tripping) 19.50.

Third Period
5. BOSTON   CARTER (unassisted)   15.02
6. EDMONTON   SIMPSON (ANDERSON, MESSIER)   18.36
Penalties: Simpson (Edm) (elbowing) 5.04; Burridge (Bos) (slashing) 12.14; Neely (Bos) (highsticking) 15.14; B. Sweeney (Bos) (fighting) 17.06; Smith (Edm) (fighting) 17.06.

Goalies: Ranford (Edm), Moog (Bos)
    Shots: Bos   7 - 11 - 7   25
              Edm   12 - 10 - 11   33

Referee: Don Koharski
Linesmen: Ron Finn, Wayne Bonney

Game #5 - May 24, 1990 - Boston Garden - Edmonton 4, Boston 1

EDMONTON: Glenn Anderson, Kelly Buchberger, Martin Gelinas, Adam Graves, Randy Gregg, Charlie Huddy, Petr Klima, Jari Kurri, Mark Lamb, Kevin Lowe, Craig MacTavish, Mark Messier, Craig Muni, Joe Murphy, Bill Ranford, Eldon Reddick, Reijo Ruotsalainen, Craig Simpson, Steve Smith, Esa Tikkanen.

BOSTON: Raymond Bourque, Randy Burridge, John Byce, Lyndon Byers, Bob Carpenter, John Carter, Dave Christian, Garry Galley, Bob Gould, Greg Hawgood, Craig Janney, Greg Johnston, Rejean Lemelin, Andy Moog, Cam Neely, Allen Pedersen, Brian Propp, Bob Sweeney, Don Sweeney, Glen Wesley.

First Period
No scoring.
Penalties: Bourque (Bos) (crosschecking) 2.56; Tikkanen (Edm) (holding) 4.32; Galley (Bos) (holding) 4.45.

Second Period
1. EDMONTON   ANDERSON (unassisted)   1.17
2. EDMONTON   SIMPSON (ANDERSON)   9.31 (GWG)
Penalties: None.

Third Period
3. EDMONTON   SMITH (MESSIER, SIMPSON)   6.09
4. EDMONTON   MURPHY (LAMB, GELINAS)   14.53
5. BOSTON   BYERS (B. SWEENEY, BOURQUE)   16.30
Penalties: Huddy (Edm) (hooking) 7.09; Bourque (Bos) (holding) 11.46.

Goalies: Ranford (Edm), Moog (Bos)
Shots: Edm 10 - 5 - 7   22
       Bos 10 - 10 - 10 30

Referee: Andy vanHellemond
Linesmen: Ray Scapinello, Swede Knox

1991
PITTSBURGH PENGUINS - MINNESOTA NORTH STARS

Game #1 - May 15, 1991 - Civic Arena - Minnesota 5, Pittsburgh 4

PITTSBURGH: Tom Barrasso, Phil Bourque, Bob Errey, Ron Francis, Jiri Hrdina, Jaromir Jagr, Grant Jennings, Mario Lemieux, Troy Loney, Joe Mullen, Larry Murphy, Frank Pietrangelo, Mark Recchi, Gordie Roberts, Ulf Samuelsson, Paul Stanton, Kevin Stevens, Peter Taglianetti, Bryan Trottier, Scott Young.

MINNESOTA: Brian Bellows, Neal Broten, Marc Bureau, Jon Casey, Shawn Chambers, Shane Churla, Ulf Dahlen, Chris Dahlquist, Gaetan Duchesne, Dave Gagner, Stewart Gavin, Brian Glynn, Brian Hayward, Jim Johnson, Basil McRae, Mike Modano, Brian Propp, Bobby Smith, Mark Tinordi, Neil Wilkinson.

First Period
1. PITTSBURGH SAMUELSSON (FRANCIS)   3.45
2. MINNESOTA   BROTEN (unassisted)   6.32
3. MINNESOTA   DAHLEN (SMITH, CHAMBERS)   9.49
Penalties: Propp (Min) (slashing), 4.17; Loney (Pit) (roughing), 7.45; Chambers (Min) (hooking), 12.32; Tinordi (Min) (highsticking), 13.45; Recchi (Pit) (interference), 15.02; McRae (Min) (unsportsmanlike conduct), 18.13; Bureau (Min) (boarding), 19.39.

Second Period
4. PITTSBURGH LEMIEUX (FRANCIS)   3.54 (SHG)
5. MINNESOTA   BUREAU (GAVIN)   6.53 (SHG)
6. PITTSBURGH YOUNG (MURPHY, JAGR)   7.43 (PPG)
7. MINNESOTA   BROTEN (MODANO)   17.01
Penalties: Roberts (Pit) (interference), 2.01; Johnson (Min) (slashing), 5.58; Bureau (Min) (holding), 10.25; Stanton (Pit) (hooking), 19.11.

Third Period
8. MINNESOTA   SMITH (DAHLEN)   1.39 (GWG)
9. PITTSBURGH MULLEN (JAGR, YOUNG)   10.35
Penalties: Jennings (Pit) (crosschecking), 4.08; Casey (Min) (slashing), 8.25.

Goalies: Casey (Min), Barrasso (Pit)
Shots: Min 9 - 12 - 8   29
       Pit 17 - 11 - 10 38

Referee: Don Koharski
Linesmen: Ray Scapinello, Wayne Bonney

Game #2 - May 17, 1991 - Civic Arena - Pittsburgh 4, Minnesota 1

PITTSBURGH: Tom Barrasso, Phil Bourque, Paul Coffey, Bob Errey, Ron Francis, Randy Gilhen, Jaromir Jagr, Mario Lemieux, Troy Loney, Joe Mullen, Larry Murphy, Jim Paek, Frank Pietrangelo, Mark Recchi, Gordie Roberts, Ulf Samuelsson, Paul Stanton, Kevin Stevens, Peter Taglianetti, Bryan Trottier.

MINNESOTA: Brian Bellows, Perry Berezan, Neal Broten, Marc Bureau, Jon Casey, Shawn Chambers, Ulf Dahlen, Chris Dahlquist, Gaetan Duchesne, Dave Gagner, Stewart Gavin, Brian Glynn, Brian Hayward, Jim Johnson, Mike Modano, Brian Propp, Doug Smail, Bobby Smith, Mark Tinordi, Neil Wilkinson.

First Period
1. PITTSBURGH ERREY (TAGLIANETTI)   14.26 (SHG)
2. PITTSBURGH STEVENS (LEMIEUX, MURPHY)   19.10 (PPG,GWG)
Penalties: Francis (Pit) (hooking) 1.07; Errey (Pit) (boarding), 9.08; Recchi (Pit) (crosschecking), 13.06; Samuelsson (Pit) (hold), 15.12; Bellows (Min) (hooking), 16.36; Chambers (Min) (interference), 18.59; Pit bench (too many men, served by Stevens), 20.00.

Second Period
3. MINNESOTA   MODANO (CHAMBERS, CASEY)   0.55 (PPG)
4. PITTSBURGH LEMIEUX (BOURQUE)   15.04
5. PITTSBURGH STEVENS (MULLEN, MURPHY)   16.32
Penalties: Duchesne (Min) (holding) 6.22; Murphy (Pit) (hooking), 6.37; Smith (Min) (interference), 9.30; Glynn (Min) (roughing), 17.27; Wilkinson (Min) (roughing), 19.58; Bureau (Min) (roughing), Loney (Pit) (roughing, fighting major), Tinordi (Min) (fighting major), 20.00.

Third Period
No scoring.
Penalties: Modano (Min) (highsticking), 5.29; Duchesne (Min) (hooking), 10.39; Samuelsson (Pit) (holding), 12.58; Bureau (Min) (roughing), Stevens (Pit) (roughing), Trottier (Pit) (misconduct), 16.20; Gagner (Min), Stanton (Pit) (roughing), 17.03; Roberts (Pit) (holding, spearing major, game misconduct), 17.34; Min bench (too many men, served by Modano), 19.41; Francis (Pit) (holding), 20.00.

Goalies: Casey (Min), Barrasso (Pit)
Shots: Min 12 - 12 - 16 40
       Pit 14 - 12 - 5   31

Referee: Andy vanHellemond
Linesmen: Kevin Collins, Gord Broseker

Game #3 - May 19, 1991 - Met Center - Minnesota 3, Pittsburgh 1

PITTSBURGH: Tom Barrasso, Phil Bourque, Paul Coffey, Bob Errey, Ron Francis, Randy Gilhen, Jiri Hrdina, Jaromir Jagr, Troy Loney, Joe Mullen, Larry Murphy, Jim Paek, Frank Pietrangelo, Mark Recchi, Gordie Roberts, Ulf Samuelsson, Paul Stanton, Kevin Stevens, Peter Taglianetti, Bryan Trottier.

MINNESOTA: Brian Bellows, Neal Broten, Marc Bureau, Jon Casey, Shawn Chambers, Shane Churla, Ulf Dahlen, Chris Dahlquist, Gaetan Duchesne, Dave Gagner, Stewart Gavin, Brian Glynn, Brian Hayward, Jim Johnson, Basil McRae, Mike Modano, Brian Propp, Bobby Smith, Mark Tinordi, Neil Wilkinson.

First Period
No scoring.
Penalties: Errey (Pit) (charging), 9.08; Francis (Pit) (holding) 13.44; Smith (Min) (interference), 16.21.

Second Period
1. MINNESOTA GAGNER (MODANO, JOHNSON) 7.21
2. MINNESOTA SMITH (BELLOWS, DAHLQUIST) 7.54 (GWG)

Penalties: McRae (Min) (boarding), 4.08; Recchi (Pit), Chambers (Min) (unsportsmanlike conduct), 5.23; Duchesne (Min) (holding), 8.38; Taglianetti (Pit) (highsticking), 12.36; Loney (Pit), Johnson (Min) (roughing), 17.28.

Third Period
3. PITTSBURGH BOURQUE (JAGR, TROTTIER) 1.23
4. MINNESOTA DUCHESNE (GAVIN, BROTEN) 2.09

Penalties: Johnson (Min) (highsticking), Bourque (Pit) (slashing), 7.20; Stanton (Pit), Bellows (Min) (roughing), 8.09; Gilhen (Pit) (holding), Gagner (Min) (roughing), 8.13; Samuelsson (Pit) (elbowing), 8.53; Dahlquist (Min) (tripping), 13.34; Stevens (Pit) (spearing major, game misconduct), 18.47; Barrasso (Pit) (slashing, served by Mullen), 19.21; Gilhen (Pit), Bellows (Min) (misconduct), 19.53; Errey (Pit) (charging), Smith (Min) (highsticking), 20.00.

Goalies: Casey (Min), Barrasso (Pit)
Shots: Pit   7 - 8 - 15   30
        Min 12 - 8 - 13   33

Referee: Kerry Fraser
Linesmen: Ray Scapinello, Wayne Bonney

Game #4 - May 21, 1991 - Met Center - Pittsburgh 5, Minnesota 3

PITTSBURGH: Tom Barrasso, Phil Bourque, Paul Coffey, Bob Errey, Ron Francis, Randy Gilhen, Jaromir Jagr, Grant Jennings, Mario Lemieux, Troy Loney, Joe Mullen, Larry Murphy, Jim Paek, Frank Pietrangelo, Mark Recchi, Gordie Roberts, Ulf Samuelsson, Paul Stanton, Kevin Stevens, Bryan Trottier.

MINNESOTA: Brian Bellows, Neal Broten, Marc Bureau, Jon Casey, Shawn Chambers, Shane Churla, Ulf Dahlen, Chris Dahlquist, Gaetan Duchesne, Dave Gagner, Stewart Gavin, Brian Glynn, Brian Hayward, Jim Johnson, Basil McRae, Mike Modano, Brian Propp, Bobby Smith, Mark Tinordi, Neil Wilkinson.

First Period
1. PITTSBURGH STEVENS (unassisted) 0.58
2. PITTSBURGH FRANCIS (STEVENS, MULLEN) 2.36
3. PITTSBURGH LEMIEUX (RECCHI, MURPHY) 2.58
4. MINNESOTA GAGNER (BELLOWS, DAHLEN) 18.22

Penalties: Samuelsson (Pit) (charging), 7.27; Stanton (Pit), Propp (Min) (highsticking), 7.44; Johnson (Min) (holding), 14.45; Samuelsson (Pit) (holding), 18.38.

Second Period
5. PITTSBURGH TROTTIER (ERREY, JAGR) 9.55 (GWG)
6. MINNESOTA PROPP (GAGNER) 13.10 (PPG)
7. MINNESOTA MODANO (PROPP, GAGNER) 18.25 (PPG)

Penalties: Modano (Min) (slashing) 4.28; Murphy (Pit), McRae (Min) (roughing), 11.22; Stevens (Pit) (holding), 11.49; Lemieux (Pit) (interference), Bellows (Min) (roughing), 12.34; Lemieux (Pit) (roughing), 13.10; Murphy (Pit) (roughing), 16.59; Errey (Pit) (highsticking), 18.06; Gagner (Min) (roughing), 18.50.

Third Period
8. PITTSBURGH BOURQUE (MULLEN, LEMIEUX) 19.45 (ENG)

Penalties: Loney (Pit) (highsticking major, game misconduct), 13.03; Casey (Min) (interference, served by Propp), 16.52.

Goalies: Casey (Min), Barrasso (Pit)
Shots: Pit 13 - 5 - 6   24
        Min 14 - 17 - 7   38

Referee: Andy vanHellemond
Linesmen: Kevin Collins, Gord Broseker

Game #5 - May 23, 1991 - Civic Arena - Pittsburgh 6, Minnesota 4

PITTSBURGH: Tom Barrasso, Phil Bourque, Paul Coffey, Bob Errey, Ron Francis, Randy Gilhen, Jaromir Jagr, Mario Lemieux, Troy Loney, Joe Mullen, Larry Murphy, Jim Paek, Frank Pietrangelo, Mark Recchi, Gordie Roberts, Ulf Samuelsson, Paul Stanton, Kevin Stevens, Peter Taglianetti, Bryan Trottier.

MINNESOTA: Brian Bellows, Neal Broten, Marc Bureau, Jon Casey, Shawn Chambers, Shane Churla, Ulf Dahlen, Chris Dahlquist, Gaetan Duchesne, Dave Gagner, Stewart Gavin, Brian Hayward, Jim Johnson, Basil McRae, Mike Modano, Brian Propp, Bobby Smith, Mark Tinordi, Neil Wilkinson.

First Period
1. PITTSBURGH LEMIEUX (MURPHY, COFFEY) 5.36 (PPG)
2. PITTSBURGH STEVENS (COFFEY, MURPHY) 10.08 (PPG)
3. PITTSBURGH RECCHI (LEMIEUX, BOURQUE) 11.45
4. PITTSBURGH RECCHI (LEMIEUX, MURPHY) 13.41
5. MINNESOTA BROTEN (TINORDI) 14.52 (SHG)

Penalties: Glynn (Min) (crosschecking), 3.38; Trottier (Pit) (crosschecking), 7.07; Tinordi (Min) (hooking), 9.54; McRae (Min) (charging, roughing, unsportsmanlike conduct), Churla (Min) (roughing), Paek (Pit) (roughing), Stevens (Pit) (roughing), 14.26.

Second Period
6. MINNESOTA GAGNER (PROPP) 6.54 (SHG)
7. PITTSBURGH FRANCIS (MULLEN) 16.26 (GWG)

Penalties: Dahlquist (Min) (hooking), 5.23; Trottier (Pit) (tripping), 10.46; Gagner (Min) (interference), Taglianetti (Pit) (holding), 14.53; Bourque (Pit) (illegal stick), 17.20.

Third Period
8. MINNESOTA DAHLEN (SMITH, DUCHESNE) 1.36
9. MINNESOTA GAGNER (PROPP, GAVIN) 7.41
10. PITTSBURGH LONEY (MURPHY, FRANCIS) 18.21

Penalties: Taglianetti (Pit) (crosschecking), 8.40; Gagner (Min) (tripping), 9.49; Glynn (Min) (crosschecking), 10.05; Tinordi (Min), Stevens (Pit) (roughing), 12.00; Gagner (Min), Lemieux (Pit) (roughing), 19.02.

Goalies: Casey, Hayward (Min), Barrasso, Pietrangelo (Pit)
Shots: Min   7 - 9 - 9   25
        Pit 18 - 5 - 8   31

Referee: Kerry Fraser
Linesmen: Ray Scapinello, Wayne Bonney

Game #6 - May 25, 1991 - Met Center - Pittsburgh 8, Minnesota 0

PITTSBURGH: Tom Barrasso, Phil Bourque, Paul Coffey, Bob Errey, Ron Francis, Randy Gilhen, Jaromir Jagr, Mario Lemieux, Troy Loney, Joe Mullen, Larry Murphy, Jim Paek, Frank Pietrangelo, Mark Recchi, Gordie Roberts, Ulf Samuelsson, Paul Stanton, Kevin Stevens, Peter Taglianetti, Bryan Trottier.

MINNESOTA: Brian Bellows, Neal Broten, Marc Bureau, Jon Casey, Shawn Chambers, Shane Churla, Ulf Dahlen, Chris Dahlquist, Gaetan Duchesne, Dave Gagner, Stewart Gavin, Brian Glynn, Brian Hayward, Jim Johnson, Basil McRae, Mike Modano, Brian Propp, Bobby Smith, Mark Tinordi, Neil Wilkinson.

First Period
1. PITTSBURGH SAMUELSSON (TAGLIANETTI, TROTTIER) 2.00 (PPG,GWG)
2. PITTSBURGH LEMIEUX (MURPHY) 12.19 (SHG)
3. PITTSBURGH MULLEN (STEVENS, TAGLIANETTI) 13.14 (PPG)

Penalties: Broten (Min) (interference), 0.09; Johnson (Min) (highsticking), 6.20; Stevens (Pit) (holding), 10.25; Roberts (Pit) (roughing), 10.59; Modano (Min) (interference), 11.17; Roberts (Pit) (interference), 13.58; Taglianetti (Pit) (tripping), 17.35.

Second Period
4. PITTSBURGH ERREY (JAGR, LEMIEUX) 13.15
5. PITTSBURGH FRANCIS (MULLEN) 14.28
6. PITTSBURGH MULLEN (STEVENS, SAMUELSSON) 18.44

Penalties: Samuelsson (Pit) (roughing), Recchi (Pit) (roughing), Tinordi (Min) (double minor, roughing), Churla (Min) (roughing), McRae (Min) (misconduct), 8.03; Gagner (Min) (roughing), 15.18.

Third Period
7. PITTSBURGH PAEK (LEMIEUX) 1.19
8. PITTSBURGH MURPHY (LEMIEUX) 13.45 (PPG)

Penalties: McRae (Min) (slashing), 12.27; Stevens (Pit), Gavin (Min) (slashing), 13.03.

Goalies: Casey, Hayward (Min), Barrasso (Pit)
Shots: Pit 11 - 9 - 8   28
       Min 16 - 7 - 16 39

Referee: Don Koharski
Linesmen: Kevin Collins, Gord Broseker

1992
PITTSBURGH PENGUINS - CHICAGO BLACKHAWKS

GAME #1 - May 26, 1992 - Civic Arena - Pittsburgh 5, Chicago 4

PITTSBURGH: Tom Barrasso, Phil Bourque, Jock Callander, Bob Errey, Ron Francis, Jiri Hrdina, Jaromir Jagr, Mario Lemieux, Troy Loney, Shawn McEachern, Larry Murphy, Jim Paek, Gord Roberts, Kjell Samuelsson, Ulf Samuelsson, Paul Stanton, Kevin Stevens, Rick Tocchet, Bryan Trottier, Ken Wregget.

CHICAGO: Ed Belfour, Rob Brown, Chris Chelios, Michel Goulet, Dirk Graham, Dominik Hasek, Mike Hudson, Igor Kravchuk, Frantisek Kucera, Steve Larmer, Jocelyn Lemieux, Bryan Marchment, Stephane Matteau, Brian Noonan, Mike Peluso, Jeremy Roenick, Cam Russell, Steve Smith, Brent Sutter.

First Period
1. CHICAGO   CHELIOS (SUTTER)   6.34   (PPG)
2. CHICAGO   GOULET (unassisted)   13.17
3. CHICAGO   GRAHAM (CHELIOS)   13.43
4. PITTSBURGH BOURQUE (TOCCHET, FRANCIS)   17.26 (PPG)

Penalties: Hudson (Chi) (interference) 2.07; Roberts (Pit) (holding) 6.27; Peluso (Chi) (hooking) 9.34; Kravchuk (Chi) (holding) 15.44; Trottier (Pit) (interference) 18.39.

Second Period
5. CHICAGO   SUTTER (LARMER, CHELIOS)   11.36
6. PITTSBURGH TOCCHET (STANTON, McEACHERN) 15.24
7. PITTSBURGH LEMIEUX (STEVENS)   16.23

Penalties: Brown (Chi) (elbowing) 2.17; Chicago bench (too many men) 13.21.

Third Period
8. PITTSBURGH JAGR (unassisted)   15.05
9. PITTSBURGH LEMIEUX (MURPHY, FRANCIS)   19.47 (PPG,GWG)

Penalties: Stanton (Pit) (hooking) 1.24; Murphy (Pit) (hooking) 17.39; Smith (Chi) (hooking) 19.42.

Goalies: Belfour (Chi), Barrasso (Pit)
Shots: Chi 11 - 11 - 12 34
       Pit 15 - 10 - 14 39

Referee: Andy vanHellemond
Linesmen: Kevin Collins, Gerard Gauthier

GAME #2 - May 28, 1992 - Civic Arena - Pittsburgh 3, Chicago 1

PITTSBURGH: Tom Barrasso, Phil Bourque, Jock Callander, Bob Errey, Ron Francis, Jiri Hrdina, Jaromir Jagr, Mario Lemieux, Troy Loney, Shawn McEachern, Larry Murphy, Jim Paek, Gord Roberts, Kjell Samuelsson, Ulf Samuelsson, Paul Stanton, Kevin Stevens, Rick Tocchet, Bryan Trottier, Ken Wregget.

CHICAGO: Ed Belfour, Rod Buskas, Chris Chelios, Greg Gilbert, Michel Goulet, Dirk Graham, Stu Grimson, Dominik Hasek, Mike Hudson, Igor Kravchuk, Frantisek Kucera, Steve Larmer, Jocelyn Lemieux, Bryan Marchment, Stephane Matteau, Brian Noonan, Mike Peluso, Jeremy Roenick, Steve Smith, Brent Sutter.

First Period
1. PITTSBURGH ERREY (PAEK)   9.52   (SHG)

Penalties: Peluso (Chi) (roughing) 2.07; Stanton (Pit) (delay of game, tripping) 7.38; Smith (Chi) (interference) 11.05; Noonan (Chi) (crosschecking) 18.36.

Second Period
2. CHICAGO   MARCHMENT (NOONAN, GILBERT)   10.24
3. PITTSBURGH LEMIEUX (TOCCHET)   12.55 (PPG,GWG)
4. PITTSBURGH LEMIEUX (TOCCHET, K. SAMUELSSON) 15.23

Penalties: Marchment (Chi) (elbowing) 12.12; Chicago bench (too many men) 19.43.

Third Period
No scoring.
Penalties: Roberts (Pit) (holding) 5.09.

Goalies: Belfour (Chi), Barrasso (Pit)
Shots: Chi 11 - 4 - 4   19
       Pit 8 - 11 - 6 25

Referee: Terry Gregson
Linesmen: Swede Knox, Ray Scapinello.

GAME #3 - May 30, 1992 - Chicago Stadium - Pittsburgh 1, Chicago 0

PITTSBURGH: Tom Barrasso, Phil Bourque, Jock Callander, Ron Francis, Jiri Hrdina, Jaromir Jagr, Mario Lemieux, Troy Loney, Shawn McEachern, Dave Michayluk, Larry Murphy, Jim Paek, Gord Roberts, Kjell Samuelsson, Ulf Samuelsson, Paul Stanton, Kevin Stevens, Rick Tocchet, Bryan Trottier, Ken Wregget.

CHICAGO: Ed Belfour, Rob Brown, Rod Buskas, Chris Chelios, Greg Gilbert, Michel Goulet, Dirk Graham, Dominik Hasek, Mike Hudson, Igor Kravchuk, Frantisek Kucera, Steve Larmer, Jocelyn Lemieux, Bryan Marchment, Stephane Matteau, Brian Noonan, Mike Peluso, Jeremy Roenick, Steve Smith, Brent Sutter.

First Period
1. PITTSBURGH STEVENS (PAEK, TOCCHET)   15.26 (GWG)

Penalties: K. Samuelsson (Pit) (highsticking) 5.43; Roberts (Pit) (tripping) 11.50; Goulet (Chi) (holding) 16.47, Jagr (Pit) (holding) 19.14.

Second Period
No scoring.
Penalties: Larmer (Chi) (crosschecking) 4.38; Stanton (Pit) (holding) 7.04; Chelios (Chi) (slashing) 10.56.

Third Period
No scoring.
Penalties: Paek (Pit) (interference) 10.05; Chelios (Chi) (fighting major, game misconduct) 19.29.

Goalies: Belfour (Chi), Barrasso (Pit)
Shots: Pit 6 - 8 - 6   20
       Chi 13 - 6 - 8   27

Referee: Don Koharski
Linesmen: Kevin Collins, Gerard Gauthier

GAME #4 - June 1, 1992 - Chicago Stadium - Pittsburgh 6, Chicago 5

PITTSBURGH: Tom Barrasso, Phil Bourque, Jock Callander, Bob Errey, Ron Francis, Jiri Hrdina, Jaromir Jagr, Mario Lemieux, Troy Loney, Shawn McEachern, Larry Murphy, Jim Paek, Gord Roberts, Kjell Samuelsson, Ulf Samuelsson, Paul Stanton, Kevin Stevens, Rick Tocchet, Bryan Trottier, Ken Wregget.

CHICAGO: Ed Belfour, Rob Brown, Rod Buskas, Chris Chelios, Greg Gilbert, Michel Goulet, Dirk Graham, Stu Grimson, Dominik Hasek, Mike Hudson, Igor Kravchuk, Frantisek Kucera, Steve Larmer, Jocelyn Lemieux, Bryan Marchment, Stephane Matteau, Brian Noonan, Jeremy Roenick, Steve Smith, Brent Sutter.

First Period
1. PITTSBURGH JAGR (LONEY)   1.37
2. CHICAGO   GRAHAM (MATTEAU, CHELIOS)   6.21
3. PITTSBURGH STEVENS (LEMIEUX, TOCCHET)   6.33
4. CHICAGO   GRAHAM (CHELIOS)   6.51
5. PITTSBURGH LEMIEUX (MURPHY, STEVENS)   10.13 (PPG)
6. CHICAGO   GRAHAM (LEMIEUX, NOONAN)   16.18

Penalties: U. Samuelsson (Pit) (interference), Stanton (Pit) (misconduct), Gilbert (Chi) (misconduct) 7.28; Chelios (Chi) (elbowing) 8.17; Roberts (Pit) (roughing) 12.44.

Second Period
7. PITTSBURGH TOCCHET (LEMIEUX, STEVENS)   0.58
8. CHICAGO   ROENICK (NOONAN, GILBERT)   15.40

Penalties: Stanton (Pit) (hooking) 2.21; Tocchet (Pit) (holding) 5.41.

Third Period
9.	PITTSBURGH	MURPHY (TOCCHET)	4.51	
10.	PITTSBURGH	FRANCIS (McEACHERN, PAEK)	7.59	(GWG)
11.	CHICAGO	ROENICK (GRIMSON, BUSKAS)	11.18	

Penalties: none.

Goalies: Belfour, Hasek (Chi), Barrasso (Pit)
Shots: Pit 12 - 9 - 8   29
Chi 8 - 14 - 7   29

Referee: Andy vanHellemond
Linesmen: Swede Knox, Ray Scapinello

1993
MONTREAL CANADIENS – LOS ANGELES KINGS

GAME #1 - June 1, 1993 - Montreal Forum - Los Angeles 4, Montreal 1

LOS ANGELES: Rob Blake, Pat Conacher, Gord Donnelly, Tony Granato, Wayne Gretzky, Mark Hardy, Kelly Hrudey, Charlie Huddy, Jari Kurri, Marty McSorley, Corey Millen, Luc Robitaille, Warren Rychel, Tomas Sandstrom, Dave Taylor, Tim Watters, Gary Shuchuk, Darryl Sydor, Alexei Zhitnik.

MONTREAL: Brian Bellows, Benoit Brunet, Patrice Brisebois, Guy Carbonneau, J.J. Daigneault, Vincent Damphousse, Eric Desjardins, Gilbert Dionne, Paul DiPietro, Sean Hill, John LeClair, Stephan Lebeau, Gary Leeman, Kirk Muller, Lyle Odelein, Ed Ronan, Patrick Roy, Denis Savard, Mathieu Schneider.

First Period
1.	LOS ANGELES	ROBITAILLE (ZHITNIK, GRETZKY)	3:30	PPG
2.	MONTREAL	RONAN (unassisted)	18:09	

Penalties: Odelein (Mtl) (holding) 2:42, Dionne (Mtl) (highsticking) 6:12, McSorley (LA) (delay of game) 11:03, Kurri (LA) (holding) 15:54.

Second Period
3.	LOS ANGELES	ROBITAILLE (BLAKE, GRETZKY)	17:41	PPG

Penalties: Granato (LA) (goaltender interference) 5:08, Taylor (LA) Muller (Mtl) (roughing) 6:23, McSorley (LA) Odelein (Mtl) (unsportsmanlike conduct) 7:16, Damphousse (Mtl) (slashing) 10:23, Millen (LA) Desjardins (Mtl) (highsticking) Brisebois (Mtl) (delay of game) 18:33, Gretzky (LA) (hooking) 19:32.

Third Period
4.	LOS ANGELES	KURRI (GRETZKY, GRANATO)	1:51	
5.	LOS ANGELES	GRETZKY (SANDSTROM)	18:02	ENG

Penalties: Huddy (LA) (hooking) 6:41, Daigneault (Mtl) (cross-checking) 18:41.

Goalies: Hrudey (LA), Roy (Montreal)
Shots: LA 11 - 20 - 7   38
Mtl 11 - 10 - 11   32

Referee: Andy vanHellemond
Linesmen: Gerard Gauthier, Ray Scapinello.

GAME #2 - June 3, 1993 - Montreal Forum - Montreal 3, Los Angeles 2 (OT)

LOS ANGELES: Rob Blake, Pat Conacher, Gord Donnelly, Tony Granato, Wayne Gretzky, Kelly Hrudey, Charlie Huddy, Marty McSorley, Corey Millen, Luc Robitaille, Warren Rychel, Tomas Sandstrom, Gary Shuchuk, Darryl Sydor, Dave Taylor, Tim Watters, Alexei Zhitnik.

MONTREAL: Brian Bellows, Benoit Brunet, Patrice Brisebois, Guy Carbonneau, J.J. Daigneault, Vincent Damphousse, Eric Desjardins, Paul DiPietro, Gilbert Dionne, Kevin Haller, Mike Keane, John LeClair, Stephan Lebeau, Gary Leeman, Kirk Muller, Lyle Odelein, Ed Ronan, Patrick Roy, Mathieu Schneider.

First Period
1.	MONTREAL	DESJARDINS (DAMPHOUSSE LEBEAU)	18:31	

Penalties: Odelein (Mtl) (roughing) 5:57, Robitaille (LA) (hooking) 6:40, Brisebois (Mtl) (interference) 7:05, Blake (LA) (tripping) 10:25, Roy (Mtl) (highsticking) 10:38, Watters (LA) (holding) Muller (Mtl) (tripping) 13:01, Sydor (LA) (holding) 14:44, Schneider (Mtl) (highsticking) 17:02, Granato (LA) (holding) 17:53.

Second Period
2.	LOS ANGELES	TAYLOR (unassisted)	5:12	SHG

Penalties: Muller (Mtl) (cross-checking) 0:35, Huddy (LA) (cross-checking) 4:20, McSorley (LA) Damphousse (Mtl) (roughing) 9:43, Robitaille (LA) Dionne (Mtl) (roughing) 16:02.

Third Period
3.	LOS ANGELES	CONACHER (TAYLOR, GRANATO)	8:32	
4.	MONTREAL	DESJARDINS (DAMPHOUSSE, SCHNEIDER)	18:47	PPG

Penalties: Brunet (Mtl) (slashing) 1:31, Damphousse (Mtl) (cross-checking) 2:30, Zhitnik (LA) (tripping) 4:17, Taylor (LA) (goaltender interference) 11:56, Brisebois (Mtl) (cross-checking) 13:16, McSorley (LA) (illegal stick) 18:15.

Overtime
5.	MONTREAL	DESJARDINS (BRUNET, RONAN)	0:51	PPG

Penalties: Blake (LA) (misconduct) 0:51.

Goalies: Hrudey (LA), Roy (Montreal)
Shots: LA 5 - 9 - 9 - 1   24
Mtl 16 - 12 - 11 - 2   41

Referee: Kerry Fraser
Linesmen: Kevin Collins, Ray Scapinello.

GAME #3 - June 5, 1993 - Great Western Forum - Montreal 4, Los Angeles 3 (OT)

MONTREAL: Brian Bellows, Benoit Brunet, Patrice Brisebois, Guy Carbonneau, J.J. Daigneault, Vincent Damphousse, Eric Desjardins, Paul DiPietro, Gilbert Dionne, Kevin Haller, Mike Keane, John LeClair, Stephan Lebeau, Gary Leeman, Kirk Muller, Lyle Odelein, Ed Ronan, Patrick Roy, Mathieu Schneider.

LOS ANGELES: Rob Blake, Pat Conacher, Gord Donnelly, Tony Granato, Wayne Gretzky, Mark Hardy, Kelly Hrudey, Charlie Huddy, Marty McSorley, Corey Millen, Luc Robitaille, Warren Rychel, Tomas Sandstrom, Gary Shuchuk, Darryl Sydor, Dave Taylor, Tim Watters, Alexei Zhitnik.

First Period
1.	MONTREAL	BELLOWS (HALLER, MULLER)	10:26	PPG

Penalties: Zhitnik (LA) (tripping) 4:23, Bellows (Mtl) (cross-checking) 5:21, Desjardins (Mtl) (interference) 7:40, Watters (LA) (tripping) 10:21, Ronan (Mtl) (goaltender interference) 13:09, Lebeau (Mtl) (slashing) 16:37, Blake (LA) (roughing) 19:59.

Second Period
2.	MONTREAL	DIONNE (KEANE, LEBEAU)	2:41	
3.	MONTREAL	SCHNEIDER (CARBONNEAU)	3:02	
4.	LOS ANGELES	ROBITAILLE (GRETZKY, SANDSTROM)	7:52	
5.	LOS ANGELES	GRANATO (unassisted)	11:02	
6.	LOS ANGELES	GRETZKY (DONNELLY, HARDY)	17:07	

Penalties: Ronan (Mtl) Taylor (LA) (slashing) 11:42.

Third Period
NO SCORING
Penalties: Lebeau (Mtl) (holding) 6:48, Sandstrom (LA) (goaltender interference) 10:50.

Overtime
7.	MONTREAL	LeCLAIR (MULLER, BELLOWS)	0:34	

Penalties: none.

Goalies: Roy (Montreal), Hrudey (LA)
Shots: Mtl 12 - 9 - 12 - 3   36
LA 10 - 13 - 10 - 0   33

Referee: Terry Gregson
Linesmen: Wayne Bonney, Ray Scapinello.

GAME #4 - June 7, 1993 - Great Western Forum - Montreal 3, Los Angeles 2 (OT)

MONTREAL: Brian Bellows, Benoit Brunet, Patrice Brisebois, Guy Carbonneau, J.J. Daigneault, Vincent Damphousse, Eric Desjardins, Paul DiPietro, Gilbert Dionne, Kevin Haller, Mike Keane, John LeClair, Stephan Lebeau, Gary Leeman, Kirk Muller, Lyle Odelein, Ed Ronan, Patrick Roy, Mathieu Schneider.

LOS ANGELES: Rob Blake, Pat Conacher, Gord Donnelly, Tony Granato, Wayne Gretzky, Mark Hardy, Kelly Hrudey, Jari Kurri, Lonnie Loach, Marty McSorley, Corey Millen, Luc Robitaille, Warren Rychel, Tomas Sandstrom, Gary Shuchuk, Darryl Sydor, Tim Watters, Alexei Zhitnik.

First Period
1. MONTREAL   MULLER (unassisted)   10:57
Penalties: Conacher (LA).(cross-checking) 1:53, Desjardins (Mtl) (highsticking) Granato (LA) (roughing) 4:24, Schneider (Mtl) (elbowing) 16:50.

Second Period
2. MONTREAL   DAMPHOUSSE (KEANE, DESJARDINS)   5:24   PPG
3. LOS ANGELES   DONNELLY (GRANATO)   6:33
4. LOS ANGELES   McSORLEY (GRETZKY, ROBITAILLE)   19:55   PPG
Penalties: Hardy (LA) (holding) 3:32, McSorley (LA) (misconduct) 5:24, Daigneault (Mtl) (roughing) Rychel (LA) (goaltender interference) 7:37, Brisebois (Mtl) Blake (LA) (roughing) 12:09, Sydor (LA) (interference) 15:58, Bellows (Mtl) (hooking) 19:10.

Third Period
NO SCORING
Penalties: Daigneault (Mtl) (cross-checking) 2:42, Schneider (Mtl) Granato (LA) (roughing) 19:30.

Overtime
5. MONTREAL   LeCLAIR (unassisted)   14:37
Penalties: none.

Goalies: Roy (Montreal), Hrudey (LA)
  Shots: Mtl   13 - 7 - 12 - 7   39
            LA   6 - 11 - 15 - 10   42

Referee: Andy vanHellemond
Linesmen: Kevin Collins, Gerard Gauthier

GAME #5 - June 9, 1993 - Montreal Forum - Montreal 4, Los Angeles 1

LOS ANGELES: Rob Blake, Jimmy Carson, Pat Conacher, Gord Donnelly, Tony Granato, Wayne Gretzky, Mark Hardy, Kelly Hrudey, Charlie Huddy, Jari Kurri, Marty McSorley, Corey Millen, Luc Robitaille, Warren Rychel, Tomas Sandstrom, Gary Shuchuk, Darryl Sydor, Tim Watters, Alexei Zhitnik.

MONTREAL: Brian Bellows, Benoit Brunet, Patrice Brisebois, Guy Carbonneau, J.J. Daigneault, Vincent Damphousse, Eric Desjardins, Paul DiPietro, Gilbert Dionne, Donald Dufresne, Mike Keane, John LeClair, Stephan Lebeau, Gary Leeman, Kirk Muller, Lyle Odelein, Ed Ronan, Patrick Roy, Mathieu Schneider.

First Period
1. MONTREAL   DiPIETRO (LEEMAN, LeCLAIR)   15:10
Penalties: Schneider (Mtl) (tripping) 4:35, Keane (Mtl) (charging) 10:46, Granato (LA) (tripping) 12:49, Blake (LA) Sandstrom (LA) Ronan (Mtl) 19:23.

Second Period
2. LOS ANGELES   McSORLEY (CARSON, ROBITAILLE)   2:40
3. MONTREAL   MULLER (DAMPHOUSSE, ODELEIN)   3:51
4. MONTREAL   LEBEAU (KEANE, LeCLAIR)   11:31   PPG
Penalties: Leeman (Mtl) (tripping) 5:52, Damphousse (Mtl) (elbowing) 7:40, Hardy (LA) (holding) 10:29.

Third Period
5. MONTREAL   DiPIETRO (DIONNE, ODELEIN)   12:06
Penalties: none

Goalies: Hrudey (LA), Roy (Montreal)
  Shots: LA   7 - 7 - 5   19
            Mtl 10 - 12 - 7   29

Referee: Terry Gregson
Linesmen: Wayne Bonney, Ray Scapinello

GAME SUMMARIES, STANLEY CUP FINALS, 1980-1995 • 203

1994

NEW YORK RANGERS – VANCOUVER CANUCKS

Game #1 - May 31, 1994 - Madison Square Garden - Vancouver 3, NY Rangers 2 (OT)

VANCOUVER: Greg Adams, Shawn Antoski, Dave Babych, Jeff Brown, Pavel Bure, Geoff Courtnall, Murray Craven, Gerald Diduck, Martin Gelinas, Brian Glynn, Bret Hedican, Tim Hunter, Nathan Lafayette, Jyrki Lumme, Trevor Linden, John McIntyre, Kirk McLean, Sergio Momesso, Cliff Ronning, Kay Whitmore.

NY RANGERS: Glenn Anderson, Jeff Beukeboom, Greg Gilbert, Adam Graves, Glenn Healy, Joe Kocur, Alexei Kovalev, Steve Larmer, Brian Leetch, Doug Lidster, Kevin Lowe, Craig MacTavish, Stephane Matteau, Mark Messier, Sergei Nemchinov, Brian Noonan, Mike Richter, Esa Tikkanen, Jay Wells, Sergei Zubov.

First Period
1. NY RANGERS   LARMER (KOVALEV, LEETCH)   3:32
Penalties: Wells (NYR) (cross-checking) 1:47, Linden (Van) (tripping) 2:27, McIntyre (Van) (roughing) 8:50, Craven (Van) (slashing) 10:35, Beukeboom (NYR) (interference) 15:54.

Second Period
NO SCORING
Penalties: Messier (NYR) (hooking) 0:20, Lidster (NYR) (tripping) 8:49, Lowe (NYR) (roughing) 8:50, Courtnall (Van) (interference) 13:18, Momesso (Van) (goaltender interference) 16:15, Beukeboom (NYR) (highsticking) 19:34.

Third Period
2. VANCOUVER   HEDICAN (ADAMS, LUMME)   5:45
3. NY RANGERS   KOVALEV (LEETCH, ZUBOV)   8:29
4. VANCOUVER   GELINAS (RONNING, MOMESSO)   19:00
Penalties: none.

Overtime
5. VANCOUVER   ADAMS (RONNING, BURE)   19:26   GWG
Penalties: Momesso (Van), Gilbert (NYR) (roughing) 9:31.

Goalies: McLean (Vancouver), Richter (NY Rangers)
  Shots: Van 10 - 5 - 7   - 9   31
            NYR 15 - 9 - 13 - 17   54

Referee: Terry Gregson
Linesmen: Randy Mitton, Ray Scapinello

Game #2 - June 2, 1994 - Madison Square Garden - NY Rangers 3, Vancouver 1

VANCOUVER: Greg Adams, Shawn Antoski, Dave Babych, Jeff Brown, Pavel Bure, Geoff Courtnall, Murray Craven, Gerald Diduck, Martin Gelinas, Brian Glynn, Bret Hedican, Tim Hunter, Nathan Lafayette, Jyrki Lumme, Trevor Linden, John McIntyre, Kirk McLean, Sergio Momesso, Cliff Ronning, Kay Whitmore.

NY RANGERS: Glenn Anderson, Jeff Beukeboom, Greg Gilbert, Adam Graves, Glenn Healy, Alexander Karpovtsev, Joe Kocur, Alexei Kovalev, Steve Larmer, Brian Leetch, Doug Lidster, Craig MacTavish, Stephane Matteau, Mark Messier, Sergei Nemchinov, Brian Noonan, Mike Richter, Esa Tikkanen, Jay Wells, Sergei Zubov.

First Period
1. NY RANGERS   LIDSTER (unassisted)   6:22
2. VANCOUVER   MOMESSO (Ronning, Hedican)   14:04
Penalties: Craven (Van) (tripping) 2:03, Lidster (NYR) (interference) 7:44, Hunter (Van) (roughing) 10:21, Hunter (Van) (misconduct) 15:26, Anderson (NYR) (interference) 16:55.

Second Period
3. NY RANGERS   ANDERSON (Messier)   11:42   SHG
Penalties: Brown (Van) (hooking) 4:27, Matteau (NYR) (holding) 6:12, Graves (NYR) (tripping) 10:35, Antoski (Van) (roughing) 13:58, Tikkanen (NYR) (goaltender interference) 17:08.

Third Period
4. NY RANGERS   LEETCH (unassisted)   19:55 ENG
Penalties: Lidster (NYR) (interference) 1:43, Diduck (Van), Kovalev (NYR) (highsticking) 4:32, Brown (Van), Matteau (NYR) (roughing) 15:29.

Goalies: McLean (Vancouver), Richter (NY Rangers)
Shots: Van   10 - 6 - 13   29
           NYR   14 - 13 - 13   40

Referee: Bill McCreary
Linesmen: Kevin Collins, Gerard Gauthier

Game #3 - June 4, 1994 - Pacific Coliseum - NY Rangers 5, Vancouver 1

NY RANGERS: Glenn Anderson, Jeff Beukeboom, Greg Gilbert, Adam Graves, Glenn Healy, Alexander Karpovtsev, Joe Kocur, Alexei Kovalev, Steve Larmer, Brian Leetch, Doug Lidster, Kevin Lowe, Craig MacTavish, Stephane Matteau, Mark Messier, Sergei Nemchinov, Brian Noonan, Mike Richter, Esa Tikkanen, Jay Wells.

VANCOUVER: Greg Adams, Shawn Antoski, Dave Babych, Jeff Brown, Pavel Bure, Geoff Courtnall, Murray Craven, Gerald Diduck, Martin Gelinas, Brian Glynn, Bret Hedican, Tim Hunter, Nathan Lafayette, Jyrki Lumme, Trevor Linden, John McIntyre, Kirk McLean, Sergio Momesso, Cliff Ronning, Kay Whitmore.

First Period
1. VANCOUVER   BURE (LINDEN, ADAMS)   1:03
2. NY RANGERS   LEETCH (unassisted)   13:39
3. NY RANGERS   ANDERSON (NEMCHINOV, BEUKEBOOM)   19:19 GWG
Penalties: Wells (NYR) (tripping) 2:54, Anderson (NYR) (roughing), Hunter (Van) (charging) 5:42, Lumme (Van) (holding) 9:57, MacTavish (NYR) (holding) 15:04, Leetch (NYR) (tripping) 17:56, Lowe (NYR), Ronning (Van) (highsticking), Messier (NYR), Momesso (Van) (roughing), Bure (Van) (highsticking major, game misconduct) 18:12.

Second Period
4. NY RANGERS   LEETCH (TIKKANEN, BEUKEBOOM)   18:32
Penalties: Lowe (NYR) (roughing) 5:34, Messier (NYR), Antoski (Van) (roughing) 16:28.

Third Period
5. NY RANGERS   LARMER (unassisted)   0:25
6. NY RANGERS   KOVALEV (GRAVES, MESSIER)   13:03 PPG
Penalties: Tikkanen (NYR) (hooking) 3:13, Hedican (Van) (holding) 5:34, McIntyre (Van) (holding) 7:58, MacTavish (NYR) (holding) 9:46, Momesso (Van) (crosschecking) 11:42, Gelinas (Van) (roughing) 16:35, Antoski (Van) (crosschecking, roughing) 19:19.

Goalies: Richter (NY Rangers), McLean (Vancouver)
Shots: NYR   11 - 5 - 9   25
           Van   9 - 10 - 6   25

Referee: Andy Van Hellemond
Linesmen: Randy Mitton, Ray Scapinello

Game #4 - June 7, 1994 - Pacific Coliseum - NY Rangers 4, Vancouver 2

NY RANGERS: Glenn Anderson, Jeff Beukeboom, Greg Gilbert, Adam Graves, Glenn Healy, Joe Kocur, Alexei Kovalev, Steve Larmer, Brian Leetch, Doug Lidster, Kevin Lowe, Craig MacTavish, Stephane Matteau, Mark Messier, Sergei Nemchinov, Brian Noonan, Mike Richter, Esa Tikkanen, Jay Wells, Sergei Zubov.

VANCOUVER: Greg Adams, Shawn Antoski, Dave Babych, Jeff Brown, Pavel Bure, Geoff Courtnall, Murray Craven, Gerald Diduck, Martin Gelinas, Brian Glynn, Bret Hedican, Tim Hunter, Nathan Lafayette, Jyrki Lumme, Trevor Linden, John McIntyre, Kirk McLean, Sergio Momesso, Cliff Ronning, Kay Whitmore.

First Period
1. VANCOUVER   LINDEN (LUMME, BROWN)   13:25 PPG
2. VANCOUVER   RONNING (BURE, CRAVEN)   16:19
Penalties: Courtnall (Van) (elbowing) 3:11, Beukeboom (NYR) (highsticking) 6:35, Graves (NYR) (holding) 13:02, Messier (NYR) (boarding major) 14:17, Linden (Van) (holding stick) 15:07, Courtnall (Van) (interference) 17:54, Tikkanen (NYR) (roughing) 18:45.

Second Period
3. NY RANGERS   LEETCH (MacTAVISH, GILBERT)   4:03
4. NY RANGERS   ZUBOV (MESSIER, LEETCH)   19:44 PPG
Penalties: Lidster (NYR) (holding) 1:13, Brown (Van) (tripping) 7:19, Lidster (NYR) (holding) 16:58, Adams (Van) (boarding) 18:55.

Third Period
5. NY RANGERS   KOVALEV (LEETCH, ZUBOV)   15:05 PPG, GWG
6. NY RANGERS   LARMER (ZUBOV, LEETCH)   17:56
Penalties: NYR bench (too many men) 3:53, Lumme (Van) (holding) 4:48, Tikkanen (NYR), Diduck (Van) (roughing) 10:42, Messier (NYR) (slashing) 11:29, Gelinas (Van) (roughing) 14:31.

Goalies: Richter (NY Rangers), McLean (Vancouver)
Shots: NYR   8 - 8 - 11   27
           Van   8 - 12 - 10   30

Referee: Terry Gregson
Linesmen: Kevin Collins, Gerard Gauthier

(NOTE: Vancouver's Pavel Bure was awarded a penalty shot at 6:31 of the second period. He was unsuccessful against NY Ranger's goaltender Mike Richter.)

Game #5 - June 9, 1994 - Madison Square Garden - Vancouver 6, NY Rangers 3

VANCOUVER: Greg Adams, Shawn Antoski, Dave Babych, Jeff Brown, Pavel Bure, Geoff Courtnall, Murray Craven, Gerald Diduck, Martin Gelinas, Brian Glynn, Bret Hedican, Tim Hunter, Nathan Lafayette, Jyrki Lumme, Trevor Linden, John McIntyre, Kirk McLean, Sergio Momesso, Cliff Ronning, Kay Whitmore.

NY RANGERS: Glenn Anderson, Jeff Beukeboom, Greg Gilbert, Adam Graves, Glenn Healy, Joe Kocur, Alexei Kovalev, Steve Larmer, Brian Leetch, Doug Lidster, Kevin Lowe, Craig MacTavish, Stephane Matteau, Mark Messier, Sergei Nemchinov, Brian Noonan, Mike Richter, Esa Tikkanen, Jay Wells, Sergei Zubov.

First Period
NO SCORING
Penalties: Hunter (Van) (elbowing) 0:49, Momesso (Van) (slashing, fighting major), Ronning (Van), Matteau (NYR) (roughing), Beukeboom (NYR) (instigator, fighting major, game misconduct), Wells (NYR) (highsticking) 12:06, Hunter (Van), Wells (NYR) (roughing) 13:20, Ronning (Van), Larmer (NYR) (holding) 17:20, Nemchinov (NYR) (elbowing) 19:32.

Second Period
1. VANCOUVER   BROWN (RONNING, ANTOSKI)   8:10
Penalties: Courtnall (Van) (elbowing major) 10:13, Messier (NYR) (hooking) 18:19.

Third Period
2. VANCOUVER   COURTNALL (LAFAYETTE, HEDICAN)   0:26
3. VANCOUVER   BURE (CRAVEN)   2:48
4. NY RANGERS   LIDSTER (KOVALEV)   3:27
5. NY RANGERS   LARMER (MATTEAU, NEMCHINOV)   6:20
6. NY RANGERS   MESSIER (ANDERSON, GRAVES)   9:02
7. VANCOUVER   BABYCH (BURE)   9:31 GWG
8. VANCOUVER   COURTNALL (LAFAYETTE, LUMME)   12:20
9. VANCOUVER   BURE (RONNING, HEDICAN)   13:04
Penalties: Kocur (NYR) (slashing) 18:41.

Goalies: McLean (Vancouver), Richter (NY Rangers)
Shots: Van   12 - 8 - 17   37
           NYR   10 - 13 - 15   38

Referee: Andy Van Hellemond
Linesmen: Randy Mitton, Ray Scapinello

Game #6 - June 11, 1994 - Pacific Coliseum - Vancouver 4, NY Rangers 1

NY RANGERS: Glenn Anderson, Jeff Beukeboom, Greg Gilbert, Adam Graves, Glenn Healy, Joe Kocur, Alexei Kovalev, Steve Larmer, Brian Leetch, Doug Lidster, Kevin Lowe, Craig MacTavish, Stephane Matteau, Mark Messier, Sergei Nemchinov, Brian Noonan, Mike Richter, Esa Tikkanen, Jay Wells, Sergei Zubov.

VANCOUVER: Greg Adams, Shawn Antoski, Dave Babych, Jeff Brown, Pavel Bure, Geoff Courtnall, Murray Craven, Gerald Diduck, Martin Gelinas, Brian Glynn, Bret Hedican, Tim Hunter, Nathan Lafayette, Jyrki Lumme, Trevor Linden, John McIntyre, Kirk McLean, Sergio Momesso, Cliff Ronning, Kay Whitmore.

First Period
1. VANCOUVER   BROWN (LINDEN)   9:42 PPG

Penalties: Beukeboom (NYR) (elbowing) 3:02, Leetch (NYR) (interference) 9:39.

Second Period
2. VANCOUVER   COURTNALL (LUMME, BURE)   12:29 GWG
3. NY RANGERS   KOVALEV (MESSIER, LEETCH)   14:42 PPG

Penalties: Momesso (Van) (interference) 2:26, Diduck (Van) (tripping) 7:27, McIntyre (Van) (interference) 13:23.

Third Period
4. VANCOUVER   BROWN (unassisted)   8:35
5. VANCOUVER   COURTNALL (LAFAYETTE, DIDUCK)   18:28

Penalties: none.

Goalies: Richter (NY Rangers), McLean (Vancouver)
Shots: NYR   7 - 12 - 10   29
       Van 16 - 8 - 7   31

Referee: Bill McCreary
Linesmen: Kevin Collins, Gerard Gauthier

Game #7 - June 14, 1994 - Madison Square Garden - NY Rangers 3, Vancouver 2

VANCOUVER: Greg Adams, Shawn Antoski, Dave Babych, Jeff Brown, Pavel Bure, Geoff Courtnall, Murray Craven, Gerald Diduck, Martin Gelinas, Brian Glynn, Bret Hedican, Tim Hunter, Nathan Lafayette, Jyrki Lumme, Trevor Linden, John McIntyre, Kirk McLean, Sergio Momesso, Cliff Ronning, Kay Whitmore.

NY RANGERS: Glenn Anderson, Jeff Beukeboom, Greg Gilbert, Adam Graves, Glenn Healy, Joe Kocur, Alexei Kovalev, Steve Larmer, Brian Leetch, Doug Lidster, Kevin Lowe, Craig MacTavish, Stephane Matteau, Mark Messier, Sergei Nemchinov, Brian Noonan, Mike Richter, Esa Tikkanen, Jay Wells, Sergei Zubov.

First Period
1. NY RANGERS   LEETCH (ZUBOV, MESSIER)   11:02
2. NY RANGERS   GRAVES (KOVALEV, ZUBOV)   14:45 PPG

Penalties: Lumme (Van) (crosschecking) 14:03, Hedican (Van), Tikkanen (NYR) (roughing) 18:50.

Second Period
3. VANCOUVER   LINDEN (GLYNN, BURE)   5:21 SHG
4. NY RANGERS   MESSIER (GRAVES, NOONAN)   13:29 PPG, GWG

Penalties: Brown (Van) (interference) 4:38, Babych (Van) (tripping) 12:36, Messier (NYR) (hooking) 16:39.

Third Period
5. VANCOUVER   LINDEN (COURTNALL, RONNING)   4:50 PPG

Penalties: Tikkanen (NYR) (hooking) 4:16, Linden (Van), MacTavish (NYR) (roughing) 10:55.

Goalies: McLean (Vancouver), Richter (NY Rangers)
Shots: Van   9 - 12 - 9   30
       NYR 12 - 14 - 9   35

Referee: Terry Gregson
Linesmen: Kevin Collins, Ray Scapinello

1995

NEW JERSEY DEVILS - DETROIT RED WINGS

GAME #1 - June 17, 1995 - Joe Louis Arena - New Jersey 2, Detroit 1

NEW JERSEY: Tommy Albelin, Martin Brodeur, Neal Broten, Sergei Brylin, Bobby Carpenter, Tom Chorske, Sean Chambers, Ken Daneyko, Bruce Driver, Bill Guerin, Bobby Holik, Claude Lemieux, Randy McKay, John MacLean, Scott Niedermayer, Mike Peluso, Stephane Richer, Scott Stevens, Chris Terreri, Valeri Zelepukin.

DETROIT: Doug Brown, Shawn Burr, Dino Ciccarelli, Paul Coffey, Kris Draper, Bob Errey, Sergei Fedorov, Viacheslav Fetisov, Stu Grimson, Mark Howe, Vladimir Konstantinov, Nicklas Lidstrom, Darren McCarty, Chris Osgood, Keith Primeau, Bob Rouse, Ray Sheppard, Mike Vernon, Steve Yzerman, Vyacheslav Kozlov.

First Period
No Scoring

Penalties: Guerin (NJ) (holding) 6:47; Konstantinov (Det) (holding stick) 11:05.

Second Period
1. NEW JERSEY   RICHER (ALBELIN, BROTEN)   9:41 (PPG)
2. DETROIT   CICCARELLI (LIDSTROM, COFFEY)   13:08 (PPG)

Penalties: Draper (Det) (roughing), 9:35; Holik (NJ) (highsticking) 11:37; Lemieux (NJ) (hooking) 13:41; Daneyko (NJ) (roughing), Ciccarelli (Det) (roughing) 15:54.

Third Period
3. NEW JERSEY   LEMIEUX (MacLEAN, CHORSKE)   3:17 (GWG)

Penalties: Brown (Det) (tripping) 4:48.

Goalies: Brodeur (NJ), Vernon (Det)
Shots: NJ   9 - 10 - 9   28
       Det 7 - 5 - 5   17

Referee: Bill McCreary
Linesmen: Brian Murphy, Kevin Collins

Game #2 - June 20, 1995 - Joe Louis Arena - New Jersey 4, Detroit 2

NEW JERSEY: Tommy Albelin, Martin Brodeur, Neal Broten, Bobby Carpenter, Sean Chambers, Ken Daneyko, Jim Dowd, Bruce Driver, Bill Guerin, Bobby Holik, Claude Lemieux, Randy McKay, John MacLean, Scott Niedermayer, Mike Peluso, Stephane Richer, Brian Rolston, Scott Stevens, Chris Terreri, Valeri Zelepukin.

DETROIT: Doug Brown, Shawn Burr, Dino Ciccarelli, Paul Coffey, Kris Draper, Bob Errey, Sergei Fedorov, Viacheslav Fetisov, Mark Howe, Vladimir Konstantinov, Vyacheslav Kozlov, Mike Krushelnyski, Nicklas Lidstrom, Darren McCarty, Chris Osgood, Bob Rouse, Ray Sheppard, Tim Taylor, Mike Vernon, Steve Yzerman.

First Period
No Scoring

Penalties: Stevens (NJ) (roughing) 0:37; Ciccarelli (Det) (slashing) 5:57; McCarty (Det) (roughing) 8:49; Broten (NJ) (highsticking) 9:27.

Second Period
1. DETROIT   KOZLOV (CICCARELLI, FEDOROV)   7:17 (PPG)
2. NEW JERSEY   MacLEAN (NIEDERMAYER, BROTEN)   9:40

Penalties: Brodeur (NJ) (delay of game) 6:56; Guerin (NJ) (slashing), McCarty (Det) (slashing) 8:58; Errey (Det) (charging) 16:01; Dowd (NJ) (interference) 18:30.

Third Period
3. DETROIT   FEDOROV (BROWN, FETISOV)   1:36
4. NEW JERSEY   NIEDERMAYER (DOWD)   9:47
5. NEW JERSEY   DOWD (CHAMBERS, ALBELIN)   18:36 (GWG)
6. NEW JERSEY   RICHER (NIEDERMAYER)   19:36 (ENG)

Penalties: Holik (NJ) (boarding) 4:58.

Goalies: Brodeur (NJ), Vernon (Det)
Shots: NJ   3 - 9 - 11   23
       Det 7 - 6 - 5   18

Referee: Terry Gregson
Linesmen: Ray Scapinello, Wayne Bonney

Game #3 - June 22, 1995 - Meadowlands Arena - New Jersey 5, Detroit 2

DETROIT: Doug Brown, Dino Ciccarelli, Paul Coffey, Kris Draper, Bob Errey, Sergei Fedorov, Viacheslav Fetisov, Vladimir Konstantinov, Vyacheslav Kozlov, Martin Lapointe, Nicklas Lidstrom, Darren McCarty, Chris Osgood, Keith Primeau, Mike Ramsey, Bob Rouse, Ray Sheppard, Tim Taylor, Mike Vernon, Steve Yzerman.

NEW JERSEY: Tommy Albelin, Martin Brodeur, Neal Broten, Sergei Brylin, Bobby Carpenter, Sean Chambers, Tom Chorske, Ken Daneyko, Bruce Driver, Bill Guerin, Bobby Holik, Claude Lemieux, Randy McKay, John MacLean, Scott Niedermayer, Mike Peluso, Stephane Richer, Scott Stevens, Chris Terreri, Valeri Zelepukin.

First Period
1. NEW JERSEY   DRIVER (BROTEN, MacLEAN)   10:30 (PPG)
2. NEW JERSEY   LEMIEUX (CARPENTER, STEVENS)   16:52

Penalties: Primeau (Det) (slashing), Lemieux (NJ) (roughing) 1:09; Konstantinov (Det) (holding the stick) 8:56; Holik (NJ) (tripping) 10:58; Lapointe (Det) (unsportsmanlike conduct), Guerin (NJ) (unsportsmanlike conduct) 16:58.

Second Period
3. NEW JERSEY   BROTEN (STEVENS, MacLEAN)   6:59 (GWG)
4. NEW JERSEY   McKAY (HOLIK, DRIVER)   8:20

Penalties: Broten (NJ) (holding the stick) 11:01; Primeau (Det) (tripping) 16:03; Carpenter (NJ) (cross-checking) 19:47.

Third Period
5. NEW JERSEY   HOLIK (GUERIN, RICHER)   8:14 (PPG)
6. DETROIT   FEDOROV (FETISOV, BROWN)   16:57 (PPG)
7. DETROIT   YZERMAN (SHEPPARD, LIDSTROM)   18:27 (PPG)

Third Period: Albelin (NJ) (highsticking) 2:30; Konstantinov (Det) (highsticking) 4:25; Draper (Det) (highsticking) 5:17; Primeau (Det) (cross-checking) 6:31; Holik (Det) (interference) 8:44; Richer (NJ) (hooking) 12:28; Ciccarelli (Det) (roughing), Taylor (Det) (roughing), Lapointe (Det) (double roughing minor), Zelepukin (NJ) (double roughing minor), Guerin (NJ) (boarding, roughing), Brylin (NJ) (highsticking, roughing) 15:37.

Goalies: Vernon, Osgood (Det), Brodeur (NJ)
    Shots: Det 7 - 5 - 12 24
            NJ 15 - 8 - 8 31

Referee: Kerry Fraser
Linesmen: Kevin Collins, Brian Murphy

Game #4 - June 24, 1995 - Meadowlands Arena - New Jersey 5, Detroit 2

DETROIT: Doug Brown, Dino Ciccarelli, Paul Coffey, Kris Draper, Bob Errey, Sergei Fedorov, Viacheslav Fetisov, Stu Grimson, Vladimir Konstantinov, Vyacheslav Kozlov, Mike Krushelnyski, Martin Lapointe, Nicklas Lidstrom, Darren McCarty, Chris Osgood, Keith Primeau, Mike Ramsey, Bob Rouse, Mike Vernon, Steve Yzerman.

NEW JERSEY: Tommy Albelin, Martin Brodeur, Neal Broten, Sergei Brylin, Bobby Carpenter, Sean Chambers, Tom Chorske, Ken Daneyko, Bruce Driver, Bill Guerin, Bobby Holik, Claude Lemieux, Randy McKay, John MacLean, Scott Niedermayer, Mike Peluso, Stephane Richer, Brian Rolston, Scott Stevens, Chris Terreri.

First Period
1. NEW JERSEY   BROTEN (RICHER, CHORSKE)   1:08
2. DETROIT   FEDOROV (LAPOINTE, FETISOV)   2:03
3. DETROIT   COFFEY (BROWN, FEDOROV)   13:01 (SHG)
4. NEW JERSEY   CHAMBERS (DRIVER, MacLEAN)   17:45

Penalties: Errey (Det) (hooking) 11:03; Daneyko (NJ) (roughing) 13:36; Primeau (Det) (goaltender interference) 15:35.

Second Period
5. NEW JERSEY   BROTEN (NIEDERMAYER, GUERIN)   7:56 (GWG)

Penalties: Daneyko (NJ) (slashing) 0:30; Lapointe (Det) (roughing), Stevens (NJ) (roughing) 10:09; Guerin (NJ) (interference) 12:43; Konstantinov (Det) (hooking) 19:12.

Third Period
6. NEW JERSEY   BRYLIN (ROLSTON, GUERIN)   7:46
7. NEW JERSEY   CHAMBERS (BRYLIN, GUERIN)   12:32

Penalties: Grimson (Det)   (roughing) 10:24.

Goalies: Vernon (Det), Brodeur (NJ)
    Shots: Det 8 - 7 - 1 16
            NJ   8 - 8 - 10 26

Referee: Bill McCreary
Linesmen: Wayne Bonney, Ray Scapinello

BACK-TO-BACK WINNERS

Many players have won consecutive championships in their careers, but few have ever accomplished the feat with two different teams. In fact, one player, Eddie Gerard, won the Cup with the 1921 Ottawa Senators, 1922 Toronto St. Pats and in 1923 with the Senators again. A total of nine different players have accomplished the feat:

Jack Marshall	1901 Winnipeg	1902 Montreal
Art Ross	1907 Kenora	1908 Montreal
Bruce Stuart	1908 Montreal	1909 Ottawa
Harry Holmes	1917 Seattle	1918 Toronto
Eddie Gerard	1921 Ottawa	1922 Toronto
Eddie Gerard	1922 Toronto	1923 Ottawa
Lionel Conacher	1934 Chicago	1935 Montreal
Ab McDonald	1960 Montreal	1961 Chicago
Al Arbour	1961 Chicago	1962 Toronto
Ed Litzenberger	1961 Chicago	1962 Toronto

WOMEN ON THE CUP

Three women have had their names engraved on the Stanley Cup: Marguerite Norris (1955) was president of the Detroit Red Wings; Sonia Scurfield (1989) was a co-owner of the Calgary Flames; and Marie-Denise DeBartolo York (1991) was president of the Pittsburgh Penguins.

EYE IN THE SKY

For the first time in NHL history, a playoff result was determined by a video replay during the 1992 Division Semi-Finals between Detroit and Minnesota. In overtime Sergei Fedorov's shot appeared to hit the crossbar. After a stop in play, referee Rob Shick consulted the supervisor of officials and video-replay official Wally Harris, who determined that the puck had entered the net, giving the Wings a 1–0 win.

CANADIENS OWN MARK FOR PRO TITLES

The Montreal Canadiens have won 24 Stanley Cups, more than any other team. The total also rates as the greatest number of championships in the history of professional sports. Major League Baseball's New York Yankees rank second to Montreal with 22 World Series titles to their credit.

GOLD MEDALLIST AND STANLEY CUP CHAMPION

New York Islanders' defenseman Ken Morrow is the only player in hockey history to win both an Olympic Gold Medal and a Stanley Cup in the same year. After helping the United States Olympic team win the gold medal at the 1980 Winter Games in Lake Placid, Morrow joined the New York Islanders and helped them win the first of their four straight Stanley Cups.